A
GLOBAL
HISTORY
OF
MAN

LEFTEN S. STAVRIANOS

Loretta Kreider Andrews · John R. McLane

Frank Safford · James E. Sheridan

ALLYN AND BACON, INC.

Boston   Rockleigh, N.J.   Atlanta   Dallas   Belmont, Calif.

A GLOBAL HISTORY OF MAN

CURRICULUM RESOURCE CENTER
South Bend Community School Corporation

All original maps by Dick Sanderson (Graf-Tech)

ABOUT THE AUTHORS

LEFTEN S. STAVRIANOS

Ph.D., Clark University; Professor of History, Northwestern University; senior author: Units One–Four, Unit Five—Soviet Union, Unit Ten—Middle East, and Unit Eleven—Our World Today.

LORETTA KREIDER ANDREWS

M.A., Northwestern University; additional year of full-time study at Northwestern's African Studies Program; author: Unit Nine—Sub-Saharan Africa.

JOHN R. MC LANE

Ph.D., School of Oriental and African Studies, University of London; Assistant Professor of History, Northwestern University; author: Unit Eight—India.

FRANK SAFFORD

Ph.D., Columbia University; Assistant Professor of History, Northwestern University; author: Unit Six—Latin America.

JAMES E. SHERIDAN

Ph.D., University of California at Berkeley; Professor of History, Northwestern University; author: Unit Seven—China.

The Acknowledgements on pages 740–742 are an extension of this copyright page.

Printed in the United States of America.

Library of Congress Catalog Card No. 70–112715.

PREFACE

In the past half century the world has moved into an era of challenge, progress, and upheaval that has no parallel. Without a basic understanding of world history, the events of these years and the current world situation are not meaningful. The purpose of *A Global History of Man* is primarily to provide both an understanding and an appreciation of the present in terms of the past. A history of Western civilization is no longer sufficient for this purpose and this text, therefore, presents today's world events in terms of our global history.

The organization of *A Global History of Man* is uniquely different from the chronological approach most commonly used today. There are four parts, each of which contributes to the composite fabric of a true global history.

Part One, consisting of one unit, gives a brief but succinct account of the geographic factors which have influenced the course of world history.

Part Two makes a rapid survey of man's history from his advent on this planet to the present day. It is divided into three units, each designed to cover a major stage in man's long journey from savagery to his first step into outer space. Unit Two covers the period of Man before Civilization and contains a discussion of the races of mankind. Unit Three covers the period from 3700 B.C. to 1500 A.D., when man lived in regional isolation. The period is divided into the ancient, classical, and medieval eras. Unit Four covers the period from 1500 to the present, when man lives in global unity as a result of Europe's overseas expansion. Its emphasis is upon the influence of Europe on the rest of the world, and it is divided into three sections: Europe Unites the World, Europe Dominates the World, and Europe's Decline and Triumph.

Part Three is devoted to a detailed analysis of six of the world's major culture regions: Soviet Union, Latin America, China, India, Sub-Saharan Africa, and the Middle East. Each of the six units in this part is divided into four sections: Basic Facts, Politics, Economics, and Culture.

Since it would require many volumes to cover each of these topics for just one of these cultural regions, the flashback technique has been employed to make the mass of detail pedagogically manageable. Present conditions and institutions are described and their explanations sought in selected historical events and forces. By using this technique, long lists of names, dates, events, dynasties, and the like are avoided and emphasis is placed upon the great forces of world history. This technique also makes the past relevant to the present, and therefore meaningful for the students.

Part Four pulls together the historical threads which make up "Our World Today." The single unit of this final part is divided into three sections: Forces Uniting the World, Forces Dividing the World, and the role of the United Nations in attempting to reduce global disunity and friction.

Several useful tools have been employed to aid the student in his study of *A Global History of Man*. Each section within a unit is followed by a series of exercises designed to test the student's recall of the immediately preceding material. At the end of each unit, there is a series of activities which require the student to interpret, compare, contrast, collate, and evaluate the material of the unit, both by itself and also with other units in the book. Each unit has a bibliography, simply annotated, to aid the student to go beyond the material in the text. The bibliographies are divided into two sections, Selected Reading and Further Reading. For the purpose of introducing the student to source material, references to the supplementary volume, *Readings in World History*, have been included on the appropriate pages of the text.

A wealth of illustrations has been included to aid the student by presenting and highlighting important points in a visual fashion. There are over 100 maps, charts, graphs, and tables in full color. There is a time line in each of the units devoted to a culture region. More than 400 pictures, many of them primary sources in themselves, have been placed throughout the book.

This edition of *A Global History of Man* has been thoroughly updated. It reflects the rapidly changing world in which we live. New pictures and an entirely new map program have been added. Graphs and diagrams include the latest statistical information. The reading lists at the end of the units have been revised and include many of the most recent popular and scholarly books on world history.

The authors are indebted to the Carnegie Corporation of New York which has generously contributed to the World History Project of Northwestern University, of which this volume is a product.

TABLE OF CONTENTS

PART **I** THE ENVIRONMENT OF WORLD HISTORY

PART **II** A SURVEY OF WORLD HISTORY

PART III THE WORLD'S MAJOR CULTURE AREAS

PART **IV** GLOBAL HISTORY TODAY AND TOMORROW

Identification of Unit Opening Photographs

Unit One: Rice Terraces at Banaue, Philippines *(D. J. Forbert, Shostal)*
Unit Two: Carving of Giraffe in a Cave in Northern Africa *(Emil Schulthess, Black Star)*
Unit Three: Scene from the South Sea Islands *(Shostal)*
Unit Four: World Map Drawn by Johann Blau in 1641 *(Courtesy of the Trustees of the British Museum)*
Unit Five: Chess Players in Gorky Park, Moscow *(Jacques Jangoux)*
Unit Six: Street Scene in Caracas, Venezuela *(Amy Lubensky)*
Unit Seven: Red Guard Marching in Peking *(Alan Band)*
Unit Eight: Street Scene in Karachi, West Pakistan *(Talbot Lovering)*
Unit Nine: Girl in Timbuktu *(Harrison Forman)*
Unit Ten: Mural of Nasser in the Bazaar, Luxor, Egypt *(Doranne Jacobson, EPA)*
Unit Eleven: Scene in Central Park, New York City, 1969 *(Margot Niederland)*

LIST OF MAPS

PART I THE ENVIRONMENT OF WORLD HISTORY

PART II A SURVEY OF WORLD HISTORY

PART III THE WORLD'S MAJOR CULTURE AREAS

PART IV GLOBAL HISTORY TODAY AND TOMORROW

THE
ENVIRONMENT
OF WORLD
HISTORY

I

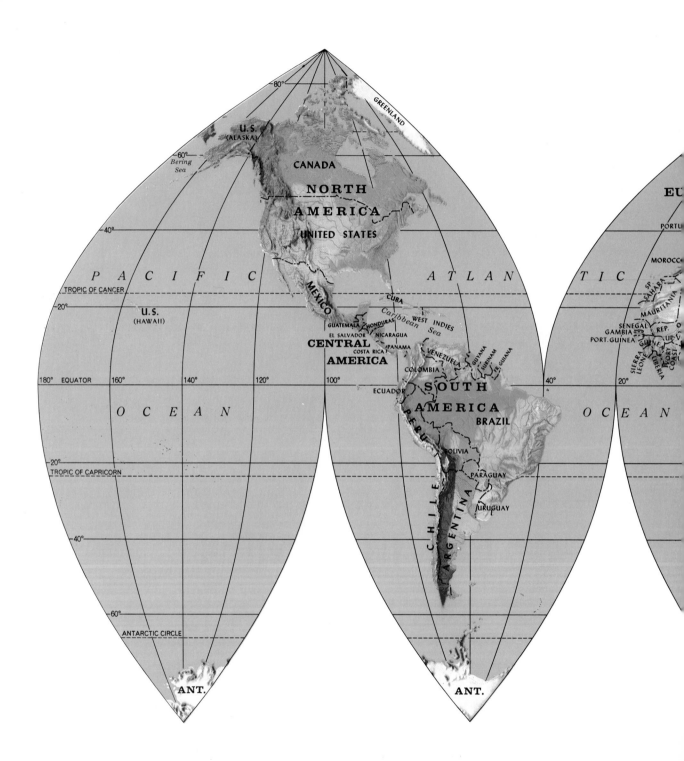

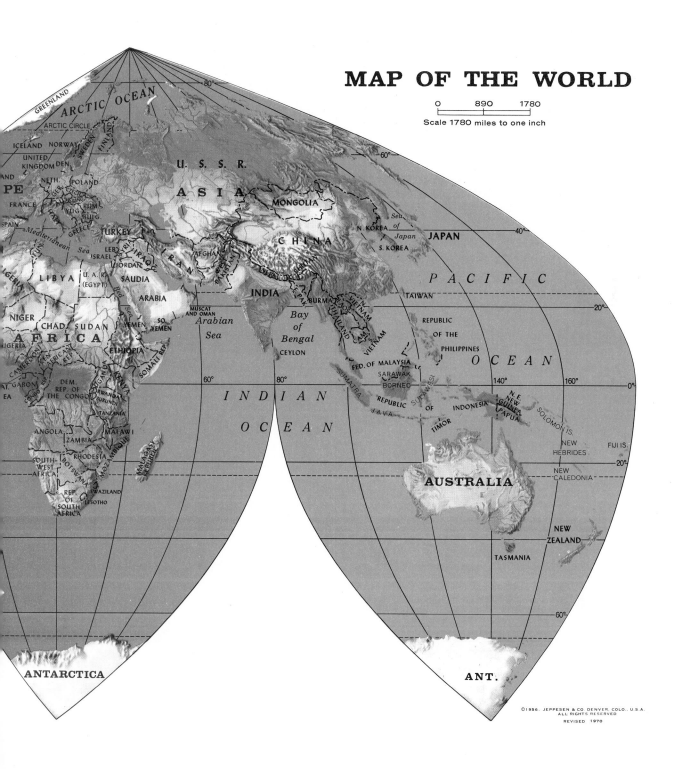

MAP OF THE WORLD

0   890   1780

Scale 1780 miles to one inch

4

MAN'S PHYSICAL WORLD

For as Geography without History seemeth a Carkasse without motion, So History without Geography wandreth as a Vagrant without a certain habitation.[1] Man is a product of the earth's surface. This means not merely that he is a child of the earth, dust of her dust; but that the earth has mothered him, fed him, set him tasks, directed his thoughts, confronted him with difficulties that have strengthened his body and sharpened his wits, given him problems of navigation or irrigation, and at the same time whispered hints for their solution. She has entered into his bone and tissue, into his mind and soul.[2]

[1] John Smith of Virginia   [2] Ellen Churchill Semple

THE CHALLENGE OF ENVIRONMENT

MAN AND GEOGRAPHY

Historical examples. The planet earth is man's home. It has mothered and fed him. It has molded his mind and body. In many ways man is the product of the earth on which he has spent the almost two million years of his existence. But at the same time he is something more than a mere product. He has indeed been influenced by the earth, but gradually he has learned to act independently of the earth and to exercise some control over it. Moreover he has always looked out beyond his earth and dreamed of other worlds in space. Today man is taking the preliminary steps to leave the earth to explore other planets.

The relations between man and his physical world are by no means simple or one-way. Man's actions cannot be explained entirely as being determined by geographic influences. Geographic influences, however, have played an important role in man's history. Therefore, the first question that we shall consider is: In what manner and to what extent has man been influenced by the planet on which he lives? Or, in other words, how has man's history been influenced by the geography of his planet, the earth?

If we look about us, we can see many illustrations of the effects of geography. It is not accidental that man's earliest civilizations developed in river valleys: the Tigris-Euphrates, Nile, Indus, and Hwang Ho or Yellow. The explanation may be found in the geographic conditions prevailing in these areas. These early civilizations were based on agriculture rather than on industry. The soil in these river valleys is some of the most fertile in the world, and the climate is warm.

It is not accidental that the most powerful countries today are the United States and the Soviet Union and that China and India are likely to rise to the top. The explanation may again be found in geography. In the modern industrial age a great power must have a large and dependable source of minerals to supply raw materials for its factories. These four countries have many of the minerals necessary for heavy industrial development.

These examples show that geographic factors have exercised a strong influence on man's history. We can also find examples which tend to prove that this is not always true. For example, the American people during the last 80 years have profited tremendously from the great iron ore deposits in the Mesabi Range of northern Minnesota. But, for thousands of years Indians fished and hunted in that area without taking advantage of the ore supply.

Another example can be seen in the case of the Hopi and Navaho Indian tribes in the southwestern part of the United States. Both tribes lived in the same locality and were exposed to the same geographic influences. Yet each has developed very different customs and ways of life. The Hopis are *pueblo* (literally village) Indians who settled in the southwest 2000 years ago. They live in towns and their houses, made of adobe or stone, may rise several stories like an apartment building. They are expert farmers who have perfected dry-farming methods to grow crops such as corn, beans, and squash. Their society is highly organized under the government of a priest-chief. The Navahos, on the other hand, came to the area from far to the north about nine hundred years ago. Their home is a single-room dwelling, called a *hogan*, which is made from a framework of poles covered with earth and dome-shaped, somewhat like an Eskimo snow house. These dwellings are individual and scattered. Al-

Permanent adobe villages in the southwestern United States testify to the stability of the highly-organized, agriculture-based Hopi society, just as the quickly built Navaho hogans in the same area indicate the independence and wanderlust of that herding tribe.

though the Navahos learned the agricultural techniques of the Hopis and became great farmers, they later turned to herding sheep and other livestock. This probably resulted from the Navahos' individuality and desire for more room. They were more warlike than the Hopis and built their herds by raiding their sedentary village neighbors and the Spanish. Although the Navahos borrowed much from the Hopis in religion and type of family relationship, they adapted them to their own needs.

Conclusions. What can we learn from these examples? Does the geographic environment control man, does it influence him moderately, or does it have no effect at all? The answer is that geographic conditions set certain restrictions and provide certain opportunities. Yet, in many ways, man himself can decide to what extent he will be bound by the restrictions and to what extent he will take advantage of the opportunities. For example, the geographic environment of the area in which he lives has forced the Eskimo to be a hunter rather than a farmer

and he has little choice of occupation if he continues to live in an area that has a polar climate. Another example of the restrictions of environment is the citrus fruit industry in the United States. Oranges can be grown in

The Challenge of Environment 7

certain favored, frost-free areas in California, Arizona, Texas, Louisiana, and Florida, not in Maine or Minnesota.

On the other hand, the geographic environment of southwestern United States permits the Navahos to make a choice of herding sheep or tilling the soil like their neighbors, the Hopis. Geographic conditions do not force any present-day citizen of the United States to mine iron ore from the Mesabi Range, nor were the original inhabitants of northern Minnesota, the Chippewa Indians, forced to fish and hunt wild game there. The natural environment of the Mesabi Range area offers man the choice of mining, hunting, fishing, lumbering, dairy farming, and many other occupations.

We may conclude that the physical environment has an important effect upon man but does not fully control him. History, in fact, is essentially the story of how man has been able to overcome *some* of the geographic restrictions and to exploit *some* of the opportunities provided by his environment. As scientific research unlocks more of the secrets of his home, the earth, man will be able to use them to exploit more of the opportunities offered by his environment. Keeping this in mind, we shall now see what the principal geographic forces are and how man has reacted to them. We shall study in turn, climate, vegetation, soils, minerals, energy, and location.

CLIMATE

What is climate? Climate is the average weather of a place or region. To determine the type of climate, it is necessary to know the total annual amount and monthly pattern of precipitation, evaporation, and temperature. An example will help to explain the interaction of these three factors. Paris, France, has an average yearly precipitation of just under 23 inches. For Bulawayo, Rho-

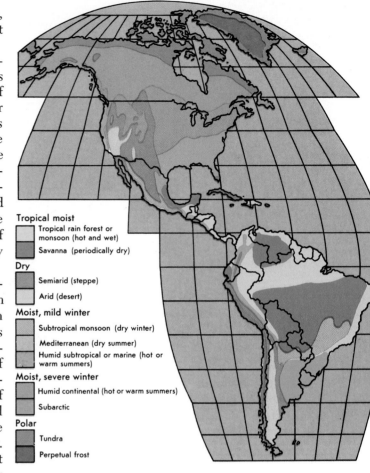

Tropical moist
- Tropical rain forest or monsoon (hot and wet)
- Savanna (periodically dry)

Dry
- Semiarid (steppe)
- Arid (desert)

Moist, mild winter
- Subtropical monsoon (dry winter)
- Mediterranean (dry summer)
- Humid subtropical or marine (hot or warm summers)

Moist, severe winter
- Humid continental (hot or warm summers)
- Subarctic

Polar
- Tundra
- Perpetual frost

desia, the total is just over 23 inches. If annual precipitation was the only factor, both cities should have the same type of climate. Yet this is not true. Paris lies in a moist climate, whereas Bulawayo falls in a semiarid climate. The explanation can be found in the monthly distribution of the precipitation and in the other two factors, temperature and evaporation. The precipitation at Paris is distributed evenly throughout the year. At Bulawayo, about two-thirds falls in the summer months when the temperature is very high while less than an inch of rain falls in

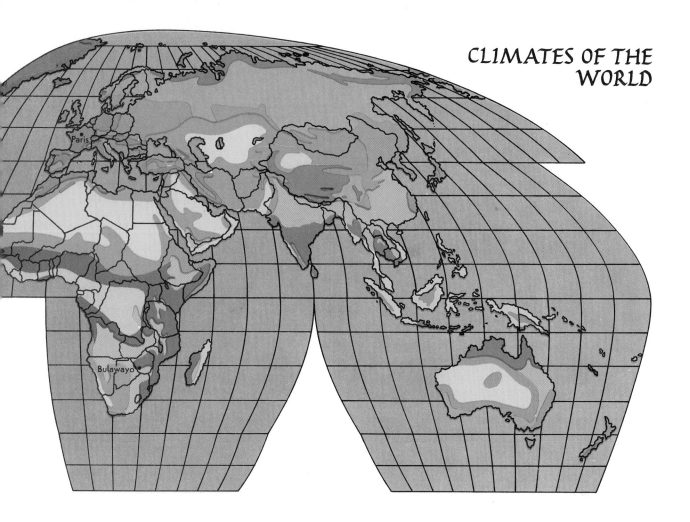

the winter months. As a result, evaporation is high in the summer when most of the rain falls and Bulawayo's effective precipitation is far less than that of Paris.

The following table will illustrate this example. The monthly precipitation is given in inches per month.

Bulawayo is located in the southern hemisphere and winter falls during our northern hemisphere summer months of June, July, and August. While it is important to know the total amount of precipitation (rain, snow, sleet, hail, dew, etc.), this example shows

	Paris	Bulawayo
January	1.54	5.81
February	1.22	4.05
March	1.61	3.03
April	1.65	.65
May	2.09	.29
June	2.32	.03
July	2.20	.04
August	2.16	.03
September	1.97	.12
October	2.32	.91
November	1.81	3.31
December	1.73	5.18
Total	22.62	23.45

that we also need to know the temperature before we can determine the type of climate in any area.

Types. There are five major types of climate, determined by moisture and temperature. These five types are: *tropical moist, dry, moist mild winter, moist severe winter,* and *polar.* The map on the two previous pages shows the extent of each of these climatic types.

Climate has a direct and strong influence on the life and general development of man. In the United States, for example, the western half of the country has been held back in its development because of inadequate rainfall. It is estimated that this aridity has reduced by at least seventy per cent the number of people who might otherwise be supported. In other words, Montana and Wyoming would be as heavily populated as Iowa and Wisconsin if they had enough rainfall for agriculture. Another example of the influence of climate may be found in the Soviet Union. The development of that country also has been slowed down by what has been described as the "too much" aspect of its climate. For the efficient production of agricultural and industrial raw materials, the north is too cold and wet, the south is too hot and dry, and the east is too cold, dry, and high. Certainly the Soviet Union would be a much wealthier country if the Himalayan Mountains did not prevent moisture-laden winds from the Indian Ocean from reaching the desert plains of the Central Asian Soviet Republics. The unproductiveness of these desert plains offers a sharp contrast to the fertile central plains of the United States. Moisture-laden winds from the Gulf of Mexico sweep northward without interruption by any mountain barriers and bring the rains which have helped to make the Midwest the greatest farming area in the world.

VEGETATION

Types. The different types of climates affect man in many ways. In the first place they determine the natural vegetation that is available to him. In the wet, hot, and humid regions tropical rain forests cover the land. Tall prairie grasses are most common in subhumid areas where the moisture is insufficient for forests. Drier, semiarid regions can support only short grasses, while arid regions have desert grasses and shrubs such as cacti that can survive with a minimum of moisture. In regions having a subarctic climate, vegetation consists of taiga or coniferous forests, mostly spruce and fir. In polar climates, agriculture cannot be carried on and only mosses, lichens, coarse grasses, and flowering shrubs can grow. Finally, in areas having an icecap climate of perpetual ice and snow, no vegetation of any kind can be found. The complete pattern of the world's vegetation zones can be seen on the map on pages 2–3.

Climate also determines to a large degree the types of plants that man grows. It permits him to produce bananas in Costa Rica, oranges in Spain, corn in Iowa, and wheat in the Ukraine. But man does not allow climate to decide completely what he will grow. It is true that he cannot grow anything in regions of perpetual frost, but for centuries he has grown bumper crops in deserts by introducing irrigation. More recently, he has extended the limits of agriculture far northward by developing cold-resistant varieties of plants and special growing techniques.

SOILS

What is soil? The soils of the world are the source of all life, of plants directly and animals and men indirectly. Considered in this light, it can be easily understood that soils have profoundly affected the life and progress of man from earliest times. When the earth first took shape, no soil covered its naked rock. Through countless eons, the rock surface was subject to weathering, the first step in the physical, chemical, and biological process that produces soil.

There are five major factors which control weathering and soil formation. They are parent rock, climate, living organisms, topography or relief, and time. The parent rock is a passive factor in the soil formation process insofar as it must be acted upon by other factors, but the character and structure of the rock has an important bearing on the soil produced from it. Limestone will produce a fertile soil because it releases plant food. Quartz will not as it releases no foods.

The climatic factors of precipitation, evaporation, and temperature function directly in the accumulation of soil materials by governing the rate of weathering of the parent rock and the decomposition of minerals in it. The living organisms such as plants, animals, insects, bacteria, and fungi serve a useful function in soil formation by adding organic matter, nitrogen, and plant nutrients. Topography or the lay of the land affects the soil formation process by acting as one of the controls of water entering the ground. Where the land has a steep slope, water runs off quickly and less sinks into the ground. A steep slope and rapid runoff means that more weathered rock residue is carried downhill than by a slower runoff on a more level slope. The last of the five major factors in soil formation, time, hardly requires explanation. Depending on the parent material, it takes from a few decades to literally millions of years for soil to form.

Soil belts. Since the variations in these five factors are numerous, it follows that the soils formed under their influence will also show many variations. There have been many systems evolved for classifying soils but most of them are too technical to be considered in the study of world history. For our purposes, therefore, the soils of the world may be divided into five broad belts.

In the far north (northern Soviet Union and Canada) the extreme cold has stopped or greatly retarded the formation of soil. Thus the soils in that zone are young, pale, shallow, coarse, and of poor quality. In the worst cases they can support only lichens and some grass and flowering plants. Further south are the light-colored soils of the northern forests. These are still relatively poor but are adequate for the forests that cover much of the Soviet Union, the Scandinavian Countries, and Canada. Still further south is a belt of mixed forests where conifers and broadleaved deciduous trees are mingled. There, the higher temperature and more varied vegetation tend to produce browner and more fertile soils. Toward the equator, the extreme heat has decayed the soils so that most of the nutrients have been washed away. These "leached" tropical soils are usually red or yellow in color and of little use for agriculture. Finally, there are the soils found in the great deserts of Africa, Asia, and Australia. These are usually red or brown, low in organic matter, but quite high in plant food. When properly irrigated they are highly productive.

Land use. Since man first learned to grow food through agriculture, most of the people of the world have lived in areas where the soil and the climate are best suited for farming. This distribution of the world's population began to change a little about two hundred years ago when man learned to make machines, construct factories, and build large industrial cities. New centers of population now appeared in industrialized regions like the Midlands in England, the Ruhr valley in Germany, and the Atlantic seaboard of the United States. Nevertheless, if we look at the world as a whole, we find that most of the people still live in the good agricultural regions. The four great population concentrations today are in eastern United States, Western Europe, the Far East, and India and Ceylon. In these areas, totaling only one-eighth of the earth's surface, live three-fourths of the world's people.

The total land surface of the world, including icecaps, mountains, and deserts, is estimated at 33,450 million acres. About twelve per cent of this total, or 4000 million acres, is generally considered to be cultivable. Four-fifths of this small area, or 3200 million acres, is now under cultivation. Of the remaining uncultivated fifth, about a third lies in Asia, one-fourth in the Americas (largely in Canada), and another fourth in Africa. But if the land now uncultivated is to be used, special skills and equipment are required. Deserts demand money and technical knowledge for dams and irrigation works. Forests and scrub may be cleared, but there are possible dangers, particularly of soil erosion. In the tropics, numerous pests and diseases must be controlled before man can grow food. Even if all these natural obstacles were overcome, and the remaining fifth of the arable land were actually cultivated, the people of the world would still not have a food surplus on their hands. Furthermore, it takes many years to make unused cultivable land into farmland. In the meantime, the world's population continues to increase at a greater rate than the world's food production.

It is true that scientists may be able in the future to increase our food supply with new techniques. One method may result from the unlocking of the secrets of photosynthesis, the mysterious process by which green plants combine dioxide and water in the presence of sunlight to produce carbohydrates (sugar and starches). Another possible method is hydroponics, or the growing of plants in vats

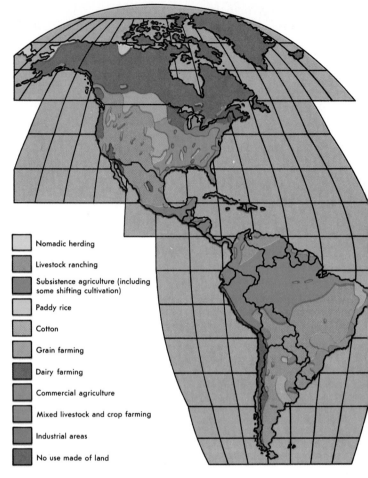

Nomadic herding

Livestock ranching

Subsistence agriculture (including some shifting cultivation)

Paddy rice

Cotton

Grain farming

Dairy farming

Commercial agriculture

Mixed livestock and crop farming

Industrial areas

No use made of land

filled with water and the minerals necessary for plant growth. A third technique is ocean farming, or the growing of edible algae (seaweeds) and other food in the ocean. But these scientific processes have not been used to any great extent and consequently have added little to man's food supply.

Meanwhile, the rapid increase in the world's population is causing the present amount of cultivable land to carry a heavier burden. A larger number of mouths must be fed by each acre of land. This increasing demand creates a temptation to overgraze or to

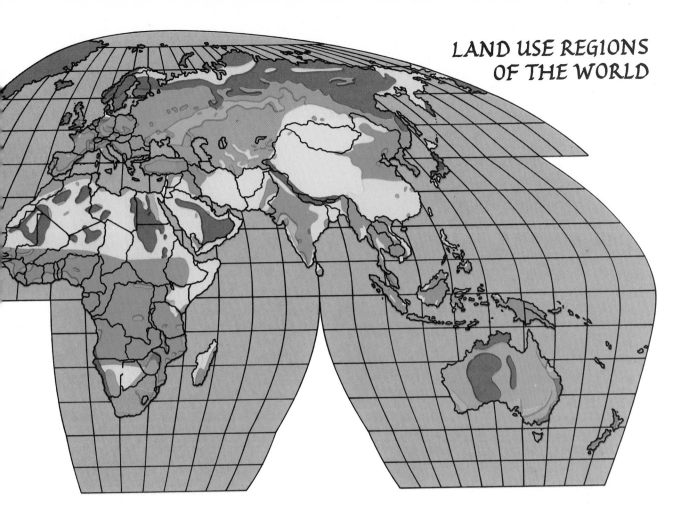

plow land that should remain in grass or forest. Once the soil of marginal land has been exposed, it becomes susceptible to erosion because its natural protective cover has been destroyed. It is then easily washed away by rains or floods or blown away by winds. Throughout the world today, cultivable land is being destroyed by erosion at a greater rate than ever before.

Erosion. The United States, where mountains of surplus grains are grown each year, has a serious soil erosion problem. Although the exhaustion and erosion of soils was recognized as early as colonial times by George Washington, Thomas Jefferson, and others, no serious attempt to cope with the problem was made until the 1930's when dust clouds, resulting from erosion of the soil of the Great Plains, were literally blown into the eyes of the national legislature in Washington. The Census of Agriculture in 1935 showed that only one acre in four of the nation's total cropland had escaped soil erosion in some form. One-eighth had been ruined for cultivation, another eighth had been severely

The Challenge of Environment 13

Dust storms are composed of finely ground topsoil which has eroded off the surface of the land, usually because of drought, overgrazing, or poor farming methods. Reclamation projects to again make such land productive have steadily increased in number since the lesson of the "Dust Bowl" in the 1930's.

damaged and was approaching ruin, and another quarter had lost one-half to almost all of its topsoil. The dust bowl mentioned above served to awaken the citizens and government of the United States to the seriousness of the problem. As a result of the work of the newly created Soil Conservation Service, the Forest Service, other national and state agencies, private conservation organizations, and many industrial firms, the erosion picture is considerably less grim today. Yet the problem persists not only in the United States but throughout the world.*

Population explosion. Meanwhile, the population of the world is increasing so rapidly that its growth has been called a "population

* See *Readings in World History,* "Man and Mother Earth," p. 2 (Boston: Allyn and Bacon, Inc., 1970).

explosion." The most important factor has been the lowering of the death rate. This has resulted from a worldwide adoption of better sanitation, the reduction of infant mortality, and the slow but steady eradication of pestilence and disease. More babies live through the first year of life, more people survive, or are protected from, plagues which formerly carried off large percentages of the population, and more people live longer due to the advances in medical science. Since the birth rate has continued to remain high and the death rate has been lowered, the world's population has increased at an extremely rapid rate. It is estimated that world population is growing by 6800 every hour or nearly 60,000,000 a year. Furthermore the rate of increase is steadily rising, so that it will be twice as fast in the second half of the present century as it was during the first. This means that world population, which rose from 1.5 billion in 1900 to 2.5 billion in 1950, will probably total 6 billion in the year 2000.

This combination of population explosion and soil erosion is creating one of the most serious problems facing mankind today. At present, about two-thirds of the world's population is considered to be seriously undernourished. For many others their diet is far from ideal. More healthful foods must be provided and the individual's average caloric total raised much higher before it can be said that the world is properly fed.

Some experts believe that despite all our technological and economic progress, there are now more poverty-stricken people in the world than there were fifty years ago. If this is the case, then what will be the condition of mankind fifty years hence, when the world population will be two and a half times greater and the world soils still more eroded?* Former President Johnson, in his State of the Union Message for 1967, told Congress: "Next to the pursuit of world peace, the really greatest challenge to the human family is the race between food supply and the population increase. That race is being lost."

* See *Readings in World History*, "Man and Food: Can They Be Balanced?", p. 8.

ALAN BAND

India has a population growth rate of almost 3% per year—and is already faced with 398 people per square mile. Calcutta exemplifies the worst aspects of this congestion and overcrowding. In the evening, when thousands of office workers make their way home, the pavement becomes almost impassable.

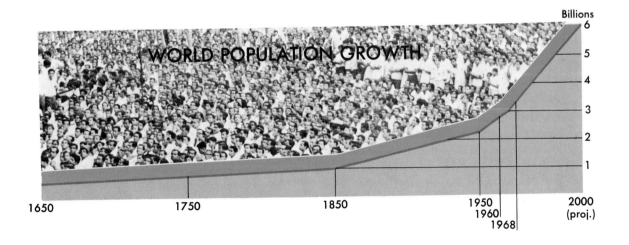

WORLD POPULATION GROWTH

Billions
6
5
4
3
2
1

1650   1750   1850   1950   2000
                          1960   (proj.)
                          1968

MINERALS

Importance. Minerals have been vital to man's development. At the very beginning man used stone to make his tools and weapons. Gradually he learned how to use metals that were better suited for his purposes. He made jewelry and other luxury objects out of gold and silver; he used bronze and iron for his swords and spears and plows.

In the 18th century man began to use minerals much more widely for his new machines and factories. Since that time the countries with large mineral deposits have had a great advantage. Great Britain, for example, could not have become the first industrial power of the world if she did not have large supplies of coal and iron. Germany was able to follow Britain because she also had plentiful mineral resources. And the super-powers of today and tomorrow, the United States, the Soviet Union, China, and India, all have tremendous mineral reserves as well as large populations and good agricultural lands. (See page 713.)

Minerals are more important in the industrial world of today than they have been at any time in the past. Unfortunately, mineral deposits are scattered unevenly about the globe so that some countries are "have countries" with respect to them, while others are "have nots." But every industrial country without exception is a "need more" in this matter. The reason is that minerals are the foundation of modern industry, and well over a hundred of them are needed for one purpose or another. No country, regardless of how large or how rich it may be, has all the minerals it needs within its frontiers. All countries have to import certain minerals from various parts of the globe.

In recent decades industry has grown so rapidly throughout the world that many experts fear that mineral depletion is as serious a problem as soil depletion. Even richly-

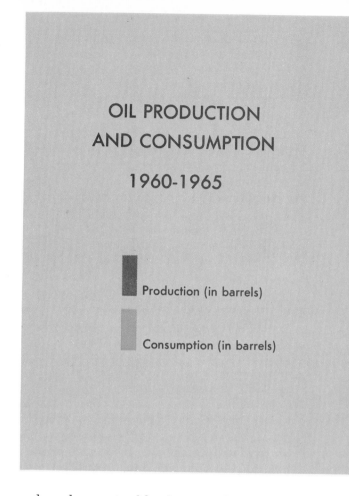

OIL PRODUCTION AND CONSUMPTION 1960-1965

Production (in barrels)

Consumption (in barrels)

endowed countries like the United States are now beginning to feel the pinch. In 1900 the United States produced some fifteen per cent more raw materials (excluding food) than it consumed. By 1950 it consumed ten per cent more than it produced. Of more than a hundred minerals that American industry now uses, about a third are fully supplied at home, another third come partly from home and partly from abroad, and the final third come largely from abroad. Our industries could not keep going without importing chrome from Africa, copper from Canada and South America, tin from Malaysia and Bolivia, oil from South America and the Middle East, and iron ore from Venezuela and Labrador.

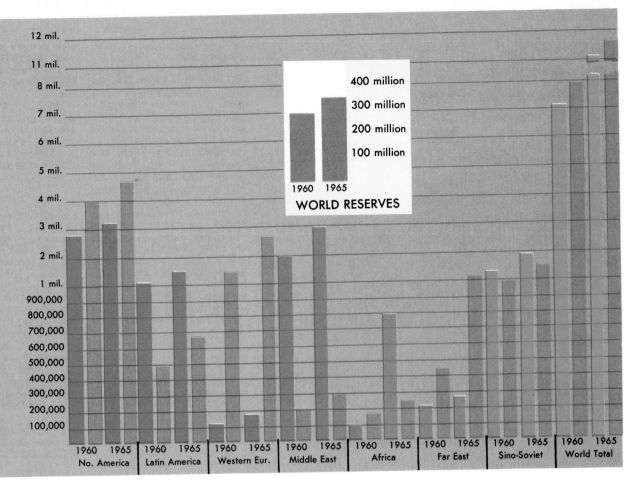

12 mil.							
11 mil.							
8 mil.							
7 mil.							
6 mil.							
5 mil.							

WORLD RESERVES

400 million
300 million
200 million
100 million

1960   1965

| 1960 1965 | 1960 1965 | 1960 1965 | 1960 1965 | 1960 1965 | 1960 1965 | 1960 1965 | 1960 1965 |
| No. America | Latin America | Western Eur. | Middle East | Africa | Far East | Sino-Soviet | World Total |

Rate of consumption. If we look at the world's proved reserves of minerals which are important as raw materials for industry, iron and aluminum seem to be available in large quantities and should last for hundreds of years. But the known reserves of lead, zinc, and tin will last only about thirty years at the rate of consumption prevailing in 1950. Since the consumption rate is rapidly increasing, these metals will soon become scarce unless new deposits or suitable substitutes are discovered.

Most experts are worried about the rapidly increasing rate of consumption of the world's supply of minerals; and the rate will undoubtedly rise much more sharply in the future as industrialization spreads to new areas such as Africa, China, and India. Experts differ as to whether we face a long-range problem or an immediate emergency. The answer depends on whether or not the rising curve of consumption can be matched by the discovery of new deposits and new substitutes.*

Optimists argue that, judging from past experience, both new reserves and satisfactory substitutes will be found. This appears to be justified, at least as far as the immediate future is concerned. Despite the rapid increase of consumption, world min-

* See *Readings in World History,* "Man's Resources: Exhaustible or Inexhaustible?", p. 11.

The Challenge of Environment 17

Between man's first harnessing animal power and his first step on the moon came increases in energy production through the control of water, wind, steam, electricity, and materials such as coal and petroleum. Each increase has in some way changed the activities of man. Today mankind has available an extraordinary amount of energy. Hopefully, this energy, which enabled man to walk on the moon, will be channelled to reduce the burden of the many still dependent on primitive types of energy.

eral reserves were higher in 1965 than in 1900; the reasons are the more efficient use of known reserves and the frequent discovery of new ones. In addition, technology has achieved, and presumably will continue to achieve, great triumphs in the development of alternatives or substitutes for known materials.

ENERGY

Muscles to horsepower. During most of the years that man has lived on this earth, his only source of energy was his own body. He was forced to depend on his muscles for transportation and for everything else he did. But his muscles are relatively weak. They supply only about one-third horsepower of energy. Gradually, however, man added to his supply of energy. He learned to harness the horse and to build water mills and windmills. More important was his invention in the 19th century of the steam engine, the

electric motor, and the gasoline engine. By the beginning of the 20th century, the automobile provided from 100 to 400 horsepower. Today we have jet planes that develop over 10,000 horsepower, and rockets for space exploration developing many million horsepower.

This tremendous increase in power production means an equally great increase in fuel consumption. Primitive man consumed no more energy than the 2000 or 3000 calories required to feed him each day. With the discovery of fire and the domestication of animals, daily energy consumption, including the wood burned for fuel and the food eaten by domestic animals, rose to about 10,000 calories. The figure jumped spectacularly with the spread of industrialization. By 1965, per capita energy consumption in the United States had reached about 192,000 calories daily.

This increase in energy is very significant because it has made possible a corresponding

NASA

increase in man's living standards. With more energy, man can produce more: more food, clothing, and housing, more of everything that goes into everyday living. That is why it is significant that since 1860 the annual amount of commercially-produced energy has been increased more than 25 times. During the same time, the world population doubled, so that the amount of energy available to each person in the world increased about 12 times.

Horsepower to megatons. This tremendous rise in energy production is a great boon for mankind, but it has created two serious problems. One is the unequal distribution of the energy now available. The Western world has been responsible for most of the great increase in the production and consumption of energy during the past century. So we find that the average man in North America today has 29 times as much energy to work for him as does a person in Asia. Even greater is the contrast between the two countries, the United States and India. The average man in the United States has 50 times as much energy at his command as a citizen of India. This explains the difference between meat once a day and meat once a month, between factories with machines and handicrafts with homemade tools, between farming with tractors and farming with oxen, between a life expectancy of over 65 years and a life expectancy of 40 years.

The other problems created by the large increase in power production is the depletion of sources of power. Until the Industrial Revolution of the 18th century, man got most of his energy from animals, wind, water, and wood. But in the past two centuries he has depended mainly on coal, oil, and natural gas. These are known as fossil fuels, having been formed in the crust of the earth millions of years ago. The consumption of these fuels has increased so sharply in recent decades that there is concern as to how long they will last. In fact, it is estimated that all the known coal, oil, and natural gas will hold out only until the year 2300.

There is no danger, however, that after 2300 all factories will close down and all homes will remain cold. A new type of energy, atomic energy, was successfully produced during World War II. This great achievement assures us that the spreading industrialization of the globe will continue. We can look forward to a second Industrial Revolution that will have much broader effects than the first, and that will be based on the atom rather than on coal. Furthermore, experts estimate that by 1975 the problem of how to harness the tremendous amount of energy produced by thermonuclear reaction, the principle on which the hydrogen bomb is based, will have been solved. When that day comes, all mankind will be able to use an inexhaustible source of power from the hydrogen in the earth's waters.

The Challenge of Environment 19

Reviewing the Essentials

Man and Geography

1. How has geography affected the history of the United States? The state in which you live? Your town?
2. Name and locate on a map the four river valleys in which man's earliest civilizations developed. Why did early civilizations develop in these valleys?
3. Give examples to show that geography does not, in all cases, influence the history of man.
4. Name five important geographic influences that affect man.

Climate

5. Name and locate on a map of the world the climate belts. How has each of these climate belts affected man?
6. Give examples of countries where development has been (a) retarded or (b) aided by climate. Give examples of countries whose people have responded to and overcome restrictions imposed by climate.

Soils

7. Name and locate on a map the major soil zones. What determines the quality of soil in any given area of the globe? Relate the soil zones to the climate belts.
8. Name and locate the largest population centers of the earth's surface. What do you conclude about soil and climate as geographic factors that influence the choice of a place to live? How much of the earth's surface do the large population centers comprise? How many of the world's people live there?
9. What percentage of the earth's surface does man cultivate? Where are the uncultivated land areas of the world?
10. What new techniques and processes is man using to increase the supply of food?
11. Cite evidence that soil depletion is a problem in the United States.
12. What is meant by "population explosion?" What is the present annual increase of the world's population? What is the world's population today? What is the projected figure for 2000 A.D.?

Minerals

13. Give examples to show how minerals have played an important role in man's development.
14. Minerals are unevenly distributed among the nations of the world. Illustrate. What minerals are essential for industrial development? What nations today have large reserves of strategic minerals? What nations face shortages?

Energy

15. Why was the shift from animal and muscle power to machine power a major achievement for man? When did this shift take place?
16. How much has commercially-produced energy increased each year since 1860? What problems have the increase in energy production created for 20th-century man? What are new sources of energy?

Explain, Identify, or Locate

hogan	energy	Hopi Indians	Himalayan Mountains
pueblo	tundra	Navaho Indians	Indo-Gangetic Plain
frost-free	cultivable	Chippewa Indians	high veld
climate	birth rate	Mesabi Range	Ruhr valley
precipitation	mineral reserves	Bulawayo	Great Plains

THE KEY FACTOR

LOCATION

Historic background. The final factor influencing the history of man is location. On first thought this would seem to be of little importance. What does it matter where people live so long as they enjoy a good climate, fertile soil, and a plentiful supply of minerals and energy sources? But the aborigines in certain parts of Australia had all these advantages, and yet they had not learned to grow food when the Europeans arrived in the late 18th century. In like manner, the Indians who inhabited the present-day United States had a very favorable physical environment but most of them lived by hunting and practiced a primitive form of agriculture, if any at all. By contrast, the peoples of the Old World, with no better climate, soil, and minerals, developed great civilizations thousands of years ago. These civilizations have spread in all directions over the globe. Meanwhile, the Australian aborigines have almost disappeared, and the Indians of the United States, now about 525,000 or a little more than half their total when the white man appeared, have been pushed aside by immigrants from the Old World who today number over 200 million.

What is the explanation for this great difference in the accomplishments of the people of the Old World compared with those of the Indians and aborigines? Is it that some peoples or races are superior to others? The answer of scientists is definitely no. In September 1952 a group of scientists from Holland, Sweden, Germany, France, England, and the United States issued a "Statement on the Nature of Race and Race Differences." This statement included the following sentence: "Available scientific knowledge provides no basis for believing

The Alaskan Eskimo was for many years excluded from the mainstream of trade and ideas. Today transportation and communication can in many ways counteract the affects of an isolated location.

that the groups of mankind differ in their innate capacity for intellectual and emotional development."[1] Thus, these scientists are saying that evidence suggests there is no such thing as superior and inferior races.

If race differences do not explain the remarkable contrasts in the achievements of various peoples, then what is the explanation? The answer is in large part location. By that we mean that the people who are likely to develop most rapidly are those who live in areas that are centrally located and who

The Key Factor 21

therefore have the opportunity to establish contacts and to exchange ideas with other people. In other words, *if other geographic factors are equal,* the key to human progress is accessibility and interaction. Those people who are the most accessible and who have the most opportunity to interact with other people will forge ahead. Those who are isolated and receive no stimulus from the outside will stand still for century after century.

EURASIA, THE HEARTLAND

Regions of Eurasia. It is not surprising, then, that the most advanced area in almost all of human history has been the great land mass known as Eurasia. This includes the continents of Europe and Asia, and also the part of Africa north of the Sahara. North Africa is included in Eurasia because it is cut off from the rest of Africa by the great Sahara Desert and therefore has usually had closer ties with Europe or the Middle East than with the southern part of its own continent.

Eurasia, as defined here, is the largest land mass on the globe. It spreads over two-fifths of the land area of the world and includes nine-tenths of the world's people. As a result there has been more accessibility and interaction in Eurasia than in other regions. Eurasia is the home of the earliest and most advanced civilizations of mankind and may be called the heartland of world history.

The other parts of our globe, those that are not Eurasian, make up three-fifths of the total land surface. They include the three principal regions of Sub-Saharan Africa, North and South America, and the continent-island of Australia. In contrast to Eurasia, all these regions are scattered and isolated. Sub-Saharan Africa is cut off by the great desert barrier, and the Americas and Australia are surrounded by the Atlantic and

Pacific Oceans. This isolation helps to explain why these three regions have had little influence on world history until about five hundred years ago. It was then that the Europeans began to expand all over the world and thus to bring the non-Eurasian regions into the main stream of world history.

In the remainder of this chapter we shall consider the historical results of the location of each of these regions in turn: Eurasia, Sub-Saharan Africa, the Americas, and Australia.

Middle East. The Eurasian heartland is so vast and all-embracing that it cannot be studied meaningfully as a unit. So we shall divide it into six areas: the Middle East, India, Europe, China, the Central Eurasian steppes, and the surrounding Seven Seas of Eurasia. The first four are important as the centers of great historical civilizations, the remaining two as channels of interaction among these civilizations.

We are dealing first with the Middle East because it is the most strategic and centrally-located area in Eurasia. The Middle East consists of the territory lying between the Soviet Union in the north, Afghanistan and Pakistan in the east, the Indian Ocean and the Sudan in the south, and Libya in the west. If you look at a map, you will see that this is a crossroads area. It is surrounded by Europe, Africa, India, and the Central Eurasian steppes. Because the Middle East, more than any other part of Eurasia, has enjoyed the advantages of accessibility and interaction, during most of human history it has been more advanced than any other part of the globe. It was in the Middle East that man first learned to till the soil, and from there the knowledge spread to other parts of Eurasia. It was in the Middle East also that man first built cities, formed governments, and learned to read and write, to do the things that distinguish civilized from

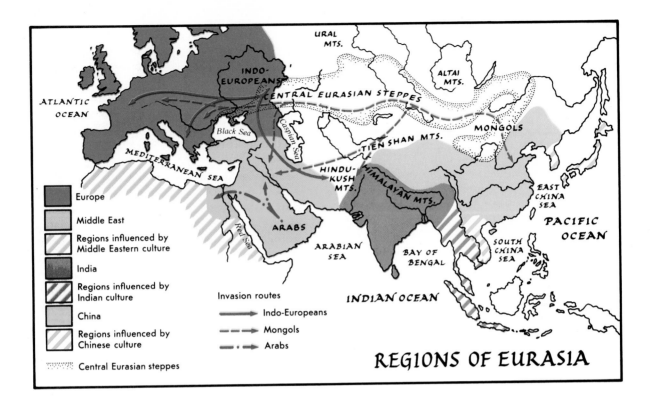

REGIONS OF EURASIA

Legend:
- Europe
- Middle East
- Regions influenced by Middle Eastern culture
- India
- Regions influenced by Indian culture
- China
- Regions influenced by Chinese culture
- Central Eurasian steppes

Invasion routes
- Indo-Europeans
- Mongols
- Arabs

uncivilized man. The Middle East also is the home of great religions, such as Christianity and Islam, which have spread not only throughout Europe but all over the world.

Because of its central location, the Middle East has served as a channel through which ideas and inventions and articles of trade have crossed back and forth from one region of Eurasia to another. We shall see later that in ancient and medieval times the silk of China and the spices of the East Indies went through Middle Eastern trade routes to Europe. In return, gold and silver were sent from Europe to the East. More recently, tea from China, jute from India, rubber from Indonesia, tin from Malaya, and oil from the Middle East itself, have passed through the Suez Canal to Europe. In the other direction, manufactured goods have been sent from

Europe. As for ideas and ways of doing things, many basic Chinese inventions such as paper, printing, gunpowder, and the compass went to Europe through the Middle East. In medieval times Europe, China, and India learned of ancient Greek and Roman writings through Arab translations of the originals.

It is true that in the modern age the Middle East has been surpassed by Europe. But this happened recently, only a few hundred years ago. We must remember that for several thousand years before that time the Middle East, largely because of its central location, led the world in the development of civilization.

India. From the Middle East we turn to India, the second most centrally located region of Eurasia. India is a vast subcontinent

Page from a bound section of the Koran, from Turkey, 16th century.

that juts down into the Indian Ocean, with the Arabian Sea on the west and the Bay of Bengal on the east. Its other borders are land bound. To the east lies Burma, separated from India by scrub and bamboo jungles and mountains. To the north are the highest mountains in the world, the Himalayas, and to the northwest are other mountains and deserts.

India's location, like that of the Middle East, has greatly affected its history. Important land and sea routes lead to other parts of Eurasia. Its central location with relation to the Indian Ocean gives it command of the sea lanes to Africa and Europe on the one hand, and to Southeast Asia and East Asia on the other. But India's land routes probably have been more important than her sea routes. In spite of desert, jungle, and mountain barriers, the subcontinent has never been as isolated as China. We shall see later that Alexander the Great invaded India in 327 B.C. and brought Greek influences in coinage, astronomy, architecture, and sculpture. Much greater was the influence of Islam which came from the Middle East about 1500 years later. Many of the people of northern India were converted to the new faith. So great were the differences between the Islamic way of life and that of the rest of India, whose religion was Hinduism, that the peninsula today is divided into the separate states of Hindu India and Islamic Pakistan.

India not only was affected by the outside world but in turn she affected it. To the Middle East and Europe she contributed knowledge of minerals, the game of chess, cotton, the domestic fowl, and probably the buffalo and rice. To China her main contribution was the religion of Buddhism. India's greatest influence was on Southeast Asia. For at least eight hundred years, from the 5th to the 13th centuries A.D., large Hindu kingdoms existed in Siam, Cambodia,

According to Indian legend chess was invented during the "Second Age of the World" to amuse the king of Ceylon. Its actual beginnings date to before the fourth century. The board above is of inlaid marble and the chessmen individually carved of ivory. Note that the elephants and camels upon which the figures sit are objects familiar to the Indian culture, just as the knights and bishops of our chessboard are more familiar to Western culture.

Java, and Sumatra. As a result, Hindu and Buddhist culture controlled Southeast Asia and left an imprint that has lasted to the present day. Southeast Asia was influenced later by Islamic culture from the Middle East and by Western culture from Europe. Nevertheless, during most of history, Southeast Asia has been a satellite of the great civilization that developed in India.

Europe. Europe is the extreme western tip of Eurasia. To the west and the north are the Atlantic and the Arctic Oceans. On the south is the Mediterranean Sea. On the east the borders cannot be clearly defined because there are no mountains or bodies of water. The Ural Mountains, the only range running from north to south, are low and worn-down; therefore, they do not serve as a barrier or a dividing line.

We of the West tend to exaggerate the size and the significance of Europe. For example, we often talk about Europe and Asia as though they were separate and comparable continents. Actually they are neither. Europe is merely a peninsula on the western tip of the Eurasian land mass. So we should compare Europe not with Asia, but rather with another Eurasian peninsula, that is, India. In fact, Europe and India are comparable to a remarkable degree. In area, the Indian Peninsula (including the states of India and Pakistan) is roughly four million

While India and the Middle East exchanged goods and learning and developed advanced civilizations, medieval European life revolved around the manor—depicted by European writers as isolated and offering little in the way of opportunity or excitement to the hard-working serf. The "Age of Exploration," however, brought drastic changes, and Europe became a part of the mainstream, and finally dominated the world.

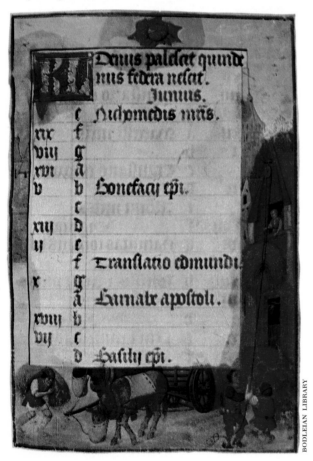

square kilometers (1,600,000 square miles), while Europe (excluding the Soviet Union) is about five million square kilometers (1,900,000 square miles). In population, the Indian Peninsula in 1966 had 616 millions and Europe 447 millions; these figures are now proportionately larger, of course. Finally, both peninsulas have a very large number of languages, but in each case about a half-dozen are spoken by the overwhelming majority of the people.

As in the case of the Middle East and India, Europe's location has greatly affected its development. Because it is on the extreme western edge of Eurasia, Europe remained until recent times an isolated, and therefore a backward, region compared to the Middle East and India. Only after 1500, when the Europeans expanded and gained control of the world ocean routes, did Europe suddenly have direct access to all parts of the world. When this happened, Europe changed overnight from a poor, out-of-the-way, and insignificant region to the wealthy and powerful center of an enormous world empire.

China. China is the most isolated of the four great centers of civilization in Eurasia. It is located at the eastern end of Eurasia, as Europe is at the western. It faces the vast Pacific Ocean as Europe does the Atlantic. In addition, China is cut off from the rest of Eurasia by great mountains, deserts, and steppes. By contrast Europe has easy access to other parts of Eurasia because the Ural Mountains present no obstacle, while the Mediterranean provides an open road to the Middle East and North Africa. This extreme isolation explains why the Chinese did not share experiences that affected other Eurasian peoples, experiences such as the conquests of Alexander and the expansion of Islam. It also explains why the Chinese never adopted the alphabet or used milk and milk products for food, as was done in the rest of Eurasia.

But China was never completely cut off as were the Americas and Australia until recent centuries. The Chinese did borrow such things as wheat, barley, the plow, the wheel, and the calendar, and in return gave some of her famous inventions, including paper, printing, gunpowder, silkworm cultivation, and the compass. Needless to say, China's isolation ended when the Europeans opened up the global ocean routes. From then on China, like Europe, had direct access to all parts of the world.

Finally, China resembles India in being the core of a broader area that it has historically dominated. This area includes Outer Mongolia, Sinkiang, Indochina, Tibet, the Korean Peninsula, and the Japanese islands. All these areas have developed under the shadow of the great Chinese civilization and have borrowed heavily from it. Chinese customs, arts, writing, and religion have left their stamp on the entire Far East to the present day.

Central Eurasian steppes. Thus far we have dealt with the four major centers of Eurasian civilization, the Middle East, India, Europe, and China. Now we turn to the Central Eurasian steppes and the Seven Seas of Eurasia. These geographic features have been extremely important because they have served as means of connection between the four Eurasian civilizations.

We shall consider first the great steppe zone which stretches from Manchuria in the Far East to the Danube valley in Central Europe. This region resembles the Great Plains of the American West. The soil is hard to cultivate, and there are climatic cycles of several wet years alternating with a run of drought years. But there is enough grass for pasture, so the steppe zone is better suited for stock raising than for farming.

Paper was made in China as early as 105 A.D., first from fish net and later from bark and rags. Printing developed in China in the fifth century, and there the first experiments with movable type were made in 1040 A.D. From China, paper and printing spread to the rest of the world.

The Eurasian steppes are divided into two parts, the separating line consisting of the Altai and the Tien Shan Mountains. To the west of that line the rainfall is sufficient for cattle raising and for some farming. The people in this western section were originally all of the Caucasoid race and spoke Indo-European languages. They spent most of their time with their herds of cattle and did a little farming on the side. Consequently they were not tied to the soil, and were always ready to pack up their great oxcarts and move into unknown country. The whole tribe participated in these migrations, women and children, as well as the warriors. The migrations naturally were towards the surrounding wealthy centers of civilization. So, as we shall see later, these Indo-European peoples repeatedly invaded India, the Middle East, and Europe.

To the east of the Altai-Tien Shan Mountains are the Mongolian plains. These are higher and drier than the steppes to the west, so the pastures can support sheep, camels, and horses, but not cattle. The people who live here are Mongoloids, rather than Caucasoids, and they speak Turko-Tatar languages rather than Indo-European. At first these Mongols were a harmless people who lived in obscurity on their broad plains. They depended on their huge flocks of sheep to provide them with milk, meat, and wool. But about 2000 B.C. they tamed the horse, a development which changed them completely, as it did the American Plains Indians when they got horses from the Spaniards. The Mongols, like the Indians, became fierce mounted warriors. They developed a type of saddle and stirrups which enabled them to control their horses perfectly while having their hands free for shooting arrows and charging with their lances. Every Mongol warrior had a string of horses; thus on a campaign he could change from one to the other and keep on riding, if necessary, at full speed for two days and nights. If provisions gave out, he could use some of his horses for food, eating their flesh and drinking their blood and fermented milk. We shall see later that these fast-moving Mongol warriors became the scourge of their neighbors, as did the Plains Indians of the United States when they acquired the horse. Thus in the 13th century under their famous leader, Genghis Khan, they conquered a vast empire stretching from the Pacific Ocean to the Black Sea.

In normal times the nomads of the Eurasian steppes were too weak to invade the centers of civilization. India, China, Europe, and the Middle East had much greater manpower and also had large walled cities which could resist attacks by raiding horsemen. But occasionally the nomads were able to overrun great empires that had existed for many centuries. Usually this happened at times when a great leader appeared to unite the nomads, and when, at the same time, a neighboring empire happened to be declining and weak. On such occasions the nomads would burst in and kill and pillage. Sometimes they would pass on, and at other times they stayed and organized new states of their own. These nomadic invaders, it should be noted, came not only from the steppes of Eurasia but also from the deserts of Arabia. In fact, the earliest human civilizations on the banks of the Nile and the Tigris-Euphrates were attacked more frequently by Arabs from the desert than by Indo-Europeans or Mongols from the steppes.

We have given detailed attention to the Eurasian steppes because they had two important effects on history. In the first place they served as a channel for interaction among the centers of civilization. This was particularly true when the nomads were able to establish large empires, such as that of Genghis Khan, which included the whole of the steppes, together with China, the Middle East, and Russia. On such occasions, both goods and ideas were exchanged back and forth along the steppe highway, from Europe to India, and from China to the Middle East. In the second place, the steppes, as well as the deserts, also affected history by introducing new peoples and establishing new empires. In this book we have divided Eurasian history into three periods, ancient, classical, and medieval. We shall see that the Mongol, Indo-European, and Arab invaders were largely responsible for this

Today the part of the "Silk Road" crossing the Hindu Kush Mountains seems barren and desolate, yet during the past 1000 years this road has seen thousands of caravans carrying goods between East and West, and invasion partys led by Alexander the Great, Genghis Khan, and Tamerlane.

division. By destroying old empires and organizing new ones, they cleared the way for the passing of one age and the coming of another.

Seven Seas of Eurasia. Just as the steppes provide land connections so the Seven Seas of Eurasia provide water connections among the Eurasian civilizations. Stretching from Europe in the west to China in the east, they are the Northeast Atlantic, the Mediterranean, the Red Sea, Arabian Sea, Bay of Bengal, South China Sea, and East China Sea. Of these seven seas, Westerners are most familiar with the Northeast Atlantic and the Mediterranean, but the other five have been more important for a longer period in the history of Eurasia. They wash the shores of ancient empires and are also free of icebergs, fog, and other hindrances found in more northerly seas. In addition, they are connected with one another. Oriental seamen could and did sail from China to India and beyond to East Africa, Mesopotamia, and Egypt.

Europeans, on the other hand, were restricted by a thin strip of sand separating the Red Sea from the Mediterranean. Before the discovery of the route around Africa in the 15th century and the building of the Suez Canal in the 19th, Europe was barred from the main routes of Eurasian trade. But after the great voyages of discovery by DaGama and others, Europeans took the lead. The result was a new era in world history. For the first time the entire globe was united. For the first time the age-old separation of the Eurasian and non-Eurasian portions of the globe was ended. Henceforth man no longer lived in regional isolation. All parts of the world were now brought together by the new ocean routes opened up by the European discoverers.

Turning now from Eurasia, we shall consider the regions of the non-Eurasian world.

REGIONS OF NON-EURASIAN WORLD

Sub-Saharan Africa. Sub-Saharan Africa was largely isolated from the Eurasian civilizations by the great Sahara Desert and by the marshes and cataracts of the Nile. This isolation prevented Sub-Saharan Africa from advancing as rapidly as North Africa. On the other hand the isolation was by no means as complete as in the case of the Americas and Australia. In ancient times the Phoenicians, Greeks, and Romans all traded with Negro Africa. In medieval times the Arabs went far into the continent, spreading the Islamic

Although in some ways isolated, Sub-Saharan Africa did share many Eurasian developments. An illustration from David Livingstone's Last Journals *shows African smiths forging iron hoes by methods learned from the Middle East.*

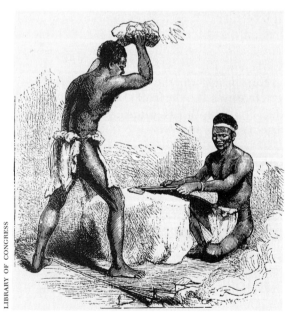

religion and establishing camel trade routes from the Mediterranean to central Africa. African people were greatly affected by these contacts with Eurasia. They learned iron manufacturing from the Middle East. They improved their agriculture with the various domesticated plants and animals that were brought to them. And the Islamic faith helped them in organizing a series of great African kingdoms in the medieval ages.

The significance of these Eurasian contacts is indicated by the fact that the level of development reached by the various African peoples depended on their proximity to Eurasia. The most primitive were the Pygmies and the Bushmen (Hottentots) at the southern tip of Africa; the most advanced were those in the Sudan, immediately to the south of the Sahara. The latter people had traded with Eurasian lands for centuries, so that they were not completely dumbfounded, as the American Indians were, when the Europeans arrived by sea. They did not look upon the white man, with his guns and horses and ships, as a god. They already knew all these objects because of their long-established contacts with the Muslim world. This familiarity made it much easier for the Africans to resist European pressures. In fact they were able to prevent the Europeans from penetrating into the interior of Africa until the late 19th century, whereas in the Americas and Australia the Europeans were able to spread far inland soon after their arrival. We shall see later that the Africans were aided in their resistance to European penetration by natural hazards such as inhospitable climate and tropical diseases. But most important was the fact that they were more advanced than the American Indians and the Australian aborigines. Thanks to their interaction with Eurasia, they were better organized and better armed, and were therefore able to keep the Europeans at arm's-length until the 19th century.

The Americas. The famous French explorer, La Salle, opened up the heart of North America in 1682 when he paddled across the Great Lakes and down the Mississippi River to the Gulf of Mexico. And 150 years later North and South America had been colonized by Europeans, and the United States had gained its independence, whereas there were still only a few European posts on the coast of Africa. We have seen that one reason for this difference is to be found in the dissimilarity of the geographic environments of Africa and North America. The climate in most of the Americas was more suitable for Europeans than the climate in most of Africa. The smooth-flowing rivers of the Americas made it easy to penetrate the continent, whereas most African rivers have waterfalls which blocked the path for explorers. But more important is the fact that, on the whole, the American Indians were not as advanced as the African peoples. And they were not as advanced because their contacts with the peoples of Eurasia had ended about five thousand years before, when the last major immigration of Mongoloid peoples had crossed the Bering Strait or the Aleutian bridge to the New World.

Despite their isolation, the American Indians can be credited with many accomplishments. Outstanding was their domestication of many plants that are now used throughout the world. The most important of these are maize or corn, beans, squashes, tomatoes, potatoes, chocolate, tobacco, and cotton. In all, about as many plants were domesticated in the New World as in all of Eurasia, a remarkable achievement for the American Indians. Equally remarkable was the high level of civilization reached by three of the Indian peoples. One was the Mayas of present-day Yucatan and Guatemala, who developed a fine architecture and sculpture and advanced far in mathematics and astronomy. The second civilization was that

Along with gold, Spanish conquistadores brought back from the New World over 50 varieties of plants domesticated by the American Indians. This Spanish manuscript illustrates methods of cultivation as well as an amazing new crop.

of the Aztecs located in present-day Mexico. They developed an advanced form of government, including a judicial and tax system, an official religion, and a periodic census for military and tax purposes. Finally the Incas of Peru were outstanding for their remarkable achievements in construction, including splendid roads, monuments, and irrigation systems.

And yet, as we shall see, all these civilizations were easily overthrown by a handful of Spaniards in the 16th century. A principal reason for this was the long isolation of the Indians which left them far behind the European newcomers. When the Spaniards arrived about 1500 A.D., the most advanced Indians had reached the level of Western

The Australian aborigine is in many ways unchanged despite the influx of Europeans. He has, however, accepted those aspects of Western life which add to his comfort and pleasure. Here a tribal headman uses Western paint to decorate such traditional tools as spears and boomerangs.

BAGLIN (MONKMEYER PRESS PHOTO SERVICE)

Europe of 1500 B.C., and of the Middle East of 3500 B.C. For example, the Indians made their tools and weapons only of stone, wood, or bone. They did work with metal, but they used it merely for ornamental purposes. The only ships they built were canoes and rafts. For land transportation they depended mostly on the human back. They did use the llama and the alpaca in the Andes, but these animals could not carry heavy loads. As for the wheel, the Indians knew about it, but they considered it a toy.

In other words the Indians lagged behind particularly in matters of technology. This, of course, was a fatal handicap when the Spaniards appeared with sailing ships, cannon, muskets, and steel swords and armor. Consequently the Spaniards easily overran the most advanced civilizations, the Maya, Aztec, and Inca. Before long the victorious white man had taken over the choicest lands and had forced the Indians into reservations. In parts of Central and South America the Indians were too numerous to be crowded

into reservations. So they remained on their land but were forced to work as virtual serfs for their new European masters.

Australia. Turning finally to Australia, we find here the most isolated large body of land on the globe. Consequently, its aboriginal population had had no contact with the outside world since about 50,000 years before when they crossed over the narrow straits from Indonesia to Australia. It is not surprising that these isolated people were far behind the American Indians in their level of development, and still further behind the African peoples and the Eurasians. The aborigines did not know how to grow food so they had to depend entirely on the animals they hunted and the plants they collected. Their weapons and tools were made entirely of wood, and they were completely ignorant of pottery. They lived in bands, consisting of families that camped together and roamed over a well-defined territory. They had no tribes, chiefs, courts, or other forms of political organization. They also had no clothes; what they wore on their bodies was for decoration rather than for protection against the weather. Because they used dogs as blankets, a chilly night was for them a "three-dog night," while a "five-dog night" meant really cold weather.

These aborigines obviously had no chance when the Europeans finally found Australia in the late 18th century. There were only about 300,000 aborigines in the whole continent, and they had no weapons to match the terrifying "fire-sticks" of the invaders. The British settlers, many of whom were lawless convicts, treated the natives with great brutality. Sometimes they even organized parties which hunted down and shot the aborigines as though they were animals. Many more of the natives died from the effects of liquor and the diseases that the white man brought with him. By 1961 the number of the unfortunate aborigines had dropped from the original 300,000 to 40,000, and most of these survivors lived in the dry interior that was of no use to the newcomers.

From this survey we can see that geographic location explains to a great extent the course of world history. It explains why the Eurasian peoples were able to develop civilizations that have lasted to the present day, while the non-Eurasian peoples lagged behind in most fields. Because of this global leadership of Eurasia, the next two units will deal mostly with Eurasian history to 1500. After that date the Europeans expanded all over the world and ended the age-old separation between Eurasia and the other continents. Consequently, global history began in 1500. After that date, man no longer lived in regional isolation as he had from the beginning of time. The European discoveries began to make neighbors of all peoples, regardless of where they lived. Since 1500, then, global unity replaces regional isolation as the distinguishing feature of world history. For this reason, Unit Four, dealing with the period after 1500, is entitled "Man Lives in Global Unity," in contrast to the preceding unit entitled "Man Lives in Regional Isolation."

Reviewing the Essentials

Location

1. Name and locate on the map the areas included in Eurasia. How much surface does Eurasia compose? Why is Eurasia referred to as the "heartland of world history?"

2. In what ways do non-Eurasian areas of the earth differ from the Eurasian? When did the non-Eurasian parts begin to influence world history?

Eurasia, The Heartland

3. Name and locate the six areas included in the Eurasian heartland. Why has the Middle East been the most advanced part of our globe for the greater part of recorded history? Give evidence of an advanced civilization in the Middle East.

4. How has India's location affected its history and made it possible for India to influence other peoples?

5. How has the location of Europe influenced its development?

6. In what ways does China's location differ from that of the other great centers of civilization? How has China's location affected its development and that of its neighbors?

7. Locate the Eurasian steppes. How have they affected history? Name and locate the Seven Seas of Eurasia. Why are they important to Eurasian civilizations?

Non-Eurasian World

8. Why did the non-Eurasian people of Sub-Saharan Africa, North and South America, and Australia have little or no influence on world history until after 1500 A.D.?

9. Describe the accomplishments of the American Indians.

Explain, Identify, or Locate

interaction	steppe zone	Aztecs	Indochina
accessibility	Australian aborigines	Bay of Bengal	Danube Valley
trade routes	Alexander the Great	Java	Aleutian bridge
Hinduism	Genghis Khan	Ural Mountains	East China Sea

UNIT ACTIVITIES

1. Individual students or groups might prepare a report on food and population pressures for presentation to class. Include in your preparation: (a) a statement of the problem with data for selected nations; (b) an analysis of the reasons for the current world problem; (c) the four transitional stages of population growth and characteristics of each stage; (d) the outlook for underdeveloped countries; (e) alternative solutions for (a) above. For information consult Philip Hauser, *Population Dilemma* (New York: Prentice-Hall, 1963); *Readings in World History* (Boston: Allyn and Bacon, Inc., 1970), "Man and Mother Earth," pp. 2–8; "Man and Food: Can They Be Balanced?", pp. 8–11; "Man's Resources: Exhaustible Or Inexhaustible?", pp. 11–25.

2. Consult *World Almanac or Information Please Almanac* for data on world population figures. Prepare a line graph showing world population for selected years, along with an analysis of the data given.

3. Prepare graphs showing population trends for selected years for these countries: United States, England, Canada, France, India, Japan. Also prepare an analysis of the data given.

4. Show on an outline map of the world the transitional stages of population growth at the present time for the following nations or regional areas: Africa, Mexico, Brazil, India, China, Indonesia, Middle East, Soviet Union, Japan, Argentina, United States, Western Europe.

5. Prepare an outline map of the world that shows the caloric intake of each of the groups given in the preceding activity. See the bibliography for sources of information.

6. Several groups of students might read supplementary materials on the following questions and present their findings to the class as a basis for class discussion:

a. Can present world resources support larger populations? Where are the resources in relation to the needs? Can science provide man with new and needed sources of food, metals, and energy?

b. Why, in spite of all our technological progress, are there more poverty-stricken people in the world today than there were fifty years ago?

Consult references listed in the bibliography under population-food problem. Also see: *Readings in World History* (Boston: Allyn and Bacon, Inc., 1970), "Man and Food: Can They Be Balanced?", pp. 8–11; and "Man's Resources: Exhaustible or Inexhaustible?", pp. 11–25.

7. "A nation writes its record on the land, and a civilization writes its record on the land." Support this statement with evidence given in the following: Fairfield Osborn, *Our Plundered Planet* (Boston: Little, Brown, 1948); *Readings in World History* (Boston: Allyn and Bacon, Inc., 1970), "Man and Mother Earth," pp. 2–8.

SELECTED READING

● The constant use of an atlas is a necessity in studying world history. Three of the best general atlases are *Goode's World Atlas* (Chicago: Rand McNally, 1964); *Advanced Reference Atlas* (New York: C. S. Hammond, 1964); and J. E. Williams, *World Atlas* (Englewood Cliffs, New Jersey: Prentice-Hall, 1958). Especially suited to this course is R. R. Palmer, *Atlas of World History* (Chicago: Rand McNally, 1957), which is available in complete and abridged editions.

● There are several general studies of geography that can be used for reference purposes, including J. H. Bradley, *World Geography* (Boston: Ginn, 4th ed., 1964); L. O. Packard, B. Overton, and B. D. Wood, *Geography of the World* (New York: Macmillan, 4th rev. ed.); and Z. A. Thralls, *The World Around Us* (New York: Harcourt, Brace & World, rev. ed., 1965).

● Illustrated studies of various aspects of man's physical world are to be found in the following series published by Garden City Books of New York City: J. Fisher, *The Wonderful World* (1956); J. Fisher, *The Wonderful World of the Sea* (1957); J. Fisher, *The Wonderful World of the Air* (1957); L. Hogben, *The Wonderful World of Energy* (1957); F. Boyd-Orr, The Wonderful World of Food (1958). Rachel L. Carson's *The Sea Around Us* (New York: Oxford University Press, 1951), is a popular and beautifully written book on the unsuspected treasures of the sea. Very interesting also is Alonzo Pond, *The Desert World* (New York: Thomas Nelson, 1962).

● For the geology and minerals of our globe, two clear accounts are given in H. and N. Schneider, *Rocks, Rivers and the Changing Earth* (New York: William R. Scott, 1952); and F. Reinfeld, *Treasures of the Earth* (New York: Sterling, 1954). The significance of atomic energy is analyzed in the pamphlet published by the Foreign Policy Association: W. B. Kaempffert, *The Many Uses of the Atom* (Headline Series No. 117).

● Biographies of atomic scientists are provided by S. R. Riedman, *Men and Women Behind the Atom* (New York, Abelard-Schuman, 1959). A good survey of the history of energy is given by L. S. de Camp, *Man and Power: The Story of Power from the Pyramids to the Atomic Age* (New York: Golden Press, 1961).

● A brief analysis of the problems caused by a rapidly expanding population and a slowly expanding food supply may be found in two articles in the September, 1963 *Scientific American:* "Population" by Kingsley Davis and "Food" by Nevin Scrimshaw. Other useful pamphlets are *World Population Problems* (Headline Series No. 174, December, 1965) by Philip Hauser; and M. S. Stewart, *A New Look at Our Crowded World* (New York: Public Affairs Pamphlet No. 393, 1966).

FURTHER READING

● Two general works which contain valuable material are J. P. Cole, *Geography of World Affairs* (Penguin, rev. ed., 1963) and O. W. Freeman and J. W. Morris, *World Geography* (New York: McGraw-Hill, rev. 1965). A mine of information concerning the globe, man, world industry, agriculture, population, etc., is W. S. and E. S. Woytinsky, *World Population and Production* (New York: Twentieth Century Fund, 1953).

● A good summary of the present world production of energy is available in Werner, Gottlieb, Helstrom, and Stewart, *Energy Does Matter* (New York: Walker, 1964); and Wilson, Mitchell, and the Editors of Life, *Energy* (Life Science Library, N.Y., Time Inc., 1963).

● On the population-food problem, there is the paperback by D. H. Wrong, *Population* (New York: Random House, rev. ed., 1961); the dramatic account of how man throughout the globe is wag-

ing war against hunger, N. W. Desrosier, *Attack on Starvation* (Westport, Ct.: Avi, 1961); W. and P. Paddock, *Hungry Nations* (Boston: Little, Brown, 1964). UNESCO has published a series of six pamphlets on "Food and People": (1) Margaret Mead, *Food and the Family;* (2) P. Kihss, *UN Sets the Table;* (3) A. Mayer, *Food and Social Program;* (4) S. Krolikowski, *Distribution of the World's Food;* (5) A. Myrdal and P. Vincent, *Are There Too Many People?;* (6) C. E. Kellogg, *Food, Soil, and People.* (These pamphlets, together with a Discussion Guide, are available from UNESCO for $1.50 plus 15¢ postage.) Also the pamphlet by A. P. Chew, *U.S. Agriculture in the World Food Situation,* is available free of charge from the United States National Commission for UNESCO, Department of State, Washington, D.C. 20520.

● On the same subject, the Food and Agriculture Organization (FAO, Rome, Italy) has published several studies, including *Development Through Food*, Basic Study No. 2, 1962; *Population and Food Supplies*, Basic Study No. 7, 1962; and *Possibilities of Increasing World Food Production*, Basic Study No. 10, 1963. The U.S. Department of Agriculture has published several useful studies including the following: *Man, Land, and Food* (Foreign Agricultural Economic Report No. 11, 1963); *The World Food Budget 1970* (Foreign Agricultural Economic Report No. 19, 1964); and *Increasing World Food Output* (Foreign Agricultural Economic Report No. 25, 1965). Finally there is much good material about food and agriculture in both its national and international aspects in the U.S. Department of Agriculture *Yearbook of Agriculture*, 1964, entitled *Farmer's World*.

A SURVEY

II OF WORLD

HISTORY

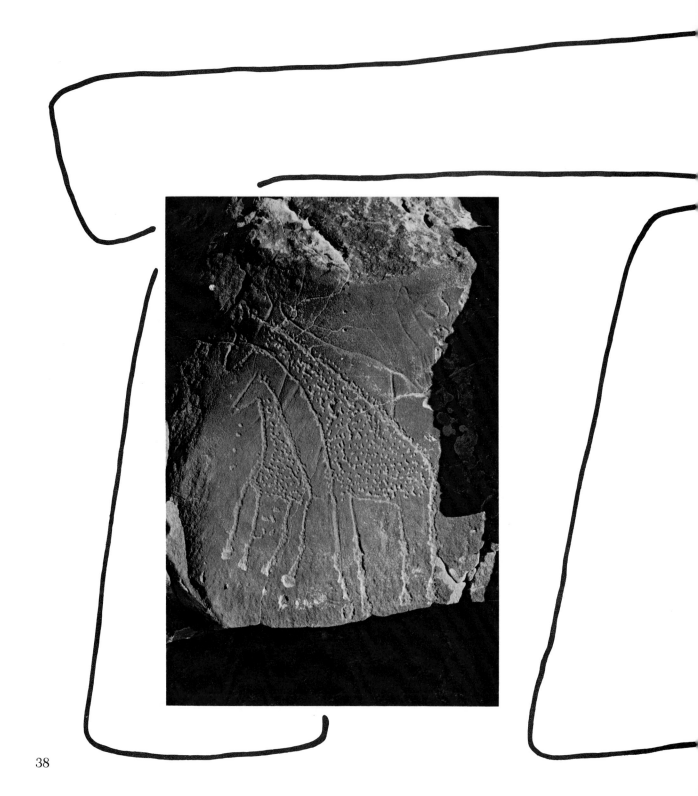

38

MAN BEFORE CIVILIZATION

However crude and ineffective primitive cultures were in their control over the forces of nature, they had worked out a system of human relationships that has never been equalled since the Agricultural Revolution. The warm, substantial bonds of kinship united man with man. There were no lords or vassals, serfs or slaves, in tribal society. . . . There were no time clocks, no bosses or overseers, in primitive society, and a two-week vacation was not one's quota of freedom for a year.

Leslie A. White

MAN, RACE, AND SOCIETY

MAN THE NEWCOMER

According to the latest estimates, man and his direct ancestors have been living on the earth for about two million years. To us, this may seem an unimaginably long period, and yet man is a very recent newcomer. The proportionate length of his existence is shown by the line drawing on this and the following page.

Our planet is probably about five *billion* years old. Yet, not until about two billion years ago did any form of life make an appearance. The first form of life consisted of single-celled creatures such as amoebas.

Only very gradually did more complex forms of life evolve from these primitive early organisms. Jellyfish and other primitive fish appeared about 400 *million* years ago. Then, about 300 million years ago living things passed from the sea to the land where they developed more rapidly. Within 100 million years dinosaurs and other giant reptiles were roaming the earth. Finally, about 150 million years ago the first mammals appeared, and then, 148 million years later (only two million years ago), man appeared.

Early man. Scientists call early men *Hominidae* or hominids. Many distinct types have been discovered. The oldest are *Zinjanthropus* (an australopithecine or near-man) and *Homo habilis*, discovered by the archaeologist Louis Leakey, in Olduvai Gorge, Tanzania. Both are hominids, but they were very different despite living in the same area at the same time, about 2,000,000 years ago. *Zinjanthropus* did not develop and died out. *Homo habilis*, by contrast, is the ancestor of later hominids, collectively known as *Homo erectus*. Examples of *Homo erectus* include Java man, Peking man, and Heidelberg man,

Earth formed 5 billion years ago

all named after the region in which their fossil remains have been found.

The next major step in the evolution of man's ancestors was the appearance of Neanderthal man, whose remains were found first in the German valley of that name. It is now known that he inhabited large areas of Europe, Asia, and North Africa. Neanderthal man developed directly into modern man or *Homo sapiens*, the species to which we all belong. The best-known prehistoric example of *Homo sapiens* is Cro-Magnon man whose bones were discovered in caves of the Dordogne Valley in France.

Cro-Magnon man, who lived around 30,-000 B.C., was probably the inventor of the bow and arrow, and carved and molded figures of bone, horn, and clay. He is the creator of the lively and brilliant wall paintings found in the caves of southern France and northern Spain. The quality and number of these works lead us to believe that the painters were specialists, freed from the necessity of hunting food. They must have worked in the pitch-black cave interiors with oil lamps and used ladders to reach the ceilings. The reds and yellows and blacks of their bison and mammoths and reindeer, drawn with great skill and feeling, glow vividly even after thousands of years.

THE RACES OF MANKIND

Cro-Magnon man is considered by anthropologists to be a member of the same species of man to which we belong, *Homo sapiens*. This name is given to all peoples with a recognizably human skeleton and a brain measuring over 1100 cubic centimeters. All hu-

COURTESY OF THE AMERICAN MUSEUM OF NATURAL HISTORY

One-celled animals
Less than
2 billion years ago

Fish appear
1 billion

700 million

500 million

400 million

Amphibians appear

Reptiles appear

Mammals appear

100 million

Man appears
2 million
years ago

mankind today belongs to the family *Homo sapiens*, but within the species it is possible to distinguish three main groups or races. These are the Mongoloid, the Caucasoid, and the Negroid. The races tend to shade into one another, and there is an infinite variety of physical types within each of the three groups.

Three major races. The Mongoloids are the most numerous race, making up roughly half the world's population. In this group are a number of types such as the Asiatic Mongoloids, the Oceanic Mongoloids, and the Indians of the Americas.

Next to the Mongoloids in number are the Caucasoids. Under this heading come many types, including the Nordic peoples of Northern Europe, the Alpine peoples of Central Europe, the Mediterranean peoples of Southern Europe, and the inhabitants of India, who have dark skin but whose other characteristics are Caucasoid. Remnants of

The line covering this and the preceding page illustrates the length of time the earth has been in existence, about five billion years. Not until two billion years ago did the first living creature appear, indicated by the change in color. Each additional change in color indicates a major development in the evolution of living things. Not until two million years ago, the very end of the line on this page, did man appear. The pictures represent a possible evolutionary sequence during that period—a very short time both in relation to the age of the earth and the age of living things.

Descending from the single species, homo sapiens, *these children illustrate some of the physical characteristics common to the three main racial groups which, because of mutation, isolation, and adaptation, evolved from that one species.*

old Caucasoid strands have been found in various parts of Siberia, and in Japan where they are called the Ainus; it is possible that certain peoples of Ceylon and Australia also sprang from the Caucasoid source. The least numerous of the racial groups is the Negroid, most of whose members are to be found in the culture region of Sub-Saharan Africa; though many are now in the Americas as the descendants of slaves who arrived with the earliest settlers.

Characteristics of races. The classification of races is based on certain physical characteristics such as hair form, and eye and skin color. Hair, for example, is usually completely straight among the Mongoloids; among the Caucasoids, it is likely to twist at intervals, making curls or waves; among the Negroids, it has a continuous curl. At the inner corner of the Mongoloid eye is an epicanthic fold of skin which gives the slant-eyed or almond-eyed appearance so often

noted. Actually, the shape and angle of placement of the Mongoloid eye are the same as the shape and angle of placement of the Caucasoid eye. The three species are also characterized by a wide variation in pigment, shown most noticeably in skin color. Brown granules are present in the skin of all peoples; it is the difference in amount that determines whether the skin will look pinkish or brownish. Hair and eye color are also the result of pigmentation. If the hair lacks brown pigment, it will be blond. Eyes are most often brown, but in the lightest eyes where the brown pigment is lacking, the color is reflected from the purple layer at the back of the iris to give the eye its blue shade.

It cannot be emphasized too strongly that not every member of each race has all the characteristics of the racial group, that all racial classification is relative and inexact. Here then is a workable definition of the term "race": A race is a group of human beings sharing a certain set of physical traits which are passed on biologically from generation to generation, and which distinguish the group from others. The important point to note about this definition is that race is a biological fact.* And yet it is often, and sometimes tragically, confused with language, religion, and nation.

What race is not. Language, for example, is a cultural rather than a biological trait, something that can be taken up, changed, and dropped from generation to generation. Language is easily passed on from one people to another by migration or conquest. Therefore a common tongue does not necessarily imply a common race, as we can see in our own country where one language is spoken by many racial strains who have gathered here from all over the world. Contrariwise, a variety of languages does not necessarily mean a variety of races. The American Indians before the coming of the white man were of one racial strain, the Mongoloid, and yet they spoke dozens of unrelated languages.

Race is also confused with religion, as is the case of the Jews, or Hebrews. You may have heard people refer to the Jewish race. This is an erroneous use of the word race, because the Jews are simply a group of people who profess Judaism, or the Jewish religion. It is true that the Jews of Biblical times resided in Palestine and belonged either to the Semitic or Armenoid branches of the Mediterranean Caucasoids. In the centuries since then, Judaism has spread widely, and now it is possible to find members of all three large racial groups who profess the Jewish faith. In the same way that there are Negroid, Mongoloid, and Caucasoid Christians, so there are Negroid, Mongoloid, and Caucasoid Jews. This is seen in a striking

way when you look at pictures of the people emigrating to the Jewish state of Israel today. There are blond Jews from northern Europe who look like Scandinavians or Slavs, and swarthy Jews from Middle Eastern countries who look like the Arabs among whom they lived for centuries.*

Race is also frequently identified with nation. Today there are English, French, and German nations, but not English, French, and German races. England, for example, was occupied in very early times by Nordics, Mediterraneans, and Alpines. Later it was invaded by Romans, Saxons, Norwegians, Danes, and Normans. Thus, instead of one physical type in England, we see there an excellent example of a mosaic of Caucasoid subraces. Similar mixtures are to be found in most parts of the world. Most striking is the case of the United States; its people are Americans, but some belong to the Caucasoid race, others to the Negroid race, and still others are members of the Mongoloid race.

The myth of racial purity. At this point we should note that just as there are no pure nations, so there are no pure races. Many people believe that at one time pure races did exist and that in recent centuries they have become mixed by intermarriage. This belief lacks support from science. Instead, most scientists agree that the different races descended from a common stock, and that all mankind belongs to the same species, *Homo sapiens*, as we have seen.

THE EVOLUTION OF MAN

If it is true that all men belong to the same species, we may sensibly ask, "Why are most people in eastern Asia Mongoloids, most people south of the Sahara Negroids, most

* See *Readings in World History*, "Are There Superior and Inferior Races?", p. 27 (Boston: Allyn and Bacon, Inc., 1970).

* See *Readings in World History*, "What We Think of Other People," p. 29.

people in Europe and the New World Caucasoids?"

Darwin's theory. One answer to this question was worked out in large part by Charles Darwin. As a young man at Cambridge University in England, Darwin did not do very well in his studies because he spent most of his time collecting and studying animals and insects. One of his professors recognized the importance of this research and found him a position as naturalist on the British government ship, *Beagle*. Between 1831 and 1836 this ship did scientific work along the coast of South America and among the South Sea Islands. Darwin collected thousands of specimens and noticed many variations of individual plants and animals. On the isolated Galápagos Islands, for example, he found species that obviously had come from ancestors on the mainland but had somehow grown different. This seemed to contradict the old theory that all forms of life were created at one time and continued unchanged thereafter. But the question remained, how and why did variation occur?

After 23 years of research and thought, he set forth his answer to the question in the celebrated and influential book, *On the Origin of Species*, published in 1859. In this work, Darwin stated that all species, including man, are not the result of separate special acts of creation. Rather they are the products of a long process of evolution, which consists of these intermediate steps: mutation, natural selection, and isolation and adaptation. There had been some attempts centuries earlier to explain the process of evolution but Darwin's was the first systematic and tenable theory.

Mutation. Mutation is a sudden and rare change in the structure in one of the genes that determine physical appearance. Genes are the factors which determine the nature of cells. A mutation might cause the child of fair-skinned parents to be born with darker skin. Since a mutation is passed on to the next generation, some of the descendants of the child would also be dark skinned. But how does mutation, which occurs in an individual, affect a whole species such as man?

Natural selection. Darwin's answer was "natural selection," by which he meant that an environment will operate to favor or "select" those physical characteristics in individuals which help them to withstand conditions of life. For instance, in a tropical climate the individual with a darker skin is better protected from the sun's rays. He has a better chance of survival. The environment operates to "select" those with dark skins. This process of natural selection could, over thousands of years, produce a predominantly dark-skinned people. This is how Darwin and those who accept his fundamental idea of evolution account for the development of racial characteristics.

Isolation and adaptation. Finally, the present-day races were probably formed, according to this theory, not only by mutation and natural selection, but also by isolation and adaptation. Primitive men had little contact with one another. Population movement and mixture were not as common as they are today. Isolation made it possible for new traits produced by mutation and selection to become predominant in today's major races. As a group lived in isolation in a given area for a long period of time, the chances are that it "adapted" itself to that area by a certain amount of physical change. If the area happened to have a very warm climate with a hot sun, then the individuals with dark skins were more likely to survive. Thus the group over thousands of years would become darker in skin color.

Darwin considered all animal life to be steps in a series of evolutionary changes from single-celled organisms. Above the theory is illustrated with reference to finches, arranged by Darwin to show their pattern of evolution.

We have seen, then, *one* explanation of how the various races of mankind gradually appeared as the result of mutation, natural selection, and isolation and adaptation. Most scientists support the basic parts of the Darwinian theory, but it must be emphasized that many questions remain unanswered. There are numerous gaps in the theoretical sequence of evolution, especially in its early phases. For such reasons, some people prefer to support the theory of direct creation.

MAN AS A FOOD GATHERER

Man's unique brain. Three abilities distinguish man from the animals about him: the ability to speak, to use fire, and to make tools. How did he learn to do these things that launched him on his fateful career of mastering the universe? The answer is that he had a superior brain. This does not mean, however, that man was born at the beginning with a brain large enough to enable him to accomplish everything that he has to the present day. Rather it was a circular process. His superior brain enabled him to learn to do new things, and as he did them he stimulated his brain and increased it in size and complexity. This increase in turn made possible new activities by man, which further developed his brain. In this manner the process continued to the present day when

Man, Race, and Society 45

man has gone on from the control of fire to the control of the atom and space travel.

The basic abilities. Why was the ability to speak, to use tools, and to control fire so important for early man? Speech enabled him to pass on his accumulated knowledge and experiences to successive generations. Fire made it possible for him to cook his food and to scare away wild beasts. Because it could be used to heat the interior of caves, man was now able to endure colder regions. Finally tools made it easier for early man to kill game, catch fish, and dig for roots and other food.

The first tools that man used consisted of any conveniently shaped stones, sticks, bones, and shells that he happened to find. Next he learned to improve these tools by changing their shape in order to make them more useful. He sharpened sticks with fire and reshaped stones by knocking and chipping. With his improved stone tools he was able to make hooks and harpoons out of bone, clothing from the skins of animals, and beads and necklaces for his ornamentation. Later he invented the bow and arrow, which was a great improvement over the spear formerly used for hunting. Now he could shoot farther and more accurately; he could carry and shoot twenty arrows in quick succession. Thus man became an efficient hunter and was able to live on animals that were much larger and stronger than he.

Man's technology. From this brief summary of the achievements of early man, we can see that the basic difference between man and the other animals about him was his ability to survive and flourish by improving his technology. He is the only creature on the globe who has been able to do this. Other animals depend on speed to run away from danger, on strength to fight against enemies, or on protective coloring to hide in

COURTESY OF THE AMERICAN MUSEUM OF NATURAL HISTORY

Pleistocene, Paleolithic, and recent Neolithic chipping tools. Note that with each period the tools became more refined.

grass or forests. Man alone has been able to use his brain to combat the difficulties and threats of his environment. For example, he learned to make clothes to protect himself against the cold; thus he has been able to live in the Arctic even though he has much less hair than other animals. He learned to use fire to frighten off animals much stronger than he. And as he improved his weapons, he not only was able to defend himself against other animals but to hunt and kill them for food.

The important point to note here is that once man began using his brain, the road was open to limitless progress. The man who developed the use of atomic power in our own age was simply continuing a process that had been started thousands of years earlier by an ancestor who discovered that he could make fire by rubbing two sticks together. And during those thousands of years the arctic rabbit has continued to depend on his white fur, the antelope on his fast legs, and the giraffe on his long neck.

Although early man had a great advantage over other animals, he also suffered a serious disadvantage. Because he was unable to grow his own food, he was forced to collect edibles wherever he could find them. He used his tools to kill animals, to unearth roots, to cut fruits, to dig clams, and to catch fish. This may seem an easy way to earn a living, but if you were to try it you would find that it is extremely hard and dangerous. Anthropologists estimate that even in fertile country with mild winters, only one or two collectors could support themselves per square mile. An area of perhaps 20 or even 30 square miles was needed for each human being in regions of cold climate, tropical jungle, or desert. Thus man could not increase in numbers so long as he remained a food collector. He had to live in small groups or bands, because only a few could find enough food in a given area. It was not possible for villages to develop, let alone cities or states. Man was largely controlled by nature, and he was to remain nature's victim until he made the great discovery that he could grow, as well as gather, food. At the moment when man ceased to be a mere food collector and became instead a food producer, a new world with limitless horizons opened before him.

MAN BECOMES A FOOD PRODUCER

The Neolithic age. About 8000 B.C., or approximately 10,000 years ago, man first learned to produce his own food. At about the same time he also learned to make better tools by grinding stone rather than chipping it. The improvement in the working of stone was such an important advance that scientists often divide the history of early man into two periods: the Paleolithic (*paleos*–old, *lithos*–stone), when man made his first tools by chipping, and the Neolithic (*neos*–new, *lithos*–stone), when man made sharper and better-formed tools by grinding.

Even though the periods take their name from the kind of tools used, the discovery of how to grow food was in reality much more significant for man's development than the discovery of how to grind stone. The Neolithic age is actually as important economically as the Industrial Revolution; in fact, it is often called the Neolithic Revolution.

The great discovery. Most authorities believe that agriculture was first developed about 8000 B.C. in the hills above the Tigris-Euphrates valley. Enough rain fell in that region to make agriculture possible. In addition, wild wheat and barley provided good crops. It was easier for early man to farm in the hills, rather than in the valley below which was periodically flooded by the river. From this center in the Middle East, the art of agriculture spread westward to Africa and Europe and eastward to India. Whether it spread as far as China or whether the Chinese developed agriculture on their own is not yet clear. We do know, however, that the American Indians discovered agriculture independently. Thus there were at least two, and perhaps three or more, centers of origin. From these centers agriculture spread until today it is practiced throughout the globe where soil and climate are satisfactory.

The shift from food gathering to food producing is one of the great turning points in history. It produced at least four major changes in the life of man. First, it raised his standard of living because he was no longer dependent on what food he could find. He could increase the supply by tilling more land and raising more livestock. Second, agriculture made possible a great increase in the numbers of man for the simple reason that a given area can support many more farmers than it can hunters. Third, agriculture enabled man for the first time to settle down permanently in one locality. No longer did he have to wander about looking for game, for patches of berries, or for beds of shellfish. Because he could depend upon a steady supply of food from his fields and his flocks, he was able to remain in one location and build himself a permanent shelter or house.

Villages develop. This brings us to the fourth and final effect of agriculture, the appearance of villages. When several farmers built their houses close together, they formed a village. These villages varied in size from 8 to 50 houses. They could not grow larger until the cultivators had invented wheeled carts and had learned to grow more food per acre. The reason was the lack of transportation. The villagers had to live close enough to their plots to transport, without too much labor, the bulky grain which was the mainstay of their diet. The number of people who could live together in a village was limited to the number who could squeeze out a living on about four square miles of surrounding land. When that number was reached and passed, the younger sons and daughters were forced to leave for another locality where they built another village and brought fresh soil under cultivation.

CULTURE OF THE FOOD PRODUCER

Village life. Life in these early villages was far from easy. Everyone, men, women, and children, had to work and work hard to produce the food and the few tools that were necessary. However, man was now able to improve his handicrafts tremendously. So long as he was a nomadic food gatherer, he could own nothing not easily transported

to the next camping site. When he learned to settle down in a village, however, man learned to make pottery in kilns, to weave cloth out of flax, cotton, and wool, and to fashion fine tools out of ground and polished stone. With improved tools, Neolithic man was able to build relatively large and solid houses. The materials that he used varied from region to region. In the Middle East, for example, adobe (sun-dried brick) was used for the walls, while in Europe the most common material was split saplings plastered with clay. The roofs were usually of thatch. Furniture was simple, beds, dressers, and tables made of wood. An open fire, usually in the center of the room, provided light and warmth; the smoke went out through a hole in the roof or a gap under the eaves.

Contacts. For many centuries these Neolithic communities were largely self-sufficient and isolated one from the other. True, there was a certain amount of trade, as we saw from the objects found at Jarmo. Staple commodities such as stone suitable for axe-heads and other tools were commonly exchanged. There was even some luxury trade, as is evident from the fact that bracelets made from the shell of a Mediterranean mussel have been found in Neolithic graves as far north as Germany.

The Neolithic villages also had some contacts other than those of trade. Driving their flocks to summer pasture, the herdsmen from one village were likely to meet their counterparts from another. The practice of seeking a wife outside one's own village required the exchange of visits. Thus the Neolithic world did not consist of a scattering of completely isolated villages. Rather there was a chain of communities among which contacts, however infrequent and irregular, were repeated. Despite these contacts, the fact remains that the villages were largely self-

This reproduction illustrates the self-sufficiency of an early Neolithic village. For years, archaeologists thought that the dwellings were actually above the waters of the lakes, but new findings prove that the houses were, in fact, along the shore. Geological changes in the lakes' shape caused the sites to be inundated.

contained units. With very few exceptions, they grew all the food they needed, used the raw materials available in their localities, and manufactured their own utensils, tools, and weapons.

Homogeneity. Another characteristic of these early villages is that they were socially homogeneous; they did not have class lines and distinctions. Some villagers did specialize in certain crafts such as carpentry, flint mining, or manufacturing of pottery, axes, and textiles. Yet they probably did not become full-time specialists but combined their crafts with the chief job of growing their own food. Basically all villagers did the same

things in the same way. An American authority on Neolithic man has written that "in the early condition of mankind what men did was customarily different from what women did, but what one man did was much like what another did . . . all men shared the same essential knowledge, practised the same arts of life, had the same interests and similar experiences."[1]

This "sameness" of the early villagers extended also to economic matters. They did not try to accumulate as much wealth as possible for personal use or for prestige. Most of the villagers were related by kinship ties and felt themselves to be essentially one large family. Natural resources such as land

The division of labor permitted by the invention of bone and clay weapons freed Cro-Magnon man to produce the cave paintings found from Europe to North Africa. Today these paintings tell historians a great deal about the tools of this period and the animals encountered and later hunted.

were owned by the village as a whole and available to everybody. Prestige and status depended not on personal riches but on the fulfillment of personal obligations. Personal property did exist, but it was very different from the personal property of the modern world because of the claims of relatives and the customs of hospitality and friendship. An early American anthropologist who studied the Indians at first hand reported that "Hunger and destitution could not exist at one end of an Indian village . . . while plenty prevailed elsewhere in the same village." Exactly the same could be said of the Neolithic village.

The Neolithic Revolution. In conclusion it should be noted that the Neolithic conditions and institutions described above did not appear at the same time in all parts of the world. Agriculture, as we have seen, was adopted at different periods by different peoples. In at least half the world it did not appear at all

before 1500 when the Europeans began to colonize vast areas and to spread agriculture all over the globe.

This was the case in most of the vast Afrasian steppe-desert belt which could support only nomadic herdsmen because of the lack of sufficient rainfall. It was the case also in large parts of the Americas and in all of Australia where the natives failed to advance beyond the food-gathering stage. And the arctic zones of North America and Eurasia also witnessed no agriculture for obvious reasons. Even in those parts of the world where agriculture was practiced before 1500, it frequently was carried on in a primitive manner. In areas where agriculture was advanced, the populations depended on it exclusively for their livelihood. But in areas where it was primitive, they depended as much upon hunting and fishing as upon agriculture.

The wide variation in the ways in which man earned his living in the various parts of the globe is very significant. Everywhere man's shift from food gathering to food producing had revolutionary effects. The more efficient man became as a food producer, the more changes in his manner of life were possible. It follows that the peoples who were most advanced in agriculture were also most advanced in their general culture. They were the ones who had enough food surplus to allow individuals to specialize in handicrafts, in trade, in religious activities, and in the work of government. It is not surprising, therefore, that it was in the great centers of agriculture that man took his next great step forward by developing civilization. Just as agriculture began in the Middle East, in Mesopotamia and Egypt, and in the Americas, so civilization also began in these centers and spread to other regions. The development and spread of ancient civilizations will be the subject of our next unit.

Reviewing the Essentials

Man the Newcomer

1. How long has the earth been in existence? How long has man been on earth?
2. Name important Hominids and describe their accomplishments.

Races of Mankind

3. Name the major races of mankind. On a map locate those parts of the world where each race predominates.
4. Define the term race. Is language a characteristic of race? Religion? Nation?
5. What traits are used by anthropologists as a basis for placing men in racial categories?

Evolution of Man

6. What contribution to scientific thought did Charles Darwin make in his *On the Origin of Species?*
7. What is meant by (a) mutation, (b) natural selection, (c) isolation, and (d) adaptation as they relate to the evolution of man?

Man as a Food Gatherer

8. What abilities distinguish man from the animals? Why have these abilities been so important in man's advancement?
9. Describe the disadvantages man suffered as a food gatherer.

Man Becomes a Food Producer

10. When did man become a food producer? Where did this take place?
11. How do anthropologists account for man's discovery of how to grow food?
12. Why is this discovery one of the great turning points in history?

Culture of the Food Producer

13. Describe a Neolithic community, including (a) homes, (b) handicrafts, (c) interaction with other people, (d) class structure, and (e) ownership of property.
14. Did the Neolithic age begin and end in all regions at the same time? Explain.
15. Why were those prehistoric people who were most advanced in agriculture also the most advanced in general culture?

Explain or Identify

Caucasoid	Cro-Magnon man	Louis Leakey	food producer
Mongoloid	Neolithic man	genes	adaptation
Negroid	Homo habilis	mutation	archaeologist
Homo sapiens	Zinjanthropus	natural selection	anthropologist
Java man	evolution	food gatherer	Charles Darwin

UNIT ACTIVITIES

1. Investigate and report on the latest discoveries and theories concerning early man. Be especially alert to differences and controversies among scientists in this area. Consult the *Readers' Guide to Periodical Literature* for the most recent findings.

2. Prepare a chart on the principal races and main physical types within these large groups. Melville Herskovits, *Cultural Anthropology* (New York: Knopf, 1955) and Ruth Benedict, *Race: Science and Politics* (New York: Compass Books, 1959) are among good sources of information.

3. Read "The Distribution of Man," by William H. Howells, *Scientific American*, September 1960, for an explanation of: (a) causes of racial development; (b) characteristics of the principal races; (c) distribution of man in three epochs or ages; (d) changes that came with the Neolithic period; (e) factors that accelerated man's distribution over the land surface of the globe.

4. Read on the life and work of Charles Darwin and prepare a report for the class which focuses on Darwin's contributions to knowledge about mankind, and the impact of his research in his own and the present time. A pertinent article is "Where Evolution Stands Today," *Life*, October 19, 1959.

5. Prepare a report or panel discussion on the Agricultural Revolution, using as a source of information "The Agricultural Revolution," by Robert J. Braidwood, *Scientific American*, September 1960. Compare and contrast the explanation given by Mr. Braidwood with that given in your text.

6. On an outline map of the world, locate the earliest cities. Prepare a statement giving reasons why cities developed in these places. Consider the factors of climate, fertile soil, natural building materials, accessibility, grazing lands, and nearness to trade routes. Which among these cities are still centers of population and which are now only ruins? Suggest reasons for both conditions for each city. For those cities which are still occupied, make a chronological list of the various peoples and civilizations which ruled them.

Which of these cities became the centers of large empires and why?

7. Several students might read and prepare for presentation to the class a report on: How the Archaeologist and Anthropologist Assemble and Interpret the Remains of the Past. Distinguish between these scientists in techniques and artifacts used, and scholarly aims. Consult the bibliography for sources.

8. Inquire about field studies conducted by archaeologists or anthropologists in your state or region. The local library, or the historical or archaeological society, may have information. What do these studies reveal about the people and animals that inhabited the region?

9. Critically examine this statement: "There are no superior or inferior races." Consult: L. C. Dunn and T. Dobzhansky, *Heredity, Race, and Society* (New York: Mentor, 1952); Ruth Benedict, *Race: Science and Politics* (New York: Compass Books, 1959); *Readings in World History* (Boston: Allyn and Bacon, Inc., 1970), "Are There Superior and Inferior Races?", pp. 27–29.

10. Prepare a written statement giving the opinions you presently hold of another people, i.e., Latin Americans, Asian Indians, Italians, English, Irish, Eskimos, etc. State the probable bases of your opinions. Determine the accuracy of your opinions and the validity of the reasons you give. What causes people to have misconceptions of other people? For information consult the topics "stereotypes" and "prejudices" in sociology and psychology textbooks; Melville Herskovits, *Cultural Anthropology* (New York: Knopf, 1955); Ruth Benedict, *Race: Science and Politics* (New York: Compass Books, 1959); *Readings in World History* (Boston: Allyn and Bacon, Inc., 1970), "What We Think of Other People," pp. 29–34.

11. From the bibliography choose one or more books on archaeology or anthropology. From your reading select appropriate evidence to support this observation: "The more we dig and find, the more clearly the main facts begin to stand out." Write a 500–700 word statement summarizing your findings.

SELECTED READING

● A good brief study of race is given in *What is Race?* (Paris: UNESCO, 1952). Other excellent studies of this subject are E. J. Alpenfels, *Sense and Nonsense About Race* (New York: Friendship Press, rev. ed., 1957); I. Block, *People* (New York: Watts, 1956); and R. L. Lehrman, *Race, Evolution and Mankind* (New York: Basic Books, 1966).

● Fascinating accounts of man before civilization are given in I. and H. Goldman, *First Men: The Story of Human Beginnings* (New York: Abelard, 1955); A. T. White, *The First Men in the World* (New York: Random House, 1953); M. Edel, *The Story of People* (Boston: Little, Brown, 1953); A. S. Gregor, *The Adventure of Man: His Evolution from Prehistory to Civilization* (New York: Macmillan, 1966); and, finally, Margaret Mead's excellent book, *People and Places* (New York: World, 1959).

● Two excellent accounts of archaeologists and their findings are by R. J. Braidwood, *Archaeologists and What They Do* (New York: Watts, 1960); and D. and J. Samachson, *Good Digging: The Story of Archaeology* (Chicago: Rand McNally, 1960).

● An interesting biography of Darwin is available by W. Karp, *Charles Darwin and the Origin of the Species* (New York: American Heritage, 1968). Also available is an abridgement of Charles Darwins's great journal of discovery, *The Voyage of the Beagle* (New York: Harper, 1959).

FURTHER READING

● Several allusions have been made in the Unit Activities to Ruth Benedict's *Race: Science and Politics* to be found in paperback (Compass Books, 1959). An international group of scientists wrote a series of pamphlets on race for UNESCO; these have been bound in a single volume, *The Race Question in Modern Science* (New York: UNESCO, 1957). An older but still useful account of early man can be found in *Mankind So Far* (New York: Doubleday & Company, 1944), by William Howells. A more recent book by the same author is *Back of History* (New York: Doubleday & Company, 1954). Both of Howells's books are very readable and well illustrated. The following paperbacks on race are also noteworthy: L. C. Dunn and T. Dobzhansky, *Heredity, Race and Society* (Mentor, 1955); and M. Wheeler, *Archaeology from the Earth* (Penguin Paperback, 1956).

● R. J. Braidwood, *Prehistoric Men* (Chicago Natural History Museum, 1967), is an authoritative and readable account of man before civilization. The latest research findings in this field have been summarized in a series of articles in the September 1960 issue of *The Scientific American*, which also has been published separately by the magazine under the title *The Human Species*. A description of primitive peoples today is given in K. Birket-Smith, *Primitive Man and His Ways* (Mentor Book, 1963).

● For the Agricultural Revolution, see the relevant chapters in the September 1960 issue of *Scientific American* mentioned above, and in S. Tax, ed., *Horizons of Anthropology* (Chicago: Aldine, 1964).

CIVILIZED MAN LIVES IN REGIONAL ISOLATION

The races of the earth are like trees. Each according to its kind brings forth the fruit known as civilization. As russet apples and pippins may grow from the same trunk, and as peaches may be grafted on a plum tree, so the culture of allied races may be transferred from one to another. Yet no one expects pears on cherry branches, and it is useless to look for Slavic civilization among the Chinese. Each may borrow from its neighbors, but will put its own stamp upon what it obtains. ... Religion, education, government, and all of man's varied occupations, customs, and institutions—his inherited culture as the anthropologists say—form a second great group of social influences whose power seems almost immeasurable.

Ellsworth Huntington

ANCIENT CIVILIZATIONS: 3700 B.C.—1000 B.C.

NATURE OF CIVILIZATION

Man first became civilized about 3700 B.C. or less than 6000 years ago. This is an insignificant period of time compared to his almost two million years on this globe. Man has been civilized about one-half of one per cent of his total career. And yet the rest of this book will be devoted to this one-half of one per cent, while the few pages you have read thus far will have to do for the remaining 99.5 per cent. Why this disproportionate emphasis on the story of civilized man as against uncivilized?

The answer is the vastly different tempo of development before and after 3700 B.C. We have seen that hundreds of thousands of years were to pass before man learned that he could make better tools by grinding rather than chipping stone. And still more thousands of years were needed before he learned that he could produce food as well as gather it. Then another four thousand years and more went by before man developed civilization. But once man became civilized he progressed so rapidly that he seemed to be leaping forward compared to his previous snail's pace. And the more time passes, the more rapid is his pace of invention and development and change.

In the field of transportation, for example, man depended on his own two legs during most of his almost two million years on this earth. Then a few thousand years ago he learned to tame the horse and other animals, and to ride them or use them to pull carriages. About a century ago man developed the bicycle, then in rapid succession the steam engine, the internal combustion engine or automobile, the airplane, and now he has even perfected spaceships which have allowed him to land on the moon. The pace of change is so fast that it has become a serious problem in itself. We do not know where we shall go from here; we only know that we shall get there in a hurry. But to return to earlier times, it is this rapidly rising curve of change that explains why the remainder of this book will deal with civilized man alone.

When man became civilized, he did so on the basis of his earlier Neolithic culture. This at once raises a question of definition. What do we mean by the terms culture and civilization? Culture may be defined as the way of life of a society, the habits, ideas, and practices of its members. This definition obviously is broad enough to cover any form of human organization. A culture, however, becomes a civilization when it reaches a further state of development. This new state cannot be defined precisely because civilizations differ widely one from the other. But we can say that a culture becomes a civilization when it develops most of the following elements: writing; arts and sciences; urban centers; formal political organization; social classes and ranks; tribute or taxation.

Transition to civilization. Not all cultures became civilizations. In fact, in the course of history, very few made the transition, and they made it at very different periods. The earliest, the largest number, and the most important of mankind's civilizations appeared in Eurasia. The chief reason for this concentration, as we noted in the first unit, was that the numerous peoples of the vast Eurasian land mass were able to interact with and stimulate each other. Such interaction and stimulation was very limited for the relatively isolated African Negroes, American Indians, and Australian aborigines.

The development of civilization allowed talented individuals the time to experiment in art. Lions, such as this bronze one dating from before 2000 B.C., appear to have been a popular subject for artists in Mesopotamia.

Because of their location, these peoples failed to develop civilizations, with the exception of the Indians of Mexico and Peru. Even these American Indian civilizations, remarkable though they were in certain respects, failed to reach the general level of over-all development that was set by the Eurasian civilizations. Furthermore it should be noted that the American Indian civilizations were suddenly wiped out with the coming of the Spaniards in the early 16th century. As a result they have left behind them few traces other than their domesticated plants such as corn, potatoes, and tobacco. All this means that today's world civilization is largely a Eurasian civilization. It is based on the four great civilizations that developed first in the Middle East, and later in India, Europe, and China.

Finally it should be noted that all these civilizations which appeared after 3700 B.C. developed largely in isolation. The most isolated, naturally, were those of Mexico and Peru. The four Eurasian civilizations had a certain amount of contact with each other, despite being separated by deserts, mountains, and oceans, which helps to explain their lead over other civilizations. But even in Eurasia, interaction in pre-modern times was limited. It is true, as we shall see later, that occasionally some conqueror such as Genghis Khan, or religion such as Christianity, or culture such as Hellenism, leaped across these physical obstacles and influenced two or three or even all four of Eurasia's civilizations. But this was the exception rather than the rule. The Middle Eastern, the Indian, the Chinese, and the European civilizations developed largely in isolation for thousands of years. They were not brought together permanently and closely until after the 15th century when the Europeans learned to cross the oceans. As soon as they did so, they could sail directly to all corners of the earth and all civilizations had direct access to each other.

But this did not happen until after 1500. World history between 3700 B.C. and 1500 A.D. is the history of regional civilizations developing along parallel but largely separate lines. This is the topic of the remainder of this unit, how civilized man lived in regional isolation for over five thousand years.

MAN'S FIRST CIVILIZATION

From hills to valleys. We have seen that agriculture made civilization possible. Since agriculture was first practiced in the hills above the Tigris-Euphrates Valley, civilization also was first developed in that region, or, rather, in the great valley below. The hilly areas could not support a dense population, so, as the villagers increased in numbers, they overflowed into the valley. There they found rich soil many feet thick that had been deposited by the river for countless centuries. But there were two big problems that had discouraged the villagers from farming in the valley before this time. One was the lack of sufficient rainfall, and the other was the periodic overflow of the river. In other words the cultivators had to discover a way to irrigate the land during the dry spell and to drain it during the floods.

This was a difficult task because the bed of the Tigris is so far below the level of the surrounding plain that the water could not be lifted for irrigation. And the Euphrates, by contrast, carries a great amount of silt from the mountains and deposits it when it slows down upon entering the flat plain. As a result the bed of the Euphrates has risen above the level of the surrounding land. Also the Euphrates has formed many branches because of the flatness of the plain. In order to irrigate the fields it was necessary to cut the banks of one of the river branches and lead the water along canals built above the level of the land. Drainage in so flat an area was even more difficult, particularly because the Euphrates tends to flood suddenly in the spring when the crops are still standing in the fields. In addition the river often changes its course, leaving densely populated areas without water. This is one reason why today we find the ruins of great cities standing in the midst of barren deserts.

Civilization developed in the Tigris-Euphrates Valley, and later in the Nile, Indus, and Yellow River valleys, because men had to plan and work together in order to cope with the formidable problems of irrigation and drainage. In the hilly areas where there was enough rain to grow crops, people could produce their food as individuals. But in the river valley whole villages had to turn out to raise dikes and dig ditches. Furthermore the dikes had to be repaired and the ditches cleared of silt each year, or they would quickly fill up and become useless. Almost as important as the need for community work was the need for community regulations. Those who lived near the ditches or reservoirs could not be allowed to take all the water and leave none for their neighbors.

All this meant that valley agriculture required control of men as well as control of water. But once the rules and the techniques of irrigation agriculture were worked out, the valley cultivators were handsomely repaid. The crops were fabulous compared to those on the relatively barren and stony hillsides.

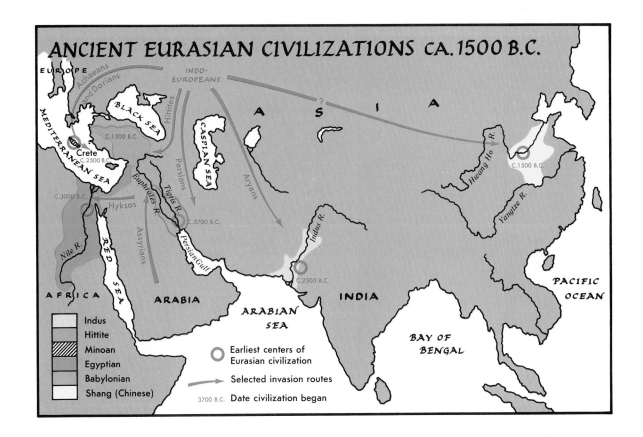

ANCIENT EURASIAN CIVILIZATIONS CA. 1500 B.C.

EUROPE

INDO-EUROPEANS

Achaeans and Dorians

Hittites

BLACK SEA

C. 1500 B.C.

A S I A

?

Crete
C. 2500 B.C.

MEDITERRANEAN SEA

CASPIAN SEA

Persians

Aryans

Huang Ho R.

C. 1500 B.C.

Euphrates R.

Tigris R.

Hyksos

C. 3000 B.C.

Assyrians

Persian Gulf

C. 3700 B.C.

Indus R.

Yangtze R.

Nile R.

RED SEA

C. 2500 B.C.

PACIFIC OCEAN

AFRICA

ARABIA

INDIA

ARABIAN SEA

BAY OF BENGAL

Indus
Hittite
Minoan
Egyptian
Babylonian
Shang (Chinese)

○ Earliest centers of Eurasian civilization

→ Selected invasion routes

3700 B.C. Date civilization began

Documents have been found dating to 2500 B.C. and indicating that the average yield on a field of barley was 86 times the sowing! The new abundance of food made it possible for the population to grow. As it grew, more land had to be flooded or irrigated, and more miles of dikes and canals and ditches had to be built. And this in turn required more community work and more controls and regulations.

This explains the rise of a ruling class of administrators who directed the work and enforced the regulations. Nct only were these administrators necessary for the complicated valley agriculture but they could now be supported because the rich valley soil produced a food surplus. This surplus also supported religious and military leaders, who soon made their appearance. In fact they often were combined in one person, the king frequently being also the priest or the military head. These governmental, religious, and military leaders gathered together in centers that developed into cities. The first cities appeared on the plain of Sumer in the lower part of the Tigris-Euphrates Valley.

The need for records. By the time the cities had taken form, the economic and administrative operations had grown to the point where the keeping of records was essential. So a system of writing was devised that made use of pictures that resembled and represented things. For example, an ox was represented by $\forall$ and the sun by $\bigcirc$. Then a simpler system (which used symbols to stand

FROM PICTURE WRITING TO THE ALPHABET

EGYPTIANS about 3000 B.C.	SEMITES about 1500 B.C.	PHOENICIANS about 1000 B.C.	EARLY GREEKS about 600 B.C.	ROMANS about 100 A.D.
Ox head	(aleph, ox)		alpha	A
House	(beth, house)		beta	B
Waves of water	(mem, water)		mu	M

for syllables) was evolved. But the Sumerians, as the people of Sumer were called, never took the final step of working out a phonetic alphabet in which each sign stands for a sound. This was developed by the Phoenicians, a people who lived in present-day Syria, Lebanon, and Israel. They perfected a phonetic alphabet of 22 letters. Each letter represented a consonant sound. The Greeks later added vowels to the Phoenician consonants and produced the alphabet that is used today by the Western world.

Nevertheless the beginning that the Sumerians had made was of major importance because writing was absolutely necessary for the new society that was developing. For example, a system of taxation was essential in order to pay for the extensive irrigation and canal systems. Obviously, written records were needed for any such taxation, as they were needed also for general administration, communications, and so forth.

A new way of life results. From this brief survey we can see that when man moved from the hills to the valleys, his whole way of life changed in many basic ways. If we examine these changes, we find that they added up to civilization as we had defined it above. Writing had been invented. Urban centers were flourishing. Formal political organization existed in the form of the new state. Social classes had developed with the appearance of kings, priests, military leaders, scribes, and numerous officials. Taxation also made its appearance in order to provide support for these ruling classes. Finally, arts and sciences were developed: architecture for the building of the temples and palaces; painting and sculpture for their decoration; astronomy to compute the time of the annual floods; mathematics to prepare plans for the numerous building projects; and medicine to safeguard the health of the rapidly growing populations. By 3700 B.C. all these basic developments had taken place on the plain of Sumer. For this reason historians generally consider that man's first civilization began at that place and at that time.*

SPREAD OF CIVILIZATION

From the Tigris-Euphrates Valley, or Mesopotamia (meaning "between the rivers"), civilization gradually spread to all parts of Eurasia. We cannot be sure about the exact course and timing, but archaeologists have worked out the general pattern. From Mesopotamia, civilization spread first to Egypt about 3000 B.C., then to the Aegean Islands and to the Indus Valley before 2500, and finally to China before 1500 B.C. These dates are all approximate and tentative. Undoubtedly they will have to be changed as more excavations are made and as dating techniques are improved. It would be more accurate if a system of double dates were used, for example 4000 to 3500 B.C. for the beginning of civilization in Mesopotamia. The above single dates are used simply because they are more convenient, but they must not be accepted as exact or final figures.

This "spread" of civilization from the original center at Sumer raises the question of exactly how the "spreading" took place. The answer is that it occurred in two ways, by direct contact and imitation, and by stimulus diffusion.

Contact and imitation. Direct contact, as might be expected, affected the regions immediately around Mesopotamia. Most contacts took place as a result of trade or war. Trade began early because Mesopotamia, although very rich in farming land, had almost no stone, minerals, metals, or timber. These commodities were essential for the

* See *Readings in World History*, "Man's Earliest Civilization," p. 36 (Boston: Allyn and Bacon, Inc., 1970)

large building projects; to secure them, trade began with neighboring regions. In return for the goods they needed, the Mesopotamians gave not only foodstuffs but also the techniques of the civilization that they had developed. The trade routes went along the Mesopotamian Valley, west to Syria, Palestine, and Phoenicia, north to Anatolia, and east to Iran and the Indus Valley. As a result this whole area developed a civilization that had a number of common basic features, though individual local characteristics were naturally kept. The common features were particularly noticeable in religion, language, and writing.

Stimulus diffusion. Civilization spread from Mesopotamia to more distant regions by stimulus diffusion. This means that the re-

Cuneiform tablets were baked for permanency after the symbols were edged in damp clay.

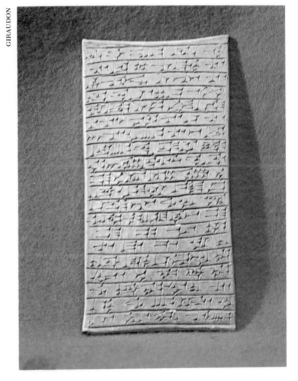

GIRAUDON

61

ceiving people did not take over completely certain specific inventions or institutions, as was the case with contact and imitation. Instead they adopted the underlying idea or principle, and then applied it in their own way to suit their own particular needs. This can be seen clearly in the case of Egypt's borrowing from Mesopotamia. The borrowing began about 3000 B.C. when Sumerian traders appeared in the area between the Nile and the Red Sea where gold was to be found. During the course of the commerce that developed, the Egyptians learned about the civilization of Sumer but did not copy it in detail. Instead they took over the *idea* of writing and developed their own writing system;* they took over the *idea* of a united state but organized one that was different from that of Sumer; they adopted the *idea* of huge temples and palaces but built their own along quite distinctive lines.

* See *Readings in World History,* "Solving the Mystery of Egypt's Hieroglyphics," p. 40.

Once civilization was firmly established in Egypt, it spread from there as it had earlier from Mesopotamia. The civilization that appeared about 2500 B.C. in the Aegean Islands, and especially on the island of Crete, was derived partly from Egypt and partly from Mesopotamia. But in this case also it was more the ideas rather than specific inventions that were borrowed. So the famous Aegean or Minoan civilization had, as we shall see later, its own distinctive characteristics that were very different from those of the mainland.

The Indus Valley. Little is know about the beginning of civilization in the Indus Valley. In fact, the very existence of this civilization was not known until the 1920's. Before that time it was believed that the Aryans, who invaded India about 1500 B.C., were the first to introduce civilization in that country. Then archaeologists were attracted to a desolate spot containing several mounds and

The discovery of the remains of Mohenjo-Daro in India proved conclusively the existence of pre-Aryan civilization. The absence of either slums or palaces seems to indicate relatively classless societies.

ALAN BAND

called by the local people Mohenjo-Daro, or Place of the Dead. Excavation revealed that Mohenjo-Daro was the site of a flourishing ancient city, or series of cities. Each one had been destroyed by floods and a new city was built upon the ruins of the old. At least seven cities were built, one on top of the other. Possibly the ruins of still other cities lie beneath those that have been dug up, but water seepage has prevented archaeologists from digging deeper to find out. Excavations in other parts of the Indus valley indicate that this civilization began before 2500 B.C., possibly as a result of stimulus diffusion from Mesopotamia. Apparently there were two routes of contact, one by sea down the Persian Gulf and across the Indian Ocean, and the other by land through Iran. But the details of the origins of this civilization remain unknown, partly because its language has not yet been deciphered.*

The Yellow River Valley. Even less is known about the beginnings of Chinese civilization on the banks of the Hwang Ho, or Yellow River. It started about a thousand years after the Indus civilization and has lasted without interruption to the present day. For long it was believed that this civilization was the product of invaders from the northwest, who brought with them knowledge of wheat and barley cultivation, bronze casting, use of horses, and writing. Since these techniques are of Mesopotamian origin, it was assumed that the roots of Chinese civilization also were to be found in the Tigris-Euphrates Valley. But today we know that horses, and also cattle and sheep, were used by the Chinese long before the appearance of the invaders. Furthermore it is very puzzling that the Chinese never have used animal milk for food, in contrast to the peoples of the Middle East and of all the lands

* See *Readings in World History,* "India's Forgotten Civilization," p. 44.

COURTESY OF THE ISABELLA STEWART GARDNER MUSEUM, BOSTON

This Chinese bear dates probably from the second century B.C. *and is one of the earliest examples of cast bronze.*

between the Middle East and China. This does not necessarily mean that Chinese civilization developed independently of any outside influence. In fact, the very sudden rise of civilization in the Yellow River valley sometime around 1500 B.C. suggests external stimulus. Perhaps the explanation is that the invaders were a small group who introduced certain new techniques but did not bring about a cultural revolution before they were absorbed by the local population. This certainly has been the effect of numerous other invaders of China from that time to the present. In any case, the scanty evidence available does not allow us to reach any definite conclusions one way or the other.

Ancient Civilizations 63

Much has been learned about Egyptian values by studying the relief on their tombs and temples. That Egyptians believed in the power of gods to control their destiny can be seen in this carving in which the god, Thonsu, (left) offers the pharaoh the emblem of life.

NATURE OF ANCIENT CIVILIZATIONS

As civilization spread from one region to another, it developed different forms, depending partly on local geographic environment. Certainly geographic location affected vitally the stability, the longevity, and even the racial basis of the various civilizations.

A crossroads civilization. Mesopotamia, for example, is located at a crossroads and was easily invaded by Indo-European mountain peoples to the north and Semitic desert peoples to the south. As a result the history of Mesopotamia was largely the history of the struggles of these two peoples for con-

trol of the region. So Mesopotamia experienced many invasions and sudden changes. Its ruling people, for example, changed several times. The people who developed the first civilization were the Sumerians, who probably came originally from Iran. But they were overwhelmed by various Semitic invaders from the Arabian Peninsula, and the latter in turn by various Indo-Europeans from Central Eurasia.

In the same way that the soil of a river delta is built up by successive inundations of the river, the human soil in Mesopotamia has been built up by repeated inundations of invading peoples. The political history of Mesopotamia was correspondingly violent.

The early city-states of Sumer gave way to kingdoms, and these in turn to empires. The empires rose and fell with repeated invasions. The Babylonian Empire which crushed the Sumerians was followed by the Hittite Empire, the Hittite by the Assyrian, and then a new Babylonian Empire which lasted until the Persian conquest in 550 B.C.

Development in isolation. In contrast to Mesopotamia, Egypt is isolated, being surrounded by the Libyan Desert on the west, the Nubian Desert on the south, the Arabian Desert on the east, and the Mediterranean Sea on the north. Egypt also is united very naturally and effectively by the Nile River. In fact Egypt is the gift of the Nile; it could not exist without the Nile water which turns the brown desert to green. So it is not surprising that Egypt has been united and comparatively peaceful through most of her history. Even the people who live there today resemble in appearance the people that we see carved and painted in temples and pyramids that were built thousands of years ago. We know that the Egyptians who lived under the pharaohs, like the Egyptians of today, were short, dark, long-headed people, with straight black hair, deep-set eyes, and slightly aquiline (hooked) noses. The political history of Egypt also lacks the violence and constant change that we noted in Mesopotamia. More than two thousand years passed between the establishment of the first empire in 2780 B.C. and the conquest of the country by the Persians in 525 B.C. During that period only three empires ruled the country, and the intervening periods of instability were comparatively short.

The island of Crete and the Indus and Yellow River valleys were as well protected from outside intervention as Egypt. Crete was surrounded by the waters of the Mediterranean, so that the Minoan civilization flourished without interruption from 3000 B.C.

until about 1400 B.C. when it was overwhelmed by invaders who crossed over from present-day Greece. Likewise the Indus civilization, protected by the lofty mountains to the north, continued peacefully from 2500 B.C. to 1500 B.C., when it also was overthrown by invaders. And the Chinese, who have been the most isolated behind a series of deserts and mountain ranges, have preserved their civilization with little intervention or change from 1500 B.C. to the present.

"Styles" develop. All these civilizations of Eurasia followed the same general pattern of evolution: the invention of individual writing systems, the development of skill in working bronze and precious metals, the growth of transport and trade, the transition from city-states to kingdoms and empires, and the evolution of architecture from mud huts to temples and palaces. But despite this general uniformity, there were profound differences among these civilizations. Each had a distinctive "style."

It seems that in this case, also, geography had considerable influence. The Mesopotamians, for example, lived in a land threatened by sudden floods, by difficult irrigation problems, and by constant invasions of barbarians. The Egyptians, by contrast, enjoyed a land protected by almost impassable deserts, and benefited from a river that flooded regularly and predictably. It is not surprising, then, that the prevailing attitude of the Mesopotamians was one of pessimism and uncertainty, while the Egyptians tended to be optimistic and confident.

This difference can be seen clearly in architecture. The uncertain Babylonians built for the moment, the confident Egyptians for eternity. The Mesopotamians normally used sun-dried bricks, even in areas where stone was easily available. They did not care that temples built of bricks would not last long; the gods probably would soon want them changed anyway. But the Egyptians, who began by imitating the Mesopotamians, soon changed from brick to stone. They built gigantic temples for their gods, and vast pyramids to house the mummified bodies of their pharaohs. The Karnak Temple at Thebes includes a hall 400 feet long, 175 feet wide, and 80 feet high. The roof is supported by rows of columns, some so large that 100 men could stand on the top of one of them. Likewise the Great Pyramid of Khufu, or Cheops, is one of the Seven Wonders of the World. It is a solid mass of limestone blocks covering 13 acres, and originally was 768 feet square

and 482 feet high. So enormous is this pyramid that its limestone blocks would build a wall 10 feet high and 9 inches wide around the boundaries of France. To the present day these huge monuments dominate the Egyptian landscape, whereas the many large structures built by the Mesopotamians have mostly crumbled away.

Style of Minoan civilization. The individuality of style can be seen also in the case of the island of Crete. It appears that the Minoan civilization of Crete was derived, as we have seen, from the older civilizations of

The massive columns of Karnak (far right) are indicative of the Egyptian outlook on life. Sheltered for many centuries by natural boundaries and a virtually immutable society, the Egyptians' sense of security was reflected in monuments built to last forever. The Ishtar Gates of Babylonia, on the other hand, had to be painstakingly reconstructed over a period of years. Built of sun-dried brick, they were easily destroyed by the elements.

Mesopotamia and Egypt. Yet the Minoans stamped everything they borrowed with their own style. Their civilization was an amphibious one, a thalassocracy, or sea civilization. They were not confined to tilling the soil of a single river valley. Instead they sailed freely from one end of the Mediterranean to the other. With their single-masted ships they served as the middlemen of the great inland sea, carrying back and forth the foodstuffs, ivory, and glass of Egypt, the horses and wood of Syria, the silver, pottery, and marble of the Cyclades Islands, and the copper of Cyprus.

Their manner of life reflected this freedom and breadth of horizons. Minoan artists never tried to impress by mere size. They did not build colossal pyramids or carve huge shapes of gods or men. Instead they reproduced the life about them on their household utensils, on the walls of their houses, and in their works of art. They found models everywhere; in natural objects such as birds, flowers, sea shells, and marine life of all types; and in scenes from life, such as peasants returning from their fields, athletes wrestling with bulls, and women dancing in honor of the Great Goddess. In architecture, the Minoans were more interested in personal comfort than outward appearance. Their palaces lacked the size and symmetry of the Egyptian buildings, but they were arranged with an eye to ventilation and shade, and had superb plumbing systems. Water for drinking and bathing was piped into the palaces, and a drainage system carried off the waste water and the rain. There is a story that a sanitary engineer, who was shown some Minoan ruins, stopped suddenly before a device for regulating the flow of drainage water from a roof and exclaimed: "But they can't use that! My firm has just bought the patent rights."

SIGNIFICANCE OF ANCIENT CIVILIZATIONS

Similarity. The civilizations of the ancient world differed from each other in their "style," their distinctive way of looking at life, or in response to their particular geographical conditions. But they were similar in one basic respect: they were much more complicated societies than the simple organization of the Neolithic era.

We have seen that during the centuries between the beginning of agriculture and the development of civilization, man lived in socially homogeneous villages. He did the

The ruins of Knossos on Crete reflect the free expression and individuality characteristic of Minoan civilization. The irregular shapes and levels and vivid colors lacked the imposing facade presented by Egyptian architecture, but provided comfortable and attractive living on a human scale.

same thing as his neighbors, lived in the same way that they did, and he farmed to feed himself and his family. But what we call civilization involves two marked changes: a tremendous increase in man's productivity, and the division of labor. He began to practice irrigation agriculture, to use various metals in place of stone, and to improve his old crafts and create new ones. These advances enabled him to build up food surpluses instead of living from hand to mouth as he had in the past. In other words, each cultivator produced enough to support others besides himself and his immediate family. This made possible specialization; some men could now devote themselves to crafts and trades, and exchange their goods for the food of the farmers. The surplus could support a ruling class; human society now developed definite levels of wealth and achievement and changed into a society in which there were rulers and ruled.

Previously, the villagers had shared common skills and knowledge and attitudes. But now a new type of society was developing in the cities: a society with scribes who knew the mysterious art of writing, priests who knew the secrets of the heavens, artists who knew how to paint and carve, and merchants who exchanged goods with lands beyond deserts and seas. So there was no longer a single culture. Instead there developed what has been called High Culture and Low Culture. The High Culture was to be found in the schools and temples and palaces of the cities; the Low Culture was in the villages. The High Culture was passed on in writing by philosophers and theologians and literary men; the Low Culture was transmitted by word of mouth among illiterate peasants.

The High Culture embraced a body of "higher learning" and the literary or learned sciences: mathematics, astronomy, and medicine. The pseudo or "near" sciences, theology and astronomy, devoted to methods of foretelling the future, were also in the High Culture domain. Ability to read and to write, the product of a long and arduous training, was a form of specialization in itself. On strictly practical grounds, a peasant, farmer, or metal-worker had very little chance of learning the skills of literacy. Literacy was confined to the special class of people who enjoyed a privileged status in Egypt and Mesopotamia. A father's advice is contained in an Egyptian papyrus in which he contrasts the possible future of a clerk or scribe who may eventually "become an official of high rank" and, of course, "exempt from all manual tasks" such as that of a metal-worker "with fingers like a crocodile's." The skills and traditions of a craft were not placed in writing; methods of workmanship and the "tricks of the trade" were passed on by word of mouth and were learned by imitation.

Although the coming of civilization removed the early equality between man and man, civilization has brought great achievements and gains. Civilized man had more control over the forces of nature and therefore was more independent of nature. For example, he no longer had to suffer from repeated floods; instead he used them to increase his food supply. Civilized man also knew how to gather and organize knowledge, and to pass it on in written form to future generations. This meant a constantly growing fund of knowledge rather than the same skills that formerly had been passed on orally from father to son for generation after generation. Finally, civilized man developed various arts that made possible new forms of human expression in addition to the traditional ones of the village.

It is true that all these advances were based to a large extent on the exploitation of the many and benefited them very little. But the important point, so far as the whole history of man is concerned, is that advances *were* made, and continued to be made with growing speed. And it was these advances that finally enabled man in modern times to gain such mastery over nature, such fantastic productivity through science and industry, that the many are now benefiting along with the few.

This means that the appearance of the scientist and the engineer during the past century or two, represents for the many the next great turning point since the coming of civilization. The Low Culture of the village during that long intervening period continued largely unchanged. But very important changes did take place in High Culture, in religion and philosophy and the arts and sciences. These changes we shall now consider in the forthcoming sections on classical and medieval civilizations. In the next unit on the period after 1500 we shall see how all mankind, both the many and the few, were profoundly affected by the scientific and economic and political revolutions.

Reviewing the Essentials

Nature of Civilization

1. "Man first became civilized in 3700 B.C., or about 6000 years ago." Exactly what does this statement mean? Why, in a study of world history, do we emphasize this 6000-year period rather than the much longer period prior to it? Why did man progress rapidly once he became civilized?

2. Explain the meaning of *culture*. When does a culture become a civilization? Do all cultures become civilizations? Give examples to support your answer. Where did the earliest civilizations appear? What factors account for their appearance? Locate early centers of civilization on a map.

3. Explain: "World civilization today is largely a Eurasian civilization."

4. Explain: "Earliest civilizations developed largely in regional isolation."

5. During what period in time did regional civilizations develop along parallel yet separate lines?

Man's First Civilization

6. Why did the agricultural revolution (around 8000 B.C.) make civilization possible?

7. What problems did the early Sumerians have to solve before they could carry on agriculture in the Tigris-Euphrates Valley?

8. What innovations, inventions, and changes are evidence of the civilization that appeared in Mesopotamia? Check these with your definition of civilization.

9. Why were the achievements of the Sumerians unknown until recent years?

Spread of Civilization

10. From Sumer, civilization spread to other parts of Eurasia. Name and locate the major areas where civilization spread, and the approximate time when this occurred.

11. How and with what peoples was *direct contact* and *imitation* an important factor in the spread of civilization?

12. Explain what is meant by *stimulus diffusion*. What people were affected by Sumerian civilization in this way?

13. What evidence is there of an advanced civilization in the Indus Valley as early as 2500 B.C.? Why is so little known about it?

14. What assumptions are made about the start of Chinese civilization in the Yellow River valley around 1500 B.C.?

Nature of Ancient Civilization

15. Explain how geographical location affected the stability, longevity, way of life, and ethnic composition: of (a) Egypt; (b) Mesopotamia; (c) Crete; (d) Indus Valley; and (e) Yellow River valley.

16. In what specific ways did early civilization follow the same pattern of development?

17. Explain: Each of the early civilizations developed a distinctive style or way of life, although all had certain things in common.

Significance of Ancient Civilizations

18. How was man's way of life different as a result of the coming of civilization? Consider economic, political, and social changes that distinguished his culture after the agricultural revolution. Describe four major changes that resulted from civilization and accelerated man's progress.

19. Differentiate between High and Low Culture. What persons or groups represented each culture? How was each transmitted?

Explain, Identify, or Locate

High Culture	Minoan	Yellow River	Sumer
cuneiform	Aryan	Mohenjo-Daro	Aegean Islands
Rosetta Stone	Tigris-Euphrates	Mesopotamia	1500 B.C.
3700 B.C.	3000 B.C.	2500 B.C.	1000 B.C.

CLASSICAL CIVILIZATIONS: 1000 B.C.—500 A.D.

BEGINNING OF THE CLASSICAL AGE

Causes. About 1000 B.C. the age of ancient civilizations came to an end and the age of classical civilizations began. This shift from one age to another was to a large extent the work of nomadic and seminomadic peoples who lived in the steppes and the deserts. These barbarians broke into the rich river valleys and completely uprooted or seriously jarred the old and outworn civilizations of Eurasia. But in doing so, they were not altogether destructive. They scattered far and wide the seeds of civilization, like a wind blowing the fluffy white seedcases of dandelions. It was in this manner that new centers of civilization developed, with new types of civilization that differed from those of the ancient period.

We saw in Unit One that there were three main groups of barbarian invaders: the Semitic Arabs of the Arabian Peninsula, the Indo-Europeans of the Central Eurasian steppes, and the Mongols of the steppes east of the Altai-Tien Shan ranges. These peoples periodically invaded the river valleys from the time of the very first civilizations. They were attracted by all the wonders of civilization: by the abundant crops, by the village barns swollen with grain, and by the manifold luxuries of the towns. This was why the earliest civilization at Sumer was overrun by Semitic tribesmen about 2650 B.C. This invasion was followed by many others, some by the Indo-Europeans from the north and others by the Semitic Arabs from the south.

The warrior horsemen. With the passage of time the nomads became more formidable and dangerous. This happened for two main reasons. The first we have already noted in the opening unit: the taming of the horse and the development of the saddle and stirrups and various weapons, which made possible the organization of cavalry armies. The second reason for the success of the nomads is their adoption of certain inventions of civilization, particularly of iron. We do not know where and when the first iron was made in quantity, though it seems to have been somewhere south of the Caucasus Mountains about the 15th century B.C. By the 12th century B.C. it was being produced in many areas

The dagger and axe head below, found in Iran, testify to the sophisticated level of bronze working reaching in ancient Luristan by the first millennium B.C.

Classical Civilizations 71

and in relatively large quantities. This was of great significance, so much so that historians write about an Iron Age replacing an earlier Bronze Age. The reason is that bronze, which is made of copper and tin, was an expensive metal, and very few could afford bronze weapons. But iron is very common and cheap, so that once the method of smelting iron ore was discovered, it could be done easily by every village smith. This meant that the barbarians now could have as good and as plentiful arms as the soldiers guarding the old centers of civilization.*

The combination of the horse and iron weapons made possible the great nomadic invasions which overwhelmed the river valley civilizations between 2000 and 1000 B.C. During the first half of this period the invaders usually arrived with horse-drawn chariots and bronze weapons; by the second half they commonly rode on horses and fought with

* See *Readings in World History,* "The Coming of the Iron Age," p. 49.

Bronze Horse, Greek Geometric Period

FOGG MUSEUM

iron weapons. In most of the old centers the conquerors uprooted the existing civilizations and replaced them with something quite different. The one exception was in the Middle East, where civilization was by now too long established to be wiped out altogether. But even there the nomads were responsible for the rise and fall of a number of empires, of which we shall note three.

The first was the empire of the Hittites, an Indo-European people who conquered and ruled a part of Asia Minor and some lands to the south, between 1900 and 1200 B.C. The second were the Semitic Assyrians who conquered a large empire that included Mesopotamia and Egypt and lasted from 750 to 600 B.C. Finally there were the Indo-European Persians, who built the first empire (550–330 B.C.) to include the entire Middle East, from India to Libya and from the Caucasus to the Persian Gulf. Some invaders also penetrated the Nile Valley, such as the Semitic Hyksos who reached Egypt about 1675 B.C. But the Nile Valley, with its natural defenses, suffered much less than did the Tigris-Euphrates.

Greater nomadic impact. In the Aegean Sea and in the Indus and Yellow River valleys, civilization was less firmly rooted than in the Middle East. Accordingly the nomadic invaders left a greater imprint in these regions and produced greater change. In the Aegean area, for example, the island of Crete and the mainland of Greece were overrun by a series of Indo-European invaders who crossed the Danube. Most important were the Achaeans armed with bronze weapons, who destroyed the Minoan civilization of Crete about 1400 B.C., and the iron-armed Dorians who, about 1200 B.C., conquered much of Greece, the islands, and southwest Asia Minor. During the next four centuries the Aegean area was primitive, tribal, and agrarian. This was the Homeric Age, so

Mounted Warrior, Greek, 550 B.C.

called because Homer's *Iliad* and *Odyssey* describe events of this era. It obviously was very different from the earlier, highly civilized, mercantile Minoan Age.

Very much the same sort of thing happened in India at this time with the invasion of Indo-Europeans who called themselves Aryans, which originally meant "nobles." With their chariots and bronze weapons they crossed the passes of the Hindu Kush Mountains from Afghanistan between 1500 and 1200 B.C. They overthrew the ancient urban civilization of the Indus Valley and replaced it with a primitive tribal society comparable to that of Homeric Greece.

Likewise the early Chinese civilization of the Yellow River valley was overrun in 1027 B.C. by charioteers with bronze weapons. The newcomers were a Chinese people who had lived in the Wei Valley on the fringes of civilization. There they had shared the language and culture of the ancient Yellow River civilization and at the same time they had borrowed the military techniques

of the neighboring barbarians. Thus they were able to overthrow the earlier Shang Dynasty and establish in its place their Chou Dynasty which was to rule China until 256 B.C.

The beginning of the classical age. It is clear from the above that all four centers of civilization in Eurasia experienced far-reaching changes as a result of the series of Indo-European and Semitic invasions. These changes spelled the end of the age of ancient civilizations and the beginning of the age of classical civilizations. For the sake of convenience we select the year 1000 B.C. as the date of the transition, though we have seen that the changes took place at different times in different regions, and that everywhere they developed for centuries instead of occurring in a single year. We shall now examine the main features of this classical age: the rise of large regional empires, the development of the classical civilizations, and the increase in interregional contacts.

Classical Civilizations 73

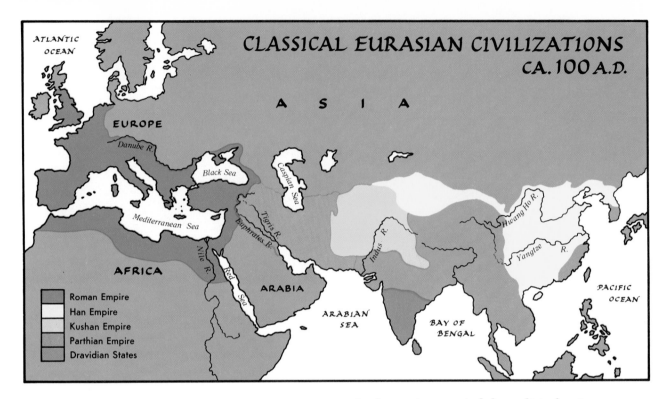

CLASSICAL EURASIAN CIVILIZATIONS
CA. 100 A.D.

Roman Empire
Han Empire
Kushan Empire
Parthian Empire
Dravidian States

FROM VALLEY TO REGIONAL EMPIRES

A glance at the maps of Eurasia about 1500 B.C. (p. 59) and 100 A.D. (above) will show that one of the chief differences between the ancient and classical periods is the size of the political units. In 1500 B.C. the Egyptian Empire was limited to the Nile Valley and the eastern Mediterranean coast, the Minoan to the island of Crete, the Babylonian to the Tigris-Euphrates basin, the Hittite to Asia Minor, the Indus to the valley of the same name, and the Chinese to the Yellow River. But by 100 A.D., when the classical age was at its height, the Roman Empire extended around the entire Mediterranean Basin, the Parthian Empire stretched across the Middle East, the Kushan Empire covered northwestern India, and the Chinese Han Empire included all the remaining territory eastward to the Pacific Ocean. So we see that

in the ancient period the political units were restricted to river valleys and were isolated from each other by wide expanses. In the classical period, by contrast, the empires extended across entire regions and had direct contact with each other.

Out from the valleys. The reason for this difference is to be found in the spread of civilization from the river valleys to the surrounding regions. This spread was partly the work of the people living in the valleys. When population pressure became too strong, they migrated to other areas. In doing so, they naturally took with them the new techniques and implements of civilization, such as the plow, the wheel, and the sickle. Traders, miners, and soldiers also penetrated into the surrounding territories, carrying on their occupations and spreading the techniques and arts of civilization in the process.

Strangely enough, civilization was extended also by the new barbarian invaders. In time they settled down, and with their efficient new iron tools they cut down forests, drained swamps, and opened vast expanses to cultivation. This was especially true in Europe where the thick forests and heavy clay soils had heretofore baffled the agriculturist. Before the Iron Age, bronze had been too expensive to use for tools, so farmers had been forced to use stone-edged axes and wooden plows. But now they were able, with strong and sharp iron axes and iron-shod plows, to transform parts of the primeval forests of Europe into a rich granary. Likewise in the Middle East, agriculture was extended far beyond its origins in the Tigris-Euphrates basin. In India the Aryan newcomers pushed southeastward and cut down the forests of the Ganges Valley. At the same time the Chinese were spreading southward from the Yellow River valley to the Yangtze Valley, where they also brought the wilderness under cultivation.

Extension by sea. Civilization was extended not only by land but also by sea. The new tools made possible the building of larger ships, and this in turn led to long-range expeditions. At first the seafarers were mostly pirates who traded only when they were not strong enough to seize what they wanted. But gradually large-scale commerce was developed on a regular basis. Soon after that, population pressure forced the seafarers to establish permanent colonies abroad.

Notable in this respect were the Phoenicians and the Greeks. The Phoenicians were a Semitic people who settled along the narrow coastal plain of the eastern Mediterranean. Because their resources were too scanty to support them they turned to commerce. By 600 B.C. they had dotted the coasts of North Africa and Spain with their trading posts. Meanwhile the Greeks were leaving the narrow valleys of their homeland and seeking their fortunes abroad. They colonized the northern shores of the Mediterranean and Black Seas. Everywhere they went, the Greeks and the Phoenicians established centers of civilization. They founded cities, built temples and amphitheaters, planted vineyards and olive orchards, and spread the use of the alphabet. Traders from western Asia Minor settled in central Italy; from their colony came the wealthy and advanced Etruscan civilization.

This combination of land and sea expansion enlarged tremendously the area of the civilized world. In 1500 B.C. it had been limited to a few river basins. By 100 A.D., when the classical age was at its height, the civilized lands stretched in a continuous band from the Scottish highlands to the Ganges Valley, and from there to the Pacific Ocean, except for a small gap in the Himalayas.

It was the vast growth of the civilized world that made possible the large empires of the classical age. Obviously it would have been impossible before 1500 B.C. to organize empires spanning the great gaps between the few centers of civilization. But once these

A Phoenician ship of about 1000 B.C. as represented by an Assyrian sculpture of that time.

gaps had been filled in, then it was very natural that empires should spread over entire regions such as the Far East, the Indian Peninsula, and the Middle East and the Mediterranean basin.

The Mediterranean basin. Considering first the Middle East-Mediterranean lands, we have already noted that the Assyrian Empire (750–600 B.C.) was the first to include both the Nile and the Tigris-Euphrates valleys. Then the Persians conquered an empire (550–330 B.C.) stretching from the Nile to the Indus Valleys, and from Central Asia to the Persian Gulf. Meanwhile the Greeks and the Phoenicians were building corresponding sea empires in the Mediterranean and Black Seas. The Phoenicians were unable to remain independent because they were located on the Asian mainland, and finally were swallowed by the huge Persian Empire. But

the Greeks, living across the Aegean Sea, were far enough away from the great land empires to keep their independence. In fact, between 500 and 449 B.C. the Greeks fought a series of wars with the Persians who tried to conquer them, as they had done the Phoenicians. The Greeks' victory over the Persians enabled them to develop their famous and distinctive civilization from which we of the West have borrowed so much.

But the great weakness of the Greeks was their lack of unity. They were organized into city-states such as Athens, Thebes, and Sparta. These cities continually fought with each other until the Macedonians came down from the north and conquered the whole country. Then the Macedonian king, Alexander the Great, used Greece as the base for the conquest of the Middle East. During his reign from 336 to 323 B.C., Alexander won an empire even greater than that of the Persians.

The ruins of Byblos, excavated in present-day Lebanon, testify to the spread of civilization throughout the Middle East. The foreground appears to be the remains of a temple or palace.

It covered the whole region from the Danube to the Indus, and from Egypt to Central Asia. But this empire was a personal creation and lasted only as long as Alexander remained alive. On his death it broke into warring fragments. The unity of this empire was never completely restored although the Romans had consolidated most of it by the first century A.D.

The Romans started with a small city-state in central Italy and steadily expanded until the Mediterranean became a Roman lake. The Roman Empire differed from the earlier Persian and Alexandrine Empires because it included most of northwestern Europe. But in the Middle East it did not extend far beyond the Mediterranean coastline; the interior was ruled first by the Parthians and then by the Sassanians. The Roman Empire was gradually reduced by the barbarian intrusions of the third, fourth, and fifth centuries. Usually historians state that these intrusions and the resulting loss of Roman control and vigor mark the beginning of the medieval age, just as barbarian invasions 2000 years before had introduced the classical age.

China. Turning to China we find a similar succession of empires, each larger than the preceding one, until finally the entire Far East and much of Central Asia were under one rule. During the classical period China was ruled by three dynasties, the Chou, the Ch'in, and the Han. We noted earlier the Chou replaced China's first dynasty, the Shang, in 1027 B.C. The Chou proved to be China's longest-lived dynasty, lasting until 256 B.C. But by the eighth century B.C. this dynasty had declined and lost control over much of the country. Barbarians from the Mongolian steppes repeatedly invaded the country. In self-protection, great noble families arose, who took over control of whole provinces and organized their own private

The Great Wall of China

armies. In fact, some of these families had more land and soldiers than the Chou emperor himself. This sort of decentralized government is known as feudalism; it appeared in Europe also about a thousand years later.

It was one of these powerful noble families, the Ch'in, that succeeded the Chou Dynasty in 221 B.C. The new Ch'in Dynasty lasted only a few years beyond the death of the founder in 210 B.C. But during this short period a centralized system of government was organized in place of the loose feudalism. The provinces were placed under bureaus or departments which were responsible to the emperor. And for the protection of the country, the Ch'in emperor built a network of military roads and also the famous Great Wall which stretched 1400 miles in-

Classical Civilizations 77

land from the coast. For centuries afterwards this tremendous wall helped to protect China against barbarian invasions from the northwest.

The great contribution of the Ch'in Dynasty was the unification of the country; the contribution of the succeeding Han Dynasty (207 B.C.–220 A.D.) was the building up of a large Chinese empire. This empire was conquered as a means of keeping the nomadic invaders in check. At this time the Chinese had much trouble with certain barbarians to the northwest. So they marched armies against them and took over some of their territory. At the same time the Chinese sent diplomatic missions to other Central Asian nomadic peoples and persuaded most of them to accept the emperor of China as their overlord. So, in the end, the Han Empire included much of Central Asia, southern Manchuria, northern Korea, provinces south of the Yangtze River, and northeastern Indochina. This great empire was the equal of the contemporary Roman Empire in area and in strength. But the Han Empire, like the Roman, became weak with the passage of time. As a result, barbarians from the northwest swept over the Great Wall into China, just as the Germanic barbarians broke through the Roman walls across the Danube and the Rhine into the Roman provinces. Thus the Han Empire collapsed in 220 A.D., and China had four hundred years of disorder and civil strife until the rise of the next great dynasty, the T'ang, in 618 A.D.

India. Considering finally India, we have seen that a fair-haired and light-skinned people, the Indo-Europeans, invaded the subcontinent between 1500 and 1200 B.C. They enslaved or drove back the earlier dark-skinned inhabitants and established a number of Aryan kingdoms in the northern part of the country. But we know little about these kingdoms because the Aryans for a long time

Monument to Asoka dating from 3000 B.C.

had no system of writing. Even after they developed writing, they kept very few records. The reason is that, in contrast to the Chinese, they were much more interested in religious and philosophical speculation than in political and administrative matters. This explains in part why Indian history is mostly one of long periods of anarchy interspersed with short periods of strong imperial rule, while Chinese history is precisely the opposite, long periods of dynastic rule interspersed with relatively short periods of anarchy.

The three principal Indian dynasties during the classical period were the Maurya (325–184 B.C.), the Kushan (50–220 A.D.), and the Gupta (320–647). The outstanding

For many years only capital letters were used in the Roman alphabet. The memorial to the Emperor Trajan, built in 114 A.D., is carved with a style of Roman lettering which many consider representative of the alphabet in its most perfect form.

EDWARD KARR

Indian ruler during these centuries was Emperor Asoka of the Maurya Dynasty. As we shall see later, in the unit on India, he is noted especially for his efforts to apply the precepts of Buddhism to his personal life and his administration. The third of these dynasties, the Gupta, came to an end similar to that of the Han of China. Central Asian nomads overran the country, and India sank into an anarchy that continued almost without interruption until the large-scale Muslim invasions in the 12th century.

DEVELOPMENT OF CLASSICAL CIVILIZATIONS

In these regional empires developed the great civilizations whose characteristics have continued to the present day. It was during these centuries of the classical age that there gradually evolved the religious, social, and philosophical systems that still distinguish the main bodies of mankind. When we think of the Chinese people or the Indians or the Europeans, we think of certain customs and beliefs such as ancestor worship, caste organization, and democratic government, or Confucianism, Hinduism, and Christianity. All these were in large part the result of the remarkable creativeness of the classical age.

Strangely enough, this creativeness arose in part from the barbarian invasions. These invasions overthrew old empires and traditional ways of life. In the confusion that followed, people naturally asked questions about the nature and purpose of life, and about the origin and working of the world. The answers that were worked out represent the great philosophies, religions, and political theories of the classical age.

A second reason for creativeness is to be found in the discovery of iron and the creation of the alphabet. Both of these increased the opportunities and the importance of the individual, and one of the chief characteristics of the classical age was the rise of the individual. Iron contributed to this, because for the first time the masses could have cheap iron tools and weapons; before, the state and a few wealthy families had monopolized the production of the expensive bronze. The alphabet also helped the individual because it made literacy much easier. Only a handful of professional scribes had been able to read and to write the complicated cuneiform script of Mesopotamia and the hieroglyphics of Egypt. But the alphabet, with its two dozen letters, made it possible for all classes to become literate. All this meant more respect for the individual and more opportunity for him to ask his own questions and to work out his own answers.

During the classical age, as during the ancient, each region of Eurasia developed a distinctive type of civilization. Each of these civilizations had its special "style" which has continued to the present day and which we can easily recognize. We shall now examine the nature of each of these "styles." We shall see that the Indians based their civilization on religion, the Chinese on propriety, the Jews on the law of God, and the Greeks on the individual.

India: Civilization based on religion. In India, the Aryan invaders who overthrew the Indus Valley civilization were typical Indo-European nomads. They were lusty, beef-eating warriors, lovers of hunting, chariot racing, and cattle raiding, men of violent action rather than thought, conquerors rather than creators. But the raiders had to settle down. Conquerors and conquered had to arrive at some way of living together. The result was a fusing of Aryan and pre-Aryan cultures, which produced a social order and a philosophy of life known as Hinduism. One feature of Hinduism is the caste system,

Belief in the "Sacred Cow" prevails. Often cows are allowed to wander freely.

which seems to have arisen partly because the fair-skinned Aryan invaders wished to preserve their status as the ruling class and remain isolated from their darker subjects.

A second important feature is the social supremacy of the priestly Brahman class which retained its power and prestige despite the opposition of the early Aryan chieftains and kings. Some authorities believe that from this class developed the highest caste and that other groups gradually assumed their respective positions under it. When Brahman ritual and ceremony became excessive, there arose the religion of Buddhism with its emphasis on meditation, brotherhood, chastity, and the preservation of life, even that of animals.

The details of these various religions and ways of life will be examined in the later unit on India. The point to note here is that they have persisted to the present day. A visitor to India today would find members of different sects eating separately because of the food taboos of their castes. He would find cows walking about freely in the streets because of the reverence for all animal life. And he would find holy men wandering about in strange costumes and treated with utmost reverence by the rest of the population. In short, the visitor would find a civilization in which extraordinary emphasis is placed upon religion and philosophy, upon an eternal spiritual life. This civilization took shape in the classical age and has persisted to the present day, dominating the lives of millions in the Indian subcontinent.*

China: Civilization based on propriety. The Indian civilization that developed in the classical age emphasized religion and philosophy; the Chinese, by contrast, laid stress on propriety, suitable conduct for human beings. The dominant body of thought in China

* See *Readings in World History,* "India: Civilization Based on Religion," p. 51.

MONKMEYER

Confucius

was that of Kung-fu-tse, known to the Western world by the Latinized name Confucius. Living in the sixth century B.C., a time of strife and anarchy, he sought to find a way out of the difficulties. In his teachings he called not for the salvation of the soul, as did India's leaders, but for good government and harmonious relations between men. These were to be gained by what he called *li,* or propriety. By this he meant that man should be concerned more about his obligations than his rights. His obligations included tolerance, charity, love of learning, obedience to parents, and reverence for elders and ancestors.

In regard to the afterlife, Confucius said, "We don't know yet how to serve men, how can we know about serving the spirits? We don't know yet about life, how can we know about death?" [1] This attitude is very different from the following expressed in a Hindu epic, "They who have lived a good life in this world will as a reward attain a good rebirth as a Brahman . . . but they who in this world have lived a shameful life will attain a shameful rebirth as a dog or a pig or an outcaste." [2]

Confucius' teachings were not widely accepted in his lifetime. But after several generations they became dominant in China and remained so until the establishment of the Communist government in 1949. The details of Confucianism will be examined in the later unit on China. The important point to note here is that Confucianism, like Hinduism, has dominated the lives of great bodies of people to the present day.* How deeply it has stamped Chinese civilization can be seen in the following proverbs of Chinese

* See *Readings in World History,* "China: Civilization Based on Propriety," p. 53.

Craftsmanship and years of study were combined to produce this 12th century Hebrew scroll.

PEABODY MUSEUM, SALEM, MASS.

peasants: "No image-maker worships the gods—he knows what stuff they are made of"; and "Work with the sunrise, Rest with the sunset, Dig the well for my drink, Plough the land for my food—What do I care for the Power above?" [3]

Palestine: Civilization based on the law of God. The third people of the classical age whose influence is felt to the present day are the Jews of Palestine. In contrast to the numerous Indians and Chinese, the Jews were a handful of tribesmen wandering along the fringes of the great empires of the Middle East. For thousands of years, between their conquest by the Assyrians in 722 B.C. and their establishment of the independent state of Israel in 1948 A.D., the Jews had no homeland. They were subject to Egyptians, Assyrians, Babylonians, Greeks, Romans, and various Arab peoples. And yet they preserved their identity and outlasted their masters. The reason is that the Jews have been a people with a Book, the Old Testament. They have been a people with a faith, belief in one God, Yahweh (Jehovah).

The Jews were typical Semitic nomads who left their original homeland in the Arabian desert and settled down in Palestine. At first they worshipped numerous deities, but about the 12th century B.C. they adopted a national god, Yahweh. In doing so, they became the first people of our Western civilization to worship only one God. The first of Yahweh's Ten Commandments was emphatic about monotheism, or loyalty to one God. "I am the Lord, thy God . . . Thou shalt have no other gods before me." This Commandment did not say that Yahweh was the only God in the world. It said, rather, that he was the only God for the children of Israel. And so the Jews regarded it as perfectly natural and proper that the Egyptians and Mesopotamians and Greeks should have their gods, just as they had their Yahweh.

The Oracle of Apollo at Delphi reflected the Greek philosophy of reason and self-study. Advice from the Oracle was usually given in vaguely-worded hints which the people then interpreted for themselves, and often the advice advocated moderation and self-control.

SVEN SAMELIUS

Furthermore the Jewish religion at this stage was more social and ethical than mystical and otherworldly. Its aim was to promote justice in this life rather than to achieve salvation in the afterlife. In the words of one of the Jewish prophets, Yahweh cares nothing for ritual and sacrifice; he cares only that men should "seek justice, relieve the oppressed, judge the fatherless, plead for the widow."

But from the sixth century B.C. onward, the Jews changed their religious ideas under the influence of the Babylonians, Persians, Greeks, and Romans who ruled them. Now the Jews saw Yahweh as the one and only God, the God for the whole human race. They also adopted a belief in an afterlife in which obedience to God's will would bring eternal happiness in heaven, and disobedience would bring eternal punishment in hell. Salvation in an afterworld now became more important than enjoyment of this life.

This new faith was to serve as the basis for Christianity. And Christianity a few cen-

turies later was to become the state religion of the Roman Empire, and eventually one of the main strands of Western civilization. To the Christian religion the Jews contributed the Commandments, the stories of the Creation and the Flood, the concept of God as lawgiver and judge, and that portion of the Bible known as the Old Testament.*

Greece: Civilization based on the individual. The other people of the classical age who influenced fundamentally our Western civilization were the Greeks. Saint Paul, whose background was partly Greek and partly Jewish, summarized the difference between these two people when he said, "The Jews require a sign, and the Greeks seek for wisdom." In other words, the Jews waited for miracles from heaven, while the Greeks wanted to find out for themselves. On their principal religious shrine at Delphi, the

* See *Readings in World History*, "Palestine: Civilization Based on the Law of God," p. 55.

Greeks inscribed the motto "Know Thyself," not "Fear God." They were concerned with man, the individual, and with this spirit they built their splendid civilization. And this civilization is, like Judaism and Christianity, one of the main elements in our Western civilization.*

Why were the Greeks able to accomplish what they did and exert the influence that they did? Geography offers a partial answer to this question. The homeland of the Greeks was in the southern part of the Balkan Peninsula where they were close enough to the ancient Middle Eastern civilizations to profit from them, and yet far enough to be able to keep their independence. Thus the Greeks were free to develop their own customs and institutions and ideas.

It must also be remembered that Greece is a relatively poor country. Hesiod, a poet of the early Greek period, describes his Fatherland as "cold in winter, hot in summer, good at no time." When the Dorian invaders settled down in Greece, they found themselves in a small country with few natural resources. Such a country simply could not support an Egyptian or Mesopotamian type of Oriental monarchy with its court and bureaucracy and pomp. Furthermore Greece is so cut up into small isolated regions by the maze of mountains that it was very hard to organize a single unified state. For all these reasons the government of Greece consisted of numerous small and independent city-states rather than a single great empire. These city-states allowed the Greek people much more freedom to do what they wished than they would have been allowed under an imperial government.

With the help of these advantages the Greeks developed their famous civilization which reached its height in the fifth century B.C. This civilization emphasized the

* See *Reading in World History,* "Greece: Civilization Based on the Individual," p. 56.

individual and his reasoning powers. The Greeks were perhaps the first people to look at the world about them with an open mind and to try to explain its operation by reason rather than by superstition or myth. For example, Greek philosophers tried to answer the question "What is the stuff of which the world is made?" One stated that it was water, because this substance was found in liquid, solid, and vapor form. Another philosopher also chose water because it was essential for both animals and plants.

With today's scientific knowledge we may smile at these efforts, but what is important is that the question was asked, and the answer was sought by the use of reason. The father of medicine, Hippocrates, also depended on reason when he said, "The fact is that invoking the gods to explain diseases and other natural events is all nonsense. In nature all things are alike in this, that they all can be traced to preceding causes." [4] This is the essence of what we call the scientific attitude. From the Greek insistence on the use of reason and the investigation of causes have come, in part, the scientific achievements of the modern world.

The rise of democracy. The Greek emphasis on the individual led also to the rise of a limited type of democracy as a form of government. In fact, our word democracy comes from the two Greek words *demos* and *kratia,* meaning rule by the people. It is true that democracy existed in classical Greece for relatively short periods. But the fact remains that for the first time in human history there was worked out a form of government in which all men except slaves and newcomers were free to participate on an equal basis. This was especially true in the city of Athens in the fifth century B.C. All adult male citizens met in an Assembly which had full power in every sphere of government, whether foreign affairs or military operations

View of the Acropolis showing the Propylaeum, Erechtheum, and the Parthenon. The Odeum of Herodes Atticus is in front.

or financial matters. Citizens also served as jurors in popular courts and in other public bodies. And to make sure that poor citizens could afford to take the time to participate in the government of their city, payments were made to all who served as jurors or in other time-consuming capacities.

This was real democracy, and it worked! The Greeks took pride in the fact that they ruled themselves instead of being subject to the whim and fancy of a despotic ruler. Their victory over the great Persian Empire made them more certain of the superiority of their way of life. This can be seen in the follow-ing speech by the famous Athenian leader, Pericles.

> We enjoyed a form of government not cop-ied from the laws of any neighboring state. Rather do other states copy ours. And since our constitution considers not the benefit of the few, but the welfare of the many, we call it a democracy. The state regards all men as equal so far as their private differences are con-cerned; but it selects for public honour those who have shown their ability in the public ser-vice, nor does poverty prevent any man from showing his worth as a citizen. . . . In brief, our city is a model for the whole of Greece.[5]

Classical Civilizations 85

INCREASED INTERREGIONAL CONTACTS

The final feature of the classical age that we shall note is the increase in contacts among the various regions of Eurasia. These contacts were of many varieties, and we shall examine here three types: cultural, commercial, and religious.

Cultural contacts. The outstanding example of cultural interaction is the spread of Hellenism from its place of origin in the Mediterranean to all regions of Eurasia. By Hellenism we mean the mixed Greek-Middle Eastern culture that developed in Alexander's far-flung empire. We have seen that the empire lasted for only a few years during Alexander's lifetime. Upon his death in 323 B.C. it was divided among his generals, and later held by Rome in the west and the Parthians in the east. But during these years many common ties were developed which together made up the new Hellenistic culture. For example, the Greek language spread through the Middle East and became the common language of all educated men and of merchants who travelled through the area.

Alexander also established at least 25 and perhaps as many as 70 new Greek cities in his empire. Several of these cities, located in Syria, Turkestan, Afghanistan, the Caucasus, and Egypt, were named Alexandria, after the great conqueror. All of them, regardless of their names, served as centers for the diffusion of Greek culture. Many Greeks emigrated from their homeland to these cities, and most of them intermarried with the local populations. As a result the Greeks dropped their attitude of superiority towards all other peoples, whom they formerly had always referred to as barbarians. In fact, a Greek of this period criticized some of his countrymen who "divided mankind into two classes, Greek and Barbarian." "It would be better," he argued, "to classify on the basis of goodness and badness; for even of the Greeks there are many bad, and of the Barbarians many thoroughly refined, such as the Indians and Iranians (Persians), not to speak of the Romans and Carthaginians with their admirable constitutions." [6]

All these developments resulted in the spread through the Middle East, and beyond, of the new Hellenistic culture that was largely Greek or Hellenic (derived from the Greek word "Hellas," meaning Greece). Most affected was Asia Minor, where the people forgot their native languages and spoke Greek. Elsewhere Greek manners, arts, amusements, and coinage were adopted. This was true as far east as India where Alexander's invasion led to Greek influence on Indian coinage, architecture, and sculpture. From India and Central Asia, the Greek influence was carried still further east to China and even to Japan. In Africa, some elements of Hellenism filtered down to Ethiopia. It also spread westward after the Romans conquered Greece and the Middle East. The Romans at this time lagged behind the Greeks in artistic and philosophical development with the result that they tended to adopt Hellenism. This is why the Latin poet, Horace, wrote,

Then captive Greece her savage conqueror
Did captivate and to the Latin boor
Gave lessons in the arts.

Despite this great diffusion, Hellenism did not leave a permanent imprint. The reason is that Hellenism affected only the cities where Greek settlers lived and where Greek dynasties had courts. Some of the native peoples were affected, of course, but they were only the small upper classes. Only in Asia Minor did the mass of the people adopt the Greek language. Elsewhere the peasant masses continued to speak their own languages and to worship their own gods. It is not surprising, then, that Hellenistic culture did not sink deep roots and did not survive through the centuries. We shall see later that when the Muslim conquerors appeared in the Middle Ages, they were able to drown the islands of Hellenistic culture with little difficulty. This is why the Greek language and culture have survived today only in the Greek homeland on the southern tip of the Balkan Peninsula.

Commercial contacts. During the classical period there was increased contact among the regions of Eurasia in commerce as well as culture. One reason for this was the development of coinage by the Greeks about 700 B.C. The coins gradually were standardized and generally accepted, making trade much easier than in the earlier days of barter.* This was especially true with the rise of the great Han Empire in the East and the Roman Empire in the West. These empires established the peace and security that was necessary in order for interregional trade to flourish.

It is significant, for example, that Alexander the Great, in the fourth century B.C., knew nothing about China, Siberia, or the Ganges part of India. However, by the second century B.C., caravans were going directly from China to the Middle East, loaded with the precious Chinese silk that was in great demand in the Roman Empire. An interesting result of this commercial tie was that numerous plants which formerly were to be found only in one region now spread to the others. For example, the Chinese now obtained for the first time the grape vine, alfalfa, chive, cucumber, fig, sesame, pomegranate, and walnut. In return the Chinese gave the orange, peach, pear, peony, azalea, camellia, and chrysanthemum.

* See *Readings in World History,* "Invention of Coinage in the Classical Age," p. 59.

Coins, while contributing to the growth of trade, also by their designs tell us much about the politics, religion, and culture of Greece.

Trade by sea also flourished among the regions of Eurasia. India was the center of this sea trade. Ships sailed to India from China, the Middle East, the coast of East Africa, and Roman ports of the Red Sea. The chief goods that were exchanged were silk and rhubarb from China, spices and aromatics from India, linen, copper, tin, and glass from the Roman Empire, and ivory from Africa. By far the most valuable commodity was silk, which was imported in huge quantities into the Roman Empire. In fact, the Romans could not export enough to pay for all this silk, so that they had to send gold and silver to make up the difference. Some historians believe that one reason why the Roman Empire later declined was that it lost too much of its gold and silver in paying for Chinese silk and Indian spices.

By the third century A.D. this interregional trade had greatly declined. One reason was the weakening of the Chinese Han and Roman Empires, which meant less order and security for the travelling merchants. At a later date, the trade declined further when the Romans at last learned the secret of the silkworm and proceeded to make their own silk. Previously they had guessed that silk was a fine down that stuck to the leaves of certain trees or flowers, or else that it was an especially delicate species of wool or cotton. The Chinese naturally tried to keep their secret, but finally, according to one story, someone in the sixth century smuggled the eggs of the silkworm to Constantinople in a hollow stick. So silk henceforth could be made outside of China, and trade between China and the rest of Eurasia declined in quantity.*

The spread of Christianity. During the classical age there was interaction among the regions of Eurasia in religious matters as well as cultural and commercial. Christianity and

* See *Readings in World History,* "Interregional Trade During the Classical Age," p. 62

Buddhism were most influential and spread farthest, probably because they were universal religions, claiming the allegiance of all men and not merely that of one group. That is why they outdistanced Judaism, which was identified with the Jews, and Confucianism, which was linked with the Chinese.

During the lifetime of Jesus and immediately after his crucifixion, all Christians were Jewish. But Paul, a Hellenized Jew who lived in the city of Tarsus in Asia Minor, boldly denied that Jesus was sent merely as the redeemer of the Jews. A loving Father had sent His only Son to atone for the sins of all mankind. Therefore Christianity was not a sect of Judaism. It was a new church, a church for Gentiles as well as for Jews. Paul's approach meant that Christianity henceforth could appeal not only to a handful of Jews, but to the millions of Gentiles who made up most of the population of the Roman Empire.

Despite fifty years of persecution, Christianity grew steadily and was finally tolerated in 313 by Emperor Constantine's Edict of Milan. Later in 339, it was made the official state religion of the Roman Empire. Then, after the fall of the Empire, Christian missionaries carried the faith to the English and German peoples between 600 and 800 A.D., to the Slavic peoples between 800 and 1100 A.D. With the expansion of Europe, both missionaries and emigrants spread Christianity to all parts of the globe.

The spread of Buddhism. The other main universal religion, Buddhism, arose as a reaction against the injustice of the caste system and the exploitation practiced by the priestly Brahman caste. The founder, Gautama (563–484 B.C.), was born Prince Siddhartha and could have lived a comfortable and pleasure-filled existence. But he was so distressed by the human suffering he saw all around him that he gave up his pleasant life and devoted family to spend many years in study and con-

These scenes, from a Chinese book originally printed in 1637, illustrate four steps in the ancient process of making silk: the care of the silkworms, actually caterpillars (above left), the selection of the better cocoons after the caterpillars have been killed by boiling (right), and the spinning and winding of the thread (above center). After several threads were twisted together for strength, it was woven into cloth on looms (above right).

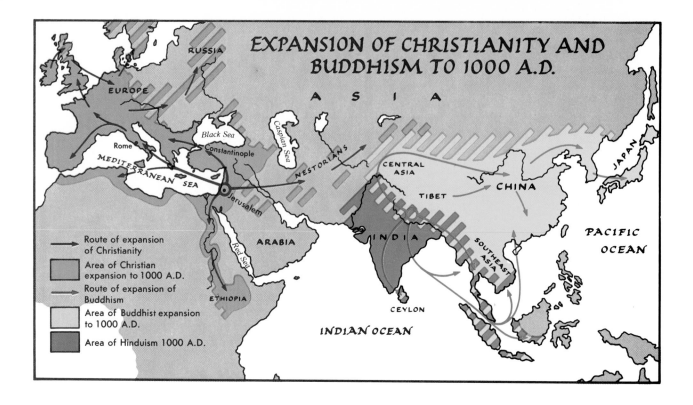

EXPANSION OF CHRISTIANITY AND BUDDHISM TO 1000 A.D.

- → Route of expansion of Christianity
- Area of Christian expansion to 1000 A.D.
- → Route of expansion of Buddhism
- Area of Buddhist expansion to 1000 A.D.
- Area of Hinduism 1000 A.D.

templation. One day when he was weary and discouraged, he sat under a pipal (fig) tree, where, in a moment of revelation, he discovered the secret of evil and suffering. The revelation is called the Enlightenment, and thenceforth Gautama was called Buddha, or the Enlightened One.

The four great truths of Buddhism are: (1) that life is sorrow; (2) that the cause of sorrow is desire; (3) that escape is possible only by stopping desire; and (4) that this can only be done by following the "Noble Eightfold Path," consisting of right belief, right intention, right speech, right action, right means of livelihood, right effort, right thinking, and right meditation. The Eightfold Path constitutes the route to spiritual perfection and, ultimately, to the achievement of Nirvana, a state in which all passion, hatred, and delusion are removed. Thus Buddhism does

not promise a "happy life" in the usual understanding of the phrase, but it does show the way to spiritual peace.

Gautama did not intend to establish a new religion, but after his death his disciples collected his teachings and preached them as the basis for the Buddhist religion. This religion grew rapidly during the reign of the great Emperor Asoka, who ruled most of India between 274 and 232 B.C. Asoka was deeply affected by the slaughter and suffering that took place during one of his campaigns. In his writings he confessed that he had deported 150,000 people and killed 100,000, and admitted that he now found this "very painful and grievous."

Because of his disgust, Asoka became a devout Buddhist and tried to apply his new religious principles in the administration of his country. He planted trees, dug wells, established rest houses for travellers, made special provisions for the education of women, and founded hospitals, including the first hospital in the world for animals. He also obeyed the Buddhist rule against taking any life. In the royal kitchens, he wrote, "formerly several hundred thousand animals were killed daily for food; but now at the time of writing only three are killed—two peacocks and a deer, though the deer not regularly. Even these three animals will not be killed in future." [7]

Asoka also wrote, "I consider my work to be the welfare of the whole world." So he sent Buddhist missionaries to Ceylon, Burma, Nepal, and even west to Greece, Syria and Egypt. In later years Buddhist missionaries carried their faith to Tibet and Central Asia, and from there it spread to China in the first century A.D. Many Chinese made the perilous journey to India to study the new religion, and when they returned they took with them thousands of Buddhist books which they translated into Chinese. In fact there are Chinese translations of Buddhist texts whose originals can no longer be found in India. From China, Buddhism spread still further: to Korea in the fourth century A.D., to Japan in the sixth century, and to southwestern Asia in the tenth century.

After these great successes, Buddhism declined in many countries. In China it seriously challenged Confucianism at one time, but in 845 A.D. it was suppressed by the government. It was not altogether wiped out, but from then on it had much less influence in China. Even in its birthplace, India, Buddhism eventually gave way to a revival of Hinduism. By the 12th century it had been completely overshadowed, and today very few traces are left in India of the religion of the great Asoka. Buddhism has remained, however, the dominant religion in Tibet, Ceylon, Burma, and Thailand. The historical significance of Buddhism is that it was a great

Statue of Buddha, Kyoto, Japan

civilizing force in Asia, as Christianity was in Europe. To many peoples it brought not only ethical principles but also a system of writing, a type of architecture, and the great civilizations of China and India which the missionaries spread together with their religion. In the same way the Christian missionaries diffused among the barbarous Germanic and Slavic peoples the civilization of Rome and Constantinople, as well as the teachings of Christ.

Persistence of regional civilizations. We have seen that interregional contacts increased greatly during the classical age. More

This statue of Buddha, located in Singapore, has been sculptured and painted in a manner distinct to the culture of Southeast Asia. People of a given culture often envisioned Buddha to be like themselves, and since Buddhism spread throughout Asia, there are many different representations. Contrast this statue from Singapore with the one on the preceding page from Japan.

than at any time in the past, the people of various parts of Eurasia were aware of each other and were affected by each other. But we should note that this interaction was not decisive. It did not lead to fundamental and permanent changes in the Eurasian centers of civilization. There is no case of one major civilization leaving at this time a permanent imprint upon another. Interregional trade declined with the fall of the Roman and Han Empires. Hellenism, which affected a wide area in Europe and Asia, petered out after a few centuries. Buddhism became a negligible force in its two most important centers, China and India. Christianity took hold in Europe and became a major element in Western civilization. But when efforts were made later to extend it to other parts of the world, there was little success except in those areas

that were settled by European emigrants. The efforts of thousands of missionaries and the expenditure of large sums of money during the past several centuries failed to Christianize Africa or South or East Asia.

Why did the extensive interregional contacts of the classical age fail to have permanent effects? In the case of trade, the reason is simply one of technology. It was hard at that time to carry on long-distance commerce by camel and caravan or by small sailing ships. Accordingly these fragile economic ties were easily snapped when empires weakened and anarchy blocked the routes of trade. Cultural and religious ties failed to continue because each regional civilization had crystallized and taken form by the classical age. Each civilization had developed its distinctive "style," and its people took pride in this "style" and refused to consider any major change in their beliefs and practices and customs. An example of this pride in regional civilization can be seen in the case of a Chinese Buddhist monk who had studied in a monastery in India and then decided to return to his country.

The monks of Nalanda (monastery), when they heard of it, begged him to remain, saying: "India is the land of Buddha's birth, and though he has left the world, there are still many traces of him. What greater happiness could there be than to visit them in turn, to adore him and chant his praises? Why then do you wish to leave, having come so far? Moreover China is a country of . . . unimportant barbarians, who despise the religious and the (Buddhist) Faith. That is why Buddha was not born there. The mind of the people is narrow, and their coarseness profound, hence neither sages nor saints go there. The climate is cold and the country rugged—you must think again."

The Master of the Law (the Chinese Buddhist) replied, "Buddha established his doctrine so that it might be diffused to all lands. Who would wish to enjoy it alone, and to forget those who are not yet enlightened? Besides, in my country the magistrates are clothed with dignity, and the laws are everywhere respected. The emperor is virtuous and the subjects loyal, parents are loving and sons obedient, humanity and justice are highly esteemed,

and old men and sages are held in honour. Moreover, how deep and mysterious is their knowledge; their wisdom equals that of spirits. They have taken the Heavens as their model, and they know how to calculate the movements of the Seven Luminaries; they have invented all kinds of instruments, fixed the seasons of the year. . . . How then can you say that Buddha did not go to my country because of its insignificance?" [8]

This feeling of regional pride, expressed so strongly by the Chinese Buddhist, explains why the individual Eurasian civilizations have persisted to the present day, and why they have not given way to one common Eurasian civilization. Today, if you were blindfolded and dropped in the midst of Paris or Delhi or Peking or Cairo, you would be able to tell very easily which city you were in as soon as the blindfold was removed. The sights and smells and sounds, the language the people speak, the clothes they wear, the food they eat, the songs they sing, the buildings they erect, the ways they worship God, all these would tell you where you were. In other words, each civilization can be distinguished by the numerous expressions of its general "style," which has continued to a large degree from the classical age to the present.

Reviewing the Essentials

Beginning of the Classical Age
1. Under what circumstances did the age of ancient civilizations come to an end around 1000 B.C.?
2. Why is the period that followed referred to as the age of classical civilizations?
3. Who were the three groups of barbarians that invaded the river valleys and scattered the civilizations they found there?
4. Why were the barbarians able to overwhelm and destroy superior and long-established civilizations?

5. Which of the ancient civilizations was changed most by the barbaric invasions? Which were changed least? How do you account for the difference?

From Valley to Regional Empires
6. The classical age was one of large empires. What is an empire? Why was it possible by 100 A.D. for large empires to encompass the lands that lay between centers of civilizations in the ancient period? What were the differences between the empires of ancient and classical periods?

7. On a map locate the empires of the classical age: in the Middle East, the Hittite, Assyrian, Persian, Greek, Phoenician, Macedonian, and Roman; in China, the Chou, Ch'in, and the Han; in India, the Maurya, the Kushan, and the Gupta.

8. Locate on a map the limits of the civilized world by 100 A.D., and contrast with the extent of the civilized world in 1500 B.C.

Development of Classical Civilizations

9. Unique ways of life developed in the regional empires because of the creativeness of the classical age. Account for creativeness in a time of confusion.

10. What were the distinguishing characteristics of the way of life that developed in India during the classical age? How did the Aryan invaders bring about change that culminated in Hinduism?

11. How does the way of life that developed in China during the classical age differ from that in India?

12. What were the teachings and beliefs that became the basis for the way of life developed by the Jewish people in Palestine during the classical age?

13. Why did the Greeks develop a way of life that emphasized the individual and his reasoning power? How did this emphasis promote the growth of democracy? How does the Greek definition of democracy in the classical age differ from our definition of today?

14. Why is a knowledge of these four ways of life essential to an understanding of the history of mankind?

Increased Interregional Contacts

15. Explain what is meant by Hellenism. Who spread Hellenistic culture? How far was its influence felt? In what ways? What effect did Hellenistic culture have on the Greeks? Non-Greeks? Why did the Hellenistic culture fail to take root in those regions to which it spread?

16. What kinds of commercial contacts were made among the regions of Eurasia during the classical age?

17. Why are Christianity and Buddhism referred to as universal religions? Summarize the teachings of each. What persons universalized Christianity? Buddhism? What parts of the world did these religions influence during the classical age? What parts of the world did they influence permanently?

18. The record of cultural, commercial, and religious contacts between regions during the classical age is impressive. Why, then, did these contacts fail to result in any permanent change in the four ways of life that developed from 1000 B.C. to 500 A.D.?

19. Give a brief account of the part silk played in classical history in reference to its affect upon trade between East and West and upon the economy of the Roman Empire.

Explain, Identify, or Locate

classical age	Jesus	Semitic Arabs	Troy
reincarnation	Confucius	Indo-Europeans	Thebes
Judaism	Asoka	Mongols	Sparta
caste	Pericles	Phoenicians	Yangtze River
Brahma	Alexander the Great	Persians	Asia Minor
monotheism	Homer	Macedonians	the Caucasus
Edict of Milan	Hippocrates	Parthians	Central Eurasia
Gautama	Dravidians	Sassanians	Kamakura
St. Paul	Hittites	Athens	Hindu Kush Mountains
449 B.C.	323 B.C.	100 A.D.	313 A.D.

MEDIEVAL CIVILIZATIONS: 500—1500 A.D.

The barbarian invasions of the Eurasian centers of civilization affected the medieval age as fundamentally as they had the classical. We have seen that the Indo-European invasions between 2000 and 1000 B.C. undermined the ancient civilizations and helped to give birth to the classical age. So it was now, during the medieval period between approximately 500 and 1500 A.D. that three great barbarian invasions dominated Eurasian history. The first were the Germanic invasions of the fourth and fifth centuries A.D., which hastened the collapse of the West Roman Empire and cleared the ground for a new civilization in Europe. The second were the Arab invasions of the seventh century, which led to the establishment of a great Muslim Empire and to the fusion of Middle Eastern and Graeco-Roman civilizations. The third wave of invasions was that of the Mongols in the 13th century, who united most of Eurasia and made possible unprecedented interaction among the regions of Eurasia. Finally we shall note that the people who responded dynamically rather than passively to these invasions were the Europeans. Between 1000 and 1500 they developed rapidly in every field and thus laid the foundation for the great European expansion overseas after 1500. In the remainder of this unit we shall consider each of these events in turn.

GERMANIC INVASIONS AND THE FOUNDING OF EUROPEAN CIVILIZATION

The West Roman Empire crumbles. During the fourth and fifth centuries A.D., several barbarian Germanic tribes overran and destroyed the West Roman Empire.* They

* See *Readings in World History*, "Rome at Its Height," p. 65.

were able to do this not so much because of their own strength, but because the West Roman Empire had become a hollow shell. It was undermined by several developments: by foreign and civil wars that drained the treasury; by inflation which ruined the middle and upper classes; by the exploitation of the farmers who lost their freedom and became virtual serfs on large estates; and by the poverty of the masses in the city who were to a large degree supported by the government. All these problems produced a very unhealthy situation. Political bickering and class conflict took the place of the former patriotism and public spirit that had made the Roman Empire a world power.

Medieval Civilizations 95

Examples of the architectural achievements of the Romans remain. The Colosseum at Rome stands as a reminder of gladiatorial contests. Le Pont du Gare at Nimes, France, recalls the vast territorial expanse of the Roman Empire.

With the decline in strength and morale, the formerly invincible Roman legions no longer were able to defend the frontiers of the empire. Barbarians were allowed to enter and serve in the legions as paid soldiers. As the empire declined still further, these barbarian reinforcements were not enough. The frontier defenses crumbled, and whole tribes of Germans crossed over into the empire. These were mass invasions, including women and children as well as the warriors. In this way several Germanic tribes settled down and occupied whole provinces of the former Roman Empire. The most important were the Visigoths in Spain, the Ostrogoths in Italy, the Vandals in North Africa, and the Angles, Saxons, and Jutes in England. This breaking-up of the Roman Empire was a gradual process, but if we wish to set a specific date, we can select 476 A.D., when a German chieftain named Odoacer overthrew the last Roman Emperor, Romulus Augustulus, ending a succession of nearly five hundred years.

The Byzantine Empire. But only the West Roman Empire collapsed in 476 A.D. By contrast the East Roman Empire, known also as the Greek or Byzantine Empire, continued to exist for another one thousand years. The dividing line between the West and East Roman Empires ran down the middle of present-day Yugoslavia. The reason the Eastern Empire managed to survive, despite

many dangers and invasions, is that it was a much older and wealthier center of civilization. So Constantinople remained as the great capital of the East Roman Empire long after Rome had fallen to the Germanic tribesmen.

The East Roman, or Byzantine, Empire continued to flourish from 476 A.D., when Augustulus disappeared, until 1453 when the Turks captured Constantinople. During this thousand-year period the eastern part of the empire made contributions of first-rate importance. It preserved the arts of civilization at a time when Western Europe had sunk into barbarism. It helped Western Europe to emerge from barbarism by purchasing its raw materials such as fish, salt, and grain, and

giving in return luxury products such as dyes, perfumes, and fine fabrics. This trade was mostly with the Italian cities, such as Venice, and as a result these cities were able to keep a much higher cultural level than the rest of Europe. The Byzantine Empire also passed on the arts of civilization to the barbarian Slavic peoples in Eastern Europe.

For this reason Slavic civilization to the present day is in many ways different from that of Western Europe. If we were to travel in Slavic countries such as the Soviet Union or Bulgaria, we would notice that many of their older buildings are patterned after Byzantine models rather than those of Rome. The religion of many Slavs is Greek Orthodox Christianity which originated in Constantinople. Their alphabet would be unfamiliar to us as they use the Cyrillic, or Slavic, derived from the Greek rather than the Roman.

Western civilization evolves. While the Byzantine Empire was preserving the great Graeco-Roman civilization in the east, a new civilization was slowly taking shape in the west. This new civilization was created by the fusion or mingling of contributions from three sources: the Germanic newcomers, the Christian Church, and the old Roman Empire. One of the German contributions was people. Whole tribes of Germans migrated into the Roman Empire and intermarried with the native peoples. This explains why today the people of northern France, where many Germans settled, are considerably lighter in complexion than the people in Southern France, where few Germans arrived. The Germans also contributed their tribal law which was personal rather than territorial. This means that the laws of the tribe governed only the persons who belonged to the tribe and not all those who lived in the area. So the German personal law usually was enforced for the German settlers, while

Monks often spent months or years painstakingly copying a manuscript. The result was often a masterpiece of calligraphy and artistic detail.

the Roman Empire, only the Church had an organization that covered a large part of the continent. The Church was carefully and tightly organized, with the pope at the top, then bishops in charge of the dioceses, and finally the priests scattered in all of the parishes. This arrangement had been built up in late Roman times, and it continued into the medieval period, and indeed down to the present day. So during the troubled times following the collapse of the Roman Empire, the Christian Church was the only institution that could operate over the whole area. It alone could receive news, send out agents, and generally serve as a cement for chaotic Europe.

In addition to its organization, the Church also made a contribution by preserving and passing on some of the civilization of the past. It did this through the monks and nuns who lived quietly in their monastic communities or monasteries. But they did not spend all of their time in prayer and religious devotion. They preserved some of the industrial skills of the past such as wood carving, metalworking, glassmaking, weaving, and brewing. They also maintained learning, for it was only the monks during these turbulent times who knew how to read and write, who copied the ancient books, kept up the libraries, and organized schools. Even in agriculture, the monks were pioneers in cutting down the forests, draining swamps, and improving methods of farming. In these ways the Christian Church, during the centuries of barbarism, helped to preserve the culture of the past and to develop a new civilization for the future.*

the Roman territorial law was continued for the native population.*

The Church binds Europe. The Christian Church also contributed much to the new civilization that was emerging in Europe. One of its contributions was organization; the Church served as a sort of cement to hold Europe together. In fact, with the collapse of

* See *Readings in World History*, "German Invaders and Their Customs," p. 67.

The inheritance from Rome. The third contributor to the emerging civilization of Europe was ancient Rome. This may seem strange since the Roman Empire long had

* See *Readings in World History*, "The Christian Church in Medieval Europe," p. 70.

been a hollow shell and finally had fallen to pieces. Yet Rome passed on a good deal that has survived to the present day. One contribution was the Latin language, from which are derived modern Romance languages such as French, Italian, Spanish, and Portuguese. Another contribution of the old empire was Roman law, which is the basis of the modern law codes of Latin nations such as France, Italy, Spain, Portugal, and the countries of Latin America. Finally, Rome passed on to the new European civilization the idea of empire and imperial unity. This may seem too vague and theoretical to have had much influence. Yet much of the prestige of the pope came from the fact that he was the bishop of Rome, the capital of the great empire of the past. Furthermore a long series of medieval kings fought endless wars in vain attempts to restore the old Roman Empire.

Charlemagne. Outstanding among these rulers was the king of the Franks, Charles the Great, or Charlemagne. He succeeded in extending his lands from their original center in France to the North Sea, the Pyrenees, central Italy, and Germany. This included all the lands that the Roman Empire had encompassed in northwestern Europe. In recognition of this fact, Pope Leo crowned Charles emperor in 800 A.D. while the people, according to one observer, shouted "To Charles Augustus, crowned of God the great and pacific Emperor of the Romans, life and victory!" This shows that the idea of the Roman Empire was far from dead in the minds of men, even several centuries after Romulus Augustulus.*

New invaders. Charlemagne's empire did not last long. It was broken up by a new wave of invasions in the ninth century by the Magyars, or Hungarians, who came from the

* See *Readings in World History,* "Recovery Under Charlemagne," p. 73.

eastern steppes; by the Norsemen, or Vikings, who came from Scandinavia; and by the Muslims who crossed over from North Africa. But gradually these barbarians also settled down and were absorbed. The Magyars settled in the Danube Valley where they finally formed the state of Hungary, while the Norsemen settled in the many lands that they had raided. In France they established the duchy of Normandy, and they also set up political structures in England, southern Italy, and Russia. Finally, the Muslims remained in control of Sicily and Spain where they developed civilizations far more advanced than those of Northern Europe.

It was in this manner that these barbarian invaders were slowly assimilated as the earlier German barbarians had been several centuries earlier. In 1001 the pope sent a golden crown to the Magyars to crown St. Stephen as their first king. At the same time Christianity, which was a powerful civilizing force, was spreading north to Scandinavia and east to Poland and Bohemia. Meanwhile the Christian churches of Western Europe and the Byzantine Empire were drifting apart because of the refusal of the Greek Patriarchs of Constantinople to recognize the spiritual authority of the pope in Rome. In 1054 a definite schism, or break, divided the Christian world into the Latin, or Roman Catholic, and the Greek, or Orthodox, Churches.

The Western "style" emerges. Because of all these developments, we can say that by 1000 A.D. a distinctive Western European civilization was beginning to take shape. This civilization was something new, something quite different from the classical Roman civilization. It differed in its political organization; in place of the one empire of the past there now were individual kingdoms arising in France, England, Scotland, Scandinavia, and elsewhere. We should note, though, that the Roman past still lingered on

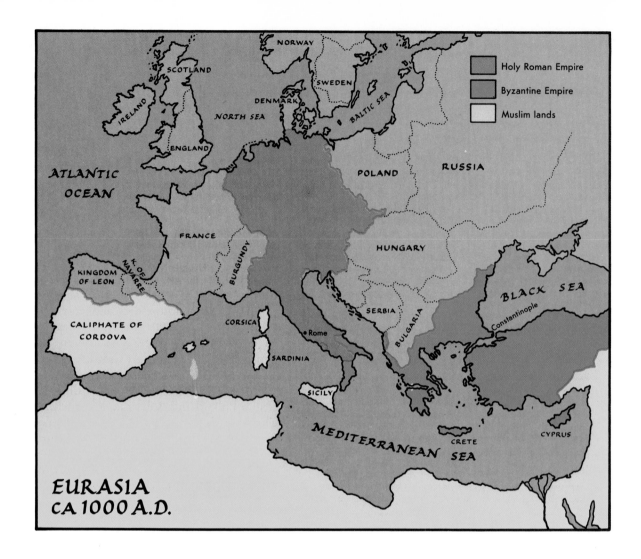

EURASIA
CA 1000 A.D.

Holy Roman Empire
Byzantine Empire
Muslim lands

in Central Europe where a large number of German and Italian states were combined to form what was called the Holy Roman Empire. And surprisingly enough, this Holy Roman Empire was to last until the 19th century.

The new Europe also differed from old Rome in the nature of its civilization. The civilization now emerging was, as we have seen, a fusion of Germanic, Christian, and Roman elements. This civilization seemed very primitive in the year 1000, certainly in comparison with the wealthy Byzantine Empire which had never succumbed to the barbarians. But we shall see later that it was the new primitive Western Europe that was to surge forward after 1000 and take the lead in overseas expansion.

ARAB INVASIONS AND THE FOUNDING OF MUSLIM CIVILIZATION

Islam. While a new civilization was slowly emerging in the West out of the anarchy of the Germanic invasions, an Islamic civilization was developing much more rapidly as a result of the Arab invasions. The Arabs were a people who, before the seventh century, had been considered barbarians by the more civilized peoples to the north. And most of them were, in fact, primitive nomadic Bedouins who wandered about with their camels in the vast desert wastes of the Arabian Peninsula. But the whole situation changed overnight when these people were given unity and a goal by the Islamic religion.

This religion was founded by Mohammed, an Arab merchant who lived in Mecca.* We shall examine the exact nature of his religion in the later unit on the Middle East. At this point we shall note that, following Mohammed's death in 632 A.D., his followers exploded out of the Arabian Peninsula like a giant bomb. Within a few years they conquered a number of ancient empires of great size and riches. How was it possible for a comparatively small number of backward desert nomads to win such dazzling triumphs?

One reason is the very fact that they were nomads, trained in the hard school of desert living and fighting. Having little to lose, these tough warriors gladly followed leaders who promised them riches in this life and paradise in the life to come. This brings us to the second reason for their successes, namely the unity and the enthusiasm provided by their new religion. Islam brought together for the first time all the peoples of the Arabian Peninsula and gave them a cause for which they were willing to fight and to

* See *Readings in World History,* "Mohammed: Founder of Islam," p. 77.

die. The third reason for the Arab victories is that, at this very moment when the Arabs were united and ready to march, the old empires to the north happened to be particularly weak. The Byzantine and Persian Empires had just fought a series of wars that left them both exhausted. Furthermore their subjects were most discontented because of heavy taxation and religious persecution. In fact, many of these subjects welcomed the Muslim invaders as deliverers who would rescue them from their hard lot. All these factors explain why the Arabs were able to win their spectacular victories, frequently against greatly superior armies.

Islam's first century. The expansion of Islam after Mohammed's death falls naturally into three phases: 632–750, 750–1000, and 1000–1500. During the first period, Islam spread in all directions, west to the Pyrenees and east to Central Asia. First they conquered the Middle Eastern lands from the Byzantines and the Persians, taking Syria in 635, Iraq in 640, Egypt in 642, and Persia in 650. Then from the Middle East the warriors of Islam fanned out westward. By 703 they had conquered North Africa, and by 715 Spain. They even crossed the Pyrenees into France, where they were finally defeated by the Franks at the Battle of Tours in 732.

Most Westerners are familiar with this Muslim invasion of Europe, but few know that at the same time the Muslims were also pushing far to the east. By 715 they had conquered Sind in northwestern India. Then they turned northward into Central Asia where in 751 they fought the battle of Talas with Chinese forces. This corresponds to the Battle of Tours in the west, with this difference: the Muslims were victorious in Central Asia whereas they were turned back in France. This fact explains why the Islamic religion is widespread in Central Asia today but did not spread north into Europe.

All these conquests enabled the Muslims to win a huge empire in little more than one century. By 750 Islam ruled over the vast territories stretching from the Pyrenees to the Indian Ocean, and from Morocco to the borders of China.

An Islamic civilization develops. The second period, from 750 to 1000, is noteworthy not for more conquests but for the development of a distinctive Islamic civilization, which was a fusion of the many old civilizations that the Muslims had won. This fusion was possible because the Muslims,

unlike the later Mongols, did not uproot the peoples and cultures they overran. The reason is that the Islamic faith did not merely provide religious doctrines and regulations. It also offered a system of law and government. It stated how people should live together in an Islamic community, and it allowed any person, regardless of his race or past religion, to join the Islamic community so long as he became a Muslim. The result was that many of the people in the conquered territories willingly accepted Islam. This in turn led to a gradual fusing of the ancient civilizations of Egypt, Syria, Iraq, Persia, and

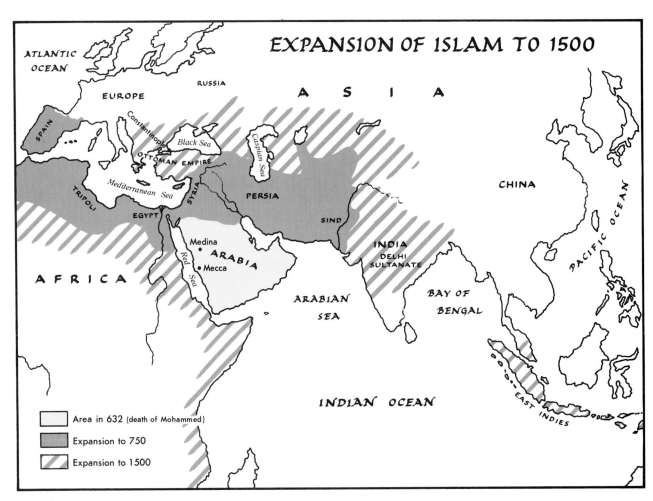

EXPANSION OF ISLAM TO 1500

Area in 632 (death of Mohammed)

Expansion to 750

Expansion to 1500

northwest India. The final product was something new and distinctive, Islamic civilization.

The civilization of Islam was not as fresh and original as, for example, that of classical Greece, because it borrowed from several earlier civilizations that were themselves splendid and inventive. As a result the Muslims found it easier to preserve and pass on, rather than to create something new. One of their scientists, for example, said, "We ought to confine ourselves to what the Ancients have dealt with and to perfect what can be perfected." [9] Despite this preoccupation with past achievements, Islamic civilization made many important contributions of its own.

Cultural middlemen. In the first place, the Muslims translated classical Greek works of philosophy and science into Arabic. Arabic translations of these works reached the West first, so that the Europeans became acquainted with this literature not in the original Greek but in Arabic. The Muslims therefore made an important contribution in preserving ancient classics and passing them on to the West. The Muslims also helped in establishing more contacts between Europe on the one hand, and India and China on the other. The Muslim world was in the center and had relations with all regions of Eurasia. This made it possible for the Muslims to serve as intermediaries or middlemen in the interchange of knowledge and techniques as well as articles of trade.

An example of this interchange may be seen in the following story left by an Arab physician and scientist who lived in Baghdad between 850 and 925.

A Chinese scholar came to my house and remained in the town about a year. In five months he learnt to speak and write Arabic, attaining indeed eloquence in speech and calligraphy (beautiful penmanship) in writing.

When he decided to return to his country, he said to me a month or so beforehand, "I am about to leave. I would be very glad if someone would dictate to me the sixteen books of Galen before I go." (Galen was a famous Greek physician of 130 to 200 A.D., whose numerous writings had been translated into Arabic.) I told him that he had not sufficient time to copy more than a small part of it, but he said, "I beg you to give me all your time until I go, and to dictate to me as rapidly as possible. You will see that I shall write faster than you can dictate." So together with one of my students we read Galen to him as fast as we could, but he wrote still faster. We did not believe that he was getting it correctly until we made a collation (a comparison or check) and found it exact throughout. I asked him how this could be, and he said, "We have in our country a way of writing which we call shorthand, and this is what you see. When we wish to write very fast we use this style, and then afterwards transcribe it into the ordinary characters at will." But he added that an intelligent man who learns quickly cannot master this script in under twenty years. [10]

This story shows how the Chinese learned, through the Arabs, about the writings of a Greek physician of the classical period. But more often it was the other way around; it was the Europeans who got Chinese knowledge through the Arabs. They learned especially about Chinese inventions such as paper, porcelain, printing, and the magnetic compass. These inventions, which reached Europe through the Muslim world, helped the Europeans to progress and eventually to expand all over the world.

In certain fields the Muslims did more than simply preserve and transmit. From India they picked up valuable knowledge in mathematics and then made contributions of their own. Our word algebra comes from a famous Arab book entitled *Hisab al-Fabr w-al-Maqabalah*, or "restoration and reduction" as a means of solving equations. We

Islamic architecture throughout the Mediterranean area documents the Muslim's wide geographical expansion. Typically Islamic is the grillwork of this minaret in Iran.

character, held together by two strong bonds. One of these was, of course, Islam, the religion of Mohammed. The other was the Arabic language, which was used for communication between such diverse peoples in the Islamic empire as Arabs, Persians, Indians, and Europeans. In other words, Arabic was the international language of the medieval Muslim world just as Latin was the international language of the medieval Western Christian world.*

Expansion and diffusion. The third period between 1000 and 1500 was again one of expansion, comparable to that which occurred from 632 to 750. But whereas the expansion in the earlier period was one of religion alone, in the later period the new Islamic civilization was diffused along with religion over wide new territories. This expansion that took place after 1000 was accomplished partly by force. The force, however, was used not by Arabs, but by peoples like the Turks and Afghans who had accepted Islam from the Arabs. The Turks, for example, expanded westward into Asia Minor, destroying the Byzantine Empire and conquering the entire Balkan Peninsula in Europe. Likewise Turks and Afghans pushed southward into India throughout the 12th century, overran the north, and established the powerful Delhi Sultanate.

Islam was spread even further by peaceful means than by force. In Indonesia, for example, Arab and Indian merchants spread the gospel of Mohammed at the same time that they traded in spices. First gaining influence in Sumatra, from there Islam spread to Java, the Moluccas, and the Malay Peninsula. As a result this whole Malaysian area is to this day overwhelmingly Muslim. In Africa, Islam spread gradually into the interior of the continent from two centers. From the

also know that Arabic numerals made mathematics easier to handle than it had been when Roman numerals were used. The Muslims also made important advances in geography. Because of their contacts with most of Eurasia, they were the first to collect systematic geographic data concerning North Africa and Asia. In medicine the Muslims began with the achievements of the Greeks, and especially of Galen. But again their wide geographical spread enabled them to learn of many new diseases and new drugs.*

The bonds of Islamic civilization. In conclusion we may say that Islamic civilization, although based on Graeco-Roman, Persian, and Indian originals, did make contributions of its own. It was a civilization of distinctive

° See *Readings in World History,* "Civilization of Islam," p. 79.

° See *Readings, in World History,* "Arab Language and Script," p. 84.

Muslim Arab colonies in the coastal towns of Kenya and Tanganyika, the faith was carried through large parts of East Africa; from Morocco the Muslim religion spread across the Sahara into West Africa.

This combination of forceful and peaceful expansion of Islam greatly enlarged the area of the Muslim world between 1000 and 1500. The extent and the unity of the Islamic world is strikingly shown by the journeys of the famous Muslim traveller, Ibn Batuta. He lived between 1304 and 1378, and journeyed more widely than any other person of medieval times. Starting from Morocco where he was born, he crossed North Africa to Syria, and then made the pilgrimage to Mecca. Afterwards he explored Arabia, Mesopotamia, Persia, and Asia Minor. Then he journeyed through Samarkand in Central Asia to India, where he lived for almost eight years at the court of the ruler at Delhi. He served as a judge, and also as ambassador to China. On the way to China he visited the Maldive Islands, Ceylon, and Sumatra. About 1350 he returned to Morocco after twenty-five years' absence. Still restless, he went north to Spain, and later crossed the Sahara and travelled in Central Africa. He reached Timbuctu and the Niger River, which he mistakenly called the Nile because he believed it flowed into Egypt. When he finally returned to Morocco and settled down, he had travelled no less than 75,000 miles. His remarkable experiences show the unity as well as the breadth of the Muslim world. As an educated Muslim he was able to serve in various capacities not only his own ruler in Morocco, but several other Muslim rulers in India, the Maldive Islands in the Indian Ocean, and elsewhere.

The expansion of the Muslim world between 1000 and 1500 has affected deeply the course of world history. The first stage of expansion to 750 had made the Mediterranean Sea a Muslim lake; the later stage of expansion made the Indian Ocean a Muslim lake. This meant that the Muslims now had control of the main trade routes of Eurasia. The great bulk of the goods that reached Europe from Asia were carried along Muslim controlled land or sea routes. In other words the Muslims had an economic strangle-hold on Europe, which they shrewdly exploited to make fat profits at the expense of the European consumer.

Another important result of the expansion of the Muslims is that it made Islam a world power. It was no longer limited to the Middle East. It was now a powerful force in India and Southeast Asia and Africa. This extension of the frontiers of Islam has affected

Moorish, or Muslim, architecture also appeared in Spain as Islam gained a foothold in the south. This scene is in Granada.

TALBOT LOVERING

105

world affairs to the present day. It explains why the Indian Peninsula is now divided into two parts, Muslim Pakistan and Hindu India. It explains why Muslim political parties are at present so influential in Southeast Asia, especially in Indonesia. It also explains why Islam today is such a powerful force on the continent of Africa. In fact it is now the fastest-growing religion in that continent. Many Africans welcome Islam as their "native" religion, and regard Christianity suspiciously as a foreign, white man's religion. The net result is that one-seventh of the people of the world today embrace Islam.

Having traced this spectacular rise of Islam, we turn now to the Mongol invasions, which at one point seriously threatened the Muslim world.

MONGOL INVASIONS AND THE UNIFICATION OF EURASIA

Genghis Khan. The third great barbarian invasion of the medieval period was that of the Mongols. Within a few decades during the early 13th century the Mongols conquered an empire even greater than that of the Muslims. The person responsible for this achievement was not a religious leader like Mohammed, but an illiterate and ruthless nomadic warrior, Genghis Khan. Genghis Khan was born about 1167 in present-day Outer Mongolia. His name at birth was Temudjin, and his father was a minor Mongol chief. When Temudjin was only twelve years old, his father was poisoned, and the young boy spent a childhood of misery. Despite these unfortunate beginnings he rose to become literally the "World Conqueror," as he was often called. Indeed, he and his offspring did conquer much of the known world; this despite the fact that Temudjin's tribe consisted of only a few thousand nomads, and the whole Mongol nation did not number more than one million.

What is the explanation for this amazing success story? One reason, as we noted earlier in the opening unit, is the rough outdoor life led by the nomads. They all learned to ride as young children and became so tough that they could ride all day long for several days in succession with a minimum of food and rest. They also learned as young children to handle weapons for hunting and, if necessary, for war. Also they were able, like the American Indians, to notice tracks and movements and signs that would altogether escape an ordinary person. An observer recently reported that the Mongol "notices a man trying to hide behind a bush or a rock five or six versts (about four miles) away. He is able to perceive the smoke of a campfire or steam of boiling water at a great distance. At dawn, when the air is transparent, he can discern figures of men and animals at a distance of 25 versts" (about 18 miles).[11]

Another reason for the triumph of the Mongols was the organizing ability of Genghis Khan. He divided his army into groups of tens, hundreds, thousands, and ten thousands, with one man in command of each group. In time of need, Genghis Khan issued orders for so many thousands of men to appear at a certain place and at a certain time. And, according to a Persian writer of that period, "they arrive not a twinkling of an eye before or after the appointed hour." [12] Genghis Khan always paid much attention to organization, as we can see from the following story that is told about him:

One day he called his sons together and taking an arrow from his quiver he broke it in half. Then he took two arrows and broke them also. And he continued to add to the bundle until there were so many arrows that even athletes were unable to break them. Then turning to his sons he said: "So it is with you also. A frail arrow, when it is multiplied and supported by its fellows, not even mighty warriors are able to break it. . . . As long, therefore,

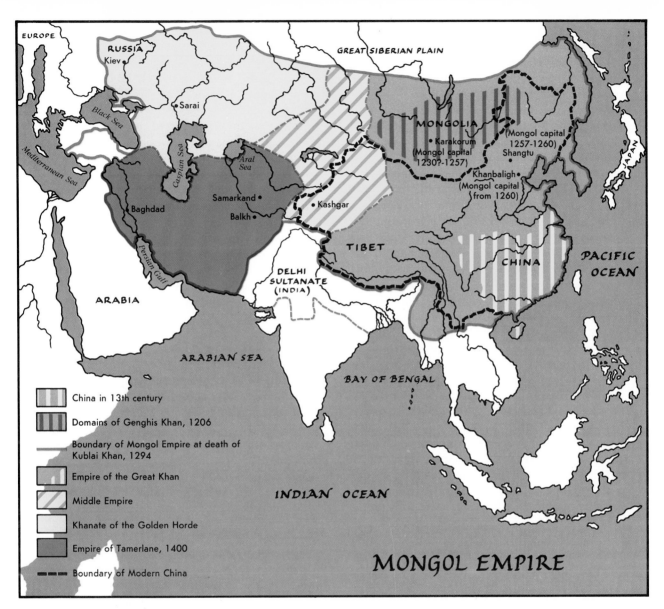

MONGOL EMPIRE

Legend:
- China in 13th century
- Domains of Genghis Khan, 1206
- Boundary of Mongol Empire at death of Kublai Khan, 1294
- Empire of the Great Khan
- Middle Empire
- Khanate of the Golden Horde
- Empire of Tamerlane, 1400
- Boundary of Modern China

as you brothers support one another and render stout assistance one to another, though your enemies be men of great strength and might, yet shall they not gain the victory over you." [13]

The Mongol warriors ride west. Once Temudjin began his career of conquest, his triumphs were as rapid and as remarkable as those of the Muslim Arabs. By 1206 he had fought his way to the top in his own country,

Mongolia. All the Mongol tribes now recognized him as their ruler, and henceforth he was called Genghis Khan, meaning "strong" and "irresistible." Between 1213 and 1215 he conquered North China, and in 1218 he overran Korea. He turned next to Central Asia which he overran between 1218 and 1224. Three years later Genghis Khan died, but his sons continued the campaigns. Between 1236 and 1241 they invaded Russia, Poland, and Hungary, and crossed the frozen Danube near Vienna. It seemed that nothing could save Europe from the fast-moving Mongol warriors, who were riding rings around the slow, heavily-armored European knights.

It was at this critical moment that Europe was saved by a lucky accident. Far away in the Mongol capital, Karakorum, the grand khan, Ogotai, died in September, 1241. The sons and nephews of the late khan, together with many of the top commanders, left the army and hastened back to take part in the election of a new ruler. After this was done, the Mongol leaders decided not to bother further with Western Europe. This seemed to them too distant an area, located on the edge of the world. So their armies, loaded down with plunder, withdrew eastward. It was this stroke of luck that saved Western Europe from becoming another province of the vast Mongol Empire. It should be noted, however, that the Mongols decided to keep the Russian lands, which they held for the next two centuries. This explains why the Russian people lived for so long under Mongol rule, whereas the Western Europeans did not.*

After their campaigns in Europe the Mongols turned to the Middle East, which was much richer and more attractive. For some time they had ruled most of Persia, and now they pushed on to the great Muslim capital of Baghdad, which they captured in February 1258. It is said that the Mongols pillaged the capital for forty days, massacring 800,000 of the inhabitants. Libraries and treasures accumulated through centuries were plundered or destroyed in a few weeks. It was not until 1260 that the Mongols were finally stopped by an Egyptian army when they were preparing to push on into Africa.

* See *Readings in World History*, "The Mongols Terrorize Europe," p. 86.

A quick decline. The Mongol Empire was now at its height. How different it was from the humble beginnings of Temudjin only a few decades earlier! The Mongols had become masters of most of the known world. It is true that they had failed in their attempts to conquer Japan and India. Nevertheless, their rule stretched from the Black Sea and the Persian Gulf to the Pacific Ocean. It included all of China, Korea, Central Asia, Persia, Mesopotamia, and the Russian lands. But this giant empire did not last long. It was too large for a single ruler to govern, especially in those days before the appearance of modern methods of transportation and communication. After 1260 it was divided into four independent Mongol kingdoms: (1) Persia and Mesopotamia; (2) Russia and Western Siberia; (3) China, Mongolia, and Eastern Siberia; (4) Central Asia.

Even within these independent kingdoms, the Mongols were soon either overthrown or absorbed by the native peoples. In China, for example, the Yuan Dynasty that the Mongols established proved to be extremely corrupt. So the Chinese revolted in 1368, chased out the Mongols, and set up their own Chinese Ming Dynasty. Also in Russia, the Mongols ruled the country from 1238 until 1480, when the Russians felt strong enough to refuse to pay any more tribute to their Mongol overlords. As the Mongols proved to be too weak to force the Russians to pay, their rule came to an end. In Persia the Mongols were not forced to leave but instead were assimilated, when, in the 14th century, they adopted the Muslim religion of their Persian subjects. In Central Asia, or Turkestan, the Mongols were also in constant conflict.

Tamerlane. One of the Turkic chieftains in this region was Timur Lenk (Timur the Lame), more commonly known as Tamerlane. Remorely related to Genghis Khan, he made himself lord of Turkestan by gangster methods and set forth on a career of conquest and destruction which almost equalled that of Genghis himself. He took Persia and Central Asia, and penetrated Russia as far as Moscow; he reached into India and captured Delhi; he defeated the Turks at the great battle of Angora in 1402. Tamerlane died in 1405 on his way to invade China. His body was embalmed, placed in an ebony casket, and sent to Samarkand, the capital of Turkestan for burial. His empire quickly collapsed as a result of family quarrels.

Reasons for collapse. Why did these great empires of the Mongols and Turks last for so short a time? One explanation is manpower shortage. Genghis Khan never was able to have more than 100 thousand Mongols in his armies because the total Mongol population, men, women, and children, was only about one million. His armies, of course, did number more than a hundred thousand but the difference was made up by recruits from among the conquered peoples. This system worked satisfactorily at the beginning, but it broke down when the Mongols had to administer vast territories with populations many times larger than their own. The few Mongols had to be spread very thinly over their great empire, with the result that they were soon either absorbed or overthrown.

Also the Mongols did not keep up with the technological progress that other people were making. They lost their hold over Russia, for example, because the Russians got cannon from Western Europe and learned how to use them, while the Mongols continued to depend on their bows and arrows and spears. So long as everybody rode horses and shot arrows, the Mongols were unbeatable because they did these things better than anybody else. But when the West developed firearms and the Mongols did not, the days of Mongol greatness came to an end.*

* See *Readings in World History*, "Mongolia and the Mongols Today," p. 88.

An illustration from a 13th century manuscript depicts the Mongols of the Eurasian steppes. Their "ferocious" natures and daring feats on horseback made them an object of fear to those making overland journeys.

BODLEIAN LIBRARY

Medieval Civilizations 109

Trade and exploration under the Mongols.
Finally, what is the significance of the Mongol invasions for world history? In the first place they made possible a great increase in trade between the various regions of Eurasia. The Mongols united most of Eurasia under their rule and, for a short time, enforced peace and security in their broad realms. Merchants soon took advantage of these favorable conditions to exchange goods back and forth from one end of Eurasia to the other. The following account, written by an Italian merchant sometime between 1335 and 1343, describes the safety of Eurasian trade routes under the Mongols, and the manner in which trade was carried on.

> . . . the road you travel from Tana (at the mouth of the Don River) to Cathay (China) is perfectly safe, whether by day or by night, according to what the merchants say who have used it. . . . You may reckon that between Tana and Sarai the road is less safe than on any other part of the journey, and yet even in this part, if you are some sixty men in the company, you may go as safely as if you were in your own house. Anyone from Genoa or Venice wishing . . . to go to Cathay should carry linens with him . . . (and) he will dispose of these well. Whatever silver the merchants carry with them to Cathay the lord of Cathay takes from them and puts in his treasury and gives that paper money of theirs in exchange . . . and with this money you can readily buy silk and whatever other merchandise you desire to buy, and all of the people of the country are bound to receive it, and you shall not pay a higher price for your goods because your money is of paper.[14]

The Mongol Empire made possible not only an increase in overland trade with China, but also an increase in land and sea trade with India and the East Indies. We noted earlier that when the Muslims expanded they gained control of the trade routes between Europe and South Asia. They took advantage of their position as middle-

men to charge high prices and make big profits. But we also saw that in 1256–1257 the Mongols overthrew the Muslim rulers of Persia. The Mongols showed no interest in the Muslim trade monopoly; they allowed European merchants to come to Persia and to go on to India and to the Spice Islands of the East Indies. Now for the first time the Europeans learned the place of origin of the spices they wanted so badly. They also learned that the original cost of the spices was low, and that it was the Muslim middlemen who made them so expensive for the European consumer.

Unfortunately for the Europeans, the new trade opportunities opened up by the Mongol conquests did not last long. As Mongol rule became weaker, the Eurasian steppes became less secure, and the overland trade with China became more difficult. Also, Persia's Mongol rulers became Muslims in the 14th century, and as soon as they did so they stopped European merchants from passing through their country on the way to India and the East Indies. So the Muslims once more had a monopoly of the main trade routes of Eurasia. The Europeans once more were blocked from direct trading with East Asia and South Asia. But, thanks to what they saw during the Mongol period, the Europeans now knew what was on the other side of the Muslim blockade. They knew what profits awaited them if they could find some way of reaching Cathay and the Spice Islands. And so they persisted in their explorations until they did discover a direct route to the East.

The Mongol Empire is significant not only because it led to a great increase in trade, but also because it led to an equally great increase in geographic knowledge. Prior to the Mongol period the people of one region of Eurasia knew rather little of the people in other regions. This was especially true of the Europeans, who were isolated at the

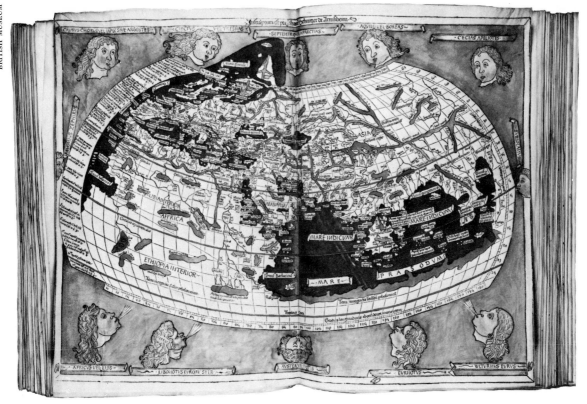

Ptolemy's map of the world reveals that part of the world Europeans knew best: Europe and the Middle East. The further one goes from the Mediterranean, the less detailed the information provided.

western tip of Eurasia. Both the Greeks and the Romans had only vague ideas about Asia and Africa. They considered the Mediterranean to be the center of the world and knew little about India and still less of China. We can see this in the outline of the world drawn by the Graeco-Egyptian, Ptolemy (A.D. 90–168), who was the greatest geographer of the classical period. During the early medieval period, geographic knowledge of the Europeans was even less, perhaps because of their intense interest in spiritual questions as opposed to earthly matters like geography. But after the Mongol conquests this ignorance was dispelled.

The Europeans were the most eager for travel and took advantage of the routes established throughout the Mongol Empire to travel back and forth from the Mediterranean to the Pacific. The Europeans also hoped to convert the godless Mongols, who had only a primitive tribal form of religion. In fact, European popes and kings thought that perhaps they could finally defeat their ancient Muslim enemies in the Middle East by converting the Mongols to Christianity and joining with them against the Muslims. So a large number of Christian missionaries went to the various Mongol kingdoms and came back with wonderful stories of what they had seen.

Medieval Civilizations 111

In the end the Mongol rulers were converted to Islam and Buddhism rather than to Christianity. Nevertheless the reports of the Christian missionaries added greatly to the geographical knowledge which was being gained about Eurasia.

Carpini. An example of such additions to geographic knowledge may be found in the case of the Italian friar, John de Plano Carpini, who led a diplomatic mission to the court of the Grand Khan in Mongolia between 1245 and 1247. He did not get the alliance he wanted, but he did come back with much new information about the extent of the Mongol Empire, the nature of its inhabitants, their manner of living, ways of fighting, religious beliefs, and method of government.

Here, for example, is a passage from the report of Carpini:

> The Mongols . . . are in appearance unlike all other people, for they are broader between the eyes, they have flat, small noses, and their heads are shaven like priests. Their hair is braided into two short locks, one behind each ear; they wear garments of skin, with the fur on the outside, but some wear jackets of woven materials, even brocade. They own vast herds —camels, oxen, sheep and goats. I think they have more horses and mares than all the rest of the world. Their emperors, chiefs and nobles have much silk, gold, silver and precious stones. Their victuals are all things that can be eaten; for we even saw some of them eat lice. Their manners are partly praiseworthy, and partly detestable; for they are more obedient to their lords and masters than any others. . . . Moreover they are disdainful of other people, and beyond all measure deceitful and treacherous towards them. They speak fair in the beginning, but they sting like scorpions in the end. . . . Whatever mischief they plan against a man, they keep it wonderfully secret. They are unmannerly also and unclean in taking their meat and drink. . . . The slaughter of other people is accounted a matter of nothing to them.[15]

The Mongolian Emperor, Kublai Khan, seems to characterize Carpini's description of the typical Mongol.

Marco Polo. Much more important and influential than this report by Carpini was the famous book written by the Venetian traveller and adventurer, Marco Polo. His father and uncle were jewel merchants who had made a trading expedition to the Mongol capital in 1266. They were so well received that in 1271 they made a second trip, taking with them this time young Marco, who was a boy of seventeen. Marco became a favorite of Kublai Khan, grandson and third successor of Genghis Khan. Kublai took the young Italian into his service and sent him on numerous missions throughout his empire. For three years Marco was the governor of Yang-chow, a Chinese city of over one million inhabitants. After 17 years' service Marco was allowed to return to his native city. On the way home he escorted a Chinese princess to Persia where she was to become the bride of the king. Finally in 1295, after an absence of 25 years, Marco returned to Venice, to the astonishment of his fellow citizens. When he told them of his adventures and of all that he had seen, they called him *Il Milione* (the man who talks in millions). Nevertheless Marco dictated his experiences, which were published in *The book of Messer Marco Polo of Venice*. The book opens with this passage, which gives some idea of what a thrilling eye-opener it was for the people of the time.

> Emperors and Kings, dukes and marquesses, counts, knights and burgesses, and all ye, who-ever ye be, who wish to know of the various races of men, and of the diversities of the dif-ferent regions of the world, take this book and have it read to you. You shall find in it all the mighty wonders, all the great singularities of the vast regions of the East—of the Greater Ar-menia, of Persia, of Tartary, and of India, and of many a country besides—set down by us clearly and in due order, as they were re-counted by Messer Marco Polo, called Mil-lione, a wise and noble citizen of Venice, who saw them with his own eyes. . . . And all who

read this book or hear it read, must believe it, as all the things contained in it are true. For I tell you that ever since the Lord our God did with his own hands mould our first Father Adam, there never was up to the present day any man, Christian or Pagan, Tartar or Indian or of any other race whatsoever, who knew and explored so great a part of the various regions of the world and of its great marvels, as this Messer Marco knew and explored. . . .[16]

Marco's stories were as exciting as this introduction promised. He told of the Grand Khan's palace with its gardens and artificial lakes, its eight square miles of enclosed ground, its guard of 12,000 men, and its 5000 elephants with harnesses of silver and pre-cious stones. He told also of roads that were paved and raised above the surrounding ground so that they might drain easily, of the Grand Canal through which 200,000 mer-chant vessels passed each year, of ports with ships larger than any known in Europe, and of lands which produced spices, silk, ginger, sugar, camphor, cotton, salt, saffron, sandal-

Marco Polo's eyewitness account of the riches of the court of Kublai Khan, written and illus-trated when he returned home after 25 years in China, astonished the Europeans.

BODLEIAN LIBRARY

wood, and porcelain. Marco described also all the fabulous countries he visited and heard about while escorting the Chinese princess to Persia: Singapore, Java, Sumatra, Ceylon, India, Socotra, Madagascar, Arabia, Zanzibar, and Abyssinia.

Marco's book suddenly doubled the size of the known world.* Europeans no longer thought only of the Mediterranean Sea; they now were aware of new continents and new oceans. They also knew now of the wealth of these foreign lands and of the profits they could make if they could find a way around the Muslim blockade. And this blockade of the Christian world was very real, as the accompanying map shows. So the Europeans felt frustrated; they had the feeling of being fenced in, and they were determined to get around that fence. They were determined to

* See *Readings in World History,* "Marco Polo Discovers New Worlds," p. 92.

regain the freedom of movement and of trade that they had enjoyed for a short while during the height of the Mongol Empire. This was one of the most important reasons why the Europeans began to feel their way across the wide Atlantic Ocean until finally they stumbled across the New World and why earlier they had discovered the route around Africa to India.

Militant Christianity. We should note, however, that the desire for trade was not the only aim of the Europeans when they sailed across the Atlantic. Religion also was very much on their minds. They were ardent Christians, and they hated the Muslims not only because they controlled the trade routes but also because they were the deadly enemies of the Christian faith. In fact, during the two centuries between 1096 and 1279 the Europeans sent eight expeditions, known as

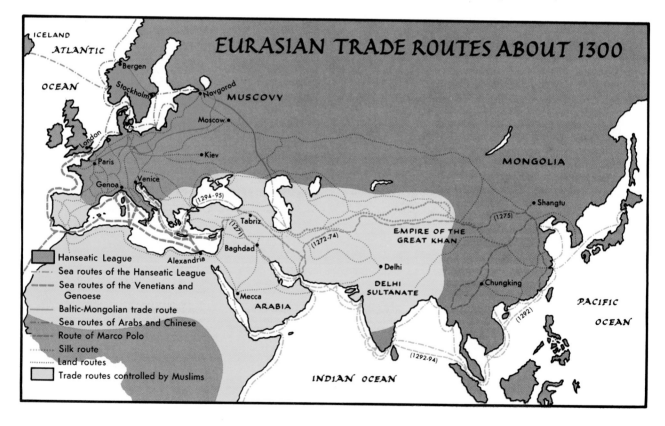

EURASIAN TRADE ROUTES ABOUT 1300

Hanseatic League
Sea routes of the Hanseatic League
Sea routes of the Venetians and Genoese
Baltic-Mongolian trade route
Sea routes of Arabs and Chinese
Route of Marco Polo
Silk route
Land routes
Trade routes controlled by Muslims

Crusades, against the Muslims in the Middle East. One of the aims of these Crusades was to win back the Holy Land of Palestine from the Arabs who had conquered it in the seventh century. At first the Crusaders did regain a part of the Holy Land, but in the end the Muslims triumphed and became once more the masters of Palestine.*

The Europeans did not give up hope of defeating their Muslim enemies. We have seen that they sent missionaries to the Mongols in the hope of organizing a giant crusade of Christian Europe and a Christianized Mongol Empire against the Islamic World. But this also failed, for the Mongols eventually were converted to Islam and to Buddhism rather than to Christianity.

The crusading spirit, however, did not die out. When the Europeans began their overseas expansion, they still had hopes of finding allies against the Muslims. They knew from Marco Polo's book that the people of India and China were not Muslims. So they hoped that the millions of Indians and Chinese might perhaps be persuaded to join forces with the Christians. Again they were disappointed, but the European discoverers did find new peoples in Africa and the New World. Since these Africans and Indians were heathens, Europeans went overseas to carry on missionary work. Usually their motives were mixed: to find treasure and to find land for settlement, as well as to find souls to save. For example, Bernal Diaz, one of the Spanish conquerors of Mexico, wrote that, "the Almighty blessed our endeavours and we baptized the men, women, and all the children born after the conquest, whose souls would otherwise have gone to the infernal regions." [17] Likewise William Bradford, one of the Pilgrim Fathers who founded Plymouth colony, wrote that among their aims was, "laying some good foundation for

* See *Readings in World History*, "The Crusades Widen Europe's Horizons," p. 95.

Christians leaving on the Crusades against the "heathen" were depicted with great detail in medieval manuscripts.

the propagating and advancing the goal of the kingdom of Christ in those remote parts of the world. . . ." [18]

WESTERN EUROPE PREPARES FOR OVERSEAS EXPANSION

At the same time that European nations were getting the urge to expand, they also were developing the know-how and the wealth necessary for expansion. Between 1000 and 1500 Europe rose from a primitive, self-sufficient, agrarian region to a bustling, confident, and militarily powerful society. It was this combination of the will to expand and the means to do so that explains Western Europe's leading role in world affairs in modern times.

Freedom from invasion. What is the explanation for Europe's all-important transformation after 1000? In the first place Western Europe suffered no more barbarian invasions. Before 1000 there had been repeated devastations by Germans, Huns, Magyars, Vikings,

Medieval Civilizations 115

and Arabs. But after that date Western Europe was left free because Eastern Europe served as a buffer. The Mongols, for example, ruled Russia from the 13th to the 15th centuries, and the Turks ruled the Balkans from the 15th to the 20th centuries. The Western Europeans, by contrast, were spared such foreign conquest and domination. They were left free to develop their economies and to work out their own institutions.

Technology. Another reason for Western Europe's transformation was its remarkable progress in technology. A distinguished American historian, Professor Lynn White, has written that, "the chief glory of the later Middle Ages was not its cathedrals or its epics or its scholasticism: it was the building for the first time in history of a complex civilization which rested not on the backs of sweating slaves or coolies but primarily on non-human power." [19] This technological progress was made partly because Europe at this time was a frontier region, mostly wooded and unoccupied. So the peasants were busy taming the wilderness, cutting down the forests, and winning farmlands. This was the same sort of work that the frontiersmen did in the United States. It was work that needed much hard labor, and there were no large numbers of slaves in medieval Europe as there had been in classical Greece and Rome. So the medieval peasant, like the American frontiersman, invented many labor-saving devices to help him in his back-breaking work.

Another reason for the technological progress was the attitude of the medieval Western European towards physical work. He did not regard hand labor with scorn, as being something that no gentleman should do. This was the case during the classical age when physical labor was looked down upon as being fit only for slaves. Plato, for example, scolded two friends who had built an apparatus to help solve a geometrical problem; manual labor, he said, hindered thought rather than helped it. This attitude was a great handicap to the growth of science and technology. It created a gap between theory and practice. The classical Greeks were excellent theorists but did not put their ideas into practice.

A medieval artist's view of peasant life.

The medieval man of Western Europe, by contrast, did not have this handicap. He found nothing degrading about physical work. Even the Western clergy did not spend all their time in prayer and meditation. They taught that work was an essential part of a good Christian life. Or, as they put it, "to work is to pray." This is why Professor White has commented that, "The monk was the first intellectual to get dirt under his fingernails." [20] And because he did so, he bridged the gap between labor and thought, which the Greeks never did, and thus laid the foundations of modern science. It is not accidental that it was a friar, Roger Bacon (1214–1294), who foresaw many of the achievements of science:

> Machines may be made by which the largest ships, with only one man steering them, will move faster than if they were filled with rowers; wagons may be built which will move with unbelievable speed and without the aid of beasts; flying machines can be constructed in which a man may beat the air with mechanical wings like a bird; . . . . machines will make it possible for men to go to the bottom of seas and rivers. . . .[21]

This attitude, together with the demands of frontier life, explains why the Europeans went beyond theory to practical application. It explains why they made more technological advances between 1000 and 1500 than the Greeks and Romans made between 1000 B.C. and 500 A.D., a period three times as long.

Much of this technological progress, as might be expected, was in agriculture. For example, the peasants now began to use the three-field rather than the old two-field system of farming. Where formerly they had allowed half their land to lie fallow or idle each year to regain its fertility, now under the three-field system only one-third was left unplanted, leaving two-thirds in production.

Much of the physical work which was a part of "the Good Christian Life" was done in the service of the Church.

Another step forward was the invention of a horse collar which rested on the horse's shoulders; the old collar resting on his neck had choked the horse when he pulled too hard. Horseshoes were another invention which aided the farmer because the horse with a broken hoof had been useless.

During this medieval period, also, water and wind mills were built to produce power for grinding grain, sawing wood, forging iron, sharpening knives, and so forth. Mills were known during the Roman period, but few were built then because there were plenty of slaves to do the work. But in medieval Europe the frontier required much work and since there were no slaves, mills were soon dotting the landscape. For the first time in history, mills made possible the use of non-human power to relieve man from much drudgery.

Increased trade. These inventions, and others like them, enabled the medieval peasant to cultivate more land and to grow more produce. This in turn led to a great increase in trade, for the peasant needed the new tools and machines, and he paid for them with the surplus produce he grew. At first the trade was small-scale, between a town and the surrounding countryside. But gradually long distance trade developed, from one part of Europe to another. And by the time of Marco Polo in the 13th century, European merchants, as we have seen, were going all the way to China to sell their goods and to get silk and other luxuries.

International trade grew rapidly because of certain technological inventions that were as important as those in agriculture. For example, the art of shipbuilding advanced

A medieval manuscript illustrates the use of a new invention: the plow.

greatly between 1200 and 1500. The tonnage of the average European ship tripled, the design of the rudder was improved, and new types of rigging and sails were developed which enabled vessels to sail into the wind.

The compass, originally a Chinese invention, was now much improved by the Europeans. Chinese navigators probably first used magnetic compasses about the early 11th century. They were simple pieces of magnetic iron, usually floated on cork or straw in a container of water. During the 14th century, the compass was marked off in 32 directional points. During the years following, navigators learned more about the deviation of compasses in various parts of the world, and came to use magnetic compasses with greater accuracy. For example, they noted that large land masses exerted a magnetism of their own and therefore, in their vicinity, the compass reading had to be slightly corrected.

Another Chinese invention, gunpowder, was taken over and used for military purposes more efficiently than had been done to that time in China. The utilization of gunpowder for military purposes was a paramount factor in enabling Europe to dominate the globe. Although Chinese, Arabians, and Indians had long known about gunpowder, it was not until 1242 that Roger Bacon at Oxford University published a book telling how to make it. The formula is usually 75 per cent saltpeter, 15 per cent charcoal, and 10 per cent sulfur. When this mixture is ignited, the gases produced equal many times the volume of the mixture. They are produced instantaneously and cause an explosion. Gunpowder's use revolutionized warfare and spelled the end of armor, castles, and all the other trappings of feudal warfare, and the end of European feudalism itself.

The end of regional isolation. We have emphasized technological progress because it explains why Europe was *able* to expand all over the world. We noted earlier why Europe *wanted* to expand; in order to end the Muslim control of the trade routes and also in order to spread the Christian faith. But this desire to expand would have been of little use if there had not been the *means* to do so. The significance of the above technological developments is that they provided the means. The inventions in agriculture made available surplus produce necessary for trade. Improvements in shipbuilding and navigation made possible international trade, and later, overseas discoveries. Finally, gunpowder and cannon enabled the Europeans to be the masters wherever their ships carried them. In this way Europe, which until 1500 had been a rather isolated and unimportant region of Eurasia, gradually became after 1500 the master of the entire globe. And this in turn meant that mankind, which hitherto had been living in regional isolation, henceforth would be living in global unity.*

* See *Readings in World History*, "Europe's Drive to Expand Overseas," p. 99.

Reviewing the Essentials

Germanic Invasions and the Founding of European Civilization

1. Examine critically the reasons for the collapse of the West Roman Empire by 476 A.D. What are the major causes?
2. Which Germanic tribes invaded the West Roman Empire? What parts of that Empire did they finally occupy? Locate these on the map.
3. What land area was included in the East Roman Empire? Why did this part survive until 1453 A.D.? What contributions did it make to civilization in the period 500–1500 A.D.? What countries were influenced by the culture of the Eastern Roman Empire?
4. What were the distinguishing characteristics of the German invaders who were changing the culture of Western Europe?
5. The Christian Church was a second important factor in the emergence of Western European civilization after the fall of Rome. What important contributions did the Church make to the civilization of Western Europe?
6. Rome itself left a legacy to Western Europe. What were its contributions?
7. By 1000 A.D. a distinctive Western European civilization was beginning to take shape. In what ways did it differ from the earlier classical Roman civilization?

Arab Invasions and the Founding of Muslim Civilization

8. Who were the Arab people and where did they live? Locate on a map. How did these people, mainly desert nomads, develop a sense of unity and goals that culminated in Muslim civilization?
9. Locate on the map the territories controlled by the Arabs in each of the three periods of their development. What do you conclude about the "spreading power" of their way of life and the reasons for it?
10. What were the distinguishing characteristics and achievements of the period of Islamic civilization?
11. In what specific ways did the expansion of the Muslim world by 1500 affect the course of world history? What areas of the earth are part of the Muslim world today? What is the appeal of Islam as a religion today?

Mongol Invasions and the Unification of Eurasia

12. Who were the Mongols? What was the extent of the Mongol Empire at its height? Compare with the Muslim Empire at its height. Why were the Mongols successful in extending their control over so large an area?
13. What did Carpini report about: (a) the kind of people found in the Mongol Empire; (b) the basis for their economy; (c) their view of foreigners?
14. How long did Marco Polo sojourn in the Far East and what were some of the countries he visited? Why is Marco Polo's report a more important source of information than the Carpini

report? What influence did Marco Polo's book have on Europe and Europeans?

15. Give reasons for the disintegration and collapse of the Mongol Empire. What contacts did Western Europeans have with the Mongols? Why is the Mongol invasion important in world history? Account for the fact that the Mongol rulers were converted to Islam and Buddhism and not to Christianity.

Western Europe Prepares for Overseas Expansion

16. Why did Europe want to expand during the period 1000–1500 A.D.?

17. Discuss each of the factors and conditions that gave Europe the ability to take the lead in uniting the globe after 1500. What was the importance of technological progress?

Explain, Identify, or Locate

Islam	Jutes	Mohammed	Mecca
Koran	Magyars	Ibn Batuta	Tours
Huns	Odoacer	West Roman Empire	Talas
Visigoths	Romulus Augustulus	East Roman Empire	Baghdad
Ostrogoths	Charlemagne	Constantinople	Karakoram
Franks	Genghis Khan	Holy Roman Empire	Samarkand
Vandals	Tamerlane	Byzantine Empire	Mongolia
Angles	Kublai Khan	732	Cathay
Saxons	Carpini	800	Pakistan
476	632	1453	Morocco

UNIT ACTIVITIES

Ancient Civilizations

1. Several students might read and prepare a report to the class on Margaret Mead's book, *People and Places* (New York: Harcourt, Brace and World, 1953), using the Eskimos, Plains Indians, the Ashanti of West Africa, the Balinese, and the Minoans as "models" of five different cultures. Their presentation should stress similarities as well as differences.

2. Have the class organize into five groups to study the civilizations that developed during the ancient period in: (a) the Tigris-Euphrates Valley (Sumer); (b) the Indus Valley (Harappa); (c) the Nile Valley (Egypt); (d) the Yellow River valley; (e) the Aegean Islands (Crete). Reports should give priority to information on the way of life that developed, the influence of geography, unique and important contributions, evidences of direct contact, imitation, and stimulus diffusion in connection with other regional civilizations.

On completion of the group presentations, a class summary should be made, with focus on similarities and differences disclosed. For information consult: Leonard Cottrell, *The Anvil of Civilization* (Mentor, 1957); J. H. Breasted, *The Conquest of Civilization* (New York: Harper and Row, 1938); *Readings in World History* (Boston: Allyn and Bacon, Inc., 1970), "Man's Earliest Civilization," pp. 36–40, "India's Forgotten Civilization," pp. 44–48; and the bibliography at the end of this section.

3. Prepare an illustrated outline map of the world showing: (a) the location of ancient valley civilizations; (b) major contributions of each; and (c) how the "spreading" of civilization from Sumer took place.

4. Read and report on the archaeological excavations at Mohenjo-Daro and the Harappa civilization in the Indus Valley. In what ways did the

Harappa civilization develop a unique character? What did it have in common with other civilizations? Why did it collapse? Consult *Readings in World History* (Boston: Allyn and Bacon, Inc., 1970), "Man's Earliest Civilization," pp. 36–40, and "India's Forgotten Civilization," pp. 44–48. Also see Jawaharlal Nehru, *The Discovery of India* (Anchor, 1959); and V. Gordon Childs, *Man Makes Himself* (Mentor, 1951).

5. Prepare a presentation, perhaps with illustrations, on the Egyptian system of writing, the problem of deciphering hieroglyphics, and Champollion's work with the Rosetta Stone and discovery of the key. Consult: J. H. Breasted, *The Conquest of Civilization* (New York: Harper and Row, 1938); *Readings in World History* (Boston: Allyn and Bacon, Inc., 1970), "Solving the Mystery of Egypt's Hieroglyphs," pp. 40–44.

SELECTED READING

● An interesting study of all the ancient civilizations is C. B. Falls', *The First 3000 Years* (New York: Viking, 1960). Among the best books on individual civilizations are H. E. L. Mellersh, *Sumer and Babylon* (New York: Thomas Crowell, 1965); L. Cottrell, *Land of the Two Rivers* (New York: World, 1962); J. Hawkes, *Pharaohs of Egypt* (New York: Harper, 1965); H. Bauerman, *The World of the Pharaohs* (New York: Pantheon, 1960); G. L. Field, *The Minoans of Ancient Crete* (New York, Thomas Crowell, 1965).

● The National Geographic Society has published an illustrated book entitled *Everyday Life in Ancient Times* (Washington: 1951). Finally there is the interesting account by M. Quennell, *Everyday Life in Prehistoric Times* (New York: 1959).

FURTHER READING

● Two lavishly illustrated surveys of past civilizations are *The Epic of Man* by the Editors of Life (New York: Time Inc., 1961): and *The Dawn of Civilization* (New York: McGraw-Hill, 1961). A scholarly analysis is provided by C. Roebuck, *The World of Ancient Times* (New York: Scribner's, 1966). Convenient paperback studies are by V. Gordon Childe, *Man Makes Himself* (Mentor, 1951); and L. Cottrell, *The Anvil of Civilization* (Mentor, 1956). For individual civilizations, see S. N. Kramer, *History Begins at Sumer* (Anchor, 1959); J. A. Wilson, *The Culture of Ancient Egypt* (Phoenix Books, 1951); S. Piggott, *Prehistoric India* (Pelican Book, 1950); W. A. Fairservis Jr., *The Origins of Oriental Civilization* (Mentor Book, 1959).

Classical Civilizations

1. On an outline map, locate and label appropriately the Semitic Arabs, the Indo-Europeans of the Central Eurasian Steppes, and the Mongols, in their successive invasions of the river valleys beginning about 2650 B.C. Consult the atlases listed in the bibliography of Unit One for accurate information.

2. As a class project, plan and develop a chart giving information indicated below for each of these empires of the classical age: Hittite, Assyrian, Persian, Greek, Phoenician, Macedonian, Roman, Chou, Ch'in, Han, Maurya, Kushan, Gupta. The chart should provide accurate information on: (a) territorial extent (boundaries of empire); (b) dates of existence; (c) leaders; (d) fields in which people excelled; (e) reasons for decline; (f) major cities.

3. On an outline map of Eurasia show the political units of the ancient period. Then on a series of outline maps show the major empires of the classical age. Prepare a summary statement which analyzes the data contained in these maps,

making clear the important aspects of the changes from period to period.

4. Each student might select one of the four ways of life described in the text: India: Civilization Based on Religion; China: Civilization Based on Property; Palestine: Civilization Based on the Law of God; Greece: Civilization Based on the Individual. Using references suggested in the bibliography and those suggested by your teacher, prepare a report describing:

> a. The distinctive ways in which the cultural universals developed.
> b. How and why this development took place.
> c. Leaders associated with the development.
> d. Its influence during the classical age and in subsequent periods of time.
> e. The areas of the world in which this way of life prevails today.

5. Prepare a paper on Hellenistic culture which deals with: (a) source of Hellenism; (b) the role of Alexander the Great in promoting the diffusion of Hellenistic culture; (c) centers and recipients of Hellenistic culture; (d) achievements of Hellenistic culture; (e) reasons for its limited impact on Eurasian civilizations.

6. Prepare a paper on commercial contacts among the regions of Eurasia in the classical age, giving emphasis to: (a) reasons for commercial contacts; (b) products traded; (c) trade routes; (d) effects of commercial contacts among the regions of Eurasia; (e) reasons for decline of trade.

7. Prepare a paper on religious contacts among the regions of Eurasia during the classical age, considering: (a) teachings of the religions involved; (b) reasons for and nature of religious contacts; (c) leaders associated with regional interaction; (d) areas involved in religious contacts; (e) reasons for decline of religious contacts.

8. Prepare a set of criteria for selecting those persons of the classical age whose influence has been world-wide and persistent. Then apply your criteria and make a selection of great world leaders. Support your selections with a 300–500 word statement.

9. Several students might prepare, as a basis for class discussion, their observations on: (a) significant achievements of the classical age as they contribute to an understanding of our world today; (b) reasons why no one region of Eurasia permanently altered and influenced the civilization of any other region.

SELECTED READING

● Interesting general surveys of the classical age are included in two of the books listed above for the ancient civilizations, *Everyday Life in Ancient Times* prepared by the National Geographic Society, and *The Anvil of Civilization* by Cottrell.

● The following books that deal specifically with Greece are all clearly written and give colorful pictures of everyday life: D. Mills, *Book of the Ancient Greeks* (New York: Putnam, 1925); M. Quennell, *Everyday Things in Ancient Greece* (New York: Putnam, 1967); W. S. Davis, *Day in Old Athens* (Boston: Allyn and Bacon, 1914); C. E. Robinson, *Everyday Life in Ancient Greece* (New York: Oxford University Press, 1933); and D. R. Barker, *The Story of Ancient Athens* (New York: St. Martin Press, 1961). Pictures of Roman life are given in W. S. Davis, *Day in Old Rome* (Boston: Allyn and Bacon, 1925); D. Mills, *Book of the Ancient Romans* (New York: Putnam, 1927); and A. Duggan, *The Romans* (New York: World, 1964). See also the interesting biographies by John Gunther, *Julius Caesar* (New York: Random House, World Landmark Book, 1959); and by C. A. Robinson Jr., *Alexander the Great* (New York: Watts, 1964).

● The religions that appeared in Eurasia during the classical age are described vividly in the paperback by J. Geer, *How the Great Religions Began* (Signet Key Book, New American Library, 1954). See also Harry Emerson Fosdick, *Jesus of Nazareth* (New York: Random House, World Landmark Book, 1959). Some of the cultural interaction in Eurasia during the classical age is set forth in the pamphlet by D. Bodde, *China's Gifts to the West* (Washington, D.C.: American Council on Education, 1942). For a fascinating description of a non-Western classical civilization that has lasted to the present, see Lin Yutang, *The Chinese Way of Life* (Cleveland: World Publishing Co., 1959). The Indian civilization is vividly brought to life by W. A. Fairservis, Jr., *India* (Cleveland: World Publishing Co., 1961).

FURTHER READING

● Recent surveys of both Greece and Rome are available in C. Roebuck, *The World of Ancient Times* (New York: Scribners, 1966); and C. G. Starr, *History of the Ancient World* (New York: Oxford University Press, 1965). For everyday life, see R. Flacelière, *Daily Life in Greece at the Time of Pericles* (New York: Macmillan, 1965); and J. Carcopino, *Daily Life In Ancient Rome* (New Haven: Yale University Press, 1940). For India, see A. L. Basham, *The Wonder That Was India* (London: Weidenfeld and Nicolson, 1961). The best general history of China is by E. O. Reischauer and J. K. Fairbank, *East Asia: The Great Tradition* (Boston: Houghton Mifflin, 1958). Pearl Buck's famous novel, *The Good Earth* (New York: John Day, 1931), provides a classic picture of peasant life and attitudes; while Lin Yutang, *My Country and My People* (New York: Reynal and Hitchcock, 1935), presents traditional upper class intellectual and aesthetic values.

Medieval Civilizations

1. On an outline map, draw the boundaries of the Western and Eastern Roman Empires; locate and label the Germanic tribes and their invasions of the West Roman Empire.

2. Several students might prepare a report on the Byzantine Empire in the period 476 A.D.–1453 A.D. Include in your report: (a) territorial extent and capital city of the empire; (b) system of government; (c) Emperor Justinian; (d) achievements of Byzantine civilization in law, literature, architecture, and art; (e) influence on western and southeastern Europe; (f) reasons for decline. Useful information may be found in T. C. Chubb, *The Byzantines* (New York: Harcourt, Brace and World, 1959); Harold Lamb, *Constantinople: Birth of an Empire* (New York: Alfred A. Knopf, 1957); C. Diehl, *Byzantine Portraits* (New York: Alfred A. Knopf, 1963).

3. Prepare a report on: the contributions of the church to the emerging civilization of Western Europe. Include information on: (a) governmental structure of the medieval church; (b) influence of the Church in the lives of medieval peoples; (c) monastic orders; (d) results of Church influence in the civilization of the Western world.

4. Several students might prepare a panel presentation for the class on Rome's contributions and continuing influence in Western civilization. Possible areas for exploration are law, architecture, language, government, religion, and literature.

5. Read on Islam in references suggested, gathering information on: (a) the teachings of Islam; (b) reasons for its rapid expansion in the periods 632–750 and 1000–1500; (c) characteristics of Muslim culture; (d) major achievements; (e) centers of learning; (f) strengths and weaknesses; (g) impact of Muslim culture on world history. See *Readings in World History* (Boston: Allyn and Bacon, Inc., 1970), "Civilization of Islam," pp. 79–84; "Mohammed: Founder of Islam," pp. 77–79; "Arab Language and Script," pp. 84–86; "The Muslim Faith," pp. 639–645. Also consult bibliography for this section.

6. Compare and contrast life in Mongolia today with life in 13th century Mongolia. Consult: *Readers' Guide to Periodical Literature* for current articles; *Readings in World History* (Boston: Allyn and Bacon, Inc., 1970), "Mongolia and the Mongols Today," pp. 88–91.

7. Compare and contrast the Muslims and Mongols as empire builders of the medieval period.

8. Prepare a report to the class on Charlemagne, ruler of the Franks. Include in your biography: (a) Charlemagne as a person; (b) extent of his empire; (c) assimilation of invading barbarians; (d) encouragement given to education, the arts, and the Church; (e) Charlemagne's place in the history of Western Europe. For sources of information consult the bibliography at the end of this section and *Readings in World History* (Boston: Allyn and Bacon, Inc., 1970), "Recovery Under Charlemagne," pp. 43–76.

9. These aspects of life in the Middle Ages should be studied as a basis for understanding why Europe was prepared to take leadership in 1500: (a) life on a feudal manor; (b) the Crusades; (c) rise of towns and cities; (d) medieval guilds; (e) the medieval Church; (f) medieval centers of learning; (g) medieval trade within Europe and with other regions. On completion the class should prepare an over-all summary.

SELECTED READING

● The decline and fall of Rome is reviewed in D. Mills, *The Book of the Ancient Romans* (New York: Putnam, 1927). The medieval civilization that developed in Western Europe after the fall of Rome is described in D. Mills, *The Middle Ages* (New York: Putnam, 1935); G. Hartman, *Medieval Days and Ways* (New York: Macmillan, 1937); and W. S. Davis, *Life on a Medieval Barony: A Picture of a Typical Feudal Community in the Thirteenth Century* (New York: Harper, 1926). More recent accounts are by R. McLanathan, *The Pageant of Medieval Art and Life* (New York: Westminster, 1966); and J. Williams, *Life in the Middle Ages* (New York: Random House, 1966).

● For the historical personalities of the medieval period, see J. H. Haaren and A. B. Poland, *Famous Men of the Middle Ages* (New York: American Book Co., 1904). One of the most famous of these personalities was Charlemagne, who is the subject of the book by T. Bullfinch, *Legends of Charlemagne* (New York: Cosmopolitan Book, 1924); and also the subject of the novel by F. Emerson Andrews, *For Charlemagne* (New York: Harper, 1949). For an interesting description of the English people's food, clothes, homes, castles, etc., during these centuries, see M. and C. H. B. Quennell, *Everyday Life in Anglo-Saxon, Viking, and Norman Times* (New York: Putnam, 1955).

● An interesting account of the exploits of the Vikings is given by F. R. Donovan, *The Vikings* (New York: Harper, 1964). One of the best-known of the Viking leaders is the subject of a biography by W. O. Steele, *The Story of Leif Ericson* (New York: Grosset and Dunlap, 1954). Also on the Vikings, there are the exciting novels by Henry Treece, *Viking's Dawn* (New York: Criterion Books, 1959); E. Dehkes, *The Young Viking Warrior* (New York: Bobbs-Merrill, 1953); and F. G. Bengtsson, *The Long Ships: A Saga of the Viking Age* (New York: Knopf, 1954).

● For the Byzantine civilization that developed in Eastern Europe, there is the brilliant and yet simply written description by T. C. Chubb, *The Byzantines* (Cleveland: World, 1959). A first-rate and clearly written account of Mohammed and his teachings is given in Florence May Fitch, *Allah, The God of Islam* (New York: Lothrop, Lee and Shepard, 1950). For the culture and achievements of the Muslim Empire, see the paperback by the authority P. K. Hitti, *The Arabs: A Short History* (Gateway Editions, 1956). On the Crusades against the Muslims, there are many books, the most interesting and clearest being by F. Hamilton, *The Crusades* (New York: Dial Press, 1965). On the Mongols, there is the fast-moving account by H. Lamb, *Genghis Khan and the Mongol Horde* (New York: Random House, 1954). Finally, for Marco Polo's adventures, see M. Rugoff, *Marco Polo's Adventures in China* (New York: Harpers, 1964); and the novel by Louise Kent, *He Went With Marco Polo* (Boston: Houghton Mifflin, 1935).

FURTHER READING

● The Cornell University Press has published several excellent paperbacks on the medieval period, including S. Katz, *The Decline of Rome and the Rise of Medieval Europe* (1955); M. W. Baldwin, *Medieval Church* (1953); and Carl Stephenson, *Medieval Feudalism* (1954). Two other paperbacks by the English authority, G. G. Coulton, bring to life medieval times: *Medieval Panorama* (Meridian, 1955); and *Medieval Scene* (Cambridge University Press, 1959). Charlemagne, first Holy Roman Emperor, is the subject of the following two colorful biographies: H. Lamb, *Charlemagne: The Legend and the Man* (Bantam Books, 1954); and R. Winston, *Charlemagne: From the Hammer to the Cross* (New York: Bobbs-Merrill, 1956).

● On the religions of the age, there are, in addition to Gaer's general work, the following convenient paperbacks: S. C. Carpenter, *Christianity* (Pelican Books, 1953); C. Humphreys, *Buddhism* (Penguin Books, 1962); M. Percheron, *Buddha and Buddhism* (Harper Men of Wisdom Books, 1957); Liu Wu-Chi, *A Short History of Confucian Philosophy* (Pelican Books, 1955). On Israel and

Judaism, see H. M. Orlinsky, *Ancient Israel* (Ithaca, N. Y.: Cornell University Press, 1954); and E. W. Heaton, *Everyday Life in Old Testament Times* (New York: Scribner, 1956). Finally there is Lin Yutang, *The Wisdom of China and India* (New York: Random House, 1942), a standard collection of selections from the literatures, religions, and philosophies of the two countries.

● On the Byzantine Empire there are two particularly interesting studies: H. Lamb, *Constantinople: Birth of an Empire* (New York: Knopf, 1957); and C. Diehl, *Byzantine Portraits* (New York: Knopf, 1927). For the Muslim world, there is available now a paperback edition of the Koran, translated by M. M. Pickthall, *The Glorious Koran* (Mentor, 1953); and also a fine survey by B. Lewis, *The Arabs in History* (London: Hutchinson's University Library, 1950).

● For an excellent brief summary of the causes, course, and results of the Crusades, see R. A. Newhall, *The Crusades* (New York: Henry Holt, 1927). Two other highly interesting studies of the Crusades are authored by Anthony West, *The Crusades* (New York: Random House, 1954); and Harold Lamb, *The Crusades* (New York: Doubleday, 1945). See also the biography by F. Gabrieli, *Muhammad and the Conquest of Islam* (New York: McGraw-Hill, 1968).

● On the Mongols, there is the paperback by Harold Lamb, *Genghis Khan* (Bantam Books), which is more detailed than his other work on the subject listed above; and also the biography by R. Grousset, *Conqueror of the World: The Life of Genghis Khan* (New York: Grossman, 1967). A more scholarly and comprehensive study is by M. Prawdin, *The Mongol Empire* (London: George Allen & Unwin, 1940). A more general survey of the nomadic peoples is given by E. D. Phillips, *The Royal Hordes: Nomad People of the Steppes* (London: Thames and Hudson, 1965). Finally, on Europe's preparation for expansion, see chaps. I and II of H. J. Wood, *Exploration and Discovery* (London: Hutchinson's University Library, 1951); and see also the paperback edition of *The Travels of Marco Polo* published by Penguin Books, which appeared in 1958.

126

CIVILIZED MAN LIVES IN GLOBAL UNITY

In the encounter between the world and the West that has been going on by now for four or five hundred years, the world, not the West, is the party that, up to now, has had the significant experience. It has not been the West that has been hit by the world; it is the world that has been hit—and hit hard—by the West.[1] The old term 'western civilization' no longer holds. World events and the common needs of all humanity are joining the culture of Asia with the culture of Europe and the Americas, to form for the first time a world civilization.[2]

[1] Arnold Toynbee   [2] Franklin Delano Roosevelt

EUROPE UNITES THE WORLD: 1500—1763

Spain and Portugal lead the way. Two countries of the Iberian Peninsula, Spain and Portugal, took the lead in Europe's overseas expansion. It was Spain that sent Christopher Columbus westward to the New World and Portugal that sent Vasco da Gama southward around the Cape of Good Hope to India. Why did these two Iberian states outstrip all the other countries of Europe in the great burst of exploration and expansion in the 15th and 16th centuries?

One of the chief reasons is that both Spain and Portugal had solid and well-organized governments, strong enough to control the nobles, to govern the people, and to collect sufficient taxes. Today we take all these things for granted, but the fact is that most European governments were not able to do these things at that time. For example, Italy was divided into nine major states and several smaller ones; these states were usually at war with each other. Germany was divided into over three hundred kingdoms, duchies, bishoprics, and free cities. As for France and England, they had been fighting each other in the exhausting Hundred Years' War, which did not end until 1453. After this period both countries were occupied at home with religious conflicts between Protestants and Catholics. England's religious problems became less acute after the defeat of the Spanish Armada in 1588 removed the threat of Spanish intervention on the side of the Catholics. In France, the religious issue was not resolved until the Edict of Nantes of 1598, which left France Catholic, though with certain guaranteed rights for the Protestants.

During this period, Spain and Portugal had been less distracted by religious conflict. They had been free to spend the time, money, and effort needed for overseas discovery and exploration. To us it may seem a simple matter to send an expedition to find out what lands exist in one direction or another. But oceanic expeditions were as complicated and difficult at that time as expeditions to outer space are for us today. It was necessary to build ships strong enough for long voyages, to fit them with the latest types of rigging and sails, and to provide them with the latest maps and navigation instruments. Captains and sailors had to be trained not to be afraid of the "Green Sea of Darkness." These men had to learn that the tropical sea was not boiling hot, and that sea monsters would not swamp their ships. All this required much time, organization, and money. For this reason, the lead in overseas exploration in the 15th century was taken by Spain and Portugal, the countries with the strongest and most efficient governments.

The discoveries of Columbus and Pizarro. Spain made the first great discovery when Columbus sailed westward and found the New World.* After leaving the Canary Islands on September 6, 1492, with three ships, Columbus sailed for five weeks with no sight of land. The crews, frightened and mutinous, demanded that he turn back. On October 9, Columbus promised to do so if they did not find land in three days. At 2:00 A.M. on October 12, just before time ran out, one of the crew saw a light flickering in the distance. On the following morning they found themselves near an island which the devout explorer named San Salvador (Holy Savior), located in the Bahama Islands and now frequently called Watlings Island. The natives flocked out to meet the newcomers and asked

* See *Readings in World History*, "Columbus Discovers the New World," p. 103 (Boston: Allyn and Bacon, Inc., 1970).

Fears engendered by this type of interpretation of the "Green Sea of Darkness" had to be overcome to inaugurate the Age of Exploration.

if they had come from heaven. The Spaniards in turn were surprised to see the Indians "as naked as when they came into the world." They also marvelled at seeing inhabitants rolling a leaf "into the form of a musket barrel but very much smaller; and lighting one end and drawing smoke into their mouths." Thus was tobacco smoking first encountered by Europeans.

Although people soon realized that this was a "new world" that Columbus had found, and not part of Asia, they considered this land mass only an obstacle in the path to the Indies. Columbus thought that he was near Asia and made two other voyages during which he tried to find the Indies and the other rich countries of the East.

Columbus died in 1506, disappointed because he had not reached the Indies. Other Spanish explorers continued to range over the Caribbean area until one of them stumbled upon a rich empire, the first prize of the Western Hemisphere. This was Hernán Cortés, who found and conquered the Aztec Empire of Mexico between 1519 and 1521. Ten years later, between 1531 and 1533, another Spanish adventurer, Francisco Pizarro, discovered the fabulous Inca Empire of Peru.* In these empires the Spaniards did not get the silks and spices they were looking for. They found something much more precious, quantities of gold and silver in hoards such as no man had ever seen. For example, when Pizarro captured the Inca emperor, he demanded as ransom that a room 22 feet long and 17 feet wide be filled as high as a man could reach, with gold and silver objects. Though Pizarro took this huge amount of treasure, he failed to keep the bargain and strangled the unfortunate emperor.

In later years the Spaniards got much more treasure from the gold and silver mines of Mexico and Peru. Between 1500 and 1660 Spain received from the New World no less than 18,600 tons of silver and 200 tons of gold. At least this was the amount that was brought in and registered at the official ports. But between 10 and 50 per cent more was

* See *Readings in World History*, "Pizarro Conquers the Inca Empire," p. 108.

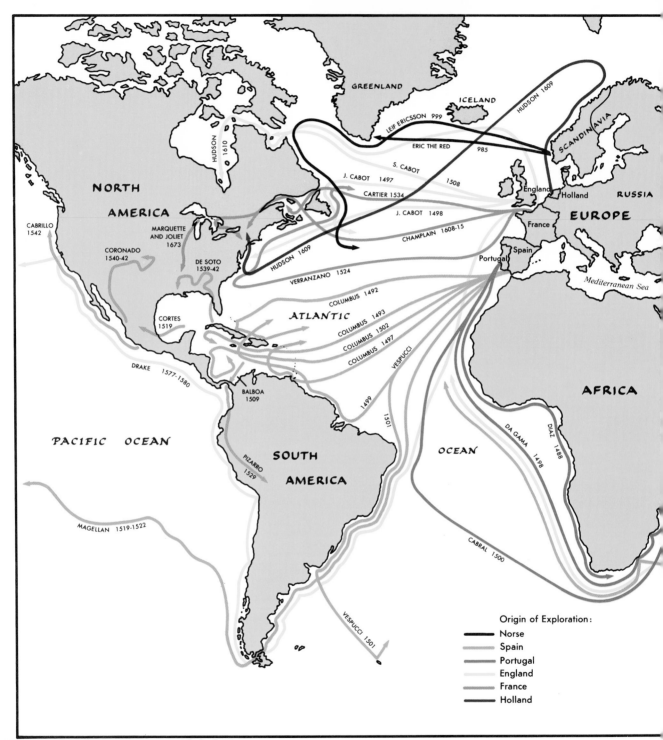

GREENLAND

ICELAND

HUDSON 1609

LEIF ERICSSON 999

ERIC THE RED 985

SCANDINAVIA

HUDSON 1610

NORTH AMERICA

S. CABOT 1508

J. CABOT 1497

CARTIER 1534

J. CABOT 1498

England

Holland

RUSSIA

EUROPE

CABRILLO 1542

MARQUETTE AND JOLIET 1673

CORONADO 1540-42

DE SOTO 1539-42

HUDSON 1609

CHAMPLAIN 1608-15

France

CORTES 1519

VERRANZANO 1524

Portugal

Spain

Mediterranean Sea

COLUMBUS 1492

ATLANTIC

COLUMBUS 1493

COLUMBUS 1502

COLUMBUS 1497

DRAKE 1577-1580

BALBOA 1509

VESPUCCI

AFRICA

PACIFIC OCEAN

PIZARRO 1529

SOUTH AMERICA

OCEAN

1499

1501

DA GAMA 1498

DIAZ 1488

MAGELLAN 1519-1522

CABRAL 1500

VESPUCCI 1501

Origin of Exploration:
Norse
Spain
Portugal
England
France
Holland

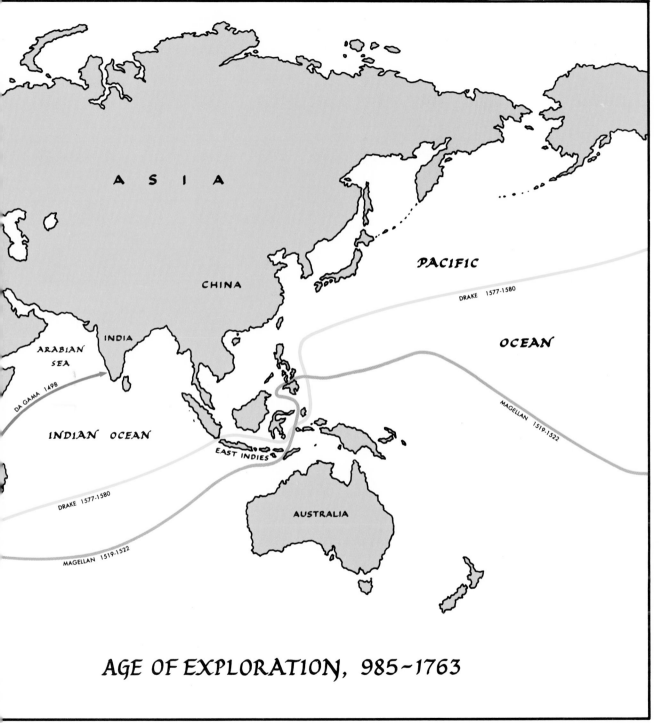

ASIA

CHINA

INDIA

ARABIAN
SEA

DA GAMA 1498

INDIAN OCEAN

EAST INDIES

DRAKE 1577-1580

MAGELLAN 1519-1522

PACIFIC

DRAKE 1577-1580

OCEAN

MAGELLAN 1519-1522

AUSTRALIA

AGE OF EXPLORATION, 985~1763

In a letter to the Spanish Crown, Columbus included this illustration of the people of the "Indies" welcoming his fleet.

smuggled in as unregistered bullion in order to avoid government taxes. All this made Spain by far the wealthiest country in Europe.

Portugal's new Cape route. Meanwhile, the Portuguese also were becoming rich because they had found a direct route to India and the Spice Islands of the East Indies. Vasco da Gama opened the route when he sailed down the coast of Africa, around the Cape of

Good Hope, and across the Arabian Sea to India.* Da Gama returned to Portugal (1498) with a cargo of spices, which were sold for a profit 60 times greater than the cost of the whole expedition. The profit was so great because the new Cape route was much cheaper than the old route through the Middle East, even though the old route was shorter. On the old route the spices had to be loaded and unloaded several times; this was a very expensive procedure. First Arab merchants picked up the spices in the East Indies and took them to India. Then other Arab merchants took them by ship from India to the Persian Gulf or to the Red Sea. At the Persian Gulf the spices were transferred to river boats which went up the Euphrates, and then to camel caravans that crossed the desert to a Mediterranean port. At the Red Sea, the spices were transferred to caravans that crossed over to the Nile River; from there river boats took the cargo down to Alexandria. Finally Italian merchants appeared at Alexandria and other Mediterranean ports, and carried the spices to the consumer in various European countries. All these loadings and unloadings added greatly to the price of the spices as did the various Arab and Italian middlemen, each of whom had to make his profit. As a result the prices paid by the European consumer for these spices were anywhere between 10 and 30 times as high as their original cost in the East Indies.

It is understandable, then, why the Portuguese were able to make such high profits from their new Cape route. They filled their ships with spices in India or the East Indies, and then sailed directly to Europe. They could sell their spices more cheaply than the Italians and still make handsome profits. So the Portuguese sent expedition after expedition to the eastern seas, and they became as wealthy as the Spaniards.

* See *Readings in World History,* "Vasco da Gama Reaches India," p. 106.

Colonies or trading stations. The 16th century was the Golden Age for Spain and Portugal.* Not only did they have great riches, but they now owned most of the world. In fact, Spain and Portugal reached an agreement by which they actually divided between them all the world outside Europe. Under the Treaty of Tordesillas of 1494, the pope drew a north-south line running 370 leagues (roughly 1300 miles) west of the Azores. All the lands west of the line belonged to Spain, and those to the east to Portugal. This did not mean that Spain and Portugal had actually conquered and ruled all the world outside Europe. The Tordesillas Treaty simply staked out the claims of the two countries so that they would not quarrel between themselves, and so that they could keep out other European countries that might wish to expand overseas.

* See *Readings in World History,* "Magellan Circles the Globe," p. 111.

Of the two empires, the Spanish and the Portuguese, the Spanish proved to be the most permanent because it consisted mainly of thinly populated lands in the New World while the Portuguese staked their claims in densely populated lands in Asia. Spain could and did send out colonists to the New World. These colonists multiplied in numbers and gradually built up a New Spain in the Americas. A visitor to New Spain could hear the Spanish language, see Spanish houses, eat Spanish food, and live under a Spanish kind of government. The civilization of Spain had been transplanted across the Atlantic with the result that the lands south of the United States are sometimes called Spanish America. They remained Spanish in character even after they won their independence from Spain in the early 19th century.

By contrast the Portuguese had no chance to build up a "New Portugal" in Asia. India and the East Indies were already too popu-

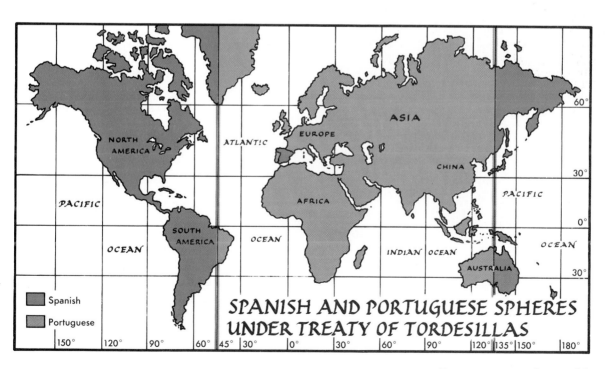

SPANISH AND PORTUGUESE SPHERES UNDER TREATY OF TORDESILLAS

The astrolobe, believed to have been invented by the Greeks about 200 B.C., may be the oldest scientific instrument in the world. From the 15th through the 19th centuries, this instrument, used with charts to determine the sun's angle, was relied on by sailors to determine time and latitude and thus guide direction. With accessories, astrolobes were used for weighing, to survey, as calendars, and as magnetic compasses.

PEABODY MUSEUM, SALEM, MASS.

lous to receive and support colonists. Thus, instead of colonies, Portugal established only trading stations in the East. In order to get a monopoly of the spice trade, the Portuguese seized strategic ports on the Indian Ocean. These included Muscat and Ormuz, guarding the passage into the Persian Gulf; Malacca, on the straits to the Far East; and ports in India and Ceylon. They failed to take Aden at the entrance to the Red Sea, but were strong enough to enter that sea at will. These were trading posts, with only a few soldiers, merchants, and officials but no permanent settlers. That is why there are no "Portuguese Indies" today as there is a Spanish America. In fact, the only remains of Portugal's empire in Asia are the tiny footholds of Macao in China and Timor in Indonesia. The rest were lost to other European powers during the 17th century when Portugal was failing in strength, or to India in the 20th century.

Decline of the Iberian empires. We have seen that the 16th century was the Golden Age for Spain and Portugal; by contrast, the 17th century was for them an age of decline and disaster. One reason for this was that both states were now involved in many wars in Europe, which wasted their money and their manpower. Another reason was that great amounts of gold and silver caused an inflation which upset the economy of the Iberian Peninsula. In addition, the Spanish and Portuguese officials were gradually corrupted by the great wealth and did not carry out their duties properly. Finally, the countries of northwestern Europe were now forging ahead rapidly and in time surpassed the Iberian states. By the 17th century they were training better sailors, building better ships, and manufacturing better goods. The end result was that Portugal lost all her colonies in Asia except for the small territories mentioned above, while Spain was forced to allow the British and others to trade with her colonies and to derive more profit from them than she herself did.

HOLLAND, FRANCE, AND BRITAIN TAKE OVER

The defeat of the Armada. In 1588 a famous sea battle marked the decline of the Iberian powers and the rise of the states of northwestern Europe. This struggle pitted the great Spanish Armada sent out by Philip II of Spain against the fleet of Queen Elizabeth of England. Philip's aim was to invade England, overthrow the Protestant Queen Elizabeth, and re-establish Catholicism as the religion of that country. As the "Invincible Armada" sailed into the narrow English Channel, it was met by Elizabeth's fleet, commanded by Lord Howard and including many tough "sea dogs" such as Sir Francis Drake. The English warships were small, but their improved design and rigging made them more maneuverable and seaworthy than the clumsy Spanish galleons. Moreover, they were armed with more and better cannon than the galleons which relied heavily on large numbers of soldiers to clear and board the decks of the enemies' ships. Keeping to the windward and engaging only at long range, the English blasted the Spaniards with heavy gunfire. The Armada broke up in disorder and fled into the North Sea with the English in pursuit. As the fleet rounded the northern part of Scotland, it was hit by a violent storm which dashed many of the ships on the rocky coasts. Most of the unfortunate Spaniards who managed to scramble to land were massacred by the inhabitants of Scotland and Ireland. More than half the ships were lost, and two-thirds of the men were dead or missing when the once-proud Armada limped back to Spain.

This catastrophic defeat was decisive in two respects. First, it guaranteed that Spain

A *seal commemorating the defeat of the Armada depicts the sinking galleons, praises British prowess, and acknowledges God's aid.*

could not forcibly reimpose Catholicism on Protestant England. Secondly, it showed that the Iberian powers were not the masters of the oceans of the world. From now on they were challenged more and more by England, France, and Holland. The Treaty of Tordesillas, dividing the world between Spain and Portugal, was henceforth completely ignored. In the scramble that followed, the Dutch first came out on top but were later surpassed by the French and the British.

A great merchant fleet. One reason for the success of the Dutch was the development of a very efficient merchant ship known as the *fluyt*, or flyboat. Before this time all merchantmen had been built with extremely thick timber so that they could carry cannon and serve as men-of-war when necessary. This was common practice at the time; the majority of the English ships that defeated the Spanish Armada were simply armed merchantmen. But the trouble with this sort of

Although the flyboat was slow and awkward, it enabled the Dutch to gain economic and political control over vast areas of the East Indies. It was a far more efficient craft than the cumbersome Spanish galleon on which the Spanish had sailed to wealth and power in an earlier century.

heavy construction was that it left little space for cargo. The Dutch now set out to build a merchant ship of maximum efficiency. They designed it with broad beam and flattened bottom, cut down the size of the cabins, and used light timber in the construction. The result was a slow and ugly but cheap and roomy freight carrier. It proved to be much more economical than all other ships, and before long the Dutch ranked first in the carrying trade of the world. As early as 1600 they had 10 thousand ships sailing to all parts of the globe; their shipyards became so efficient that they could turn out one vessel each day.

The success of the Dutch flyboat brought rich profits to Holland and is important because it gave the Dutch the opportunity to see how weak the Portuguese had become in the East Indies. In 1602 their Dutch East India Company was established to challenge the Portuguese monopoly in the Spice Islands. Since the Dutch proved more efficient in business and stronger in sea power, they soon won out, and the Portuguese East Indies became the Dutch East Indies. As we

saw above, Portuguese holdings in Asia were reduced to the tiny footholds which Portugal holds to the present day.*

When the Dutch became the masters of the East Indies, they were not content merely to hold a few trading posts along the coast. Gradually they extended their rule into the interior until they became the owners of entire islands rather than of only the coastal fringes. In this way the Dutch, in a much stronger position than the Portuguese had been, were able to hold the islands from the 17th to the mid-20th century. Only after World War II were the Dutch forced to give up the East Indies because of the strength of the native Indonesian nationalist movement.

During the centuries of Dutch rule, the East Indies became known for many products other than spices. For example, the Dutch introduced the coffee plant and in 1711 harvested 100 pounds of coffee. As the coffee habit swept Europe, coffee production

* See *Readings in World History,* "Holland Challenges Portugal," p. 113.

rose sharply until by 1723 the Dutch were selling 12 million pounds a year. In addition to coffee, the Dutch developed a profitable trade in other products such as rubber, rice, sugar, and palm oil. Later they discovered and exported in large quantities such natural resources as tin, oil, coal, and copper. In this way the Dutch exploited the great natural wealth of the Indies and made rich profits for themselves.

We should note that during the 17th century the Dutch were busy in many other parts of the globe beside the East Indies. For example, they monopolized the whaling industry in the Arctic waters and controlled most of the rich trade in the Baltic Sea. In the New World the Dutch founded New Amsterdam on Manhattan Island in 1623; it served them as a trading center until it was taken by the British in 1664. Also in the Western Hemisphere, the Dutch controlled for a few decades much of the northeast coast of present-day Brazil. But in 1654 they were forced out of most of the area by the Portuguese, though to this day they still hold Surinam (or Netherlands Guiana) and a small group of islands in the West Indies. Finally, the Dutch established a colony on the Cape of Good Hope in South Africa in 1652, for the purpose of providing fuel, water, and fresh provisions for Dutch ships on the long voyage to the East. The settlers took root and thrived, even though this colony was taken over by Britain in 1815. The present-day Boers, or Afrikaners, of South Africa are the descendants of these original Dutch settlers and comprise 57 per cent of the total European population of the country.

Decline of Dutch fortunes. The 17th century was the Golden Age for the Dutch, but during the following century they lost their position of leadership. One reason was that they were entangled in a series of wars with the French and British which left them ex-hausted. Another reason was that other countries passed laws to protect their ships against Holland's tremendous merchant marine. England, for example, required that all goods being imported should be in "English bottoms," that is, in English ships. Perhaps the main reason for Holland's decline is that she lacked the manpower and resources of her rivals. Little Holland could not hold her own against Britain and France in the 18th century for the same reason that Britain and France today cannot hold their own against continental powers like the United States and the Soviet Union. It is true that Holland managed to keep her rich East Indies until after World War II. But during the 18th century her navy and her merchant marine sank from first place, and Amsterdam no longer held first position as the banking center of Europe.

Rivalry between Britain and France. With the decline of Holland, the British and French fought for supremacy in the overseas world. Most of the fighting took place in India and North America where both countries had colonies. The British had trading posts in the Hudson Bay area for carrying on the fur trade, and they also had several colonies along the Atlantic coast. The first of these had been planted at Jamestown, Virginia, in 1607.* Once tobacco plantations were started, this colony prospered, although the English king, James I, stormed and ranted against the use of tobacco. "This precious stink," as he called it, "is a custom loathsome to the eye, hateful to the nose, harmful to the brain, and dangerous to the lungs. . . ." Despite these protests the pleasures of smoking proved too strong and Virginia prospered as a tobacco producer. Further to the north was the colony of Plymouth established in 1620. This also pros-

* See *Readings in World History,* "John Smith at Jamestown," p. 116.

pered, with codfish and trim Yankee ships taking the place of tobacco. Other English colonies were established along the Atlantic until they numbered 13 in all. All grew rapidly as immigrants poured in from the British Isles and from other European countries. In fact, by the time of the American Revolution, these colonies had a population equal to one-half that of Britain.

Meanwhile, the French also had founded colonies in North America, the most important being on the banks of the St. Lawrence River. Established in 1608 by Samuel de Champlain, this settlement grew slowly but steadily. The descendants of the original French settlers today number over four million people and comprise one-fourth of the total population of Canada.* In addition to their colony on the St. Lawrence, the French also established a string of fur-trading posts deep in the interior of the continent. Taking advantage of the great natural waterways, the French soon made their way up the St. Lawrence River, along the Great Lakes, and then down the Ohio and Mississippi Rivers to the Gulf of Mexico. The explorer, Robert de la Salle, reached the Gulf as early as 1682 and thus gave France a claim to the heart of the continent. The French backed up their claim by building forts and fur-trading posts along these rivers and lakes.

Rivalry becomes conflict. The expansion of the French to the Gulf of Mexico inevitably led to conflict with the English. The French forts had fenced in the English and trouble began when the English colonists began to cross the Appalachian Mountains. The Anglo-French wars in North America were fought not only because Britain and France were at war in Europe but also because there was a basic clash of interests in the New World itself.

* See *Readings in World History,* "Beginnings of New France in North America," p. 114.

During these wars, both sides showed certain strengths and weaknesses. The French had the great advantage of strategic location; a network of forts effectively surrounded the English on the Atlantic seaboard. The French also had the advantage of cohesion and discipline, since they were ruled by officials sent out from Paris, who were accustomed to giving orders and being obeyed. By contrast, the English colonies were divided by political factions and feuds because these colonies had elective assemblies as well as officials appointed from England. The officials frequently were at loggerheads with the delegates in the assemblies who had been elected by the colonists.

But the English did have the important advantage of great superiority in numbers. One reason for this is that the French government allowed only Catholics to emigrate to the colonies, but in England there was no such restriction. In fact, many religious dissenters, including Pilgrims, Puritans, Quakers, and Catholics left England for the colonies in order to find religious freedom. Religious considerations, then, reduced emigration to the French colonies and increased it to the English. By 1688 there were 300,000 English settlers concentrated along the Atlantic seaboard but a mere 20,000 Frenchmen scattered over the vast areas of the St. Lawrence and Mississippi Valleys.*

India a prize. Meanwhile the British and the French were gaining footholds in India, where the native population was far too dense to permit the planting of European colonies. Instead, the British and the French established trading posts along the coast, which they were allowed to build only with the consent of the powerful Mogul emperor of India. During the 16th and 17th centuries, the Moguls controlled a large part of India

* See *Readings in World History,* "Frontier Life in the Thirteen Colonies," p. 118.

and had little trouble keeping the Europeans in hand. In the unit on India, we shall see that Emperor Akbar, who ruled between 1556 and 1605, was one of the world's greatest monarchs. At this time European merchants had to beg to be allowed to carry on their trading in the ports of India.

In the late 17th century, however, Mogul power declined rapidly for reasons which we shall note in the unit on India. With this decline, India split into a large number of states which frequently were at war with each other. In place of the strong Mogul Empire there was now a weak and divided India. The British and French took advantage of this opportunity and extended their holdings. They also fought against each other and attempted to find allies among the various Indian rulers. Just as the British and French found allies among the Indian tribes of North America, so they found them among the Indian princes in Asia.

The Seven Years' War. Whenever the British and French were at war in Europe, they also fought in the colonies. In fact, each of the four wars between the two countries is known by two names, one for the war in Europe and the other for the war in the American colonies:

War of the League of Augsburg	
King William's War	1689–1697
War of the Spanish Succession	
Queen Anne's War	1701–1713
War of the Austrian Succession	
King George's War	1743–1748
Seven Years' War	
French and Indian War	1756–1763

The Seven Years' War or French and Indian War, which began in America two years before it started in Europe, was the most important. The British government chartered a land-exploitation company to operate in a part of the Ohio Valley claimed by the

Akbar's policies gave India the military and political strength to resist the British.

French. Colonists and British troops were defeated in their attempt to dislodge the French. Following this clash, negotiations began in Europe; these broke down and fighting spread over North America, the continent of Europe, and India. In the colonies the deciding factor was the superior strength of the British Navy. The French had brilliant commanders such as the Marquis de Montcalm in America and Joseph Dupleix in India. But these men frequently could not get supplies and reinforcements from France because of the British Navy. This points to one of the main reasons why General James Wolfe finally was able to defeat Montcalm at Quebec,* and why Robert Clive defeated Dupleix in south India.

* See *Readings in World History*, "England's Triumph in North America," p. 120.

When the Treaty of Paris in 1763 ended this war, Britain had become the most powerful colonial power in the world. In America, France surrendered to Britain the St. Lawrence Valley and all the territory east of the Mississippi. Spain, who had fought on the side of France, was forced to cede Florida to Britain. In India, France was required to destroy all her fortifications and to restrict herself thenceforth to commerce. These provisions of the Treaty of Paris had a tremendous effect on future world history. They determined, first of all, that the Mississippi Valley, the heart of the North American continent, was to develop as part of the English-speaking world rather than of the French. The other great effect of the Treaty of Paris is that it paved the way for British rule in India. The agreement did not hand India to the British, who still had only a few coastal footholds. It did drive out the French, freeing the British gradually to extend their rule in the following decades until they were masters of the entire peninsula.

We may conclude that it was these terms of the Treaty of Paris that enabled Britain to be the greatest colonial power between 1763 and 1914; she had already secured maritime supremacy, which was the deciding factor in maintaining and expanding her empire.

RUSSIA EXPANDS OVERLAND *

While the Western European states were expanding overseas, Russia was quietly expanding overland. In fact the Russians, like the Americans, have long been a frontier people, with the difference that they pushed their frontier *eastward* to the Pacific while we pushed ours *westward* to the Pacific.

Freedom from Mongol rule. The Russians could not begin their overland expansion

* See *Readings in World History*, "Russian Overland Expansion," p. 122.

until they had freed themselves from their Mongol masters. We noted earlier that the Mongols had conquered Russia in 1237. For almost 250 years the Russians remained under Mongol domination. During those years the Russians were ruled by their own princes, but these in turn had to pay tribute to the Mongol overlords. Finally, in 1480 one of the Russian princes, the prince of Muscovy, was strong enough to discontinue payment to the Mongols. And later on, in 1552, another Muscovite ruler, Ivan IV or Ivan the Terrible, attacked the Mongol settlements in the Volga Valley. He was completely successful, so that the Russians now took the Volga Valley and pushed on to the Ural Mountains.

When the Russians reached the Urals, they were like the American frontiersmen who had reached the Allegheny Mountains. Beyond stretched relatively empty lands, the vast plains of Siberia. So the Russians eagerly pushed eastward just as the Americans went westward. There was one big difference: the Russian frontiersmen, with a longer distance to cover, reached the Pacific much sooner than did the Americans. One reason for this is that the Siberian natives offered less resistance than did the American Indians. Another reason is that the land east of the Urals is all flat, a huge plain stretching on and on for thousands of miles. Furthermore great rivers crisscrossed this plain, so that the Russians were able to paddle from one to the other with short portages (carrying of boats overland between navigable waters). Like the French and English in America, the Russians kept advancing across Siberia in search of furs. As early as 1637, only 50 years after they had crossed the Urals, they reached the Pacific Ocean.

Russia in the Pacific Northwest. The fogs and storms of the Pacific did not stop these rough and ready frontiersmen. Instead they

The dome and Byzantine cross of this Russian Orthodox church in Juneau, Alaska are similar to those of St. Basil's cathedral in Red Square.

pushed ahead; for in the very waters of the North Pacific they found more furs, the precious pelts of the sea otter. Just as they had pursued the sable across Siberia, so now they pursued the sea otter across the Pacific to the Aleutian Islands and to North America. The Russians organized the Russian-American Company, which established trading posts in the territory which is now the state of Alaska. The big problem for the company was the transportation of supplies several thousand miles from Moscow to Alaska. It tried to establish a colony in California, but the settlement did not take root, and California ultimately became a part of the United States rather than of Russia.

Alaska became a possession of the United States when the Russians sold the area in 1867. They were willing to sell because the sea otters were practically exterminated by this time and the fur trade was not yielding any revenue. They also felt that it would be necessary to organize an expensive colonial government in order to hold on to a colony which was located so far from the center of home government, especially since American settlers were already spreading out over the Pacific Northwest. Rather than be forced out, they sold Alaska to the United States for $7,200,000, which amounts to the remarkable real estate bargain of less than two cents an acre. Within a few years the United States got its money back many times over with the discovery of gold and the beginning of the gold rush.

Despite the sale of Alaska, the Russians still held the tremendous land mass stretching from the Ural Mountains to the Pacific Ocean. This gave them plenty of room for growth in an area comparable to the western frontier available to Americans. This fact is of great significance, for it enabled Russia to become one of the great powers of the world. Because of the vast natural resources of Siberia, Russia today is not just another European state like Poland or Germany, but rather a world power comparable to the United States.

SIGNIFICANCE OF THE PERIOD FOR WORLD HISTORY

The significance of the period between 1500 and 1763 is that it paved the way for Europe's domination of the globe in the 19th century. In the field of politics, for example, the European states during these years gained control over the vast underpopulated regions of the globe: Siberia, the Americas, and Australia. It is true that the Europeans had not fully explored and opened up these regions by 1763. But they had made such inroads that it was only a matter of time before they would completely take over and populate these great continents. We shall see later that tremendous mass emigration from Europe in the 19th century filled the empty spaces of the globe. That is why people of European origin occupy a far larger portion of the globe today than any other people.

We should note, however, that the European countries in 1763 had few colonies outside of the relatively empty lands that they were beginning to settle. In Africa the Dutch had established a settlement on the Cape of Good Hope, and the Portuguese had organized the colonies of Angola and Mozambique. Elsewhere in Africa there were only scattered European trading posts along the coasts. Likewise in India the British had a foothold in Bengal, but the rest of the peninsula still was under native rulers. In the East Indies and in Ceylon the Dutch held the key

positions, while in the Philippines the Spaniards were establishing their rule. But further north, in China and Japan, the Europeans held no area whatsoever. They were allowed to carry on trade, but they were not permitted to establish any colonies or permanent trading stations.

It is clear then, that the political map of the world was very different in 1763 from what it was to be in 1914. By 1763 Europe had a firm grip on the underpopulated regions, but only a few holdings in the rest of the world. If we compare maps of the world in 1490, in 1763, and in 1914, we can see that by 1763 Europe had begun her expansion over the globe, but was not yet the ruler of the earth, as would be the case by 1914.

Turning from political to economic conditions, we find very much the same situation. By 1763 Europe had consolidated the world economically but did not yet dominate it. Oceanic routes were open; world-wide trade

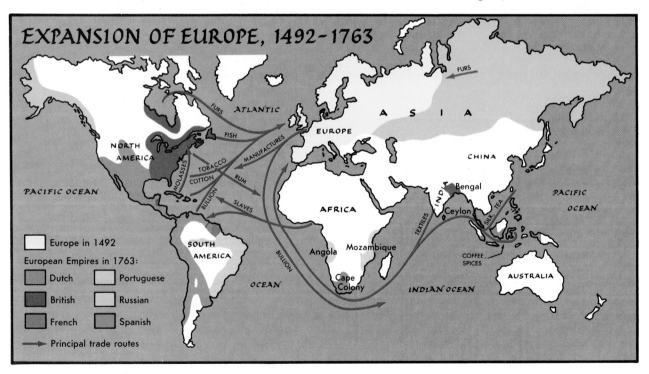

EXPANSION OF EUROPE, 1492–1763

Europe in 1492

European Empires in 1763:
Dutch
British
French
Portuguese
Russian
Spanish
Principal trade routes

had been established. Before 1500 commerce had been carried on only within Eurasia: between Europe, the Middle East, China, and India. There was a tiny trickle of trade with Africa South of the Sahara, and none at all with the Americas, Australia, or Siberia. After the voyages of Columbus and Vasco da Gama, this trade pattern changed at once. Goods were shipped back and forth from all parts of the word. Some of the most important goods were cotton textiles from India, tea and silks from China, coffee and spices from the East Indies, sugar from the West Indies, slaves from Africa and furs from North America and Siberia.

But because the Europeans traded only at seaports and did not penetrate to the interior of the continents, they could not be said to dominate the economy of the whole world. Before 1763 they only shuttled between continents, yet this traffic was enormously lucrative. With the profits realized they were able to open and exploit larger areas by building roads, railways, and canals. Thus the commerce before 1763 laid the basis for later global mastery.

The period between 1500 and 1763 is one of transition between the regional isolation of the pre-1500 era and the global domination of the 19th century.* This was the period when Europe united the globe, and in doing so, gained the strength to become its master. We turn now to this period of mastery between 1763 and 1914.

* See *Readings in World History,* "Limits of European Power," p. 124.

Reviewing the Essentials

Spain and Portugal Lead the Way

1. Why were Spain and Portugal able to take the lead in overseas expansion?

2. What problems posed by overseas expansion in the 15th century are similar to those faced by 20th-century nations in exploring outer space?

3. Using a map, trace the following voyages: (a) Columbus' voyage to the New World; (b) Vasco da Gama's Cape route; (c) Magellan's route around the world. What were the immediate and long-range results of these expeditions?

4. Locate on a map those parts of the New World discovered and claimed by Pizarro and Cortés.

5. What were the provisions of the Treaty of Tordesillas, 1494? Locate on a map those lands designated as Portuguese; as Spanish. What was the purpose of this division?

6. What were the reasons for the decline of Spain and Portugal in the 17th century?

7. Locate on a map the overseas lands ruled by Spain and Portugal in the 17th century.

Holland, Britain, and France Take Over

8. Why was the defeat of the Spanish Armada a major event in world history?

9. Give reasons why the Dutch took the lead after 1588. Name and locate on a map lands acquired by the Dutch in the 17th century. Why did the Dutch lose leadership to France and England in the 18th century?

10. During the 17th century, England emerged as the major overseas power. Give reasons for this development.

11. What part did Samuel de Champlain and Robert de la Salle play in the building of New France? Name and locate the settlements established and lands claimed by France in North America during the 17th century.

12. Compare and contrast life in the English and French settlements in North America. Why was conflict between France and England in North America inevitable?

13. Explain this statement: The Seven Years' War, 1756–1763, fought on two continents, determined in large measure England's leadership in the colonial field for the next century and a half.

14. What were the provisions of the Treaty of Paris, 1763? What were the consequences of the treaty for (a) Spain; (b) France; (c) England; (d) English colonists in the 13 American colonies?

Russia Expands Overland

15. Trace the steps in the eastward overland expansion of the Russians to the Pacific. In what ways was the overland expansion of the Russians similar to the Americans' westward expansion? How did it differ?

16. Why were the Russians willing to sell Alaska? Why is it considered a "real-estate bargain?"

Significance of the Period for World History

17. Compare the map of the world in 1500 with that in 1763. What changes had taken place that indicate shifts in the location of political and economic power? How did the developments occurring in the period 1500–1763 pave the way for Europe to dominate the globe in the 19th century?

18. Explain: The period 1500–1763 is one of transition from regional isolation to the global unity of the 19th century.

19. What persons played major roles in the period of transition from regional isolation to global unity?

Explain, Identify, or Locate

1492	1519	1588	1607
Dutch East India Company	Sir Francis Drake	Azores	Dutch Guiana
Edict of Nantes	Queen Elizabeth I	Philippines	Antilles
Treaty of Tordesillas	Philip II	Angola	Quebec
Spanish Armada	James I	Mozambique	Jamestown
Incas	James Wolfe	Macao	Plymouth
Aztecs	Marquis de Montcalm	Cape of Good Hope	Bengal
Vasco da Gama	Robert de la Salle	San Salvador	Baltic Sea
Cortés	Samuel de Champlain	Iberian Peninsula	Aleutian Islands
Pizarro	Joseph Dupleix	Red Sea	Siberia
Magellan	Robert Clive	Alexandria	Ural Mountains
Columbus	John Smith	St. Lawrence River	Indonesia
1608	Volga Valley	New Amsterdam	Treaty of Paris
	1620	1763	

EUROPE DOMINATES THE WORLD: 1763—1914

EUROPE'S GROWING STRENGTH

During the years between 1763 and 1914 Europe became mistress of the world, controlling not only ocean routes and half-empty territories, but also the ancient and densely-populated centers of civilization in Africa and Asia. This was, indeed, a most extraordinary development. Never before in the history of mankind had one small portion of the globe dominated the remainder.

How did this unprecedented situation come about? The answer is to be found in the development in Europe of certain attitudes, dating from long before 1763, but culminating at that time.

The primary characteristic of Europe in the years following the decline of Rome had been structuralism. The predominant institution, the Church, had provided in that period of chaos a feeling of continuity, a pattern for life based on age-old and unquestioned religious teachings. The social and political system of feudalism and the economic system of manorialism had reinforced and been reinforced by the structuralism of the Church. The peasants or serfs worked on the manor owned by a vassal or lord. The serf owed unquestioning obedience to the lord, as well as part of his crop and certain traditional duties in return for the protection of the lord and the right to live on the manor. The system was one of mutual obligation, each person knowing his place and accepting it, each performing the duties of his station and receiving the privileges of his station in return. The Church, with its emphasis on faith and obedience to authority, supported this system for hundreds of years.

The Renaissance. By the 15th century, however, the feudal system had broken down.

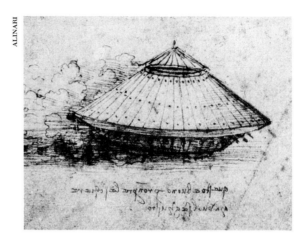

ALINARI

Leonardo da Vinci epitomized the "Renaissance Man." His paintings included the Last Supper *and the* Mona Lisa; *his scientific designs, a flying machine and a "tank" (above), powered by hand.*

As trade developed and man learned more of the world, he became less ready to accept serfdom and lack of social and economic mobility, and more ready to question many age-old explanations and beliefs. New attitudes developed. *Humanists,* curious about man, his search for happiness, and his place in the universe, placed strong emphasis on the worth and uniqueness of the individual. *Rationalists,* rejecting superstition and theology as sources for explanations of natural occurrences, instead urged man to use reason to solve the problems posed by his surroundings. The concern for man and use of reason led to scientific enquiry in the fields of astronomy, energy production, gravitation, and many others. It led to new outlooks in art and literature, emphasizing life on earth rather than spiritual life. *The Prince,* by Machiavelli, spoke of practical rather than

Three paintings of the Madonna and child, from the Byzantine period (above left), the early Rennaissance (above), and the late Rennaissance (left), illustrate the movement toward realism in art.

moral reasons to rule kindly and wisely. The art of Michaelangelo placed a new emphasis on the human form. Questioning of the long-accepted practices of the Catholic Church led to the Protestant Reformation; such men as Luther, Calvin, and the two Wesleys broke from the Catholic Church and founded separatist sects which are the basis of present-day protestantism.

By the 18th century, the humanism and rationalism of the Renaissance had consolidated a base for the three great revolutions which took place in Europe: the Economic, Scientific, and Political Revolutions. These revolutions gave Europe both the desire and the means for mastering the world.

Economic revolution. When Europe began her expansion about 1500, she was not a particularly wealthy or economically advanced region. Vasco da Gama found this out when he reached India in 1498 and tried to sell some cloth he had brought with him. One of his companions wrote "We did not effect these sales at the prices hoped for ... for a very fine shirt which in Portugal fetches 300 reis, was worth here ... only 30 reis, for 30 reis in this country is a big sum." [1] So the Portuguese discovered that the Indians were producing cheaper and better cloth and other manufactured goods than they did. This raised a very serious problem. How were the Portuguese to get the textiles of India and the spices of the East Indies if they could not produce anything that was wanted in return? This was a problem not only for the Portuguese but for all Europeans, since all wanted the goods of the East.

The Europeans were lucky because the problem was solved with the discovery of the treasures of the newly discovered lands. The gold and silver mines of the Incas and Aztecs provided bullion to pay for the spices, textiles, and other goods from the East. The Europeans also found that African slaves could be used to work on plantations in the New World. Slaves were shipped to the Americas where they were set to work growing sugar cane, tobacco, cotton, and other crops. In this manner the Europeans were able to exploit all the continents of the world. A golden stream of raw materials and profits poured into Europe.

All this meant a great boom in Europe's industries as well as in commerce. Europe now began to supply the world with such goods as woolens, firearms, hardware, trinkets, ships and ships' accessories, including lumber, rope, sails, anchors, pulleys, and navigation instruments.* As world trade in-

* See *Readings in World History*, "First Factories in England," p. 126.

TO BE SOLD & LET
BY PUBLIC AUCTION,
On *MONDAY* the 18th of *MAY*, 1829,
UNDER THE TREES.

FOR SALE,
THE THREE FOLLOWING
SLAVES,
VIZ.

HANNIBAL, about 30 Years old, an excellent House Servant, of Good Character.
WILLIAM, about 35 Years old, a Labourer.
NANCY, an excellent House Servant and Nurse.
The MEN belonging to "LEECH'S" Estate, and the WOMAN to Mrs. D. SMIT

TO BE LET,
On the usual conditions of the Hirer finding them in Food, Clothing and Medical once,
THE FOLLOWING
MALE and FEMALE
SLAVES,

ROBERT BAGLEY, about 20 Years old, a good House Servant.
WILLIAM BAGLEY, about 18 Years old, a Labourer.
JOHN ARMS, about 18 Years old.
JACK ANTONIA, about 40 Years old, a Labourer.
PHILIP, an Excellent Fisherman.
HARRY, about 27 Years old, a good House Servant, used to House Work and the Nursery.
LUCY, a Young Woman of good Character, used to House Work and the Nursery.
ELIZA, an Excellent Washerwoman.
CLARA, an Excellent Washerwoman.
FANNY, about 14 Years old, House Servant.
SARAH, about 14 Years old, House Servant.

Also for Sale, at Eleven o'Clock,
Fine Rice, Gram, Paddy, Books, Muslins, Needles, Pins, Ribbons, &c. &c.
AT ONE O'CLOCK, THAT CELEBRATED ENGLISH HORSE,
BLUCHER,

Note that three West Indian slaves are to be sold outright, and that eleven more are "to be let," as if they were work animals.

creased, the demand for these goods also increased. But the craftsmen who made the articles in their little shops could not turn them out fast enough to meet the demands of the growing world market. This created an incentive to devise ways to increase productivity, or, in other words, an incentive to invent labor-saving machinery. In fact, in 1754 there was founded in London the Society for the Encouragement of Arts, Manufacture, and Commerce. This organization gave money, medals, and other awards for achievements such as the invention of machinery that would increase the output of nails or speed up the spinning of thread or the weaving of cloth.

Europe Dominates the World 147

INDUSTRIAL REVOLUTION

1733	John Kay developed the "flying shuttle" which doubled the speed of weaving.
1767	James Hargreaves invented the spinning jenny, decreasing by eight the time needed to spin thread.
1768	Richard Arkwright made use of water power to run spinning machines. Since his frames were too large to use in homes, he developed the factory system.
1768	Edmond Cartwright developed a loom run by water power.
1769	James Watt perfected the steam engine.
1793	Eli Whitney developed the cotton gin which mechanically separated the seeds from the fibers.
1800	Alessandro Volta invented the electric current battery.
1807	Robert Fulton launched the first successful steamboat.
1814	George Stephenson adapted the steam engine to power a railroad locomotive.
1831	Michael Faraday used electric power to operate machines.
1834	Cyrus McCormick developed the reaper.
1837	John Deere built the first steel plow advancing both agriculture and industry.
1839	Charles Goodyear developed a way to vulcanize rubber allowing it to stand up to extremes of temperature.
1844	Samuel Morse developed the first practical electrical telegraph.
1856	Henry Bessemer and William Kelly developed a means of mass production of steel by blowing air through molten iron.
1866	Cyrus Field laid the Atlantic Cable.
1867	George Westinghouse invented the air brake.
1876	Alexander Graham Bell invented the telephone, electric light.
1879	Thomas Edison invented the incandescent lamp.
1880	George Eastman perfected photography.
1887	Gottlieb Daimler constructed the first successful automobile.
1897	Guglielmo Marconi invented the wireless telegraph.
1897	Rudolf Diesel perfected the internal combustion (diesel) engine.
1903	Wright Brothers made the first successful heavier than air flight.
1939	Hans von Ohain developed the jet engine.

It was the necessity to satisfy the expanding world market that led to the series of remarkable inventions in the 18th and 19th centuries. In industry after industry, new machines and new processes for increasing productivity were developed. These inventions, together with the systems of manufacturing, transportation, and distribution which resulted from them, constitute the Industrial Revolution.* As an example of the radical change in the European economy, Great Britain, who took the lead in the Industrial Revolution, increased production of two key commodities as follows:

	1770	1800	1861
Coal (in million tons)	6	12	57
Iron (in thousand tons)	50	130	3800

The Industrial Revolution began in Great Britain about 1770, spread to the continent by 1815, and to the United States by 1830; the result was that, during the 19th century, Great Britain, Western Europe, and the United States achieved a near-monopoly of world industrial production. From Europe's industrial strength came Europe's colonial drive in the late 19th century. As the Industrial Revolution spread from Britain to Belgium, France, Germany, and other European countries, fierce competition developed among these countries. They competed with each other for markets in which to sell the goods pouring out of their factories. They competed for cotton, rubber, tin, copper, oil, and other raw materials needed for their factories. They competed also for markets where they could invest the profits from their industries. In other words, as the various European countries became industrialized, they became rivals all over the world. In order to win in this contest, they began grabbing colonies; because there would be no economic

* See *Readings in World History,* "Beginnings of the Industrial Revolution," p. 127.

Fear that Hargrave's spinning jenny would create unemployment led to attempts to destroy the jenny. More often, however, the jenny created employment and increased numbers of children were brought into the labor force to satisfy greater demand for the improved product. This led to abuses which were not corrected until the 20th century.

threat from other countries in their own colonies. In this way, the Industrial Revolution was one of the chief reasons for the burst of imperialism and colonialism in the late 19th century. There were other reasons, especially the rise of nationalism, which we shall consider later. In summary, the industrialized countries of Europe became imperialistic, and, within a few decades, divided almost the entire globe among themselves.

Europe Dominates the World 149

Scientific Revolution. Side by side with the Economic Revolution came the Scientific Revolution.* The two developments were closely connected, for technology and science depend on each other. Technology emphasizes know-how; science emphasizes know-why. Inventors like James Hargreaves with his "spinning jenny" were technicians. Because they were faced with the problem of speeding up the production of a certain commodity, they built machines to do the job. But the scientist is interested in the principles on which the machine operates, in cause and effect. When he has discovered the

* See *Readings in World History*, "The Place of Science in Western Civilization," p. 130.

laws and the sequence which they follow, he can apply this knowledge to many other fields beside the production of cotton textiles.

To illustrate the basic difference between technology and science, we might consider the Indian boy who fishes with a spear. He is taught by his father always to aim below the fish in order to hit it. Once he has learned this, he is satisfied. But the scientist wants to know why the human eye sees the fish at a different point from the place where it actually is. He carries on experiments, from which he learns that light rays follow one course in air and another in water. The light ray "bends" when it hits the water; thus the fish appears to be where it is not. Having

Edward Jenner's invention of vaccination, particularly his use of cowpox serum to prevent smallpox, was a major scientific contribution. His thesis was not readily accepted, however, as is seen in this caricature of the results of the injections.

CONTRIBUTIONS TO THE SCIENTIFIC REVOLUTION

Nicolaus Copernicus (1473-1543)	**SIXTEENTH CENTURY** Developed the heliocentric theory — the earth revolves around the sun and the earth also revolves on its own axis.
Galilei Galileo (1564-1642)	Constructed a telescope with which he confirmed Copernicus' theory. Measured the acceleration of gravity.
Sir Francis Bacon (1561-1626)	**SEVENTEENTH CENTURY** Developed the scientific method of research and experimentation.
Johannes Kepler (1571-1630)	Discovered the exact movement of the planets.
René Descartes (1596-1650)	Developed analytic geometry. Refined the scientific method and applied it in experimentation.
Anton van Leuwenhoek (1637-1723)	Developed the microscope and described the properties of germs.
Sir Isaac Newton (1642-1727)	Explained the law of gravity and its affect on the movement of the solar system.
Benjamin Franklin (1706-1790)	**EIGHTEENTH CENTURY** Proved the basis of electricity.
Joseph Priestly (1733-1804)	Isolated oxygen and explained its role in burning and breathing.
Antoine Lavoisier (1743-1794)	Explained the chemical nature of combustion.
John Dalton (1766-1844)	**NINETEENTH CENTURY** Stated the theory that all matter is composed of tiny particles or atoms.
Sir Charles Lyell (1797-1875)	Computed the age of the earth and showed it had been formed by natural forces.
Charles Darwin (1809-1882)	Developed the theory of evolution — that all animals and plants are the product of gradual evolution since the first cells of life appeared millions of years ago.
Gregor Mendel (1822-1884)	Discovered the principles of heredity.
Louis Pasteur (1822-1895)	Formulated the theory that germs are the basis of many diseases.
Wilhelm Wundt (1832-1920)	Created modern experimental psychology.
Sigmund Freud (1856-1939)	Developed psychoanalysis, the study of the subconscious.
Albert Einstein (1879-1955)	**TWENTIETH CENTURY** Developed the theory of the relationship between matter and energy.
Wilhelm Roentgen (1845-1923)	Discovered the uses of X-rays.

learned this principle of light rays, the scientist can apply it for purposes other than catching fish. In fact, he has applied the principle, and as a result he has been able to construct lenses in eyeglasses, microscopes, and telescopes. There are many more examples; even such recent developments as radar and television are based on principles concerned with the behavior of light rays.

In this manner, the Economic and Scientific Revolutions developed together, each stimulating the other.* For example, as factories increased in number and size, vast quantities of coal and other minerals were needed to fill their requirements for raw materials. This led to a great increase in mining, which in turn led to the discovery of metals such as bismuth, zinc, and cobalt. It became necessary to devise new techniques for separating and processing these metals, and as a result, the science of chemistry was advanced. Scientists learned about chemical processes involved in mining, which could then be applied in other fields. Today science has advanced so far that it is usually industry that learns from science rather than the opposite. The work of Thomas Edison has made possible the electric light and motion-picture industries, and the work of Alexander Graham Bell, the telephone industry.

Science tended to advance in spurts in individual fields during various periods. For example, in the 16th and 17th centuries, major progress was made in physics and mathematics. In the 18th century there was important progress in chemistry. During the 19th century, sweeping progress was made in several fields, including biology, geology, medicine, and psychology.

The most influential scientific work of the 19th century was that by the English naturalist, Charles Darwin. In 1859 he published his world-famous *On the Origin of Species*

setting forth the theory of evolution. This holds that all animal and vegetable species in their present innumerable forms were not created a few thousand years ago; rather they are the products of gradual evolution that has been going on since the first cell of life appeared on this planet millions of years ago. This theory naturally created a furor between the scientists who supported it and the churchmen who attacked it as a challenge to Biblical teaching.

In conclusion, the Scientific Revolution is significant for world history for two reasons. One is that it made a tremendous impression on people all over the globe. Science, together with technology, are the only products of Western civilization that all peoples are anxious to learn. Few of them care for such European achievements as Graeco-Roman philosophy or the Christian religion or Renaissance art. But they are all determined to master European science and technology because these are the means for developing their economies and their military power.*

The second reason why the Scientific Revolution is significant is that it helped Europe to expand over the globe. Europe could not have exploited vast continents without railroads, canals, and steamships. Europe could not have tamed the tropics had not medical science shown how to control tropical diseases. Equally important were the rifles, machine guns, and cannon, which enabled the Europeans to have their way, whether in the American plains, the Siberian steppes, the Chinese coast, or the African interior. As an English writer put it during the war with the Zulus in 1893:

> Whatever happens we have got
> The Maxim † gun and they have not.

* See *Readings in World History,* "Science in the Modern World," p. 134.
† A recoil-operated machine gun named after its inventor, the American-born Hiram Maxim (1840–1916).

* See *Readings in World History,* "Science Aids the Economic Revolution," p. 133.

July the 13th, 1789, the citizens of Paris took to the streets to begin the French Revolution. Since its completion, this liberal revolution has served as an inspiration to people throughout the world living under oppressive governments.

Political Revolution. The Economic and Scientific Revolutions went hand in hand with the third great revolution, the Political. The Political Revolution was essentially a basic change in the relations between government and people. Up to this time government had been regarded as something above the people, and people as something below the government. Throughout the world there was this sharp cleavage between rulers and ruled. In some areas people believed that their monarchs had been appointed by God to rule and that they were required to obey. Authority resided in the government, and there was no redress against its acts however tyrannical. But with the coming of the Political Revolution these beliefs were shaken. Now the idea gradually spread that government and people were not entirely different and separate; that government depended upon the people; and that the people had the right and the duty to control their government. This was indeed a revolutionary idea, and its revolutionary effects are being felt throughout the world to the present day. The African and Asian peoples fighting against foreign domination are moved by this idea as strongly as were our own ancestors.

Europe Dominates the World 153

One of the chief reasons that the Political Revolution started in Western Europe in modern times was the growth of commerce accompanied by the rise of a merchant class. This new middle class was dissatisfied with the old feudal classes which had controlled politics in the earlier medieval period. As the merchants increased in numbers and in strength, they demanded a share in government. They wanted to participate in the election of a parliament, and they insisted that the country should be governed by this parliament rather than by the nobles or the king. Generally they insisted on freedom of the press and the right of assembly. These ideas are commonly known as liberal ideas or liberalism. This attitude toward government was the driving force behind the great political revolutions that changed Europe in the period to 1914.*

The first of these revolutions took place in England. The Puritan leader, Oliver Cromwell, expressed the aims of the English Revolution when he declared: "The People are,

* See *Readings in World History*, "The Rise of Liberalism," p. 135.

under God, the Original of all just Power," and the Commons [of Parliament] "being chosen by, and representing the People, have the supreme Power in this Nation." [2] In the civil war that followed, the Puritans were victorious, and King Charles I was executed in 1649. The Puritan victory established the supremacy of Parliament, and England has had parliamentary government ever since. At first, representatives were elected only by persons whose income was above a certain level, but the First and Second Reform Bills passed in 1832 and 1867 extended the vote to most of the people.

The next political revolution took place in America where the colonists protested against "taxation without representation." In the Declaration of Independence in 1776 they expressed typical liberal ideas: ". . . all men are created equal . . . Life, Liberty and the pursuit of Happiness . . . Governments are instituted among Men, deriving their just Powers from the consent of the governed." The victory of the colonists assured the establishment of a state based upon liberal principles.

"The wrath of God has visited itself upon you," exclaimed Cromwell to Charles the First.

CONTRIBUTIONS TO THE POLITICAL REVOLUTION

Nicolo Machiavelli (1469-1527)	One of the first men to view government realistically, without the aura of divine right or the natural superiority of the monarch. In *The Prince* he stated that the good ruler was one who was successful and powerful; to achieve this the ruler must have the support of the people; and to gain this support must rule in the best interests of the people not the personal interest of the ruler.
Thomas Hobbes (1588-1679)	In the *Leviathan* he discussed types of government. Although placing authority in the hands of the soverign, he formulated the doctrine that subjects can and must abandon a ruler who no longer protects them.
Benedictus Spinoza (1632-1677)	In his writings offered the thesis that man would be a better citizen if allowed to freely speak his mind, and that just government offers the maximum freedom possible. One of the first advocates of freedom of speech.
Baron de Montesquieu (1689-1755)	In *Spirit of Laws* he developed the idea of separation of the powers of government into executive, legislative, and judicial branches, thus preventing the growth of tyranny.
John Locke (1632-1704)	His *Two Treatises on Government* stated that according to natural law all people are equal and have the right to life, liberty, and the protection of property. To protect these rights men *voluntarily* form governments, based on the consent of the governed. Thus if the ruler is harsh or arbitrary, the people have the right to remove him.
(Francois Marie Arouet) Voltaire (1694-1778)	A strong critic of authoritarian society, he demanded freedom of expression for all, freedom for each man to follow his own reason as long as he does not interfere with the rights of others. He offered the idea of a "benevolent despot," a sovereign ruling in the best interests of his people.
Jean-Jacques Rousseau (1712-1778)	Believing in the inherent goodness of the nature of man, Rousseau felt man was corrupted by society, was "in chains" forged by governments denying men freedom. He formulated the "social contract" theory which held that governments were formed voluntarily by men and should be overthrown if they disregard the wishes of men. Rousseau along with Locke and Montesquieu strongly influenced the founders of the United States Republic.
Marquis de Condorcet (1743-1794)	One of the first to declare in favor of the French Republic and against the monarchy, he believed that men must work toward the end of inequality between nations and classes. An advocate of freedom in all areas: speech, press, and religion.
Jeromy Bentham (1748-1832)	In a treatise on efficient and ethical government, he stated that the object of all legislation must be the greatest good of the greatest number, thus helping to formulate the idea of representative government.
Thomas Jefferson (1743-1826)	Author of the *Declaration of Independence*, he synthesized the ideas of many political thinkers which later became part of the United States Constitution, and influenced and provided a pattern for many of the political revolutions.
The Federalists (1787-1788)	Written by Hamilton, Madison, and Jay, this series of articles explaining the United States Constitution provided a blueprint for a government embodying all the liberal concepts and insured the acceptance of the Constitution, thus aiding in the inauguration for the first time of a government based on and testing the viability of these concepts.
Karl Marx (1818-1883) **Friedrich Engels** (1820-1895)	Assuming an economic basis for historical events, these two men formulated the dialectic theory of government. The repressed proletariat, deprived of rights and the fruits of their labor, would revolt against their bourgeoisie masters, and continue to revolt until the bourgeoisie is destroyed, thus creating a classless society. Then all people would reap the benefit of their production. And, each person, producing to the best of his ability and deriving from the community only what he needed, would no longer need to be ruled by an organized government. At this point, government, whose purpose was the protection of property, would no longer be necessary and would disappear. The philosophy of Marx and Engels affected large groups in many countries, becoming the basis for Socialism and Communism.

A few years after the American Revolution, the French people also rose up with similar demands. In 1789 the French National Assembly adopted the "Declaration of the Rights of Man and Citizen." This declaration included the following principles: "Men are born and remain free and equal in rights.... The aim of all political association is to preserve the natural rights of man. These rights are liberty, property, security, and resistance to oppression." The French revolutionaries were as successful as the English and American had been. In 1793 they executed Louis XVI and established a republic that has persisted despite occasional relapses into monarchy.

These three revolutions have provided inspiration for people everywhere who are oppressed by tyrannical governments. On every continent, in Europe and Latin America in the 19th century, in Asia and Africa in the 20th, the battle cries of liberalism have been repeated: "...Supremacy of parliament.... All men are created equal.... Liberty, Equality and Fraternity...."

Nationalism. The Political Revolution consisted not only of the liberalism which we have described but also of another "ism" that was just as explosive, nationalism. By nationalism we mean the doctrine that advocates national interests, unity, and independence. We tend to accept nationalism as a standard attitude, yet it has developed only in modern times. Before that, an individual's loyalty was given to a tribe or feudal lord or church. For example, if a peasant in medieval France had been asked what he was, he would never have thought to say that he was a Frenchman. Rather he would have said that he came from such-and-such a village, and that Lord So-and-So was his master. The effect of nationalism, then, has been to make people feel that they are members of a nation, a larger community with mutual in-

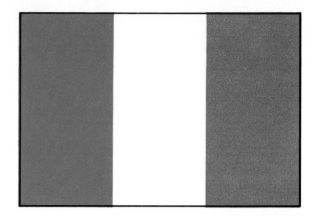

The Parisians storming the Bastille wore badges of red and blue, the colors of the city of Paris. In creating a flag, white, the symbol of the Bourbons, was added to symbolize the unity of king and people. In European tradition, any tricolor symbolized revolution, and the blue, white, and red of the French also came to symbolize republicanism.

terests and institutions, whether they be French or Italian or Arab or Chinese.*

Nationalism, like liberalism, began first in Western Europe. It gained great momentum during the French Revolution. The French government at that time organized *national* armies in which all young Frenchmen fought for *la patrie*, their nation. The government established *national* schools in which children were taught love of country. The use of nationalist symbols such as the national flag and the national anthem began during the French Revolution. With the help of these devices, Parisians and Burgundians and Normans were transformed into nationalists, into Frenchmen. How strong the feeling was at this time can be seen in the following excerpt from a letter written in 1793 by a young French soldier to his mother: "When *la patrie* calls us to her defense, we should rush to her as I would rush to a good meal. Our

* See *Readings in World History*, "The Rise of Nationalism," p. 137.

life, and our talents do not belong to us. It is to the nation, to *la patrie*, that everything belongs. . . . the principles of love for *la patrie*, for liberty, for the republic are engraved on my heart. . . ." [3]

Gradually nationalistic fervor spread to other parts of Europe. It caused bloody revolution in areas where the people who were becoming nationalistic happened to be under foreign rulers. In those areas the nationalists demanded independence, and usually they had to take up arms in order to win their independence. That is why there were so many revolutions on the continent of Europe throughout the 19th century. A few of these were liberal revolutions, for example, the uprisings by French citizens against their own government because it allowed only a few citizens to vote in elections and to take part in public affairs. But most of the revolutions were nationalistic rather than liberal. They were uprisings against foreign rulers: the Greeks against the Turks in 1821, the Belgians against the Dutch in 1830, the Poles against the Russians in 1830 and 1863, the Italians against the Austrians in 1830 and 1848, and others.

During the 20th century nationalism spread from Europe to all parts of the world. We shall see in later units how this idea has aroused people so rapidly that 58 countries won their independence between 1945 and 1969. Today the strongest political force in the world is the idea of nationalism which originated in Europe.

Socialism. In addition to liberalism and nationalism, the Political Revolution contained the ideas of socialism or communism. These two terms were used interchangeably until the 1917 Bolshevik Revolution in Russia, after which the term "socialist" was used to refer to those who believed that capitalism could be replaced by peaceful means, and the term "communist" was used to refer to those who believed that force would be necessary. But both socialists and communists drew their main ideas from Karl Marx and Friedrich Engels, who wrote in the mid-19th century. These two men taught that the competitive capitalist society based on private ownership of the means of production should be replaced by a cooperative Socialist society based on public ownership of the means of production.*

* See *Readings in World History*, "The Rise of Socialism," p. 138.

Giuseppe Garibaldi, a fiery advocate of unification for Italy, was one of the most exciting figures in this nationalistic revolution.

BROWN BROTHERS

This doctrine naturally appealed strongly to those who owned little private property, that is, the workers. By 1914 socialism had won a wide following among the workers of the industrialized European countries. In fact, the Socialist parties had more parliamentary strength by 1914 than any other single parties in Germany, France, and Italy. Nevertheless socialism still remained only an "ism," only a theory. Nowhere had it actually been tried out and tested. This changed with the Bolshevik Revolution, which established the first Communist state, the Soviet Union. We shall see later that it also led to the establishment of the Communist International, whose aim was to spread communism throughout the world. Today, communism, like nationalism, is a powerful international movement. It is supported by great powers such as the Soviet Union and China, and it has strong parties in such countries as France, Italy, and India.

SIGNIFICANCE OF THE THREE REVOLUTIONS

The Economic, Scientific, and Political Revolutions had two great effects upon the development of man. One was that they changed man's whole way of life. To understand why they did so, we need to go back over five thousand years to the beginnings of civilization. We noticed in Unit Three that with civilization came the rise of classes, the rulers and the ruled. Civilization ended the equality that had existed among villagers in Neolithic times. In its place came the division between the ruling classes in the cities and the peasant masses in the countryside. This division lasted until modern times, when it began to disappear under the impact of three great revolutions.

These revolutions created a new and constantly changing world. The Economic and Scientific Revolutions produced new industrial and urban centers with the result that the masses no longer were tied to their fields as hewers of wood and drawers of water. They were able to move from place to place, and from one position in society to another. Likewise the Political Revolution brought new ideas that awakened the masses and challenged the old organization of society, which consisted of a few rulers at the top and the great mass of subjects below. This, in turn, meant the end of the old division between the High Culture of the upper class in the cities and the Low Culture of the peasant mass in the country. This division is disappearing in the modern world in which the same schools, books, newspapers, and radio and television programs are available to all. In conclusion, it is clear that the three revolutions affected man so deeply and in so many ways that they created an entirely new way of life.

The second great effect of the three revolutions was that they enabled Europe to dominate the globe in the 19th century. The Economic Revolution contributed to imperialism by creating a need for markets and for raw materials. The Scientific Revolution gave strength to European imperialism by providing new machines, new weapons, and new means for communication and transportation. Finally, the Political Revolution encouraged imperialism because, as each European people became nationalistic, they demanded their "place in the sun." That is, they demanded a colonial empire as large as that of their neighbors because they felt that their nation should not be surpassed by any other nation.*

In this way the Economic, Scientific, and Political Revolutions were largely responsible for the tremendous imperialist drive of Europe in the late 19th century. This was the period of the greatest land-grabbing in

* See *Readings in World History,* "Europe Turns to Expansion," p. 142.

the history of mankind. Nothing like it has been seen before or since. The result was that almost the entire globe came under the direct or indirect rule of Europe. The Chinese and Ottoman Empires, for example, did not become European colonies, but they were so dominated by European banks, military missions, and gunboats that they certainly were semicolonies. Even if we consider only the full colonies, in 1914, seven European countries owned 115 colonies which were almost three times larger in population and almost 30 times larger in area than the mother countries.

EUROPEAN EMPIRES IN ASIA

India. Asia was one of the areas in which the European states built great empires in the period between 1763 and 1914. The first part of Asia to fall under European rule was India. There were many reasons for India's vulnerability. By 1763 the Mogul Empire had become weak and could not prevent European aggression. By the Treaty of Paris in the same year, the French were forced to leave India, allowing the English a free hand. The great wealth of the country encouraged the English to push out from their original

base in Bengal and to conquer the entire peninsula. They met little resistance from the people of India, who had no feeling of nationalism. If the Indians had invaded Britain, the English would have drawn together and fought to the end to protect their nation. But when the British invaded India, the people of that country showed little concern. Since they were not nationalistic, it made little difference to them whether they were ruled by English kings or Mogul emperors. Many of them joined the English as mercenaries and helped them conquer the country, a fact which helps to explain why a few thousand English soldiers were able to win a vast country like India with a population of hundreds of millions.

In the following unit on India we shall see how the British had effectively conquered the subcontinent by the middle of the 19th century. We shall also see how they ruled India, and what the effects of this rule were. Here we should simply note that throughout the 19th century there was no concerted opposition to British domination. This is borne out by the fact that in 1914 there were in India, a country of over 300 million people, only 7000 British administrators and 75,000 British troops. In other words there was only one

Photograph of an Englishman in India, about 1860.

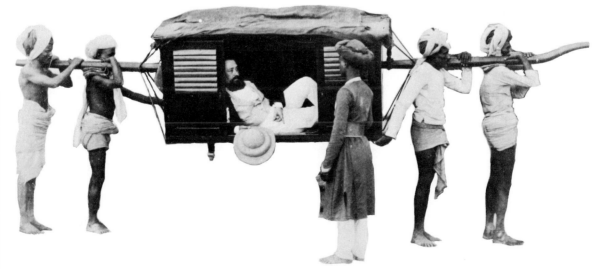

Englishman for every 4000 Indians, yet with this small force, the English succeeded in controlling the country.

The explanation for this surprising situation is, again, the lack of strong nationalistic feelings. Because of this lack, the great majority of the people did not care whether or not they were governed by foreigners. But the spirit of nationalism gradually filled the Indian masses, and after World War II the British could no longer hang on. They left India in 1947. Despite its desire to be rid of British rule, India has remained a member of the Commonwealth of Nations.

Southeast Asia. Once the British had established themselves solidly in India, they used this colony as a base for expansion into other parts of Asia. First they moved into Southeast Asia, where they conquered Burma by stages during three wars in 1824, 1852, and 1886. They took the Malay Peninsula in stages and built strategic Singapore.

Meanwhile the Dutch were entrenching themselves in the East Indian islands from which they had ousted the Portuguese. The Dutch, in their zeal to exploit these wealthy islands to the fullest, treated the native Indonesian people with cruelty and injustice. In fact Jan Coen, who was governor of the Indies between 1617 and 1630, specifically said that the natives were the "cattle" of their Dutch masters. "May not a man in Europe do what he likes with his cattle? Even so does the master here do with his men, for everywhere, these with all that belongs to them are as much the property of the master, as are brute beasts in the Netherlands." [4]

France also seized territory in Southeast Asia, using as a pretext the murder of a French missionary in Annam. French troops were landed in 1858, with the explanation that they were "to avenge the insults to our sacred religion and our pious missionaries."

After capturing the excellent port of Saigon, the French gradually expanded their foothold until they had carved out the large colony of French Indochina.

By this time the only independent territory left in Southeast Asia was Siam, or Thailand. And the main reason Siam was spared was that the British in Burma and the French in Indochina could not agree on the division of the little kingdom that lay between them. Instead they allowed it to remain independent in order to serve as a buffer.

China. At the same time that the European powers were carving up Southeast Asia, they were pressing upon the giant country of China to the north. China, however, was not conquered and made into a colony, as were India and Southeast Asia. One reason was that China traditionally had a strong centralized government whereas India did not. Furthermore the Manchu Dynasty which came to power in China in 1644 was strong and vigorous. Because the Manchus had full control of the whole country, the Europeans were not able to seize footholds along the coast and expand inland, as they had done in India. Instead the Chinese kept the Europeans at arm's length, allowing them to trade only at the port of Canton under strict regulations.

By the middle of the 19th century, the Manchu Dynasty had fallen into decline and the Chinese no longer could hold back the Europeans. By that time the European powers were much stronger because of the Industrial and Scientific Revolutions. They now had warships which could steam up and down the Chinese coast and bombard fortifications and cities at will. The Chinese could do little to defend themselves because they had not developed the steam engine or modern cannon. The contrast between the two civilizations became clear when war broke out between China and Britain in 1839. A certain general, who was the cousin of the Chinese emperor, came forth with a plan for defeating the British and their warships. He proposed tying firecrackers to the backs of monkeys, which should then be thrown on board the English warships anchored off the coast. The plan was approved and 19 monkeys were brought to the Chinese headquarters. No one dared, however, go near enough to the warships to carry out the plan.

Since the Chinese had to depend on such fantastic schemes, it is not surprising that they were easily defeated by the English in the first war between 1839 and 1842. They were just as easily beaten in a second war with Britain and France between 1856 and 1858. And, worst of all, they were defeated by the Japanese in 1894–1895, because the Japanese in the meantime had learned the secrets of Western science and technology.

Despite these defeats China did not become a colony like India. By this time several European powers, as well as Japan and the United States, were interested in China. No one power had a free hand and China escaped conquest. Although China did not become a colony, she did become a semi-colony. We shall see in the later unit on this country that China was forced to accept various "unequal treaties" which gave special privileges to foreigners. Also the whole country was divided into spheres of influence, in which individual foreign powers had special rights. The British, for example, had a free hand in the Yangtze Valley, the Russians in Manchuria, the French in Yunnan province bordering Indochina. Thus China was controlled and exploited by European imperialism, even though she was not actually conquered.

The little industry which the Chinese had was located on the coast and thus was easily accessible to attack. The factories of Canton and much of the city were destroyed in war.

PEABODY MUSEUM, SALEM, MASS.

Laying the tracks of the Trans-Siberian Railroad over the ice of Lake Baikal.

Central Asia. At the same time that China was becoming a semicolony of the Western European Powers, Central Asia was becoming a part of the Russian Empire. We noted earlier that the Russians had pushed rapidly across Siberia, reaching the Pacific Ocean as early as 1637. Immediately to the south of Siberia was the steppe country in which roamed the Kazakh nomads. Still further south began the great desert, dotted with rich oases. The oases supported the ancient Muslim khanates or kingdoms of Bukhara, Khiva, and Kokand. These khanates were well organized and much stronger militarily than the scattered tribes of Siberia. This was one reason why the Russians did not advance southward into Central Asia after conquering Siberia. Another reason was that the Russians did not feel at home in the hot deserts of the south; they much preferred the familiar forests and snows of Siberia.

In the 19th century, however, the Russians were able to conquer Central Asia bit by bit. The explanation again is the Economic and Scientific Revolutions. The steam railway enabled the Russians to transport men and supplies across the deserts; the machine gun and the cannon gave them a great advantage over the Muslim warriors. First the Russians won the Kazakh steppes between 1825 and 1850. Then they pushed southward, taking Bukhara in 1868, Khiva in 1873, and Kokand in 1876. During the 1880's and 1890's the Russians were on the borders of India, an advance which created a number of crises with Britain. But the distances were so great and the mountains so high that war was almost impossible in that area before the invention of the airplane. Agreements were worked out by Britain and Russia which drew the boundaries that have continued to the present day.

Japan. Japan, the great exception of Asian countries, did not become a colony like India or a semicolony like China. At first it appeared that Japan would not escape the fate of her neighbors. Japan, like China, had a policy of keeping out all Europeans except for a few Dutch traders. But an American fleet under the command of Admiral Perry appeared in Tokyo Bay in 1853 and compelled the Japanese to open their ports. During the next few years unequal treaties, similar to those which had been forced upon China, were forced upon Japan. The country seemed doomed to outright conquest or to division into spheres of influence.

At this point the Japanese did something that no other Asian people were able to do in the 19th century. They managed to unite against the Westerners and at the same time to copy those aspects of Western civilization which would give them the strength to resist.* Instead of depending on monkeys and firecrackers, they studied Western science and technology, built industries, and organized a modern army and navy. By using Western knowledge and techniques, they were able to force the revision of the unequal treaties in 1894. In the same year they copied the Western Powers in another fashion by embarking on imperialist adventures of their own.

First the Japanese fought and defeated the huge but antiquated Chinese Empire. As a result of their victory, they annexed Formosa and some other islands off the coast of China. Then the Japanese faced the Russians who were pushing down from Siberia into Manchuria and Korea. Since the Russians were getting too close for comfort, Japan made Russia a proposal: Russia should have a free hand in Manchuria and Japan a free hand in Korea. The Russians refused the offer because they were sure they could defeat

* See *Readings in World History*, "Europe's Impact On Japan," p. 144.

A Japanese woodcut depicting Admiral Matthew Perry, 1853.

BETTMANN ARCHIVE

Japan. In fact they scornfully called the Japanese *makaki*, or little monkeys, and they seriously argued whether one Russian soldier was worth one and a half, or two Japanese soldiers.

The Japanese settled that question by attacking suddenly on February 5, 1904, without a declaration of war, as they were later to do at Pearl Harbor. To everybody's surprise, the Japanese beat the Russian Goliath. By the Treaty of Portsmouth (New Hampshire) in 1905, they made various gains, including the southern half of Sakhalin Island and a free hand in Korea. Five years later the Japanese added Korea to their growing empire.

Under the auspices of Theodore Roosevelt, officials for both sides met to settle the Russo-Japanese War in 1905.

BROWN BROTHERS

More important than these territorial gains was the psychological effect of the Japanese victory over the Russians. For the first time an Asian people had beaten the Europeans. The white man was not invincible, and a thrill of hope swept over the colonial peoples of the globe. Typical was the reaction of Jawaharlal Nehru, who was then a fourteen-year-old boy. "Japanese victories," he wrote, "stirred up my enthusiasm, and I waited eagerly for the papers for fresh news daily. I invested in a large number of books on Japan and tried to read some of them. I felt rather lost in Japanese history, but I liked the knightly tales of old Japan. . . . Nationalistic ideas filled my mind. I mused of Indian freedom and Asiatic freedom from the thralldom of Europe. I dreamed of brave deeds, of how, sword in hand, I would fight for India and help in freeing her." [5]

The Japanese victory caused other Asians also to feel nationalistic and to dream of freedom. For this reason the Russo-Japanese War stands out as a landmark in modern world history. It represents the beginning of the awakening of the colonial peoples and the beginning of the decline of the European empires.

EUROPEAN EMPIRES IN AFRICA

Africa before 1914. The European Powers did not penetrate into the interior of Africa until the end of the 19th century. This delay is surprising since the African people were not as numerous and as advanced as those of India. One reason for the delay is the geography of Africa: the Sahara Desert, the steaming jungles, the tropical diseases, and the waterfalls on the lower courses of the rivers. All these will be considered in the unit on Africa. Another reason for the late penetration is that Africa did not offer easily available riches, such as the spices of the East or the gold and silver of the Americas. The Europeans decided that Africa was not worth bothering with, except for one useful commodity, slaves. But it was not necessary to go into the interior for slaves; they could be bought from native slave traders along the coast. For centuries the Europeans were satisfied to have only a string of slave stations along the west coast of the continent.

The only exceptions to this general picture were in the north and in the extreme south. We have seen that in the south the Dutch had planted a colony of settlers at the Cape. The settlers took root and gradually spread inland. But they were few in number and counted for little until the 20th century. In North Africa (north of the Sahara) were ancient Muslim states inhabited by Caucasoid rather than Negroid peoples. These states were theoretically a part of the Ottoman Empire, but by the 19th century this empire was disintegrating and could offer no protection. The French had little trouble in occupying Algeria in 1830 and Tunis in 1881. Three years later the British occupied Egypt, which had suddenly become important because of the completion of the Suez Canal in 1869.

Even with these annexations, most of Africa was still untouched. The map of Africa in 1884 shows that, even at that late date, the Europeans had only a thin outer fringe. By contrast, the map of Africa in 1914 shows the continent carved up and occupied from north to south and from east to west. Within three decades the imperialist powers of Europe had divided among themselves almost an entire continent.*

Leopold starts the scramble. Seeking an opportunity for profit, the Belgian king, Leopold II, sent agents into the Congo basin where they persuaded unsuspecting native chiefs to sign treaties handing over huge

* See *Readings in World History*, "An African View of European Expansion," p. 146.

The evils of the Arab slave trade were first brought to Europe's attention in the writings of such explorers as David Livingstone. This engraving from one of Livingstone's journals vividly portrays how the Arabs treated slaves who escaped or were rebellious.

tracts of land. Then Leopold built roads, established trading posts, and forced the natives to work for him. His methods were so unbelievably brutal that it is estimated that the population of the Congo declined by one-half (from 20 to 10 millions) between 1885 and 1908. If the Africans did not bring in the required amount of rubber and ivory, they were mutilated or shot. News of these atrocities leaked out, and Leopold was forced to hand his Congo possessions over to the Belgian government in 1908. Before that date they had been his private property; afterwards they became a Belgian colony, known as the Belgian Congo. The government immediately ended the atrocities and introduced reforms, though forced labor continued. Despite the moral condemnation of the world, Leopold died an immensely wealthy man. His riches encouraged other countries to stake out their claims in the interior of the continent.

Europe Dominates the World 165

EUROPE AND THE WORLD 1914

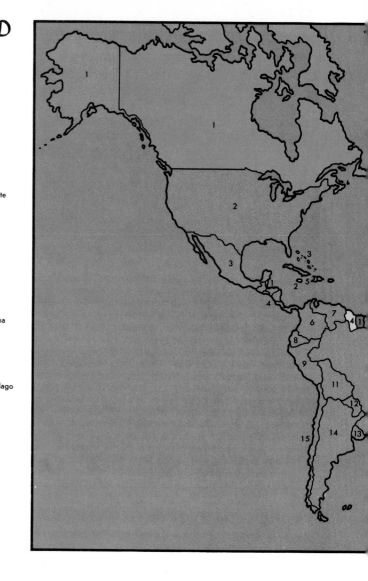

European Nations

1 Norway	5 Netherlands	9 France
2 Sweden	6 Belgium	10 Spain
3 Denmark	7 England	11 Portugal
4 Germany	8 Ireland	12 Italy

British Colonies

1 British Honduras	9 Egypt	17 Aden Protectorate
2 Jamaica	10 Anglo-Egyptian Sudan	18 India
3 Bahamas	11 British Somaliland	19 Ceylon
4 British Guiana	12 Kenya	20 Malay States
5 Gambia	13 Uganda	21 Sarawak
6 Sierra Leone	14 Nyasaland	22 New Guinea
7 Gold Coast	15 Rhodesia	23 Solomon Islands
8 Nigeria	16 Bechuanaland	24 New Hebrides

French Colonies

1 French Guiana	4 French Equatorial Africa	7 French Indo-China
2 Algeria	5 French Somaliland	8 New Caledonia
3 French West Africa	6 Madagascar	9 New Hebrides

German Colonies

1 Togo	4 German East Africa (Tanganyika)	6 Bismark Archipelago
2 Kamerun	5 New Guinea	
3 German Southwest Africa		

Belgian Colonies

1 Belgian Congo

Portuguese Colonies

1 Portuguese Guinea	2 Angola	3 Mozambique

Dutch Colonies

1 Dutch Guiana	3 Sumatra	5 New Guinea
2 Dutch East Indies	4 Borneo	

Spanish Colonies

1 Spanish Morocco	2 Rio de Oro	3 Spanish Guinea

Italian Colonies

1 Tripoli	2 Eritrea	3 Italian Somaliland

Danish Colonies

1 Greenland	2 Iceland

British Dominions

1 Canada	3 Australia
2 Union of South Africa	4 New Zealand

Russian Empire

European- derived States

1 Alaska	7 Venezuela	13 Uruguay
2 United States	8 Ecuador	14 Argentina
3 Mexico	9 Peru	15 Chile
4 Central America	10 Brazil	16 Philippines
5 West Indies	11 Bolivia	
6 Colombia	12 Paraguay	

Non-European States

1 Liberia	5 Persia	9 Japan
2 Abyssinia	6 Afghanistan	10 Siam
3 Ottoman Empire	7 China	
4 Arabia	8 Korea	

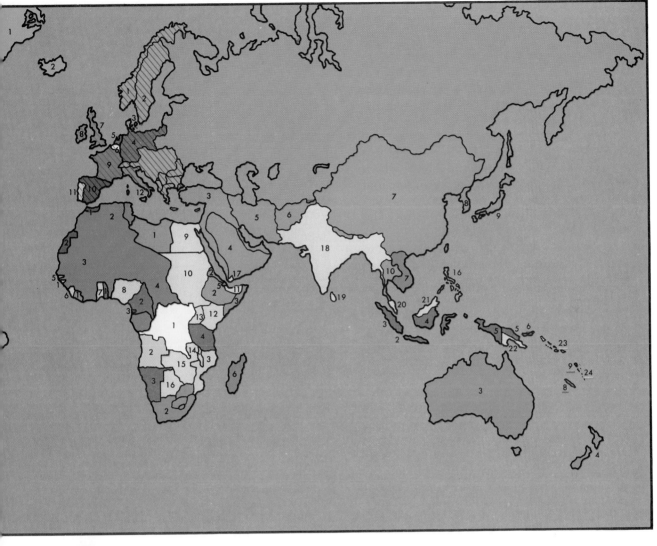

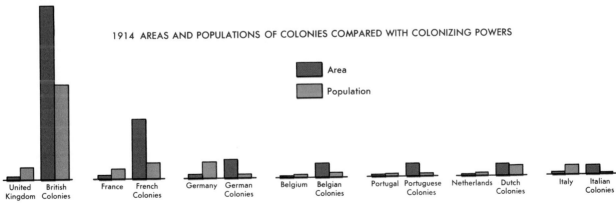

1914 AREAS AND POPULATIONS OF COLONIES COMPARED WITH COLONIZING POWERS

Area

Population

United Kingdom — British Colonies — France — French Colonies — Germany — German Colonies — Belgium — Belgian Colonies — Portugal — Portuguese Colonies — Netherlands — Dutch Colonies — Italy — Italian Colonies

British and French acquisitions. North of the Congo basin is the large and fertile Niger Valley. The British in the lower part of the valley defeated their French competitors and carved out the colony known as Nigeria. The lands north of Nigeria were taken over by the French, who moved down from Algeria. These territories became known as French West Africa and included a large part of the Sahara Desert. The French also moved into French Equatorial Africa, which included a part of the Congo basin north of the Congo River, and expanded westward from Algeria to take over the Muslim state of Morocco.

Meanwhile the British and French were also competing in the Sudan, the British going up the Nile from Egypt and the French moving overland from French Equatorial Africa. After a sharp crisis in 1898 which almost led to war, the French gave way, and the British became the masters of the Sudan, although it was called the Anglo-Egyptian Sudan.

German and Italian latecomers. The Germans and the Italians were late in joining the imperialist drive because Germany and Italy were not fully united as national states until 1870. They did not have old footholds in Africa similar to those of Britain and France. Once they got started, the Germans and Italians worked hard to make up for lost time. Most energetic was young Dr. Karl Peters, who landed secretly in East Africa in 1884. Within 10 days he had persuaded the chiefs to sign away more than 60,000 square miles, an area almost a third as large as his German homeland. When the natives realized what was happening and began to resist, Dr. Peters followed a policy which he called *Schrechtlichkeit*, or frightfulness. The result of this frightfulness was the killing of 200,000 Africans who rose in rebellion. In this way Germany gained control of the colony of

Emperor Menelik of Ethiopia

German East Africa, now the country of Tanzania. The British, who had been alarmed by Peters' activities, also got their share, British East Africa (Kenya and Uganda). The French were satisfied with the large island off the coast, Madagascar. In addition to their holdings in East Africa, the Germans managed to pick up three other pieces of African real estate: the Cameroons, Togoland, and South-West Africa. In the latter colony, the Germans were so brutal that in 1904 they killed 65,000 of the 80,000 native Herero people.

Meanwhile the Italians had also been on the hunt for territory, but with less success. They got two small barren colonies on the Red Sea coast, Eritrea and Somaliland. Later, in 1896, they sent an army into the large kingdom of Ethiopia. The Ethiopians were not a primitive tribal people; their emperor Menelik had an army of 80,000 men trained by French officers and armed with French weapons. He easily defeated the small Italian army of 10,000, and Ethiopia remained free. In fact, by 1914, Ethiopia, the Union of South Africa, and the small republic of Liberia on the west coast were the only independent states on the whole continent. The Italians were more successful in 1911 when they acquired Libya from the weak Ottoman Empire. Because Libya was mostly desert, the French and British had not bothered to take it for themselves.

South Africa. In South Africa the situation differed from that of the rest of the continent because of the large number of European settlers. There were two groups, the original Dutch, or Boers, and the English who arrived after Britain took over the Cape Colony from Holland in 1815. The Boers were dissatisfied with British rule, especially when they were forced to free their slaves in the 1830's. They migrated northward and established two independent republics, the Orange Free State and the South African Republic. Unfortunately for the Boers, gold and diamonds were found in their new lands, and thousands of English poured in. Friction between the Boers and the English newcomers brought on war with England in 1899. The Boers fought hard but were overwhelmed by 1902. The British gave generous terms, allowing the Boers self-government and recognizing their language as equal to English. In 1910 the Boer and British states were combined to form the Union of South Africa.

The new Union had a total European population of 1.2 million, but they were outnumbered by 4.1 million Africans. And this large majority was exploited as ruthlessly in

"Commandos" came into prominence during the Boer War. A commando was a swiftly-striking, hit-and-run unit employed to disrupt enemy communications and destroy supplies. An old "view-master" slide depicts Boer commandos in action.

BETTMANN ARCHIVE

South Africa as anywhere else on the continent. Allowed no political rights, they were forced to work in European-owned mines and farms for miserably low wages. Imperialism was present in South Africa, the difference being that it was the imperialism of the local white settlers rather than of the European governments. We shall see in the later unit on Africa that this difference has made South Africa the main trouble spot on the continent. In the face of rising African nationalism, European governments have granted independence to their African colonies. On the other hand, the white minority in the Republic of South Africa is not willing to give equal political rights to the Negroes because they would be hopelessly outvoted (South Africa became a republic in 1961). The danger areas in Africa today are those with white minorities in control, chiefly South Africa, Rhodesia, and Portuguese Angola and Mozambique.

EUROPEANIZATION OF THE AMERICAS, AUSTRALIA, AND ASIATIC RUSSIA

At the same time that Europe was conquering empires in Asia and Africa, the empty lands of the Americas, Australia, and Asiatic Russia were also being Europeanized. By Europeanization is meant the wholesale transfer of European peoples, economies, and cultures to these territories. Obviously Europeanization is something much more permanent than the mere conquering of a colony. Usually colonies are lost after their inhabitants become nationalistic, whereas an area which is Europeanized is very likely to remain culturally and politically tied to the mother country.

Racial Europeanization. One aspect of the Europeanization process is the mass emigration of European caucasoids, or racial Europeanization, which took place for a variety of reasons. One was the tremendous increase in Europe's population from 140 million in 1750 to 401 million in 1900. Another reason was persecution of various types. For example, anti-Semitic persecution in Russia forced 1.5 million Jews to emigrate to the United States between 1900 and 1914. The development of the steamship made it physically possible to transport large numbers of Europeans overseas. Tens of millions of people could not have crossed the seas in the days of the *Mayflower* and the *Santa Maria.*

These and other factors led to the greatest movement of peoples in all history. The human tide grew ever larger as the 19th century progressed. The high point came between 1900 and 1914 when almost one million emigrants left Europe *each year.*

The result of this mass emigration was the racial Europeanization of large parts of the earth.* Today we tend to take this for granted. We are accustomed to the fact that Caucasoids or peoples of European origin are distributed throughout the world. Siberia is inhabited by Russian-speaking people, Latin America by Spanish- and Portuguese-speaking peoples, North America by English- and French-speaking peoples, and Australia and New Zealand by English-speaking people. But all this has taken place since 1500, and especially since 1800 when most of the emigration occurred. Before those dates the Caucasoids were confined to Europe, North Africa, the Middle East, and India. By contrast the Mongoloids were then spread over Siberia, the Far East, and the whole New World. Today, however, the distribution is altogether different. Because of the tens of millions of Europeans who emigrated in the 19th century, the Mongoloids of the New World and the Australoids of Australia are now a small minority.

* See *Readings in World History,* "A New Life in the New World," p. 150.

The net result is a racial map of the world today that is very different from that of 1500. This difference is of tremendous significance for world history. If technology and nationalism had developed first in an area other than Europe, the great population movements would have been out of China, Africa, or India rather than out of Europe.

Economic Europeanization. Hand in hand with racial Europeanization went economic Europeanization. By this is meant the extension of European economic control and methods to all parts of the globe. Before 1763 the Europeans had gained control of the ocean trade routes, but had not penetrated into the interior of continents. After 1763 they were able to open up and exploit whole continents because of the weapons, equipment, and knowledge provided by the Economic and Scientific Revolutions.

The rifle, machine gun, and cannon enabled the Europeans to become world masters, from the deserts of Central Asia to the pampas of Argentina, and from the jungles of Africa to the rivers of China. Steel plows and farm machinery permitted the use of the vast prairies for farming, while railroads and steamships transported farm products from one end of the world to the other. By 1914 there were 30,000 steamships on the ocean trade routes, as well as several railway systems spanning the continents. The first transcontinental railway in the United States was completed in 1869; the first in Canada in 1885; and the Trans-Siberian in 1905. By 1914 another great transcontinental line, the Berlin-to-Baghdad railroad, was almost finished, and the Cape-to-Cairo railroad had several sections completed.

Europe was the center of this world-wide economic system. Europe provided the money by serving as the world's banker. Even in the United States, which was more advanced than most countries, Europe had

Although independent, some former British colonies still fly the "Union Jack" as a symbol of their status in the British Commonwealth. The wide geographical area encompassed by the Commonwealth testifies to the "Europeanization" of the globe.

invested no less than 7.2 billion dollars by 1914. Europe also served as the workshop of the world. By 1870, 65 per cent of the world's manufactured goods were produced there. These goods were shipped to all corners of the globe, and in return came raw materials and food such as rubber and tin from Malaya, tea and silk from China, jute and cotton from India, gold and diamonds from South Africa, and beef, wheat, wool, and mutton from Argentina, Canada, Australia, and the United States.

Cultural Europeanization. Cultural Europeanization followed racial and economic Europeanization. The cultures that developed in the new lands were generally similar to those of Europe. This was true even though all the new lands, except those belonging to Russia, won independence from their mother countries. The first to break away was the United States in 1776. Then the various Latin-American states followed one after the other during the course of the 19th century. Finally a number of British colonies won self-government although they remained within the British Empire. These colonies became Dominions and were given the right to run their own affairs. Canada became a Dominion in 1867, Australia in 1901, New Zealand in 1907, and South Africa in 1910.

Despite this cutting of political ties with Europe, the new lands developed cultures that were basically European, though with many local variations. In Latin America, for example, the people of European origin are a minority as against the Indians and Negroes. And yet Latin-American culture is essentially Spanish and Portuguese culture. The reason is that the great majority of the people speak the Spanish or Portuguese languages, belong to the Catholic Church, and share the same customs and attitudes. It makes little difference whether they are whites, Negroes, Indians, or a mixture of the three. They *feel* themselves to be Latin Americans, and it is this feeling that counts.

The culture which has developed in the United States is essentially European also, although it is closer to that of the British Isles than to that of the Iberian Peninsula. America continued to look to England for guidance in cultural matters long after winning political independence. Early American writers such as Washington Irving and Nathaniel Hawthorne lived in Europe for long periods and wrote in the style of English authors. Perhaps the first really American book, in theme and the use of the idiom, was Mark Twain's novel *Huckleberry Finn*, published in 1884. Since that date the United States has produced distinguished works and outstanding leaders in every field: William James in philosophy, John Dewey in education, William Prescott in history, Grant Wood in art, Louis Sullivan and Frank Lloyd Wright in architecture, and many others.

But it is true that Englishmen coming to the United States do not feel that they are in an altogether foreign country. They understand our "American" English, they read our literature, they enjoy some of our movies, and they find our religions the same as theirs. In fact, American culture in the past few decades has increasingly been imitated in Britain, from hot dogs to jazz, and from supermarkets to chromium-plated cars. So strong has been this reverse influence across the Atlantic that the English humor magazine *Punch* published a satirical article (April 13, 1960) entitled "Our American Heritage" which stated, "We like to imagine the Americans thinking sentimentally of the British ancestors from whom they derive their language, their culture, their tea-bags. Actually it is the British who should be looking gratefully to the Americans for their enduring influence on our way of life." Whether the British should look to the Americans or the Americans to the British, the important point is that the culture of the United States, like that of Latin America, has many close ties with Europe.

This is even more true when we turn to the British Dominions. These Dominions have kept their political connections with Britain, as well as many cultural ties. At the same time they also have been influenced in recent years by the United States. This is especially true of Canada and Australia, where many examples can be found of both British and American links. For example, the Englishman who visits Canada soon finds that he gets blank stares when he talks of petrol, silencer, boot, and demister, and so he switches to gas, muffler, trunk, and windshield wiper. On the other hand, there are other areas where the Englishman will feel quite at home. Most Canadians say blinds, taps, and braces rather than shades, faucets, and suspenders. Finally, there are cases where the Canadians have maintained their individuality against both the English and the Americans. If you go to a department store in England and ask for a chesterfield, you will get a man's coat; in the United States you will get a pack of cigarettes; but in Canada you will get an overstuffed sofa.

We may conclude that the Americas and Australia and South Africa are far from being carbon copies of Europe. Special local conditions, a variety of ethnic mixtures, and strong native cultures have combined to produce many overseas variations of European civilization. And yet the variations are insignificant compared to the similarities. This becomes clear if we compare the languages, clothes, foods, buildings, and customs of London, Madrid, and Paris with those of Peking, Delhi, and Cairo, and then with those of New York, Montreal, and Melbourne. The basic similarities between the European cities on the one hand and the American and Australian cities on the other arise from the process of cultural Europeanization that accompanied the racial and economic.

SIGNIFICANCE OF THE PERIOD FOR WORLD HISTORY

In conclusion, the period from 1763 to 1914 stands out as the age of European domination. In the field of politics this domination was evident in Europe's direct rule over Africa, India, and Southeast Asia, and indirect rule over China and the Ottoman Empire. In the field of economics, Europe was the center of a new global economy and provided the money and the know-how that kept this economy running smoothly. Europe also affected directly and intimately the everyday lives of millions of ordinary people throughout the globe. The inhabitants of a village in India, for example, might find their thousands of years of isolation suddenly ended by a railroad built with European money and under the direction of European engineers. Soon afterwards the villagers would see their ancient handicrafts destroyed by cheap, machine-made, European goods brought in on the railroad. And before long the villagers would also discover that they no longer were working to feed themselves and their neighbors but rather to grow industrial crops, such as jute, cotton, and indigo, for factories in far-off Europe. The effect of all these developments was to change very drastically the lives of almost all these villagers.

The hundreds of millions of villagers scattered throughout the globe were not affected during this period by European art or literature or political theory. Since they were almost all illiterate they had no chance to learn about such things. However, their small ruling classes did have both the time and the money to learn European languages, to travel in European countries, and to attend European universities. Almost all these people were tremendously impressed by what they saw and learned. Indeed they carried their admiration for things European to absurd lengths. "Our fathers," writes a political leader in India, "were violently pro-British. They could see no flaw in the civilization or the culture of the West. They were charmed by its novelty and its strangeness. . . . Everything English was good—even the drinking of brandy was a virtue. . . . A man who did not drink was hardly entitled to be called educated. . . . Everything not English was to be viewed with suspicion." [6]

In the 20th century this worship of the West gradually gave way as local nationalism developed. But during the 19th century, "Europe" and "civilization" were considered to be one and the same thing. Never before in the history of man had one small portion of the globe so completely dominated the remainder.* This domination lasted until the outbreak of World War I in 1914. After that date, Europe's influence declined in one respect, though in another it continued to grow. This is the main characteristic of world history in the period since 1914, to which we now turn.

* See *Readings in World History,* "The New Imperialism," p. 153.

Reviewing the Essentials

Europe's Growing Strength
1. What areas of the world did Europe control by 1914? Locate them on a map.
2. How and why did Europe gain control of these territories and ocean routes during the period 1763–1914?

Economic Revolution
3. In 1500 the Europeans were unable to compete in quality and price of goods with the Indian and Chinese merchants. What problem did this pose for the Europeans? How were the Europeans able to solve the problem? With what results?

4. Discuss this statement, citing examples from the period: "Necessity is the mother of invention."
5. What were the immediate and long-range results of the inventions described on p. 148 of your text?
6. How did industrialization lead to colonialism in the 19th century?

Scientific Revolution

7. Explain: "Technology emphasizes know-how; science emphasizes know-why." Describe the relationship of technology and science.
8. Support this statement, giving examples of scientists and their discoveries from the 16th through the 19th centuries: "Science tended to advance in spurts in individual fields."
9. Why did science flourish in the West? Why are the people of the rest of the world more interested in science and technology than in other Western achievements?
10. In what ways did the Scientific Revolution make possible European domination of the globe, 1763–1914?
11. What was the effect of Charles Darwin's *On the Origin of Species?*

Political Revolution

12. What changes in the relations of people and government resulted from the Political Revolution?
13. Why did the Political Revolution start in the West?
14. Formulate a definition of liberalism. Are the Declaration of Independence and the Declaration of the Rights of Man and of the Citizen "liberal" in terms of your definition?
15. Formulate a definition of nationalism. How does nationalism differ from nationality? Trace the historical development of nationalism in Western Europe, giving examples of nationalistic uprising from the 18th through the 20th centuries.
16. What appeal did Karl Marx and Friedrich Engels make to the working class? What did they mean by socalism and communism? (Note that these terms were used interchangeably.) What fact indicates the strength of the socialist parties?

Significance of the Three Revolutions

17. How did the Economic, Scientific, and Political Revolutions change man's way of life? Contrast with his way of life during the medieval period.
18. How did the three revolutions help Europe to dominate the globe during the 19th century?

European Empires in Asia

19. Into what part of Southeast Asia did (a) England; (b) France; (c) the Netherlands; and (d) Portugal extend their control?
20. Why was Thailand able to maintain its independence? Why was China able to avoid becoming a European colony?
21. Why was Russia able to extend her control over Central Asia in the 19th century, even though she had made no advance after her acquisition of Siberia in the 17th century? Locate on a map those additions made by Russia.
22. Japan's fate might have been the same as that of India and China. Why wasn't it? In what ways did the West influence and change Japanese life?
23. What territory did the Japanese gain as a result of their victory over China in 1894? Over Russia in 1905?
24. Explain: More important than these territorial gains was the psychological effect of the Japanese victory over the Russians.

European Empires in Africa

25. European nations bypassed the interior of Africa until the end of the 19th century. Give reasons.
26. Under what conditions and circumstances did Belgium, Germany, and Italy acquire colonies in Africa? Compare with Britain and France.
27. Name and locate the two oldest independent states of Africa.
28. Review the events that brought about the establishment of the Union of South Africa. Why was there increasing friction between the Boers and the British prior to 1910?

Europeanization of the Americas, Australia, and Asiatic Russia

29. What is racial Europeanization? What conditions caused it to take place? When did the mass emigration of people reach its height? What countries were the most important source of emigrants, 1846–1932? Why these particular nations? What nations were the major recipients of European emigration after 1800?

30. In what ways is the racial map of the world today very different from that of 1500? What is the importance of the mass movements of people after 1500 to world history? Why did they come from Europe instead of Asia and Africa?

31. What is economic Europeanization? What accelerated this phenomenon after 1763?

32. "Cultural Europeanization followed racial and economic Europeanization." Discuss this statement, giving examples for the U.S., Latin America, and the British Commonwealth.

Europeanization of the Americas, Australia, and Asiatic Russia

33. Support this statement: "The period from 1763 to 1914 stands out as the age of European domination." Give specific examples.

34. Conquered peoples emulated the West during the 19th century because they equated "Europe" and "civilization." Why did this happen? Why did the same people respond differently in the 20th century?

Explain, Identify, or Locate

socialism	rationalism	Reformation	humanism
communism	Galileo	Copernicus	Manchuria
Dominion status	Newton	Marx	Korea
psychoanalysis	Mendel	Leopold II	Singapore
evolution	Pasteur	Boers	Saigon
imperialism	Freud	Sahara Desert	Thailand
sphere of influence	Darwin	Union of South Africa	Congo River
Renaissance	Cromwell	Ethiopia	Nigeria

EUROPE'S DECLINE AND TRIUMPH: 1914—

WORLD WAR I: BEGINNING OF DECLINE

Origins of World War I. World War I undermined Europe's domination of the globe. The war began in 1914, although the background and more important causes can be traced to events which occurred even as far back as the latter half of the previous century.

One of these background causes was the economic rivalry among the Great Powers, especially Britain and Germany. We have noted that Britain was the pioneer and leader in industrialization in the late 18th and early 19th centuries. After 1870, however, other countries began to catch up to and surpass Britain. This produced a trade war, par-

ticularly between Britain and Germany. American manufactured goods were sold largely in the great domestic market within the United States, but Germany competed with Britain in most of the markets of the world, and this rivalry poisoned the relations between the two countries and helped to bring on the war.

Per Cent of Total World Economic Production		
	1870	1913
Britain	31.8	14.0
U.S.A.	23.3	35.8
Germany	13.2	14.3

Another cause for World War I was the race for colonies. We have seen that, for various reasons, the European powers in the late 19th century competed with each other all over the globe in a scramble for empire. This led to many disputes and crises:

Britain vs. France over the Nile Valley and Siam
Germany vs. France over Morocco and the Congo
Britain vs. Germany over East and West Africa
Russia vs. Britain over Persia and Afghanistan

A third background cause was the division of the European powers into hostile alliance systems, the Triple Alliance and the Triple Entente. The first to be formed was the Triple Alliance, which originated in the Dual Alliance of 1879 between Germany and Austria. In 1882 this agreement was transformed into the Triple Alliance when Italy also signed. These three powers did not band together in order to start a war; their alliance agreement was a defensive pact to prevent war. They agreed to fight beside each other only in the event that one of them was attacked by an outside power. The other great European powers doubted the sincerity of the Triple Alliance. They feared the great strength of this bloc and reacted by forming a counterbloc. First France and Russia signed an alliance in 1894; then Britain and France signed an entente (agreement) in 1904 which settled their colonial disputes but did not require them to aid each other in case of war; Britain and Russia made a similar entente in 1907.

In this way the chief European powers were organized into two rival alliance systems by 1907. However, these alliances proved to be a menace to peace rather than a preserver of peace. If power A and power B had a dispute, then at once the allies of the two powers also were involved. This meant that every little quarrel became a great crisis and involved all the powers of Europe.

In fact, when World War I broke out, a German official said, "It all came from this d——d system of alliances, which were the curse of modern times." [7]

The fourth and final background cause for World War I was nationalism. We saw earlier that nationalism began in Western Europe and then spread to Eastern Europe and to other parts of the world. When it reached Eastern Europe, it caused serious political trouble because it challenged the old multinational empires of Austria-Hungary, Germany, and Russia. In Germany, for example, there were not only Germans but also Poles, French, and Danes. On the western frontiers of Russia there were not only Russians but also Finns, Latvians, Estonians, Lithuanians, Poles, and Romanians. The most diverse patchwork of nationalities could be found in Austria-Hungary. In addition to the ruling Austrians and Hungarians, there were Czechs, Slovaks, Poles, Ruthenians, Romanians, Italians, and South Slavs (or Serbs, Croats, and Slovenes). It is obvious that as soon as the spirit of nationalism infected these peoples, there was bound to be an explosion in Central and Eastern Europe.

The explosion came in 1914 when the Serbian nationalist, Gavrilo Princip, made a desperate attempt to end Austro-Hungarian rule by assassinating the Archduke Franz Ferdinand in the Bosnian town of Sarajevo.* The Austrians were determined to smash Serbian nationalism, and, when the Serbs refused to accept an ultimatum designed to destroy Serbian autonomy, attacked Serbia in late July. At once the alliance system began to operate. The Russians supported their fellow-Slav Serbs, while the Germans supported their Austrian ally. Then the French and British came to the aid of their Russian ally. The Italians, however, refused to do the same for their German and Austrian

* See *Readings in World History*, "Serbian Nationalism Triggers World War I," p. 155.

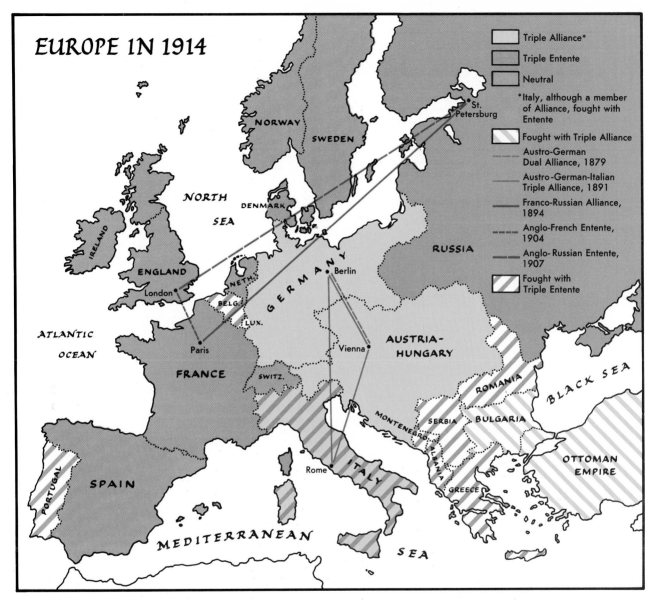

EUROPE IN 1914

Triple Alliance*

Triple Entente

Neutral

*Italy, although a member of Alliance, fought with Entente

Fought with Triple Alliance

Austro-German Dual Alliance, 1879

Austro-German-Italian Triple Alliance, 1891

Franco-Russian Alliance, 1894

Anglo-French Entente, 1904

Anglo-Russian Entente, 1907

Fought with Triple Entente

NORWAY

SWEDEN

NORTH SEA

DENMARK

IRELAND

ENGLAND

London

NETH.

BELG.

LUX.

ATLANTIC OCEAN

Paris

FRANCE

SWITZ.

St. Petersburg

RUSSIA

G E R M A N Y

Berlin

Vienna

AUSTRIA-HUNGARY

ROMANIA

BLACK SEA

MONTENEGRO

SERBIA

BULGARIA

Rome

ALBANIA

OTTOMAN EMPIRE

SPAIN

PORTUGAL

ITALY

GREECE

MEDITERRANEAN

SEA

allies, preferring to remain on the sidelines until it became clear which side would win. Finally Italy joined the Entente in 1915. Other nations soon entered the conflict until much of the rest of the world was involved.

Course of World War I. In the first two years of the war, the Central Powers had the advantage. Because they were better pre-pared, they conquered large areas of Allied territory. In 1914 the Germans overran most of Belgium and a part of northern France, and almost captured Paris. The French, with British help, were able to stabilize the battle lines, and the western front became the scene of continuous trench warfare from Switzer-land to the North Sea. In the following years the Central Powers concentrated on their

Europe's Decline and Triumph 179

Travellers intending to embark on the Atlantic voyage are reminded that a state of war exists between Germany and her allies and Great Britain and her allies; that the zone of war includes the waters adjacent to the British Isles; that, in accordance with formal notice given by the Imperial German Government, vessels flying the flag of Great Britain, or of any of her allies, are liable to destruction in those waters and that travellers sailing in the war zone on ships of Great Britain or her allies do so at their own risk.

Imperial German Embassy
Washington, D.C., April 22, 1915

The warning on the left was printed in American newspapers at the request of the German Embassy. The headlines of May 8, 1915, on the right, tell the story of the torpedoing and sinking of the Lusitania. *This incident played a large role in the decision of the U.S. to enter the war.*

northern and eastern fronts. They won a part of northern Italy, occupied all of Serbia and Romania, and a part of Greece, and drove the Russians back hundreds of miles. By 1917 Germany and her allies dominated a large part of the continent of Europe, yet they could not win a decisive victory. The war dragged on in bloody stalemate.

The main campaigns were fought in northern France, where hundreds of thousands of men were repeatedly sacrificed for the sake of a few square miles. The combination of machine-gun nests, barbed-wire entanglements, and elaborate trenches made it impossible to carry on the open maneuvering and fighting of past wars. The defense proved stronger than the offense; year after year the bloodletting continued. In 1916, for example, the Germans made a desperate attempt to capture the stronghold of Verdun in northeastern France. For 10 months they battered the French defenders and finally had to admit failure. The Germans lost almost as many men as the French, 330,000 to 350,000.*

* See *Readings in World History,* "Trench Warfare: Exercise in Futility," p. 156.

In an effort to break this terrible deadlock, the Germans in February 1917 began unrestricted submarine warfare, using their U-boat fleet to sink ships carrying food to Britain. In this way they hoped to starve the British and force them to drop out of the war. The Germans expected that they could then easily defeat a France deprived of British support. But in carrying out a campaign of unlimited submarine warfare, the German U-boats sank American ships and American lives were lost. When the protests of the United States government were ignored, this country, convinced that Germany was a threat to its security, entered the war on the Allied side in April 1917.

In the same year Russia was driven out of the war. In the unit on Russia, we shall see that this occurred for two reasons: the catastrophic defeats suffered by Russian armies and the outbreak of revolution behind the Russian front. The loss of Russia was more than made up by the entry of the fresh and powerful United States. In the month of March 1918, 85,000 American troops arrived in France. By July the number had jumped to 306,000. And behind this flood of manpower was an even greater flood of food, arms, and munitions. The Central Powers were overwhelmed and, one by one, they were forced to surrender, first Bulgaria, then Turkey and Austria-Hungary, and finally Germany on November 11, 1918. Never before in the history of man had such a war been fought. About 10 million men had been killed, 20 million wounded, and the direct cost was 180.5 billion dollars.

Peace settlement. World War I was ended with the signing of peace treaties with each of the defeated Central Powers: Versailles Treaty with Germany (January 18, 1919); St. Germain Treaty with Austria (September 10, 1919); Trianon Treaty with Hungary (March 22, 1919); Neuilly Treaty with Bulgaria (November 27, 1919); and Sèvres Treaty with Turkey (August 20, 1920), which was replaced by the Lausanne Treaty of July 24, 1923. From the viewpoint of world history, this peace settlement is notable for three reasons: (1) the establishment of the League of Nations; (2) the triumph of nationalism in Europe; and (3) the ignoring of nationalism in the non-European world.

The League of Nations was the first worldwide organization of nations pledged to the preservation of international peace. Its mem-

Entrenched for safety, opposing armies faced each other across a mined and barbed-wire "no-man's-land." Advances and retreats were measured in feet in some parts of the battle area, and casualty figures were enormous; only by rushing directly into enemy fire could any gains be made. Terms such as "trench mouth" and "over the top" became common expressions during the war.

bers bound themselves to help each other against aggression, to submit disputes to arbitration, and to refrain from war until three months after the decision of the arbitration body.* In addition to this primary concern with peace, the League of Nations also devoted itself to such problems as reducing armaments, improving labor conditions, combatting disease, and checking abuses such as slavery. The League had some success in coping with these problems, but, as we shall see later, it was not able to prevent the outbreak of World War II in 1939.

The triumph of nationalism in Europe can be seen clearly by comparing the map of the continent before and after World War I. The old multinational empires of Germany and Austria-Hungary disappeared following the war, while Russia lost all her subject-nationalities along her western frontier. In place of the old empires appeared a number of new countries: Poland, Czechoslovakia, a greatly enlarged Romania, and Yugoslavia which consisted of prewar Serbia and Montenegro and the former south Slavic provinces of Austria-Hungary. All these countries were established by the Allies on the basis of the principle of self-determination which was set forth originally in President Wilson's Fourteen Points.† This principle holds that each nationality should have the right to set up a government of its own choosing rather than be forced to accept foreign rule.

This principle was not followed in every single case. In Europe after World War I there were a considerable number of Germans in Italy, Czechoslovakia, and Poland, and a considerable number of Hungarians in Czechoslovakia, Romania, and Yugoslavia. The fact that the various nationalities in Central and Eastern Europe are so inter-

mingled makes it impossible to draw frontiers without leaving some minorities on one side or another. Nevertheless there were fewer minorities in Europe after the war than before. The principle of self-determination was followed more closely in Europe after 1918 than at any time in the past.

By contrast, self-determination was completely ignored in the world outside of Europe. For example, the Allies kept all their colonies scattered around the globe. No one extended the principle of self-determination to these colonies by asking the Indians or the Burmese whether they wanted to remain under British rule or by asking the Indochinese whether they wished to continue under French rule. Furthermore the Allies divided Germany's overseas colonies and Turkey's Arab provinces south of Asia Minor. Again no one asked the people of German East Africa or South-West Africa or the Cameroons or Togoland whether they wanted to exchange German rule for British rule or no foreign rule at all. As for the Arab provinces, they were divided and parcelled out as League of Nations mandates to Britain and France. Britain took Iraq, Palestine, and Transjordan, while France received Syria and Lebanon.

It is true that all these colonies and provinces were given to the victorious Allies as League mandates rather than as outright possessions. This meant that the mandatory power (the country that received the mandate) promised to look after the welfare of the mandate's population and to report annually to the League of Nations. But the League did not have the authority or means to take action against a mandatory power which failed to live up to its obligations. As a result, the mandatory powers did pretty much what they wished with their mandates. Self-determination was largely a forgotten principle outside the borders of the continent of Europe.

* See *Readings in World History,* "The League of Nations," p. 167.
† See *Readings in World History,* "Wilson's Fourteen Points," p. 159.

EUROPE AFTER WORLD WAR 1

Boundaries of Germany,
Austria-Hungary, Russia and
Ottoman Empire in 1914

New nations created by
Treaty of Versailles

Territory ceded by the Ottoman Empire

Territory ceded by Bulgaria
(to Greece)

Rhineland

Europe's economic supremacy ends. World War I is a great turning point in world history because it began the weakening of Europe's domination of the globe. One of the principal reasons for this is that it ended Europe's economic supremacy. Before the war, Europe was the banker and the workshop of the world. We have noted that in 1870 Europe was turning out 65 per cent of the world's manufactured goods and that by 1914 Europe had vast sums invested abroad. But the war was so expensive and destructive that the European states had to sell many of their overseas holdings. Thus Britain lost a quarter of her foreign investments, France a third, and defeated Germany the entire amount. Within a few years after the war, the great creditor nation of the world was not Britain but the United States. In 1914 the United States owed European investors 7.2 billion dollars, but by 1919 various European countries owed the United States 3.7 billion dollars, and this figure was to increase steadily over the next several decades.

Point One of Wilson's Fourteen Points called for "open covenants openly arrived at." The Treaty of Versailles which ended the First World War, however, was drawn up in secret meetings by the "Big Four:" Lloyd George of Britain, Orlando of Italy, Clemenceau of France, and Wilson of the U.S.

A similar reversal took place in industry because many European factories were destroyed during the war. At the same time scores of new factories were being built in the United States and other non-European countries in order to meet the needs of the war. Thus European industries were now challenged and even surpassed by industries in Pittsburgh, in Osaka, and in Bombay. By 1929 the United States alone was producing 42.2 per cent of the world's total industrial output, which was more than that of all the European countries combined.

The rise of Communist power. World War I also led to the establishment of a Bolshevik Russian government which immediately tried to spread communism throughout Europe and the world. Before the war Russia was almost a semicolony of Western Europe. Many of the Russian banks and industries were owned by Western European companies, and the tsarist Russian government

was heavily in debt to France and other European countries. When the Bolsheviks under Lenin came to power, they repudiated the tsarist debts and seized all the banks and major industries. In addition they at once began a campaign to spread communism abroad.* With this aim in mind they organized in 1919 the Communist International or Comintern. The first meeting of the Comintern proclaimed, "Proletarians of all lands! In the war agains imperialistic barbarity, against monarchy, against the privileged classes, against the bourgeois state and bourgeois property, against all forms and varieties of . . . oppression—UNITE!" In its second meeting in the following year the Comintern was equally violent: "The Communist International has proclaimed the cause of Soviet Russia as its own. The world proletariat will not sheathe its sword until Soviet Russia is incorporated as a link in the World Federa-

* See *Readings in World History,* "Bolshevik Revolution and World Communism," p. 161.

tion of Soviet Republics. . . . Working men and women! On this earth there is only one banner which is worth fighting and dying for. It is the banner of the Communist International!" [8]

Bolshevik propaganda had much influence, particularly because of the war-weariness and misery of many people in Europe. President Wilson's adviser, Colonel House, wrote in his diary on March 22, 1919: "Rumblings of discontent every day. The people want peace. Bolshevism is gaining ground everywhere. . . . We are sitting upon an open powder magazine and some day a spark may ignite it." The explosion which Colonel House feared did not occur. Bolshevik revolts broke out in several places, such as Hungary and Bavaria, but they were crushed. On the other hand the Soviet government in what was now the Union of Soviet Socialist Republics managed to survive after a hard struggle against anti-Bolshevik Russian groups and against Allied forces that invaded the country. By 1920 the fighting was over, and during the following years the Soviet government gradually was recognized as the official government.

The new Union of Soviet Socialist Republics was very different from the old tsarist Russia. Instead of being a semicolony of Western Europe, it was an ever-present challenge to the rest of Europe. And we shall see that the challenge became increasingly serious as the Soviet Union gained economic and military strength with its Five-Year Plans.

The war brings colonial unrest. Finally World War I weakened Europe's world position by arousing the subject colonial peoples. Before 1914 the white man had great prestige in Asia and Africa. He was regarded almost as the divinely-appointed ruler of the globe. This prestige was badly shaken during the war years as the colonial peoples saw their

Karl Marx

European masters butchering each other. A large number of Asians and Africans were drafted into the various armies, especially those of the Allies. Their experiences in Europe opened their eyes, and gave them new ideas. Inevitably they heard the Allied slogan of self-determination, and they asked why it should be applied only to the continent of Europe. This attitude caused a French colonial administrator to remark that, "The 175,000 [African] soldiers, enrolled during the years 1914–1918, dug the grave of the old [colonial] Africa in the trenches of France and Flanders." [9] Some of the colonial peoples even heard the Bolshevik appeals for a world Communist revolution, and began looking to Moscow for leadership rather than to Paris or London.

Europe's Decline and Triumph   185

These experiences and attitudes produced a wave of unrest and even of revolt against European domination. The movement was strongest in the Arab world, where there were uprisings against French rule in Syria and Lebanon, and against British rule in Egypt and Iraq. In the end the French and the British were able to retain the Arab mandates. They did so partly by using their superior force and partly by allowing the Arab nationalists a certain amount of self-government. Likewise in India, the British were seriously embarrassed by Mahatma Gandhi's passive resistance campaign. For the first time India's peasant millions joined the movement against foreign rule, and Britain was forced to grant a considerable degree of self-government. Finally, in China the postwar years saw the triumph of local nationalism. Under the leadership of Chiang Kai-shek the nationalist Kuomintang party partially united the country and began a campaign against the old unequal treaties and foreign intervention. The new attitude of the Chinese people toward European is described in the following report of the American ambassador in the mid-1920's:

> Chinese who were heretofore most friendly and congenial with foreigners are now stirred to intolerance and pour out of their memories long stored-up recollections of abuses . . . on the part of foreigners toward their people—instances of jostling off the sidewalks, of the kicking of rickshaw coolies, and the like. Even though it expresses itself in political terms, the present crisis of feeling, it seems to me, is . . . a revulsion against what the individual Chinese feels to be the offense to his personal dignity and self-esteem, implicit in the overbearing attitude of the white man towards the Chinese.[10]

Despite all this agitation and turmoil, the European powers managed to keep their colonial possessions. A map of the world in the 1920's does not look very different from a map of the world before 1914. The only significant change is in Europe where new states appeared as a result of the Versailles Treaty. Everywhere else the old colonial empires still were in existence. The German colonies were gone, but they were taken over by France and Britain. In other words, Europe still *seemed* to be the master of the globe, and to a certain extent she was. Underneath the surface, however, there were great stirrings, and Europe was barely hanging on.* This was very different from the old days when European rule was practically unchallenged. Now Europe was on the defensive and was to remain on the defensive until everything was swept away during World War II.

A TWENTY–YEAR TRUCE

The recovery of Europe. At the end of World War I the future of Europe seemed dark. Much of the continent was infected by the virus of communism. Wide areas were devastated, there was much unemployment following the demobilization of the armies, and the controversial problem of reparations continued the wartime bitterness. The Versailles Treaty held Germany responsible for the war and required her to make payments to the Allies for the damages they had suffered. In 1921 the Allies demanded a total of 33 billion dollars. The Germans protested that they were in no condition to pay such an amount and systematically attempted to avoid payment. The French countered by occupying the Ruhr Valley, Germany's great industrial center. The Germans resorted to strikes, passive resistance, and covert violence; the result was a complete stalemate.

Europe also faced the problem of security. Theoretically, the League of Nations pro-

* See *Readings in World History,* "Unrest in European Colonies," p. 163.

tected its members against aggression. But the League had no armed forces; European powers made their own arrangements for self-protection. France, for example, built up a system of alliances designed to keep in check both Germany and the Soviet Union. She allied herself with the new states that had the same aim: Poland, Czechoslovakia, Yugoslavia, and Romania. Because both felt isolated by these alliances, Germany and the Soviet Union came to an understanding and signed the Rapallo Treaty of 1922. Italy, disappointed when all her territorial claims were not satisfied and feeling isolated by the French alliance system, tried to build up a counterbloc of countries such as Austria, Hungary, Bulgaria, and Albania, who wished to revise the peace settlements in their favor. As a result of these diplomatic maneuverings, Europe was divided into a number of rival and mutually suspicious diplomatic blocs.

During the late 1920's Europe appeared to make a good recovery and to settle these various problems. Scattered Communist revolts in Central Europe were put down. The Soviet Union was too weak during those years to spread communism by force. The war devastation was gradually repaired with the help of American loans. The wheels of industry once more began to turn, and unemployment was reduced. The reparations problem was settled when Germany and the Allies agreed upon the Dawes Plan in 1924 and the Young Plan in 1930. The first plan set up a schedule of annual payments, while the second plan reduced Germany's total reparations bill from the original 33 billion dollars to 8 billion.

The world's need for security seemed to be answered by the Locarno Pact of 1925 and the Kellogg-Briand Pact of 1928. According to the terms of the Locarno Pact, Germany agreed to accept her western frontiers with France and Belgium (where she had lost terri-

tory by the Versailles Treaty), and, in return, was allowed to enter the League of Nations. In other words, the pact brought together the former enemies of World War I.* Along the same line, the Kellogg-Briand Pact obliged its signatories to "renounce war as an instrument of national policy." No effective means were provided for enforcing this pact, but it was signed by over 60 nations, with the hope that the moral pressure of world public opinion would hold back any would-be aggressor.†

All these achievements and agreements were very encouraging. By the late 1920's Europe seemed to be well on the road to recovery. The continent was peaceful and prosperous, and the future looked promising. But then came the Great Depression, and within a few years fear and insecurity had replaced the optimism of the '20's.

Great Depression. Depressions are by no means uncommon; many have occurred in modern times. But the Great Depression which began in the fall of 1929 was unprecedented in both duration and severity. Between 1929 and 1932, world industrial production fell 36 per cent, and world international trade fell 60 per cent. By contrast, the greatest decline in both industrial production and international trade in any previous depression had been only a little more than 7 per cent.

This economic breakdown meant heavy unemployment. By 1933 the United States had 13 million unemployed, or a quarter of all its workers (as late as 1938, one-fifth of the American workers were still unemployed). Unemployment was equally severe in other countries, especially in those that were highly industrialized, such as Britain and Germany.

* See *Readings in World History*, "The Locarno Pact," p. 168.
† See *Readings in World History*, "The Kellogg-Briand Pact," p. 169.

Thousands of unemployed were forced to join "bread lines" and wait in "soup kitchens" in order to survive the worst periods of the Depression. By 1933 more than one-fourth of U.S. workers were unemployed, and conditions were more severe in other countries. Attempts to find solutions to the severe economic depression brought Franklin Roosevelt and the "New Deal" into power in the United States and also consolidated the power of Hitler in Germany and Mussolini in Italy who were then able to inaugurate their philosophy of Fascism.

High unemployment in turn meant much suffering and misery. In the United States, for example, 5000 banks closed their doors between 1929 and 1932. These were years of bread lines, soup kitchens, of apple-selling on street corners, and of veterans marching on Washington to pressure Congress into providing relief. In countries less wealthy than the United States, the suffering was more severe. A whole generation of men grew up in Great Britain without ever having a chance to work at a job. They kept body and soul together with the small payments they received from the "dole," as the relief system was called in Britain. Much worse off were the people of Eastern Europe and of most of the rest of the world. Living standards in these regions were always low, and the governments made no attempt to provide relief. So the unemployed of most countries could either starve on city streets or could go to live with relatives in the country, where they could eke out an existence on a small plot.

Mass suffering of this sort inevitably produced political unrest and political change. In the United States the depression swept the Republican Herbert Hoover out of office, and Franklin Delano Roosevelt came in with his New Deal program of social and economic legislation to cope with the crisis. In Great Britain the Labor Government was forced to give way to a National Government which included representatives of all parties and which tried desperately to restore economic health. Across the channel in France, cabinets rose and fell even more frequently than in normal times.

The most startling and ominous of all was the political revolution in Germany that brought Adolf Hitler to power. The depression certainly was not the only factor that explains Hitler's triumph. Many circumstances combined to produce this political upheaval, including Hitler's own talents, the divisions among his opponents, and the tradition of authoritarian rule in Germany. Yet it is safe to say that without the depression Hitler never would have gotten near the top. This is made clear by the results of the various elections in which Hitler's National Socialist (Nazi) Party participated. The following figures give the percentage of the total number of votes that his party received in the various elections:

> 1924 May—6.6%
> 1924 Dec.—3%
> 1928—2.6%
> 1930—18.3%
> 1932—37.3%

These figures show that before the depression the Nazis had little following, and that support was steadily decreasing. But with the depression they at once attracted many voters and became a major party. It was only when one out of every five workers was unemployed that the Germans began turning in desperation to the Nazi Party. Obviously Hitler had no chance of becoming the master of Germany so long as his party won 6 per cent or less of the total vote. But it was a very different situation when it had over a third of the popular vote.

These political changes brought about by the Great Depression are most important for world history. They affected deeply the relations between countries and contributed greatly to the coming of World War II.*

Drift to war. In February 1932 the British statesman, Sir Austen Chamberlain, delivered a speech in which he said:

> I look at the world today and I contrast the conditions now with the conditions at that time, and I am forced to acknowledge that for some reason or other, owing to something upon which it is difficult to put one's finger, in these last two years the world is moving backward. Instead of approaching nearer to one another, instead of increasing the measure of goodwill, instead of progressing to a stable peace, it has fallen back into an attitude of suspicion, of fear, of danger, which imperils the peace of the world.[11]

In retrospect we can see that this "something" that Sir Austen could not put his finger on was the Great Depression. It was the economic collapse that poisoned the relations between countries in various ways. For example, all governments tried to help their economies by importing as little as possible from the outside. They raised high import tariffs and also set quotas which prohibited altogether the importation of certain foreign goods above a certain amount. These restrictions, and many others like them, led to fierce economic warfare among the nations

* See *Readings in World History*, "The Great Depression," p. 170.

of the world. In time the economic warfare damaged the political relations between countries that formerly were friendly.

Another effect of the Great Depression was to bring to power certain governments with aggressive military policies. These governments tried to solve unemployment by building up huge armies and armament industries, which could be used for foreign conquest. In Germany, for example, Hitler demanded *lebensraum,* or living space, for his people.* It soon became clear that by *lebensraum* Hitler meant a large part of Europe, especially Eastern Europe. His book, *Mein Kampf* (My Battle), is filled with statements about Germany's need to expand eastward. "We turn our eyes towards the land in the East. . . . If we speak of land in Europe today, we can only think in the first instance of Russia and the border states under her influence. Fate itself seems to point the way forward for us. . . . The giant State in the East is ripe for collapse."

Open aggression. Likewise in Japan there were certain military leaders, industrialists, and ultranationalistic groups who favored territorial expansion. They argued that Japan, with her limited natural resources, had to conquer foreign lands or else she would be hopelessly surpassed by large and wealthy countries such as the United States and the British Empire.† With the coming of the depression Japan suffered severely because her economy was largely dependent on foreign markets and these markets now shrank alarmingly. The militarists took advantage of the unemployment and distress, insisting that there would be no such problems if Japan had her own empire. This reasoning was scarcely justified in view of

* See *Readings in World History,* "Hitler's Plans for Conquest," p. 173.
† See *Readings in World History,* "The Tanaka Memorial," p. 172.

the fact that unemployment was even more severe in England and in the United States than in Japan. Nevertheless the militarists won more and more key positions in government until they were strong enough to do as they wished. Then they set out to conquer an empire in Asia just as Hitler later was to do in Europe.

The same thing happened in Italy where Premier Benito Mussolini, who had seized power in 1922, urged his people to be warlike and expansionist. Only by creating another Roman Empire, said Mussolini, could Italy solve her economic problems and fulfill her destiny.* As a step in this direction Mussolini invaded the African kingdom of Ethiopia, or Abyssinia, in 1935. An Italian engineer at the time justified the invasion as follows: "In Abyssinia there is gold and platinum and it costs next to nothing to recover. But it is all locked up in the earth. Nobody does anything except loaf in the sunshine. When you look at it properly it is immoral to think that a people, from sheer laziness, can put an embargo on an incalculable treasure, while others have to fight against all the forces of nature in sterile ground." [12]

We see, then, that the Great Depression was to a considerable degree responsible for acts of aggression in Europe, Asia, and Africa. The depression also made it difficult to stop these attacks because each country was fully occupied with its own domestic problems. Each country tended to look the other way when Japan invaded Manchuria, when Italy invaded Ethiopia, and when Hitler invaded one European state after another. This was one of the chief reasons why the League of Nations failed to keep the peace.

Another cause for failure was that the Great Powers had become highly suspicious of each other. They were divided into three

* See *Readings in World History,* "Mussolini's Plans for Conquest," p. 176.

antagonistic camps. One consisted of the democratic Western powers, Britain and France, together with France's allies in Central and Eastern Europe. This group wanted to keep the status quo in Europe; they wished to maintain the frontiers drawn at the end of World War I because they had been the victors and the beneficiaries. The second camp consisted of the authoritarian or dictatorial governments, Germany, Italy, and Japan, called the Axis powers because the alliance had originated in an agreement termed the Rome-Berlin Axis. These countries were opposed to the status quo; they wanted to change the frontiers so that they would get more land in Europe and more colonies abroad. Finally in the third camp was Communist U.S.S.R., who was distrusted and feared by the other two camps, and who distrusted and feared them in return.

With all this hostility and lack of unity, it is not surprising that the League failed in its task of preventing World War II. However, it was not so much the League that failed, as it was the powers that failed to use the League because they were divided and mutually suspicious. So the 1930's were years of continual crisis and drift to war.

First Japan invaded the Chinese province of Manchuria in 1931. The League sent a commission to investigate and later condemned Japan for her aggression. But no attempt was made to force Japan to withdraw; she stayed on in Manchuria and a few years later took over the other provinces in North China. The next move was by Mussolini, who invaded Ethiopia in 1935. This time the League tried half-heartedly to stop the aggression by applying economic sanctions against Italy. That is, it called on its members to refuse arms to Italy, to stop buying her goods, and to deny her financial aid. But these sanctions were not enough to check Mussolini; in less than a year Italian troops had conquered Ethiopia.

CULVER PICTURES

For a time, to many people of Italy, the nationalism and economic progress preached by Mussolini were a welcome change from the fear and unemployment of the post-World War One era. Here Mussolini gives the Fascist salute also used by Hitler in Germany.

Europe's Decline and Triumph 191

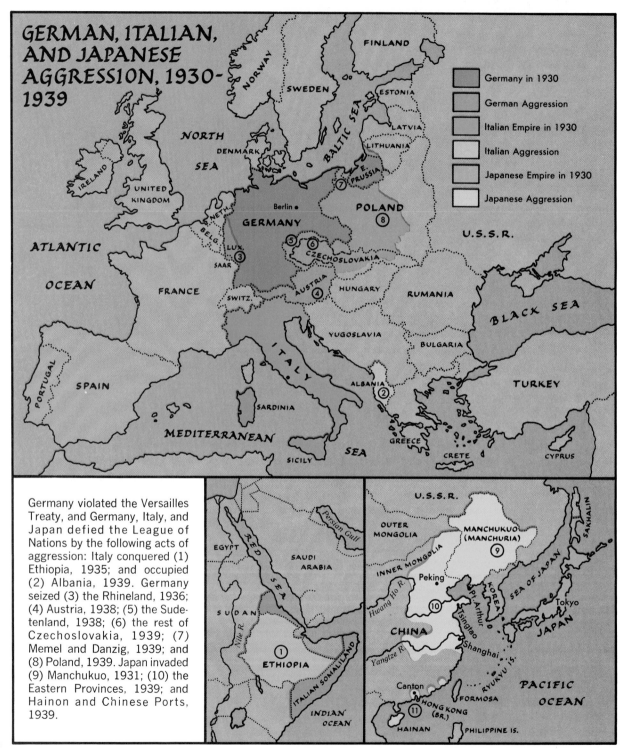

GERMAN, ITALIAN, AND JAPANESE AGGRESSION, 1930–1939

Germany in 1930
German Aggression
Italian Empire in 1930
Italian Aggression
Japanese Empire in 1930
Japanese Aggression

Germany violated the Versailles Treaty, and Germany, Italy, and Japan defied the League of Nations by the following acts of aggression: Italy conquered (1) Ethiopia, 1935; and occupied (2) Albania, 1939. Germany seized (3) the Rhineland, 1936; (4) Austria, 1938; (5) the Sudetenland, 1938; (6) the rest of Czechoslovakia, 1939; (7) Memel and Danzig, 1939; and (8) Poland, 1939. Japan invaded (9) Manchukuo, 1931; (10) the Eastern Provinces, 1939; and Hainon and Chinese Ports, 1939.

192

Hitler moves in Europe. The successes of Japan and Italy and the ineffectiveness of the League encouraged Hitler to move in Europe. First he rearmed Germany in defiance of the Versailles Treaty. Then he sent German troops into the Rhineland, another breach of the Versailles Treaty as well as of the Treaty of Locarno. These moves protected his western frontiers against any interference by France. The democracies hesitated, and Hitler was ready for action in the east.

In March 1938 he annexed Austria with virtually no opposition. The justification he offered was that the people of Austria were Germans and should be part of the German state. He used the same argument in September 1938 when he forced Czechoslovakia to hand over the border provinces of the Sudetenland, in which a German minority lived. But in March 1939 he took over the remainder of Czechoslovakia, and this time the excuse of uniting Germans could not be used because the Czechoslovaks were a Slavic people. In the next month Mussolini invaded and annexed the state of Albania in the Balkans.

By this time both the Western Powers and the Soviet Union were alarmed by Hitler's acts of aggression. Germany and Italy now dominated Central Europe, while their ally Japan was swallowing up more of North China. Britain and France tried to reach an agreement with the U.S.S.R., but mistrust on both sides caused the negotiations to fail. In August 1939 the Soviets turned to the other camp and signed a nonaggression pact with Germany. This agreement left Hitler free to do what he wished without fear of having to face both the Western Powers and the Soviet Union. He moved swiftly. On September 1, 1939, he attacked Poland despite warnings from Britain and France, who had promised to come to Poland's aid. The two Western Powers fulfilled their obli-

gation and declared war on Germany on September 3. Thus World War II began, only a little more than two decades after the end of World War I.*

WORLD WAR II

New methods of warfare. Unlike the First World War, the Second was a war of movement rather than one of static trench fighting, in which offense proved stronger than defense. In World War I the defense was stronger than the offense and the armies of both sides were bogged down because the elaborate trench systems, machine-gun nests, and barbed-wire entanglements could delay or completely halt any offensive action. During World War II, defenses of the same type were easily shattered by a combination of two offensive weapons, the tank and the plane. Both had been used in the later stages of World War I but were not decisive weapons because they were of primitive design and commanders had not learned how to employ them in battle.

During the interwar years the Germans realized the potentiality of these weapons. Hitler's defiance of the Versailles Treaty allowed the German military leaders to develop the potentiality to such an extent that they gave Germany an immense advantage at the outbreak of World War II. The *Wehrmacht* (German Army) developed the panzer (armored) divisions composed of large numbers of tanks supported by infantry. The tanks were larger, more heavily armored, and armed with heavier artillery pieces than any others in the world. The *Luftwaffe* (Air Force) developed new types of planes designed to support ground troops. The German General Staff devised tactics to make use of the new weapons. Instead of trying to break through defense lines with waves of

* See *Readings in World History,* "The Coming of World War II," p. 177.

charging infantrymen, the Germans used dive-bombers to blow up enemy communications centers, troop concentrations, and fortifications. The bombing was followed by tank attacks that pierced enemy lines. In the wake of the tanks came the infantry, motorized in many cases, which mopped up scattered enemy resistance. These were the tactics of the famous German *blitzkrieg*, or lightning warfare. They help to explain the spectacular German victories in the first two years of the war, a period during which the Western Powers depended too much on the weapons and techniques of World War I.*

* See *Readings in World History,* "The Nature of Blitzkrieg Warfare," p. 180.

Course of the war. In September 1939, the German panzers and *Luftwaffe* crushed the Polish Army in less than a month. In April 1940, the German forces smashed Denmark and Norway. Belgium and the Netherlands fell in the following month. The greatest shock came when the Germans overwhelmed the French armies in a brief seven-week campaign and forced the French government to surrender on June 22.

After these stunning victories, Hitler sent airfleets of the *Luftwaffe* over Britain in the late summer and early fall of 1940 to prepare the way for invasion. This was the famed Battle of Britain, in which the Royal Air Force, armed with the Hurricane and new

Many Germans, made desperate by the collapse of their economy and resenting the blame for World War One, gradually grew more and more willing to accept the policies of the demagogue, Adolf Hitler. A brilliant orator, Hitler told the Germans exactly what they wanted to hear and led them into the most catastrophic period ever to plague mankind.

194

Spitfire fighters, and aided greatly by their system of radar, held its ground and knocked down many *Luftwaffe* planes. England was badly battered, but its civilian population held firm. The significance of the defeat of the *Luftwaffe* over Britain was indeed great. First, Britain was saved from invasion. Second, the myth of German invincibility was broken. Lastly, it forced Hitler to turn to the south and the east. Therefore, he moved against the U.S.S.R., reasoning that if his eastern frontier were secure, he would then be safe to attempt the conquest of Britain. He issued his fateful order for attack upon the Soviet Union the following spring. "The sooner Russia is crushed the better. . . . If we start in May 1941, we would have five months to finish the job in." [13]

In preparation for the Soviet campaign, Hitler set out to control the Balkans in order to eliminate trouble from that quarter. Romania and Bulgaria had already joined his camp, but Yugoslavia and Greece held out. He attacked these two countries on April 6, 1941. In less than three weeks his panzer divisions had reached southern Greece, despite British attempts to aid the defenders. The island of Crete was captured by an airborne invasion, but the German drive to reach Middle Eastern oil and outflank the Suez Canal by jumping into Iraq from Crete was foiled by the British. Hitler then moved his armies eastward, and, on June 22, 1941, the campaign against Russia began.

Allied victory in Europe. The year 1941 is the great turning point of World War II. During that year the Soviet Union and the United States became involved; the U.S.S.R. as a result of Germany's attack on June 22, and the United States by Japan's attack at Pearl Harbor on December 7. The tremendous economic and human resources of the United States and the Soviet Union in the end decided the outcome of the war. At first both

A recruiting poster for Hitler's National Student Organization depicted a handsome Nordic youth proudly holding a National Socialistic flag. Posters of this type exerted a strong influence on German youth.

countries suffered serious defeats because of surprise attacks. Both sides were not as well prepared as their enemies. Yet the U.S.S.R. finally contributed greatly toward Germany's defeat in Europe, and the United States was chiefly responsible for Japan's defeat in Asia and a principal contributor to the defeat of the Axis in Europe.

In the Soviet Union the Germans at first conquered a tremendous amount of territory. In the north they reached the gates of Leningrad, in the center the suburbs of Moscow,

Prior to the United States' entrance into the war, Roosevelt and Churchill signed the Atlantic Charter, setting forth their joint war aims and the common principles on which "they base[d] their hopes for a better future for the world."

and in the south the Caucasus Mountains. The high point of the German advance came in November 1942 when panzer divisions reached the outskirts of the city of Stalingrad on the Volga River. Hitler declared at the time, "Here I stand and here I shall remain." But the Soviet defenders resisted desperately until reinforcements came from the east and surrounded the besiegers. Hitler lost no fewer than 300,000 men in this epic battle of Stalingrad, which proved to be the turning point of the Russo-German war.*

From then on the Soviets pushed their attack relentlessly, and despite strong German counterattacks, drove Hitler's armies back. The British and the Americans in a coordinated effort cleared the Germans from

* See *Readings in World History,* "Stalingrad and Okinawa," p. 181.

Africa. The British Eighth Army, led by General Montgomery, decisively defeated the German-Italian forces, under the famed Desert Fox Rommel, at El Alamein and drove them out of Egypt, across Libya, and into Tunisia. In November 1942 American and British troops landed in French North Africa to aid the British attack from Egypt. They pushed rapidly across Morocco and Algeria and into Tunisia. Rommel made a stand, but the pressure from north and south brought surrender of another 300,000 in May 1943.

The greatest amphibious landing in history took place on D-Day, June 6, 1944, when Allied forces under General Eisenhower invaded Normandy. A massive Soviet attack in the east followed, and the Soviet army drove the Germans from Russian soil and began advancing across Poland. Hitler's armies were caught in a vise and relentlessly squeezed. By September 1944 the Western Allies were on German soil, and the Soviets had reached eastern Germany. When the Allies reached the Elbe River, the Soviets were crossing the Oder and beginning the siege of Berlin. On April 30 Hitler and other German officials committed suicide, and a week later, on May 8, Germany surrendered.

Allied victory in Asia. The pattern of war was roughly the same in Asia. There the Japanese also won spectacular victories at the beginning. After attacking Pearl Harbor, they quickly conquered Hong Kong, French Indochina, the Philippines, the Dutch East Indies, British Malaya, and Burma. Within five months the Japanese had become the overlords of a fabulously rich empire with a population of nearly 150 million people. But the tide began to turn with the Battles of the Coral Sea (May 7, 1942) and of Midway (June 4–7), which stopped the Japanese steamroller. From then on the vast output of America's factories gradually brought victory in the Pacific.

More incomprehensible, and thus more horrifying, than the combat deaths resulting from World War II, was the annihilation of six million Jews in Nazi occupied areas. Jews were interred in concentration camps where the group murders took place. Hitler's policies included the "hardening" of his own officers, the S.S., by making them watch and take part in the mass extinction.

Beginning in August 1942 American forces began attacking the outposts of the Japanese Empire at Guadalcanal in the Solomon Islands, and New Guinea. Two great offensives were aimed at Japan: one from Hawaii and the Central Pacific under the command of Admiral Nimitz; the other from Australia and the Southwest Pacific under General MacArthur. During 1943 and 1944 these forces were able to advance to the Marshall Islands, the Marianas, and then to the Philippines. In the spring of 1945 the war was carried to the doorstep of Japan with the conquest of the islands of Iwo Jima and Okinawa.* From these two bases the United States Army Air Force and the carrier-based planes of the Navy between May and August launched a great air offensive against the Japanese islands. At least a fourth of the population was affected by the explosives.

* See *Readings in World History,* "Stalingrad and Okinawa," p. 181.

The climax came on August 6 with the atomic bombing of Hiroshima. The following day President Truman announced in a radio address, "Sixteen hours ago, an American plane dropped one bomb at Hiroshima, an important Japanese army base. That bomb had more power than 20,000 tons of TNT. It had more than 2000 times the blast power of the British 'Grand Slam,' which is the largest bomb ever used in the history of warfare." This one atomic bomb demolished three-fifths of the city of Hiroshima and killed 78,150 of its inhabitants.* On August 9 a second atomic bomb was dropped upon the city of Nagasaki, with results as catastrophic as at Hiroshima. The next day Radio Tokyo broadcast Japan's acceptance of the Allies' terms. On September 2 the formal surrender documents were signed by Japanese officials on board the U.S. battleship *Missouri* in Tokyo harbor.

Cost of the war. World War II was even more destructive of human lives and property than World War I had been. It is estimated that over 15 million soldiers were killed or missing. Many millions of civilians lost their lives, including 6 million Jews alone, who were murdered at Hitler's order. The military operations cost approximately 1.5 trillion dollars. If this sum were divided equally among all the people of the world, every man, woman, and child would receive $600. Furthermore this amount does not include the many billions of dollars lost in damage to property of all kinds, buildings, railways, roads, bridges, ships, livestock, factories, and mines.

Peace settlement. The peace settlement was delayed and left incomplete because of the postwar conflict between the Soviet Union and the Western Powers. (See following section on the Cold War.) Only after long

* See *Readings in World History,* "Hiroshima," p. 187.

negotiations were they able to agree on peace treaties with Italy and the smaller Axis countries: Hungary, Romania, Bulgaria, and Finland. The treaties were signed in Paris in February 1947. The defeated nations were required to pay heavy indemnities, most of which went to the U.S.S.R., and they were required to give up certain territories. Italy surrendered her colonies in Africa; Hungary returned Transylvania to Romania; and Finland gave to the U.S.S.R. Petsamo, its warm water port on the Barents Sea, and an area stretching southward for almost 150 miles. The treaty with Finland confirmed the 1940 losses of Karelia and an area in Central Finland. Earlier, in 1939–1940, the U.S.S.R. had annexed Bessarabia, the eastern part of prewar Poland, and the Baltic states of Estonia, Latvia, and Lithuania.

Despite repeated conferences the Western Powers and the Soviet Union were unable to agree upon a peace treaty for Germany. The former German republic remained divided into four occupation zones: the British, American, French, and Soviet. In 1947 the British and American zones were merged; the French was joined to them in 1948. A central government for the three zones was formed. In 1949 the Federal Republic of Germany, consisting of the three former occupation zones, came into existence. Gradually this Republic was given full self-government and was even allowed to rearm and to ally itself with the Western Powers against the U.S.S.R. Meanwhile the Soviet Union was doing the same thing in her zone, where the German Democratic Republic was organized. The division of Germany into two rival republics was a part of the larger division of Europe into two hostile camps, the Communist and the Western.

The conflict between the U.S.S.R. and her former allies also blocked a peace treaty with Japan. However, Japan was occupied solely by United States forces under General Mac-

Military Casualties of the Chief Countries in World War II		
Country	Number	Fraction of Total Population
U.S.A.	295,904	$\frac{1}{500}$
United Kingdom	305,770	$\frac{1}{150}$
British Commonwealth (including U.K.)	452,570	$\frac{1}{1250}$
U.S.S.R.	7,500,000	$\frac{1}{22}$
France	200,000	$\frac{1}{200}$
Germany	2,850,000	$\frac{1}{25}$
Italy	300,000	$\frac{1}{150}$
China	2,200,000	$\frac{1}{200}$
Japan	1,506,000	$\frac{1}{46}$

Arthur as Supreme Commander, rather than under joint control of the wartime allies. When agreement with the Soviet Union about a Japanese peace treaty could not be reached, the United States took the lead in preparing one which was acceptable to the Japanese government and to most of the nations of the world. It was signed in 1951, to take effect in 1952. The Soviet Union attended the conference but refused to sign; moreover, there were no representatives of either Communist or Nationalist China. By this treaty, Japan gave up all her recent conquests and also her older colonies of Korea, Manchuria, Formosa, and the southern half of Sakhalin Island. Japan also agreed to pay reparations to the nations which she had attacked.

We can see that as late as 1951, six years after the end of World War II, the peace settlement was still in the process of negotiation. The former allies were competing with each other in wooing and even in arming their former enemies. The explanation for this strange outcome can be found in the activity of the Cold War, to which we now turn.

THE COLD WAR

Wartime cooperation. World War II was followed not by peace, security, and relaxation but by what is known as the Cold War. A state somewhere between peace and war, it has been characterized by deep mistrust among the former allies, by piling armaments of the terrible new atomic variety, and by outbreaks of small wars in scattered parts of the globe.

The Cold War was a bitter disappointment to the peoples of the world, particularly because the Allies had cooperated effectively during the war years. Under the pressure of a common foe and a common danger, they had come closer together than at any time in the past.[*] The United States shipped vast quantities of arms, munitions, food, and transportation equipment to Britain and the Soviet Union. Then in May 1942 a twenty-year mutual-aid pact was signed by Great Britain and the Soviet Union. A year later, in May 1943, the Soviets abolished the Communist International which they had established in 1919 in order to overthrow the governments of the world. In view of their friendly relations with the Western Powers, the Soviets decided that the Comintern had outlived its usefulness.

An agency which developed from Allied wartime cooperation was the United Nations Relief and Rehabilitation Administration, called UNRRA for short. During its brief existence from 1943 to 1948 it distributed millions of tons of essential supplies: food, clothing, seeds, farm equipment, and industrial machinery. UNRRA's swift help saved many lives and speeded the world's economic recovery. The Allies also held a series of wartime conferences at Casablanca, Cairo, and Teheran in 1943, at Yalta in February 1945, and at Potsdam in July–August 1945.

[*] See *Readings in World History*, "Allied Wartime Cooperation," p. 189.

The purpose of these conferences was to make plans for the peacemaking and for the postwar period. At Yalta, for example, the allies agreed to assist the liberated peoples of Europe to hold "free elections" and to establish "governments responsive to the will of the people."

The most important foundation stone for the postwar world was laid when the United Nations was organized in the summer of 1945. Representatives of all the nations at war with the Axis met in San Francisco and prepared the charter for the new international body. The organization and functioning of the United Nations will be considered in the final unit. The main point to note here is that, like the League of Nations, it is a voluntary organization of sovereign nations. Its success, therefore, depends on the cooperation of its members, especially the Great Powers.

Coming of the Cold War. As World War II neared its end, the differences between the Allies became sharper and more open. The reason, of course, was that the more their common danger lessened, the more they could afford to quarrel among themselves. Most of the disputes arose out of certain policies followed by the Soviet leaders. These leaders were determined to gain control over strategic surrounding territories in order to prevent another devastating invasion such as the one they had just suffered. Specifically, they used the Red Army to put puppet governments into office in Eastern European countries such as Bulgaria, Romania, Poland, and Hungary. They tried to force concessions from Iran and Turkey in order to gain access to the Persian Gulf and also to the Mediterranean.

These policies at once brought the Soviet Union into conflict with the Allies. Britain and France were strongly opposed, for strategic reasons, to the extension of Soviet

National Flags of the members of the United Nations.

power to the Persian Gulf and the Mediterranean. The Western powers also reminded the Soviets that puppet governments in Eastern Europe violated the Yalta agreement for "governments responsive to the will of the people." The reply of the Soviet leader, Joseph Stalin, was brutally frank: "A freely elected government in any of these countries would be anti-Soviet and that we cannot allow." [14] So Stalin made and unmade governments in Eastern Europe and ignored the protests of the West.

President Truman's plan for the containment of communism included providing economic aid to those countries threatened with disruption.

In this way the relations among the former allies became steadily worse. Wartime cooperation gave way to what was called the Cold War. Britain's great leader, Winston Churchill, brought this Cold War out into the open in a speech which he made in Fulton, Missouri, on March 5, 1946.* It was on this occasion that Churchill first used the expression "iron curtain," which immediately became popular throughout the world. "From Stettin in the Baltic to Trieste in the Adriatic," declared Churchill, "an iron curtain has descended across the Continent. . . . Nobody knows what Soviet Russia and its communist international organization intends to do in the immediate future, or what are the limits, if any, to their expansive and proselytizing tendencies. . . . I do not believe that Soviet Russia desires war. What they desire is the fruits of war and the indefinite expansion of their power and doctrines. . . ."

* See *Readings in World History,* "Cold War," p. 190.

Course of the Cold War to 1953. Two stages are noticeable in the course of the Cold War. The first dates from the immediate postwar period to 1953 when the Cold War became steadily sharper and more serious. The second is from 1953 onward, when the conflict began to ease somewhat, although there have been many up and downs during that time.

During the first period the Soviets tightened their grip on their East European puppet states, while the United States quickly bolstered the other European countries against pressure from the East. For example, when Communist-led guerrillas threatened the pro-Western government of Greece, President Truman rushed money and arms to its defense. This was the occasion (March 12, 1947) when the President proclaimed the so-called Truman Doctrine: "I believe it must be the policy of the United States to support free people who are resisting attempted subjugation by armed minorities or by outside pressures."

A few months later, in June 1947, the United States launched the European Recovery Program, or Marshall Plan. During the next four years, from 1948–1952, the United States sent to Europe approximately 12 billion dollars' worth of supplies, including food, raw materials, farm machinery, and industrial equipment. This tremendous assistance put the Western European countries back on their feet. Living standards rose, and the strength of the large Italian and French Communist Parties declined. Finally the United States bolstered its European allies militarily by organizing the North Atlantic Treaty Organization (NATO) in 1949. It included the United States, Canada, Great Britain, France, Italy, and seven smaller nations. These members coordinated their defenses and agreed to aid one another in case of outside attack. Greece and Turkey joined in 1952 and West Germany in 1955.

This combination of economic and military measures successfully stopped the spread of communism in Europe. In Asia, however, the story was different. It proved impossible to raise the living standards of Asia's teeming millions as had been done in Europe. Too often the local governments were corrupt and inefficient and lost popular support. In China, after continued fighting from 1945 to 1949, the Nationalist government led by Chiang Kai-shek was overthrown by the Communists led by Mao Tse-tung. A year later, in 1950, the Communist government of North Korea attacked the non-Communist government of South Korea. The United States brought this aggression before the United Nations and obtained quick action in support of South Korea. Troops were sent by more than a dozen UN members, and the North Korean armies were driven back over the old border almost to the Yalu River, the boundary between North Korea and Red China. At this point China entered the war, and the UN forces were driven back. The war dragged on until 1953, when it was agreed that the old frontier should be restored with a few modifications. Finally in Indochina the French were forced in 1954 to withdraw, and the former colony was divided into four separate countries. North Vietnam came under Communist control, South Vietnam was strongly supported by the United States, and the other two countries, Laos and Cambodia, tried to remain neutral in the Cold War.

These violent developments led the United States to try to construct a security system in the Far East similar to NATO in Europe. In 1954 it organized the Southeast Asia Treaty Organization (SEATO), consisting of the United States, Great Britain, France, Australia, New Zealand, Pakistan, Thailand, and the Philippines. These members agreed to aid one another in case of an attack by the Communists.

Chiang Kai-shek (left) and his son, Chiang Wei-kuo (right)

WIDE WORLD

Course of the Cold War since 1953. In 1953 the Cold War began to ease a little. One reason for this was the death in April 1953 of the suspicious and dogmatic Soviet dictator, Joseph Stalin. His successor, Nikita Khrushchev, was just as much a Communist, but he called for peaceful coexistence rather than Cold War with the rest of the world.* Another reason for the improvement was the ending of the Korean War in July 1953 and the Indochina War in August 1954. Perhaps more important was the growing feeling on all sides that war had become an impossible way of settling international disputes. On March 1, 1954, the United States had exploded at Bikini a hydrogen bomb equal to 15 million tons of TNT. This was 750 times more powerful than the Hiroshima atomic bomb which

* See *Readings in World History,* "Peaceful Coexistence," p. 191.

killed 78,000 people. Winston Churchill, with his usual insight, saw that this terrible new weapon transformed international relations as well as warfare. In a House of Commons speech in 1955, he pointed out that the hydrogen bomb threatened the existence not only of little countries like England but also of large countries like the United States and the Soviet Union.

There is an immense gulf between the atomic and the hydrogen bomb. The atomic bomb, with all its terror, did not carry us outside the scope of human control. . . . With the hydrogen bomb, the entire foundation of human affairs was revolutionized and mankind placed in a situation both measureless and laden with doom.

However, a curious paradox has emerged. Let me put it simply. After a certain point has been passed, it may be said, the worse

FRANK COU (BLACK STAR)

For the people of Korea, the horror and destruction of the Korean War was not easily forgotten. In this scene, a few minutes of comparative safety allow Korean shoeshine boys to make extra money from an American G.I.

204

things get the better. The broad effect of the latest developments is to spread ... to a vast extent the area of mortal danger. This should certainly increase the deterrent upon Soviet Russia by putting enormous spaces and scattered population on an equality, or near equality, of vulnerability with our small, densely populated island and with Western Europe.... The hydrogen bomb, with its vast range of destruction and the even wider range of contamination, would be effective also against nations whose populations hitherto has been so widely dispersed over large land areas as to make them feel that they were not in any danger at all.

It may well be that we shall, by a process of sublime irony, have reached a stage in this story where safety will be the sturdy child of terror....

Churchill's interpretation of the new world situation created by the hydrogen bomb was generally accepted. In the Soviet Union, Premier Khrushchev declared, "Only lunatics want war." In the United States, General Douglas MacArthur said, "Sooner or later, if civilization is to survive, war must go." Once the fighting ended in Korea and Indochina, international relations improved substantially. It is true that there were many ups and downs. In 1956, for example, there was a serious setback because of two outbreaks of violence. One was the use of Soviet troops to crush a revolt in Hungary against the Communist government of that country. The other was the British-French-Israeli invasion of Egypt because of a dispute over Premier Nasser's seizure of the Suez Canal. (See unit on the Middle East.)

The anxiety caused by these events gradually lessened, and new attempts to reduce tensions were made. These were set back when, in May 1960, an American U–2 plane was shot down while taking pictures deep inside Soviet territory. The Soviets reacted violently and cancelled President Eisenhower's planned visit to their country. Much more serious was the 1962 Cuban crisis, precipitated when American air reconnaissance revealed that Soviet missile bases were under construction in Cuba and that a large part of the United States soon would be within range. In a dramatic broadcast President Kennedy proclaimed a quarantine to halt Soviet ships carrying offensive weapons to Cuba, demanded the removal of the Soviet strategic missiles, and began preparations for an invasion of Cuba. When Khrushchev announced that he had ordered Soviet missiles withdrawn and all Soviet bases in Cuba dismantled in return for a pledge not to invade Cuba and the ending of the U.S. blockade, it became clear that neither country wanted war.

The confrontation during the Cuban crisis so appalled responsible statesmen that they renewed their efforts to alleviate world tensions. On August 5, 1963, the United States, Britain, and the Soviet Union signed a test ban treaty prohibiting nuclear explosions in the atmosphere, in outer space, and under water. Most of the countries of the world promptly signed the pact along with the original three. In February 1967, 14 Latin American countries signed a treaty banning the manufacture, use, or possession of nuclear weapons in their countries. In the same year 98 countries signed a treaty prohibiting the placing of weapons of mass destruction in orbit around the earth, the installation of such weapons on the moon or other celestial bodies, and the national appropriation of these bodies by any country. All of these treaties were hailed enthusiastically by most of the countries of the world.

These treaties helped to lessen international tensions, but at the same time other developments were having the opposite effect. One was the growing crisis in Vietnam where the United States became increasingly involved following the defeat and departure of the French in 1954. Beginning with eco-

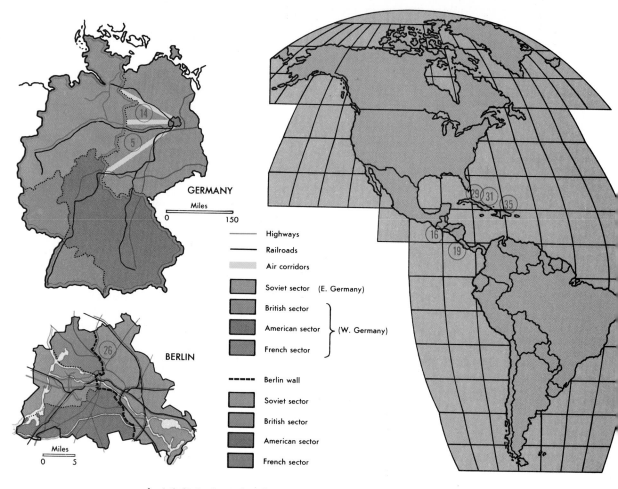

GERMANY

Miles
0   150

BERLIN

Miles
0   5

Highways

Railroads

Air corridors

Soviet sector   (E. Germany)

British sector

American sector   } (W. Germany)

French sector

Berlin wall

Soviet sector

British sector

American sector

French sector

WORLD TROUBLE SPOTS SINCE 1945

1	1945-62	Algerian war for independence
2	1946	Soviet troops invaded Iran, forced to withdraw by UN
3	1947	Communist uprisings in Greece and Turkey
4		Muslims and Hindus clash in South Asia
5	1948	Berlin airlift as result of Soviet blocking of corridor to West Berlin
6	1948, 56, 67	Arab-Israeli clashes in Middle East
7	1950-53	Korean War
8	1950	Dutch driven from Indonesia after much bloodshed
9		Chinese Nationalists vs. Taiwanese enabled Chinese to control island
10	1951	Chinese clash with India, Burma and North Vietnam
11		Tibet "liberated" by Chinese Communists — Dalai Lama fled to India

12	1953	US Navy bomber shot down by Chinese over Manchuria
13		Mau Mau rebellion in Kenya to drive out British
14		British plane shot down by Soviets in Berlin Corridor
15	1953-55	Chinese communists, with Soviet aid, invade Burma
16	1954	Guatemalan government overthrown by US armed exiles
17		French driven from Indochina
18	1955	Taiwan bombed by Chinese Communists
19		Nicaraguan rebels invaded Costa Rica
20	1955-62	Indonesians clash with Malaysians over territorial dispute
21	1956	British, French and Israelis invade Egypt after nationalization of Suez Canal
22		Uprisings in Poland and Hungary suppressed by Soviet troops
23	1958	US and British troops suppress uprising in Lebanon

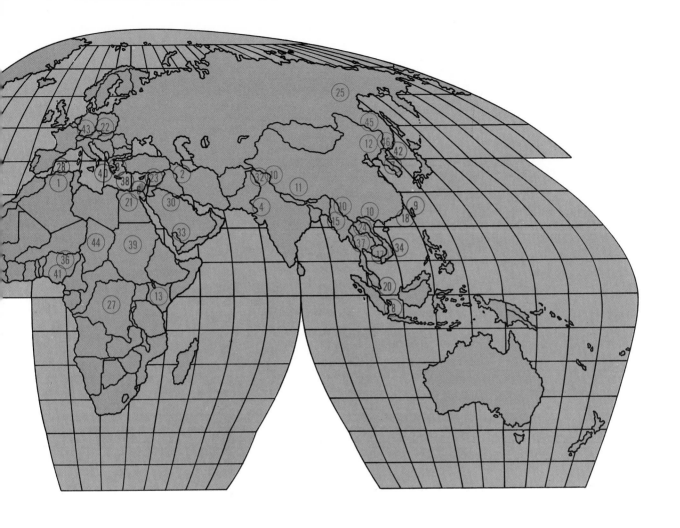

24	1959	Civil War in Laos
25	1960	US U-2 plane (espionage) shot down over USSR
26	1961	Berlin wall constructed
27		Civil war in Congo — Katanga province declares independence
28		French and Soviet planes exchange shots
29		With help from US, Cuban exiles invade Bay of Pigs in Cuba
30	1961-69	Iraq and Kuwait clash of territory
31	1962	US forces the withdrawal of Soviet missiles from Cuba
32	1962-67	India and Pakistan clash over Kashmir and Jammu
33	1962-68	Civil War in Yemen
34	1963	US troops sent to Vietnam

35	1965	US troops invade the Dominican Republic to suppress an attempted overthrow of the military regime
36	1966	Civil War in Nigeria
37	1967	Martial law declared in Thailand as Communist uprisings increase
38		Greece and Turkey clash over Cyprus
39		Civil War in Sudan
40		Greek government overthrown by military junta
41	1968	Biafra declares independence from Nigeria as civil war continues
42		USS Pueblo captured by North Korean
43		Soviet invasion of Czechoslovakia
44		Civil War in Chad
45	1969	Sino-Soviet border clash
46		US plane shot down over North Korea

To prevent defections to the West, the "Berlin Wall," a complex of concrete and barbed wire, was built in 1962 and is continually manned by East German guards. Although some have escaped, many have lost their lives trying to clear the wires. In past years the gates have been opened during holiday seasons to allow visits to family and friends.

nomic aid and military advisors, the United States deemed it necessary to step up its assistance to South Vietnam by sending over half a million men by 1968, as well as bombing strategic targets in North Vietnam. Peace negotiations began in Paris in March 1968, but to date no real progress in the discussions has been made. However, in 1969, a small number of U.S. troops began to be withdrawn.

Another source of tension was in the Middle East where the creation of the independent state of Israel in 1948 was never accepted by the surrounding Arab countries. The result has been a succession of wars between the two sides. The first was in 1948 when the Arab countries attacked the newly-created state of Israel and were repulsed. The second was in 1956 when Israel, together with Britain and France, invaded

Egypt, but was forced to withdraw under pressure from the United Nations, the Soviet Union, and the United States. The third war came in 1967 when Israel, in response to what she considered dangerous threats by her neighbors, attacked and defeated them in a stunning six-day campaign, and occuped the Sinai Peninsula and the west bank of the Jordan River. Since then there has been deadlock in the Middle East, with continual raids and counter-raids. Israel refuses to evacuate any territory until after negotiations and settlement with her neighbors, while the Arabs refuse to negotiate until after evacuation.

A third source of tension was the invasion of Czechoslovakia in August 1968 by the Soviet Union, together with four of its East European allies. The cause for the invasion was the launching of a "Democratic Socialist Revolution" in Prague in January 1968 by a group of Communist progressives led by Alexander Dubcek. For the first time since World War II, the Czechoslovak people enjoyed a free press, free public discussion, and free travel abroad. A main reason for the intervention by the Soviet Union and its allies seems to have been the fear that the new freedom in Czechoslovakia might strengthen popular demand throughout Eastern Europe for similar freedom and thus endanger the existing Communist regimes.

These and other dangers to world peace led United Nations Secretary General U Thant to include the following warning in his annual report to the General Assembly on September 26, 1968:

A young Czech shot during the Soviet invasion of Czechoslovakia in August 1968 is carried away in the fore of Soviet tanks.

I regret to have to report that little progress, if any, has been recorded toward the growth of international order based on law and justice. On the contrary, there has been a serious decline in the standards of international differences.

This tendency to return to force as a means of national policy strikes at the very basis of the United Nations; just settlement is sacrificed to superior might, and international tensions are consequently heightened. If this trend is not reversed, and if the principle of nonintervention in the free destiny of nations is not re-established, the future of international peace and security itself is indeed a very dark one.[15]

Europe's Decline and Triumph 209

DECLINE AND TRIUMPH OF EUROPE

The decline of Europe began with World War I. It was speeded up tremendously by World War II. Europe's influence in world affairs has decreased in almost every field: political, economic, military, and colonial.

Political decline. Europe no longer dominates world politics as was the case before 1914; the continent has come to be divided into two parts, each of which is allied with non European powers. The eastern part consists of Easy Germany, Poland, Czechoslovakia, Hungary, Romania, and Bulgaria. These countries are dependent upon, and under the influence of, the Soviet Union. Albania has lined up with Communist China. The only country in Eastern Europe that has managed to remain relatively independent is Yugoslavia, although it, too, has a Communist government. Turning to Western Europe, we noted earlier that this part of the continent was dependent upon the United States for economic and military support immediately after the war. Today, thanks to the great success of the Marshall Plan, the Western European countries have recovered and can stand on their own feet. Consequently they are able now to take a more independent position in world affairs than they had been able to do in the 1940's. However, this independence should not be exaggerated. In the final analysis, political strength depends on the amount of supporting economic and military power. And in these respects Europe today is overshadowed by both the United States and the Soviet Union.

Economic and military decline. Until the late 19th century, Europe was the workshop of the world. European factories turned out more goods than the rest of the world combined. This economic leadership also gave Europe the military leadership of the world. But today the situation is very different.* In economic, political, and military strength, it is increasingly evident that Europe has fallen behind. In fact, the first three economic powers of the world today are all non-European: the United States, the Soviet Union, and Japan.

Colonial decline. By far the most spectacular decline of Europe after World War II was in colonial affairs. We noted above that European countries managed to keep their colonial empires after the First World War. But in less than two decades after the second war, the European powers were forced to surrender almost all their overseas possessions. This was an extraordinary development which changed radically the map of the world within a very short period. One reason for this sudden upset was that the subject peoples were awakened much more by World War II than by World War I. This was especially true of the colonies in Asia, most of which were overrun by Japan. The prestige of the white man was badly damaged when Japanese forces easily drove the British out of Malaya and Burma, the French out of Indochina, the Dutch out of Indonesia, and the Americans out of the Philippines. Furthermore the Japanese deliberately encouraged local nationalist movements during the few years of their rule. They tried to develop a feeling of Asian unity against the former European masters. When the Japanese were forced to give up their conquests, they frequently left arms with local nationalist groups.

Hence it is not surprising that when the Europeans tried to return to their colonies, they discovered that their former subjects were not at all willing to accept them. Instead they began a struggle for full independ-

* See *Readings in World History,* "Economic Decline of Europe," p. 193.

ence. In this struggle they were helped by the fact that the old colonial powers (Britain, France, and Holland) had been greatly weakened by World War II. All these circumstances enabled most of the colonial peoples to win their freedom in the years after 1945.

New independent states appeared not only in Asia, but also in Africa, the Middle East, and Latin America. They appeared so rapidly that 58 countries won independence between 1944 and 1969, and the list is still growing. These 58 countries have a 1969 population of over 1 billion, or one-third of the world's total. Never before in history had a change occurred so rapidly. The map on page 212 shows that the world in 1969 was very different from that of 1914.*

Triumph of Europe. Despite the disappearance of the great colonial empires, the period since World War II has been one of European triumph as well as of decline. The reasons for the triumph is that during those years, European ideas, techniques, and institutions have spread throughout the world more rapidly than at any time in the past.

We noted earlier that in the modern period since 1500, Europe became prominent because of three great revolutions, the Economic, Scientific, and Political. These revolutions gave Europe the power, the drive, and the knowledge to expand all over the world and to conquer great empires. By the 19th century, Europe had become the mistress of the world. Then, after 1914, and especially after 1945, Europe lost her position of leadership. She fell behind, as we have seen, in political influence, in economic and military power, and in colonial possessions. But the reason she fell behind is that her three great revolutions have been steadily spreading throughout the world.

* See *Readings in World History*, "End of European Empires," p. 194.

The Economic Revolution, for example, began in England, spread to Western Europe, and then to the United States, U.S.S.R., Japan, the British Dominions, and other overseas territories. Today a great number of countries all over the world have their own Three- or Four- or Five-Year Plans, by which they hope to industrialize themselves as rapidly as possible. As a result, Europe today is producing 25 per cent of the world's industrial output compared to 72 per cent in 1860.

Science has also spread rapidly from Europe and has become the one body of knowledge that all peoples are anxious to learn. Consequently science is no longer a European monopoly. Indeed, more scientific work is now being done in the United States and in the Soviet Union than in any European country.

Finally, Europe's political revolution also is sweeping the entire globe. Nationalism and communism are of European origin, and both these "isms" are awakening millions of people in all parts of the world. In Africa, European rule is being fought with such European slogans as "freedom," "independence," and "one man, one vote." It is largely this spread of European political ideas and movements that undermined and swept away the European colonial empires.

In conclusion we see that behind Europe's decline is Europe's triumph. The one led naturally and inevitably to the other. If Europe is no longer the dominant force in the world, the chief reason is the diffusion throughout the world of Europe's three great revolutions.*

SIGNIFICANCE OF THE PERIOD FOR WORLD HISTORY

Looking back over this period since 1914, its significance for world history is that it

* See *Readings in World History*, "Triumph of Europe," p. 197.

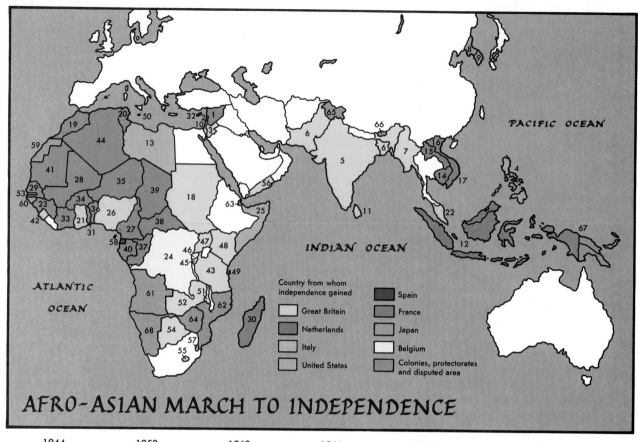

AFRO-ASIAN MARCH TO INDEPENDENCE

Country from whom independence gained

- Great Britain
- Netherlands
- Italy
- United States
- Spain
- France
- Japan
- Belgium
- Colonies, protectorates and disputed area

1944
1. Syria
2. Lebanon

1946
3. Jordan
4. Philippines

1947
5. India
6. Pakistan

1948
7. Burma
8. N. Korea
9. S. Korea
10. Israel
11. Ceylon

1949
12. Indonesia

1952
13. Libya

1954
14. Cambodia
15. Laos
16. N. Vietnam
17. S. Vietnam

1956
18. Sudan

1957
19. Morocco
20. Tunisia

1957
21. Ghana
22. Malaya*

1958
23. Guinea

1960
24. Rep. of the Congo
25. Somalia
26. Nigeria
27. Cameroon
28. Mali
29. Senegal
30. Malagasy Rep.
31. Togo
32. Cyprus
33. Ivory Coast
34. Upper Volta
35. Niger
36. Dahomey
37. Congo Rep.
38. Central African Rep.
39. Chad
40. Gabon
41. Mauritania

1961
42. Sierra Leone
43. Tanganyika**

1962
44. Algeria
45. Burundi
46. Rwanda
47. Uganda

1963
48. Kenya
49. Zanzibar**

1964
50. Malta
51. Malawi
52. Zambia

1965
53. Gambia

1966
54. Botswana
55. Lesotho

1967
56. Southern Yemen

1968
57. Swaziland
58. Equatorial Guinea

Colonies, protectorates and disputed areas

Spain
59. Spanish Sahara

Portugal
60. Portuguese Guinea
61. Angola
62. Mozambique

France
63. French Somaliland

United Kingdom
64. Rhodesia†

India, Pakistan
65. Jammu and Kashmir

66. Bhutan (regulated by India only in external affairs)

United Nations
67. New Guinea (with Australia)
68. Southwest Africa

*Combined in 1963 with Singapore, Sarawak, and Sahab to form Federation of Malaysia. Singapore withdrew in 1965.

**Combined in 1964 to form Tanzania

†Claimed independence in 1965 but unrecognized by Britain until discontinue policy of apartheid.

212 *Civilized Man Lives in Global Unity*

marks both the triumph and decline of Europe. The triumph is shown on the map, "Europe and the World, 1914" (pages 166–167). This makes clear the extent of Europe's influence upon the world in which we live. The entire globe can be divided into regions of greater or lesser connection with Europe. First there is Europe itself, together with the Soviet Union and its vast empire in Asia. Then there are the European colonies, greatly shrunken since 1914, but still of considerable size and number. Also there is the Commonwealth of Nations, with its original member states consisting largely of peoples of European origin, and its new member states with African and Asian populations. In the Americas are the independent European-derived states, that is, states that are fully independent but which have peoples and cultures of European origin. Finally there is the rest of the world which is also independent, but whose peoples and cultures are non-European in origin. But even in these states, Europe's influence is still all-important. China, for example, is today being rapidly changed by a government which is using two "isms" of European origin, industrialism and communism.

We see, then, that the entire globe has been profoundly affected by Europe. This is why the British historian, Arnold Toynbee, has written the following:

> Future historians will say, I think, that the greatest event of the twentieth century was the impact of Western Civilization upon all the living societies of that day. They will say of this impact that it was so powerful and so pervasive that it turned the lives of all its victims upside down and inside out—affecting the behavior, outlook, feelings, and beliefs of individual men, women and children in an intimate way....[16]

But the years since 1914 have also seen the decline of Europe as a political, economic, and military force. Europe no longer rules the globe as she did in the 19th century. However, this domination of the world by one small region was entirely unprecedented. For thousands of years prior to the beginning of European expansion in 1500, each region of the globe went its own way. Since there were comparatively few contacts among the various regions, each developed its own way of life. There was no possibility of any one region imposing its way of life on the remainder, for the obvious reason that continents and oceans could not be crossed. All this changed when Europe experienced its three great revolutions. These made it possible for Europeans to expand all over the world and dominate it. But their domination lasted only about two centuries. As soon as non-European peoples learned the secrets of the three revolutions, European mastery was finished.

Now Europe is merely one region of several, rather than *the* ruling region of the globe. In a sense, we are now returning to an earlier pattern of world organization. In the past, each region was independent and normally was not dominated by any other region. Something like this may develop in the future. The various regions will probably be more independent in the political sense, even though spreading industrialization will create increasing conformity in ways of living. Now that European domination is broken, we can expect the Africans South of the Sahara to go their way, the Muslims of the Middle East to go theirs, and so on with the Indians in South Asia, the Chinese in East Asia, and Latin Americans in the New World.

In the remaining part of this book, we shall consider each of these regions in turn. First we shall see what is happening in these areas today. Then we shall travel backward and trace the historical roots of these conditions. We shall explore the historical events, the forces, and the personalities that help to explain our world of today.

Reviewing the Essentials

World War I

1. What is economic rivalry? Why was it a cause of World War I? Who were the major economic rivals preceding World War I? What nations were competing for colonies?

2. What is an alliance? Why do nations enter into alliances? What two systems of alliances were organized before World War I? Why were these arrangements a cause of World War I?

3. How did the assassination of Archduke Franz Ferdinand set in motion events that culminated in World War I?

4. Name and locate on a map the Allied Powers and the Central Powers. What were the advantages and disadvantages of each side at the beginning of World War I? How did these shift during the course of the war?

5. How was World War I different from all previous wars? Describe the major strategy of each side. Why did the Central Powers lose? What were the results of the war in (a) cost in human life and (b) direct cost?

6. What problems confronted the Allied statesmen at the end of the war? What program for a peace settlement did President Wilson submit in his Fourteen Points?

7. Describe the organization of the League of Nations and the role it played in the world after 1919.

8. What is the principle of self-determination? Name and locate the new nations that appeared on the map of Europe as a result of the peace treaty settlements. Why was the principle of self-determination largely ignored outside of Europe? Where was the principle compromised in Europe and in non-European areas?

9. What is a mandate? What is its relationship with the mandatory nation? What mandates were assigned to Great Britain? To France?

10. How did World War I affect Europe's industrial output and investments? What nations emerged from the war to challenge the industrial leadership of Europe?

11. How did World War I lead to the establishment of a Bolshevik government in Russia in 1917? Why was the Comintern set up?

12. How did World War I promote the development of nationalism among colonial people? In what areas was this feeling most pronounced? What persons are associated with resistance to European control?

Twenty-Year Truce

13. What problems confronted Europe during the early 1920's?

14. Why did European nations resort to alliances when a League of Nations had been organized to keep the peace? Who were the parties of the Rapallo Treaty, 1922? What was the purpose of this treaty?

15. Give evidence to show that the Great Depression was in fact an economic breakdown. Explain how the depression affected conditions within nations and relations between nations. What events in Great Britain, France, Germany, and the United States are evidence of change and unrest produced by the depression? How did the nations of the world cope with the problem of unemployment?

16. The nations in the period 1929–1939 can be divided into three power blocs, each antagonistic to the other. Identify the members of these power blocs and their objectives. Why was the League of Nations unable to resolve the differences between the power blocs which resulted in World War II?

17. Describe the series of crises created by aggression in the period 1933–1939. How did (a) England, (b) France, and (c) Russia respond to the acts of aggression? Include in your consideration of this question the Munich settlement of 1938. What events were an immediate cause for a declaration of war on Germany on September 3, 1939?

World War II

18. What were basic differences between World War I and World War II? What were the advantages of the Allied Powers? Of the Axis Powers?

19. Describe the German blitzkrieg. What spectacular victories did Germany win during the first two years of the war?

20. Why was 1941 the turning point of World War II?

21. On a map locate the extent of German penetration of the Soviet Union. What were the disadvantages of the military achievement?

22. How did the strategy of the Western Allies relate to that of the Russians to bring about the surrender of Germany?

23. Why was Japan able to conquer so large an area in so short a time? At what point was the Japanese advance checked? By whom? What important victories accompanied the American offensive in the Pacific? What was the effect of the use of the atomic bomb in the offensive against Japan?

24. Compare the costs of World War I and II in terms of human lives and direct cost. In what ways were peace settlements made after World War II different from those made after World War I? What settlement was made with Germany? With Japan?

The Cold War

25. In what specific ways had the Allies cooperated during World War II? Why did differences develop? Over what policies?

26. Under what circumstances was the United Nations organized? For what purposes?

27. How did the Truman Doctrine, the Marshall Plan, and NATO stop the spread of communism in Europe? What developments in Asia during the first stage of the Cold War (1945–1953) indicate that communism had expanded there? What steps were taken to stop the spread of communism in Asia? Why did the Cold War subside after 1953?

Decline and Triumph of Europe

28. How does the division of Europe into two parts contribute to its decline? What countries belong to the eastern section? To the western section?

29. Explain: "In the final analysis, political strength depends on the amount of supporting economic and military power." Where does Europe stand today in respect to these criteria of strength?

30. What new nations are maintaining some relation with the former colonial power? How do you explain this? What newly free states are members of the Community (French) and the Commonwealth of Nations (British)? Why did the Union of South Africa withdraw from the Commonwealth of Nations?

31. If Europe has been in a state of decline since 1914, is it accurate to say that the period since World War II has also been one of triumph for Europe? In what ways is European influence being felt in the winds of change that blow over Asia and Africa?

Explain, Identify, or Locate

open covenant	economic sanctions	Benito Mussolini	Normandy
Bolshevik	bloc	Adolf Hitler	Dunkirk
Comintern	iron curtain	Franklin D. Roosevelt	Berlin
Triple Alliance	Cold War	Neville Chamberlain	Elbe River
Triple Entente	summit conference	Chiang Kai-shek	Oder River
Fourteen Points	Truman Doctrine	Joseph Stalin	Ruhr Valley
reparations	Marshall Plan	Harry Truman	Okinawa
ultimatum	Lenin	Rommel	Iwo Jima
collective security	Lloyd George	Montgomery	Pearl Harbor
Mein Kampf	Georges Clemenceau	Khrushchev	Bataan
"have and have not nations"	Vittorio Orlando	Nimitz	Hiroshima
lebensraum	Woodrow Wilson	MacArthur	Nigeria
appeasement	Aristide Briand	Verdun	Burma
fascism	Winston Churchill	Warsaw	Vietnam
1914	1929	Stalingrad	Yalu River
	1939	1945	1953

UNIT ACTIVITIES

Europe Unites the World: 1500–1763

1. Prepare a report on the Italian city-states. Include in your presentation information on: (a) location and accessibility to the outside world; (b) centers of wealth and culture; (c) nature and extent of trade in selected products; (d) trade routes with the Orient and Africa; (e) reasons for failure to find an all-water route to the Orient; (f) impact of exploratory activities of Atlantic nations in the period 1500–1763.

2. Consult several historians in addition to the author of your text for explanations of why Europe expanded overseas after 1500. Note similarities and differences in the explanations given. Can you account for the differences in interpretation?

3. Do additional reading and report on the Renaissance and the Reformation, relating them to the economic, political, and social conditions of the time. Describe the changes brought about in the organization of European society during these two periods.

4. Consult the bibliography for this section for additional readings on the lives and achievements of the great explorers. Several students might present a symposium comparing the explorers of the 15th and 16th centuries with the space explorers of the 20th century.

5. Prepare a report on the joint stock company as a business organization which raised capital funds for overseas expeditions of discovery and settlement. What was the structure of a joint stock company? How were funds raised? Who invested? What were the important stock companies that participated in exploration and colonization? What were the advantages and disadvantages of this kind of organization? What were the contributions of joint stock companies in promoting Europe's mastery of the globe?

SELECTED READING

● The story of how European discoverers explored the world is told in these three books: Joseph B. Icenhower, *Man Against the Unknown: The Story of Exploration* (Philadelphia: Winston, 1957); Mary S. Lucas, *Vast Horizons* (New York: Viking Press, 1943); and Harold Lamb, *New Found World* (New York: Doubleday, 1955). The various types of ships used by man, from the earliest dugouts to modern liners, are described in words and in drawings by Edwin Tunis, *Oars, Sails and Steam* (Cleveland: World, 1952).

● There are many accounts of the lives and achievements of the great explorers, some of the best being: Samuel E. Morison, *Christopher Columbus, Mariner* (New American Library, 1955); Seymour Pond, *Ferdinand Magellan* (New York: Criterion Books, 1959); I. R. Blacker, *Cortes and the Aztec Conquest* (New York: Harper and Row, 1965); and Ronald Syme, *Captain Cook, Pacific Explorer* (New York: William Morrow, 1960). There is an interesting novel on the struggle for the spice trade: Agnes Hewes, *Spice Ho!* (New York: Knopf, 1947).

FURTHER READING

● The question of why Europe expanded and Asia did not is analyzed by J. R. Levenson, *European Expansion and the Counter-Example of Asia, 1300–1600* (Englewood Cliffs, N.J.: Prentice-Hall, 1967). The best short study of the age of exploration in all its aspects is the splendid work by the English scholar, J. H. Parry, *The Age of Reconaissance* (Mentor Books, 1963). See also the lavishly illustrated book edited by H. Trevor-Roper, *The Age of Expansion: Europe and the World 1559–1660* (London: Thames and Hudson, 1968). Some information on Russia's overland expansion is given in Emil Lengyel, *Siberia* (New York: Random House, 1943); in E. Lessner, *Cradle of Conquerors: Siberia* (New York: Doubleday, 1955); and T. Armstrong, *Russian Expansion in the North* (Cambridge, England: Cambridge University Press, 1965). The decisive battle which assured the naval supremacy of the northwest European states instead of Spain is told with fascinating detail by Garrett Mattingly, *The Armada* (Boston: Houghton Mifflin, 1959). For the effect of Europe's expansion on Europe itself, see the stimulating study by Walter Prescott Webb, *The Great Frontier* (Boston: Houghton Mifflin, 1952).

● The nature of the people and societies that the European explorers discovered is usually overlooked. Information on this important subject is given in George Alexander Lensen, *The World Beyond Europe* (Boston: Houghton Mifflin, 1960), Part 1; Basil Davidson, *The Lost Cities of Africa* (Boston: Little, Brown, 1959); John Collier, *Indians of the Americas: The Long Hope* (Mentor paperback); and A. M. Josephy, Jr., *The Indian Heritage of America* (New York: Alfred A. Knopf, 1968). Works concerned with the impact of Europe on the various overseas regions are given in the Readings of the relevant units which follow.

Europe Dominates the World: 1763–1914

1. This section poses important questions for you as young historians to ponder:

   a. Why did the *Industrial Revolution* take place in 18th-century England?
   b. Why did 18th-century man have confidence in his ability to fathom the unknown and arrive at an understanding of natural laws, thereby bringing about the *Scientific Revolution?*
   c. Why did 18th-century man believe that he had the right to create his own political institutions?
   d. Why were *liberalism, nationalism,* and *socialism* products of the 19th century?

   Working individually or in small groups, read in references suggested by the bibliography or by your teacher, and prepare answers to the above questions. Develop definitions of the terms italicized with explanations and evidence drawn from your reading. In each case, acknowledge sources used and be prepared to point out instances of agreement and disagreement among historians cited in your explanation.

   Finally, as a class, discuss these questions: What have been the results of the Economic, Scientific, and Political Revolutions in the life of man? How would our lives differ if they had not taken place? What has been their global impact?

2. Among men whose ideas have influenced the life of man are: Montesquieu, Voltaire, Rousseau, Copernicus, Galileo, Sir Isaac Newton, John Locke, Adam Smith, Karl Marx, and Charles Darwin. You may wish to add others to this list. Read for information about their influence on the world's development. Several students might prepare a presentation for the class on why these men might, in fact, be labeled "Thinkers Whose Ideas Shook the World."

3. The French and American Revolutions can be studied as "models" of great political revolutions of modern history. Prepare a report on each, giving reasons why the French overthrew the *ancien régime* (old system) and why American colonists separated from the mother country. Consult the sources listed in the bibliography. Attention should be given to the phases of each revolution and the significance of each in world history.

4. Develop a clear definition of the term "imperialism" after consulting sources listed in the bibliography. Discover reasons why certain nations became imperialistic in the 19th century. Assess or evaluate the results of imperialism for (a) the European nations that followed imperialistic policies and (b) the colonial peoples in Asia and Africa.

5. Study the Declaration of Independence as a document that gave expression to the ideas em-

phasized in the 18th-century Political Revolution, namely, the "social contract" theory of government and the doctrine of human rights. Trace the source of the ideas expressed in the Declaration. Why were they viewed as revolutionary at the time when they were written? How do these ideas give meaning to our national purpose today? What other peoples of the world have been influenced by them and sought to implement them in their political institutions?

SELECTED READING

● The inventors and the inventions that produced the Industrial Revolution are described vividly and simply in the following three books: Gertrude Hartman, *Machines and the Men who Made the World of Industry* (New York: Macmillan, 1939); Elizabeth R. Montgomery, *The Story Behind Great Inventions* (New York: Dodd, Mead, 1953); and Robert J. Forbes, *Man, the Maker; A History of Technology and Engineering* (rev. ed., New York: Abelard-Schuman, 1958).
● The exciting story of the discoveries and progress made in various fields of science is told in the following books: R. Burlingame, *Scientists Behind the Inventors* (New York: Harcourt, Brace, and World, 1960); Patrick Moore, *Story of Man and the Stars* (New York: Norton, 1955) for the history of astronomy; Elizabeth R. Montgomery, *The Story Behind Great Medical Discoveries* (New York: Dodd, Mead, 1945); Keith Gordon Irwin, *The Romance of Chemistry* (New York: Viking, 1959); and the fascinating illustrated books by Lancelot Hogben, *The Wonderful World of Mathematics* (New York: Garden City Books, 1955); and *The Wonderful World of Energy* (New York: Garden City Books, 1957).
● The Scientific Revolution can also be studied through biographies of the great scientists, such as the following: Emily Hahn, *Leonardo da Vinci* (New York: Random House, 1956); Elma E. Levinger, *Galileo* (New York: Messner, 1952); Beulah Tannenbaum and Myra Stillman, *Issac Newton* (New York: Whittlesey House, 1959);

Sarah R. Riedman, *Antoine Lavoisier* (New York: Nelson, 1957); Charles Darwin, *The Voyage of the Beagle* (New York: Harper, 1959); Harry Sootin, *Michael Faraday: From Errand Boy to Master Physicist* (New York: Messner, 1954); Madeleine P. Grant, *Louis Pasteur* (New York: Whittlesey, 1959). The connection between the Industrial and Scientific Revolutions is made clear in Roger Burlingame, *Scientists Behind the Inventors* (New York: Harcourt, Brace, 1960).
● A good introduction to the Political Revolution is given in Albert Carr, *Men of Power: A Book of Dictators* (New York: Viking, 1956) which has chapters on the English leader Cromwell, the French leader Napoleon, and the German leader Bismarck. The colorful career of the Italian nationalist revolutionary, Garibaldi, is vividly described in Marcia Davenport, *Father of Modern Italy* (New York: Random House, 1957). For the American Revolution, see Francis R. Bellamy, *The Private Life of George Washington* (New York: Crowell, 1951); and Edmund S. Morgan, *The Birth of the Republic 1763–1789* (University of Chicago Press, 1956). A lively account of the execution of King Charles I is given by Hugh R. Williamson, *The Day They Killed the King* (New York: Macmillan, 1957). Finally there is Charles Dickens', *A Tale of Two Cities,* in numerous editions, which pictures the abuses in old France and the terror during the revolution.

FURTHER READING

● An excellent collection of essays presenting various interpretations of the Industrial Revolution is in the paperback by Philip A. M. Taylor, *The Industrial Revolution in Britain: Triumph or Disaster?* (Boston: D. C. Heath, 1958). The best short study of the subject is by T. S. Ashton, *The Industrial Revolution 1760–1830* (London: Home University Library, 1948).
● On the Scientific Revolution, the best overall survey is the paperback by William Cecil

Dampier, *A Shorter History of Science* (Meridian, 1957). A clear analysis of the nature of science is given by the British physicist, Norman Campbell, *What is Science?* (Dover, 1959).

● A useful summary of nationalism, with appended readings, is given by Hans Kohn, *Nationalism: Its Meaning and History* (Anvil Book, Van Nostrand, 1957). There is a fine collection of essays on various phases of nationalism by several authorities in the paperback by Urban G. Whitaker Jr., *Nationalism and International Progress* (San Francisco: Chandler, 1960).

● On liberalism, a convenient summary and collection of readings are given in J. Salwyn Schapiro, *Liberalism: Its Meaning and History* (Anvil Book, Van Nostrand, 1958). A stimulating analysis of the English, French, and American Revolutions is available in Crane Brinton, *The Anatomy of Revolution* (Vintage paperback, 1957). A famous history of the French Revolution is now available in paperback: Georges Lefebvre, *The Coming of the French Revolution* (Vintage, 1957). Finally on the American Revolution, see Edmund S. Morgan, *The American Revolution: A Review of Changing Interpretations* (Washington: Service Center for Teachers of History, 1958).

● On imperialism, the best descriptive account remains Parker T. Moon, *Imperialism and World Politics* (New York: Macmillan, 1939). See also part 2 of George Alexander Lensen, *The World Beyond Europe* (Boston: Houghton Mifflin, 1960). For works on Europe's impact on the various overseas territories, see the relevant units.

Europe's Decline and Triumph: 1914–

1. Prepare a report on Otto von Bismarck, the German statesman whose foreign policies made Germany a major European power and increased international tension after 1871. Show in what ways Bismarck's program influenced the course of world history.

2. Consult several historians for their explanation of the causes of World War I. Among the many possible sources are Bernadotte E. Schmitt, *The Coming of the War,* 2 vols. (New York: Scribner's, 1930); Sidney B. Fay, *The Origins of the World War,* 2 vols. (New York: Macmillan, 1929); and C. R. M. F. Cruttwell, *A History of the Great War, 1914–1918* (Oxford University Press, 1934). Prepare a summary of the explanations given. Note points of agreement and disagreement and cite supporting evidence given by the authors.

3. Support these statements:

a. "The rigidity of the great alliances forced the leading states into an 'all or nothing' situation in which war, once it came, could not remain an isolated, localized affair."
b. "The First World War is still the great turning point of the 20th century, in spite of all that has happened since."
c. The period following World War I was a time of crisis for democracy and the liberal-democratic principles of Woodrow Wilson.
d. World War I and World War II were alike in that both demonstrated that "warfare had outstripped man's ability to make use of it for his own ends."

4. The Paris Peace Conference, 1919–1920, was the largest and most distinguished assemblage of diplomats and statesmen since the Congress of Vienna (1815). Read in supplementary materials for information on: (a) problems confronting the peace conference; (b) the Big Three; (c) reasons why Wilson's principles given in the Fourteen Points were unacceptable to the Allies; (d) compromises Wilson was induced to make to save the League of Nations; (e) immediate and long-range effects of compromise settlements on Europe and non-European areas involved.

5. Compare the absolutism of the one-party, totalitarian state that developed in Italy, U.S.S.R., and Germany after World War I with the divine-right monarchies of an earlier period. Why did the new kind of absolutism develop in Western Europe and receive support from the people in these countries?

6. Several students might prepare for a discussion or debate on the question: Europe:

Decline or Revival? Their talks should serve to stimulate class discussion of this important question on which historians and observers hold differing views.

7. In Vera M. Dean's *The Nature of the Non-Western World* (Mentor, 1956), read chap. xii, "West and Non-West: The Heart of the Matter," for examples of non-Western peoples stimulated by contact with the West. Then, write a concise explanation concerning how these contacts have greatly influenced the pattern of world organization.

SELECTED READING

● One of the best introductions to the world of the 20th century is Vera M. Dean's *The Nature of the Non-Western World* (Mentor, 1963, rev. ed.). Another important source is the pamphlets published in the Headline Series of the Foreign Policy Association in New York City. Among the many pamphlets in this series are Philip M. Hauser, *World Population Problems* (No. 174, 1965); Lincoln P. Bloomfield, *The UN at Twenty and After* (No. 173, 1965); P. E. Mosely, *The Soviet Union Since Khrushchev* (No. 175, 1966); J. W. Lewis, *Communist China: Crisis and Change* (No. 179, 1966); A. Rivkin, *The New States of Africa* (No. 183, 1967); P. G. Hoffman, *The Rich and the Poor: Economic Development in Perspective* (No. 191, 1968); and M. H. Kerr, *The Middle East* (No. 192, 1968).

● For international relations an excellent source is the series of pamphlets published in the Foreign Relations Series of North Central Association (River Forest, Illinois: Laidlaw), *America's Role in the Middle East; Southeast Asia and American Policy; America's Stake in Western Europe; The United States and World Affairs; Chinese Dilemma; The United States and the Soviet Challenge; The United States and the United Nations; Africa and the World Today;* and *Concepts of International Relations.*

● Another useful pamphlet series, entitled *Background,* is published by the United States Department of State. The pamphlets in the series cover a wide range of topics from individual countries to a discussion of the Berlin problem. A typical example is *Geopolitics and Foreign Relations* (1964). For current problems see *Great Decisions,* prepared annually by the Foreign Policy Association. Eight booklets each year provide a study and discussion program of key international issues. A typical example for 1968 is *The Middle East: What Prospects for Enduring Peace?;* and for 1969 is *Czechoslovakia, Russia, and Eastern Europe: What Outlook for East-West Co-existence?* (Boston: Allyn and Bacon, 1968, 1969, 1970).

FURTHER READING

● For the geographic forces influencing the world during the 20th century, see J. P. Cole, *Geography of World Affairs* (Penguin, 1963). The best interpretative studies are G. Barraclough, *An Introduction to Contemporary History* (Pelican Book, 1967); D. Thomson, *World History from 1914 to 1950* (New York: Oxford University Press, 1954); and the various studies by Barbara Ward, such as *The Interplay of East and West* (New York: Norton, 1957); and *Five Ideas that Changed the World* (New York: Norton, 1959).

● Comprehensive surveys of developments since World War II are provided by H. W. Gatzke, *The Present in Perspective* (Chicago: Rand McNally, 1961, 2nd ed.); G. Bruun and D. E. Lee, *The Second World War and After* (Boston: Houghton Mifflin, 1964); P. Calvocoressi, *International Politics Since 1945* (New York: Praeger, 1968); and G. F. Hudson, *The Hard Bitter Peace* (New York: Praeger, 1967).

● An excellent survey of the colonial revolution is provided by R. Emerson, *From Empire to Nation: The Rise to Self-Assertion of Asian and African Peoples* (Cambridge: Harvard University Press, 1960). Of the numerous studies of global economic imbalance, outstanding are R. L.

Heilbroner, *The Great Ascent* (New York: Harper, 1963); and Barbara Ward, *The Rich Nations and the Poor Nations* (New York: Norton, 1962).

● For the most recent developments, see the periodic publication *Contemporary Civilization* (Chicago: Scott Foresman), each issue consisting of readings and essays on topics of prime concern to the contemporary world.

IMPERIAL WAR MUSEUM

THE III
WORLD'S
MAJOR CULTURE
AREAS

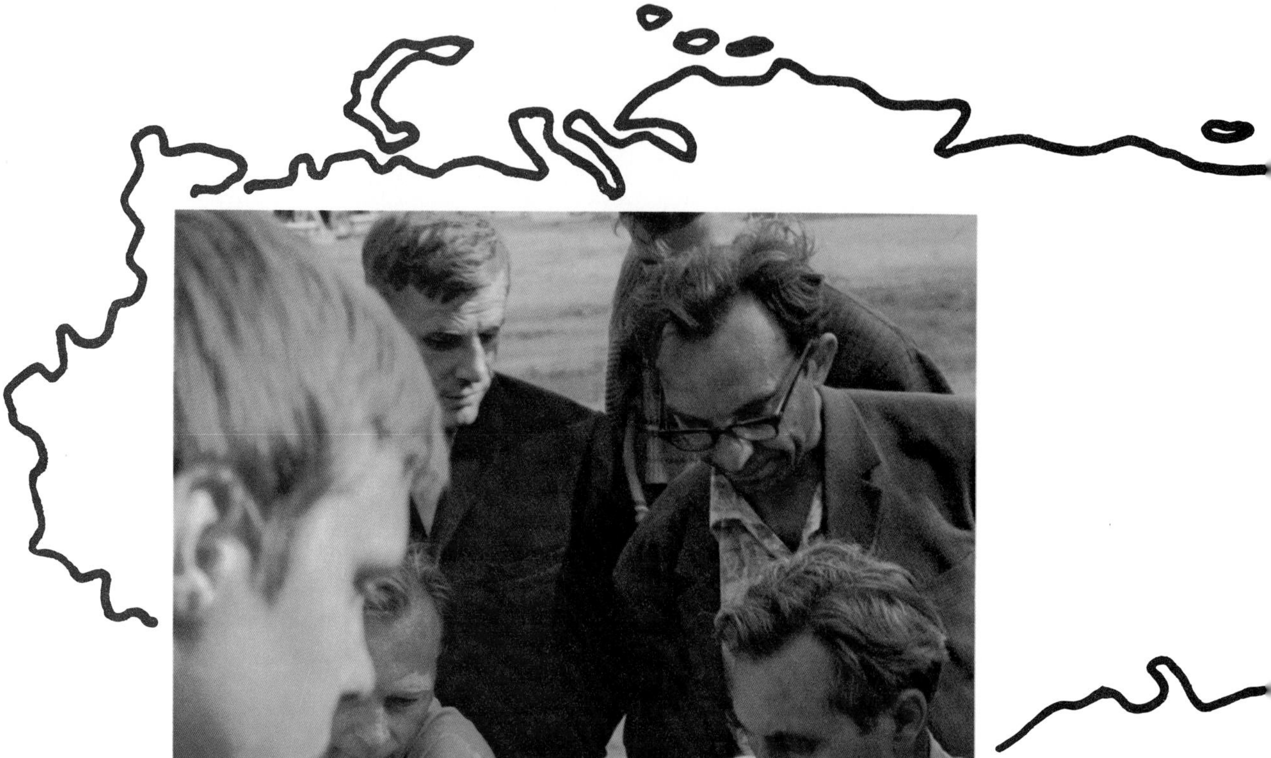

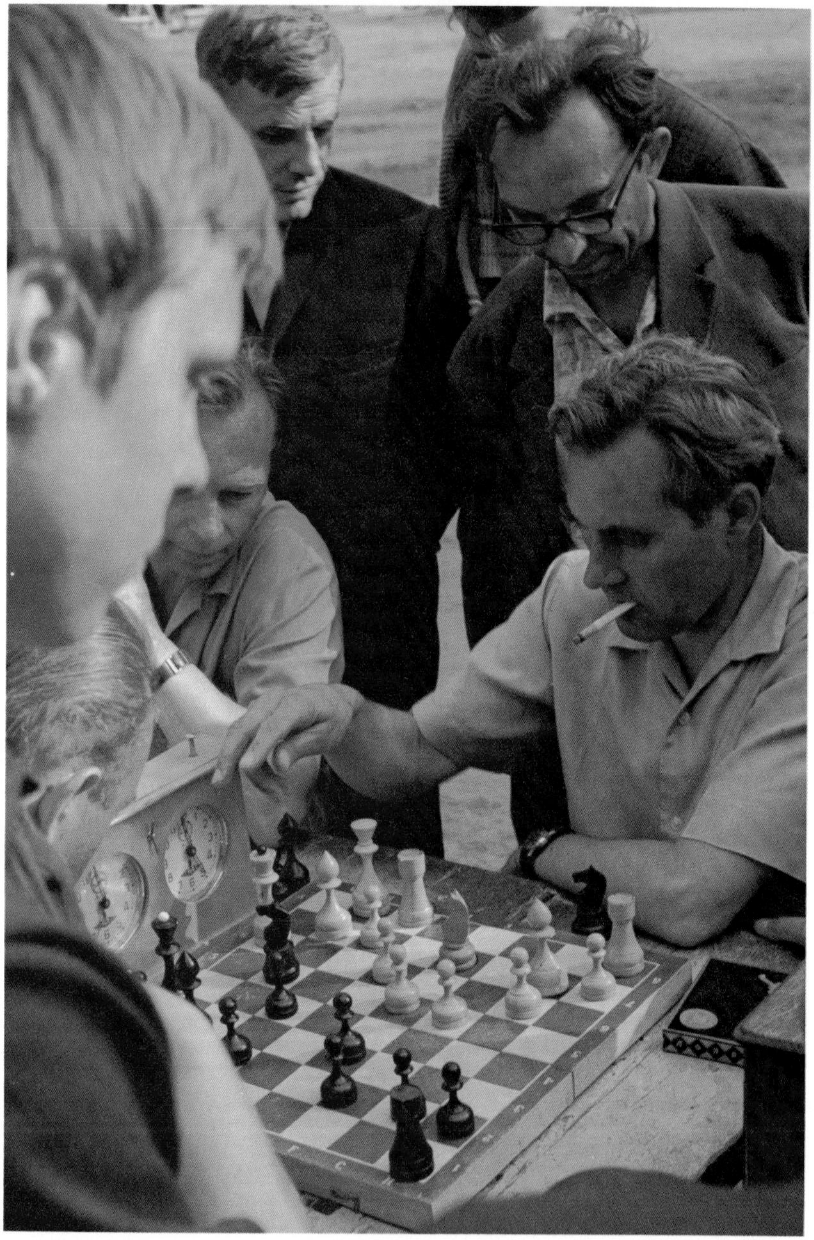

SOVIET UNION

There are...two great nations...which seem to tend toward the same end, although they started from different points: I allude to the Russians and the Americans. ... The American struggles against the natural obstacles...the adversaries of the Russian are men...the conquests of the one are therefore gained by the ploughshare; those of the other by the sword. The Anglo-American relies upon personal interest to accomplish his ends, and gives free scope to the unguided exertions and common sense of the citizens; the Russian centres all the authority of society in a single arm: the principal instrument of the former is freedom; of the latter servitude...each seems to be marked out by the will of Heaven to sway the destinies of half the globe.

Alexis de Tocqueville

BASIC FACTS: The Immensity and Variety of "Mother Russia"

GEOGRAPHY

Area. If you were to travel in the Union of Soviet Socialist Republics (often shortened to the Soviet Union or U.S.S.R.), you would probably be most impressed by the tremendous size of the country.* An old Russian peasant proverb says, "Russia is not a country, it is a world." In fact, the Soviet Union is the largest country in the world, covering one-sixth of the land surface of the globe. It is larger than the United States and Canada combined. The distance across the Soviet Union is about 5400 miles, compared to 3000 miles across the midcontinental United States. During certain seasons of the year, when night is falling at Leningrad near Russia's western frontier, dawn is breaking at the East Cape across from Alaska. As a final point on understanding the immensity of the Soviet Union, remember that many parts of the U.S.S.R. are closer to the United States than they are to the Union's capital, Moscow.

Coastline. Despite its huge size, the Soviet Union has a very short usable coastline. The map shows that the coast along the Arctic Ocean is one of the longest in the world, but much of it is useless because the polar seas are frozen for long periods in the year. The Arctic port of Murmansk on the Barents Sea is the only harbor that is ice-free all year long. All other ports, whether located on the Arctic Ocean, the Baltic Sea, the Black Sea, or the Pacific, are blocked by ice for some period during the year.

Along with the problem of icebound ports, the Soviet Union is faced with the problem of limited access to the open oceans of the

* See *Readings in World History* (Boston: Allyn and Bacon, Inc., 1970), "The Russian Land," p. 202.

world. There are several good Soviet ports on the Baltic Sea, but the narrow straits between Denmark and Norway must be passed before the open sea can be reached. These straits can be easily blocked by a potential enemy.

The same is true regarding the Black Sea where the narrow straits leading to the Mediterranean are controlled by Turkey, although their use is controlled by international convention. Even on the Pacific coast, the approaches to Vladivostok, the only large Siberian port, are blocked to some extent by the main Japanese islands. In summary, the Soviet Union is a large country with a relatively short coastline and hampered by poor access to the open oceans of the world. This should be remembered because it helps to explain why the Russians frequently have fought wars in an attempt to gain warm water ports. Long before the Communists seized power, the Russians fought the Turks several times in the hope of reaching the Mediterranean.

Topography. The most noticeable characteristic of the land of the Soviet Union is its flatness. It is true that there are mountains in the U.S.S.R. Some of them, such as the Pamir and Altai Mountains, are amongst the highest in the world. But the topographical map shows that the Soviet Union's mountains are almost all along her borders: for example, the Caucasus in the southwest, the Pamirs and Altai in the south, and the Stanovoi in the east. Inside the mountain ranges the land is mostly a flat plain. The Ural Mountains run north and south down the center, but they matter little because they are low and easily crossed.

Only in the extreme south, in the area of the Crimean, does the Soviet Union have a continually mild climate. Thus this area has become a vacation center for people throughout the Soviet Union.

Climate. The climate of the great plains of the U.S.S.R. is classified as continental, that is, a climate with long, cold winters and short, hot summers. The winters are long because almost all of the Soviet Union is located north of the latitude of Chicago. Heavy snows come early and stay for long periods of time, while cold, piercing winds sweep unhindered over the frozen plains. To protect themselves, the people wear heavy fur jackets and caps and thick sheepskin boots. They remain indoors during most of the winter and heat their houses with woodburning stoves. The only exceptions to this severe continental climate are to be found in the desert areas of Central Asia and in a few spots along the Black Sea where a mediterranean type of climate prevails. This explains why the Black Sea coast is the great vacation area of the Soviet Union.

Since the plains are surrounded by mountains, the winds from the oceans lose much of their moisture before they reach the interior of the Soviet Union. The winds from the Pacific, for example, drop a good deal of their moisture when they hit the maritime ranges of Siberia. The winds from the Indian Ocean lose all of their moisture when they rise over the lofty Pamirs. Only in the west is the Soviet Union open to rain-producing winds from the Atlantic. But these winds are not strong enough to spread over all the plains. That is why many parts of the Soviet Union suffer from shortage of rain. The driest are the desert areas north of the high mountain barriers between India and Central Asia, where nothing can be grown except with the help of irrigation. Many other regions are semiarid, which means that in some years there is enough rain for crops but in other years there is drought which kills off the crops. Only in the extreme western part, near the Black and Baltic Seas, can farmers be fairly sure of getting sufficient rainfall, as do the farmers of Illinois and Iowa.

The Soviet Union, then, has a smaller proportion of land suitable for agriculture than has the United States. If there were a mountain range as high as the Pamirs stretching along the Gulf of Mexico, then we would

Basic Facts 227

U.S.S.R. ~ CLIMATE

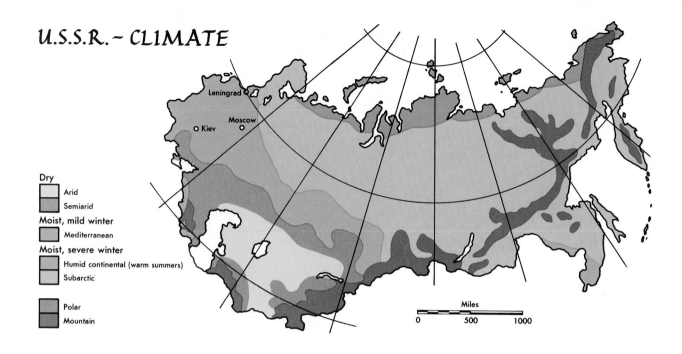

Dry
- Arid
- Semiarid

Moist, mild winter
- Mediterranean

Moist, severe winter
- Humid continental (warm summers)
- Subarctic

- Polar
- Mountain

Miles
0   500   1000

have the same difficulty as the Soviets. The warm, moisture-laden winds from the Gulf of Mexico would not be able to sweep north and bring rain to our southern and mid-western states. Instead all the rain would fall along this imaginary coastal range, and the central part of the United States would be desert or simiarid rather than the fertile granary that it is now.

Vegetation zones. The climate of the Soviet Union has produced four main vegetation zones. In the far north, along the arctic shore, is the tundra, frozen all year round, except for a short, six-to-eight week growing period. The natives of this region depend on the reindeer for transportation, and hunt the sable, fox, marten, and other fur-bearing animals.

South of the tundra is the great coniferous forest zone called the taiga, which contains no less than one-fifth of the forest area of the world. It was in these forests that the early

Russians made their home. There they hunted animals, collected honey and wax, and carried on a primitive type of agriculture, as did our own frontiersmen. They used the timber from the forests in many ways: to build cabins, make furniture, provide fuel, fashion plows and other tools, and carve fine objects of art.

Below the forests lies the open, grassy, steppe zone. Here we find the fertile black earth formed by millenniums of decayed grass. For many centuries the open steppe was the highway along which Asiatic nomads galloped out of Central Asia and invaded Russia and the rest of Europe. During those centuries the Russians found refuge in the deep forests where the nomads on their horses could not follow. Today the steppe country is the Soviet Union's main agricultural area. The famous black earth is extremely fertile and produces rich crops if there is enough rain. In the southern and eastern parts of the steppe, the rainfall steadily decreases until finally the steppe becomes desert.

The desert zone in the far south extends from China across Central Asia to the Caspian Sea. The Russians did not feel at home in the deserts of Central Asia, just as our own frontiersmen did not feel at home in the deserts of southwestern United States. For this reason the Russians did not conquer Central Asia until the late 19th century, whereas they won huge areas farther north centuries earlier. Today great irrigation projects are being completed in the desert regions. Cotton, fruits, and vegetables are growing in the former wastes of Central Asia, as they also are now growing in Arizona, New Mexico, and eastern California.

Rivers. Since the U.S.S.R. is largely a plains country, most of its rivers are long, wide, slow-moving, and without rapids. These qualities make them useful, in contrast to the short and swift rivers of mountainous countries such as Norway and Greece. The Russians have used their rivers in various ways: to conquer new lands, to colonize open territories, and to carry on trade. In the summer they go up and down their rivers in boats; in the winter they skim over the ice in sleds drawn by horses.

In the part of the country west of the Ural Mountains, the rivers flow in three directions, north to the Arctic, west to the Baltic, and south to the Black and Caspian Seas. The northern rivers are of little importance be-

The Yenisei River at Tura, U.S.S.R.

229

cause they flow into arms of the Arctic Ocean which are frozen for most of the year. The other rivers, as we shall see, have played important roles in Russian history. The chief of these are the Dvina and the Neva emptying into the Baltic, the Dnieper into the Black Sea, and the Volga into the Caspian. The largest of these is the Volga, which flows through the heart of the Soviet Union and in many respects resembles our Mississippi.

In Siberia, the vast territory to the east of the Ural Mountains, there are some of the longest rivers in the world. We rarely hear of them because they flow north to the Arctic Ocean and have been little used. The only exception is the Amur (1780 miles), which winds its way eastward to the Pacific. Three of the Arctic rivers are worth noting. From west to east they are the Ob (2500 miles), the Yenisei (2800 miles), and the Lena (3000 miles). These rivers, with the exception of the Amur, are longer than the mainstream of the Mississippi (2470 miles) although the Mississippi-Missouri is much longer.

Resources. During the tsarist period, before the Communists seized power in 1917, it was known that Russia was rich in natural resources. But no one knew exactly how rich, because most of the country had not been surveyed. Once in power the Soviet government sent out prospecting parties to all regions of the Soviet Union. They have discovered so many mineral deposits that the Soviets now claim that their country is first in the world in many mineral resources. For example, resources of iron ore were estimated in 1917 to be 2 billion tons, but by 1960 over 35 billion tons had been located, according to Soviet claims. Before 1917 the only oil fields in Russia were located in the Caucasus, but under the Soviet regime additional rich oil fields have been discovered in seven widely scattered regions. Similarly, large

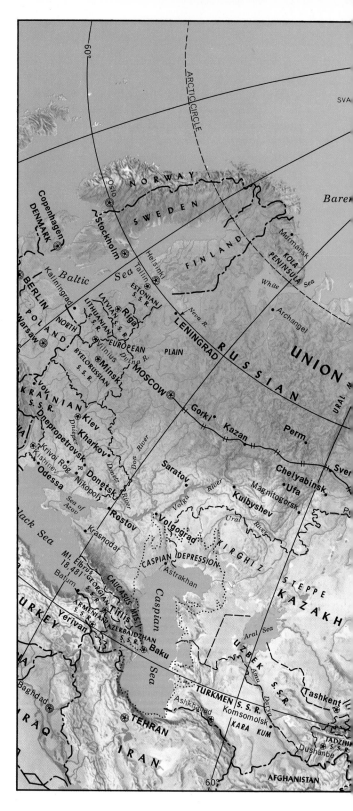

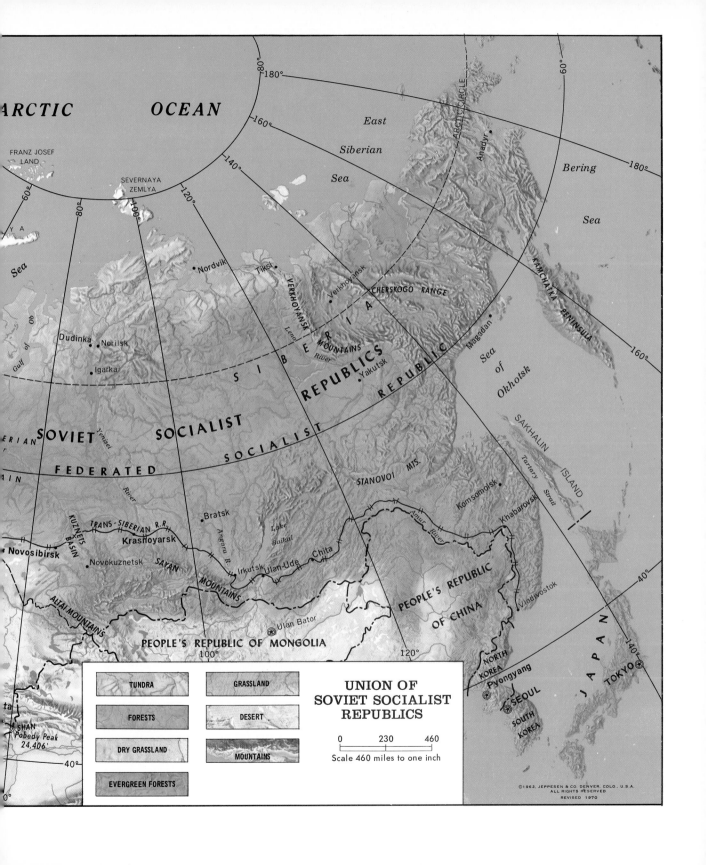

ARCTIC OCEAN

FRANZ JOSEF LAND

SEVERNAYA ZEMLYA

East Siberian Sea

Bering Sea

ARCTIC CIRCLE

KAMCHATKA PENINSULA

Anadyr

Nordvik   Tiksi

Verkhoyansk

CHERSKOGO RANGE

VERKHOYANSK

Sea

Y A

Sea

Gulf of Ob

Dudinka   Norilsk

Igarka

Lena River

MOUNTAINS

S I B E R I A

REPUBLICS   REPUBLIC

Yakutsk

Magadan

Sea of Okhotsk

SAKHALIN ISLAND

SOVIET   SOCIALIST

Yenisei

SOCIALIST

FEDERATED

SOCIALIST

STANOVOI MTS.

Komsomolsk

Tartary Strait

River

KUZNETS BASIN

TRANS-SIBERIAN R.R.

Bratsk

Krasnoyarsk

Angara R.

Lake Baikal

Amur River

Khabarovsk

Novosibirsk

Novokuznetsk

SAYAN

MOUNTAINS

Irkutsk Ulan-Ude

Chita

PEOPLE'S REPUBLIC

OF CHINA

Vladivostok

ALTAI MOUNTAINS

Ulan Bator

PEOPLE'S REPUBLIC OF MONGOLIA

JAPAN

ta

SHAN

Pobedy Peak
24,406'

NORTH KOREA

Pyongyang

TOKYO

SEOUL

SOUTH KOREA

TUNDRA	GRASSLAND	
FORESTS	DESERT	
DRY GRASSLAND	MOUNTAINS	
EVERGREEN FORESTS		

UNION OF
SOVIET SOCIALIST
REPUBLICS

0   230   460

Scale 460 miles to one inch

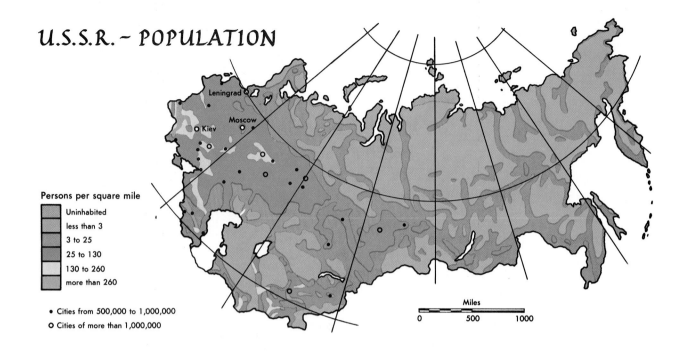

U.S.S.R. - POPULATION

Persons per square mile

Uninhabited
less than 3
3 to 25
25 to 130
130 to 260
more than 260

● Cities from 500,000 to 1,000,000
○ Cities of more than 1,000,000

Miles
0   500   1000

deposits of numerous other resources have been found. At present the Soviet government is claiming that the U.S.S.R. possesses the world's largest reserves of coal, iron, manganese, copper, lead, zinc, nickel, bauxite, tungsten, and mercury. It is not certain to what extent these boasts are justified, but there is no doubt that the Soviet Union is very well supplied with natural resources. It is important to remember that these resources have made it possible for the Soviet Union to become a great industrial power. And in the world of today, industrial power also means military power.

PEOPLE

The Soviet Union is today a great power, not only because of its vast natural resources but also because of its large population. The first country in the world in area, it is the third in the world in population. Only China and India have larger populations than the Soviet Union. In mid-1968 the Soviet people numbered 238 million, compared to 202 million in the United States.

The Soviet republics. The average person assumes that all the citizens of the Soviet Union are Russians, but this is not the case at all. No less than 169 different ethnic groups live within the Soviet frontiers. This is true also of the United States, where we find living side by side people named Smith (English), Romano (Italian), Novak (Czech), Murphy (Irish), Erickson (Swedish), Polavsky (Polish), Petrich (Yugoslav), Pappas (Greek), and Takahashi (Japanese).

Although the Soviet Union and the United States both have many ethnic strains, there is one big difference between them. In the United States all the ethnic groups live together. In your classroom and in your neighborhood you will find not only Irish or Italians or Poles, but all these, and many more. The reason may be found in the fact

A child wearing the traditional dress of Bukhara, and a young boy of Mongol extraction from Kirghiz, illustrate the mosaic of ethnic groups which make up the U.S.S.R.

that all our ancestors, who came from many countries in Europe, Africa, and Asia, settled together in various parts of our country and became thoroughly mixed. That is the reason why the United States is often called a melting pot of peoples.

In the Soviet Union there has been less melting or mixing. Instead one people, the Great Russians, spread out, conquered dozens of surrounding peoples, and combined them forcefully into a great empire. But the conquered peoples did not become Russians. They remained what they were; they kept their languages and their customs. So the Soviet Union today is like a mosaic rather than like a melting pot. The various ethnic groups of the Soviet Union have not been melted together; rather they have been welded together, while keeping many of their national characteristics.

This historical development of the Soviet Union helps to explain why it is called the U.S.S.R., or Union of Soviet Socialist Republics. It is, in fact, a union of 15 republics, each including a major ethnic group. The United States, of course, also is a union of many states, but these states are simply convenient divisions of land. By contrast, the Soviet republics are based on ethnic groups, or nationalities, as the Soviets call them. It would not have been practical to set up a separate republic for each of the 169 ethnic groups in the Soviet Union. Instead the 15 major groups each have a republic, and, within each republic, several minor ethnic groups as well as the major one can be found.

Basic Facts 233

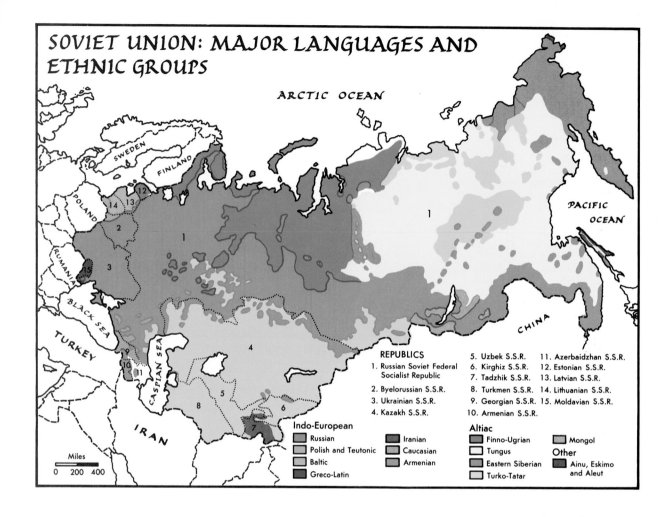

SOVIET UNION: MAJOR LANGUAGES AND ETHNIC GROUPS

ARCTIC OCEAN

PACIFIC OCEAN

SWEDEN

FINLAND

POLAND

RUMANIA

BLACK SEA

TURKEY

CASPIAN SEA

IRAN

CHINA

Miles
0   200   400

REPUBLICS

1. Russian Soviet Federal Socialist Republic
2. Byelorussian S.S.R.
3. Ukrainian S.S.R.
4. Kazakh S.S.R.

5. Uzbek S.S.R.
6. Kirghiz S.S.R.
7. Tadzhik S.S.R.
8. Turkmen S.S.R.
9. Georgian S.S.R.
10. Armenian S.S.R.

11. Azerbaidzhan S.S.R.
12. Estonian S.S.R.
13. Latvian S.S.R.
14. Lithuanian S.S.R.
15. Moldavian S.S.R.

Indo-European
Russian
Polish and Teutonic
Baltic
Greco-Latin
Iranian
Caucasian
Armenian

Altiac
Finno-Ugrian
Tungus
Eastern Siberian
Turko-Tatar
Mongol

Other
Ainu, Eskimo and Aleut

The drift to the cities. Finally, we should note that an ever-increasing percentage of the population of the Soviet Union, as in the United States, is living in cities rather than in the countryside. The explanation in both cases is the growth of industry. In 1897 only 15 per cent of Russia's people were in cities. By 1913 there were 18 per cent, by 1939, 33 per cent, and by 1960, 50 per cent. By contrast, the United States, which is more highly industrialized, has over 70 per cent of its population in cities. In the Soviet Union now, people are drifting to the big cities in increasing numbers; as members of the various nationalities come together, differences begin to disappear under the impact of mass urban culture. This "homogenizing" process will be discussed more fully in the section on culture.*

HISTORICAL PERIODS

The Russian civilization is very young compared to the ancient civilizations of

* See *Readings in World History*, "The Russian People," p. 208.

China, India, the Middle East, and Europe. Consequently, we cannot divide Russian history into the familiar ancient, classical, medieval, and modern periods, as we do the histories of the other regions. Instead we shall use as divisions the five periods in which five cities were the capitals of the country. The cities and the periods are: (a) Kiev, 878–1237; (b) Sarai, 1237–1472; (c) Moscow, 1472–1703; (d) St. Petersburg, 1703–1917; (e) Moscow, 1917 to the present.

Kiev, 878–1237. This was the period when the first Russian state was organized around Kiev on the Dnieper River. The Russians were an eastern Slavic people who long before had spread out from their place of origin in the Pripet Marshes in present-day Byelorussia. They pushed northeast toward the Arctic, east toward the Volga, and southeast toward the Black Sea. Like our own frontiersmen, they earned their living by hunting, fishing, primitive farming, and some trading along the rivers. They were not politically united but instead were divided among a number of separate tribes who were ruled by local leaders.

All this changed with the appearance from the north of the Vikings, sometimes called the Varangians, or *Rus*. It was from this word that *Russia* was derived. Using the principal river and lake routes from the Baltic, the Varangians penetrated among the east Slavic peoples and slowly established political control over them. A semihistoric or legendary chieftain, Rurik is thought to be the first to organize the east Slavs into small principalities. This occurred sometime about 860 or shortly after. Although historical evidence about this period is fragmentary, Rurik is frequently referred to as the founder of the Kievan state. A Varangian chieftain named Oleg ruled Kiev about 878, and under his rule Kiev became the center of the first unified Russian state.

The Kievan state remained in existence for over four centuries, and during that time the Russians carried on a flourishing trade with the nearby Greek Byzantine Empire. It was only natural that in the course of this trade the Russians learned and borrowed a good deal from the more advanced Greeks. We noted earlier that they borrowed their alphabet, which is mainly Greek and still in use. They accepted the Greek Orthodox religion, which, as we shall see, still remains the religion of many Russians. They borrowed, finally, various arts, such as church architecture, icon painting, and church music.

Sarai, 1237–1472. The Kievan period of Russian history came to an end when the Mongols conquered Kiev in 1237. For the next two and a half centuries, the Mongols ruled Russia from their capital at Sarai on the Volga River near present-day Volgograd. This period of Russian history is important for two reasons. In the first place, the domination of the Mongols restricted the Russians so that they fell far behind the Western Europeans in their development. During these years the Western Europeans were in the midst of the Renaissance and rapidly forging ahead in all the arts and sciences. But the Russians could not keep in touch with these advances because they were behind the iron curtain of Mongol rule. The Mongol conquest cut them off from contact with Greek Byzantine influences from the south, while the heathen Finns and Lithuanians and the Roman Catholic Poles, opposed to Orthodoxy, cut off Western influences. The Russians stood still, while the West was developing science and an advanced economic system and preparing for its great expansion overseas.

The other important development during the Mongol period was the rise of a new Russian center at Moscow. The old center

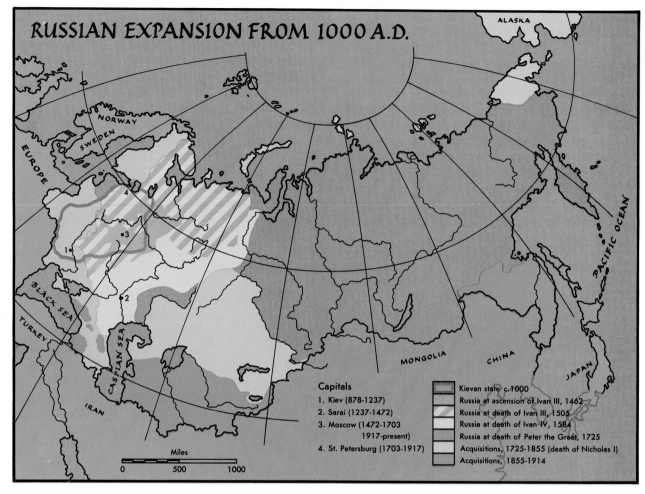

RUSSIAN EXPANSION FROM 1000 A.D.

Capitals
1. Kiev (878-1237)
2. Sarai (1237-1472)
3. Moscow (1472-1703
          1917-present)
4. St. Petersburg (1703-1917)

Kievan state c. 1000
Russia at ascension of Ivan III, 1462
Russia at death of Ivan III, 1505
Russia at death of Ivan IV, 1584
Russia at death of Peter the Great, 1725
Acquisitions, 1725-1855 (death of Nicholas I)
Acquisitions, 1855-1914

Miles
0   500   1000

---

at Kiev was located in the treeless steppe country, exposed to raids by Mongol horsemen. Moscow was much further north in the forest zone, a difficult region for the Mongols to penetrate. Furthermore, the rulers of Moscow were able, hard-working, and thrifty. Like all Russian leaders, they were forced to pay tribute each year to the Mongol khan. The Russian princes met the payments, built up their strength, and bided their time. Finally in 1472 a ruler named Ivan III refused to pay tribute any longer. The Mongols sent their army up to the Oka River near Moscow. Ivan drew up his army

on the other side of the Oka. His forces were so strong that the Mongols dared not cross the river and instead turned back. Their retreat was the beginning of the end of Mongol rule, and a powerful Russian state gradually developed with Moscow as its capital.

Moscow, 1472–1703. During this third period, Russia developed some of the basic characteristics which have lasted to the present day. The outstanding ruler was Ivan IV, who is commonly known as Ivan the Terrible because he did not hesitate to kill thousands of nobles, including his own son, in order to make himself the absolute ruler of Russia. Ivan IV established the autocratic form of government that has continued in Russia to the present.

Another important development during this period was that the peasants lost all their rights and became mere serfs. Henceforth they could not move from the village in which they were born. They had to work the land of the nobles, receiving only enough to keep body and soul together. The great majority of the Russian people lived as serfs until their liberation in the mid-19th century.*

The third important event during these years was the beginning of the great Russian Empire. Ivan conquered the remaining Mongols in the Volga Valley,† and cleared the way for Russian expansion over the Ural Mountains into Asiatic Russia, or Siberia. A Russian frontiersman named Yermak crossed

* See *Readings in World History,* "Nobles and Serfs in Tsarist Russia," p. 218.
† See *Readings in World History,* "Ivan the Terrible Conquers the Mongols," p. 213.

the Urals in 1581. By 1637 the Russians had reached the Pacific Ocean, thus winning a great empire stretching five thousand miles across Eurasia. Later, in the 19th century, the Russians completed their empire by turning southward and conquering the desert territories of Central Asia.

St. Petersburg, 1703–1917. The outstanding characteristic of this period is that Russia was greatly changed by the influence of the West. This era began when Tsar Peter the Great moved his capital from Moscow to the coastal city which he founded on the Baltic. Peter made this move because, as he said, he wanted "a window to the West." That is, he wanted to open the way for Western ideas and techniques to come into his country. Peter was determined that backward Russia should catch up to the West, and he spent his time and his great energy to that purpose.* We shall see later in this unit that Peter had

* See *Readings in World History,* "Peter the Great Westernizes Russia," p. 215.

Ivan III (lower left) consolidated the independence of Russia, and Ivan IV (center), its autocratic nature.

Peter the Great (right), employing harsh and unscrupulous methods, made Russia a powerful force in modern Europe.

SOVFOTO

237

a good deal of success in forcing his people to drop their old habits and adopt new ones from the West. We shall also see that this Western influence continued and even increased after Peter's reign. Western ideas such as liberalism and Marxism came into the country. Western money poured in and helped to open mines and to build railways and factories. This in turn led to the rise of new classes and of political parties that were dissatisfied with the autocratic tsarist regime dating back to Ivan IV. This discontent steadily increased during the 19th century until finally the Bolsheviks were able in 1917 to seize power and to establish the Soviet government.

Moscow, 1917 to the present. One of the first things the Bolsheviks did was to move the capital from St. Petersburg back to Moscow. They felt safer in the interior of the country than on the western border where the threat of counterrevolution and foreign intervention was strongest. The Bolsheviks then proceeded to establish an entirely new type of society. They changed the name of the country from Russia to Union of Soviet Socialist Republics, or U.S.S.R. We shall see that they changed much more: the political system, economic organization, religious beliefs, literature, art, and education.

Probably this period since 1917 has seen more deep and far-reaching changes than did

Modern Soviet soldiers of the current regime present a sharp contrast to St. Basil's Church in the background which dates from the earlier "Moscow" period.

any of the four earlier periods. It is true that certain aspects of Russian culture remain the same as in the Kievan period. But it is also true that the new Soviet leaders have forced the people to change their ways of living and thinking more than at any time in the past.

Comparison with United States history. From this brief summary we can see striking similarities and differences between Russian and American history. Perhaps the most important single experience that both peoples have in common is that of the frontier. Both the Russian and American people have faced a vast untamed wilderness. Generation after generation of American and Russian frontiersmen fought the wilderness with rifle and axe and plow. In doing so, both have developed certain common characteristics. Both tend to be more interested in material things than in cultural refinements. Both are likely to be rough and ready, with little patience for traditions that may stand in the way of getting things done. Both are usually direct, forthright, outspoken, and energetic. An American authority on the Soviet Union has written: "In many ways, the Soviets resemble the Americans more than any other people. Like Americans, they are eager to ask questions and learn new things; they are not afraid to make mistakes; they have an attitude of breezy but not annoying self-confidence, born of the knowledge that they have vast spaces and great material resources at their disposal; and they adjust themselves readily to new and entirely untried conditions." [1]

Looking at the other side of the coin, we find that the most important single difference between American and Soviet citizens is in their relations with their governments. Throughout American history the individual has been all-important; throughout Russian history the government instead has counted most. We Americans have always controlled

AREA COMPARISON U.S. ~ U.S.S.R.

Miles
0   1000   2000

our government to suit our needs. As Lincoln put it, we have government "of the people, by the people, for the people."

In Russia, however, a government of this type has never existed. During the centuries of tsarist rule, no political parties were allowed. The tsar was called the "Little Father," and all Russians were his children and were expected to obey him. The Bolshevik Revolution established a Communist dictatorship and it has now been in power since 1917. Therefore, we are now at a sufficient distance to form some judgment of its performance. The Revolution did not bring any political freedom, despite its slogans and promises. In place of the Little White Father came the Communist Party. We shall see later how this Party rules the Soviet people as autocratically as any tsar. It decides what the children shall learn in school, what the people shall read in their newspapers, what they shall hear on the radio, what they shall see on television, what wages they will receive for their work, and what goods they will be able to buy with their wages. In short, the average American thinks of government and people as one and the same thing; the average Soviet thinks of government as something above the people and their master. This basic difference arises from the different historical experiences of the two people.

Reviewing the Essentials

Geography

1. Compare and contrast the Soviet Union and the United States in respect to: (a) size; (b) distance from east to west; (c) distance from north to south; (d) coastline; (e) topography; (f) climate.

2. How has the fact that the Soviet Union has a very short usable coastline affected Russian history?

3. Why is a smaller proportion of the Soviet Union than of the United States suitable for agriculture?

4. Name, locate, and describe the characteristics of the four main vegetation zones in the U.S.S.R.

5. Name and locate the Soviet Union's major rivers. How have they influenced the country's development?

6. What are the Soviet Union's most important natural resources? Why are these resources particularly important to the Soviet Union in the mid-20th century?

People

7. What is the present population of the Soviet Union? Compare with the populations of China, India, and the United States.

8. How many ethnic groups live in the Soviet Union? Name and locate the fifteen major ethnic groups. Point out important differences between these groups in the Soviet Union and in the United States, comparing their influence on the development of each nation.

9. What percentage of the Soviet Union's population today is (a) urban and (b) rural? Compare with the United States.

Historical Periods

10. Name the periods into which Russian history is divided. Why are these divisions used rather than the usual designations of classical, medieval, and modern?

11. What events influenced Russia's development and culture during the Kievan period? When did this period end? Under what circumstances?

12. Why is the Mongol rule of the Sarai period important? What event marks the beginning of the end of Mongol rule?

13. During the Moscow period, 1472–1703, Russia developed certain basic characteristics that have continued to the present. What are they?

14. In what ways was Russia influenced by the West during the St. Petersburg period?

15. What changes came to the Soviet Union during the second Moscow period?

16. What characteristics common to Americans and Soviets can be attributed to the influence of the frontier? What are basic differences between the two peoples?

Explain, Identify, or Locate

878	Ivan IV	Vladivostok	Altais
steppe	Peter the Great	Volgograd	Arctic Ocean
taiga	Catherine the Great	Moscow	Baltic Sea
tundra	Alexander I	Ukraine	Black Sea
Rurik	Murmansk	Caucasus	1637
Ivan III	Kiev	Urals	1917
1237	Leningrad	Pamirs	

POLITICS: The State That Refuses to Wither Away

PRESENT STATE

On the surface, the political system of the Soviet Union resembles that of the United States. Both countries have constitutions. Both have periodic elections in which the people vote for two houses. In the United States they are the House of Representatives and the Senate; in Russia they are the Soviet of the Union and the Soviet of Nationalities. In both countries there are supreme courts that interpret the law, judges who enforce the law, and police who keep order.

But if we look underneath the surface we find the two political systems not at all similar to each other. The chief difference is that there is only one political party in Russia. Its official title is the Communist Party of the Soviet Union. This party completely controls the country and the people. Someone has said: "There can be several parties in the Soviet Union, but on the sole condition that one is in power and the others in jail."

Elections Soviet-style. Exactly how does this one-party system work at election time?[*] In the first place, every effort is made to get every Soviet citizen to vote. The press, the radio, television, street meetings, and parades are all used to get the voters out. Failure to show up at the polling station is regarded as unpatriotic and almost as treasonable. It is not surprising, therefore, that in the 1958 elections, 99.97 per cent of the 134 million voters cast ballots.

When the citizen reaches the voting place, he is handed a ballot on which there is only one name, that of the official candidate. The ballot needs no "X." It can be put as printed in a box that is out in the open. If this is done,

[*] See *Readings in World History,* "A Soviet Election," p. 230.

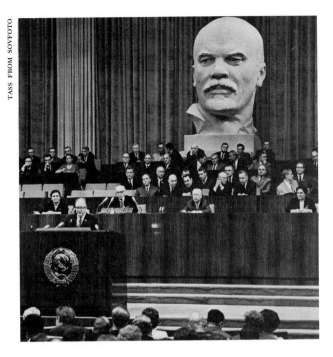

A bust of Lenin dominates the chambers of, and perhaps inspires, the presidium of the Supreme Soviet of the Soviet Union.

it means a vote for the official candidate. Since almost all the voters use the box in plain view, it takes a brave man to step into the secret polling booth that is nearby. The assumption is that anyone who does so intends to cross out the name of the official candidate and write in another. So we find that of the nearly 134 million who voted in 1958, only half a million failed to vote for the official candidates.

Not all the official candidates on the ballots are Communist Party members. In fact, the official name for the list of candidates is the "Bloc of Communist and non-Party People." Nevertheless the great majority of the candidates are Communists, and those who are not have been either selected or approved by the Communists. Indeed the Soviet Premier, Nikita Khrushchev, declared during the 1958 elections that, "the Communist Party organization plays a major role in selecting candidates" and that all nominations were made by "reliable persons." [2]

The Communist Party. How is the Communist Party able to control not only the elections but also almost everything else that happens in the Soviet Union? Surprisingly enough, the Party is not particularly large. It does not include all Soviet citizens, or even a majority of them. In 1968 it had about 12.5 million members, or less than 5 per cent of the total population. In addition there were about 30 million young people enrolled in the Communist Youth organizations.

Despite its small size, it is the Communist Party that really rules the U.S.S.R. The Party includes many of the most able, energetic, and ambitious people of the country; one must belong to the Party to rise to the top. This attracts many opportunists as well as those devoted to the ideology. But whatever the motive in joining, the Party member must work hard and efficiently, or else be expelled. In fact, there are periodic housecleanings when the Party throws out thousands of what are called "radish Communists," that is, Communists who are red outside and white inside. In this way, the Party is kept small deliberately, in order to be sure of a hard-working and completely dependable membership.

A second reason for the Party's success in controlling the Soviet Union is its discipline and unity in following a common "Party line." This line is determined by the top leaders, and all members are expected to support it or be expelled. This means that every Party member is saying the same thing and

working for the same thing, whether it has to do with Soviet policy towards the West, the lack of housing, or the working conditions in the local factory. The fact that all Communists are always supporting a common "line" makes them much more effective than if they were acting independently of each other and at cross purposes.

The Party controls the state. Perhaps the most important reason for the Party's grip on the Soviet Union is that its members occupy the key positions in the armed forces, police, courts, bureaucracy, and educational institutions. We have seen that the majority of the delegates who are elected to the Soviet of the Union and the Soviet of Nationalities (which together are known as the Supreme Soviet of the U.S.S.R.) are Communists. These Communists naturally elect only Communists to the Presidium of the Supreme Soviet which acts for the Supreme Soviet when the latter is not in session, and to the Council of Ministers which is the executive organ of government, comparable to our cabinet. This means that many of the same Communist leaders are in the Presidium and the Council of Ministers as are in the top Communist Party bodies, the Central Committee, and Presidium. In the chart of the Soviet Government and Communist Party we see that these two Communist bodies are elected by the All-Union Party Congress, which in turn is elected by Communist Party members throughout the Soviet Union.

The chart shows that the government and the Party are two parallel organizations in the Soviet Union. The government theoretically and officially runs the country. But the government is completely controlled by the Party, because the top Communists hold key posts in the government as well as in their Party. So the real center of power in the present-day Soviet Union is the Presidium

USSR

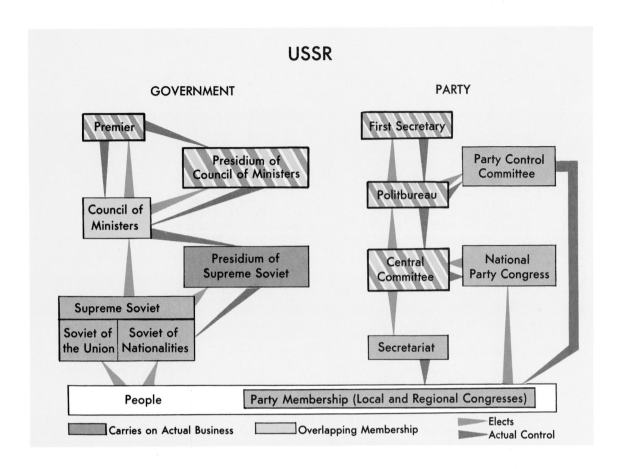

GOVERNMENT

Premier

Presidium of Council of Ministers

Council of Ministers

Presidium of Supreme Soviet

Supreme Soviet

Soviet of the Union | Soviet of Nationalities

PARTY

First Secretary

Party Control Committee

Politbureau

Central Committee

National Party Congress

Secretariat

People

Party Membership (Local and Regional Congresses)

Carries on Actual Business   Overlapping Membership   Elects   Actual Control

of the Central Committee of the Party. For example, if there is a question whether more or less housing should be built, it is the Party Presidium that first discusses the matter and reaches a decision. Only then will the Council of Ministers or the Presidium of the Supreme Soviet, both of which are headed by these same Communist leaders, issue official government decrees for carrying out the housing decision.

We may conclude that although the elected Supreme Soviet is, theoretically, the source of all power in the Soviet Union, actually it is merely a "rubber-stamp" body. It meets for only a few weeks each year and approves automatically the proposals that are set before it. The Supreme Soviet cannot propose and pass its own laws, as do legislative bodies in the West. All this means that the Soviet people do not really govern themselves. There is no democracy in the Soviet Union, as we understand democracy. If any citizens tried to change their present leaders or the system, they would be labelled traitors and clapped into prison, or worse.

On the other hand, the Soviet citizens are encouraged to complain if the manager in their factory is inefficient, if their clothes are poorly made, or if there is too much red tape in a government office. Soviet newspapers publish thousands of "Letters to the Editor" filled with complaints on all sorts of subjects.

"Loggers Union Committee Report: 'Today in our new clubhouse a festival concert took place.'"

They also publish cartoons, such as that shown here, which point up defects in all aspects of Soviet society. In other words, the people are allowed and urged to criticize how the Soviet socialist system works, but they are absolutely forbidden to suggest scrapping the system and trying another. They are free to criticize a factory manager or a store clerk, but they cannot say a word against the Party leaders who run the country.

HISTORICAL ORIGINS

We have seen that the Soviet Union today has an authoritarian government in which a few Communist leaders make all the decisions. This type of government is not something new for the Soviet people. They have lived under authoritarian rule from the time of the rise of the Moscow state in the 15th century to the present day. This is a major difference between the Soviet Union and Western Europe where democratic governments developed in modern times.

There are at least three reasons for this long history of authoritarian government in Russia. One is the traditional alliance between the Orthodox Church and the tsarist government; the second is the lack of a middle class; the third is the presence, real or imaginary, of foreign danger.

The Church, an arm of the tsar. The alliance between church and state began in Russia about one thousand years ago when Orthodox Christianity was adopted by the Russian people. In contrast to the churches in Western Europe, most of which remained independent of their states, the Russian Orthodox Church was from the beginning closely connected with the tsarist regime. The Church received financial support from the state, and also was aided in missionary efforts to win the various peoples of Russia to the Orthodox faith. In return the Church officials

urged the people to be loyal at all times to the government. In fact, the 1832 Imperial Code of Laws specifically required the parish priest to "warn his parishioners against false and dangerous rumors, to strengthen them in good morals and in submission to their masters, and to try by all means to prevent the disturbances of the peasants." The priest faithfully obeyed this order in his sermons in church and in his teachings in school. For example, the Church prepared in 1895 a catechism for school use which read as follows: [3]

Question: What says the Fifth Commandment?
Answer: Honor thy father and thy mother.
Question: Should we honor only our parents?
Answer: Besides our parents, we should respect all those who in any way fill their places for us.
Question: Whom, then, should we honor?
Answer: 1. First and most of all, the Tsar.
  2. Pastors and spiritual teachers.
  3. Kindly persons, our superiors and teachers.
  4. Our elders.
Question: Why should we especially respect the Tsar above all others?
Answer: Because he is the father of the whole people and the anointed of God.
Question: How should we show our respect for the Tsar?
Answer: 1. We should feel complete loyalty to the Tsar and be prepared to lay down our lives for him.
  2. We should without objection fulfill his commands and be obedient to the authorities appointed by him.
  3. We should pray for his health and salvation, and also for that of all the Ruling House.

Weak middle class. The power and money of the middle classes in Western European nations were the prime forces which ended the supremacy of the monarchies and nobles and established parliamentary governments. In Russia, however, the middle class was in-

Cathedral of the Annunciation, the Kremlin, Moscow

significant because trade was insignificant. Trade was insignificant because Russia, as we have seen, is almost landlocked. In contrast to a country like Britain, which has easy access to world trade routes, Russia has a very poor location for trade. For this reason, Russian commerce was always slight, and, consequently, the Russian middle class correspondingly weak. This left only the kings and nobles at the top and the peasants at the bottom. The peasants were the great majority, but they were downtrodden, illiterate, and helpless. The tsars and nobles were able to rule without challenge until the mid-19th century when a middle class and a working class began to appear.

Fear of invasion. Foreign danger also helps to explain the long tradition of authoritarian rule in Russia. Today it seems strange to talk about outside danger since the Soviet Union is a great world power. But the Muscovite state of the 15th century was very small, so small that it included only a small percentage of the Russian people. The rest were un-

Fountains decorating the entrance to the Summer Palace, St. Petersburg, were created by the toil of thousands of serfs.

JACQUES JANGOUX

der foreign rule, the rule of Poland, Lithuania, the German Teutonic Knights, and the Mongol Golden Horde. The very existence of Moscow was threatened by these powerful surrounding states. Almost every year the Mongols invaded the Russian lands and took thousands of prisoners whom they sold into slavery. That is why a famous historian of Russia has written that, "constant and cruel blows from enemies on all sides implanted in the least intelligent of Russians an instinct of national defence and of the value of a national dictatorship." [4]

Early Muscovite rulers such as Ivan III and Ivan IV (the Terrible) established the "national dictatorship" that was necessary for survival. They crushed the formerly powerful nobles and made them mere servants of the state. They also changed the formerly free peasants into serfs, unable to move from the estates in which they worked. This strengthened the state because the serfs were now readily available when soldiers were needed for the army and taxes for the treasury. In order to carry out his wishes, Ivan IV organized a force that was very much like the secret police of the Soviet Union today. It consisted of men who wore black clothes, rode on black horses, and who swore that they would obey Ivan "before any man or even God." With these followers, Ivan ruled Russia with an iron hand. A contemporary writer described Ivan's government as follows: "Throughout the Russian land, through his entire realm, there is one faith, one weight and one measure! He alone rules; whatever he orders is carried out, and whatever he prohibits remains prohibited. No one contradicts him. . . ." [5]

Precisely because no one could "contradict" them, Ivan III and Ivan IV were able to defeat their enemies and to enlarge greatly the size of Russia. Likewise when Peter the Great decided that Russia had to Westernize in order to hold her own, he plunged ahead without asking anyone's permission. He *forced* thousands of serfs to work on the building of St. Petersburg; he *forced* thousands of nobles to leave their estates, shave their beards, enter government service, and send their sons to Western universities. These and other measures aroused much opposition, but Peter replied that he was "an absolute monarch who does not have to answer for any of his actions to anyone in the world." [6]

These policies of Ivan III, Ivan the Terrible, and Peter the Great made Russia a strong power. Later rulers, such as Catherine the Great and Alexander I, expanded the frontiers until Russia became a great empire stretching from the Baltic to the Pacific. Obviously the Russian people no longer needed to fear foreign enemies. Yet their autocratic government remained, and the reason is the continued absence of a middle class. Russia still was a country of tsar and nobles at the top and of serfs at the bottom. The serfs did rise periodically in terrible revolts during which they killed many nobles and government officials. But because they lacked organization and knowledge, they were always defeated in the end.

Pressure against autocracy. During the 19th century this situation began to change.* In 1861 Tsar Alexander II liberated the serfs, who now became peasants with civil rights. But the newly freed serfs did not get much land with their liberty, and, as they increased in numbers, their little plots became increasingly inadequate for their needs. Unable to support their families properly, they turned against the tsarist government. They demanded more land and were ready to take up arms to get it.

At the same time Russia gradually was becoming industrialized. Mines were being

* See *Readings in World History*, "Russian Revolutionaries Look to the United States," p. 220.

opened, and factories and railroads were being built. This meant the rise of new classes of workers, industrialists, and merchants, all of whom were dissatisfied with the tsarist regime. The middle class of industrialists and merchants, the bourgeoisie, were dissatisfied because of the political conditions. They had wealth but no say in running the country, since there were no elections and no parliament until 1905. So, industrialists and merchants were eager for political reform.

The workers' dissatisfaction came from economic reasons. During these early days of industrialization they had the same grievances as the workers of Western Europe did during the early 19th century. They suffered from low pay, long hours of work, and poor working and housing conditions. Like workers elsewhere, they began to organize unions to demand better pay and working conditions. Like workers in other industrial countries they also began to learn about Marxism, which called for the overthrow of the government and the establishment of a socialist

state. A political party was organized, the Social Democratic Party. This split into two groups: the Mensheviks (meaning minority) who wanted to bring about socialism by peaceful means, and the Bolsheviks (meaning majority although they were actually a minority within the party) who believed that violence and revolution would be necessary. The Bolshevik leader, N. Lenin, was exiled for revolutionary activities but later returned to seize power and establish the Soviet government.

Lenin in Red Square shortly after the Revolution

Each year thousands of Soviet citizens queue up outside the Kremlin in Moscow to visit the tomb of Lenin.

What Communists believe. How could an exiled revolutionary seize the reins of government of the largest and one of the most populous countries in the world? Lenin was able to accomplish this by building an ideology from the writings of Karl Marx and Friedrich Engels and then using it to fashion a hard core of disciplined revolutionaries.

The key to Marxist doctrine is the theory of surplus value. According to this theory, the value of any commodity depends on the amount of labor necessary to produce it. A forest of trees, for example, is valueless, but if the trees are chopped down, transported to mills, sawed into lumber and made into furniture, then this final product has a value because of the labor spent in producing it. But the price at which the furniture is sold is higher than the value based on the labor, because it also includes the profit exacted by the capitalist. This means that the workingman who provides the labor receives less in wages than the price paid by the consumer.

Marx argued that this difference between labor provided and wages received is the Achilles' heel of capitalism, because the workers as a class cannot buy with their wages what they produce. In the long run this will lead to overproduction due to inadequate purchasing power because of inadequate wages. This in turn will lead to closing of factories, unemployment, a further decline of purchasing power, and, finally, a full-scale depression. Furthermore, Marx prophesied, the depressions would become more frequent and more severe until finally the unemployed proletariat would be driven in desperation to revolution. Thus capitalism, according to Marx, was bound to be replaced by socialism. And the new socialist society would be depression-proof because the government would own the means of production, and therefore there would be no private employers, no profits, and hence no lack of purchasing power.

The course of events since the mid-19th century when Marx wrote has not followed the pattern he forecast. It is true that depressions were a problem until World War II, but today they seem to have been eliminated by a variety of economic policies followed by Western governments. Thus the poor are not becoming poorer as Marx prophesied. Rather they are becoming better off. An automobile in 1914 cost 2,753 hours of work at average pay in the United States, while in 1948 it cost only 953 hours. A pound of rib roast cost 48 minutes of work in 1914 but less than 30 minutes in 1948. Likewise a man's suit cost 64 hours of work in 1914 compared to 24 hours in 1948.

Organizing a revolution. Despite these facts, Marx's doctrines became very popular throughout the world, especially in countries such as pre-World War I Russia where

The Russian autocracy first experienced revolution in 1905—an attempt by the middle class to wrest a degree of political power from the tsar. As a result the Duma (parliament) was created. The tsar, however, set immediately to work recapturing the power he had ceded.

BROWN BROTHERS

many elements of the population were dissatisfied. In that country Lenin taught that, in order to bring about a revolution, the workers should wage a political as well as an economic fight. They should not be satisfied merely with economic gains such as higher wages, but should also make political demands for democratic rights such as a free press, free elections, and free trade unions.

Alexander Kerensky

BROWN BROTHERS

But he made it clear that these democratic rights should then be used to overthrow the tsarist regime. Lenin also taught that his Social Democratic Party could not overthrow the government unless it consisted only of professional and disciplined revolutionaries who would be able to resist the tsarist secret police. As a result a split occurred between the Bolsheviks and the Mensheviks. Lenin's Bolsheviks were tightly organized and disciplined, and this strength enabled them to overcome their Socialist rivals as well as the tsarist government.

All these developments meant a very different Russia from that of the old days.* Instead of bound and helpless serfs who were easily kept down, the tsar and the nobles now were confronted by land-hungry peasants, a discontented middle class, and revolutionary workers. The more time passed, the more the opposition movement grew. The last tsar, Nicholas II, was a weak ruler, unable either to smash the opposition or to satisfy it with adequate concessions.

World War I. With the outbreak of World War I in 1914, the revolutionary movement in Russia became increasingly widespread. The Russian Armies were badly defeated, and the civilian population suffered from shortages of food and fuel. The tsarist regime was blamed for everything, until finally it collapsed in March 1917. It was succeeded by an essentially middle-class government headed by Alexander Kerensky. This government wished to establish in Russia a democratic parliamentary regime similar to those in Western Europe. For this reason it was warmly welcomed by the Western countries, including the United States. It was believed that since Russia had finally gotten rid of her tsarist autocracy, she would now follow in the path of her democratic allies.

* See *Readings in World History*, "Russian Revolutionaries Sentenced to Siberia," p. 223.

Red Guards and students wait for the St. Petersburg police, October 1917.

But this hope was soon to be blasted. The Kerensky government was able to stay in power only from March to November 1917.

One reason for the short life of the Kerensky government is that the middle class in Russia still was very small compared to the workers and peasants.* The workers and peasants were not especially interested in parliamentary democracy. They wanted land, but Kerensky was unwilling to divide up the large estates. They also wanted peace, but

* See *Readings in World History*, "On the Eve of Revolution," p. 226.

Kerensky again was unwilling to drop out of the war and leave Russia's Western allies in the lurch. Meanwhile the Bolsheviks under Lenin were campaigning up and down the country with their slogan of "Land, Peace, and Bread." This was what many of the peasants and workers wanted; they turned against the Kerensky government. This shift enabled the Bolsheviks to seize power in November 1917 and to establish the Soviet Union that has lasted to the present day.*

* See *Readings in World History*, "Triumph of the Bolsheviks," p. 227.

Soviet period. The Soviet Union has had three main leaders: Lenin from 1917 until his death in 1924, Joseph Stalin from 1926 until his death in 1953, and Nikita Khrushchev until 1964. After Khrushchev, the Soviet Union was not ruled by any one man, but by the small group of top Communist Party officials in the Presidium of the Central Committee of the Communist Party. But regardless of who its leaders might be, the Soviet government has been as autocratic as the tsarist. In fact it has been more autocratic, and it has sent to Siberia more political prisoners than any previous government. It is true that elections are held periodically, but we have seen that they mean little when only one party is allowed. The Communists argue that parties represent classes, and since there is only one class in the Soviet Union, only one party is needed.* But the fact is that under that one party, millions of people have suffered persecution or exile or even death. This was particularly true during the rule of Stalin, who became increasingly dictatorial and tyrannical in his later years.†

On the other hand, it should be noted that the Soviet government has been gaining in popularity, especially since World War II. One reason is that over three-fourths of the present population have been born and raised under Soviet rule and know no other form of government. Also living conditions improved considerably after Khrushchev came to power. He provided much better housing and more food and clothing. In addition Khrushchev and his successors reduced the numbers in the prison camps and eased up on the force and terrorism. There is less fear now than there was under Stalin. Many Soviet citizens are becoming more satisfied with their government and are looking forward to a better life in the future.

* See *Readings in World History,* "Premier Khrushchev on Soviet Democracy," p. 231.
† See *Readings in World History,* "Premier Khrushchev on Stalin's Tyranny," p. 233.

When, for example, an American correspondent interviewed five hundred "men in the street" in the Soviet Union, he found that many grumbled about specific defects in their system, but only one favored changing the system itself. And this one person did not believe that change of the system would be possible because of the strength of the government.*

In the absence of free elections or public opinion polls, we cannot be certain about the attitude of the Soviet people towards their government. Probably it varies according to age, nationality, and occupation. Some of the nationality groups, such as those of the Baltic states and of Central Asia, undoubtedly are less satisfied with the present government than are the Slavs. Most outspoken, however, are the young intellectuals: students, writers, scientists, engineers, and professionals of all kinds.†

These young people have enjoyed in recent years a modest amount of freedom, so that they are more forthright than their fathers who had been forced to knuckle under to the brutal Stalin. They have been openly demanding more freedom, less censorship of the press and of the universities and of writers. The Soviet government does not know how to deal with these critics. The natural reaction of the old Communist leaders is to restore the terror, but this is no longer as simple and as easy to do as in the days of Stalin. The Soviet Union today is a complex society with a sophisticated industrial and scientific establishment that needs the active support of millions of highly educated specialists. If these specialists are put in prison or sent off to Siberia to dig coal or cut down trees, what will happen to Soviet industry and science?

* See *Readings in World History,* "Soviet Citizens and Their Government," p. 234.
† See *Readings in World History,* "A Soviet Poet's Plea for Freedom," p. 236.

Stalin used coercion and terror to collectivize agriculture and nationalize industry.

Soviet leaders are in a dilemma, which explains their wavering back and forth, sometimes easing the pressure and at other times cracking down hard. In fact, some experts believe that a major reason for the Soviet invasion of Czechoslovakia in August 1968 was the fear that the freedom recently gained in Czechoslovakia might prove contagious and make it impossible to control Soviet intellectuals any longer. This opinion may be held by some Soviet citizens as well, as is shown in a letter written by a Soviet worker just before his arrest for anti-government activity: *

> ... if Czechoslovakia were really able to organize a democratic socialism, then there would be no justification for the absence of democratic freedoms in our country, and then, for all we know, our workers, peasants, and intelligentsia might demand freedom of speech in fact and not merely on paper.[7]

Finally, an English authority on the Soviet Union has described the present political situation as follows:

> It is reasonable to ask whether, after 50 years of Soviet dictatorship, we are witnessing the first stirrings of another revolution. The future alone can tell. But as far as rebellious youth is concerned, nothing is further from their thoughts than revolution.
>
> Many of them are Party members and think of themselves as convinced Communists. They are Soviet patriots. They do not seek to overturn the system, only to improve it. As far as the writers and artists are concerned, they are concentrating on freedom of conscience and expression, the pursuit of truth, the defeat of corruption and lies. They want to purge, not destroy.[8]

* See *Readings in World History,* "A Soviet Worker's Political Protest," p. 239.

Reviewing the Essentials

Present State

1. In what respects do the Soviet and United States political systems appear to resemble each other?
2. Who and how many belong to the Communist Party in the U.S.S.R.? Explain how the Party operates at election time. How does the Party control the Soviet Union? Where is power concentrated?
3. Why, under the Soviet political organization, is there no democracy as we define democracy in the United States?
4. What are the basic differences between socialism and communism?

Historical Origins

5. Describe the changes that came to 19th-century Russia.
6. What events brought the Kerensky government to power in Russia? How did the goals of this government differ from those of the tsars? Why did it fail to win the support of the Russian people?
7. How is the Soviet period of political history divided? What have been the prevailing characteristics of this period?
8. Why, in spite of its authoritarianism, has the Soviet government gained in popularity with the people?

Explain or Identify

serfdom	capitalist	"Land, Peace, and Bread"	Joseph Stalin
Duma	Bolshevik		Karl Marx
proletariat	Menshevik	"radish Communist"	N. Lenin
bourgeoisie	Marxist	Alexander Kerensky	Nikita Khrushchev

ECONOMICS: "The World Shall Rise on New Foundations"*

PRESENT STATE

Nature of Soviet socialism. The chief difference between the American economy and the Soviet is that the American is run mostly by private individuals and the Soviet mostly by the government. That is why the official title of the Soviet Union is the Union of Soviet Socialist Republics. The word "socialist" has been included in the title because the Soviet economy is socialistic. This means that the government owns and operates the main parts of the economy; for example the government maintains control over banks, mines, railroads, factories, farms, and foreign trade.

* From the *Internationale*, communism's anthem.

The Soviet government, however, does not own all property, down to the last toothbrush and last hairpin.* In fact there are three types of property in the Soviet Union. First, and most important, is the state property owned by the government. Second is the cooperative property owned by groups of Soviet individuals. Most of this cooperative property consists of small factories and collective farms. The third type of property is private and includes all kinds of personal belongings such as a home, furniture, car, or bank account.

* See *Readings in World History,* "Private Bank Accounts in the Soviet Union," p. 248.

Under private property would be included small farms and small shops which individual citizens may operate so long as they do not hire anyone to work for them for wages. Individual farmers or shopkeepers must work by themselves; if they wish to add others and to enlarge their operations, then they must form a cooperative in which the members divide the profits among themselves. So it is impossible under the Soviet Socialist economy for any one person to become wealthy by hiring thousands of workers, paying them wages, and keeping any profits that are left over. But this does not mean that all Soviet citizens have equal incomes. We shall see shortly that the differences in income are as great in the Soviet Union as they are in the United States.

Despite the existence of the cooperatives and of private shops and farms, the Soviet government completely controls the Soviet economy. It does so because it owns practically everything that is economically important. The state owns all the land and other natural resources such as mines and oil fields. It carries on all trade with foreign countries. It owns all heavy industry, all power plants, all banks, all railroads and telegraph and telephone systems, all retail and wholesale distribution facilities in cities, and all gas and water works. The state also owns almost all farms, including the type of Soviet farms which are known as collectives. We shall see later that these are operated by co-operatives, yet the title to the land actually belongs to the state. (The other type of Soviet farm is the state farm, which is both owned and operated by the government.) Cooperatives also run small enterprises such as handicrafts, trapping, or fishing. They also carry on wholesale and retail trade in rural areas. But the operation of all cooperatives is supervised by the state.

The Soviet government also controls the entire economy because it decides what

goods will be produced each year and in what quantity. The government has this control because of its Five-Year Plans. These plans are prepared by the State Planning Commission, or *Gosplan*. This is a body of statisticians, engineers, and other experts, who are appointed by the Council of Ministers. The Gosplan receives a vast amount of statistical data from all over the Soviet Union, so that it knows exactly how many workers there are in the country, how much machinery, and how much raw material. With all this information, the Gosplan draws up the Five-Year Plans along the lines ordered by the government, which means, as we have seen, the Communist Party. The Party leaders decide what should be the chief goals of each plan, and the Gosplan prepares its figures with these goals in mind.

The first Five-Year Plan (1928–1932) was to build up heavy industry as soon as possible in order to make the Soviet Union economically independent. The second Plan (1933–1937) emphasized, among other things, the development of the Far Eastern provinces because war with Japan was feared at that time. The plan for 1966–1970 aimed at raising the low level of agricultural production by means of big capital investments in farm machinery, fertilizers, and roads. It also sanctioned experiments which freed factories from centralized control.

At present, the great majority of Soviet citizens work either on collective farms or in state factories. The farms so far have proven less successful than the factories, as we shall see from the following descriptions.

Collective farms. In 1966 there were approximately 36,000 collective farms, or *kolkhozy*, compared to 12,000 state farms, or *sovkhozy*, and a handful of small private farms in isolated and infertile areas. The *sovkhozy* average 121,000 acres with 651 workers, while the *kolkhozy* average 31,000 acres

Virgin grassland in 1954, by 1968 Kazakh S.S.R. produced over 82 million acres of grain per year.

In a Moscow free market, a peasant woman sells vegetables from her private plot.

U.S.S.R.– LAND USE

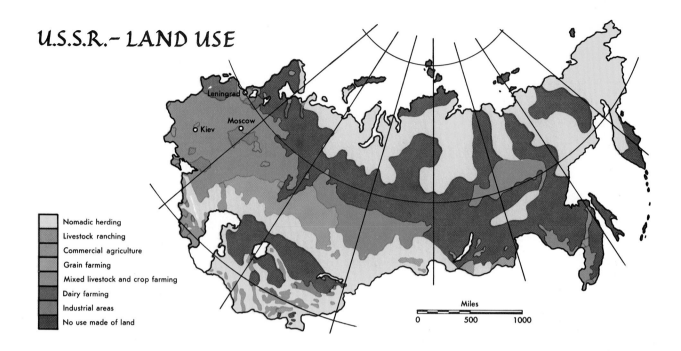

Nomadic herding
Livestock ranching
Commercial agriculture
Grain farming
Mixed livestock and crop farming
Dairy farming
Industrial areas
No use made of land

Leningrad
Kiev
Moscow

Miles
0   500   1000

with 417 workers. Since the *sovkhozy* are owned by the state, its workers are paid wages as if they were factory workers. By contrast, the *kolkhozy* are cooperatively operated, though not cooperatively owned. Each *kolkhozy* family owns its house, furniture, tools, and a surrounding garden of one-quarter to two and a half acres. In this garden each family can grow whatever it wants. The harvest from the garden may be consumed by the family or else sold at any price in the market place of the nearest town. Each family may also privately own one cow, one pig, ten sheep and goats, and unlimited poultry.

Most of the land on the *kolkhozy* is worked cooperatively by the farmers who work together in brigades. There are cow-milking brigades, hog-feeding brigades, tractor brigades, seeding and cultivating brigades, and the like. The produce from this cooperative work is sold partly to the state and partly on the open market. From the money received are deducted certain sums for such

things as taxes, crop insurance, a new school or clubhouse, farm machinery, and so forth. Whatever is left over is the profit for the year, which is divided among the *kolkhozy's* members.

Resistance to system. The Soviet agricultural system has not worked well so far. This is proven by the fact that the 38 million workers on Soviet farms produce only about 80 per cent as much as do the 4 million workers on American farms. We noted earlier that one reason for this extraordinary difference in productivity is that the climate of the Soviet Union is much less favorable for agriculture than that of the United States. Where there is enough heat, as in the south, the rainfall is inadequate, and where there is enough rainfall, as in the north, the temperature is too low.

Another reason for the difference in productivity is that Soviet farmers do not have as much machinery and fertilizers as do the

American. The Soviet government has been interested mostly in developing industry and therefore has starved agriculture. It has taxed the farmers heavily and given very little in return, so that Soviet agriculture has been primitive and unproductive.

Probably the chief reason for the inefficiency of Soviet agriculture, however, is that the farm workers have never been satisfied with collectivized farming. Government taxes have been so heavy, and agricultural prices so low, that at the end of each year they receive very little for their work in the collective fields. Thus, they prefer to work hard on their own private garden plots and to sell any surplus produce in the open market where they receive high prices. This explains why these plots, although comprising only 3 per cent of the cultivated land, produce about one-third of the Soviet Union's total farm output, including 76 per cent of all eggs and 42 per cent of all vegetables.

Khrushchev tried to raise productivity in various ways. He bought large amounts of American hybrid corn that produces higher yields than ordinary seed. But few parts of the Soviet Union have the combination of abundant rainfall and heat necessary for good corn crops. Also, he sent thousands of settlers to the "virgin lands" of Central Asia. But these lands have too little rain and become dust bowls when the natural sod is plowed up.

One of the main reasons for Khrushchev's fall from power in 1964 was this failure in agriculture. His successors have made various changes in the hope of increasing output. Farm workers now are allowed to have larger private plots and to keep more livestock on these plots. They also are now taxed less heavily, and no longer pay higher prices for consumer goods than do people living in cities. Most important, farmers are now guaranteed a minimum amount each month for their work in the collective fields, the rates

being based on those being paid to the *sovkhozy* workers. This gives the *kolkhozy* workers an incentive which they lacked so long as they were paid only what was left at the end of the year, usually very little because of the high taxes and low prices. With the new system, the *kolkhozy* farmers are encouraged to work harder in the hope of having something extra to divide at the end of the year, in addition to the guaranteed monthly minimum. Finally, farm workers henceforth will be paid pensions when they retire, as is done for the workers in industry.

On a state farm near Kiev women work in the cucumber fields, thus freeing men for work with the heavier tractors and grain equipment.

JACQUES JANGOUX

Women in urban areas make up a high percentage of the industrial workers. Here a young girl works a mechanized loom at a textile factory in Tashkent.

What all this means is that the Soviet leaders at last have decided to invest in agriculture in order to make it more productive. The income of collective farmers rose by 10 per cent in 1965 and 16 per cent in 1966. The Soviet leaders are gambling that farm workers will be encouraged to raise their output with the knowledge that their incomes will rise correspondingly.

State factories. We have seen that most Soviet farms are cooperatively run. By contrast, most Soviet factories are operated as well as owned by the government. Therefore the workers in these factories are paid wages by the government rather than by dividing the profits among themselves. But again the workers do not all receive equal wages. Like the collective farmers, they are paid according to the skill and the amount of their work. A lathe operator, for example, will receive

much more than a janitor. And he will receive still more if his output is above the quota that has been set for his job. Wage differences in a Soviet factory are at least as great, if not greater, than in an American factory. Soviet socialism, therefore, does not mean equal pay; rather it means government ownership of most of the means of production.

Soviet workers are allowed to have trade unions, as are American workers. These trade unions do many of the same things that unions do elsewhere. They protest to the manager if the machines are not safe, if the lighting is poor, or the food in the cafeteria is unsatisfactory. But Soviet unions lack the one freedom that Western unions prize most highly, the freedom to strike. The government argues that if the workers want higher wages, they should work harder, surpass the quota, and then receive a bonus. This means, of course, that the government completely controls the wage scales, and that the worker can do nothing except work harder if he wants to earn more.

Soviet factories are run by managers who are appointed by the government. The managers receive higher wages than the workers, but they also are prodded by a system of quotas and bonuses. The manager whose factory produces more than the set quota receives a bonus. But if his factory repeatedly fails to meet the quota, then he is fired.

In conclusion we see that Soviet factories, like the American, operate on the principle of pay according to the skill and quantity of work. Soviet workers and managers have the same incentive to work hard and to learn new skills as do the American. Nevertheless there still remain two great differences between American and Soviet industry. One is the government ownership of most Soviet factories. The other is the inability of the Soviet workers to strike in order to get what they want. This means that they do not have the independence of American workers. They have no choice but to accept the wage scales set by the government.

The consumer waits. This lack of freedom to strike is one reason why Soviet industry is growing so rapidly. It has enabled the Soviet government to keep wages very low. This in turn means that Soviet workers have never been able to buy many commodities that American workers take for granted, commodities such as automobiles, television sets, refrigerators, and washing machines. Consequently, the Soviet planners did not have to concentrate on turning out such consumer goods. Rather they concentrated on what are called capital goods, that is, dams, power plants, railroads, steel mills, and factories of all types. The emphasis was on building industry for future production rather than turning out consumer goods for present use.* This meant a low standard of living, and the people had no choice but to accept it. The great difference in the treatment of American and Soviet consumers is shown in the following table. It compares the Soviet output of three consumer items with the United States output.

	Soviet Union 1964	U.S. 1964
Radio and television sets		
Production	7,700,000	19,000,000
In use	76,000,000	246,000,000
Passenger cars	184,000	7,752,000
Shoes	474,000,000	621,000,000

* See *Readings in World History*, "Soviet Efficiency: Myth or Fact?", p. 245.

TASS FROM SOVFOTO

It is true that Soviet citizens get many social services inexpensively or free of charge, including free medical care, education, and pensions, and pay rent averaging only 4 to 5 per cent of wages. Nevertheless nearly all Soviet women work not only because they are expected to do so but also because their wages are needed to fill out the family *bumajnik* or pocketbook. And, this pocketbook is not very full, as is clear from the fact that a Soviet citizen must spend about half his income on food, while an American spends only about one-fifth.

Soviet plans continue to stress capital goods. About 70 per cent of the total Soviet industrial output is now spent on capital goods and 30 per cent on consumer goods, whereas in the United States the ratio is exactly the other way around. As a result, Soviet industry has grown rapidly under Soviet rule. By 1940 it was eight and a half times larger than in 1913, and by 1958 it had jumped to 36 times larger than in 1913. Or, to put it in another way, Russia was fifth in the world in industrial output in 1913, coming after the United States, Germany, Britain, and France. Today the Soviet Union is in second place, though her industrial output is only half that of the United States, which is in first place.

HISTORICAL ORIGINS

Today the Soviet government is using every propaganda means to urge its citizens to work hard in order to catch up with the United States. This is an old story for the Russian people. In fact, their history is largely a series of frantic efforts to reach the level of the more advanced Western countries.

A "backward" country. Why has Russia always lagged behind in her economic and technological development? One reason was that she had suffered more than two centuries of Mongol rule. During those long years she had stood still, while the West had moved rapidly ahead. Another reason is to be found in her location in Eastern Europe, far from the ocean trade routes. She could not take part in the great overseas commerce that brought so much wealth to Britain, Holland, and other Western states. Instead Russia remained an agricultural country of nobles and serfs. Her trade and industry and technology were all feeble and backward.

Peter the Great's remedies. Tsar Peter the Great was one of the first to realize how dangerous this backwardness was for Russia. In his youth he had met English, Dutch, and German merchants. From them he learned how superior were the Western ships, cannon, muskets, and manufactured goods. He saw that Russia had to catch up if she was to survive and hold her own. In fact, he moved his capital from Moscow to St. Petersburg in order to be closer to the West. He brought thousands of skilled Western craftsmen to Russia, and sent thousands of young Russian students to the West. He imported many books dealing with the new arts and sciences, and had them translated into Russian. He himself set an example by working and learning along with his subjects. During his lifetime he became fairly expert in many fields, including shipbuilding, navigation, dentistry, astronomy, engraving, bootmaking, and metalwork.

Peter was well fitted for the task he had assumed. He was seven feet tall and tremendously strong, being able to bend a coin with his bare hands. He never seemed to tire, so that he could spend all night drinking and carousing with his friends in his palace, and then, the following day, pound an anvil like a blacksmith or pull the teeth of some unfortunate subject so that he might learn dentistry. He allowed nothing to stand in the

Peter the Great visits a British shipyard.

way of his goal to modernize his country. Like Ivan the Terrible, he even went so far as to execute his own son because he had joined the group that opposed modernization. The combination of energy, determination, and ruthlessness produced the results he wanted. By his death in 1725, Russia was making more iron than any other European country. Also, Russian factories were turning out the cannon, muskets, and uniforms needed by the army.

Although Peter did much to industrialize his country, he did little for the great majority of his people who were downtrodden serfs. These serfs were tied to the land which they cultivated. They belonged to the owner of the land, whether the owner happened to be a noble or the government. The job of the serf was to till the plot of land that was assigned to him, and to hand over a portion of his produce to the landowner. It made no difference if a serf was dissatisfied with his occupation or his master. He could not move from the village in which he was born, and he had no rights as a citizen. If he was abused by a noble or by a government agent, he could not turn anywhere for protection. He had no choice but to accept orders and carry them out.

Serfdom in modern times. We come here to an important difference between Western Europe and Russia. In Western Europe, serfdom existed in the Middle Ages and disappeared in modern times. In Russia it was the other way around; serfdom did not exist in the Middle Ages but appeared in modern times. The explanation for this difference is that in the medieval period there was too much land and too few people in Russia to make serfdom possible. So long as there was plenty of land on all sides, no Russian peasant would stand for any abuse from his landowner. A peasant simply picked up his belongings and moved off to the empty lands of the nearby frontier.

However, a remarkable change took place in modern times with the coming of rulers such as Ivan the Terrible and Peter the Great. These men wanted to make Russia strong, and to do this they needed a big army and plenty of money. But they could get neither so long as the peasants were free to run off to the frontier whenever they saw a recruiting officer or a tax collector. So the government cooperated with the nobles in forcibly tying the peasants to the land they tilled. Laws were passed which steadily took away the peasants' freedom of movement. In this way the formerly free peasants were changed into serfs who were bound either to private noble estates or government lands.

And these serfs comprised well over 90 per cent of all the people of Russia.

Late industrialization. This system of serfdom is very important because it helps us understand why Russia fell behind the West with the coming of the Industrial Revolution. We have seen that the Industrial Revolution began in England in the late 18th century and spread to Western Europe in the early 19th. But it did not continue eastward to Russia until the very end of the 19th century. One of the main reasons for this lag is to be found in serfdom. After all, the Industrial Revolution was nothing more or less than the invention and use of machinery in order to save labor. But there was no need for labor-saving machines in Russia at this time because there were plenty of serfs who could be ordered to do any work. So why should the nobles spend their money on machines and factories when all their needs were taken care of by the serfs? Why should anyone in Russia offer prizes for labor-saving inventions as was being done at this time in England? Not only were there plenty of workers, but also there was no need to turn out more and more goods because Russia did not have the world-wide markets that England did. Whereas the English were selling their manufactured goods in North and South America, in Africa, in India and in China, the Russians could sell their products only in their own country. And the market in their own country was very small, since nearly all Russians were serfs who could buy almost nothing.

For these reasons Russia during the 19th century fell far behind the West in her economy and technology. This became clear when Russia fought England, France, and Turkey in the Crimean War in 1853–1856. The French and British fought with steam warships while the Russians still depended on warships propelled by sail. The rifles of the British and French soldiers shot four times as far as the rifles of the Russians.

Russia lost the war but learned a lesson. During the following years the government initiated a number of basic changes. The most important were the abolition of serfdom and the pushing of industrialization. The government had little choice so far as serfdom was concerned because by this time the serfs were becoming more and more restless. Each year numerous revolts were breaking out in various parts of the country. The government had the choice of either revolution from below or reform from above. It chose the latter, and in 1861 it issued the famous Emancipation Edict liberating the serfs.

The edict gave them legal freedom and almost the same civic rights as other citizens. They received the land that they tilled, but they had to pay for this land over a period of 49 years. The land was not given outright to individual peasants as private property. Rather it was given to the village communes, or mirs, which consisted of all the peasant families of each village. The commune in turn distributed the land among the various families according to the size of each family. And every few years the land was redistributed in order to take into account the changes in the size of families.

This system meant that the land was divided evenly on the basis of need. There was no chance for a particularly hard-working family to get more and more land and to become rich. This continued until 1906 when another law was passed allowing the individual peasant to leave the commune and to have a private plot of his own. A considerable number of peasants took advantage of this, and there soon appeared a new class of wealthy peasants who were known as kulaks.

After the Crimean War the Russian government also pushed industrialization. It did so by various ways, such as setting up high

Russian peasants, released from serfdom, still faced starvation and oppression through the early twentieth century.

tariffs against the importation of foreign manufactured goods, and also borrowing large sums from foreign countries in order to buy machinery and build factories. As a result, Russia's industrial output more than doubled between 1900 and 1914. By 1904 Russia had completed the great Trans-Siberian Railroad stretching 5000 miles from Chelyabinsk to Vladivostok. By that date, Russia had a total of 40,000 miles of railroad. But there was still far to go to catch up with the West. Despite the fact that Russia had much greater resources and manpower than Germany, France, or England, she was far behind all three in industrial output.

Disaster in World War I. This economic backwardness proved fatal during the First World War which began in 1914. The Russian soldiers fought bravely on the side of the Allies against the Germans and the Austrians. But their bravery proved useless because they did not have enough guns, munitions, and other supplies. Their industry was too small; they simply lacked the factories to turn out the weapons and supplies that their army needed.* There were cases of Russian soldiers fighting in the snow of the Carpathian Mountains without boots on their feet. Even worse off were the men who had to go into battle without rifles. A Russian general told the French ambassador at the time: "Imagine, in several infantry regiments which took part in the last engagements, one third of the men had no rifles! The poor devils waited patiently, in a storm of shrapnel, until they could pick up the rifles of their fallen comrades. It was a miracle that under such conditions there was no panic. . . . How long will our soldiers bear the trial? At all costs we must have rifles." [9]

Such handicaps naturally led to terrible defeats. In the year 1915 alone, the Russians lost 2.5 million men. The civilians suffered along with the soldiers. Over 5 million fleeing refugees clogged the roads before the advancing enemy. Railroad service broke down under the strain of the war, so that

* See *Readings in World History*, "Russia in World War I," p. 225.

Russian peasants were encouraged to celebrate collectivization, which according to the Soviet government would bring progress and plenty. Soon the celebrations turned to anger and demands for the end of collectivization.

BROWN BROTHERS

the cities were left without sufficient food and fuel during the bitterly cold winters. This combination of military defeat and economic collapse turned both soldiers and civilians against the tsarist regime. Mass discontent finally led to the 1917 revolution.

The collective system. When the Communists came to power, they had the same ambitions as Peter. They wanted to develop the economy quickly and to catch up with the West. As Lenin put it, "Either perish, or overtake and outstrip the capitalist countries." The Communists, however, wanted to create a new type of economy, a socialist economy, but the problem was how to do it. At first they thought that it would be very simple. Lenin said that it needed only "the extraordinarily simple operations of watching, recording, and issuing receipts, within the reach of everybody who can read and write and knows the first four rules of arithmetic . . ." [10]

The Communists soon learned, however, their task was not an easy one. They tried "workers' control," by which the workers took over the factories and ran them, but this experiment ended in chaos. After some years of floundering, they decided that a socialist economy could be built only by careful planning from the center. So they began a series of Five-Year Plans in 1928 and have continued them to the present day.

The stubborn kulaks. We have seen that the Soviet economy built up by the Five-Year Plans is based largely on state ownership of factories and collective farms. The Bolshevik leaders did not have much trouble taking over the factories because their owners were too few to resist and the factory workers did not object. But the Bolsheviks had much more trouble setting up the collective farms. Many peasants did not want to give up their private plots and join the collectives.

TIME CHART FOR THE SOVIET UNION

PRE-RUSSIAN PERIOD	1000 B.C.-500 A.D.	Slavic migrations into Russia.
	650 A.D.	Khazars control southern Russia.
	862	City of Novgorod invites Viking rule.
	989	Vladimir I accepts the Greek Orthodox Church.
	1223-1480	Mongols rule Russia.
	1584-1613	Time of political instability.
	1613-1917	Romanov dynasty rules Russia.
	1689-1725	Peter the Great partially Europeanizes Russia.
	1801-1825	Alexander I adopts policy of Russification. Nicholas I crushes Decembrist uprising.
	1812	Napoleon invades and retreats from Russia.
	1853-1856	Crimean War with Turkey, Great Britain, and France.
	1905	Russia defeated in Russo-Japanese War. 1905 revolution and formation of the Duma.
	1914	Russia enters World War I against Germany.
KIEV PERIOD 878 AD-1237	1917-1920	Russian revolution ends tsarist rule, brings Communist rule under Lenin.
	1928	First Five-Year Plan begins.
	1936-1938	"Great Purge" within Communist Party.
	1939	U.S.S.R. signs nonaggression pact with Germany. Invades Finland.
SARAI PERIOD 1237-1472	1941-1945	Germany invades U.S.S.R. U.S.S.R. sustains tremendous losses but drives Germans back to Berlin.
	1950	Mutual-aid alliance signed with Communist China.
MOSCOW PERIOD 1472-1703	1953	Stalin dies. Malenkov becomes premier, replaced by Bulganin in 1955. Khrushchev begins rise to power.
	1955-1956	"De-Stalinization" causes unrest.
	1957	Soviet scientists launch first successful satellite, Sputnik I.
ST. PETERSBURG PERIOD 1703-1917	1958-1964	Khrushchev as Premier promotes policies of peaceful coexistence. Increasing rift with Communist China.
	1964	Khrushchev replaced by Brezhnev and Kosygin.
SOVIET STATE 1917-Present	1968	Soviet invasion of Czechoslovakia.
	1969	Sino-Soviet border clashes.

Resistance came from the kulaks, or wealthy landowners. They saw no reason why they should hand over to the collectives all the lands and goods for which they had worked so hard. It particularly galled them to enter the collectives on the same terms as the poor peasants who brought nothing with them. So the kulaks fought against the new system tooth and nail. In some cases they burned the buildings of the collectives and poisoned the cattle. They also spread rumors in order to incite the peasants. For example, they whispered that those who joined the collectives would have to surrender not only their land, but eventually they would also have to give up their wives and children.

The Soviet government crushed this opposition of the kulaks without mercy. It encouraged the poor peasants to strip the kulaks of their property. Then Soviet police stepped in and took away the kulak families to prison or to labor camps. No one knows how many hundreds of thousands of families were uprooted from their villages and scattered around the country. The government did not care what happened to them so long as they were destroyed. The Soviet newspaper, *Red Star*, wrote on January 16, 1930, "What will become of the kulak after his liquidation as a class? To us it is all one, let him fall under the first passing automobile or spend the rest of his life in exile, anything provided he disappears from our midst." [11] In the end the Soviet leaders had their way. The kulaks did disappear from their midst. The collective farms gradually took root, partly because of the government's force and partly because of the government's tractors that began to pour out of the factories.

"Produce or perish." The Soviet socialist economy grew larger and stronger as one plan followed another. The Communist leaders drove the people ever harder, to work longer hours and to turn out more

goods. In order to get what they wanted the leaders used a combination of the carrot and the stick. Workers who did not fill their quotas were first warned and then hauled up before public meetings to account for their failures. But those who passed their quotas were given various rewards: better housing, higher wages, special vacation privileges, and assorted decorations and awards. At the height of the first Five-Year Plan, the Soviet leader, Joseph Stalin, made a speech in which he explained why he was setting such a furious pace:

It is sometimes asked whether it is not possible to slow down the tempo a bit, to put a check on the movement. No, Comrades, it is not possible! The tempo must not be reduced! On the contrary, we must increase it as much as it is within our powers and possibilities. To slacken the tempo would mean falling behind. And those who fall behind get beaten. . . . One feature of the history of old Russia was the continual beatings she suffered for falling behind, for her backwardness. She was beaten by the Mongol Khans. She was beaten by the Turkish beys. She was beaten by the Swedish feudal lords. She was beaten by the Polish and Lithuanian gentry. She was beaten by the British and French capitalists. She was beaten by the Japanese barons. All beat her—for her backwardness: for military backwardness, for cultural backwardness, for political backwardness, for industrial backwardness, for agricultural backwardness. She was beaten because to do so was profitable and could be done with impunity. . . . That is why Lenin said during the October [1917] Revolution: "Either perish, or overtake and outstrip the advanced capitalist countries." [12]

During these Five-Year Plans the Soviet people received little in return for their hard work. The emphasis was on future rewards rather than present satisfactions. The plans concentrated on building more factories and more machines rather than on turning out more clothes, shoes, furniture, and other commodities that would have made life easier and pleasanter. But this sacrifice paid off, for the Soviet Union quickly became the strong economic and military power that Stalin wanted. Between 1928 and 1932, which was the period of the first Plan, the Soviet Union's share of the total world industrial output rose from 4 to 14 per cent. This moved her up from the fifth to the second greatest industrial country of the world.

But then came a great setback with World War II. The Germans overran a large part of the U.S.S.R. and caused tremendous damage. They destroyed factories, blew up dams, flooded mines, and burned towns and villages. By the end of the war, one of every ten Soviet citizens was dead, and one of every seven was homeless. Despite these terrible

losses the Soviets won out and their armies beat back the Germans and invaded Germany. This was very different from World War I, and one reason for the difference was that the Soviet Union received many more war supplies from her allies, and especially the United States, during the Second World War than during the First. But another important reason for the difference was that, thanks to the Five-Year Plans, the Soviet economy was much stronger by 1941 than it had been in 1914. Soviet factories now were able to turn out many more tanks, planes, and guns for the soldiers at the battlefront.

When World War II ended, the Soviet government resumed its plans. A Seven-Year Plan, which ran from 1959 to 1965, aimed at making the Soviet Union as productive as

The 1969 Soviet May Day Parade was the first not to display Soviet armaments.

TASS FROM SOVFOTO

COMPARISON OF OUTPUT / U. S. AND U.S.S.R.

1966		UNITED STATES	SOVIET UNION
Gross National Product		743 billion U.S. dollars	337 billion U.S. dollars
GNP Per Capita		3760 U.S. dollars	1450 U.S. dollars
Agriculture (in short tons)	Wheat:	39,319	110,781
	Corn:	114,893	9,277
	Meat:	16,591	10,845
lbs. of meat per capita		170	93
Mineral Products (in short tons)	Cement:	74,039	88,185
	Iron Ore:	57,551	102,486
	Steel:	134,101	106,814
lbs. of steel per capita		1,470	873
electricity (in million Kw hrs.)		1,248,232	544,566

the United States in *absolute* output by 1965. Khrushchev also claimed that the Soviet Union would surpass the United States in *per capita* output by 1969 or 1970. What were the results of this plan?

Instead of catching up to the United States, the Soviet economy slowed down during this Seven-Year Plan. The head of Gosplan has stated that whereas the Soviet economy grew 8.2 per cent annually from 1956 through 1960, its rate was 6 per cent during the 1960's. Western experts estimate that the decline was from 6 to 4 per cent during those periods. Whatever the figures might be, the fact remains that there was a slowdown. Thus, whereas in 1960 the total output of the Soviet economy was 44 per cent of the American,

by 1966 it had increased only to 45 per cent instead of the 100 per cent by 1965 as had been planned by Khrushchev. Furthermore, the Soviet work force at the end of 1966 totalled 108 million as against 74 million in the United States, which means that the output of the average Soviet worker was only about one-third of the American.

The Soviet slowdown is due partly to the casualties and low birth rate during the war years, which are now affecting the labor supply. It is also due to a willingness to spend more on consumer goods and to the increasing complexity of the Soviet economic system. So long as it was merely a matter of turning out more steel, coal, and oil, it was not too difficult to increase production sharply.

But it is a very different matter now, when Soviet factories must produce complicated equipment as well as goods that will satisfy the consumer.

Changes Since Khrushchev. The slowdown in the 1960's reflected a crisis in the entire Soviet planning system, as is proven by the fact that changes were made in the Soviet economy that were as basic as the introduction of the Five-Year Plans in 1928. In September 1962, Professor Yevsei G. Liberman of Kharkov University published an article in the Communist Party newspaper, *Pravda*, in which he stated that production could be increased if factories geared their output to profit and to demand rather than the orders of Gosplan.

Under the old system, all profits went back to the state, which made most of the decisions in the running of each industry. Liberman proposed that this be changed by: (1) giving the managers more autonomy in running their plants; (2) rating the managers not on the basis of output but of profit, so that they would be forced to produce quality goods that customers would be willing to buy (The old system had encouraged managers to fulfill their quotas by turning out vast quantities of goods "for the shelf" rather than for the consumer.); (3) allowing managers to keep a larger percentage of their profits to use for reinvestment, or higher salaries, or bonuses, or for any way the manager thinks best.

This proposal did not mean the end of communism and the return of capitalism. All enterprises still were to be owned by the state or by cooperatives rather than by private capitalists. Nevertheless the new emphasis on profit and on satisfaction did mean a sharp break with the past. So Liberman's proposals caused a great debate until finally, in mid-1964, two large clothing plants were switched to the new system. In January 1965

BROWN BROTHERS

Khrushchev's failure to solve the problems of agriculture was one issue responsible for his dismissal.

the experiment was broadened to include 400 plants in light industry. By 1968, 26,000 industrial plants, accounting for almost three-fourths of total industrial output, were operating under the new system. The profits of the new-type plants in 1966 had risen 24 per cent compared with an increase for all factories of only 8 per cent. For this reason Premier Kosygin announced in 1967 that all industries would soon be on the new plan.*

The outlook for the Soviet economy. We have seen that Soviet industry expanded so

* See *Readings in World History*, "New Soviet Economic Policy," p. 259.

GUM, Moscow's largest department store, appears to be a shopper's paradise. However, although more consumer goods are now becoming available, shortages are still common and it is necessary to wait in long lines several times before a purchase can be completed.

rapidly because the Communists spent 70 per cent of their industrial output on capital goods and 30 per cent on consumer goods, whereas our ratio is roughly the opposite. This difference exists because in the Soviet Union a small group of men can decide what shall be produced, whereas in the United States it is the consumer who finally decides. If the United States were to follow the Soviet ratio in industrial development, it would mean much higher taxes and much lower living standards. This, of course, would arouse a storm of protest that would have to be heeded. Americans have a free press, free trade unions, and a choice of parties for which they can vote. The Soviets, by contrast, have government-controlled unions and press, and a choice of only one party. The leaders of that party can do as they wish, without paying much attention to the Soviet man in the street.

The Soviet consumers, however, are grumbling against producing so little for the present.* An anonymous "Letter to the Editor" of a Moscow youth newspaper states:

> . . . Doesn't it seem to you that the craze for these Sputniks . . . is untimely . . . we're still up to our necks in earthly matters . . . goods are expensive. And that rocket, I don't doubt, eats up so much money that everybody would probably groan if they knew the cost of it.
>
> Tell any worker: Now you look here, Ivan, if we don't launch this rocket your little Volodya would start going to a kindergarten, that a yard of cloth would cost not 4 rubles, but half that, that you could buy an electric iron in a store—and I'm certain that he'd say: "For God's sake, don't launch those rockets."
>
> Rockets, rockets, rockets!—who needs them now! To hell with the moon for the time being, give me something better for the table. . . .

* See *Readings in World History,* "Soviet Consumer Complaints and Responses," p. 252.

In other words, this Soviet citizen is asking for more consumer goods and less capital goods. Newspapers frequently carry letters like this and cartoons satirizing the items offered as "first quality products" in Soviet stores. (See above.)

An observer of trends in public opinion in the Soviet Union has noted that the overwhelming majority of the people are preoccupied with the material aspects of everyday life, such as the prospect of earning more money from their job or profession, the opportunity of obtaining a new apartment, or the improvement of the health and diet of their families. They considered these things more important than world problems such as the future of Berlin, or conditions in Vietnam or Cuba.

> Why should we meddle all over the world? It only antagonizes other nations. If I had my way I would concentrate on making this country (the Soviet Union) the richest and most powerful on earth. Let the rest of the world look after itself.

Widespread education will inevitably encourage more and more people to think for themselves. So long as most citizens were illiterate peasants, they could easily be ordered around by the Communist leaders. But now, more and more, Soviet citizens are becoming physicians, teachers, scientists, administrators, and engineers. These well-educated people are demanding not only more political freedom, as noted earlier, but also higher living standards.

Despite the progress of recent years, life in the Soviet Union remains mostly drab and joyless. The average city dweller has only about 70 square feet of apartment space, less than the 1920 level. The new apartment buildings that are appearing everywhere are notorious for their poor construction. A cartoon in the humor magazine, *Krokodil,* shows a housewarming party in a new apartment;

KROKODIL (SOVFOTO)

A SOVIET COMMENT ON POOR CONSUMER GOODS

AS MADE.   AS LABELED.

all the gifts are tools and materials for repairing cracks in the floor, walls, ceiling, and windows.

Another chief complaint of Soviet citizens is the endless waiting for everything. A mother of two children told an American correspondent:

> The Soviet housewife's problem is time— time to go six times to the department store looking for children's coats, time to go from one end of town to the other looking for a store selling potatoes, time to hunt through store after store looking for a simple sweater set, time to go and buy fur-lined boots in July because they won't be there when it gets cold!! [13]

If the housewife is fortunate enough to find what she wants, then more waiting is necessary before she can buy the article. First she waits in line to choose the sample she prefers, then she waits in another line to pay for it, and then she goes back through the first line to turn in a receipt and pick up her parcel.

In response to growing complaints against such conditions the Soviet government is taking various steps. Self service stores are being opened to reduce the waiting in lines. The new emphasis in industry on profit is aimed to encourage quality rather than quantity in the goods produced. Articles are published in the official press demanding that restaurants be made more pleasing to both the eye and the palate; "give us not only calories, but interesting impressions as well." * The government has signed contracts with foreign automobile companies to increase the supply of cars for private citizens. For example, a 333 million dollar contract with the Italian Fiat Company provides for the construction of a large plant in the Volga region which will turn out 600,000 light cars per year by 1970.

Under popular pressure, this trend towards the satisfaction of consumer needs is likely to continue. It is significant that the Soviet budget for 1968 was the first one to call for a higher rate of increase in consumer goods than capital goods, 8.6 as against 7.9 per cent.*

* *Pravda*, April 2, 1968

* See *Readings in World History*, "Soviet Living Conditions," p. 261.

To cope with the housing shortage, single family dwellings are slowly being replaced by modern apartment buildings. However, it will be many years before Soviet cities can provide adequate living space, and "urban renewal" scenes such as this are common.

MAYER (BLACK STAR)

Reviewing the Essentials

Present State

1. What are the fundamental differences between the economic systems of the United States and the Soviet Union?

2. Name three kinds of property in the Soviet Union and give examples of each.

3. How and why does the Soviet government control the entire Soviet economy?

4. What is a Five-Year Plan? What were the major goals of the first, second, and present Plans?

5. How is agriculture organized in the Soviet Union? Differentiate between the collective (*kolkhoz*) and the state farm (*sovkhoz*). Why is agriculture the weakest point in the Soviet economy? What is the government doing to correct the situation?

6. How are the Soviet factories operated? Who determines what and how much will be produced and how much the workers will be paid?

7. Explain: "Soviet socialism does not mean equal pay. . . ." What are representative wages for unskilled and skilled workers? Why the difference?

8. What is the purpose of trade unions in the Soviet Union? How do Soviet trade unions differ from those in the United States and Western Europe? With what effect?

9. What social services are provided free or at low cost to Soviet citizens?

10. What percentage of Soviet industrial output is spent on capital goods (heavy industry) and on consumer goods? Compare with the United States.

Historical Origins

11. Why has Russia lagged behind the West in economic and technological development? What did Peter the Great do to industrialize and modernize 18th-century Russia?

12. Why did serfdom develop in Russia at a time when it was disappearing from the countries of Western Europe? How did the existence of serfdom cause Russia to lag behind in economic and political development?

13. What changes were made in Russia after the Crimean War? With what results?

14. Cite evidence of Russia's economic backwardness in World War I.

15. What were the goals of Lenin and the Bolsheviks for the Soviet economy?

16. Why did the government deal harshly with the resistance and opposition of the kulaks?

17. What reasons did Joseph Stalin give for driving ahead with the Five-Year Plans? Where did the Soviet Union stand in industrial output at the end of the first Five-Year Plan (1928–1932)? In what ways was World War II a setback for the Soviet economy?

18. What goals were set forth in the Seven-Year Plan (1959–1965)? What prevented the fulfillment of this Plan?

Explain, Identify, or Locate

collectives	Gosplan	kulak	state factory
sovkhoz	ruble	trade union	village commune
kolkhoz	quotas	consumer goods	Seven-Year Plan
produce or perish	"free markets"	*Pravda*	Trans-Siberian Railroad
"workers' control"	brigades	capital goods	
cooperatives	household plots	Emancipation Edict	

CULTURE: How New Is the Soviet Man—or Woman?

PRESENT STATE

Ideology. The Soviet Union's Communist leaders believe that they can change human beings as well as the organization of society. In fact they claim that they are doing just that. They boast that in their socialist society a new man is appearing, the "Soviet man," as they like to call him. What is this "Soviet man" like? To what extent is he the product of Soviet communism, and to what extent is he similar to his ancestors who traded in ancient Kiev or struggled to build Moscow into a world empire or cowered beneath the knout of an autocratic landlord?

Anyone visiting the Soviet Union will find that, on the surface at least, the Soviet peo-

ple are like people everywhere else. Indeed, many visitors have reported that the Soviets resemble the Americans quite closely. Like Americans, they are warm, friendly, energetic, and sports-conscious. But if we look beneath the surface, we find some basic differences between the average American and the new "Soviet man." The major difference is in ideology, the theories, aims, and attitudes on which each operates. There is a certain uniformity in the thinking of all Soviet citizens because they are subjected to propaganda almost every waking hour, from the day they are born until the day they die. The aim of this propaganda is to persuade the

Soviet people of the superiority of Soviet society and of communism.

We have seen that communism is the ideology or the body of ideas worked out by Marx and Lenin. According to this philosophy, mankind is continually changing from one form of social organization to another. Just as capitalism took the place of feudalism, so now socialism and communism will inevitably take the place of capitalism. So far as we can tell, most citizens of the Soviet Union accept this ideology.

Americans believe in the superiority of their way of life and system of government just as Soviet citizens believe in communism. But because the Soviet Union is an authoritarian state, the propaganda for communism is many times more thorough than the propaganda for American democracy. The Soviet government uses every means to drive home Communist theory, not only the schools, radio and television, and newspapers, but also the total artistic production: including such things as plays, films, novels, poems, painting, and music.

This relentless indoctrination has inevitably left its mark on the mind of the Soviet people. It has given them a common stamp, so that their thinking is usually predictable and almost automatic. This does not mean that all, or even most, Soviet people approve everything their government does. We shall see that with the spread of higher education, more and more of the younger generation in the Soviet Union, as in other countries, are challenging their elders and their society. Yet very few challenge communism itself, and can hardly imagine living under another system. Those Soviet citizens who have grievances usually want reform of their existing society rather than revolution to overthrow it.

This conclusion is supported by a report of the views held by 3000 former Soviet citizens who fled from the U.S.S.R. during and after World War II.* Since these people have refused to return home, they presumably are more critical of Soviet society than most Soviet citizens. A group of American scholars used detailed questionnaires and held long interviews with these former Soviet citizens in order to learn their views. They found that the former citizens hated such things as police terror, the collectivization of the land,

* This data is from a book by Raymond A. Bauer, Alex Inkeles and Clyde Kluckhohn, *How the Soviet System Works* (Harvard University Press, 1956).

Young Pioneers practice a Russian folk dance for a pioneer camp program.

JACQUES JANGOUX

overwork in the factories, and poor housing conditions. But at the same time they favored the system of free education, the public health program, medical insurance, and government ownership of heavy industry. The scholars concluded that the former Soviet citizens "accept the system and reject the regime." In other words, they accept a socialist type of society but reject its present leaders and their policies.

Education and science. Another characteristic of the new "Soviet man," in addition to his ideology, is his tremendous interest in education and especially scientific education. The Soviet school system was studied in 1958 by a group of American experts headed by Dr. Lawrence G. Derthick, then United States Commissioner of Education. The group was surprised by the amount of money and attention being spent on education in the Soviet Union.* Soviet leaders have been willing to make this great outlay because

* See *Readings in World History*, "The Soviet Educational Challenge," p. 264.

they realize education is essential in their race to surpass the United States. Dr. Derthick reported as follows: "The slogan we saw most in posters, films and everywhere was 'reach and overreach America.' We did not find among children and teachers any evidence that this fierce sense of competition was other than of peaceful intent.... They are convinced that time is on their side and they can win world supremacy through education and hard work." [14]

Exactly what are the Soviet leaders doing in the field of education? First, they have made education available to everybody. There are now 54 million students in elementary and secondary schools as against less than 10 million in 1915 under the tsars, and 4 million in higher education as against 127,400 in 1915. Education now is compulsory from the first grade, which children enter at age seven, through the eighth grade. Plans are under way to make ten-year schooling compulsory, although Soviet educators admit that it will be some years before this will be possible outside the large cities.

JACQUES JANGOUX

The Soviet Union provides year-round recreation programs for Young Pioneers. The red pioneer scarf is a symbol of great prestige; the threat of its loss for behaving in a manner unfit for "pioneers helping to build the Soviet Union" is taken very seriously.

Second, Soviet leaders are requiring their students to work harder than American students do.* Schools are open 6 days per week rather than 5. Homework assignments and examinations are considerably more difficult than in the United States. Since the aim of the Communist leaders is to make the Soviet Union the foremost industrial country in the world, their secondary schools take 53 per cent of the students' time for science and mathematics. When the Soviet students graduate from secondary schools, they have had 5 years of physics, 4 of chemistry, 5 of biology, 1 of astronomy, and a 10-year program of arithmetic, algebra, geometry, and trigonometry. Few American college students study as much science and mathematics as a Soviet secondary graduate. Finally, Soviet education is free. Many scholarships are provided for the best students so that they may go on to college and graduate school.

The heavy investment in education has paid rich rewards to the Soviet government. It has provided literate workers for Soviet factories and skilled scientists for Soviet laboratories. Yet Soviet education faces many problems and criticisms.† The Soviet Minister of Education, M. A. Prokofiev, said in 1967: "The number of school hours devoted to compulsory subjects is too great and our curriculum is too rigid. There is no scope for reasonable initiative." [15] It was not until the 1966–67 school year that students in the 9th and 10th grades were allowed four hours of elective courses.

Soviet educators also complain of what they call "formalism," that is, dull recitation of assignments that are memorized. "We are too concerned," wrote one of these educators, "with *what* to communicate to pupils, and we devote too little attention to *how to* communicate it." [16]

* See *Readings in World History,* "Rules for Soviet School Children," p. 265.
† See *Readings in World History,* "Soviet Education: Myths and Facts," p. 270.

A science student in Moscow spends twice as much time in class as his American counterpart.

Finally there is another drawback that is not discussed by Soviet teachers, namely, the lack of an open and questioning mind outside the physical sciences. Free inquiry is very limited in the humanities and social sciences because the basic ideology was set forth long ago by Marx and Lenin, and the current official line by the Communist Party leaders in Moscow. This regimentation is increasingly resented and rejected by the younger generation. "We don't go in for political slogans," said a coed at Moscow University, "because by themselves they are meaningless. Few of us read the papers. There's too much pure propaganda. They pound us with slogans and outworn political clichés as if we couldn't understand anything else. The government must prove what it says, or we will not listen."

Yet despite all these weaknesses, the fact remains that the Soviet Union has established an efficient educational system, and in today's world this is as essential as efficient factories or efficient guns.

Position of women. Soviet leaders claim that they have created a new "Soviet woman" as well as a new "Soviet man." It is true that almost all visitors are surprised by the sight of women doing heavy work such as cleaning streets, driving buses and trucks, digging excavations, painting on high scaffolds, and directing traffic at city intersections. It is true that Soviet women have always done hard work, but in the tsarist period it was almost always unskilled work. In the countryside they did various chores on the farms. In the cities, more than half of all working women before 1917 were simply domestic workers. What is new today is that women have the same opportunity as men to get an education and to enter any profession. And what is significant is the remarkable degree to which Soviet women have taken advantage of this opportunity.[*]

Three-fourths of all Soviet physicians, teachers, and lawyers are women.
Nearly one-third of all Soviet engineers are women.
More than half of all Soviet economists are women.
Over one-third of all Soviet agricultural technologists are women.

[*] See *Readings in World History*, "The Soviet Woman," p. 274.

ALAN BAND

280 *Soviet Union*

Also, Soviet women hold 45 per cent of the jobs in industry, 30 per cent in construction, and 28 per cent in transportation. All in all, women make up 45 per cent of the entire labor force in the Soviet Union. By contrast, in the United States only 4 per cent of the physicians and surgeons are women, 3 per cent of our dentists, and 1 per cent of our engineers.

These statistics mean that almost no Soviet women stay at home; almost all are employed in one occupation or another. To make this possible, the Soviet government has passed laws giving women equal opportunity and guaranteeing them equal pay where they perform the same work as men. The government also has set up a nation-wide system of day nurseries and kindergartens where mothers may leave their children while at work. All this is a far cry from the pre-Soviet days when women were expected to work hard, but at menial jobs. The peasants used to say, "the hair is long, but the mind is short." And so women were regarded as inferior, simply because of their sex. Today they are considered as equals and, more important, treated as equals.

One exception to this rule is in politics. Women account for only 20 per cent of the Communist Party membership, and 27 per cent of the Supreme Soviet. As for the Presidium of the Supreme Soviet and the Presidium of the Communist Party, where the real power lies, these have always been men's clubs. A Mrs. Yekaterina Furtseva was a member of the Party Presidium, but she was the exception to the rule.

Nationalities under the tsar. As important as the Soviet treatment of women is the Soviet treatment of nationalities. We noted earlier in this unit that there are no less than 169 different ethnic groups living within the frontiers of the Soviet Union. By far the largest group is that of the Slavs, consisting of about 125 million Great Russians, 40 million Ukrainians or Little Russians, and 8 million Byelorussians or White Russians. In addition to these Slavic peoples, who form the large majority of the total population, there are many others, including Baltic peoples (Latvians, Estonians, and Lithuanians), Uzbeks, Kazakhs, and Armenians, Georgians, and Azerbaidzhanians. Tsarist treatment of these nationalities varied widely from period to period. At times they were simply ignored; at other times they were severely oppressed by attempts to Russify them. This was done by pressing them to accept the Russian language and the Orthodox religion. The nationalities naturally resented this pressure, and therefore they took a leading part in the 1905 and 1917 revolutions against the tsarist government. In fact, tsarist Russia often was referred to at that time as "the prison house of nations."

Soviet treatment of nationalities. The Bolsheviks from the beginning set out to win these discontented nationalities to their side. As early as 1913, Joseph Stalin wrote an essay entitled *Marxism and the National Question,* in which he stated that each nationality should have the right of self-determination, including even full independence if it so desires. But after the Bolsheviks seized power they interpreted this right of self-determination in such a way that it meant very little. They reserved the right to workers and peasants, and since the Bolsheviks considered themselves to be the spokesmen of the workers and peasants, there could be no justifiable demand for independence. In other words, if any groups of Ukrainians or Armenians or Kazakhs came out for independence, they were automatically branded as bourgeois counterrevolutionaries and ruthlessly suppressed. So there was self-determination in theory but not in practice. The Bolsheviks were quite as determined to hold their em-

Although in theory minority groups are allowed to have their own newspapers and cultures, in practice more and more pressure is being exerted to "Russify" all the peoples of the Soviet Union. Special pressure is being placed on Jews, with the inference being that to adhere to the Jewish faith is to be disloyal to the Soviet Union. Here a Soviet Jew reads one of the few newspapers still printed in Hebrew.

pire together as were the tsars. And they did hold it together, so that the Union of Soviet Socialist Republics, as we have seen, consists of 15 republics representing 15 nationalities as well as many minor ones.

How have the Soviet leaders governed all these nationalities that they kept under their rule? The Soviets themselves have summarized their policy with the slogan, "National in form but Socialist in content." In accordance with this slogan, the nationalities were allowed to keep their own languages, litera-

tures, arts, crafts, music, dancing, and so forth. School classes could be held in Tadjik or Lithuanian or Armenian, and books and newspapers could be published in these and all other languages. This was the "national in form" part of the Soviet slogan.

To carry out the "Socialist in content" part required that whatever was written in books or newspapers and whatever was taught in schools, had to be Socialist, or Communist. In other words, the newspapers in Tashkent, Riga, or Yerevan were published in the native languages, but their content was essentially the same as the Communist papers in Moscow and Leningrad. Likewise schools in Samarkand, Batum, or Tallin used textbooks written in the native languages, but the content again was essentially the same as that of the Communist textbooks used in the Russian part of the Soviet Union. In this way the "national form" was strictly controlled by the "Socialist content."

Even this restricted "national form" was whittled down during the 1930's. One reason was that some of the educated leaders of the nationalities were becoming too nationalistic and anti-Russian. Another reason was that the Five-Year Plans needed a disciplined and uniformly educated population in order to push ahead with industrialization. It would be hard, for example, to train the large number of scientists and technicians that were needed if the students did not understand the Russian language in which the scientific and technical journals were published. So in 1938 the government required the teaching of Russian in all non-Russian schools. This meant that the students in those schools had to learn two languages. At about the same time the government abolished the national divisions in the army. Soldiers of all nationalities were now mixed together, and Russian was made the language of instruction and command. Similar regulations were issued in other fields, all designed to lessen national differences and to make all Soviet people as disciplined and homogeneous as possible.

Displacement of nationalities. During World War II most of the nationalities remained loyal to the Soviet government though there were important exceptions. Many Ukrainians welcomed the German invaders and joined their ranks. Many more would have done so if the Germans had not acted as brutally as they did. Also there were

small Turkic ethnic groups in the Crimea and in the Caucasus that collaborated extensively with the Germans. The Soviets, in retaliation, uprooted almost all those peoples from their ancestral homes and scattered them through Central Asia. They did the same with a small colony of Germans on the Volga River, fearing that they would join the Nazi invaders who were advancing from the West.

Since the end of World War II the most important development affecting the nationalities has been the heavy emigration of Slavic peoples (Great Russians, Ukrainians, and Byelorussians) to all parts of the Soviet Union. Many spread out during the war when whole industries were moved from the European part of the U.S.S.R. to escape the German Armies. These industries, together with most of their workers, were transplanted east of the Urals, and most of them were allowed to remain permanently in their new sites. Many new industries were established in Siberia and in Central Asia after the war, and again many Slavic workers went east to work in the newly built factories. Finally the Soviet government under Khrushchev launched a campaign for the farming of the "virgin lands" of the east, especially in the Kazakh Republic. Once more this meant hundreds of thousands of young Slavic men and women crossing the Urals to settle permanently in what had been non-Slavic lands. The result of all these migrations is a much greater mixture of the various nationalities. In the Kazakh Republic the Kazakhs are now a minority, and in the other republics the Slavic newcomers are steadily becoming more numerous and more influential.

Survival of ethnic groups. What is the future of the nationalities in the Soviet Union? Some believe that the non-Russian peoples will become increasingly restless and anti-Soviet. It is argued that educated young

Kazakhs and Azerbaidzhanians and Latvians will turn against the Russians just as educated young Africans and Asians turned against their European rulers. On the other hand, other authorities believe that this analogy is not justified for two reasons. One is the large-scale settlement of Russians in all the non-Russian republics, so that it is much easier for Moscow to maintain its rule in the Central Asian or Baltic republics than for London or Paris to hold their colonies.

The other reason is to be found in the intensive industrialization which is tending to make all the Soviet peoples more and more alike, despite their varied origins. In the Soviet Union, as in the rest of the world, industrialization means urbanization. People are concentrating in cities, where they are all subject to the same mass culture and mass indoctrination. This is especially true of the young people who know that in order to get ahead they must accept the Soviet system and must get a higher education, which is given in the Russian language. This pressure for uniformity, together with the actual physical mixing of peoples, will, according to some authorities, slowly weaken the various nationalities. Eventually they will lack both the power and the desire to resist the Moscow government, and will become an integral part of Soviet society just as the Spanish Americans in our Southwest have become an integral part of United States society.

In Tashkent, a Uzbekstan craftsman works to perfect a Dukar, an instrument used to accompany traditional Uzbekstan folksongs and dances.

JACQUES JANGOUX

HISTORICAL ORIGINS

We have seen that the Soviet leaders are changing the Soviet Union with their Communist ideology, their Communist system of education, and their treatment of women and of the nationalities. Does this mean that Soviet Russia today is altogether different from the Russia before 1917? The answer is definitely not. Many aspects of present-day Russian culture can be traced back for centuries, not merely to 1917.

Russia's conversion to Christianity. Much of the culture of today's Soviet Union has roots going back one thousand years to 990 A.D. when the Russians first became Christians. It was the ruler of Kiev, Vladimir the Saint, who decided at that time that his pagan Russian people should become Christians. The story of how he made this important decision is interesting. First the Muslims tried to persuade Vladimir to accept their Islamic religion. But he decided against them, partly because Islam prohibited wine, and the Russians, he felt, were too fond of wine to be willing to give it up. Then the Jews used various arguments to win Vladimir to their religion. After listening to their speeches, Vladimir asked them where their country was. "Jerusalem," they replied, "but God in His anger has scattered us over the whole world." "Then you are cursed of God," cried the king, "and yet you want to teach others: begone! we have no wish, like you, to be without a country." Finally appeared a Greek priest, who, after briefly criticizing the other religions, set forth the nature of Christian teachings. He began with the creation of the world and ended by promising paradise to those who were baptised and led good Christian lives.

Vladimir was most impressed by the Greek priest, and yet he hesitated to make a final decision on so important a matter. So he called together his boyars (nobles), and, after telling them of the various religions, asked them for their advice. "Prince," they replied, "every man praises his own religion, and if you would make a choice of the best, send wise men into the different countries to discover which of all the nations honors God in the manner most worthy of Him." So Vladimir sent his wisest men to foreign lands to report on what they found. These envoys reported that the Muslims worshipped in mean-looking mosques and in a manner that was gloomy and discouraging. They were unfavorably impressed also by the Jewish synagogues and the Catholic Christian churches and services.

At last Vladimir's envoys reached Constantinople, the glorious capital of the Byzantine Empire. There they were taken to the magnificent church of Santa Sophia, where the Patriarch, clad in his pontifical robes, was celebrating Mass. The splendor of the cathedral, the ornaments of the altars, the sweet odor of the incense, the reverent silence of

Mosaic in St. Sophia Cathedral in Kiev

the people, and the mysterious solemnity of the ceremonies all filled the Russian visitors with wonder and amazement. They were convinced that this church must be the dwelling of the Most High. On their return to Kiev the envoys had little praise for the Islamic, Jewish, and Catholic faiths. But they were enthusiastic in their praises of the Greek Orthodox church. "Every man," they said, "who has put to his lips a sweet draught [drink] henceforth abhors anything bitter; wherefore, we having come to the knowledge of the faith of the Greek Church desire none other." [17]

With this report, both Vladimir and his *boyars* decided in favor of Greek Orthodox Christianity. After they were baptized, they ordered their subjects also to receive baptism. And so, hundreds of thousands of Russians waded into the Dnieper River while the Christian priests on the bank offered up their prayers.

This conversion of Russia to Christianity meant much more than a simple change in religion. The Greek priests from the Byzantine Empire brought with them not only their Christian faith but also their rich Byzantine culture. This is why visitors today find that the Russian alphabet is derived from Greek rather than Latin. The explanation is that the Russians got their alphabet together with their religion from the Byzantine Greeks. Visitors also find that the old Russian churches are very different from the old churches in Western Europe. In contrast to the straight lines and soaring spires of Western Gothic cathedrals, many Russian cathedrals are built after Byzantine models, with several onion-shaped domes and cupolas.

Religion today. In these old cathedrals the people today worship as they did in Kievan days. Particularly on special occasions, such as Easter and Christmas, the churches are crammed with worshippers. The Orthodox, as well as the other religious faiths, conduct their services with no interference by the government. These faiths have estimated their numbers as follows:

Russian Orthodox............30 to 50 million
Muslims .... 25 million
Roman Catholics .... 12 million
Greek Catholics ....4.5 million
Jews.............................3.4 million
Baptists......................... 2 million
Lutherans........................ 1 million

The Soviet government is strongly antireligious or atheistic. It allows citizens to worship but uses every means to persuade them not to do so. All the schools, from the elementary level to the university, teach the students that religion is a superstition that has no place in a modern scientific world. On the other side, no church may give religious teaching to anyone under the age of 18. This means that there can be no parochial schools in the Soviet Union as there are in the United States and many other countries. The government has a monopoly of all education and uses it to fight against religion.* If an individual wishes to join a church he is free to do so. But such an individual cannot hope to rise in the Communist Party or in the Soviet government.

What is the result of all these pressures against religion? It is difficult to be sure because the evidence is contradictory. On the one hand the churches are frequently crowded. On the other hand, the congregations usually consist largely of old men and women. Also it should be remembered that today there are only 55 churches in Moscow compared to 1000 in 1917; thus it is not surprising that the 55 are crowded. A distinguished old priest sadly told an American correspondent in 1957: "Religion is dying and will never again be a vital force in the Soviet Union. The young simply are not interested." [18]

On the other hand, a two-year official survey made in the late 1960's in the large city of Kazan revealed that 21 per cent of the population believed in one religion or another, though only 3 per cent of these believers were 30 years old or younger. Also it is significant that the Soviet press constantly complains of the continued influence of religion and calls on all Communists to fight it with all their power. Perhaps there is something to the old Russian saying that religion is like a nail; the harder you hit it, the deeper it goes.†

* See *Readings in World History*, "Soviet Antireligious Propaganda," p. 279.
† See *Readings in World History*, "The Future of Religion in the USSR: Two Views," p. 281.

Family life. Turning from religion to the family, we again find much of old Russia still present in the Soviet Union. In the early days of the revolution, many Communists felt that the family was outdated. They argued that it was a relic of the past, like private property, and that it should be thrown overboard together with private property. So the Bolshevik revolution was hardly a month old when the government passed laws making both marriage and divorce easier. A couple merely had to register at a government office to make their marriage legal. Likewise either partner could obtain a divorce by applying at the government office and paying a small fee. It was not uncommon for a husband or wife to receive a postcard from his or her mate announcing that their marriage was ended. This looseness led to many abuses, and the women complained the most.

The government gradually made the laws more strict. The fee to obtain divorce has been raised from a few rubles to between five hundred and two thousand. Either one or both partners might be required to pay this fee. Also both partners must now appear before a court, and judges are very slow and reluctant about granting divorces. In fact a divorce is harder to get in the Soviet Union now than in almost any country in Europe. The government has been carrying on a propaganda campaign against what it calls the "light-minded attitude towards the family." Furthermore, the date of each divorce is entered in the passport which each individual carries wherever he goes. Since divorce is so much frowned upon, each date is a serious black mark against the passport holder and will hold him back in whatever career he chooses. Finally, the government is trying to promote the size of each family as well as its solidarity. Women with ten or more children are given the title of "Mother Heroine," others with five or more offspring earn "The Order of Motherhood" and "Glorious Motherhood." Special financial grants and allowances are given to families depending on the number of children.

We may conclude that the Soviet government definitely has turned its back upon the earlier notion that the family is an outdated social institution that should be abandoned. Instead the family now is as much the basic unit of society as it had been in the tsarist period.

Another change that has occurred in recent years is the stress on femininity. Formerly

It is becoming increasingly more difficult to distinguish young people in Moscow from their counterparts in the U.S. or Europe.

JACQUES JANGOUX

Symphony No. 13, with music by Dimitri Shostakovich (left) and words by the poet Yevgeny Yevtushenko (right), performed for the first time in Moscow in 1962, received unprecedented acclaim from the Russian people who feel art and music to be an intimate and important part of their lives.

women worked alongside men and as hard as men. They wore shapeless dresses and heavy shoes, pulled their hair into knots on the back of their heads, and scorned jewelry and cosmetics. Now they follow clothes fashions, wear high-heeled shoes, go to beauty parlors, and look after their figures.*

Finally, the lives of Soviet women, and of their families, are now being transformed by television.† Antennas are sprouting from houses and apartment buildings all over the Soviet Union. Because of the shortage of space, the television sets usually are put in kitchens. "Everybody I know gathers in the kitchen," said a Moscovite recently, "because the television and the refrigerator are there." [19]

Artistic life. In the field of literature we again find the legacy of old Russia to be all important in the modern Soviet Union. The Soviet people are perhaps the world's greatest readers. There are reported to be 400,000

* See *Readings in World History,* "The Soviet Woman," p. 274.
† See *Readings in World History,* "Television in Soviet Life," p. 286.

libraries in the country; bookstores and sidewalk bookstalls are to be found everywhere in the streets. The surprising thing about the Soviet readers is that they prefer the old pre-1917 classics, not only those by Russian authors such as Pushkin, Turgenev, and Tolstoy, but also by foreign authors such as Shakespeare, Mark Twain, and Victor Hugo. These classics are published in huge editions to meet the popular demand. Since 1917, almost 50 million copies of Pushkin's works have been published, five million of Victor Hugo's, and two million of Shakespeare's. The Soviets do read, of course, the writings of Soviet authors, but not so eagerly and intensely. They read them and set them aside; the classics they read again and again.

Why is there less interest in the modern Soviet works than in the classics of all literatures? Perhaps the main reason is to be found in the following resolution passed by the Central Committee of the Communist Party on August 14, 1946: "Soviet literature neither has nor can have any other interests except those of the people and of the State. Its task is to help the State to educate the youth." [20]

In other words, literature, like everything else, is to be used for political purposes. That is why there are no comics nor mystery stories published in the Soviet Union. These would be too frivolous; they would not contribute to the education of the new Soviet man and woman.

Instead the government urges the writing of novels, plays, and poems which are politically useful but unbearably boring. When boy meets girl in Soviet literature, they talk about increasing factory production and surpassing the United States. In the past few years even the Communists have realized that this may be good propaganda, but that it is unappealing literature. A Communist magazine recently stated: "Art is not just another form of political propaganda." It also criticized Soviet authors who "write standard plays about boy and girl on a collective farm in which both are more attached to their tractors than to each other." [21]

Not all Soviet literature is dull and inferior. A few authors of genius have produced great works despite the controls of the government. Among them was the late Boris Pasternak, whose novel of life during and after the Revolution, *Doctor Zhivago*, was published outside the Soviet Union. Pasternak was forced to refuse the Nobel prize for literature in 1958 under pressure from the Soviet government. Mikhail Sholokhov has written many novels admired in the U.S.S.R. and abroad, among them *And Quiet Flows the Don*, which has sold 10 million copies in the author's homeland. But these are special cases; so long as literature is required to serve the interests of the state, so long will Soviet citizens prefer the classics of the 19th century.

In other arts also Soviet citizens depend on pre-1917 creations. This is especially true of ballet, which all Soviet people love. No less than 32 Soviet cities have their own ballet troupes, who regularly perform a repertoire almost entirely classical. Also popular in the Soviet Union and throughout the world are folk-dancers such as the Moiseyev troupe,

A Soviet audience enjoys the circus.

who have met with enormous success in the United States. As for music, the famous composers of the tsarist period: Tchaikovsky, Rimski-Korsakov, Moussorgsky, and Borodin, all remain great favorites; but there have been remarkable achievements under the Soviet regime. The compositions of Dimitri Shostakovich, Aram Khatchaturian ("Sabre Dance"), and the late Sergei Prokofiev ("Classical Symphony") are widely played. Soloists such as the violinist David Oistrakh and the pianist Emil Gilels are rated as superior artists on the world's concert stages.

The new Soviet man. In conclusion, we can now try to answer the question of how new

Cosmonaut Yuri Gagarin, an example to all the U.S.S.R. of the potential accomplishments of the "new Soviet Man."

WIDE WORLD

is the "new Soviet man." The answer seems to be that he is largely new, but not altogether so. His acceptance of Communist ideology, his passion for education and science, his acceptance of women as equals, and his determination to keep learning and working until the Soviet Union becomes the foremost power in the world, all these are new features of the Soviet man. Yet at the same time some of the old Russian remains in him: his love of ballet, his preference for the literary classics, his attendance at church services, and his celebration of the Christmas holiday, even though the Christmas trees are called New Year's trees, and the robust, red-cheeked, white-bearded Santa Claus is known as Grandfather Frost.

In recent years the "new Soviet man" has become too new and too different for the liking of the country's leaders. The younger generation in the Soviet Union, as in many other countries, is striking out on new paths. Many call themselves the "Fourth Generation." The three generations before them were those which had won the 1917 Revolution, worked in the great industrialization drives, and fought in World War II. But all this is ancient history for young Soviets today. Not having endured the trials, privations, and terrors of their parents, they are more gay, uninhibited, and forthright. "The present young generation," complained the Communist Party leader, Leonid Brezhnev, "does not have the severe schooling of revolutionary struggle and is not hardened as the older generation has been." By contrast, a visitor to the Soviet Union will hear young people say, "We just want to live. We want to be left alone to lead the lives we choose." [22] Thus the generation gap is as much of a problem in the Soviet Union as in the United States. And it is bound to affect profoundly the future development of the country, since half the present population is under 27 years of age.

Reviewing the Essentials

Present State

1. Describe the new "Soviet man" who is emerging in the U.S.S.R. What kind of person is he? What does he value, approve, and disapprove in his way of life? How does he view the United States and our way of life? What are the sources of his opinions?

2. Why does the Soviet Union give high priority to education? Cite evidence in support of the emphasis placed on education. Describe the favorable and unfavorable aspects of the Soviet educational system.

3. Describe the new "Soviet woman." How has the status of women changed since the tsarist period?

4. What was the policy of (a) the tsars and (b) the Bolsheviks on self-determination for nationality groups?

5. What do Soviet leaders mean by their policy of "national in form but socialist in content," as it relates to nationalities?

6. What changes were made immediately before, during, and after World War II which tend to "neutralize" the importance of nationality groups within the Soviet Union?

7. What is the outlook for the future of nationalities in the Soviet Union?

Historical Origins

8. How did Vladimir, ruler of Kiev, finally decide that pagan Russia should become Orthodox Christian?

9. What is the position of the Soviet government on religion, religious instruction, and church attendance? How do the Russian people respond?

10. How has the Soviet government reversed its position on the family? What steps is the government now taking to strengthen the family?

11. How is literature used to serve the purposes of the state? Why do people in the U.S.S.R. appear to prefer classic works of the period prior to 1917?

Explain, Identify, or Locate

"prison house of nations"	Tchaikovsky	Vladimir	Constantinople
ethnic group	Boris Pasternak	Borodin	Dnieper River
Mikhail Sholokhov	Pushkin	Prokofiev	Kiev
	Tolstoy	Santa Sophia	

UNIT ACTIVITIES

1. On an outline map of the Soviet Union locate the major rivers, cities, nationalities, and republics of the R.S.F.S.R. Also prepare a resource map, locating major natural resources, vegetation zones, the Trans-Siberian Railroad, hydroelectric power centers, and industrial centers. A useful source is George Kish, *Economic Atlas of the Soviet Union* (Ann Arbor: University of Michigan Press, 1960).

2. Read in suggested sources and others on the Soviet people today. Look for information on: (a) the major nationality groups in the Soviet Union and their way of life; (b) values the Soviet people hold important; (c) how the Soviets feel about their government, Five-Year Plans, missile and rocket development, and the non-Soviet world. Consult several of the following useful source materials: "USSR: The New Regime," *Current History,* September, 1965; Louis Fischer, *Russia Revisited;* Edward Crankshaw, *Khrushchev's Russia;* Charles W. Thayer and the Editors of Life, *Russia* (New York: Time, Inc., 1960); *U.S.S.R.,* a magazine published by the Embassy of the Union of Soviet Socialist Republics in the

U.S.A., for Russians' statements on their way of life; *Readings in World History,* "Soviet Citizens and Their Government," pp. 234–236; "Complaints of Soviet Consumers," pp. 252–256; "The Soviet Educational Challenge," pp. 264–265; "The Future of Religion in the U.S.S.R.: Two Views," pp. 281–283.

3. Prepare for class a panel discussion on the topic: Soviets Ask Questions about the United States. For background information, consult the sources listed in the preceding activity and check *Readers' Guide to Periodical Literature* for recent pertinent articles. Compile a list of questions that Soviets frequently ask about the United States and its citizens; show how these questions reveal aspects of their own culture. Make explicit your conclusions about the Soviet people and the outlook for the United States-Soviet relations.

4. Prepare a report for presentation to class on the U.S.S.R.'s political system. Include in the report information on the following questions:

a. In what ways were these goals reinforced or changed by Stalin?
b. What changes were introduced by Khrushchev?
c. What appear to be reasons for shifts in Soviet policy?
d. What are implications for the U.S.S.R., the U.S.A., and the Free World?

For information see: *The United States and the Soviet Challenge* (Foreign Relations Series); Thomas P. Whitney, *Has Russia Changed?* (cited); *Readings in World History,* "Premier Khrushchev on Soviet 'Democracy,'" pp. 231–233.

5. Develop visual material, i.e., charts and diagrams, to illustrate the features of the U.S. and Soviet economic systems. Similarities and differences should be identified and explained. Consult the *Readers' Guide to Periodical Literature* for current information. Also see: H. Heymann, "Storm Signals for the West," *Saturday Review,* January 21, 1961; *Readings in World History,* "Soviet Efficiency; Myth or Fact?" pp. 245–247; "An Appraisal of the Soviet Economy," pp. 241–244; "Complaints of Soviet Consumers," pp. 252–256; "The Soviet Economic Challenge," pp. 256–259.

6. Prepare a report on the process of developing a Five-Year Plan in the Soviet Union, indicating the kind of problems involved in comprehensive planning of this type. Consult: Harry Schwartz, *Russia's Soviet Economy;* "Inside the Soviet Economy," *Saturday Review,* January 21, 1961.

7. Read on the Seven-Year Plan, and prepare for a class discussion of its implications for the Soviet Union and the non-Soviet world. A good source is Gregory Grossman, "Khrushchev's Plan for Seven Fatter Years," *The Reporter,* December 25, 1958; also consult *Readers' Guide to Periodical Literature* for sources of latest data.

8. Study Soviet agriculture as a major problem in the country's economy, noting: (a) organization of Soviet farms; (b) problems that have plagued planners in meeting goals for agricultural output; (c) causes of these problems; (d) goals and policies of Lenin, Stalin, Khrushchev, Kosygin, and Brezhnev. Consult: *Current History,* September 1965 (cited); Charles W. Thayer, *Russia* (cited), chap. v, "Trial and Error on the Farm"; *Readings in World History,* "The Russian Peasant and His Government," pp. 250–252; "Soviet Efficiency: Myth or Fact?" pp. 245–247.

9. Identify from your study of the Soviet Union those things that have (a) changed and (b) not changed since the death of Stalin. What are the implications in the situation for (a) Russia and (b) the West? See E. R. Platig, *The United States and the Soviet Challenge* and other sources listed in previous activities and the bibliography.

10. A major emphasis in the course is on understanding the way of life that is developing in certain regional areas of the world. In the case of the Soviet Union, identify and explain what you now regard as important and significant developments that characterize the Soviet way of life. Include political, economic, and cultural aspects. In class discussion, consider what these developments mean to (a) the United States and its allies, (b) the Sino-Soviet bloc, and (c) the underdeveloped nations.

11. Have the class prepare for discussion: Current Problems and Issues in United States-Soviet Relations. Groups might prepare statements of the policy problem, alternative solutions, and

recommended action. The following can be guiding questions:

    a. What action can the United States take to reduce Soviet influence in satellite countries?

    b. Should the United States continue to work for a united Germany?

    c. How can the United States reduce or block Soviet influence in the Middle East?

    d. What can the United States do to end the arms race and establish an effective program of arms control?

    e. How can the United States deal most effectively with the Sino-Soviet bloc?

    f. How can the United States meet the Soviet offensive in the underdeveloped countries?

Questions of this scope demand wide reading and deep thought. A few of the many possible sources are suggested here: *Goals for Americans: The Report of the President's Commission on National Goals* (Englewood Cliffs, N.J.: Prentice-Hall, 1960), pp. 299–331; Eliot Zupnick, *Primer of U.S. Foreign Economic Policy* (Headline Series No. 169, 1965), "The Communist Economic Challenge"; "The Question of U.S. Economic Aid for Latin America," *Congressional Digest,* February 1961; "The Question of Outlawing Nuclear Weapons: Pro and Con," *Congressional Digest,* October 1958; Vera M. Dean, *The Nature of the Non-Western World;* E. R. Platig, *The United States and the Soviet Challenge* (cited).

SELECTED READING

● For an excellent introduction to the geography of the Soviet Union, see A. Nazaroff, *The Land and People of Russia* (Philadelphia: Lippincott, 1966, rev. ed.). A very useful atlas which illustrates the geography, history, and economy of Russia is *Philips' Soviet Atlas: History, Geography, Resources* (Chicago: Denoyer-Geppert, 1954).

● Excellent general histories of Russia are by H. E. Salibury, *Russia* (New York: Macmillan, 1965); W. Habberton, *Russia: The Story of a Nation* (Boston: Houghton Mifflin, 1965); and M. E. Petrovich, *The Soviet Union* (Boston: Ginn and Co., 1964). For recent developments, see P. E. Mosely, *The Soviet Union Since Khrushchev* (Foreign Policy Association, Headline Series, No. 175).

● Biographies of Ivan the Terrible and Peter the Great have been written by the highly regarded Harold Lamb, *The March of Muscovy: Ivan the Terrible and the Growth of the Russian Empire*

1400–1648 (New York: Doubleday, 1948); and *The City and the Tsar: Peter the Great and the Move to the West 1648–1762* (New York: Doubleday, 1948). See also the biography by J. Archer, *Man of Steel: Joseph Stalin* (New York: Julian Messner, 1965).

● For a brief analysis of Soviet-American relations, see the pamphlet by E. R. Platig, *The United States and the Soviet Challenge,* Foreign Relations Series (River Forest, Illinois: Laidlaw). A clear explanation of communism is given in Andrew Gyorgy, *Communism in Perspective* (Boston: Allyn & Bacon, 1964).

● Generations of Russian children have been brought up on the fables of the writer, Ivan Krylov. His *Russian Fables* have now been translated by Sir Bernard Pares (Penguin Books, 1942). Also enjoyable are the illustrated Georgian folk tales by G. and H. Papashvily, *Yes and No Stories, A Book of Georgian Folk Tales* (New York: Harper, 1946).

FURTHER READING

● Three excellent general histories of Russia are available in paperback form: Sir Bernard Pares, *Russia* (New York: Mentor Book, 1949); John Lawrence, *A History of Russia* (New York: Mentor Book, 1962); and Hans Kohn, *Basic*

History of Modern Russia (Van Nostrand, Anvil Book, No. 25). A more detailed account is available in N. V. Riasanovsky, *A History of Russia* (New York: Oxford University Press, 1963).

● There are some excellent collections of source

materials on many aspects of Russian history. They are *Reading in Russian History* (Syracuse University Press, 1965) by W. B. Walsh which places its emphasis mostly on the Tsarist period; *Soviet Society: a Book of Readings* (Boston: Houghton Mifflin, 1961) by Alex Inkeles and K. Geiger, which concentrates on the period since the 1917 Revolution; *Readings in Russian Civilization* (Chicago: University of Chicago Press, 1964, 3 vols.), Thomas Riha, ed. (available in paperback); and *The Soviet Union, 1922–1962: A Foreign Affairs Reader* (New York: Praeger, 1963, paperback), Philip E. Moseley, editor.

● The most detailed and authoritative history of Russia up to the Soviet period is *Russia: A History and Interpretation* (New York: Macmillan, 1954, 2 volumes), written by Michael T. Florinsky. There is also a shortened version of this text now available: *Russia: A Short History* (New York: Macmillan, 1964). Florinsky is also the editor of the *Encyclopedia of Russia and the Soviet Union* (New York: McGraw-Hill, 1961). Good surveys which cover both the Tsarist and Soviet periods are given by G. Vernadsky, *A History of Russia* (New Haven: Yale University Press, rev. ed., 1961); and M. C. Wren, *The Course of Russian History* (New York: Macmillan, 2nd ed., 1963). All these histories are chronological in approach and organization. A contrast to this approach can be found in *Russia: Tsarist and Communist* (Princeton, New Jersey: Van Nostrand, 1962) by A. G. Mazour which provides a topical analysis of various historical topics, such as church and religion, state, foreign affairs, industry, and the arts.

● William Chamberlin, *Russian Revolution* (New York: Macmillan, 1935) is an authoritative source for the story of that earth-shaking event. For the Soviet period, there are two competent studies, one by Hugh Seton-Watson, *From Lenin to Khrushchev* (New York: Praeger, 1960); the other by Edward Crankshaw, *Khrushchev's Russia* (Penguin Books, 1960). An important analysis of what makes the Soviet Union run is W. W. Rostow, *The Dynamics of Soviet Society* (Mentor Book, 1967). For the most recent period, see A. Dallin and T. B. Larson, *Soviet Politics Since Khrushchev* (Englewood Cliffs, N.J.: Prentice Hall, 1968); and H. Salisbury, ed., *The Soviet Union: The Fifty Years* (New York: Harcourt Brace, 1968).

● Soviet-American relations are expertly discussed by George F. Kennan, *On Dealing with the Communist World* (New York: Harper, 1964); the same author's *Russia and the West Under Lenin and Stalin* (Boston: Little, Brown, and Co., 1961); and Isaac Deutscher, *Great Contest: Russia and the West* (New York: Oxford University Press, 1960).

● A fine source on the Soviet economy is Harry Schwartz, *Russia's Soviet Economy* (Englewood Cliffs: Prentice-Hall, 1960, 2d ed. with appendix 1954–1958); and his *Soviet Union: Communist Economic Power* (Chicago: Scott Foresman and Co., 1963). Also useful are Alec Nove's two books. They are *Soviet Economy* (New York: Praeger, 1961, paperback); and *Economic Rationality and Soviet Politics* (New York: Praeger, 1964).

● For the historical background of relations between the United States and the Soviet Union, see *American-Russian Relations 1781–1947* (New York: Rinehart, 1952) by W. A. Williams. For analysis and discussion of the present relationships between the two countries, there are three excellent paperbacks: *The Kremlin and World Politics* (Vintage Russian Library, 1960) by P. E. Mosely; *Russia and America* (Mentor Book, 1956) by H. L. Roberts; and *U.S. Foreign Policy and the Soviet Union* (Santa Barbara, California: Box 4068, Center for the Study of Democratic Institutions) by F. W. Neal.

● There are many biographies of the past and present leaders of the Soviet Union. Among the most authoritative are the following: *The Prophet Armed* (Trotsky) (New York: Oxford University Press, 1954) by Isaac Deutscher; *Stalin: A Political Biography* (New York: Vintage Book, Random House, 1960), also by Deutscher; *Lenin: A Biography* (New York: Doubleday, 1948) by D. Shub; *Life of Lenin* (New York: Harper & Row, 1964) by Lewis Fischer; *Khrushchev, the Making of a Dictator* (Boston: Little, Brown and Co., 1960) by George Poloczi-Horvatti; *Karl Marx: The Red Prussian* (New York: Grosset & Dunlap, 1958) by Leopold Schwartzchild; and *Three Who Made a Revolution* (New York: Dial, 1964) by Bertram D. Wolfe.

● A sympathetic portrait of the Russian people may be found in Wright Miller's *Russians as People* (New York: Dutton, 1961). Education is covered by Nigel Grant, *Soviet Education* (Baltimore: Penguin Books, 1964). Sports are covered by Henry W. Morton, *Soviet Sport, Mirror of Soviet Society* (New York: Collier, 1963).

● The Sino-Soviet rift is discussed by Harry Schwartz, *Tsars, Mandarins, and Commissars: A History of Chinese–Russian Relations* (Philadelphia: Lippincott, 1964); Edward Crankshaw, *New Cold War: Moscow versus Peking* (Baltimore: Penguin Books, 1963); and Klaus Mehnert, *Peking and Moscow* (New York: G. P. Putnam's Sons, 1963).

● The life story of a colorful Russian woman who married an American journalist is Willie Snow Ethridge, *Nila: Her Story* (New York: Simon & Schuster, 1956), the portrait of Nila Magidoff. For a deeper insight into the mentality of the Soviet elite, read Arthur Koestler's superb novel of Communist terror, *Darkness at Noon* (Modern Library).

● Finally, there are some excellent paperback surveys of Russian literature which mirror many aspects of Russian history. Among them are the following: *An Outline of Russian Literature* (Mentor Book, 1958) by M. Slonim; and *A History of Russian Literature from its Beginning to 1900* (Vintage Books; 1958) by D. S. Mirsky.

LATIN AMERICA

...unless necessary social reforms, including land and tax reforms, are freely made, unless we broaden the opportunity of all of our people, unless the great mass of Americans share in increasing prosperity, then our alliance, our revolution, our dream, and our freedom will fail. But we call for social change by free men—change in the spirit of Washington and Jefferson, of Bolívar and San Martín and Marti—not change which seeks to impose on men tyrannies which we cast out a century and a half ago. Our motto is what it has always been—progress yes, tyranny no—progresso si, tirania no!

John F. Kennedy

BASIC FACTS: Old Empires, New Nations

GEOGRAPHY

Latin America stretches more than 10,000 miles south and east from the borders of Texas to the tip of Cape Horn. Latin America reaches so far to the south that there is no European capital, not even Moscow, which is farther away from Chicago, than is Buenos Aires, the capital of Argentina.

The area of Latin America is more than twice that of the United States. Within this area there are 20 separate independent countries which are "Latin American," that is, which developed from Spanish, Portuguese, or French colonies and perpetuate Spanish, Portuguese, or French language and culture. In addition to these 20 Latin American countries, there are nearby a number of British and Dutch colonies, as well as Guyana (formerly British Guiana), Trinidad-Tobago, Barbados, and Jamaica. These small former British colonies, though in the same zone as Latin America, are usually not considered part of Latin America.

The 20 Latin American countries vary greatly in size. Brazil is the fifth-largest country in the world. The area of the United States is slightly greater than that of Brazil, only because the United States includes the enormous state of Alaska. Argentina, the second-largest nation in Latin America, is almost five times the size of Texas. Mexico, the third-largest country in Latin America, is three times the size of Texas.

At the other extreme, Latin America contains some very small countries. Haiti, the Dominican Republic, Cuba, and the other Caribbean islands are most comparable in area to the New England states.

Most of the Andean republics, those located at least partially in the Andes Mountains, fall into a medium-sized category. Peru, Colombia, Bolivia, Venezuela, and Chile are each bigger than Texas. These Andean countries seem even larger when one travels in them, because their large, steep mountains make ground transportation so slow and difficult.

Population Distribution. Although many of the Latin American countries extend over large expanses, their populations are not yet very great. The population of all of Latin America is only a little bigger than that of the United States, though the area is double. Brazil, the giant of Latin America, does have more than 80 million people. But only three other countries in the region: Mexico, Argentina, and Colombia, can as yet claim more than 15 million citizens. Eleven of the twenty countries have populations of five million or less.

Although the populations of many Latin American countries are quite small, this does not mean that they are all "underpopulated." Two of the smallest countries, Haiti and El Salvador, have high population densities (more than 325 persons per square mile), comparable to that of India. Most of the other Latin American republics do have low population densities, from 20 to 60 persons per square mile. The average for the whole region is 33 per square mile. (In the United States the average is 50 per square mile, and in Europe it is 152.)

To find comfort in these figures, however, would be a delusion. As the Latin American countries are much less industrialized than the United States or Western Europe, the bulk of their populations must support themselves on the land. And cultivable land is relatively scarce in Latin America. Whereas

12 per cent of the land in the world as a whole can be cultivated, and in the United States almost 20 per cent; in Latin America only about 4 per cent of the land is arable. Most of the great Amazon basin, as well as frequently-inundated areas in southeastern Mexico, and parts of Colombia, Venezuela, Ecuador, and Peru, are not good for agriculture because flood-waters or an overabundance of rain leach the soils. The western coasts of Peru and northern Chile on the other hand, get almost no rain, and, in most places, are a complete desert. Many other areas, such as the northern half of Mexico, the lowland plains of Colombia and Venezuela, and much of southern Argentina, can be used only for grazing widely-scattered sheep and cattle.

Thus, if we consider Latin America's population density in relation to usable land, the picture is not encouraging. Whereas the world average of persons per square mile of arable land is 560, five Latin American countries (Haiti, Peru, El Salvador, Costa Rica, and the Dominican Republic) have more than 1,200 persons per square mile of land under cultivation. Of the 20 countries in the region, 14 have a greater density of population in relation to arable land than the world average. Only two Latin American countries, Argentina and Nicaragua, have fewer persons per square mile of arable land than the United States.

The problem of unusable land is best exemplified by Brazil, which has only 23 persons per square mile of its total area, but almost 1,000 persons per square mile of arable land. In Brazil, as in most of Latin America, some of the land not now used for farming could be made usable through flood

The Precordillera Mountains, Tarapaca, Chile

control, irrigation, heavy fertilizing, and other devices. But all of these require large investments of capital. With the possible exception of oil-rich Venezuela, the Latin American countries do not have the capital required for large-scale development of their now-useless lands.

The problem of population pressure on usable land is aggravated by the high birth rate in most of Latin America. In recent years Latin America as a whole has had an annual birth rate of 40 per thousand, double

Basic Facts 299

the rate in the United States. Despite this high rate, the rate of population increase in Latin America, until the 20th century, remained relatively moderate because of high death rates, and particularly frequent infant mortality. But as medical facilities and treatment have been extended to larger numbers of people, the mortality rates have tended to decline. As a result, in the last few decades, the Latin American population has been expanding rapidly. In the more developed countries of the region, such as Argentina, Cuba, and Chile, rates of population increase have been relatively low, about 1.6 per cent per annum. But the populations of 10 of the 20 countries have increased at rates of more than 3 per cent. The Latin American average net population growth is close to 3 per cent per year, the highest of any region of the world.

Latin America's high birth rate means that its population is extraordinarily young. In the countries with high rates of population increase, about 45 per cent of the people are under 15 years of age, and well over half are under 20. (In contrast, less than 40 per cent of the United States' population is under 20.)

In part because so large a proportion of Latin America's population is young (and so small a proportion is adult), it has been especially difficult to extend education. In nine of the 20 countries, more than half the people over 15 years of age were illiterate in 1960, and in four more at least a third were illiterate.

Another obstacle to the spread of education has been the fact that a great proportion of the population has lived in rural areas. In rural Latin America it has been difficult to establish schools, partly because competent teachers do not want to live in the country. This problem is being remedied, however, by the large-scale migration to the city.

School children waiting for class to begin in Rio de Janeiro, Brazil, reflect the varied racial makeup of Latin America.

CARL E. OSTMAN

The massive migration to the cities began only recently. Until 1940 the Latin American population was overwhelmingly rural. Since 1940, however, peasants have moved into the cities in increasing numbers. In 20 years (1940–60) São Paulo in Brazil doubled in size. In the same period, Lima and Mexico City tripled their populations. And in *ten* years (1950–60) Cali, Colombia, doubled, and Caracas in Venezuela *tripled*. There are now well over one hundred cities with more than 100,000 people. Twelve metropolitan centers have more than one million inhabitants. As of 1965, the metropolitan areas of Rio and São Paulo each contained close to five million people, Mexico City more than five million, and Buenos Aires seven million. Today about half of Latin America's population lives in urban areas, communities of more than 2,000 people. And, in the more advanced countries of Latin America, between 20 and 40 per cent live in large cities (with populations of more than 100,000).

Barriers to progress. The geography of Latin America has been less helpful to economic development than that of the United States. Most Latin American countries are in the tropics. This has meant that, historically, it has been difficult to inhabit the extensive lowland regions. Before the European conquest of America, some lowland regions in the tropics apparently had large populations. But with the European and African came malaria and yellow fever, which, spread by the mosquito, made it dangerous to live in the tropical lowlands. Thus from the colonial period Latin Americans have shied away from these areas. Today the tropical diseases are no longer a threat, because of the widespread use of DDT and other pesticides, as well as because of advances in tropical medicine. But, well into the 20th century, and in most cases still today, the majority of the people have lived in the highlands where

Caracas, Venezuela

the temperatures are cool and comfortable and the fevers did not threaten. One reflection of this is the situation of many capital cities at high elevations. Eight of the capital cities are above 3,000 feet, and four are at altitudes of more than 7,500 feet.

While the mountains have offered a safe and comfortable place in which to live, they also have presented certain problems, particularly in obstructing transportation. In the United States there are no mountain ranges, not even the Rockies, which are as extensive, as high, or as difficult to cross as those of Latin America. Central Mexico, the area around Mexico City, is a jumble of high mountains. Hernan Cortés dramatized this fact when, on his return to Spain from conquering Mexico, he was asked what the country looked like: Cortés simply took up a piece of paper and crumpled it in his hand. Guatemala also has difficult mountains. One 30-mile stretch in northern Guatemala is called *el Tapón* (the stopper) because almost daily landslides make the stretch of the Pan American Highway running through it virtually impassable.

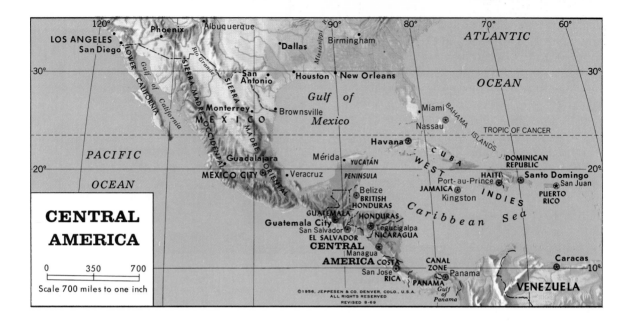

In South America there are two major mountain formations. The Brazilian Highlands divide the highland plateau of the Brazilian interior from the strip of lowlands along the coast. Until the end of the 19th century this barrier greatly obstructed trade between the interior and the coast. And in part because of this range, the Brazilian population tended to remain on the coast and the development of the interior was retarded.

The most formidable mountains in South America are the Andes, a system of ranges which runs unbroken for 4,400 miles along the western edge of South America, from northern Venezuela to the southern tip of Chile. In southern Chile, it consists of only one steep range, but in Bolivia, Peru, and Ecuador there are two high parallel ranges, and in Colombia three ranges, all running north and south. The passes over the central ranges are usually well over 10,000 feet above sea level. The most important pass between Chile and Argentina is 12,600 feet up, and the major mountain highway and rail routes in Peru and Bolivia go over passes

13,000 to 15,800 feet above sea level. Fourteen Andean peaks reach heights of over 20,000 feet, all of them higher than the United States' loftiest peak, Mt. McKinley in Alaska.

The mountains have greatly obstructed communications within and among the Latin American countries, as well as with the outside world. During the colonial period and most of the 19th century, almost all cargo travelled along mere paths, carried by mules, horses, oxen, or, in many cases, by human bearers. Even these mule paths were often in terrible shape, because frequent torrential rains gutted them. After a rain, or if the paths were not well-maintained, they were often impassable. Transportation over these mule paths was very slow and very expensive, in the 19th century about 40 times as costly as sending goods by rail.

If transportation has been difficult within most Latin American countries, it has been equally so, of course, between the various countries. Central Mexico is completely separated by mountain ranges from Guatemala and the rest of Central America. Each

CENTRAL

Caribbean Sea

AMERICA

Barranquilla
Maracaibo
Caracas

TRINIDAD AND TOBAGO
Port-of-Spain

ATLANTIC

10°

10°

PANAMA CANAL

PANAMA

VENEZUELA

Orinoco R

Georgetown
Paramaribo
Cayenne

OCEAN

GUYANA

SURINAM
FRENCH GUIANA

Bogotá
COLOMBIA

GUIANAN HIGHLANDS

Río

EQUATOR

Otávalo Ibarra
Quito

MARAJÓ ISLAND

EQUATOR

0°

0°

Guayaquil

Mt. Chimborazo
20,577

AMAZON

Negro

Río Amazon

ECUADOR

Amazon

Manaus

Rio Pará Belém

Iquitos

Río

BASIN

A
N
D
E
S

SOUTH AMERICA

BRAZIL

10°

Trujillo

P
E
R
U

10°

Lima

PAN-AMERICAN HIGHWAY

La Paz
BOLIVIA

Brasília

BRAZILIAN HIGHLANDS

PACIFIC

20°

ATACAMA

Sucre

20°

OCEAN

TROPIC OF CAPRICORN

DESERT

PARAGUAY

Río Paraná

SÃO PAULO

RIO DE JANEIRO

Santos

Asunción

ATLANTIC

Mt. Aconcagua
22,834

Mendoza

Río Paraná

URUGUAY

PAN-AMERICAN HIGHWAY

OCEAN

30°

C
H
I
L
E

Santiago

30°

A
R
G
E
N
T
I
N
A

Montevideo

BUENOS AIRES

La Plata R.

PAMPAS

40°

Río Negro

40°

STEPPE

PATAGONIAN

FALKLAND IS.

50°

TIERRA DEL FUEGO

50°

LATIN AMERICA (SOUTH)

0   300   600

Scale 600 miles to one inch

ICE AND SNOW	DESERT
FORESTS	SAVANNA
PRAIRIE	TROPICAL RAIN FORESTS
DRY GRASSLAND	MOUNTAINS

LATIN AMERICA CLIMATE

Tropical moist
- Tropical rain forest or monsoon
- Savannah

Dry
- Arid
- Semiarid

Moist, mild winter
- Subtropical monsoon
- Humid subtropical or marine
- Mountain

Miles
0   1000

throughout Europe and the United States. But the railroad was not as helpful to the mountainous lands of Latin America. Construction costs there were high, at least double those in lowland regions. (And railroads were constructed in the tropical lowlands at a cost of thousands of deaths from tropical diseases.) In addition, railroads had certain limitations. They could be run up a maximum grade of about 5 degrees. In many places they were too expensive to construct, given the limited freight they might carry. Therefore, the Andean countries were slow to undertake railroad building. During the era of the railroad they fell farther and farther behind Europe and the United States in overland communications.

For the mountainous countries of Latin America, the 20th century has brought two important breakthroughs in transportation, the automobile and the airplane. Automotive transportation has been a boon to the mountain countries because roads can be built and trucks driven through many areas where it would be impossible, or too expensive, to construct a railroad. The airplane also presented an obvious solution to the obstacle of the mountains. It is noteworthy that an Andean nation, Colombia, had a commercial airline in 1919, one of the first to be established anywhere in the world. Today a large proportion of Colombia's internal freight haulage is by airplane. And a bank in Bogotá, Colombia, even runs an "aereo-bank," a branch bank carried by airplane to areas of the country too remote to be reached in any other way.

Rivers. Not only have Latin American mountains obstructed communications, but the region's river systems have done little to compensate. In the United States the development of the great Mid-western breadbasket was facilitated by easy transportation down the Ohio, Missouri and Mississippi rivers.

of the Andean countries also has been almost completely cut off from the others.

Finally, the mountain-bound countries were, until recently, to a great extent cut off from trade with Europe and the United States. For the majority of people who lived in the mountain regions, transportation costs made it difficult to export any product to the major world markets. Each of the highland regions, therefore, stagnated in its own little pocket. As landowners in the most isolated regions could obtain little cash for their crops, they tended to operate outside a cash economy, investing as little capital as possible in their holdings and depending heavily on the low-paid, unproductive, and unskilled labor of their peons.

In the 19th century a major improvement in land transportation, the railroad, spread

In contrast, the rivers in Latin America have been of relatively little help, either because they are not navigable or because they pass through places which have been difficult to farm.

No important river runs through the highlands of Central Mexico where most Mexicans live. In South America, there are four important river systems, the Amazon, the La Plata, the Orinoco, and the Magdalena. All four are to some extent navigable, but this does not necessarily make them very useful. The Amazon in Brazil can be navigated by ocean-going ships for more than 2,000 miles. But the Amazon basin is not a hospitable place in which to live; it is not good for farming because excessive rain and flood-waters leach the soil. As not many people live in the Amazon basin, there is little for ships to carry upon its vast waters.

Similarly, the Orinoco flows through the hot tropical backlands of Venezuela, where few people live. There is little for it to transport along most of its course. An important

iron-and-steel development has been built near Ciudad Bolivar, and this provides important cargo for the lower third of the Orinoco system. But the upper reaches of the river remain mostly unused.

Mention should also be made of the several dozen small rivers which rush down from the Andes to the Peruvian coast. These are too small and plunge too steeply down the mountains to be usable for navigation. However, for centuries their waters have been used to irrigate Peru's coastal desert, providing a basis for intensive agriculture there. In addition, in the 20th century these rivers have become important sources of hydroelectric power.

Aids to progress. While much of Latin America's territory is taken up by tropical jungles or inundated plains, by mountains, deserts and other waste areas, it is also blessed with some exceptionally fine land resources. The most important of these is the Argentine *pampa*, which, fanning out from Buenos

With the aid of mosquito control and modern tropical medicine, Brazil's vast Amazon wasteland is now being developed.

Aires in a radius of 300 to 500 miles, covers about one-fifth of the country. The pampa of Argentina is a fantastically fertile agricultural area, in many places being covered by 20 feet or more of rich topsoil. In addition to being flat, well-watered, and fertile, the pampa also offers very easy communications with the port of Buenos Aires. The pampa region, therefore, has been an important producer of meats and cereals for world markets. It has enriched the Argentine families who own its large *estancias* and provided the basis for a relatively high standard of living for most of the Argentine people.

Most of the mountainous countries of Latin America are blessed with rich deposits of minerals. In fact, Latin America has been renowned in the world as a producer of minerals practically since Columbus discovered America. Mexico, Peru, and what is now

Bolivia became famous in the 16th century as the world's largest producers of silver. So much silver and gold were produced in Spanish America that the world supply of these precious metals was multiplied by six during the 16th century. And Latin America produced even more silver and gold during the next two centuries of the colonial period.

In modern times Mexico and Peru have continued to be leading sources of silver, and Colombia of gold. But these precious metals have become much less important to the Latin American economies than oil and the industrial ores. Venezuela since the 1920's has been one of the world's leading exporters of oil.

Mexico and the Andean countries have been important suppliers of industrial metals. Chile has been the source of quantities of nitrate and one of the biggest producers of copper. Latin America as a whole provides one-fifth of the world supply of copper. During the first half of the 20th century Bolivia was the leading producer of tin ore. But its deposits now are seriously depleted, and for the past 15 years the Bolivian tin mines have been struggling to survive.

Since World War II, other, not previously exploited, metals have come to the fore. For example, good supplies of bauxite, used in making aluminum, exist in Venezuela, Cuba, and Brazil. Brazil itself is manufacturing aluminum.

Brazil, Venezuela, Chile, and Peru are now major suppliers of iron ore to the world market. In the state of Minas Gerais in Brazil, there are mountains of ore whose iron content is greater than 65 per cent. Venezuela also has great hills of rich iron ore in the Orinoco basin, which are being exploited by American steel companies as well as by the government of Venezuela. These countries also possess important deposits of scarce metals used as alloys with iron in making steel.

LATIN AMERICA POPULATION

Miles
0   1000

Persons per square mile

less than 3
3 to 25
25 to 130
130 to 260
more than 260

• Cities from 500,000 to 1,000,000
○ Cities of more than 1,000,000

Despite these rich supplies of iron ores and alloys, Latin America did not begin to develop its own iron and steel industries until the 20th century. Mexico built the first important steel mill, at Monterrey, just before World War I. Elsewhere steel industries were started only after World War II. This delay may be attributed to a number of factors. But one important problem has been the lack of good supplies of coal needed for iron and steel production. Most of the coal reserves in Latin America are of low quality and are also badly located for exploitation.

PEOPLE

Racial and cultural groups. The total population of Latin America in 1965 was about 240 million. The population is composed primarily of the descendants of three main racial groups: the American Indians, sometimes called Amerinds; the Afro-Americans; and the descendants of Europeans. Over the past four and a half centuries there has been considerable inter-mixture among the three groups. In most countries of Latin America most of the people are descended from at least two of the major contributing groups.

Insofar as people in Latin America are divided into "racial" categories, it is on the basis of social behavior as much as by skin color or some other racial characteristic. A man is considered an "Indian" if he wears typically Indian or peasant clothing and speaks an Indian language. If the same man puts on shoes and adopts Spanish as a primary language, he becomes known as a *cholo* or *mestizo*. And if he graduates from the university and becomes a lawyer or a physician, he is considered "white." Thus "racial" categories in Latin America are to a great extent really social or cultural categories.

Five countries in Latin America today are thought of as "Indian" lands. In Guatemala

A tin mine in Bolivia reflects optimism in the new facilities provided for its workers. Bolivian tin supplies, however, are rapidly being depleted, and the future of this community as of many similar ones seems dim.

and Bolivia the "Indians" amount to roughly half the population. In Peru the Indians make up about 40 per cent of the population. In Ecuador about one-third are Indian, and in Mexico somewhat less than one-third. But in all of these countries the proportion of Indians in the population is continuously declining, as more and more of them migrate to the towns and cities, put on urban clothing, speak Spanish, and thus become *mestizos*, or simply ordinary citizens. In Mexico, Peru, and Ecuador these *mestizos* account for half or more of the population, and in Guatemala and Bolivia for more than one-third.

RACIAL DISTRIBUTION OF LATIN AMERICA

Predominantly Indian areas

Predominantly Caucasoid areas

Predominantly Negroid areas

Predominantly Mestizo areas:

Indian and Caucasoid

Negroid and Caucasoid

Intermingled Indian, Mestizo, Negroid and Caucasoid

The Indian contribution to these five countries has been strong for a number of reasons. All of these countries had great concentrations of Indian populations in highland regions at the time of the Conquest. In the highlands the toll of European diseases was often terrible. But it was not so totally devastating as in the Caribbean. Malaria and yellow fever could not affect the mountain regions which were too cool for the survival of the mosquito. In addition, the pre-Conquest Indian cultures of Central Mexico, Guatemala, and the Inca-controlled Andes were highly developed. The Indian peasants of these places were accustomed to regular labor service in support of their Indian lords. Thus when the Spanish made similar, though harsher demands, many more of these In-

dians survived than in the Caribbean and Brazil.

Outside of the above mentioned countries, the Indian population is not very great. In much of Central America, in Paraguay and parts of Chile, Colombia, and Venezuela, the Indian contribution to the population is evident. But in these countries *mestizos* are the most numerous group and almost everyone, whether *mestizo* or white, is essentially Spanish in culture.

Negroes, or people of partially-African descent, make up a sizable proportion of the population in some parts of Latin America. Afro-Americans are concentrated in the Caribbean islands, in the coastal regions of the mainland countries surrounding the Caribbean (Venezuela, Colombia, Panama, Costa Rica, etc.), and along the coastal belt of northern Brazil.

The Afro-American populations were brought to the Caribbean and to Brazil because of the annihilation of the Indians who inhabited these lands in the 16th century. When the Europeans came, they carried with them diseases to which the Indians had no immunity. In addition, the Spaniards and Portuguese made severe demands on the Indians for labor. As the Indians of these regions were hunters and gatherers and were not accustomed to steady, hard labor, the European demands came as a shock. The Indian populations in the Caribbean and in Brazil therefore rapidly died, and their places were taken by African slaves imported to work the sugar plantations.

Some parts of Latin America, particularly in the temperate zone south of the Tropic of Capricorn, are quite markedly European in racial as well as cultural makeup. Unlike the rest of Latin America, Argentina, Uruguay, southern Brazil, and Chile have received large numbers of European immigrants. During the colonial and early republican periods the Indians in these lands were virtually wiped out. Particularly in Argentina, the Indians were wild nomads, whom the Spanish found impossible to use as laborers (as they had done in Mexico and the Andean countries). The Spanish, and later the Argentines in the republican period, therefore drove the Indians out so that the land could be safely used for grazing cattle. Later on, in the middle of the 19th century, when Argentina began to develop, it turned to Europe for the necessary laborers. The Argentine pattern of settlement in these respects was very similar to that of the United States. Southern Brazil, Uruguay, and Chile also have received substantial numbers of European immigrants.

Between 1880 and 1915 most immigrants came from Italy, Spain, and Portugal. But in the 20th century they also have come from Central and Eastern Europe. In Brazil there have been significant numbers of Japanese immigrants. The countries of southern South America, particularly Brazil, have been racial and cultural melting pots as much or more than the United States.

Race and class. Most Latin Americans are much less concerned about racial differences than people in the United States have been. Latin Americans are conscious of color differences. But they do not give them as much importance as North Americans. In the United States, newspapers frequently identify individuals by race or cultural origin, referring to Negro lawyers or black students or Mohawk Indian construction workers. In Latin American newspapers these same individuals would be called simply lawyers or students or construction workers.

There are some exceptions to this lack of emphasis on race; Argentines tend to be hysterically proud of their whiteness. But in many Latin American countries, while some racial prejudice exists, it does not take an absolute or rigid form. Individuals are classified as much by the amount of education or money they possess and by the way they dress and behave socially as they are in racial terms. Race is a consideration in social ranking, but not the only one or even the primary one. This is illustrated in the case of a lower middle-class Brazilian whose first daughter married a white mechanic and whose second daughter married a black lawyer. To his third daughter he gave the following instructions regarding marriage: If the man is white he can be a mechanic, if he is black he has to be a lawyer. A common saying in Latin America is that "money whitens." So, as this example shows, does education. Thus, society in many Latin American countries is more fluid with regard to race than it is in the United States.

Class divisions. While Latin Americans are less rigid about race than North Americans, Latin American society is very much split by *class* divisions. In most countries there is a great social gap between a very small rich, well-dressed, and university-educated upper class and a much larger struggling white-collar class. And between these two urban groups, on the one hand, and the peasants, on the other, there is an enormous gulf in wealth, education, and dress. In practice the upper-class tends to be "white" while the peasants at the bottom are Indian, Negro, or *mestizo*. But this division does not reflect systematic *racial* discrimination. Rather these divisions have persisted because people in the lower classes have not had the educational or economic opportunities which would permit gifted individuals to rise easily in the social scale. Thus, while a Negro who becomes a lawyer or an Indian who becomes wealthy may enter the upper class, it is very hard for anyone at the bottom in Latin America to obtain the education or the job opportunities needed to rise in society.

RELIGION

Latin America is overwhelmingly Roman Catholic. The Roman Catholic Church plays an important part in the cultural, social, economic, and political, as well as the religious, life of Latin America. This role is much more pronounced there than is the influence of any religious organization in the United States. Protestant, Jewish, and other religious groups exist in all Latin American countries, but they constitute tiny minority groups. Although religious intolerance has existed in the past and occasionally reappears for short periods, the practice of most religions is generally permitted throughout Latin America today.

HISTORICAL PERIODS

The history of Latin America can be divided into four major periods. These are (a) the pre-Hispanic period to 1500; (b) the conquest and the colonial era, 1500 to 1800; (c) the wars of independence, 1800–1825; and (d) the national period since 1825.

Toltec Civilization flourished in Mexico from the 10th through 12th centuries. The excavation of the Temple of the Two Griffins in 1940 began study which is still going on.

Pre-Hispanic period to 1500. When the Spanish and Portuguese came to America at the beginning of the 16th century, the land was inhabited by American Indians who had reached several quite different levels of development. In the lowest category were the natives of Patagonia who went about naked (despite the freezing cold of their abode) and lived off shell-fish. Others at a low level were the seed-gathering and hunting nomads who roamed the plains of Argentina and the arid regions of northern Mexico.* At a higher level were the Indians

* See *Readings in World History* (Boston: Allyn and Bacon, Inc., 1970), "Pre-Columbian Cultures: The Primitive Fuegians," p. 289, and "Pre-Columbian Cultures: The Nomadic Chichimecs," p. 292.

who practiced a primitive type of agriculture in the tropical forests of Brazil and in the Carribbean region. In these cultures the men usually hunted and fished, while the women cultivated patches of maize and manioc. The most advanced American Indians were the peoples who developed the remarkable civilizations which the Spanish found in Mexico, Guatemala, and the Andes.

The best-known of these advanced peoples are the Aztec of Central Mexico, the Maya of Yucatan and Guatemala, and the Inca, who at the time of the Spanish conquest controlled almost all of present-day Ecuador, Peru, and Bolivia, and some of Argentina and Chile. It should be made clear, however, that these three famous cultures were not

Machu Picchu, "the lost city of the Incas," stood atop a 6750-foot mountain. The stone terraces were used for structural support and for growing food.

the only highly-developed ones in Mexico and the Andes. They were simply the beneficiaries of thousands of years of cultural evolution, carried forward by a host of different Indian groups. When the Aztecs appeared upon the historical scene in the Valley of Mexico (now Mexico City) two hundred years before the Spanish conquest, they at first were a relatively primitive people. They came to have a highly-developed society by conquering other more advanced

cultures which had lived in the region for centuries. Similarly, the Incas in Peru appear to have been a rather backward people, until little more than a century before the Spanish came, when the Incas began to conquer their neighbors. As the Incas absorbed other more highly civilized peoples into their empire, they learned from them. By combining the advances made by others they developed the magnificent civilization which became known as Inca.

The Indians of Mexico and the Andes achieved a high degree of civilization mainly because they were pioneers in developing agriculture. They were extraordinarily successful in domesticating many plants that are now grown all over the world. The most important crops were corn, beans, squashes, tomatoes, potatoes, tobacco, cotton, and chocolate. In all, the Indians domesticated over one hundred plants, as many as the Old World developed. This was truly a remarkable achievement and represents by far the most important contribution of the American Indians to civilization.

Thanks to this progress in agriculture, the Mayas, Aztecs, and Incas were able to accumulate the food surplus necessary to support cities, priesthoods, elaborate governments, costly public projects, and all the other institutions that together constitute civilization. Furthermore their productive agriculture enabled them to increase in population far more than the less advanced Indian peoples. Scholars today are hotly debating the question of how many Indians may have lived in these highly-developed cultures before the Spanish conquest. Recent estimates suggest that Mexico may have contained from 15 to 20 million people (almost as many as lived there 10 years ago). It is possible that the Inca empire contained an equal number.

While the major pre-Columbian civilizations had in common a high level of agri-

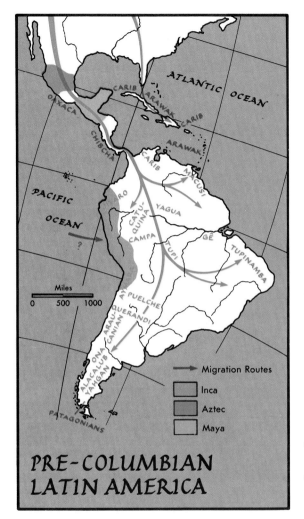

PRE-COLUMBIAN LATIN AMERICA

warlike than the Maya. They paid more attention to military organization and their state was somewhat more organized. One of the most striking peculiarities of the Aztecs was the extraordinary extent to which they practiced human sacrifice in their religious rituals.*

* See *Readings in World History*, "Pre-Columbian Cultures: The Advanced Aztecs," p. 294.

BRITISH MUSEUM (TOP); UNIVERSITY MUSEUM, PHILADELPHIA (BOTTOM)

cultural development, each of them had its own unique strengths. The Mayan culture was outstanding for its extraordinary development of the arts and sciences. A culture at its height before 1000 A.D., its accomplishments included a primitive form of writing, a sculpture that ranks among the world's great art, and the development of mathematics and astronomy to a point equal to that reached by Europeans at the time.

The Aztecs and other peoples of Central Mexico, by contrast, seem to have been more

The peoples of the Andes performed much less human sacrifice than those in Mexico. But in some other ways they were less developed. Whereas the advanced Indians of Mexico were able to write (using pictures and symbols), none of the cultures of Peru had writing in any form. The Inca did have a device for recording numbers of objects called the *quipu*, which was a collection of cords with different kinds of knots in them, the knots representing numbers. But for this device to be used it was necessary to have a *quipu* specialist who had to memorize what objects all the different cords and knots stood for.

The strongest points of the Incas were in engineering and architecture and in the organization of their state. They built remarkable roads, fortresses, and temples out of great blocks of stone so perfectly joined that

The intricate and remarkably constructed stonework of Machu Picchu

FRANK SAFFORD

even now, nearly five hundred years later, a knife cannot be inserted between them. They also developed an extensive irrigation system, parts of which are still in use. The Incas' marvelous works in construction were closely related to their achievement in organizing their empire. It was the efficient organization of the imperial state which permitted the Incas to mobilize the tens of thousands of workers needed for their larger projects. The Inca political system was arranged in a tightly-knit hierarchy, with the Inca as a divine symbol at the top. The idea of the Inca's divinity was impressed upon the people through many devices: he supposedly never set foot on the ground, being always carried in a palanquin; his clothes were of a special quality, and after they had been used they were burned so that no one else might use them; the Inca married his sisters so as to preserve the purity of his descendance from the Sun; and the most beautiful girls in the empire were selected for his service, or for him to distribute as favors or rewards to the chief nobles in the empire. But people gave their loyalty and their service to the Inca not only because they were awed by him and the prowess of his armies, but also because Inca rule offered some advantages. The Inca had granaries which in time of local crop failure were used to feed people who might have starved if left to their own devices.* The Incas' amazing institutions have such various aspects that their empire has been termed everything from an "oriental despotism" to an example of primitive socialism.

Conquest and colonial era, 1500–1800. During this period the Spaniards and Portuguese dismembered the Indian civilizations and carved out colonial empires covering most of the Western Hemisphere. Imme-

* See *Readings in World History*, "Pre-Columbian Cultures: The Ingenious Incas," p. 298.

17.

Belief that the sun required human nourishment resulted, some experts believe, in the sacrifice of 20,000 victims annually during the Aztec Maize Ritual. The victim was first lashed to a scaffold and shot with an arrow. The heart was then removed with the sacrificial knife (below).

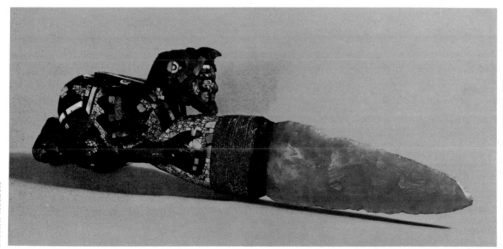

Basic Facts 315

"We Spaniards," said the conquistador Hernán Cortés, "have a disease which only gold can cure."

diately after Columbus' first voyage Spain began to establish outposts in the Caribbean Islands. Expeditions in search of Indian slaves for the first settlements at Santo Domingo and in Cuba led to the exploration and seizure of the coastal areas on the surrounding mainland. In 1510 the first major mainland settlement was established on the isthmus of Panama under the leadership of Vasco Nuñez de Balboa. In 1518, Hernán Cortés led an expedition into Mexico. In the course of three years of fighting Cortés destroyed the Aztec Confederacy, and the core of Mexico fell under Spanish control. In 1535, the Mexican colony was organized as the Viceroyalty of New Spain. From this base, Spanish forces moved southward to conquer Central America, and also northward into the present Southwest United States.

Balboa's discovery of the Pacific Ocean in 1513 opened the way to Peru. Under the leadership of Francisco Pizarro, the Spanish *conquistadores* arrived in Peru in 1532. They found the Inca Empire disastrously torn by a bloody civil war between two claimants to the throne. This division seriously weakened the Incas and helped the Spaniards in their campaign. Thus the Inca Empire became a Spanish possession, known as the Viceroyalty of Peru.

The Spaniards built strong bases in the Caribbean islands, Mexico, and Panama. Yet control of this Caribbean area continued to be uncertain until the 18th century. French, Dutch, and English privateers (with the tacit or open approval of their government) raided Spanish shipping and attacked coastal settlements during most of the colonial period.

The region of La Plata (Argentina and Uruguay), now one of the most developed in Latin America, was neglected by Spain until late in the colonial period. Initial efforts to conquer the area failed because the nomadic Indians of the pampa would not submit to the Spaniards and labor for them, as had the more docile indigenes of Mexico and the Andean regions. Even after Spanish settlements were established in northern Argentina between 1550 and 1580, the region remained a backwater in the empire. The silver-producing areas of Mexico and Peru were much more important to the Spanish Crown and were consistently favored by it over such marginal areas as La Plata. During the 18th century, however, Spain recognized the economic potential of Buenos Aires and the pampa. In 1776 it established the Viceroyalty of La Plata, with Buenos Aires as its capital, and at about the same time granted the region greater freedom of trade.

The most discussed aspect of Spanish colonial rule has been the treatment of the Indians. From the 16th century onward Spain's European rivals propagated a "Black Legend," which emphasized the Spaniard's cruelty toward the Indians during the conquest and afterward. Some historians, particularly in the 20th century, have developed a counter-interpretation of Spanish actions which has been called the "pink legend." This stresses that while the Spanish did subjugate the Indians and exploit their labor, at least the Spanish crown and certain clergy (most notably Fray Bartolomé de Las Casas) were much concerned about the treatment of the Indians. During the 16th century the Indian question was periodically de-

A Spanish priest, Bartolomé de Las Casas, the "apostle of the Indians," provided this illustration in his 16th-century treatise condemning the treatment of the Indians by the Spanish conquerors.

bated by jurists before the Spanish court and throughout the colonial period frequent orders were sent to the New World to restrain the Spanish colonists' excessive demands on the Indians. Though these orders were often not enforced, they at least stand as testimony of the Spanish crown's desire to rule humanely.* No other contemporary imperial power, neither England, France, nor Portugal, demonstrated so much concern for the welfare of its conquered peoples.

At the same time that the Spanish were conquering Peru and the rest of Andean South America, the Portuguese began to settle Brazil. In the Treaty of Tordesillas (1494) the Spanish Crown had agreed to respect Portugal's right to colonize this part of the Western Hemisphere. Portugal, however, did little to establish effective control over the region until 1530. One reason for the delay was that Portugal's manpower, shipping, and capital were all heavily engaged in the pepper trade with India and Southeast Asia. In this early period the Brazilian coast was visited only by Portuguese traders in brazil wood, from which the country got its name. After 1530 the Portuguese crown, fearing the encroachment of the Spanish and French, made serious efforts to colonize Brazil. Portugal was a small country and the effort of maintaining its empire along the coasts of Africa and Asia had severely weakened it. Therefore, the job of colonization was turned over to a dozen private entrepreneurs called *donatarios* (much like the proprietors in the English colonies in the following century). Most of the *donatarios* failed in their efforts to establish an economic foundation for colonies and in their struggles against the Tupi Indians. (One *donatario* wrote the king: "We have had to conquer by inches what your majesty has granted us by leagues.") But the

Portuguese settlements in Brazil remained largely under the control of local landowners and merchants, in contrast with Spanish America where the royal bureaucracy quickly became very important.

The scarcity of Portuguese manpower in the 16th and 17th centuries had an important effect in shaping Brazilian society. Needing labor for their plantations, the Portuguese first enslaved the Tupi Indians. Since the Tupis died in great numbers, the Portuguese, like the Spanish in the Caribbean, replaced the Indians with African slaves. As in every part of the Americas where slavery existed, there was considerable miscegenation between master and female slave, but with different results in Brazil than in the United States. In the United States masters generally did not recognize their mulatto offspring as their children and kept them in slavery. But in Brazil, where there was a scarcity of white manpower, mulatto sons of plantation owners often were brought into the middle and upper ranks of society as clerks, foremen, and priests. Many thus became more identified with the white upper-class than with the mass of slaves. This helped to establish in Brazil a tradition of at least partial racial integration.*

The most important settlements in Brazil in the 16th and 17th centuries were at Pernambuco and Bahia on the Northeastern coast. These Portuguese communities, and others on the coast of Brazil, were sustained by the production and export of sugar to Europe. In the 16th century the Brazilian sugar industry boomed. But during the 17th century competition from newer plantations in the Caribbean began to undermine the Brazilian planters, and the Brazilian Northeast fell into a long period of economic stagnation. When the *bandeirantes* (slave-hunters from the region of São Paulo) began

* See *Readings in World History*, "American Indians under Spanish Rule," p. 306.

* See *Readings in World History*, "Race Relations in Brazil," p. 309.

to discover gold and diamonds in the central interior of Brazil at the end of the 17th century, masters and slaves from the decaying Northeast moved south *en masse* to the mine fields of Minas Gerais.

The economic and political center of the Portuguese colony moved with them. Rio de Janeiro grew up as a port serving the mines, and in 1763 the Captain-General of Brazil moved his headquarters from Bahia to Rio. Rio served as Brazil's chief administrative center from that time until 1960, when the city of Brasilia, newly created in the undeveloped interior state of Goiaz, became the country's capital.

Wars of independence, 1800–1825. The first country in Latin America to break away from its European possessor was Haiti which had been the French colony of Saint Domingue. Stimulated by the egalitarian ideology of the French Revolution, Haitian mulattos and blacks in 1804 overthrew their French masters. Despite Napoleon's efforts to reclaim the colony, Haiti succeeded in winning its independence.

Napoleon also played an important role in the independence of Spanish and Portuguese America. In 1807, in the course of the Napoleonic Wars, French troops invaded Spain and Portugal and Joseph Bonaparte, Napoleon's brother, was proclaimed King of Spain. Most of the Spanish American independence movements started in response to the Napoleonic invasion, with the leaders proclaiming their loyalty to the dethroned Spanish Bourbon, Ferdinand VII, and refusing to recognize the Bonaparte regime in Spain.

Although Spanish America moved decisively for independence only after it no longer had a legitimate king, Spanish American creoles had found some cause for discontent before that time. Through most of the colonial period, the most important

LATIN AMERICA IN 1802

offices in government administration and in the Church had been reserved to the Spanish-born. The creoles (members of the white upper-class born in the Americas) resented being excluded from the higher offices. Creole merchants also agitated for the right to trade more freely with nations other than Spain. In such commercial centers as Buenos Aires and Caracas, many in the creole upper-class were becoming acutely aware that Spanish rule was contrary to their economic interests. Finally, to some degree creole leaders in Spanish America were influenced by the examples of the American and French revolutions.

With the Napoleonic invasion of Spain in 1808, the empire lost its king, its source of authority. The response of the Spanish colonial bureaucracy was to attempt to continue exercising power, while the creoles, through their city councils, or *cabildos*, attempted to establish autonomous, locally-controlled governments. In 1810, in Caracas (Venezuela), Bogotá (Colombia), and Buenos Aires (Argentina) the *cabildos* set up autonomous governments, though they did not declare independence. Buenos Aires was effectively independent from this date onward. After a number of unsuccessful attempts to liberate Bolivia, the Argentines, under the command of José de San Martín, crossed the Andes to free Chile in 1817–18, and then went on to begin the battle to end Spanish control of Peru.*

In the northern tier of South America (Venezuela and Colombia) the struggle was hard-fought and bloody and went on for more than a decade. The creole regimes in Colombia and Venezuela were weakened by internal conflict over who would lead and what cities would dominate in the new states being formed. When, after Napoleon's overthrow, Ferdinand VII returned to the Spanish throne, it was relatively easy for Spanish forces to crush the new creole governments. By 1816 the Spanish armies had retaken control of most of Venezuela and Colombia, after which they executed a substantial number of the creole upper-class leaders. The severe repression served simply to harden creole hatred of Spanish rule. Under the leadership of Simón Bolívar, the Colombians and Venezuelans secured their independence by 1821. Bolívar's troops then moved south and between 1822 and 1825 liberated Ecuador, Peru, and Bolivia.

Independence everywhere in Spanish America was led by the creole upper-class, who wanted to take the place of the Spaniards in control of government, but were not social revolutionaries. The conservative char-

* See *Readings in World History,* "San Martín Fights for Independence," p. 313.

acter of Spanish American independence is particularly evident in Mexico. There the first revolutionary movement in 1810 was a peasant rebellion led by a parish priest, Miguel de Hidalgo. The upper-class creoles in Mexico were frightened by Hidalgo's Indian and *mestizo* hordes, and rallied to the support of the Spanish bureaucracy. The Spanish army defeated and executed Hidalgo and then his successor José María Morelos. When independence finally came to Mexico in 1821, it was brought about by the reactionary upper clergy and the professional army who feared a new revolutionary republican government in Spain (1820–1823) which would perhaps strip away their special privileges.

Brazilian independence was achieved with little bloodshed. When French troops occupied Portugal in 1807, the Prince-regent João VI and his court left Lisbon, under the protection of the British fleet, to establish a Portuguese government-in-exile at Rio de Janeiro. Brazil in effect was the center of the Portuguese Empire until 1821, when João returned to Lisbon. On leaving Rio, João left his first son, Dom Pedro, as regent of Brazil. The Portuguese parliament, rightly fearing that Brazil under Dom Pedro might become independent, ordered him to return to Portugal and moved to bring Brazil back into a strictly colonial relationship. Dom Pedro refused to return and in 1822 put himself at the head of a new Empire of Brazil. Armed resistance by a few Portuguese garrisons was quickly overcome. Brazil's peculiar, royally-led independence helped the country to have a more stable beginning than her Spanish-American neighbors. In most of the Spanish American countries the post-independence governments found it difficult to establish their authority and were frequently overturned by armed revolution. In Brazil, however, Dom Pedro and his son Pedro II provided a sense of continuity and legitimacy which tended to reduce political unsteadiness in Rio for most of the 19th century.

National period since 1825. During the national period the independent nations of Latin America gradually developed their present characteristics. As most of the remainder of this unit is devoted to the national period, little is said about it here. It should be noted, however, that one of the major characteristics of the national period has been the political sub-division of much of Spanish America.

Bolívar had dreamed of a Latin America that was to be united as well as free. But a large number of new states appeared in the place of the former colonies. One reason was the mountain and jungle barriers separating one region from another. Added to this was the lack of communication and transportation facilities among the regions. Fragmentation also was caused by the centuries of isolation under Spain, which developed separatist traditions. Finally there were the personal ambitions of individual leaders who preferred prominence in a small state to obscurity in a large union.

The end result was that eight Spanish-American colonies became *eighteen* separate countries. During the Wars of Independence, the former Viceroyalty of the United Provinces of the Rio de la Plata disintegrated into the separate republics of Argentina, Paraguay, and Bolivia. Later, in 1828, Uruguay emerged out of the wars between Argentina and Brazil. Likewise the former Viceroyalty of New Granada split into the separate countries of Colombia, Venezuela, Ecuador, and, much later, Panama. And, during the course of the 19th century, the once relatively united Captaincy-General of Guatemala broke up into the separate states of Guatemala, El Salvador, Nicaragua, Honduras, and Costa Rica.

WHO (ALMASY)

Statue to Simón Bolívar, Bogotá, Colombia.

Reviewing the Essentials

Geography

1. On a map distinguish among Latin, South, and Central America. Name and locate the political divisions of South and Central America.
2. Compare the countries of Latin America with the United States in respect to: (a) size and (b) population density and (c) relationship of population to the amount of arable land. What is the significance of Latin America's high rate of population growth?
3. How has the geography of Latin America been both an obstacle and an aid to the development of the area and the progress of the people?
4. Name and locate the major river systems of South America. How have these (a) promoted and (b) retarded the development of the continent?

People

5. In which countries do Indians form a large proportion of the population? In which are there many people of African descent? Where do people of European origin predominate? What countries are considered basically mixed or *mestizo*? Locate each of these countries on the map. Explain why some countries remained largely "Indian," while others became predominantly European or Afro-American.
6. How do racial relations in Latin America differ from those in the United States? How do Latin American class systems differ from that of the United States?

Historical Periods

8. In what ways did the various Indian groups of the pre-Hispanic period differ in their levels of development? What were the principal achievements of the Indians of Mexico and Peru which give evidence of advanced civilizations? Why is the domestication of plants such an important achievement? In what ways did the leading Indian cultures of pre-Hispanic America (those of Mexico and Peru) differ from each other? How did the Incas maintain control of their vast empire?
9. How did the kings of Spain differ from the kings of England in their attitudes toward the American Indians?
10. In what ways did colonial Spanish America and colonial Brazil under the Portuguese differ from each other? What effect did Portugal's shortage of manpower have on Brazil's development?
11. What caused Spanish America to become independent from Spain between 1808 and 1825? Name the revolutionary leaders associated with the Wars of Independence in Spanish America, and the countries which they helped to liberate. Why, after obtaining independence, did Spanish America divide into 18 different countries?

Explain, Identify, or Locate

mestizo	Magdalena	Pizarro	Simón Bolívar
pampa	La Plata	*donatarios*	José de San Martín
Andes	Aztecs	Bahia	Miguel de Hidalgo
Patagonia	Incas	Rio de Janeiro	João VI
Caribbean	Mayas	Caracas	Dom Pedro
Amazon	Balboa	Bogotá	Ferdinand VII
Orinoco	Cortés	Buenos Aires	

POLITICS: The Paradox of Centralized Authority and Instability

PRESENT STATE

At first glance, Latin American politics are somewhat similar to those of the United States. Latin American countries are republics, as is the United States. Most of them have constitutions similar to our own. Almost all have presidents at the heads of these countries, along with the familiar division of authority among the executive, the legislative, and the judicial branches of government.

Centralism. Beyond these general forms, however, there are a number of differences between the governments of Latin America and of the United States. Politics in almost all Latin American countries is highly centralized. In all but a few of the Latin American republics provincial governors are not elected, but appointed by the President. Four Latin American countries (Argentina, Brazil, Mexico, and Venezuela) supposedly have "federal" constitutions, with elected state governors, as in the United States. But even in these countries governors frequently are chosen or removed by the national president.

As a corollary of Presidential power, electoral politics is also highly centralized. A party's candidates for office are chosen not by primary elections but by party directorates. Sometimes one national directorate will ultimately decide the list of their party's candidates for every region of the country. Once elected to office, a Latin American politician maintains little contact with the region which supposedly elected him. His primary concern is not the local election district but the party directorate. After all, it is the directorate, much more than his electoral district, which determines his

General Rafael Trujillo in Santiago

political career. In its tendency to party centralism, Latin American politics is more comparable to that of Western Europe, particularly France and Italy, than to that of the United States.

While political power in Latin America tends to be centralized, at the same time, paradoxically, governments tend to be rather weak and ineffective. There is often a wide gap between the letter of the law and its application. In many countries taxes have been evaded on a grand scale. And almost everywhere there is a tendency to believe that the law exists to be ignored.

Government employees frequently are arbitrary administrators. In some countries favorable government action can be obtained with a bribe, and without a bribe decisions may be delayed indefinitely. In Mexico the bribe, called the *mordida* (bite), is expected by many officials, even for routine matters.

In most countries officials' decisions also are affected by friendship or personal relations. Bureaucrats will bend the rules for someone they know or who impresses them. Others may well be turned away.

Personalism. Personal relations are the key to many aspects of Latin American politics. Many Latin Americans attach themselves to a patron, a man of power or influence, in the hope of obtaining government jobs or benefiting from government connections. At the national level these patrons are called *caudillos*. Often whole parties are built around these *caudillos*, the parties being known simply by the names of their patron-leaders. (For example, the followers of General Manuel Odría in Peru are called *Odristas*.) When the party patron wins, his followers live well; when the *caudillo* dies, his party usually collapses and disappears.

The *caudillo* or patron is an important figure in Latin America because of the class structure. Since the Conquest a small upper class has dominated a large peasant mass. As the upper class has most of the wealth and controls the economy, the livelihood of the peasants, and also many city people, has depended on winning the favor of some rich man. The peasant's survival has depended upon the will of the estate-owner; the white-collar worker knows he must curry favor with the upper-class merchant. In the republican era this habit of looking to a powerful man for employment or favors has found expression in politics. Now the *caudillo* simply uses his control of the government to reward and support his dependents.

Instability. Another characteristic of Latin American politics is the pronounced instability of most states. So-called "revolutions" frequently upset one government and establish another. Actually these are not true revolutions, but generally mere *coups d'état* executed by the military. A true revolution produces a fundamental change in a system, a basic reorganization of the social and political order. A revolution in this sense has only very rarely occurred in the history of Latin America.

Why Latin America has suffered so much political instability is not easily explained. A simple answer would be that people who are out of power overthrow the existing government because they want government jobs and control of government revenues. This is certainly an important factor behind many political upheavals. But other problems, to be discussed later on, have also been involved.

The tropical dictators. There are some Latin American countries which experience little political flux, not, however, because they are firmly founded democracies. Particularly in some of the small countries of the Caribbean and Central America, regimes controlled by one man, or one family, have lasted for decades.

In these one-man, military-backed regimes, the reigning dictator makes no distinction between the interests of his family and those of the country. All that the country has to offer, whether it be political office or property, is absorbed by the ruling family and its hangers-on. When the Somoza family, which has controlled Nicaragua since 1939, was accused of taking over a large proportion of the best property in the country, one of them replied that, after all, the family was acting in the best interests of the country: what was good for his family was good for the country.

Youths in Buenos Aires flee a blanket of tear gas used by police on June 29, 1969 to disperse demonstrators protesting New York Governor Nelson Rockefeller's visit to Argentina.

One of the hallmarks of these dictatorial regimes is a tendency to glorify the ruling strongman as a Great Benefactor. Rafael Trujillo, who ran the Dominican Republic as his personal fief from 1930 until his assassination in 1961, had himself officially titled "The Benefactor of the Fatherland." The name of the capital city was changed from Santo Domingo to Ciudad Trujillo. Thousands of monuments to Trujillo were sprinkled about the country, and a neon sign in Ciudad Trujillo constantly flashed the motto "God and Trujillo."

These regimes have not been as beneficial as their leaders insist. Repressive measures are used in all of them. In the Somozas' Nicaragua, people have long been accustomed to seeing soldiers armed with submachine guns stationed at numerous checkpoints on the highways. In one of the worst cases, the Dominican Republic under Trujillo, opponents of the regime frequently were tortured and murdered. In 1956, one critic of the Trujillo government, a professor at Columbia University in New York, was abducted and apparently murdered by Trujillo agents.

Latin Americans frequently accuse the United States government and American companies of supporting and sustaining these despots. The United States government, they contend, has aided them with military equipment, military training, and economic aid. And American companies, it is widely believed, have made large financial payments to some of Latin America's strongmen in order to obtain economic concessions.

Although American support may have helped some of these dictators, a more important factor in their rise to, and maintainance of, power has been the internal condition of the country. Almost all the dictatorships of this type have occurred in the smaller countries of Latin America. In many of these smaller countries the underdeveloped economies have not created the strong urban business, white-collar, and working-class groups which might effectively oppose the rule of one strongman or his family.

The military in politics. While there have been numerous examples of simple dictatorships in Central America and the Caribbean islands, they are not really representative of Latin America today. The small countries of the Caribbean and Central America make up a very small proportion of the people of Latin America. The bulk of the population of Latin America lives in the medium-to-large countries. Most of these larger countries have a style of politics somewhere between the more-or-less successful democracies in Chile, Uruguay, and Costa Rica, on the one hand, and the petty despotisms of the Caribbean area, on the other.

In a number of the larger or medium-sized countries such as Argentina, Brazil, Venezuela, Bolivia, and Peru, there is a strong tradition of military intervention in politics. Even when the armed forces do not seize outright control of the government, the ever-present possibility that they may do so makes the army an important political force which every civilian administration must take carefully into consideration.

There are also, however, organized, articulate urban groups which may (or sometimes may not) assert the desirability of civilian rule. But the political parties which represent these urban groups frequently are divided into numerous ambitious, quarreling, uncooperative political factions. As a result, civilian governments often are weak. When the civilian politicians become excessively divided and ineffectual, or when the government party carries out policies which the military considers dangerous, the army takes over. Often military *coups* have the approval of the urban upper class and businessmen, particularly when army intervention stops any movement toward popular revolution. After the military government rules for a while, however, people in the big cities grow tired of the army officers' rigidity and lack of political sensitivity, and a movement of civilian revulsion occurs. When the ruling military group becomes very unpopular, others in the armed forces displace them and restore civilian rule. Then the cycle begins again.

Not all military governments in Latin America have been completely reactionary. Some have combined repressive measures with the execution of unpopular, but perhaps necessary, economic reforms which civilian governments have been too weak to carry out. Still other army-dominated governments have been notably progressive and popular. Some of these have made important social reforms in order to head off the possibility of violent revolutionary upheaval.

Not all military governments are one-man dictatorships. Particularly in the period since 1930 there have been many examples of collective leadership through a military *junta*, usually representing each of the branches of the armed forces. In these *juntas* one man may be dominant, but he finds it necessary to consult various groups within the services. In most countries the armed forces are not a simple organism with one will, but a collection of factions with differing views on policies. If important groups in the armed forces become disaffected, the military government can fall, just as a cabinet in a parliamentary system falls when the ruling party becomes divided.

A few countries in Latin America have had relatively little military intervention or other forms of political disruption during the 20th century. Costa Rica has no national army (only a national police force), and the money which many countries use for maintaining the armed forces in Costa Rica goes for education. Uruguay and Chile are also countries which in the past few decades have been free from military *coups*, and have in most respects been stable. In Mexico the military played a dominant role in politics for more than a century of its national history. But by 1940 Mexico's Revolution of 1910 had created a system which has been remarkably stable and in which the military has been completely loyal and subservient.

Students in politics. The participation of students in Latin American politics as an important pressure group, acting through strikes, demonstrations, and even riots, at one time amazed Americans. As students in the United States have begun to play a similar role, however, the activities of Latin American students have seemed less surprising. In both cases, students have represented an idealistic conscience, calling the attention of their elders to social ills which the latter have found it convenient to ignore. In Latin America, students have viewed themselves as spokesmen for the poor who, because they are inarticulate and unorganized, do not have their interests represented within either the parties or the military.

Emiliano Zapata organized and led the peasants during the Mexican Revolution of 1910.

HISTORICAL ORIGINS

We have discussed three notable characteristics of Latin American politics: a combination of centralism and weakness in administration; a pronounced tendency to instability; and the direct involvement of the military in politics. What historical explanation can be given for these political characteristics?

Royal authority. At the time Columbus sailed to the New World, Spain was becoming consolidated under absolute royal authority. Long before this time, however, the kings of Castile had begun to infringe upon the independence of the municipal governments. Ferdinand and Isabella (whose marriage had led to the creation of a unified Spain) brought the process of subjugating the local governments to a successful conclusion. They also seized complete control of other previously independent centers of social power: the Church, the nobility, and the rich military orders.

Ferdinand and Isabella further monopolized power by undermining the *cortes*, the Spanish parliament. In Spain the history of representative government was the reverse of that in England. In Great Britain the kings, needing revenues from parliament, had to concede this assembly increased powers and privileges. In Spain on the other hand, the *cortes*, once strong in the medieval period, withered under Ferdinand and Isabella and their successors because the Spanish kings did not need to call upon the *cortes* for money. The immense amounts of gold and silver sent to Spain from America helped concentrate power in the hands of the Spanish crown and allow the crown to ignore the *cortes*.

The enlargment of Spain's empire tended to strengthen royal authority in other ways. The effort required to hold its vast empire together spurred the Spanish monarchy to establish a tightly-controlled bureaucracy. The machinery of this centralized state was established in Spanish America on as grand a scale as in Spain itself. All important officials in the New World were appointed by the king and almost all of them came from Spain. (Of 170 viceroys in the three centuries

of Spanish America's colonial period, all but four were born in Spain.)

The bureaucracy in the New World had many tentacles. The viceroys were the chief administrative officers, but they shared some of their powers with a group of judges called the *audiencia*. The crown also sent out special inspectors to check up on the behavior of the other royal officers. In addition, all of the Church hierarchy was appointed by the crown and was responsible to it.

This elaborate bureaucracy was organized so as to concentrate decision-making in the hands of the king and his advisers in Spain. Several different officials often had jurisdiction over the same area; as a result, they frequently came into conflict. When such disputes arose, each official would send elaborate reports to Spain, where the question would be decided. The result was that the king's councillors made decisions on numerous local colonial questions, no matter how trivial they might be.

"I obey but..." While the Spanish crown strongly asserted centralized control from Spain, it was frequently unable to make its decisions effective. This was partly because of the huge size of Spain's possessions in America. Royal authorities certainly made their weight felt in Mexico City and Lima, but it was another matter to control ranchers on Mexico's northern plains or landowners isolated in the Peruvian Andes. The size of the empire also meant diversity. And this meant that laws made in the interests of one area or group would be vigorously resisted by others with opposing interests. As a result, it was common for laws to go un-enforced. Officials receiving unenforceable royal orders performed the ritual of placing the decree on their heads and announcing "I obey but do not enforce." That is, I respect the king's authority but cannot enforce his law. In many ways this tradition is still alive.

TIME CHART FOR LATIN AMERICA

PRE-COLUMBIAN **To 1500**	500-1000 A.D.	Mayan culture at highest level.
	400-1532	Incan civilization flourishes.
	1375-1519	Duration of the Aztec Empire.
	1492-1504	Four voyages of Columbus.
	1496	Neuva Isabela (now Santo Domingo), the oldest European-founded city in the Western Hemisphere established by Bartholomew Columbus.
	1519-1522	Cortés conquers Aztecs.
	1531-1533	Pizarro subdues Incas.
	1538	Oldest university in the Western Hemisphere, Santo Domingo, established in Nueva Isabela.
	1551	Universities of Mexico, Mexico City, and San Marcos, Lima, established.
	1763	Rio de Janeiro becomes capital of Brazil.
PERIOD OF CONQUEST AND COLONIZATION **1500-1800**	1804-1825	Independence movements.
	1810-1825	Bolívar liberates Venezuela, Colombia, Ecuador, and Peru.
	1816-1822	San Martín liberates Argentina and Chile.
	1835-1852	Rosas rules as tyrant of Argentina.
	1846-1848	Mexican War with the United States.
	1879-1883	Chile fights and wins the War of the Pacific against Bolivia and Peru.
	1889	Brazil becomes a republic.
	1889-1890	First Pan American Conference.
	1903	Panama becomes independent of Colombia, leases Panama Canal Zone to the United States.
WARS OF INDEPENDENCE 1800-1825	1933-1936	United States adopts Good Neighbor policy. President Franklin Roosevelt abrogates Platt Amendment Controlling Cuba.
	1946	Perón becomes dictator of Argentina, overthrown in 1955.
NATIONAL PERIOD **1825-Present**	1948	Organization of American States (O.A.S.) established.
	1959	Batista overthrown by Castro in Cuba.
	1961	Brazil moves capital into the new interior city of Brasília. Trujillo assassinated. Latin American Free Trade Association formed. Alliance for Progress formed. Economic development speeds up.

The Spanish bureaucracy also was riddled with corruption. In Spain government jobs were very prestigious, and there was a great deal of competition for them. Generally offices could be obtained only through the influence of some noble patron, and frequently people had to bribe their way into office. As the jobs paid very little, and the office-holders had made considerable investments in bribes, they generally tried to use their offices in illegal ways to build their fortunes. This Spanish administrative heritage also lives on in modern Latin America. Middle-class Latin Americans still tend to seek their fortunes in government jobs. They still need patrons or influence to get them; the jobs still pay little; so there is still a strong temptation to misuse the office to earn a little extra.

Comparison of the English and Spanish colonies. Unlike the colonists in English America, the American-born creoles of Spanish America had little part in colonial government. Many members of the creole upper class served in town councils (*cabildos*). These, however, were not elected as democratically as in the English colonies. Each town coucil chose its successors, and some councillors held office by royal appointment. Furthermore, the *cabildos* dealt only with local matters. There were no colonial assemblies as in British America. So the Spanish-American upper class had no experience in the give-and-take of parliamentary decision-making on problems of more than local significance.

What are the reasons for the differences between the English and Spanish colonial governments? One already has been mentioned. The parliamentary bodies in Spain were being whittled to nothing at the time of Spanish colonization. But, when the English colonies were being established a century later, the British parliament was growing stronger and stronger. Therefore, the establishment of parliamentary bodies in the British colonies seemed appropriate to both governors and governed.

Another important factor is the different economic character of English America and Spanish America. The Spanish at the very beginning of the Conquest discovered substantial supplies of gold and silver. Many royal agents were thus sent to America; the precious metals were too important to the Spanish treasury and the Spanish war effort to be left to colonial self-government. It is significant that the greatest degree of local autonomy, the greatest freedom from bureaucratic supervision in colonial Spanish America occurred in those regions which produced no precious metals.

In contrast with the great silver lodes of Mexico, Peru, Bolivia, and Chile, and the gold of the Caribbean and Colombia, North America in the 17th and 18th centuries offered almost no precious metals. Nothing in New England or Virginia made it necessary or worthwhile to create an elaborate bureaucracy. Partly for this reason, the British permitted a substantial amount of colonial self-government.

Brazil—some differences. A comparison has been made between the centralism of colonial Spanish America and the greater local autonomy which characterized English America. Portuguese Brazil differed somewhat from colonial Spanish America in having more effective local autonomy. In Brazil, as in North America, no precious metals were discovered for almost two centuries. Partly for this reason, and partly because of the weakness of the mother country, the Portuguese crown tended to dominate and control its American territories less than the kings of Spain. Though Portuguese governors were sent out, planters in Brazil, as in English America, were permitted to exercise considerable control over local affairs. Only with the discovery of gold and diamonds in the Brazilian interior (1693–1725) did the Portuguese crown move to assert more effective central control, and then primarily in the mining regions. Today the Brazilian political system remains somewhat more federal and loosely-strung than in the Spanish American countries. This may be because of its larger size and diversity as much as for any other reason. But it is possible also that differing institutional traditions have something to do with it.

Why political instability? In a certain sense, Latin America ever since independence has been searching for an adequate replacement for the king. In the colonial period the king stood at the center of the system. It was his ultimate, unchallenged authority which tied the state together. Whenever interest groups came into conflict, the king decided the issue. Thus, when the king was suddenly removed, the whole structure fell apart.

The leaders of the Latin American movements for independence were aware that their peoples were not prepared for representative government, and some of them hoped for this reason that new monarchies could be created in the New World. In Brazil an independent monarchy was successfully established. This was possible because the Portuguese king, João, himself had come to Brazil, fleeing Napoleon. When King João returned to Portugal, his son, Dom Pedro who assumed the new throne of Brazil, could make some claim to a legitimate right to rule. Under Dom Pedro and his son, Pedro II, Brazil enjoyed relative stability from 1822 until the empire collapsed in 1889.

Most attempts to establish monarchies failed, however, partly because it was virtually impossible to find a ruler whose authority would be accepted as legitimate beyond question. Agustín Iturbide, the general who made Mexico independent of Spain, proclaimed himself emperor in 1822. He was thrown out after less than a year. Later, in 1864, Archduke Maximilian of Austria was brought to Mexico as emperor. He was executed after only three years. Once the thread of royal legitimacy had been broken by separation from Spain, it proved impossible to replace it.

Another reason it was hard to re-establish monarchy was that the example of the United States' republican system was so compelling. The United States had succeeded so remarkably that many Latin American leaders believed that the republican system was the magic key to all progress and goodness. Simón Bolívar realized that, because of the attraction of the United States' model, monarchy probably could not survive in Latin America. On the other hand, Bolívar, like the monarchists, believed full-fledged democracy could not work because Latin America was so plagued with illiteracy and political inexperience. Bolívar therefore supported a kind of monarchy in republican dress. In the constitution he wrote for Bolivia in 1826 he proposed that the President hold power for life and that he choose his successor. The new states of the Americas, he said, needed "kings with the name of presidents." *

Bolívar's compromise solution, however, also failed. The appeal of the fully-republican North American and French models was too strong to be resisted. By 1830, the government of every Spanish American country was republican *in form.*

What kind of republic? Adoption of republican government did not end uncertainty over the proper form of political organization. In many countries Liberals, who favored a federal government like that of the United States, fought with Conservatives, who

* See *Readings in World History,* "Bolívar: How to Organize the New Nations," p. 316.

The peasants of Latin America have traditionally felt strong ties to the Catholic Church, often because the priests lived and worked closely with the people. In a peasant village a barefoot priest leads his poor parishioners.

wanted a centralized republican system which would conform better to Spanish traditions. In such countries as Mexico, Venezuela, Colombia, and Ecuador this was an issue over which civil wars were fought through much of the 19th century.

While republican systems were adopted almost everywhere after 1830, there remained nevertheless a need for a figure with the authority of a king. To some extent the generals of the independence period and other military *caudillos* filled this need. Nevertheless, the *caudillos* were not an entirely satisfactory substitute. A *caudillo* who seized power by force lacked an aura of legitimacy. It was always tempting, therefore, for rival leaders to challenge the power of the *caudillo*-president, thus throwing their country into civil war.

The problem of the Church. Another problem which emerged as Spanish America moved from a monarchical system to a republican one was that of the Church. In the Spanish colonial period, the Roman Catholic Church not only had a religious monopoly, but also had been an integral part of the government. Church officials were appointed by the king, and often served as civil administrators as well as dealing with church matters. The Church also had great social and economic power. Church institutions were the largest landowners and the most important moneylenders in the colonial period. The Church ran almost all philanthropic institutions, such as orphanages and hospitals. Finally, as almost all Spanish Americans were devout Catholics, the Church could command the primary loyalties of the greater part of the people. The Church reached into every aspect of social life, and its representatives, whether archbishops in the capital cities or parish priests in provincial towns, were listened to with respect, and usually obeyed, on any question on which they chose to speak.

After Independence, this situation created trouble in a number of ways. The Church's great power and privileges upset many Spanish American politicians. Those who looked to the United States as a political model believed the Church must be separated from the state. Many, hoping to attract European immigrants, wanted at least a guaranty of religious toleration to all creeds, which the Church opposed. Civilian politicians also worried that the Church's power would permit it to overthrow any secular government at will. The problem then was how to trim the Church's powers and privileges, when the Church, hallowed by belief and centuries of social action, was so much stronger than a republican system which was new, unfamiliar, and ineffective, and which had neither a broad nor a strong base of support.

The Church problem in several cases was resolved only after prolonged violent conflict. In Mexico the question of Church power was fought over for more than a century, from the 1830's through the 1930's. Colombia and Ecuador were also torn by civil wars involving the political power and the status of the Church.

In some countries, like Argentina, Uruguay, Chile, Bolivia, and Peru, civilian politicians managed to establish the supremacy of the state over the Church without resorting to violence. The success of the civilian politicians in these countries seems to be due to the fact that they did not press the Church question hard in the first decades of independence while the state was still weak. In most of these countries, pressure for secular supremacy was applied gradually until the time, particularly after 1880, their governments had acquired enough strength to compete effectively with the Church.

The military in politics. As indicated earlier, one of the most prominent features of Latin American politics has been the frequent seizure of power by the military. This characteristic stems not from Spanish colonial tradition so much as from the Independence period. During the wars for independence large armies had to be created. When the wars were over and independence was won, these armies became powerful pressure groups which insisted on having their salaries and pensions paid in preference to any other government obligations. When civilian politicians sought, by decreasing the size of the army, to lighten the heavy financial burden which it represented, military officers frequently revolted and overthrew their governments.

The wars of independence were important not only in creating a new and virtually irresistible pressure group, but also in bringing generals to the fore as national leaders. For the first several decades of the republican era, the heroes of the wars of independence in Mexico and the Andean countries were, with only a few exceptions, the men who occupied the Presidency. By the time the independence heroes began to pass from the scene there were numerous younger generals, created by later civil wars, waiting to step into their places. Thus army officers came to assume that the presidency was by right theirs. This often led to trouble, particularly because there was usually a surplus of generals. When one general took power by force, it was easy for others to be persuaded that they had more legitimate claims to the presidency and that they should take to the field to prove it.

The military—from amateur to professional. The 19th century military was not professional by present-day standards. Many were upper-class politicians who were made generals not because of military prowess or service but because their political and social importance seemed to require that rank. Most of these men served only in time of civil war and fought only in behalf of their political party, or of their own political aspirations.

Toward the end of the 19th century there occurred a movement toward the professionalization of the Latin American military. For a while it was thought that this would have the effect of removing the military from politics. This has not been the case. In the more developed countries of Latin America, the professional military has stood on the sidelines to some extent. Twentieth century military officers, however, also have tended to develop a sense of superiority to civilian politicians whom they consider opportunistic and corrupt. When civilian governments seem too weak to handle a crisis, or are hostile to the military, the army will step in, as it has proven repeatedly throughout the period from 1930 to the present.

Instability since 1930. One of the principal causes of instability in contemporary Latin America has been the economic stress which the region has been undergoing since 1930. By 1900 the major problems of the 19th century: the question of the proper form of government, the role of the Church, the transgressions of the wilder sort of *caudillo*, had been resolved in many countries. In addition, in the early decades of the 20th century much of Latin America was enjoying temporary economic prosperity. As a result, some countries (Argentina, Uruguay, Brazil, Colombia) were remarkably stable between 1900 and 1930. In 1930, however, the world depression cut Latin America's export earn-

ings by two-thirds. As a result of the economic crisis, military *coups* and revolutions occurred in several countries. Since then the larger countries have been attempting to industrialize. Industrialization has brought new pressure groups, such as industrialists and urban labor unions. In most countries civilian governments have found it necessary to appease these pressure groups by making special concessions (for example, subsidies for industrialists, higher wages for organized labor). These concessions have brought inflation which has heightened tensions in the big cities. In addition, the rapid development of urban slums since 1940 has created the potential for radical mass revolution. In many instances the civilian political parties have been unable to cope with these new pressures. As a result the period since 1930 has witnessed numerous military coups, and governments are continually faced with demonstrations and an occasional revolution.

Considering the continuing instability south of the Rio Grande, many people have been tempted to blame some fundamental weakness in Latin American culture. For example, instability is often attributed to Latin authoritarianism, or Latin anarchism, or Latin extremism. But this kind of explanation seems too simple and abstract to be very useful in understanding real political events.

Why is political instability a continuing influence south of the Rio Grande? Perhaps the best way to understand is to hold in mind that the region has somewhat different mechanisms for making political changes. In the United States, government decisions are influenced by elections, by court cases, and by the action of pressure groups on the legislatures and executives of the nation and the states. All of these processes also operate in Latin American countries. But in Latin America there are also other accepted instruments of political change, among them student riots and military coups.

A May Day celebration in Havana in 1961 drew displays of support for Cuban communism. Fidel Castro was portrayed on countless signs as an ally of Mao and Khrushchev.

"Revolutions" and revolutions. Despite all of the political turmoil which Latin America has suffered, in most "revolutions" little social change has occurred. In most cases, it has simply been a question of one faction in the upper-class throwing out another.* But Latin America has had a few genuine social revolutions, in which important changes did occur. The two most significant social revolutions have been the Mexican Revolution (1910–1940) and the Cuban Revolution (1959–?).†

The Cuban Revolution led by Fidel Castro has proven much more radical than the Mexican; but both revolutions shared certain common characteristics. Both started in reaction to military-supported personal dictatorships: of Porfirio Díaz (1876–1910) in Mexico, and of Fulgencio Batista (1952–1959) in Cuba. In both cases, with the violent struggle to overthrow these dictators, broad

masses of the population were mobilized and made politically aware as never before. At the same time the violence tended to weaken the established powers in the society. In each country, the army supporting the dictatorial government became demoralized and collapsed, the large landowners were intimidated, and urban politicians were displaced by revolutionary warrior-heroes.

These warrior-heroes, with the support of a large popular following, carried out sweeping changes which aimed at increasing social and economic equality. In Mexico and Cuba alike the revolutions devoted particular attention to the plight of the peasants. The revolutionary governments seized control of the large landed estates and placed them under new systems of government ownership which were to benefit the peasants. In both countries there also occurred massive campaigns to spread literacy among the peasants, so that they might play a more active role in the political life of the nation and share more equally in its economic and social benefits. Both revo-

* See *Readings in World History,* "A Typical 'Revolution,'" p. 321.
† See *Readings in World History,* "Two Social Revolutions," p. 324.

Politics 335

lutions promoted a change in social attitudes toward peasants and poor people in general. Before the revolutions, peasants in both countries were not only exploited economically but also looked down upon and generally excluded from social consideration. Both revolutions sought to bring the peasant, and the poor in general, more fully into national life.

Another important aspect of both the Mexican and Cuban revolutions has been their insistence on political and economic independence from foreign powers. In both Mexico before 1910 and Cuba before 1959 United States economic power was very great. In Mexico in 1910 American companies controlled more than half of the oil business and three-quarters of mining and smelting, and they dominated many other economic activities. In Cuba in 1959 American companies dominated the sugar industry, railroads, mining, oil, and banking, and entirely owned the telephone and electric power companies. This excessive eco-

BLACK STAR

To demonstrate the need for Cuban economic independence, particularly in the production of sugar on which the Cuban economy depends, Fidel Castro went into the cane fields and cut sugar with the workers, thus encouraging them to make sugar production a success.

nomic control by a foreign power stirred up strong resentment against the United States companies, and the United States government which represented their interests. This anti-American feeling provided revolutionary leaders in both countries with a convenient means of unifying their countries during the periods of severe economic and social stress which occurred during the revolutions. By attacking the United States government and economic interests as "foreign devils," the revolutionary governments were able to focus social discontent on a foreign enemy and thus rally support for the revolution. As a part of this anti-foreign nationalism, both revolutionary governments seized substantial economic interests of American and other foreign companies. In Mexico, almost all large foreign-owned landholdings and, in 1938, foreign-owned oil companies were nationalized. In Cuba, Fidel Castro's revolution made a clean sweep of all foreign properties. These acts of seizure brought reaction and retaliation by the United States government, particularly against Cuba which, since 1960, has suffered an almost total embargo of trade with the United States. But the seizures of foreign property also served the revolutions as important symbols of national independence and helped to build mass support for the revolutionary government. Finally, as a part of their drive for national economic independence, both Mexico and Cuba have sought to promote the development of nationally-controlled industry.

Hemispheric impact of the Cuban revolution. Castro's revolution in its first years caught the imagination of Latin America's youth. The Cuban government also has made vigorous efforts to propagate the revolution in other Latin American countries. As a result, pro-Castro groups have sprung up, particularly among students, in most of the Latin American republics. Their efforts, however, have been fruitless. Only in the Dominican Republic in 1965 has a movement like the Cuban one come close to taking power. Rather than bringing about revolution, Cuban efforts in most cases have provoked right-wing reaction. Partly because of fears aroused by Castro-oriented agitation, the military during the 1960's has seized power in one country after another.

The military is still the ultimate arbiter of Latin American politics. If the army becomes demoralized or divided as it did in Cuba in 1958, revolution is possible. But, as long as the military remains united in its hostility to revolution, it appears that the forces of social revolution in Latin America will be repressed.

THE UNITED STATES AND LATIN AMERICAN POLITICS

The frequent revolutions, the military dictatorships, and the general political instability of Latin America have posed difficult foreign-policy problems for the United States. Because of the weakness and instability of many Latin American republics, the United States government at various times has feared that they might be dominated either by a European power or by some national party hostile to the United States. Particularly in the 20th century when the United States had become the overwhelmingly predominant force in the hemisphere, the State Department has had to confront the problem of *whether* the United States should intervene in the internal affairs of Latin America, and if so, in what ways.

The Monroe Doctrine. In the early 19th century, the United States welcomed revolutions in other American countries. In this period (1801–1825) the United States was generally friendly to the movements for independence from Spain, and offered at least verbal support against intervention by other European powers. This policy was strongly stated in the Monroe Doctrine. In 1823, President James Monroe warned the European monarchies to keep their hands off the Western Hemisphere:

> The American continents, by the free and independent condition which they have assumed and maintain, are henceforth not to be considered as subjects for future colonization by any European powers.

Monroe went on to assert that any effort by a European power to control a Latin American state would be considered an unfriendly act by the United States.

Although in the United States the Monroe Doctrine is usually thought of as a policy of generous protection, in Latin America it has been intensely disliked. Latin American leaders long have viewed the doctrine not so much as a protective device as an assertion of United States imperialism. They point out that in the 19th century the United States in fact often failed to protect them from the European powers. Beyond that, the United States, which was supposedly protecting the Latin American countries, itself seized half of Mexico in 1848 and Puerto Rico in 1898. In addition, United States' power was used to take the state of Panama away from Colombia in 1903, and to dominate Cuba from 1898 into the 1930's. Viewing these actions, Latin Americans have wondered not so much how they would be protected from the European powers as from the United States itself. To Latin American critics, Monroe's motto, "America for the Americans," has really meant "the Americas for the Anglo-Americans."

Latin American hostility to the Monroe Doctrine was sharpened by the addition to it of the Roosevelt Corollary. In 1904 President Theodore Roosevelt asserted the right of the United States not merely to protect Latin American states from European powers but also to intervene to establish order in

A Colombian interpretation of Theodore Roosevelt's Latin American Policy. Roosevelt had engineered Panamanian independence from Colombia so that Panama, when independent, would allow the building of the canal on terms profitable to the United States.

them. The Roosevelt Corollary held that if the United States were going to prevent the European powers from intervening in Latin America to collect debts, the United States logically would have to guarantee that the Latin American republics would behave responsibly. The Roosevelt Corollary provided one rationale for widespread American intervention in Central America and the Caribbean between 1909 and 1933.

Because of vigorous Latin American objections to American interventionism the administrations of Presidents Herbert Hoover (1929–1933) and Franklin Roosevelt (1933–1945) repudiated the Roosevelt Corollary. Nevertheless "Monroe Doctrine" remains a dirty word south of the Rio Grande.

To interfere or not to interfere? The problem of European penetration in Latin America is only one of the spiny issues which has confronted the State Department. A more frequently faced question is whether the United States should use diplomatic and economic pressures to influence the course of domestic politics in Latin American countries. And, if it should do this, for what purposes and in what ways should the United States exert its influence? Should it attempt to uphold constitutionally-elected governments? If so, in the pursuit of this aim, should it deny recognition to military governments which have seized power by force?

Another question is whether and in what ways the United States may seek to influence the economic and social policies of Latin American countries. Should it give special support to governments promising progressive reforms, such as land redistribution? Or, alternatively, should it retaliate against governments which expropriate American companies, or show particular favor to conservative regimes which promise not to rock the boat with progressive reforms or nationalist economic policies?

AREA COMPARISON
U.S. –LATIN AMERICA

Miles
0   1000

These questions continually arise. And, as there are strong differences of opinion, both in the United States and in Latin America, about the proper aims and the proper instruments of American policy, these issues never have been, and never will be, settled to the satisfaction of everyone. If the United States government tolerates military dictatorships with reactionary social policies, liberals on both sides of the Rio Grande are unhappy. On the other hand, if it encourages progressive reform and tolerates expropriation of foreign-owned property, conservatives become equally unhappy. As a result, United States policy has wavered back and forth: sometimes attempting to encourage democracy and reform; at other times intervening against revolutionary change; and, most rarely, keeping hands off to let each country work out its own destiny.

Politics 339

Both Presidents Theodore Roosevelt (1901–1909) and William Howard Taft (1909–1913) interfered in the affairs of the Caribbean countries in order to obtain stable governments. The most wide-ranging intervention in domestic politics occurred, however, under President Woodrow Wilson (1913–1921). Wilson tended to view himself as a kind of democratic messiah; he was determined to extend constitutional democracy as practiced in the United States to the other nations of the globe. For this reason, Wilson intervened in the Mexican Revolution, refusing to recognize the counter-revolutionary government of General Valeriano Huerta and several times sending troops to aid the revolutionaries. Despite Wilson's good intentions, even the Mexican revolutionaries resented his interference, and Wilson is now treated as an interventionist villain in Mexican history.

During the 1920's the United States continued to interfere in Latin America in an effort to enforce stable democracy. In this period the United States Marines governed Nicaragua, Haiti and the Dominican Republic. But again American interference backfired; the result in each of these countries was more dictatorship rather than constitutional democracy. In addition, American interference involved the United States in innumerable complications and earned it the resentment of many Latin Americans. Presidents Herbert Hoover (1929–1933) and Franklin Roosevelt (1933–1945) therefore tended to abandon Wilson's democratic imperialism. They gradually withdrew the Marines, and Roosevelt in treaties signed in 1933 and 1936 agreed to the principle of non-intervention in the internal affairs of other American republics. Non-intervention became the foundation stone of Roosevelt's Good Neighbor Policy; because of this policy Franklin Roosevelt was greatly admired throughout Latin America.

The United States, however, proved unable to resist interfering. At the end of World War II, for example, the United States' ambassadors in Brazil and Argentina openly attacked the dictators in these countries, hoping to contribute to their overthrow. This tactic backfired in Argentina, where Juan Domingo Perón made United States' interference in Argentine affairs an effective election issue in 1946 and was elected overwhelmingly.

After the Argentine fiasco, the United States lost some of its reformist impulse. Secretary of State James F. Byrnes returned the United States to a policy of recognizing whoever had established effective power, whether the government was a dictatorship or a constitutionally-elected democracy. This was a sensible policy, among other reasons because the United States has found that withholding recognition is generally ineffective anyway. Unfortunately, in the 1950's the policy of treating democracies and dictatorships alike was carried too far. The United States supplied arms to dictators, and frequently American officials were photographed smiling in the embrace of some petty tyrant. During the 1950's Latin Americans severely criticized the United States for its apparent friendliness to such dictators as Rafael Trujillo in the Dominican Republic, Anastasio Somoza in Nicaragua, and Fulgencio Batista in Cuba.*

With the election of John F. Kennedy to the Presidency, the pendulum of policy toward dictators briefly swung to the reformist side again. Kennedy, committed to a program of progressive reform and social democracy in Latin America, for a time resurrected Woodrow Wilson's policy of not recognizing governments which took power by force. When military juntas seized power in Peru in 1962 and in the Dominican

* See Readings in World History, "Hostility to the United States," p. 347.

Republic and Honduras in 1963, President Kennedy refused to recognize them and suspended all aid programs. This policy failed to stop the military juntas, however. After the assassination of President Kennedy, the administration of Lyndon B. Johnson returned to a policy of recognizing military governments without question, though it waited until these governments had first been recognized by several Latin American countries.

The question of Communism. With the development of the Cold War, the question has arisen of how to treat Latin American governments which drift toward (or into) Communism. Anxiety about Communist influence has caused the United States on several occasions to break its pledges of 1933 and 1936 not to intervene militarily in other American republics. On three occasions during the 1950's and 1960's the United States has engaged in military intervention. The first case was in Guatemala which had an anti-United States and increasingly pro-Communist government under President Jacobo Arbenz (1951–1954). The Arbenz government was overthrown in 1954 by an armed invasion of Guatemalan exiles. They were supplied and otherwise helped by the United States.

The second case involved Cuba. In 1961 a group of Cuban exiles, aided by the United States, invaded their country in an attempt to destroy the pro-Communist regime of Fidel Castro. They were disastrously defeated at the Bay of Pigs.

The third case came in the Dominican Republic in 1965. In April of that year a rebellion of younger military men, backed by substantial numbers of the population of Santo Domingo, suddenly erupted. Their apparent aim was to break the power of the military establishment built up by the dictatorial Trujillo regime, and to return power

A North American soldier searches a Santo Domingan boy for weapons during the U.S. invasion in 1965.

to Juan Bosch, the elected president deposed by the military in 1963. The United States' ambassador decided that the rebellion, if successful, would establish a Castro-type regime. When the conservative military proved unable to suppress the revolution, the United States sent in some 22,000 marines and paratroopers. To give this act of unilateral intervention the color of legality, the United States later induced the Organization of American States to send an Inter-American Peace Force. Token troops were sent from Brazil and Central America. But the fact was that in the first instance the United States had intervened single-handedly in disregard of its treaty obligations.

Many people in the United States believe that this resumption of military intervention might be a justified weapon in the "Cold War" against Communism. But many progressive Latin Americans are indignant, believing that the practical effect of American intervention, despite the official explanations, is to block necessary and long overdue social reform.*

* See *Readings in World History,* "The United States and Latin American Revolution," p. 351.

Reviewing the Essentials

Present State

1. In what ways are Latin American political systems similar to that of the United States? Why are the "federal" governments in Latin America not really federal in the sense of that of the United States? In what other ways does politics in Latin America differ from politics in the United States?

2. Describe the various types of military government in Latin America and the social conditions in which each type tends to appear. Why does the military often seize power in Latin American countries?

3. What is the role of students in Latin American politics? Does it differ from the role of students in the United States?

Historical Origins

4. What are the historical origins of Latin America's tendency to political centralism? Does it seem strange to you that the Latin American political tradition should be at once one of centralized government and ineffective administration? How can one explain this combination?

5. In what ways, and why, did Spanish rule fail to provide a firm foundation for republican government in the post-Independence period?

6. Considering Latin America's continuing instability over a period of a century and a half, does it seem more reasonable to look for the explanation in some fundamental feature of Latin American cultural attitudes, or is it more helpful to look at the particular problems which Latin Americans faced in each period? What problems contributed to the political instability of Latin America in the 19th century? In the 20th century?

7. Discuss two true revolutions which have occurred in Latin America in the 20th century. What made these revolutions different from most political upheavals in Latin America?

The United States and Latin American Politics

8. Why have Latin Americans disliked the Monroe Doctrine?

9. In what periods has the United States tended to intervene in the domestic politics of Latin American countries, and in which periods did it tend not to intervene? Why did the United States intervene during one period and not intervene during another?

10. What should the United States do when a Latin American political group comes to power which promises to carry out necessary social and economic reforms, but which may also turn out to be Communist? Should the United States intervene? Why or why not? What should it do instead?

Explain, Identify, or Locate

mordida	Agustín de Iturbide	Roosevelt Corollary	Rafael Trujillo
caudillo	Maximilian	Good Neighbor Policy	Anastasio Somoza
cortes	Pedro II	Juan Domingo Perón	Fulgencio Batista
cabildo	Monroe Doctrine	James F. Byrnes	

ECONOMIC AND SOCIAL STATISTICS FOR SELECTED LATIN AMERICAN COUNTRIES

1967 Figures	Per Capita Income (US Dollars)	% of GNP Derived from Agric.	Per Capita Caloric Intake	% of Dwellings with Piped Water	% of Dwellings with Electricity	Drs. per 10,000 People	Illiteracy Rate (Over 15 Years)
Honduras	$226	41%	2,070	24.9	14.6	1.6	64.8
Bolivia	$176	23%	1,860	37.5	32.3	2.9	67.9
Brazil	$273	30%	2,950	21.0	38.7	4.0	39.3
Venezuela	$935	8%	2,240	67.1	78.4	7.8	34.2
Argentina	$758	15%	3,230	53.1	77.6	14.9	8.6

ECONOMICS: The Struggle to Develop

PRESENT STATE

An "underdeveloped" country is one with little capital, and therefore with low productivity. Since productivity is low, income is also low. This in turn means low living standards, few schools, poor health conditions, and a scarcity of doctors and health services.

Most Latin American countries have many or all of these characteristics as is indicated in the graphs shown above. The per capita income in Bolivia is only one-twentieth that of the United States, and the country shown with the highest per capita income (Venezuela) is only one-quarter.

As an "underdeveloped" area, Latin America is not as badly off as some regions of the world. As a whole it is much poorer than the United States or Western Europe, but it is markedly better off than most of Asia or Africa.

Within Latin America itself, however, the wealth and standard of living of the different countries vary a great deal. The richer ones (Venezuela, Argentina, Uruguay) have per capita incomes of more than 800 dollars, about half as high as the leading European nations. In the poorer countries (Haiti, Bolivia, Ecuador, Honduras), the per capita incomes are less than 250 dollars, close to Asian standards.

While per capita income is widely used as a shorthand device for measuring wealth and development, it is a very rough measure indeed. Per capita income statistics cover over the great differences in incomes and levels of living within each nation. Venezuela, for example, has the highest per capita income in Latin America. Yet most of this wealth is concentrated in the hands of a relatively-small group of big businessmen, professionals, and skilled workers employed in the oil and iron industries. Venezuelan small farmers, and the hordes of urban unemployed around Caracas, are as badly off as almost anyone in Latin America. Thus, while the national *average* may be high, the majority of the people are quite poor. Similarly, in Brazil, wealth is not only ill-distributed across classes but is also badly-distributed geographically. While southern Brazil, particularly in and about São Paulo, is as industrialized and rich as almost any area in the world, Northeastern Brazil is very poor. Brazil is therefore both rich and poor, something the national averages tend to obscure.

Thus, although the Latin American republics are not as poor as most Asian countries, still a considerable proportion of their population is very poor by any standard. Millions of people in Latin America, in some countries many more than half the population, live in hovels on tiny plots of ground in rural

areas, or in pasteboard or other makeshift shacks in slums surrounding the big cities. As a rule, neither the peasants nor the city poor have clean water or sanitation facilities near their homes. Consequently, many are afflicted with intestinal diseases. The diet of the poor is certainly inadequate, and many are never sure where their next meal will come from. In sharp contrast, the upper classes live in great comfort, in large houses with numerous servants.

Land tenure. The differences between rich and poor have been particularly marked in rural areas. The great bulk of the land is concentrated in large estates owned by landlords who usually do not work, or live on, their land themselves. These large landholdings or *latifundia* are known by different names in different countries. But with the exception of only a few countries, the economic pattern is essentially the same. In 1950, less than 2 per cent of the landowners controlled more than two-thirds of the culti-

This peasant village in Peru could be any one of a thousand like it in Latin America. Lacking sanitation facilities, running water, and electricity the inhabitants are continually subjected to disease and early mortality. To subsist at all the peasants must work for meager wages, for many others, equally poor, are waiting to take their place.

vated land. Not only do these large land-owners own most the land, they also have the *best* land, the flat, fertile valley lands.

At the other end of the scale there are the peasants, many of whom cultivate small plots of two, five, or ten acres of hilly or even mountainous land. Almost three-quarters of the landholdings in Latin America are these small plots or *minifundia;* yet they contain only 4 percent of the land under cultivation. The peasants holding this land are extraordinarily poor. But there are many, even poorer, people in rural areas, the landless laborers who attempt to support themselves by working for a pittance on the big estates.

Programs to redistribute the land have been carried out on a large scale in Mexico and Bolivia. Nevertheless, almost everywhere else the *latifundia* dominate the scene. A description of an estate near Trujillo in northern Peru illustrates the point. The estate is one of the largest sugar-producers in Peru. But its owner lives in Lima and only occasionally visits the estate. His main interest in the estate is in his herd of bulls which he breeds for the bullfights in Lima. It is primarily his love of the bull ring which leads him to leave the capital city, rather than a concern to increase sugar production. The workers living on the estate, called *peones,* work for it five days a week. Each *peon* is provided with housing, clothing, and a small bit of land on which he can grow crops for his own use. He also is paid a small amount in cash wages, only five dollars per week. On many estates, particularly in the Andean highlands, the *peones* are even more poorly paid.*

Such a land system gives rise to at least two questions. The first is a matter of social justice. Is it right for a few men to own so much land, while many remain poor and landless? The second question concerns

* See *Readings in World History,* "The Hacienda," p. 365.

Because of the lack of steelmaking facilities and the high cost of replacement parts, many farmers of the Andean countries must continue to cultivate their land with oxen and wooden plows.

economic development. Not all estate-owners are as uninterested in commercial farming as our Peruvian bull-breeder. Nevertheless, absentee ownership and, as a result, inefficient operations, are very common. Studies have shown that large estates in Latin America are much less productive than smaller farms. This is because on the large estate neither the absentee owner nor the *peones* who work for him take an interest in production. Small farmers who farm their own land, on the other hand, have more incentive to produce.

The rich and the poor. While the difference between rich and poor is most striking in rural areas, the distance between classes is quite marked everywhere, whether in the country or the city. As of 1965 the wealthiest 5 per cent in Latin America received almost one-third of all personal income. The bottom *half* of the society got only one-sixth of all income. (In the United States the top 5 per cent were receiving just under one-fifth of personal income, and the bottom half were earning only a little more than one-fifth. Thus, the differences between rich and poor, while great in the United States, are still greater in Latin America.)

Even though the upper 5 per cent in Latin America control a fantastic *proportion* of the wealth in their societies, it should be made clear that few are wealthier than "upper middle class" Americans. The standard of living of most in Latin America's upper class is comparable to that of moderately successful doctors, lawyers, or businessmen in the United States. Their relative wealth contrasts shockingly, however, with the widespread poverty around them. Equally shocking are the attitudes of many members of the upper class. Many wealthy Latin Americans not merely ignore the lower classes but also feel that poverty is entirely the fault of the poor themselves and nothing can (or should) be done about it.

Latin American society today consists not only of the few rich and many poor, but also of middle groups, typically skilled laborers and office-workers in the cities. Their standards of living are higher than those of peasants and unskilled urban labor. But still many of them would fall well below what is considered the poverty line in the United States. Because Latin America suffers from a desperate housing shortage, almost all of this urban middle group is badly and expensively housed. A young accountant, with his family, may live in a tiny one-room apart-

ment; and this may consume 40 or 50 per cent of his income. In addition, this middle group must confront the high cost of education in Latin America. They want their children to receive as much education as possible so as to be able to rise economically and socially. But in many Latin American countries there are rather few public secondary schools, and these are often not very good. As a result, many office-workers are faced with the impossible financial burden of sending their children to private secondary schools. Some middle group children manage to get into the universities. But usually for lack of money they fail to finish.

When the Latin American upper class is criticized for the unequal distribution of wealth in their countries, the usual reply is that the problem is not one of spreading the wealth but of increasing it. They point out that if all the money of the wealthy few was taken away and distributed over the whole population, there would be no noticeable improvement in the income of the masses. Heavy taxes on wealthy people, they like to say, would make the rich poor, but they would be of no noticeable help to the masses of the poor. This argument is faulty, in that the money taxed away from the rich may be used by the governments in ways which will benefit the whole society. But there is also some truth in the point. In Latin America, the problem is not merely that the wealth is badly distributed but also that the national economies need to produce more for all classes.

The two questions of distribution of wealth and productivity are closely intertwined. The Latin American economies are less productive partly because the proceeds of the economy are so unevenly distributed. Two per cent of the people are wealthy enough to own a sumptuous house, and a car, and to travel (and purchase their clothes) in Europe and the United States. Yet the poorer groups who might buy clothes and necessities produced in the country's own factories, can do so to only a limited degree because of their low incomes. Badly distributed income, by restricting the consumer base, discourages national industry and slows economic growth.

Poor distribution of wealth has been only one cause of economic retardation in Latin America. Other factors which have tended to slow economic development have been topographical obstructions; the lack of large internal markets; political instability; and the lack of skilled labor, capital, technological knowledge, and business initiative. These various problems will be discussed in the following survey of the economic history of Latin America.

HISTORICAL ORIGINS

At first glance it seems paradoxical that Latin America has been a region of poverty. In the 16th and 17th centuries the British and French envied the Spanish because Spanish America produced such a great wealth of silver and gold. Actually, however, Latin America has never really been rich. Even in the colonial period, when Mexico, Bolivia, and Peru were mining great quantities of silver, these were poor countries. While a few miners, landowners, and merchants became wealthy, the great mass of the population remained poor. Latin America's unequally distributed wealth, inefficient ways of working the land, and low living standards have their origins in the colonial period.

The Iberian heritage. When the Spanish came to the New World, they brought with them customs and attitudes which tended to hold back economic development. During seven hundred years of warfare between Spanish Christians and Muslims (711–1492), the development of a Spanish Christian merchant class was slowed and society was

Rio de Janeiro

LATIN AMERICA LAND USE

Miles
0   1000

Livestock ranching

Subsistence agriculture (including some shifting cultivation)

Grain farming

Commercial agriculture

Mixed livestock and crop farming

Industrial areas

No use made of land

dominated by a warrior nobility. The Spanish nobles lived as absentee owners of large estates, many of which were used for sheep-raising or cattle ranching while others were farmed by a subjugated peasant population. Most of the Spanish conquistadors were relatively poor men and not nobles. But they shared noble attitudes and were anxious to establish themselves as a new landed aristocracy, living a life of ease, in the New World. It proved possible to do this because of the nature of the Indian population they encountered.*

The Indians and the land. The Indians in Central Mexico, much of Central America

* See *Readings in World History,* "Social Attitude Toward Labor," p. 355.

and in the Andes were very highly developed. They were accustomed not only to steady agricultural labor, but also to supporting a class of Indian overlords. As a result, in these places it was relatively easy for the conquistadors to dominate the population, using the remnants of the old Indian ruling class as their agents. Because the Indians of Mexico and the Andean region were so docile, the Spanish were able to force them to work in the mines and on their estates, giving them only token pay.

At the same time that the Spanish colonists were exploiting Indian labor they took more and more Indian land. The Spanish crown issued repeated orders to protect land occupied by Indian communities. Nevertheless these orders were largely ignored. Often Spanish cattle herds would trample the Indians' crops, forcing them off the land. In many places disease and overwork decimated the Indian population making it possible for Spanish landowners to seize land formerly belonging to the weakened Indian communities.

When the Spanish took over the land they commonly ran cattle and sheep on it rather than cultivating crops. To some extent the strong Spanish ranching tradition encouraged this. But it also occurred because the Spanish population in most of the New World was too small to provide a market for crops and the poor Indians either grew their own or starved. On the other hand, there *was* a market for cattle hides, which were used for carrying ore in the mines, and for wool for clothing. As a result, in the 16th and 17th centuries there developed a pattern of absentee landowners casually grazing cattle rather than carefully cultivating their large estates.

During the republican era the exploitation by large landowners and the poverty of the Indian peasants seems to have become worse even than in the colonial period. The new republican governments abandoned the colonial policy of protecting Indian lands. They split up the Indian community lands and encouraged the peasants to sell their land to the large estate-owners. At the same time that the Indians were losing more and more land, their numbers were growing larger. For by the beginning of the 19th century the Indians had developed some immunity to European diseases. Thus while the Indian peasant population was increasing in numbers, the amount of land it controlled was decreasing. The peasants thus found themselves in an ever poorer bargaining position in dealing with the big landowners. The less land the Indians had to support themselves, the more they had to depend on work for the *haciendas*. And the more they needed work, the less they were able to demand adequate wages from the big landowners. Consequently, in many places the real wages of peasants dropped by about two-thirds during the 19th century.*

Exploitation and backwardness. Because of their depressed situation, the peasants were reduced to an attitude of fatalistic hopelessness. With no hope of rising economically, all initiative was discouraged. They did not try experiments with new seeds or fertilizers because on their small plots of land they could not risk failure. They did not send their sons to school because they believed their labor was needed to help support the family. It may well have been true that the sons could not be spared and the new experiments were risky. But there also was a psychological factor, the psychology of hopelessness in the culture of poverty.

The oppressive situation in which the peasants found themselves also produced what might be called an exploitation syndrome. As the landowners paid the peasants miserable wages, the peasants also took an

* See *Readings in World History*, "Rural Poverty: Mexico, 1900," p. 371.

exploitative attitude, stealing from the *hacendado* (landowner) when they could get away with it, or allowing the *hacendado's* property to be destroyed by acts of more-or-less deliberate carelessness. Thus the maldistribution of land and wealth tended to foster attitudes harmful to economic cooperation, and therefore to economic development. For example, when landowners finally began to become interested in using new agricultural machinery, they were often afraid to buy it, assuming that their laborers, either through ignorance or through malice, would wreck it. The persistence of this feeling of mutual suspicion between classes in Latin America has had a destructive effect not only on agriculture but also on urban industry. Even today and in an urban context, worker reliability continues to be a difficult problem.

European South America. The oppression and poverty just described have been true particularly of the peasants in the "Indian" areas of Mexico, Guatemala, and the Andes. But in those parts of South America where few Indians have survived, the laboring population has been better treated. In the plains regions of Argentina, Uruguay, and southern Brazil, the nomadic Indians were driven out or killed off in the colonial period and in the 19th century. When these regions began to produce meats, wool, and wheat, many European farm laborers flocked to them. Unlike the Indian peasants in the Andes, the European immigrants were able to defend themselves against excessive exploitation. This was partly because, in the boom conditions of 1880–1914, their labor was in great demand. Also the immigrants, being Europeans, were culturally better equipped to defend themselves. If a landowner were too harsh, they quickly moved on to another estate, or to Buenos Aires or some other city, or else they returned to their mother country. Thus the immigrant workers were able to demand higher wages than the Andean Indian peasants, who, not knowing Spanish well or knowing much about the outside world, were afraid to venture very far from the land of their birth.

The cultural preparation of the European immigrants helped Argentina, Uruguay, and southern Brazil to become more developed than most other parts of Latin America. The higher wages received by immigrant laborers helped to provide a better market for national manufacturers in these places. The immigrants also often brought with them technical and business skills which further helped economic development in "European" South America.

Some common economic problems. Despite great differences between the poor Indians of Peru and Bolivia and the much better off European populations of Argentina, Uruguay, and southern Brazil, all of the Latin American countries have shared some common economic problems. Before 1930 they all depended too heavily on the export of raw materials and delayed too long in developing industry. And in the past 30 years, most of Latin America has attempted to industrialize under the severe handicaps of capital shortage, galloping inflation, and the population explosion.

Raw material exports. During the 19th century, all of the Latin American countries concentrated on exporting foodstuffs and raw materials: Brazil on cotton, sugar, cacao, and coffee; Argentina and Uruguay on beef, hides, mutton, and wheat; Cuba on sugar and tobacco; Mexico and the Andean countries on silver, tin, and copper.

The export of primary products promoted internal economic development in only a limited way. Only improvements which helped exporting were undertaken. Some

railways were built to haul out ores, and banks were established to handle commercial operations. But the export economies stimulated few other improvements.

The Latin American countries' concentration on foreign trade also made them very vulnerable to price changes in world markets. In some of the smaller countries more than 40 per cent of all economic production was for the export trade. This meant changes in prices had a drastic effect on their economies.

Vulnerability was further increased by the fact that many countries depended on the export of only one or two products. During much of the 20th century coffee has made up 70 to 80 per cent of the exports of Guatemala, El Salvador, and Colombia. In Cuba, sugar has produced 70 to 80 per cent of foreign exchange. Even huge Brazil, with its varied exports, has depended upon coffee for from half to two-thirds of its export income. Copper has accounted for more than three-fifths of Chile's exports, and tin for two-thirds of Bolivia's. In Venezuela, petroleum has been responsible for more than 90 per cent of all exports. With each country depending on one product for half to three-quarters of its foreign income, any sudden fall in the price of this commodity was felt sharply.

Despite the disadvantages of relying so heavily on the export of primary products, Latin American leaders before 1929 did little to diversify their economies. They were on the whole satisfied with exporting raw materials and were not particularly bothered that their countries depended so much on one or two commodities. Primary products exports were profitable for the upper class, and few Latin American leaders worried about the fact that their societies as a whole remained poor. Most of the upper class was convinced that this was Latin America's unalterable economic destiny. They believed nature had decreed that Europe and the United States would provide Latin America with the manufactures it needed, and that Latin America would supply the industrial nations with tropical foods and minerals.

Retarded industrialization. The few individuals who did attempt to establish factories generally failed. Early factories were hurt by poor communications as it was very costly to import machinery and raw materials over the mountainous mule-paths. Poor roads also meant that a factory's goods could reach only the immediately surrounding regions. Often it was cheaper to transport goods from England than from a factory in a nearby province.

Partly because of the frequent civil wars of the 19th century, Latin American factory owners received little effective help from their governments. Numerous civil wars caused national revenues to be spent on military expenditures, rather than being used for road and railroad construction. As a result road systems in 19th-century Latin America could barely be maintained, let alone improved. Chronic civil war also disrupted trade and marketing. Factory owners could never be sure when their workers might be drafted. Fear of forced contributions to political armies, and the general economic disruption brought by civil wars, discouraged businessmen and caused potential investors to send their money abroad.

Latin American industry was also retarded by lack of technical know-how. In the United States labor scarcity induced Americans to rely wherever possible on machines. North Americans became used to working with machines and inventing better ones. In contrast, in Latin America, where cheap peasant labor was available, labor-saving machinery was not introduced.* As a result, neither the

* See *Readings in World History*, "Cheap Labor Hinders Development," p. 356.

Each coffee-growing country feels that it produces "the best coffee." A professional taster in Brazil tests whether the blend is just right.

upper class nor the laboring class in Latin America developed the technical skills of their northern neighbors.

Finally, industrialization was held back by Latin America's passion for exporting primary products. As long as communications remained poor, governments unstable, and workers unskilled, it was much less complicated to produce and export coffee or beef than to establish a cotton mill. As long as European markets for raw materials remained attractive, the Latin American upper class invested in agriculture rather than in manufacturing. Similarly, as the Latin American upper class was convinced that exporting raw materials was more profitable than manufacturing, most Latin American governments provided little tariff protection for local industry.

The move to industrialize. Latin American complacency about depending on raw material exports was rudely disrupted by the world Depression of the 1930's which sharply reduced the demand for raw materials. Between 1929 and 1932, the value of Latin America's exports as a whole dropped by about 65 per cent. As export earnings disappeared, Latin American leaders recognized that emergency action had to be taken. In the early 1930's, therefore, many countries established controls restricting the importation of foreign goods. This encouraged Latin American entrepreneurs to undertake manufacturing, to fill the vacuum.*

World War II further stimulated manufacturing, but for quite different reasons than the Depression. During the war Latin America's export earnings rose again. In wartime, however, the Latin American countries could no longer obtain the manufactured goods formerly supplied by the United States, England, France, and Germany. Thus the unavailability of foreign manufactures also caused industries in Latin America to expand. Mexico suddenly found herself producing manufactures not merely for herself but also for Central America. Colombia's textile industry began to supply not only

* See *Readings in World History,* "The Move to Industrialize," p. 375.

An effort is being made to refine or manufacture locally raw materials produced in the area. A sugar factory in Colombia helps develop the economy and also provides employment.

WHO (ALMASY)

Colombia, but also Venezuela, Ecuador, and Peru. Similar industrial expansion occurred in Argentina, Brazil, and Chile.

By the end of World War II, the industrialization of the larger countries of Latin America was under way. An irreversible process had been started, as the United States discovered at the Chapultepec Conference in Mexico City in 1945. At this conference, the United States' representative urged the Latin American countries to eliminate the import restrictions thrown up during the 1930's. To his surprise, the Latin American delegates angrily refused. During the war important industrial interests had emerged in their countries. No Latin American government was willing to jeopardize the newly-established industries by subjecting them to competition from the United States and other industrial powers.

In addition, Latin American economists pointed out a distressing fact: since the 1920's the prices paid for Latin America's raw materials had risen only slightly, while the manufactured products which Latin America imported from the United States had doubled in cost. For several reasons moreover, it seemed likely that this trend would continue. For one thing, the world markets for foodstuffs are relatively static. In the rich countries of the world increases in consumer power have tended to go not into more food but into fancier gadgets. No matter how rich they become, the people of the United States and Western Europe can drink only so much coffee or eat so many bananas. This means that consumption of these tropical foodstuffs will increase only gradually, at about the same rate as the populations of the industrial countries. Secondly, while the market is static, more and more tropical countries are producing for it. In particular, the many coffee and cacao-growing Latin American countries have felt heavy pressure from emerging

Colombian women must hand sort processed coffee beans to remove those with imperfections or of poor quality.

African competitors. Latin America's share of world trade has declined from 11 per cent in 1950 to 5.1 per cent in 1968. African competition has been one factor in this decline and the competition has kept prices of tropical products down. Finally, Latin American economists fear that the industrial countries will develop substitutes for Latin America's raw materials. Colombians, for example, shudder at the thought that American technology may create a *synthetic* coffee. This, of course, would have a disastrous impact not only on Colombia but also Brazil and most of Central America.

Defensive industrialization—some problems. It seems likely that the terms of trade will continue to turn against Latin America. The Latin American countries, therefore, have been trying to industrialize not so much be-

Great strides have been made in Latin American industry since World War II. Moreover, more and more industry is domestically owned rather than controlled by foreign companies.

cause internal conditions favor it as because they have no alternative. Each step toward industrialization has been taken in self-defense. In the 1930's manufacturing was promoted because they could not afford foreign goods. During World War II it was because foreign manufactures were unobtainable. And since the war it has been because they again cannot afford foreign manufactures. In a sense then Latin America has backed into industrialization.

Partly because of this defensive approach, Latin American industrialization has lacked organized goals. In the rush to make consumer goods, many Latin American countries neglected the development of electric power or domestic agriculture. This has led to acute shortages of the electric power needed to keep the new factories going, and also to food shortages. Galloping inflation has created considerable social stress in the industrializing countries.

Ironically, the development of manufacturing has not rid Latin America of its dependence on raw material exports. Most of the new factories require large quantities of imported machinery and replacement parts to keep running. Only through continued sales of its coffee, copper, and oil can Latin America supply her factories with the steel, the machinery, and parts they need.

The current state of industry. Despite these problems, almost every Latin American country now makes some light consumer goods. Between 6 and 8 per cent of the world's production of cotton textiles, cigarettes, and beer is in Latin America. This is close to Latin America's share of the world population (about 9 per cent). But in heavy industry the region lags badly. It forges less than 2 per cent of the world's pig iron and steel, less than Canada alone. Moreover, manufacturing, and particularly heavy industry tends to be concentrated in the largest countries. Seven Latin American republics now have large steel complexes. But the three largest countries (Brazil, Mexico, and Argentina) produce five-sixths of the steel made in Latin America. Mexico, Brazil, and Argentina have been assembling automobiles for more than a decade, and are now moving to make parts themselves. But in the medium size countries, such as Peru and Colombia, automobile assembly is just beginning, and in some of the smallest countries such as Haiti, Ecuador, and Paraguay, there is practically no factory manufacturing.

The need for a common market. Many problems have hindered the development of heavy industry in Latin America. But an important one is that most of the countries are too small to provide the large markets needed to support automobile or other elaborate industries. One way to open up larger markets to Latin American industrialists would be to create a Latin American Common Market, to break down barriers to trade among the various Latin countries so that products made in each could sell freely in all. A Latin American Common Market has been discussed for more than a decade. But so far few concrete steps have been taken to establish one. All of the larger countries now have the same specially, protected industries, and no one wants to face competition even from other Latin American countries. In addition, the smaller countries like Ecuador and Paraguay fear that any factories they might try to establish would be annihilated by competition from already-established factories in the larger countries (Mexico, Brazil, Argentina). The prospects of a full Common Market, therefore, seem rather dim at the moment.

Shortage of capital. Latin American economic development is also held back by a shortage of capital. Despite vigorous efforts to reduce their dependence on imported goods, the Latin American countries continue to lose much of their economic life-blood in foreign trade. Latin America still imports much more than it exports. Between 1956 and 1960 its trade deficit was over one billion dollars per year, and in the 1970's this may well increase to more than 1.5 billion dollars per year.

The resulting capital shortage is made worse by the fact that many rich Latin Americans invest some of their money abroad. They do this because of economic instability and possible revolution at home, and also to avoid paying taxes. Whatever their reasons, their countries are deprived of badly needed capital.

Inflation undercuts capital development. Even the money which remains in Latin America is not always productively used. One of the main reasons for this is inflation. About half the countries in Latin America have suffered severe inflation since World War II; in some of them prices have often doubled in the space of a year. In this situation rich Latin Americans tend to invest in land, and particularly in urban real estate. Investments in land are safe and profitable in periods of acute inflation. Unfortunately they do not help to develop the economy.

Inflation also has discouraged saving. With the currency constantly losing value, people are inclined to rush out and buy consumer goods before their *pesos* decline in value. As people deposit little money in the banks, the banks have little to lend to productive enterprises.

The population explosion. The effects of Latin America's capital shortage are greatly aggravated by the population explosion. In Latin America as a whole the population is increasing at close to 3 per cent annually.

In most countries more than half the population is under the age of 21. This means that tremendous numbers of youths have to be fed, clothed, and educated; yet there are relatively few people of a productive age to feed, clothe, and educate them. Because of Latin America's staggering population increase, education continues to lag in the region. Each year every Latin American country educates more children than it did the year before. But because of the constantly increasing numbers of children, each year there are also more children not going to school. Given its present rate of population expansion Latin America cannot staff the government and business enterprises and simultaneously provide enough teachers to educate its youth. In economic terms, if a Latin American country's economy grows by 3 per cent per annum and its population grows at the same rate, it has gotten nowhere. It has not accumulated capital. And it certainly has not narrowed the gap between itself and the more developed countries.

Migrants to the cities and land reform. Latin America not only is falling farther behind the most advanced countries, what development it has achieved has been unbalanced and has aggravated some of its serious social problems. In general the upper classes and people in the cities have benefitted from the economic changes of the past 30 years, but the poor and people in rural areas have gained very little. The peasants are increasingly aware that their countries' money and other benefits of development are in the city. Seeking higher wages, better medical services, and education, peasants since about 1940 have been flooding into the cities at a faster and faster rate. These peasant migrants generally lack the skills needed for city jobs. In addition, many of Latin America's new factories use highly-automated American machinery, and therefore do not need much labor. As a result, many of the migrants remain unemployed or find menial, unproductive jobs such as shining shoes or selling lottery tickets.* In 1968, one-quarter of the adult labor force of Latin America was unemployed, as many as in the United States in the worst years of the Great Depression. Many of the unemployed turn to theft. Upper-class Latin Americans fear that the increasing number of urban poor may well lead to mob violence or to full-scale social revolution.

Faced with this danger, some Latin American leaders now see the need for land reform. So long as it was merely a question of social justice they did little. But now that there is a threat of violent revolution, even some moderate or conservative governments are starting on land reform. They hope that this will make rural life attractive enough to stop the flight to the cities. Thus, Latin American leaders realize at last that, if violent upheaval is to be avoided, something must be done about the fundamental problem of badly-distributed land.†

THE UNITED STATES AND LATIN AMERICAN ECONOMIES

Whatever happens in Latin America, the United States will be involved because of its close ties to the economies of most of the countries. The United States is the largest single market for most of the Latin republics; about 40 per cent of Latin America's exports go to the United States. American companies also operate many of the oil fields, and own many of the mines, public utilities, and factories in Latin America.

Many Latin Americans resent their economic dependence on the United States. As a high proportion of their goods are sold

* See *Readings in World History,* "Urban Poverty: Sao Paulo, Brazil, 1955," p. 378.
† See *Readings in World History,* "Land Reform," p. 384.

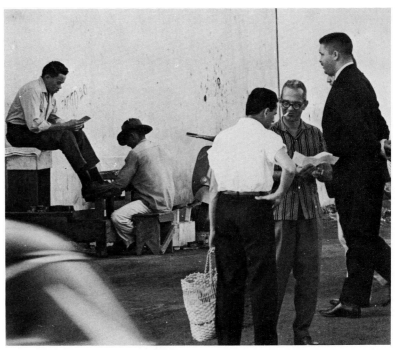

A street scene in the new capital city of Brasília illustrates a cross-section of new immigrants, established businessmen, and tourists.

in American markets, often they blame the United States when the prices of their products fall. During the 1950's Latin American leaders severely criticized the United States government for failing actively to support trade agreements which would help to sustain and stabilize the prices of coffee and other commodities. One of the most important acts of President John F. Kennedy, in the eyes of Latin Americans, was his agreement to use the United States' power as the world's largest buyer of coffee to help stabilize the price of this product.

American companies in Latin America. Latin Americans also have often been unhappy about the activities of some American companies in their countries. In the past, United States investments have been concentrated in extractive industries (mining and oil). Many Latin Americans think that the oil and mining companies are seizing valuable raw materials, taking big profits out of the country, and leaving nothing behind. This feeling is expressed in a slogan common to many Latin American countries: *Nos roban el petróleo* (They are stealing our oil). This belief was behind the seizure of American oil facilities in Mexico and Bolivia in 1938, in Argentina in 1963, and in Peru in 1968. In other countries, increasingly restrictive policies toward oil and mining companies have been adopted.

Another sore spot with Latin Americans is foreign ownership of public utilities. Since the 1930's American and other foreign utilities companies have not expanded telephone or electricity services as fast as the rapid growth of Latin America's cities required. This was in part because the Latin American governments held rates down so low that it was not profitable for the companies to increase services. The people in Latin America's cities, however, have been bitter about

Many United States companies do derive huge profits from their investments in Latin America. Some, however, have also accepted a great share of social responsibility. Above, housing for workers in Chile.

not getting better telephone, electric, or public transportation services. The utilities companies, therefore, frequently have come under attack and often are nationalized.

Latin Americans also sometimes resent American companies because they believe the companies are taking excessive profits out of their countries. Many Latin Americans are acutely aware that their countries desperately need capital, and they hate to lose any. Latin American governments therefore often impose restrictions on sending profits abroad. To United States companies this attitude seems unreasonable; unless the companies can send profits back to their stockholders, they will not invest in Latin America. The continuing struggle between foreign companies and the Latin American governments over this question is a frequent cause of contention between the United States and the other American republics.

United States aid. Despite the considerable friction that foreign companies often produce, the United States government until the end of the 1950's insisted that the North American contribution to Latin American development should be made primarily by private investment. Between 1945 and 1960, the United States did provide Latin America with some technical assistance, loans, and surplus food. But the region received much less aid from the United States in this period than did other parts of the world. In 1960, however, United States aid to Latin America began to increase, primarily because Castro's revolution in Cuba raised fears in Washington of widespread Communist revolution in Latin America.

The Alliance for Progress. The first promise of a major effort to help Latin America was given by President John F. Kennedy (1961–63) in his proposal for an "Alliance for Progress." President Kennedy committed the United States government to provide Latin America with more than a billion dollars per year, almost entirely in loans, for a decade. Under Kennedy's program, however, the Latin Americans also were to help themselves. Of the 100 billion dollars in development capital to be invested in Latin America during the 1960's, 80 per cent was to come from Latin America itself. In fact, Latin America in the 1960's has provided closer to 90 per cent of the capital invested in the region.

The Alliance for Progress differed from most previous aid programs in strongly emphasizing the need to invest in social improvement rather than simply in new factories. The program aimed not merely at erecting steel mills, but also at building badly-needed housing, improving education, health, and sanitation, carrying out agrarian reform, and strengthening the collection of progressive taxes. The social reform aspects of the program have created some controversy. Latin American conservatives have resented United States' pressure for tax reform. On the other hand, American leaders have sharply criticized the Latin American governments for not moving more quickly toward tax and land reform. Some Latin American countries have made a start on agrarian and tax reform, but at the cost of some irritation and resentment in the Latin American governments. No matter how well intentioned the United States' insistence on reform, Latin American leaders sometimes grow tired of being told how to run their affairs.

To many Latin Americans the Alliance has been a disappointment because it has not brought as much foreign capital to the region as had been expected. In the first five years of the Alliance, United States private investments in the region increased by less than a seventh while they almost doubled in Europe and Africa. And since 1965, partly because of the financial drain of the war in Vietnam, the United States government's contributions also have fallen below expected levels. By 1968 only three countries (Brazil, Colombia, and Chile) were receiving more than token loans from the United States, and the programs in these countries were under heavy attack by the United States Congress.

Latin America remains very short of capital. Nor does it appear that foreign loans will provide more than a short-term solution. Already 75 per cent of the loans now being made to Latin America is used to pay off previous loans. Economic growth remains slow, barely keeping ahead of the rapid increase of population. Food production,

in fact, is falling *behind* population expansion.* It is still possible that many Latin American governments, unable to handle their economic and social problems, will be pulled into the turbulent currents of violent revolution.

* See *Readings in World History,* "Economic Growth Remains Too Slow," p. 388.

The Chilean Ministry of Housing is establishing a number of self-help community development programs under the auspices of UN technical assistance. Housing developments comprise a major proportion of this program. The newsstand at Patria Vieja is the center of activity of that project.

UNITED NATIONS

Reviewing the Essentials

Present State

1. In terms of per capita income, which are the poorer countries of Latin America and which are the richer ones? Locate each on a map.

2. Why is per capita income an inadequate or not very accurate measurement of economic development?

3. What effects does extremely unequal division of wealth have on economic development?

Historical Origins

4. In what respects did Spanish traditions tend to slow economic development in colonial Spanish America? What did the existence of a large, disciplined Indian population have to do with Spanish America's economic backwardness in the colonial period and the 19th century?

5. How and when did the Indians lose their land? What were the consequences of their losing the land?

6. In what ways, and why, has the economic development of "European" South America differed from that of the "Indian" areas of Latin America? Locate the "European" countries and the "Indian" ones on a map.

7. What have been the principal exports during the 20th century of Colombia, Cuba, Brazil, Chile, and Bolivia? Roughly, what proportions of their total exports did their single largest item represent? In what ways has Latin America's dependence on the export of raw materials been disadvantageous? How has heavy dependence on one export product made the problem more acute?

8. Why did industrialization come more slowly to Latin America than to the United States? When and why did Latin America begin to move decisively toward industrialization? What kind of manufacturing did the Latin American countries first establish? What is the current state of industry in Latin America?

9. What are some of the problems which continue to make economic development difficult in Latin America?

10. What are the connections between population growth, migration to the cities, and land reform?

The United States and Latin American Economies

11. What has been the role of the United States in the Latin American economies? Why do many Latin Americans resent United States economic activities in Latin America?

12. Why did United States aid to Latin America expand after 1960? Under the Alliance for Progress, in what form was foreign financial aid primarily to be given?

13. Under the Alliance for Progress, how much of Latin America's development capital was to come from foreign sources and how much was to be generated by Latin America itself? How much has Latin America in fact provided?

14. How did the Alliance for Progress differ from previous United States government aid programs in Latin America?

15. Why have many Latin Americans been disappointed by the Alliance for Progress?

Explain, Identify, or Locate

latifundia	*peon*	Caracas	Alliance for Progress
minifundia	*hacendado*	São Paulo	

CULTURE: Two Classes, Two Worlds

PRESENT STATE

If you were to visit a Latin American country, you would soon realize that in culture, as in economics and politics, there is a great gap between the small and wealthy ruling class at the top and the masses of the people at the bottom. You would discover that your upper-class acquaintances know a good deal about the things generally regarded as "culture." They would be widely read in art, music, and philosophy, frequently much more so, in fact, than many college-educated Americans. But you might also notice that they knew little about scientific or mechanical things. They would think it degrading to stoop to work with their hands. If anything went wrong with a piece of machinery, as, for example, an automobile, very likely they would know much less than you would about how to replace a spark plug or to make other minor repairs.

On the other hand, if you were to leave the large cities and travel in the rural areas where the peasants live, you would encounter a quite different kind of people. You would find that the great majority of the lower classes were unable to read and write, either in Spanish or in Indian languages. You might find gifted "primitive" artists among the peasants, people who did not study art formally but who nevertheless show great natural talent in the things they paint and draw. You might also run across "primitive" musicians, talented people without formal study or training in music.

Practically all of the people of Latin America are strongly religious Catholics, but the peasants in a different way from your upper-class acquaintances. You would find in the Indians strong superstitions dating back to before Columbus, as well as some

WHO (ALMASY)

A Guatemalan peasant weaves in the traditional manner. Objects decorating her home reflect both Catholic and Indian culture.

imported by the Spaniards after the Conquest. But with these superstitions would be a warm and intimate love of the Church. Although they would know much less about the dogma and theology of the Church than would the upper class, the Indians would in most cases be more loyal and obedient Catholics.

Many of the Indians have an intimate and somewhat mystic or religious love of the soil they work and of their local communities and villages. For most, it is difficult to conceive of permanently leaving the communities in which they were born. Though many peasants, including Indian ones, travel about a good deal to markets in the surrounding area, most of them rarely venture very far from their native villages.

In conclusion, the culture you would find in Latin America is very different from that of the United States. Everywhere it is a culture that is divided into two parts. The few in the highly-cultivated Latin American upper class live in an entirely different world from the many in the peasant culture at the bottom. This is not true of the United States where the great majority, regardless of income, shares essentially the same culture.

One reflection of this difference can be seen in the fact that in the United States most people consider themselves "middle-class," whether they are industrialists, surgeons, skilled workers, or farmers and no matter how great the differences in their incomes. In contrast, in Latin America people in the

middle ranks of society have no clear conception of a class identity. There is a clearly visible upper class and a clearly identifiable lower class. But the people in the middle, the clerks, the skilled workers, have no developed sense of a common class identity. They are rather individuals who are "not lower-class," but live with the ever present fear that they may be thought so. Most individuals in this middle group have only a very limited hope of attaining the prize of upper-class status. Nevertheless, in their anxiety not to be thought "lower," they strive diligently to imitate the upper class insofar as possible, in dress, speech, and social manners. Thus, while the United States is a "middle-class" society, with everyone blending in either from above or below, Latin American society is upper-class dominated, with an anxious and aspiring, but also rather hopeless, middle sector.* These differences have their roots in the historical experiences of the Latin American people, to which we now turn.

HISTORICAL ORIGINS

Pre-Columbian Indian cultures. Compared to the Indians north of the Rio Grande, those of Latin America were much more numerous and much more advanced. It is true that the cultures of some were very retarded because the people remained simple food-gatherers. This was the case with the tribes in the southern part of South America. But the great majority lived in Mexico and the Andean highlands, and it was these Indians who developed the remarkable Mayan, Aztec, and Inca civilizations. It was these Indians also who survived the Spanish conquest and who today make up a large percentage of the population of Mexico, Guatemala, Ecuador, Peru, and Bolivia.

The literary and cultural orientation of upper-class Latin American culture is reflected in the preponderance of bookstores.

JACQUES JANGOUX

* See *Readings in World History*, "Cultural Values," p. 392.

The Hapsburg Eagle, symbol of Philip II of Spain, attracted the attention of 16th-century Peruvian Indians who incorporated it into their designs.

In Mexico and the Andean countries, therefore, the influence of Indian culture is much more marked than in the United States. In these countries Indian traditions remain strong among the peasant population. A traveller would see hundreds of examples of Indian influence on all sides. Most common is the use of adobe for building purposes, also unmilled pine logs as beams. Of Indian origin also is the blanket or *sarape* that is draped over the shoulders; likewise the *poncho* consisting of two blankets sewn together with a slit left open for the head. Another conspicuous example of Indian influence is to be found in Mexican cooking. *Tamales, tortillas,* and the various chili dishes are based on the two great Indian staples, beans and corn. Finally there can be seen in the market places numerous ex-amples of Indian folk art, including beautifully woven cloth, straw baskets, mats and hats, copper pots, pitchers, and bells, and wood carving of all types: plates, bowls, spoons, canes, trunks, and masks.

Iberian culture. Despite all these examples of Indian influence, Latin American culture today is basically of Iberian origin. The Spanish conquerors, and the millions of immigrants from Spain and Portugal who followed them, brought the civilization of their homelands with them. Of course it was not transplanted without change. Inevitably it had to be adjusted to the specific local conditions existing in the New World. Nevertheless the civilization they developed in the Americas was fundamentally Iberian in origin, and it remains Iberian to the present

Culture 363

Latin American music, from the Cuban pachanga *to the Brazilian* bossa nova *and the Caribbean* calypso, *is deeply influenced by African drum rhythms.*

front flush with the street or sidewalk all are Spanish architectural forms found everywhere in Spanish America. The mark of the Spaniard can also be found in town planning. Throughout Spanish America towns are built not along a main street but around a square central plaza, from which all the streets lead off in strictly-ruled right-angles. This distinctive city plan is found everywhere in Spanish America because the Spanish crown ordered that all towns were to be laid out in this way, according to one carefully-prescribed plan.

The attitudes and customs of the people in urban areas are also very Spanish or Portuguese. In family organization there is the typical Spanish pattern of male dominance and of close supervision of girls. Until recently young people of the upper and middle classes were not permitted to have dates without chaperones. The Latin American upper and middle classes also are influenced by the Spanish tradition of regarding physical labor as unsuitable for a gentleman. The great ambition of many young Latin Americans is to become white-collar workers and thus avoid the disgrace of having to work with their hands.

day. Proof of this can be seen on all sides by anyone who travels through the region.

Most obvious are the languages, Portuguese in Brazil and Spanish in the rest of Latin American except in isolated Indian communities. As important as language is religion, Roman Catholicism brought by the Spaniards and Portuguese. (We shall see later that Catholicism has been considerably modified in the Indian villages by the ancient tribal religions.) In addition the Spanish and Portuguese imposed their law codes which were Roman in origin.

Spanish and Portuguese cultural influence is particularly marked in Latin America's cities and towns. Spanish origins can be seen in houses and other buildings. The use of the patio or courtyard, the barred window, tiles for wall decoration, and the house

African contributions. Although Latin American culture today is basically Spanish or Portuguese, there is also a notable African contribution, brought by the millions of slaves who were imported to work on plantations. This African influence is strongest in the Caribbean area and on the northern coast of Brazil where most people of African descent now live. But examples of their influence can be found throughout Latin America, especially in music.

Cultural variety. Music is a good example of the co-existence of European, African, and native Indian elements. The music of the Indians before Columbus' time was played at a slow tempo on high-pitched wood-wind instruments. Prominent among these were the *quena* or flute, and the *rondador* which resembled Pan-pipes. With these instruments the Indians played music using a five-tone minor scale and sounding, to Western ears at least, like melancholy, high-pitched wails. The Africans, by contrast, use the drum which in Africa had been their means of sending messages as well as making dance music. They use drums of various sizes to beat out innumerable rhythms of warmth, vitality, and intensity. Finally there is music of European origin, from Spanish folksongs to Renaissance Masses to the works of Stravinsky. With this rich musical background, a traveller in Latin America can hear African ceremonial drums in Brazil, the central European polka in Paraguay, the rapid strumming of the Mexican guitar, the melancholy piping of the ancient *quena* in the Bolivian highlands, contemporary dissonance in the opera of Buenos Aires, and American rock-and-roll everywhere.

European and Indian cultural contributions are even more closely mixed in Latin American foods. In the tropical countries of South America everyone eats manioc or *yuca* root, as well as maize, beans and chocolate, all of Indian origin. And in the Andean countries, there is a heavy use of potatoes, as there was before the Conquest. But in the same countries plantains and bananas, rice and sugar, and beef and chicken, all brought by the Spaniards, figure importantly in the diet. In the *pucheros* and *sancochos* of Colombia or in the *papas huancayos* of Peru, these "European" and "Indian" foods are intermingled to make national dishes with centuries of tradition behind them. The upper class and peasants alike eat these foods which form their common heritage.

Mixtures of Spanish and Indian patterns, however, are most frequently found among

JACQUES JANGOUX

The mournful sound unique to Latin America is produced by these Bolivian flute players.

the peasants. One example of combined Spanish and Indian influences is in peasant clothing. Much of the clothing now considered typically "Indian," because the Indian peasants wear it, originally came from Europe. The jackets and knee breeches worn by Guatemalan Indians are essentially an Indian adaptation of European peasant dress of the 18th century. Similarly the felt hats worn in the Andean countries stem from Europe, but the Andean peasants use them in their own way, the women as well as the men wear bowlers or fedoras.

Indian peasants turn European-style felt hats to their own uses.

Many common peasant beliefs also are Indian adaptations of Spanish beliefs of the 16th century. In many parts of Spanish America peasants divide diseases, medicines, foods, and many other things into categories of "hot" and "cold." That is, these objects are believed to carry "hot" or "cold" spirits or qualities. In Mexico a man who is strong is thought to have "hot" blood. In some places foods which are considered digestible are "hot," indigestible ones are "cold." These beliefs at one time were thought to be entirely of indigenous origin. But anthropologists now believe that they stem in part from medieval European medical doctrines, though of course with some Indian adaptations.

The mixture of Indian, Spanish, and African cultures appears in the rituals of the Roman Catholic Church in some parts of Latin America. The character of the Church in the cities, of course, is predominantly Spanish. But in rural areas native Indian religious beliefs and practices have been mixed in. In Mexico, the shrine of the national patron saint, the Virgin of Guadalupe, is located on the site of a pre-Columbian temple to Tonantzin, a goddess of fertility. And as late as the 19th century it was not uncommon for Mexican Indians to dance before the altar as they had done in religious ceremonies before the Conquest. In present day Guatemala some Indian communities still practice both pre-Columbian pagan and Christian religious rituals simultaneously, and mixed together. In the town of Chichicastenango, Indian priests conduct pagan rituals inside the Roman Catholic

Church and before Roman Catholic images in public processions. Similar accommodations have been made by the Church in Peru and Bolivia.

To some degree, pre-Columbian and European Roman Catholic practices have become mixed together through deliberate policy of the Church. For example, missionaries in the 16th century built churches on the sites of pre-Columbian religious centers in order to take advantage of established patterns of worship. For the same reason they permitted the Indians to dance as a part of religious ritual because they were accustomed to it. In many cases, however, pre-Columbian pagan rituals have persisted despite Church disapproval.

In the Caribbean area and in Brazil, African religious practices have persisted along side, and blended with, Roman Catholic rituals. Even in some of Brazil's largest cities one can still see the *candomblé*, a spiritualist rite involving African gods. These rites also are widely practiced in Haiti under the name *vodun* (or voodoo, as it has been called by foreigners).

The Church. Despite the survival of some striking Indian and African rituals, the Church in Latin America conforms fundamentally to the Iberian model. Many Church leaders, and the Spanish crown as well, took very seriously the mission of converting the Indians and Africans to Christianity. In almost every expedition of Conquest a Spanish friar went along to begin the conversion process. After the conquest of Mexico, one of the first acts of the Spanish king, Charles V, was to send over Franciscan missionaries. The first group of 12 Franciscans carried on an incredibly energetic campaign of conversion, baptizing thousands of Indians and giving them elements of religious instruction. Later on their activities were reinforced by those of the Dominicans, Jesuits, and other orders.

Their efforts were quite effective, for most of the Indian peasants of Spanish America soon became, according to their lights, Roman Catholics. African slaves also were quickly converted to Christianity, by order of the king. One Jesuit priest in Cartagena, Colombia, San Pedro Claver, was canonized for his work in ministering to African slaves.

Many friars, Bartolomé de Las Casas the most famous among them, also attempted to defend the Indian peasants against exploitation by Spanish colonists. In part because of the innate religiosity of the Indians, in part because of the friars' work as protectors, the missionaries were able to exercise an extraordinary degree of influence over the Indians. One reflection of this can be seen in the impressively large and ornate colonial churches built by the Indians in communities which even today are rather small rural villages and towns.

In the building of these structures the Church itself placed a heavy burden on the unfortunate Indians. In the 16th century, Archbishop Alonso de Montúfar complained

The struggles of Las Casas resulted in laws regulating fairer treatment for the Indians.

Las Casas unter seinen Schützlingen.

about the onerous exactions made by the friars for the purpose of constructing churches:

> The excessive costs and expenditures and personal services, and the sumptuous and superfluous works which the friars are erecting in the Indian villages at the Indians' expense, should be remedied. With respect to the monasteries, in some places they are so grandiose that although they are designed to accommodate not more than two or three friars, they would more than suffice for Valladolid. . . . It is nothing for a friar to begin a new work costing fifty to sixty thousand dollars . . . and bring Indians to work on it in gangs of five hundred, six hundred, or a thousand, from a distance of fifteen to twenty miles, without paying them any wages, or even giving them a crust of bread.[1]

It is noteworthy, however, that the friars had to use little physical coercion to get their sumptuous churches built. This suggests the extent to which the friars gained the respect and loyalty of the Indian peasant population.

Later in the colonial period when many Indian communities were taken from the friars' control and turned over to secular parish priests, the latter continued to be leading authorities among the Indian peasants. In many cases the parish priests used their influence over the Indians to exploit them, demanding not only payment for all the sacraments but also unpaid personal services. In addition, parish priests often induced (or required) their flocks to celebrate religious festivals elaborately; in most cases the parish priest made money from these festivals not only by collecting for celebration of the sacraments, but also by selling the peasants all the paraphernalia for the festivals. Nevertheless, despite what seemed like exploitation to outside observers, the Indians did not appear to mind this clerical domination. When the rebellion of Tupac Amarú occurred in Bolivia and Peru in 1780, the Spanish civil administrators were slaughtered, but the Indians did not harm the parish priests. Today in the Andean countries the parish priests continue to have an incredible amount of influence and power in peasant communities. Peace Corps workers have found that when peasants elect committees to guide the development of their villages, the priest almost invariably is elected to all the committees, and he generally heads them.

The Church has dominated not only the peasants but also has shaped the ideas of the upper-class and other urban elements. In the colonial period all art and the most impressive architecture were Church-inspired. All holidays were religious festivals, and most public celebrations had a religious character. All charitable institutions, such as hospitals, asylums, and orphanages, were run by Church organizations. This is still true to a great extent.

The Church also controlled colonial education. The Dominicans and the Jesuits ran most secondary schools and universities in colonial Spanish America. Higher education in the colonial period was largely restricted to the study of theology and canonical law. Not until the latter part of the 18th century were significant efforts made to introduce scientific courses into the university curricula. Most university graduates went into the Church, or, to a lesser degree, and in the later period, became physicians and lawyers.

This colonial tradition in education has profoundly affected Latin American upper-class culture. Through the 19th century and into the 20th the educational systems tended to emphasize religious, philosophic, humanistic, and legal studies, and to be rather weaker in the natural sciences. In the 19th century, some Latin American leaders tried to establish studies in the natural sciences and technology. But this proved difficult to do. The colonial universities, emphasizing religious and legal education, had prepared very few men capable of teaching the sci-

To attract Indian support, many traditional customs and beliefs were incorporated into Catholic religious doctrine. In Mexico today, the festival of the Virgin of Guadalupe reflects this fusion of spiritual beliefs.

ences. In addition, students tended to resist going into technical fields because the traditional professions of law and the priesthood seemed to offer more secure social status.

In the present century, male students have gravitated much more to the fields of engineering and medicine. Very few men now study liberal arts in the university; students in the humanities are mostly women. Nevertheless, the traditional preference for the law as a profession for males continues strong. In the last few decades departments of economics, sociology, and other branches of the social sciences have been established in the leading universities. But these new departments have been fought by the entrenched law faculties, which formerly taught these subjects, if at all, in an amateurish way. In some cases sociology departments have also been attacked by traditionalist Church leaders, who tend to view social scientists as dangerous prophets of secularism and Marxism.

Impact of other cultures. In addition to the early and basic molding by Spaniards, Portu-

guese, American Indians, and Africans, there have been newer influences from Europe and from other parts of the globe. At the end of the 18th century, in the decades just before Latin American independence, upper-class creoles began to visit Europe. In addition, the Spanish crown began to permit various French and German scientists and mining technicians to journey through the countries of Spanish America. Independence further intensified cultural contacts between Latin America and the whole of Western Europe. In the first decades of the 19th century British merchants and mining entrepreneurs came to Latin America, seeking their *el Dorado* in the markets and resources of the continent which for so long had been monopolized by Spain and Portugal. At the same time artisans and skilled workers from Western Europe and the United States arrived. All of these, of course, had some impact on upper-class culture, particularly those who remained in Latin America and married into notable families.

For their part the Latin American upper classes began to enter more actively into the export-import trade. The export-import trade provided these upper-class merchants with the wealth, and also offered them the excuse, for travel abroad. If they were to import cottons and woolens from Great Britain and silks and other luxury items from France, they must visit the country of manufacture to learn about the latest fashions and to make commercial contacts. While in Europe they also generally made sure to take in the opera, to meet French intellectuals, and to visit the Vatican. By the middle of the 19th century travel to Europe had become not only a vogue, but almost a requirement for upper-class status.

Increased cultural contacts with Western Europe and the United States brought important improvements in Latin America's material culture. European adventurers introduced the Latin American upper class not merely to pianos, patent medicines, and artificial dentures, but also to new techniques and industries of fundamental importance to the economy. British immigrants, mainly Irish, developed the sheep industry in Argentina. British, American, and German businessmen brought steamboats, and ultimately the railroad, to other countries. Similarly, the foreign travels of the Latin American upper classes resulted not only in a taste for the opera, new standards in clothing, and a blessing from the Pope, but also in many technical advances. Often they brought back better plows, seeds, or livestock breeds to advance their country's agriculture.

While there were certain economic and cultural advantages in the increased contact with Western Europe which occurred in the 19th century, there was also a negative side. As the upper classes began to use imported furniture, imported clothes, and imported ideas, they became more clearly and definitely separated from the peasants and other lower groups. At the end of the colonial period, class differences were apparent, but the upper class in many parts of Spanish America nevertheless ate the same foods and in some places used much the same kind of clothing as the peasants. But in the 19th century, the consumption habits of the upper classes changed markedly as they followed the European mode, while the peasants' manner of living changed much less. As a result, the distance between upper and lower increased culturally as well as economically.

Mass immigration after 1870. As individuals, the merchants and artisans from Western Europe and the United States who came to most of the Latin American countries in the early part of the 19th century had an important influence on the Latin American upper class. But they did not constitute a mass migration. Many countries did attempt to encourage European immigrants to come in great numbers. But most of them failed because their Indian or other peasant populations could be made to work for wages much lower than any European would accept. For this reason, Mexico and the Indian lands of the Andes never were able to attract substantial numbers of immigrants.

Massive European immigration did occur, however, in Argentina, southern Brazil, and to a lesser extent in Uruguay and Chile, in the latter part of the 19th century. Between 1860 and 1914, about two and one-half million immigrants came to southern Brazil and about five million to Argentina. Not all of them stayed. Many of those who came to Argentina were migratory workers, who were called *golondrinas* (swallows) because they came to work for only one or two harvests and then returned to Europe. Nevertheless by 1914 more than two million people had entered Argentina and stayed there. In 1914 almost one-third of the Argentine population had been born in Europe, and in Buenos Aires three out of every four adults had been born abroad.

All immigrants to Latin America did not become wealthy or even middle class. This Colombian family barely lives at a subsistence level.

European immigration to Argentina and Brazil was interrupted by World War I and again by the Depression and World War II. But after each of the world wars it began again, though on a smaller scale than before 1914.

The British and Germans were most prominent among the immigrants to Argentina, Brazil, and Chile before 1860. But by the end of the 19th century the Italians, Spanish, and Portuguese became the dominant immigrant groups. Together these three groups accounted for more than three-quarters of all immigration to Argentina and Brazil before World War I.

The immigrants who came between 1880 and 1914, therefore, were predominantly of Mediterranean culture, Roman Catholic religion, and Latin tongues. Unlike the earlier German immigrants, who formed separate German-speaking communities, the people who came from lands of Latin culture assimilated quite easily.

Since World War I many new European immigrant groups have come to Latin America seeking safety from political or religious persecution. Spanish liberal refugees of the Spanish Civil War came in the latter part of the 1930's, particularly to Mexico, where the government was sympathetic to them. During the 1930's and 1940's many German and Eastern European Jews came, fleeing Hitler's campaign to exterminate the Jews of Europe. The Jewish refugees settled in every part of Latin America; but by far the largest Jewish community is in Buenos Aires. With the defeat of Germany in 1945, many Nazis in turn sought refuge in Argentina, Brazil, Bolivia, and elsewhere. (The fact that both Jews and former Nazis have come in numbers to Argentina is one factor underlying the development of violent anti-Semitic persecu-

Culture 371

tion in this country during the 1960's.) Since World War II, refugees from the Communist governments of Eastern Europe also have found a haven in Latin America.

Asian influence. Immigrants have come to Latin America from Asia as well as from Europe. In the second half of the 19th century, Chinese laborers were brought to Peru to dig fertilizer on the coast, and later to build railroads into the Andes. In the 20th century almost a quarter of a million Japanese have come to Brazil, primarily as agricultural laborers. The Japanese are the fourth largest immigrant group in Brazil. All over Latin America, particularly in the cities, there are immigrants from Lebanon and other parts of the Middle East.* (These people from the Levant everywhere in Latin America are somewhat inaccurately called *Turcos*.) With the exception of the *Turcos*, almost all the immigrants from Asia came as agricultural or construction laborers. Many of the Japanese in Brazil have remained in rural areas as farmers. But the Chinese and Japanese in Peru have tended to move to the cities, where they engage in commerce and manufacturing.

Immigrant Contributions. The contributions of the 19th and 20th century immigrants have been most important in the economic sphere, the British as merchants and developers of railroads and mining, the Germans and Japanese as farmers, the Italians and others as industrial entrepreneurs. All of the immigrant groups contributed not only business leaders but also great numbers of skilled workers needed to develop modern agriculture and industry. Thus in Argentina and Brazil, and to a lesser degree in the other countries of Latin America, much of the industrial progress and economic growth of the

* See *Readings in World History,* "Variations on the Norm: I. The Recent Immigrant," p. 401.

20th century can be attributed to the leadership and skills of the European and Asian immigrants.

The immigrants also have had some influence on social patterns. In Argentina and Brazil the native upper class in many ways tried to ape the English and French who lived among them. Under British influence, horse racing came into vogue in the early 19th century and men's clubs modeled after those in London were established. (Often they even have English names, as in the case of the Jockey Club in Buenos Aires.)

While the British and French have left their marks on the upper class, the Italians have had a much broader impact. Their ways of life, in Buenos Aires and São Paulo, have become those of much of the working and middle classes, of which their descendants form a considerable part.

> The Italians changed Argentine habits: they added macaroni, spaghetti, and vermicelli to the national diet; they brought Italian expressions and words into the spoken language; they created *lunfardo,* a dialect of the slums and underworld of Buenos Aires; and they revolutionized urban architecture.[2]

Other immigrant groups have had a lesser, but still notable, impact on mass culture. In Peru, for example, Chinese food is widely consumed in Lima and other cities.

Some immigrants have made important contributions to the intellectual life of both the upper and middle classes in Latin America. In the 19th century, when few native-born intellectuals knew much about the natural sciences, university courses in these subjects often were taught by immigrant scientists. In the 20th century many refugees from Germany and Central Europe have provided intellectual and artistic leadership, teaching the natural and social sciences in universities, running good bookstores, playing in the symphony orchestras.

In part because of continued immigration of educated Europeans, and travel of Latin Americans to Europe, Latin America's contacts with the cultural currents of Europe have been broadened and reinforced. There is hardly a new development in the religious, artistic, literary, musical, and philosophical life of Europe which does not quickly become known to Latin American intellectuals. Buenos Aires, with a first-rate opera, a vital theatre, *avant-garde* filmmakers, and such writers as Jorge Luis Borges and Julio Cortázar, ranks as one of the world's cultural capitals.

Art and architecture. European influence is also quite marked all over Latin America in the fields of art and architecture. In every Latin American country one finds young (and not-so-young) artists painting in variants of the contemporary abstract style. And in every major city of Latin America, as in the United States, high glass-walled buildings in the current cosmopolitan style have been going up for two decades.

This is not to say that Latin American artists and architects have merely copied ideas developed abroad. Oscar Niemeyer in Brazil is world-famous as an architect of great originality. Brasília, the new capital of Brazil, is a monument to the imagination of Niemeyer and other Brazilian architects. Mexico also can boast some superb achievements in modern architectural design. One of the most notable is the University City in Mexico City, which blends pre-Columbian artistic themes with new techniques and shapes made possible by steel and concrete.

Art in 20th-century Latin America has been of such variety and originality as almost to defy description. Probably the most famous Latin American painters of the 20th century have been José Clemente Orozco, Diego Rivera, and David Siqueiros. These three Mexican painters, greatly influenced by the

Mexican Revolution, believed that their life mission was to teach their countrymen of their national traditions and to instill a sense of national pride. Consequently, their murals of the life of the Indians, and of the dramas of the Conquest and the Mexican Revolution, were presented in a simple, straight-forward, powerful style. They wanted their patriotic message to get across to all Mexicans, from Indian peasants up.

Though the painters of the Mexican Revolution have been the most well known, they are not really typical of 20th-century art in Latin America. Most of the younger artists in Mexico and elsewhere have turned away from the traditional representational styles used by Rivera and Siqueiros. Much of the

A statue to "The Builders" pays tribute to the magnificent modern architecture of Brasília.

WHO (ALMASY)

In isolated areas of Latin America, many Indians never go beyond their villages or even see other people for long periods of time. One of the tasks of the Peace Corps is to bring education, modern work methods, and medical attention to the people of these areas.

374 *Latin America*

recent work is abstract and contains no specifically "national" characteristics. But, expressing themselves as modern individuals rather than as Latin Americans, many painters have demonstrated great talent. They have earned respect in international exhibits as well as in world art markets.

Effect of modernization. At the present time the culture of Latin America is rapidly changing under the impact of modernization. By this is meant the complex process by which underdeveloped countries become developed. This includes the more intensive exploitation of natural resources by the construction of railways and factories, and the opening of mines and power plants and irrigation works. But it also includes the more efficient use of human resources by improved educational and medical services, and by bringing all classes of the population into the development process.

In the "Indian" countries of Latin America, one task of modernization is to involve the Indians who in the past have been largely isolated in their villages. The extent of their isolation is difficult for us to imagine. It is due in part to the long neglect and exploitation of the Indians by the ruling white class. Owning most of the good land, the whites have looked upon the Indians simply as a source of cheap labor. They have assumed almost no real responsibility for the Indian's welfare in any sense, whether in earning a living or getting an education or keeping in good health. The Indian, on his part, kept his dignity by living his life in his own way and turning his back on the white man.

Why should he not be allowed to continue living in his traditional manner without interference from the outside? A Guatemalan anthropologist has answered this question as follows: "It is not for us to say whether the Indian cultural tradition is good or bad, but we are justified in saying it is less productive,

efficient, and healthful than what the country needs if it is to advance. From this point of view, the Indian undoubtedly is a problem."[3]

Latin American countries now are trying more and more to bring their Indians into national life. In the case of Indian villages located near large cities, this often is being done by the expansion of the cities and the building of roads. The Indians are then able to go back and forth from the city easily and quickly. They can sell their produce in the city and even find work there. In this way they gradually become a part of city and national life.[*]

THE UNITED STATES AND LATIN AMERICAN CULTURE

> Latin Americans all know that North Americans are rather naive, childish people, impatient with delay, uninterested in the finer things of life, and absorbed only by amusements and money-making.
>
> North Americans all know that Latin Americans are impatient about practical details, uninterested in efficiency, and absorbed only by poetry, women, and revolutions.

These two statements express some of the stereotyped ideas which Latin Americans and North Americans have of each other. Latin Americans and North Americans have understood little of each other's culture.[†]

One reason for this is that the cultural differences between the two really have been considerable. The United States has been a Protestant country, in that Protestant values have been adopted, consciously or unconsciously, by the great majority of the population. In addition, United States society has been relatively open to economic and social mobility, at least for whites. Consequently,

* See *Readings in World History,* "Variations on the Norm: II. The Indians," p. 404.
† See *Readings in World History,* "Low Marks for the United States," p. 408.

there has been heavy emphasis on individual achievement and on economic productivity. North American society also has been characterized by a high degree of territorial mobility; it is not at all abnormal to move from one city to another every five years. Because of this extraordinary mobility the North American family has tended to become much more fragmented than has been the case in more traditional, static societies, such as those of Latin America. In the United States parental authority is outgrown by adolescence, each younger generation shaking off parental controls as quickly as possible. Also, because of the tendency to mobility, the social style of the United States has been rather impersonal by Latin American lights. People from the United States are viewed by many, but not all, Latin Americans for their readiness to establish superficial social relations with strangers, and for their willingness to drop their new friends when it seems convenient to do so.

Latin Americans have found these characteristics unsettling. From the perspective of their much more static and more clearly hierarchical societies, Latin Americans have tended to view the United States as frighteningly chaotic. In Latin America the family is strong, its ties are binding, and they are constantly reinforced by daily or weekly contact. (Among middle- and upper-class Latin Americans, the Sunday visit of the sons and their families to the revered Mother is considered more or less imperative.) Relations between fathers and sons are often more distant than in the United States; but fathers are almost invariably treated with respect. Defiance of parents, relatively common in the United States, is not (yet) tolerated in Latin America.

Similarly, Latin Americans, as products of a completely Roman Catholic culture, have found the great number of American religious sects disturbing. Most Latin Americans

have had little contact with and therefore know very little about either Protestantism or Judaism. (Some Latin American peasants, for example, think that Protestants are the same as Communists; both, after all, are non-Catholic.) The existence of dozens of religious denominations in one society seems to them yet another example of the essentially anarchic character of North American society.

In Latin America things move more slowly than in the United States. Many Peace Corps workers have been distressed to find that it takes much longer to get things done in Latin America than they expect. People simply have a different time sense. From the Latin American point of view, North Americans rush around too much and work too hard. They don't know how to sit back and enjoy life.

Latin Americans, particularly upper-class Latin Americans, also consider the United States a society completely dominated by materialism. Since the middle of the 19th century many upper-class Latin Americans have believed that North Americans think of nothing but making money. Business success has so dominated United States' values, in their view, that there is no interest in or knowledge of, literature, music, or the fine arts.

While the older generations of the Latin American upper class commonly hold this view, there are many signs that the younger generations are developing a new perspective on North American culture. As more and more Latin American students and other visitors come to know the United States, they tend to have a more accurate, though perhaps no more flattering, picture of the United States. They still think of North Americans as brusque and arrogant. And many have become increasingly aware of, and disgusted by, the racism in the United States. But they also are discovering that some of the old stereotypes are not true. An Argentine visitor to the United States found to his surprise that some people were interested in religion and the arts:

> Browse through the museums [of the United States]. They rival those of Europe, and will teach you how unjust it is of us to regard this nation as uncultured. Every day and at all hours the art galleries and libraries are filled with people—families, students, tourists. And as the guides explain the pictures in detail, these "uncultured" visitors faithfully take notes.
>
> Don't fail either to go to Mass one Sunday at St. Patrick's Cathedral, as fine a temple as most of Europe's. This will clear up another misconception—that people here are interested solely in material things.[4]

Much still needs to be done to correct the ignorance and misunderstanding on both sides. Perhaps the greatest need is to realize that sweeping generalizations are dangerous. We have seen that Latin American culture varies tremendously. It can be that of the Indians, going back centuries before the arrival of the white man, or it can be the culture of a proud university in Mexico or Peru, older than any in the United States. Or it might be a culture brought by a recent immigrant from Italy, India, or Japan.

We have also seen that Latin Americans are far from resting content with past glories or achievements. They are fully aware of their many problems, including the underprivileged Indians, the inequitable land distribution, and the inadequate medical and educational services. And there are Latin Americans who are striving just as earnestly to cope with these problems as there are North Americans striving to cope with problems such as unemployment, spreading slums, and race discrimination.

A sidewalk art exhibit in Mexico City.

Reviewing the Essentials

Present State

1. Compare the cultures of upper- and lower-class Latin Americans.
2. What are some of the notable differences between the cultures of Latin America and of the United States?

Historical Origins

3. In what countries of Latin America has the influence of pre-Hispanic Indian cultures been strongest? In what ways has the Indian cultural contribution been most evident? Why has culture in these countries been influenced more by the Indians than in the United States?
4. In what respects has Latin America followed Spanish cultural patterns?
5. Where is African cultural influence in Latin America strongest?
6. What peoples migrated to Latin America in the 19th and 20th centuries? To which countries did most of these immigrants go? How have they influenced and modified the cultures of Latin America?
7. Why did friars and priests become especially influential with the Indians of Latin America? In what ways can the influence of the Roman Catholic Church on the upper classes be seen?
8. What changes have taken place in Latin American universities in the past few decades?
9. Why are the governments of Mexico and the Andean countries concerned about integrating the Indians into national life?

The United States and Latin American Culture

10. What common conceptions of the United States do Latin Americans have? What concep-

tions of Latin Americans are often held in the United States? In what ways are the two cultures really different? What factors have contributed to these differences?

11. In what ways are Latin American views of the culture of the United States beginning to change? Are North American ideas about Latin Americans changing?

Identify or Explain

candomblé	Jockey Club	Jorge Luis Borges	Jose Clemente Orozco
golondrinas	Brasília	Julio Cortázar	Diego Rivera
Turcos	University City, Mexico	Oscar Niemeyer	Bartolomé de Las Casas

UNIT ACTIVITIES

1. On an outline map of Latin America show the natural and human resources of the region. Locate and label: (a) major river systems; (b) mineral deposits; (c) agricultural areas; (d) racial groups; (e) concentration of population.

2. Prepare a chart on pre-Hispanic Indian cultures in which you give information on: (a) approximate population; (b) area occupied; (c) way of life; (d) achievements; (e) Spanish conquest; (f) influence on Latin-American culture. Good sources of information are: Elizabeth C. Baity, *Americans Before Columbus* (New York: Viking Press, 1961); Julian Steward and Louis Faron, *Native Peoples of South America* (New York: McGraw-Hill Co., 1959); Eric Wolf, *Sons of the Shaking Earth* (Chicago: University of Chicago Press, 1959); J. Eric Thompson, *Mexico Before Cortés* (New York: Scribners, 1933); and *Readings in World History* (Boston: Allyn and Bacon, Inc., 1970), "Pre-Columbian Cultures: The Primitive Fuegians," pp. 289–291; "Pre-Columbian Cultures: The Nomadic Chichimecs," pp. 292–293; "Pre-Columbian Cultures: The Advanced Aztecs," pp. 294–297; and "Pre-Columbian Cultures: The Ingenious Incas," pp. 298–306.

3. Prepare a report on: The Indians Under Spanish Rule. Include information on: (a) ways in which the Spanish dealt with the Indians; (b) reasons for this treatment; (c) grievances of the Indians; (d) policy of the Madrid government; (e) immediate and long-range effect on the economy, politics, and social structure of Latin-American countries. Useful information is given in: *Readings in World History* (Boston: Allyn and Bacon, Inc., 1970), "American Indians under Spanish Rule," pp. 306–309; Charles Gibson, *Spain in America* (New York: Harper and Row, 1966); *The Spanish Tradition in America* (New York: Harper, 1968); and *The Aztecs under Spanish Rule* (Stanford: Stanford University Press, 1964); and Lewis Hanke, *The Spanish Struggle for Justice in the Conquest of America* (Boston: Little Brown and Co., 1966).

4. Read in sources suggested on the independence movement in 19th century Latin America. Prepare a comparison of Latin and Anglo-American independence movements which focuses on: (a) causes; (b) ideology; (c) leaders; (d) results. Consult: Bernadine Bailey, *Famous Latin-American Liberators* (New York: Dodd Mead and Co., 1960); Elizabeth D. Waugh, *Simón Bolívar* (London: Collins, 1946); R. A. Humphreys and John Lynch, *The Origins of the Latin American Revolutions, 1808–1826* (New York: Alfred A. Knopf, 1966); John J. Johnson, *Simón Bolivar and Spanish American Independence, 1783–1830* (Princeton: Van Nostrand Press, 1968); and *Readings in World History* (Boston: Allyn and Bacon, Inc., 1970), "San Martín Fights for Independence," pp. 313–315; and "Bolívar: How to Organize the New Nations," pp. 316–321.

5. Consult United States History texts for information on the circumstances which led to the issuance of the Monroe Doctrine as a statement of United States foreign policy. What were its immediate and long-range effects on: (a) Latin-American countries; and (b) the United States? For a full treatment see Dexter Perkins, *The Monroe Doctrine* (New York: Peter Smith, Volumes I–III, 1927–1937).

6. Several students might prepare a report for the class on "Population Growth: A Basic Social Problem for Latin America," as a basis for class discussion on population trends and implications for economic development. Consult: *The Economic Development of Latin America in the Post-War Period* (UN Economic Commission for Latin America, New York, 1963); Philip Hauser, *World Population Problems* (Headline Series No. 174, Foreign Policy Association, 1965); Katherine and A. F. K. Organski, *Population and World Power* (New York: Alfred A. Knopf, 1961).

7. After reading for background information in the sources suggested below examine critically the question: "Why is Latin America an Underdeveloped Area Today?" Consult: *Readings in World History* (Boston: Allyn and Bacon, Inc., 1970), "Social Attitude Toward Labor," pp. 355–356; "Cheap Labor Hinders Development," pp. 356–364; "Economic Growth Remains Too

Slow," pp. 388–391; and "Land Reform," pp. 384–387. See also Henry L. Williams, *Fantastic South America: Continent of the Future* (New York: Horizon Press, 1958), the sections on culture and natural resources. Also see the magazine *Current History*, for December, 1965, and January, 1966, for causes of unrest.

Formulate a statement on completion of class discussion stating conclusions arrived at concerning factors basic to Latin America's economic development.

8. Prepare a report on the land reform problem in Latin America. Give attention to the following: (a) prevailing system of land ownership; (b) productivity; (c) Mexican Land Reform of 1915; (d) recent land reform programs in Latin America; (e) relation to effective economic development. Useful sources: *Readings in World History* (Boston: Allyn and Bacon, Inc., 1970), "Land Reform," pp. 384–387; Thomas F. Carroll, "The Land Reform Issue in Latin America," in Albert Hirschman, *Latin American Issues* (New York: Twentieth Century Fund, 1956), pp. 161–201; and Howard Cline, *The United States and Mexico* (Cambridge: Harvard University Press, 1963). See Also *Economic Development of Latin America in the Post-War Period* (New York: United Nations, 1964); and "Population Growth in Latin America: Problem and Challenge," *Latin American Business Highlights* (New York: Chase Manhattan Bank, Third Quarter, 1964).

9. Read on programs to develop the Amazon region and to promote the industrial development of Brazil. Consult: *The Amazon: A New Frontier* (Headline Series No. 45, 1944); *Reader's Guide to Periodical Literature* for current articles on Brazil's Five-Year Plans; on Brasília.

10. Prepare for presentation to the class your observations, based on selected readings, on the topics: (a) Barriers to Understanding Another People's Culture; (b) Proposals for Improving Our Understanding of Latin America. For useful information see: *Readings in World History* (Boston: Allyn and Bacon, Inc., 1970), "Hostility to the United States," pp. 347–351; and "The United States and Latin American Revolution," pp. 351–354; John P. Gillin, "Some Signposts for Policy," in Richard N. Adams, *et. al. Social Change in Latin America Today* (New York: Harper and Row, 1960); Frank Tannenbaum, "Toward an Appreciation of Latin America," in Herbert L. Matthews, *The United States and Latin America* (Englewood Cliffs, N.J.: Prentice-Hall, 1963); the magazine *Saturday Review*, March 25, 1961; and Harlan Cleveland *et. al.*, *Overseas Americans* (New York: McGraw-Hill, 1960).

11. Do selected reading as a class or in working groups in preparation for drafting a policy statement on the question: What shall be United States policy in responding to new trends in Latin America? It is suggested that the class first identify major changes and the problems arising from them. In working groups, students will propose alternative policies which the United States might follow in dealing with these changes. The consequences of alternative policies should be noted. Finally, following critical examination of proposed policies, the class should, with the assistance of a drafting committee, prepare a policy statement. For information consult: Herbert L. Matthews, "Diplomatic Relations," *The United States and Latin America* (Englewood Cliffs, N. J.: Prentice-Hall, 1963); Richard N. Adams *et. al.*, *Social Change in Latin America* (New York: Harper and Row, 1967); John G. Gerassi, *The Great Fear* (New York: Macmillan, 1963); and Mildred Adams, editor, *Latin America: Evolution or Explosion?* (New York: Dodd, Mead, and Co., 1963). See also *Current History* for December, 1965, and January, 1966; "Development Financing and the Alliance for Progress," U.S. Department of State, 1965; and Lyndon B. Johnson, address at the "Third Anniversary of the Alliance for Progress," U.S. Department of State, 1964. The State Department has various pamphlets available on request.

SELECTED READINGS

● There are a number of good general books about Latin America. William L. Schurz has written *This New World* (New York: E. P. Dutton, 1964), dealing with the development of Latin American society in the colonial period; and *Latin America* (New York: E. P. Dutton, 1964), providing a descriptive survey of contemporary Latin America. Two general books on the Indians of Latin America may be recommended: Elizabeth C. Baity, *Americans Before Columbus* (New York: Viking, 1951) is the story of the Indians from pre-Hispanic times through the period of the *conquistadores,* while John Collier, *Indians of the Americas* (New York: Norton, 1947) deals with the Indians during the national period. Anne M. Peck's two books, *The Pageant of Middle American History* (New York: Longmans, Green, 1947) and *The Pageant of South American History* (rev. ed., New York, Longmans, Green, 1958) divide between them the story of Latin America from pre-Hispanic to recent times. Robert Alexander, *Today's Latin America* (Garden City, N.Y.: Doubleday, 1962) is a good, brief survey of contemporary problems.

● Many excellent books have been written about the Spanish discovery and conquest of the New World. Only a few can be mentioned here. Louise A. Kent's *He Went With Christopher Columbus* (Boston: Houghton Mifflin, 1940) is a fictionalized account of Columbus' voyage. Samuel Eliot Morison, *Christopher Columbus, Mariner* (Boston: Atlantic-Little, Brown, 1955) is a biography of the celebrated "Admiral of the Ocean Sea." Felix Riesenberg, Jr., *Balboa,*

Swordsman and Conquistador (New York: Random House, 1956) is an account of the adventure-filled life of the discoverer of the Pacific Ocean.

● The story of the great *conquistadores* is set forth in fiction form in the following books: Helen Lobdell, *Golden Conquest* (Boston: Houghton Mifflin, 1953) and Samuel Shellabarger, *Captain from Castile* (Boston: Little, Brown, 1945); and Albert J. Nevins, *The Young Conquistador* (New York: Dodd Mead, 1960). A collection of firsthand accounts of the conquest is presented in the pamphlet by John Francis Bannon, *The Spanish Conquistadores: Men or Devils?* (New York: Holt, Rinehart and Winston, 1960).

● Latin America's struggle for independence is described in the following biographies of the revolutionary leaders: Bernardine Bailey, *Famous Latin-American Liberators* (New York: Dodd Mead, 1960); and Elizabeth D. Waugh, *Simón Bolívar* (New York: Macmillan, 1941). For the national period there are two books by Delia Goetz: *Half a Hemisphere* (New York: Harcourt, Brace, 1943) and *Neighbors to the South* (rev. ed., New York: Harcourt, Brace, 1956) with vivid thumbnail sketches of contemporary life in each of the Latin-American countries.

● All students will find especially useful the many materials published by the Pan American Union (Washington, D.C.) and their beautifully illustrated monthly magazine *Americas,* their *American Nations Series, Special Series for Young Readers, Commodity Series,* and *Art, Folklore, and Music.*

FURTHER READING

● The two standard works on the geography of Latin America are Preston E. James, *Latin America* (3rd rev. ed., New York: Odyssey, 1959); and G. J. Butland, *Latin America* (New York: John Wiley & Sons, Inc., 1960). A number of general histories are available. The best probably is Hubert Herring, *History of Latin America* (2nd edition, New York: A. A. Knopf, 1961). Donald

Worcester and Wendell Schaeffer, *The Growth and Culture of Latin America* is less factual and more interpretive. Others of more-or-less comparable quality are John E. Fagg, *Latin America: A General History* (New York: Macmillan, 1963); and Helen M. Bailey and Abraham P. Nasatir, *Latin America: The Development of Its Civilization* (Englewood Cliffs, N.J.: Prentice-Hall, 1960).

Donald M. Dozer, *Latin America: An Interpretive History* (New York: McGraw-Hill, 1962) divides the history of Latin America into short chronological periods, using brief segments of the histories of various countries for illustrative purposes.
● Few events have inspired more books than has Hernán Cortés' conquest of Mexico. Maurice Collis, *Cortés and Montezuma* (New York: Harcourt, Brace, 1955) re-examines the careers of the two great leaders. Bernal Díaz del Castillo, *The True Story of the Conquest of New Spain* (published in many editions) has been a popular favorite for centuries. Díaz del Castillo was one of Cortés' soldiers and described from firsthand knowledge the conquest of Mexico in the vivid and simple language of a soldier. An abridged version of Bernal Díaz's account has been published by Shirley Glubock under the title, *The Fall of the Aztecs* (New York: St. Martin's Press, 1965). The same theme is covered in an American Heritage Junior Library publication: Irwin R. Blacker, *Cortes and the Aztec Conquest* (New York: Harper and Row, 1965). The Aztecs' view of the Conquest appears in Miguel Leon-Portilla, *The Broken Spears* (Boston: Beacon Press, 1962). For two conquistadors' accounts which show sympathy for the Indians, see the fascinating report of Cabeza de Vaca, *Adventures in the Unknown Interior of America* (New York: Collier Books, 1961) and Pedro Cieza de Leon, *The Incas* (Norman, Okla.: University of Oklahoma Press, 1959).

● On race relations, colonial and modern, see Frank Tannenbaum, *Slave and Citizen: The Negro in the Americas* (New York: Knopf, 1946); Gilberto Freyre, *The Masters and the Slaves* (New York: Knopf, 1964); Marvin Harris, *Patterns of Race in the Americas* (New York: Walker, 1964); and Magnus Mörner, *Race Mixture in the History of Latin America* (Boston: Little, Brown, 1967).

● For politics and government, see Martin C. Needler, *Latin American Politics in Perspective* (Princeton: Van Nostrand Press, 1963); Robert D. Tomasek, *Latin American Politics* (Garden City, (N.Y.: Doubleday, 1966); and Peter G. Snow, *Government and Politics in Latin America* (Holt, Rinehart and Winston, 1967). Historical perspectives are presented in Hugh Hamill, *Dictatorship in Spanish America* (New York: Knopf, 1965); John J. Johnson, *Political Change in Latin America* (Stanford: Stanford University Press, 1958); and A. Curtis Wilgus, ed., *Dictators of South America* (Washington: George Washington University Press, 1937).

● In recent years there have been several good books on economic development in Latin America. One of the best is William Withers, *The Economic Crisis in Latin America* (Glencoe and London: The Free Press of Glencoe—Macmillan Ltd., 1964). Also useful are Reynold Carlson, "The Economic Picture," in Herbert L. Matthews, *The United States and Latin America* (Englewood Cliffs, N.J.: Prentice-Hall, 1963): *The Economic Development of Latin America in the Post-War Period* (United Nations, New York, 1964); and *Economic Survey of Latin America* (Published for the Organization of American States by Johns Hopkins Press, Baltimore, 1964).

● The following histories of individual countries, emphasizing social and economic patterns, are James R. Scobie, *Argentina: A City and a Nation* (New York: Oxford University Press, 1964); Rollie Poppino, *Brazil: The Land and People* (New York: Oxford University Press, 1968); and Charles C. Cumberland, *Mexico: the Struggle for Modernity* (New York: Oxford University Press, 1968). The Mexican Revolution is treated from contrasting points of view by Frank Tannenbaum, *Mexico: The Struggle for Peace and Bread* (New York: Knopf, 1962); and Howard Cline, *The United States and Mexico* (New York: Atheneum, 1963). Details on the background and course of the Cuban Revolution can be found in Wyatt MacGaffey and Clifford Barnett, *Twentieth Century Cuba* (Garden City: Doubleday, 1965). The dynamic of the Cuban Revolution is interpreted by Theodore Draper, *Castro's Revolution* (New York: Praeger, 1962).

CHINA

Grey-haired China has one foot in the grave, while a youthful China is ... conceived. ... Now, when things are dying, yet being born, when they are being ruined, yet being completed, destroyed, yet constructed, decaying, yet blossoming, ... every sound evokes an echo, and every echo awakes a dream, so that the self-awakening of each individual leads to the self-awakening of an entire people. Let everyone arise resolutely and march forward courageously without looking back, to demand ... an ideal China.

Li Ta-chao, Chinese Marxist, 1916

BASIC FACTS: A Continuum of Thirty-five Centuries

Over half a century ago an American Secretary of State declared that, "Whoever understands China has the key to world politics for the next five centuries." [1] Probably few Americans were impressed by that statement when it was made. Our grandfathers considered China a strange nation where things were done all wrong: where men wore skirts and sported pigtails and women walked about in trousers, where people talked in sing-song, and where books were read from back to front and up and down instead of across. Not only was it viewed as a quaint nation, but a weak and backward one, with little capacity to influence world affairs.

Today, however, few would deny that what happens in China in the next generation will affect the rest of the world for the next century. For, in modern times, the most populous and oldest living civilization in the world has been transformed. Revolutionary changes have thrust China into the modern world, and the only thing that seems strange now is the speed with which she has developed into a dynamic world power.

The modern transformation of China is a superb example of acculturation, which means the modification of one culture through contact with another. This process is important when so many formerly traditionalistic and isolated societies are, like China, changing as a result of contact with the West. To understand this process we must first examine the characteristics of Chinese society at the time Westerners arrived. Some of these characteristics are the product of geography.

GEOGRAPHY

Isolation. In the centuries before the existence of modern transportation, oceans, high mountains, and wide deserts cut China off from the rest of the world. To the southwest and west are the highest mountain ranges in the world. To the east is the great Pacific Ocean, impassable until fairly recent times. To the north and northwest are deserts and steppe lands that offer considerable protection, though not as much as the mountains and the ocean.

These natural barriers prevented sustained contact between China and other civilizations. By contrast, the several ancient civilizations in the Middle East had close contact with each other and even with India. China's civilization was the most isolated. Therefore it was the least influenced by others, and in many ways the most distinctive.

Variety. China is a huge country, surpassed in area only by the Soviet Union and Canada. It is also a country of rich diversity, with great mountains, arid deserts, fertile valleys, and broad steppes.

Despite many local and regional variations, there are broad differences between north and south China, with the Yangtze River marking the approximate dividing line between them. South China is semi-tropical, with cool winters and hot moist summers. Because of its mild climate and heavy rainfall, the growing season is long, and two or three crops can be grown during the year. The water buffalo is the chief agricultural animal. Much of south China, seen from an airplane, looks very green and very wet. North China, on the other hand, is brown and dry, for there is far less rainfall. Even more important, rainfall in the north is very irregular, so that the north is the scene of floods and droughts, sometimes in the same year. Because of the limited and uncertain rain-

The Wushui River

fall, agriculture in the north has always been a precarious business, and every year crop failures produce famine in various districts.

Rivers. A third aspect of China's geography that has deeply influenced her historical development is her river system. The main rivers of China have acted as foes as well as friends to the people. The two greatest river systems, the Yellow River in the north and the Yangtze River in central China, have provided the water for the necessary irrigation of the fields. The canals linking the many waterways have served as an important communications system. At the same time, these great rivers have overflowed their banks at frequent intervals to ruin the crops and bring death to millions from the resulting famine.

The Yellow River flows rapidly in a big loop through the hills of western China, where it picks up huge quantities of silt. The river then flows eastward across the north China plain, which is almost at sea level. The water flows so slowly on this flat plain that much of the silt collected earlier falls to the bottom. The bottom of the river is therefore constantly rising, and a heavy rain can easily cause the river to spill its banks in a disastrous flood. So frequently has this happened that the river is called "China's Sorrow."

The majestic Yangtze, one of the world's longest rivers, flows from the lofty mountains of Tibet eastward to the sea, a distance of about 3200 miles. Unlike the Yellow River it is navigable by ocean-going vessels for 600 miles inland while river boats can reach over 1600 miles upstream. The Yangtze is China's main river, comparable to our Mississippi. Along this important waterway one-tenth of all mankind lives today. But the Yangtze, too, is hard to control and an elab-

CHINA - CLIMATE

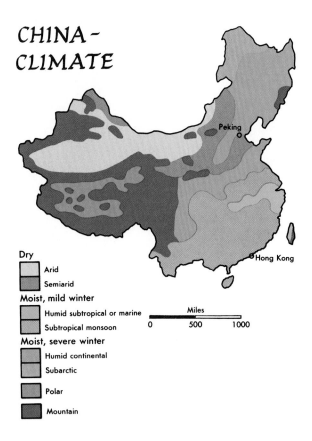

Peking

Hong Kong

Dry
- ☐ Arid
- ☐ Semiarid

Moist, mild winter
- ☐ Humid subtropical or marine
- ☐ Subtropical monsoon

Moist, severe winter
- ☐ Humid continental
- ☐ Subarctic

- ☐ Polar

- ☐ Mountain

Miles

0   500   1000

orate system of levees has not been enough to prevent periodic floods. The disastrous consequences of the flooding of these two great rivers has concerned all governments of China. Today the Communist government has begun a vast program of dam and reservoir building in order to prevent floods and to harness the waters for electric power. "China's Sorrow" may yet be converted to "China's Joy," and these great rivers may become reliable friends of the people.

Seacoast. The coastline of China has evidently not played as crucial a role in Chinese development as the river systems, although it seems clear that some of the southern ports conducted a flourishing international trade for many centuries. Canton in particular was

a bustling commercial city at least as early as the eighth century, and in subsequent centuries continued to be the natural destination, the first great gateway to China, for merchants and travellers coming from Southeast Asia and the world beyond. But this trade did not modify the fundamental agrarian character of China, nor did it stimulate cultural innovation.

The seacoast did gain importance in the 19th century, when Hong Kong, Shanghai, and other great ports developed under the stimulus of Western enterprise in China. Western culture first penetrated China through the seaports, for it was here that Westerners and their enterprises were centered. The nucleus of a modern Chinese business class came into being in the ports, and from the port cities Western cultural influences gradually spread throughout the country. Western trade also gave the ports unprecedented importance in the Chinese economy. After 1949 the Communist leaders shifted China's trade policies to reduce the role of the Western maritime nations, and the seaports consequently declined in economic importance. This, however, is probably a temporary phenomenon, and it is likely that the future will see a resurgence of the leading Chinese seaports to world prominence.

The paradox of China. Several things stand out from this survey of China's geography. In the first place, isolation has given China protection and security, so that a distinctive culture was able to develop and to endure down to the modern age. Secondly, within China there is as much variety in land and climate as is to be found in a whole continent. The climate, mountains, and rivers have divided China into many distinctly different areas. The variety is great and the divisions are important, but, despite all this, China has always been a single cultural unit. Indeed, cultural unity has been a distinguishing feature of China's history from the beginning. Since this unity was clearly not the result of geography we must look to other factors to get our explanation.

PEOPLES

The most impressive thing about the people who live in China is that there are so many of them. In area China is the third largest country of the world, but in population she far surpasses any other nation. China has often counted her numbers but never very accurately until recent years. In 1953 the Chinese Communists conducted a nation-wide census and reported the population of mainland China to be 583 million.* This is accepted as the most trustworthy figure ever reported of China's population. But every year this huge figure is increasing at the rate of between 13

* The U.S. Government estimated China's population in 1967 to be approximately 760,300,000.

and 20 million. This means that there are now about 780 million people living in China. In other words, every fourth human being is a Chinese! If China keeps on growing as it is growing now, there will be over a billion Chinese some time in the 1980's, and these billion Chinese will comprise one-third of the human race!

The huge population of China is distributed unevenly throughout the country. Less than 15 per cent lives in cities, in contrast to over 70 per cent in the United States. The remaining 85 per cent of the Chinese live in rural areas, especially in the northern plain and along the major rivers and the coastline. These regions have attracted most of the population because they have good soil or plenty of rainfall or both. By contrast the population is much sparser in the arid plateaus, deserts, and steppe lands of the western border regions.

About 6 per cent of the people of China are non-Chinese and are referred to by the

A Chinese scroll depicting the varied faces of the Chinese people.

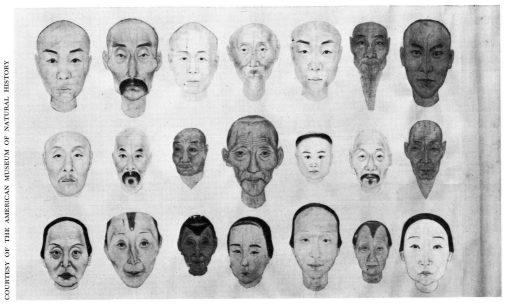

COURTESY OF THE AMERICAN MUSEUM OF NATURAL HISTORY

Tracing over already printed characters is the first step in the long years of study necessary to learn the complicated Chinese writing system.

present government as "minority nationalities." These include Tibetans, Uigurs or Eastern Turks, Mongols, Manchus, Koreans, and others. The government has set aside certain "minority nationality areas" for these non-Chinese peoples. These minority nationality areas are all located in the outlying border regions, to the northwest, west, or southwest. Although these minority peoples are not Chinese, they are almost all closely related to the Chinese. They also belong to the Mongoloid race and, like the Chinese, have straight black hair, dark eyes, narrow eyelids, and relatively flat faces. Thus China has much more racial unity than do countries such as India, the United States, or the Soviet Union, nations whose populations include not only Caucasoids but also Negroids, Mongoloids, or both. This racial unity has contributed greatly to the impressive cultural unity of China.

LANGUAGES

More people speak Chinese than any other language. But the Chinese language has many different dialects, some of which are as different from each other as Italian is from Spanish or German is from Swedish. Yet no matter what dialect is spoken by the Chinese, there is only one written language, and it is one of China's great triumphs. In the past, the written language was known only to a small percentage of the population, those of the upper classes, but the Communist government has vigorously promoted various programs designed to create universal literacy. Unquestionably, substantial progress has been made toward that goal.

The written form of Chinese is quite different from the written form of any other language. It does not employ an alphabet. Instead, it uses thousands of symbols, commonly called graphs or characters. Each character is different from all the others, and each is roughly the equivalent of a word in English. Probably this writing system originated in remote antiquity when pictures were drawn to represent things or ideas, but the majority of characters in use today cannot be traced to a pictorial origin. In an unabridged dictionary, there are 40,000 or more characters, although a knowledge of only about 3,000–5,000 is adequate for reading a newspaper. Each character must be individually memorized, and this is one of the reasons why Chinese is difficult to learn, even for the Chinese.

Characters are pronounced in different ways in different parts of China, but the meaning of any character is the same no matter how it is pronounced because the meaning depends upon its appearance and not upon how it sounds. It is as if an Italian, Swede, and Englishman took a figure eight and pronounced it in their various tongues; the meaning to each of the three would still be the same.

This common written language has been one of the great unifying forces in Chinese history, for through it people in all parts of the vast country shared the same cultural heritage. Moreover, since the written form of the language does not depend upon pronunciation, it does not change as pronunciation changes. Consequently the written language of the 19th and early 20th centuries was essentially the same as that used two thousand years earlier. Thus the language has contributed to a unity in time as well as space.

On the other hand, once China began to modernize there arose pressures to reform the written language so it would be easier to learn and be a more efficient instrument for a technological society. Reform was suggested as early as the 19th century, but not until the Communists came into power was a compre-hensive reform program undertaken with state backing. The ultimate goal of the program is to replace the characters with an alphabet similar to that used in English. There are many difficulties involved in such a change, and it may not be realized for another decade or two. In the meantime, preliminary reforms have been completed, including the use of simplified characters and printing from left to right.*

RELIGIONS

It is difficult to obtain reliable information about religion in China today. However, we know that the present government is unsympathetic to religion, and its policies have apparently been rather successful in reducing the social importance of religious thought and institutions.

Even in pre-modern China, religion was never as powerful as in India or in the Christian world. Chinese intellectuals were usually more concerned with the proper conduct of affairs in this world than with speculations about the supernatural, and a powerful priesthood never emerged. Confucianism, Taoism, and Buddhism are often spoken of as the three religions of traditional China. But that is misleading; Confucianism and Taoism were basically schools of philosophy, although with some religious aspects. Confucianism was primarily concerned with the question of social harmony, the proper relations between man and man.† Taoism was also concerned with harmony, although its focus was more on man and nature.

Even original Buddhism was not fundamentally a religion. However, it ultimately divided into two great branches, and the branch that took root in China created a huge

* See *Readings in World History* (Boston: Allyn and Bacon, Inc., 1970), "The Chinese Writing System," p. 414.
† See *Readings in World History*, "The Thought of Confucius," p. 418.

pantheon of gods and goddesses, and all the other aspects of a genuine religion. Buddhist beliefs and attitudes pervaded all areas of Chinese life. By the eve of the modern period, there was virtually no Chinese whose ideas and values were not shaped in some way by Buddhism. But while Buddhism was of enormous importance in terms of its cultural, moral, and spiritual influence, it never succeeded in creating a strongly organized church that could compete with the political and intellectual influence of the state. All Chinese religions have been organizationally weak except Confucianism, and Confucianism's organizational strength lay in its political and social implications, not its religious overtones.

Folk religion. Until modern times, the mass of the Chinese people held a complex mixture of religious ideas that derived from Confucianism, Taoism, and especially Buddhism, but also included belief in a variety of other spirits and gods and supernatural forces. Sacrifices were regularly made to the spirits of mountains, rivers, and the soil. The success of any venture, from building a hut to arranging a marriage, depended upon the good will of the spirits. Therefore every village had its expert on local spirits, and his advice was sought, for a fee, whenever an important action was contemplated.

The common people also practised ancestor worship, although this was widespread in other classes as well. Among the educated, the veneration of ancestors often only symbolized respect for the memory of the dead, and underlined the importance of filial relations generally. But the uneducated believed that the ancestors were living in the world of the spirits, and could therefore influence those spirits to help people still in this world. They made sacrifices to the ancestors in the hope that they would influence the spirits in desired ways.

HISTORICAL PERIODS

Chinese history presents problems because of its great length. It is true, as we have seen, that civilization began about two thousand years earlier in the Middle East than it did in China. But China's civilization has continued without a break from its beginnings, about 1500 B.C., to the present. By contrast there have been many sharp breaks in the history of the Middle East, such as Alexander's conquests which spread the new Hellenistic culture, and the Muslim conquests, which brought radical changes in racial makeup, language, and culture as well as in religion

China's isolation from other centers of civilization protected her from such disruption. Until modern times, the invaders of China were invariably at a lower level of civilization, therefore adopting Chinese culture rather than modifying it, except in matters of detail. China has continued for over 35 centuries with the same race, the same language, and the same culture. And, because of this continuity, the various periods of Chinese history have not been so different from each other as has been the case in other parts of the globe.

Beginnings of Chinese civilization. The earliest Chinese written records date from about 1500 B.C. This was during the Shang Dynasty, which lasted until the 11th century B.C., when it was overcome by invaders. The written records are in the form of animal bones and tortoise shells. Peasants in north China often came across such "dragon bones" while plowing the fields, and sold them to local druggists to be ground into medicinal powders. Then, at the end of the 19th century a Chinese scholar discovered that many of these bones were inscribed with a very early form of Chinese writing, which scholars subsequently learned to read.

EAST ASIA

SAVANNA

GRASSLAND

DRY GRASSLAND

DESERT

FOREST

MOUNTAINS

ICE AND SNOW

0   145   390   390

Scale 390 miles to one inch

©1962, JEPPESEN & CO. DENVER, COLO., U.S.A.
ALL RIGHTS RESERVED
REVISED 1969

PACIFIC   OCEAN

REPUBLIC OF THE PHILIPPINES

U. S. S. R.

MONGOLIAN   PEOPLE'S   REPUBLIC

GOBI

Ulan Bator

ALTAI MOUNTAINS

NAN SHAN

Yumen

TURFAN DEPRESSION

Urumchi

TIEN SHAN

Kashgar

Tarim River

TARIM BASIN

TAKLA MAKAN

PAMIRS

KUNLUN SHAN

Ulugh Muz Tagh 25,340'

TIBET

Lhasa

KASHMIR

PAKISTAN (EAST)

NEPAL

Mt. Everest 29,028'

SIKKIM

BHUTAN

INDIA

I N D I A

C H I N A

TSINLING SHAN

Hsinging

Lanchow

Sian

Taiyuan

Yinchuan

Hwang Ho

Paotou

Huhohaote

Hwang Ho

PEKING

Tangshan

TIENTSIN   DAIREN

Shihkiachwang

Tsinan

Tzupo

Tsingtao

Yellow Sea

Grand Canal

Suchow

Chengchow

Hofei

Nanking

SHANGHAI

Hangchow

Ningpo

East China Sea

WUHAN

Nanchang

Changsha

Tungting Lake

Foochow

Amoy

Swatow

CANTON

VICTORIA

HONG KONG

South China Sea

HAINAN

Holhow

Nanning

Si River

Kueiyang

CHUNGKING

RED BASIN

Chengtu

Minya Konka 24,900'

Amne Machin 23,490'

Koko Nor

Yangtze River

Mekong River

Salween River

Salween R.

BURMA

THAILAND

NORTH VIETNAM

Red River

L A O S

Mekong R.

Kunming

Yangtze River

Koko Nor

Red River

TAIWAN (FORMOSA)

Taipei

Formosa Str.

RYUKYU ISLANDS

Naha

TROPIC

S. KOREA

N. KOREA

Pyongyang

SEOUL

Inchon

Taegu

Pusan

Yalu River

Fukuoka

Kitakyushu

Nagasaki

KYUSHU

Kobe

Osaka

Kyoto

SHIKOKU

Sea of Japan

J A P A N

Sapporo

HOKKAIDO

Harbin

Tsitsihar

Kirin

Changchun

Fushun

FouShun

Mukden

Aigun

Amur River

Aigun River

40°

100°

80°

120°

100°

80°

20°

CHINA - POPULATION

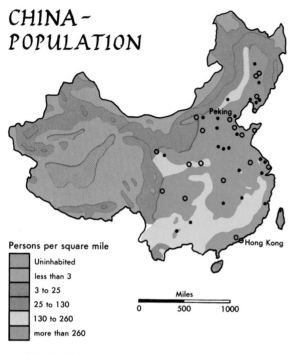

Persons per square mile

Uninhabited
less than 3
3 to 25
25 to 130
130 to 260
more than 260

• Cities from 500,000 to 1,000,000
○ Cities of more than 1,000,000

Miles
0   500   1000

It turned out that the "dragon bones" were really oracle bones, that is, bones on which questions were written so the gods could answer "Yes" or "No." All sorts of questions were asked: about sickness, dreams, hunting, the weather, or the harvest. These questions were inscribed on a polished bone or turtle shell, and then incisions were made carefully at various points. Red-hot sticks were pressed at these points, producing cracks. The shape, arrangement, and direction of these cracks were interpreted for the "Yes" or "No" answer, just as teacups and palms are "read" today for answers to similar questions about the future.

Fortunately these shells and bones were carefully buried. As a result many have survived to the present day. From many thousands of inscriptions we have learned a good deal about the way of life of these early Chinese. We have learned that they lived by hunting, fishing, and farming and that they had primitive handicrafts. Since the writing consists of pictorial characters, we know from the appearance of the characters for "fish" and "to fish" that the Shang people used pole and line, bait and net. Similarly we know from the varying forms of the character for "hunting" that arrows and double-headed spears were the instruments of the chase. Historians and archaeologists also have learned that these early Chinese people already had learned to make silk from the silkworm, had mastered the art of creating beautiful earthenware and bronze vessels, and also had developed an elaborate religious system in which ancestor worship played an important part. The details of Shang political organization are still obscure, but it is clear that it was an authoritarian and monarchical society. The Shang state was not large, although the culture called Shang extended over much of north China and even beyond, embracing the other political units of the time, about which little is yet known.

The Multi-state period. In 1027 B.C., a vigorous people from the western borders of the Shang moved eastward to establish political control over large areas, including the Shang domain and others. This marked the beginning of the Chou era, which lasted for almost eight centuries, until 256 B.C. It was the longest dynastic period in Chinese history, and in many ways the most significant.

The Chou conquerors divided their newly-won lands into many small units, and put at the head of each a lord who acknowledged himself a vassal of the Chou ruler. This arrangement was similar to that of Western feudalism, where regional political control was also in the hands of vassal lords. Consequently, the Chou is often called China's feudal period, although this usage is misleading because the word feudalism properly denotes a complex of other characteristics which did not exist in China. Moreover, after the eighth century B.C., even the vassal relation was more nominal than real.

The small vassal states created by the Chou gradually grew stronger and larger, casting off Chou control and engaging in war with their neighbors. As victors absorbed the defeated, the number of states decreased, the size of the states increased, and the once-vassal rulers became absolute monarchs. Moreover, the China culture area was expanding as peoples in the Yangtze valley gradually adopted the chief elements of Chinese civilization, and they also established new and powerful states. By the sixth century B.C., what is today north and central China was the site of nearly a dozen independent countries, a system of sovereign states much like present-day Europe. This process of struggle and absorption continued until 221 B.C., when the state of Ch'in conquered the last of the remaining states and thus created a single country: China.

The second half of the Chou era was a time not only of warfare and conquest, but of economic and social transformation. Technological advances, such as the discovery of iron metallurgy and the development of new irrigation and fertilizing techniques, increased agricultural productivity. This stimulated population growth. The communal land-holding system of the early Chou gradually gave way to a system of private ownership, with landowners paying fixed taxes to the state. Trade flourished, and copper coins came into use.

These changes, within states ever growing in size, required expanded governmental administrative organizations. The governments became increasingly bureaucratized. And as monarchs sought everywhere for bureaucratic and military talent that would give them an edge over their neighbors, earlier class barriers to social advancement fell by the wayside.

Caught in the turmoil of constant warfare and accelerating social change, late Chou thinkers struggled to understand and to explain what was happening. Even more important, they wanted to define the kind of sociopolitical order best designed to preserve and cultivate important human and cultural values. This effort produced several centuries of great intellectual creativity in China at almost the same time that the classical Greek philosophers created a golden age of thought in the West. This period in China is known as the Age of the Philosophers, or the Hundred Schools of Thought. In the long run Confucius (551 B.C.-479 B.C.) was the most influential philosopher of that time.*

Han unity and empire. The unification of China by the Ch'in involved far more than the mere conquest of all other states. Genuine unity was achieved by imposing a centralized bureaucratic government over the entire country, with impersonal laws that applied to all, and by standardizing coinage, weights and measures, and the written language. These measures were generally in accord with the chief trends of the late Chou, but their embodiment in formal institutions was of enormous significance for this created the basic outlines of the sociopolitical organization that was to dominate China for the next two thousand years.

The Ch'in Dynasty came to an end only a few years after the death of the first emperor of united China in 210 B.C. However, before his great work of unification and standardization could be undone, the Han Dynasty was established, and preserved the major Ch'in achievements for the next four centuries. Thus, while the Ch'in Dynasty can be said

* See *Readings in World History,* "The Thought of Confucius," p. 418.

to have unified China, it was the Han Dynasty that maintained the unity long enough so that it became the norm to which China ever afterwards aspired, no matter how fragmentized the country at times became.

The Han Dynasty also extended the boundaries of the nation northward into Korea, westward into Central Asia, and southward into what is now North Vietnam. However, in much of the southern and western regions under Han political authority, Chinese culture was only beginning to take root. For a thousand years after the Han, Chinese people, institutions, and values steadily moved into these areas to make them, finally, genuinely Chinese.

This great empire of the Han was fully equal to the Roman Empire in size, military power, and cultural achievement. However, they were so remote from each other that neither empire had substantial knowledge of the other. Despite this, Chinese silk shipped across Central Asia to the Mediterranean was in such demand among the Romans that it played a significant role in the Roman economy.

Besides perpetuating the basic organization of the Ch'in, the Han Dynasty made its own contributions to subsequent Chinese civilization. One of the most far-reaching was its acceptance of Confucianism as state-supported orthodoxy. This was achieved by honoring Confucius and the ideas attributed (often mistakenly) to the Confucian school, by giving imperial favor to Confucian scholars, and by establishing a Confucian university and channelling many of its graduates into state service. This early link between Confucianism and the bureaucracy was gradually elaborated into the celebrated civil service examination system, which reached its full development by about the 10th century.*

* See *Readings in World History,* "The Civil Service Examinations," p. 419.

TRADITIONAL CHINA

The Han Dynasty came to an end in the third century, when the Roman Empire was also nearing its fall. The Han was destroyed by internal conflict and corruption, by peasant rebellions, and by the desire of leading generals to seize power from the faltering Han rulers. However, there were profound differences in what followed the collapse of the two empires.

In the West, the fall of Rome led to several centuries of disorder out of which a radically different type of society emerged. A Roman coming into the Europe of 1000 or 1500 or 1900 would have been astonished by strange new German people in many parts of the old empire. He would have found the Latin language replaced by several new Germanic and Romance languages; the Roman togas replaced by blouses and trousers; the ancient Roman gods cast aside for the new Christianity; the Roman imperial structure replaced by many new nation states; and the old ways of earning a living rivalled by new agricultural techniques, commerce with hitherto unknown parts of the globe, and new crafts with strange machines that saved labor and ran without the traditional horse, water, or wind power.

In China, the disintegration of empire was also followed by a period of disorder and disunion; from the third to the sixth century, China was divided into many states, small and large. In addition, during these centuries barbarian invaders ruled portions of north China, and Buddhism, which had entered the country in the middle of the Han period, became widely accepted in both north and south. But despite the entry of these alien elements, when China was finally reunited in the late sixth century it differed far less from Han and pre-Han China than post-invasion Europe differed from the classical Roman order. Moreover, the history of China

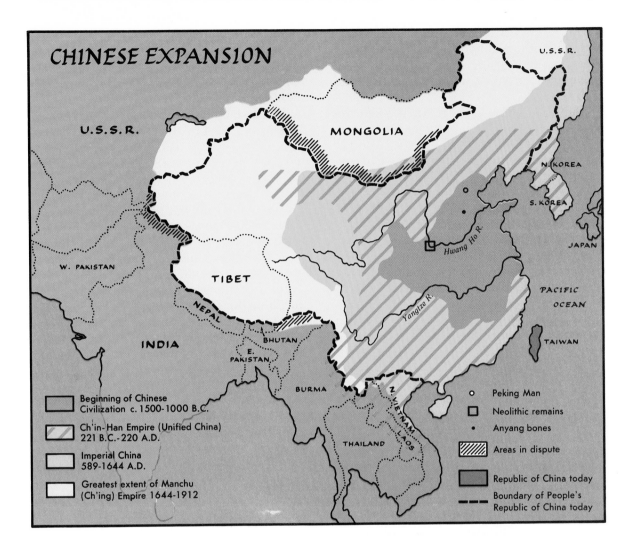

CHINESE EXPANSION

Beginning of Chinese
Civilization c. 1500-1000 B.C.

Ch'in-Han Empire (Unified China)
221 B.C.-220 A.D.

Imperial China
589-1644 A.D.

Greatest extent of Manchu
(Ch'ing) Empire 1644-1912

○ Peking Man

□ Neolithic remains

• Anyang bones

Areas in dispute

Republic of China today

--- Boundary of People's
Republic of China today

U.S.S.R.

MONGOLIA

U.S.S.R.

N. KOREA

S. KOREA

JAPAN

Hwang Ho R.

PACIFIC
OCEAN

W. PAKISTAN

TIBET

TAIWAN

NEPAL

BHUTAN

INDIA

E.
PAKISTAN

Yangtze R.

BURMA

V I E T N A M

L A O S

THAILAND

---

after the sixth century was more along the lines of the growth and maturing of earlier tendencies than of the development of new departures.

Division by dynasties. The Chinese have always written their history in dynastic slices, and this has led Westerners to think of Chinese history in the same way. Each dynasty is customarily described in terms of a few distinctive features which seem to have characterized it. For example, the Sui Dy-

nasty (589–618) is notable for having achieved the reunification of China, and also for having created a great system of canals in central China. The T'ang and Sung Dynasties, which ruled from 618 to 1279, represented the high point of Chinese civilization. During those centuries, China's cities were the greatest in the world,* poetry and the arts flourished, China was in advance of the West in many fields of science, the civil service

* See *Readings in World History,* "Urban Life in 13th Century China," p. 422.

system was perfected, and Confucianism was gradually modified by various Buddhist ideas to produce the final version of Confucian orthodoxy that was accepted until the 20th century.

During the Yuan Dynasty (1279–1368), the Mongols ruled China, but Mongol culture differed so much from that of the Chinese, and Mongol policies antagonized the Chinese to such a degree, that the entire century of Mongol rule was marked by hostility and resentment between the two peoples. Indeed, the conservatism and despotism that are thought characteristic of the following Ming Dynasty (1368–1644) are often explained as a reaction to the unhappy period of foreign rule. The Ming is also celebrated for having despatched seven great maritime expeditions between 1405 and 1433. The largest of the ships measured 444 feet long and 180 feet wide, and the average was 370 by 150 feet. Many such vessels—the first expedition consisted of at least 62 ships with 28,000 men—sailed around Southeast Asia, across the Indian Ocean to India, and on to the Persian Gulf and to East Africa. These were remarkable maritime achievements, but, curiously, we do not know precisely why they were sent or why they were suddenly terminated.

The last dynasty was the Ch'ing, which ruled from 1644 to 1912. It was another non-Chinese dynasty, consisting of Manchus who swept down from their northern homeland. The Manchus adopted Chinese ways much more completely than the Mongols, and Manchu rule was thus much longer and more stable. In fact, the Manchus justified their authority by ruling in accord with Chinese tradition, and this may have made it more difficult for them to respond to the new type of challenge which the West presented to China during this dynasty.

At the beginning of their reign, the Manchus were able to regulate Western activities in China. By the middle of the 19th century, however, Western technology had become much superior to that of China; the rifles, cannon, and steamships of the "long-nosed barbarians" were infinitely superior to the

The Dragon Robe was worn only by the imperial emperor and his princes.

spears and junks of the Chinese.* Consequently, when friction over the conditions of trade and intercourse led to war, China was defeated time after time. These defeats, coupled with domestic rebellion, brought the Ch'ing Dynasty to an end in the early 20th century.

The dynastic cycle. When the history of traditional China is viewed in terms of this sequence of dynasties, a cyclical pattern emerges. Each dynasty was founded amidst social disorder, political fragmentization, and civil war, when one leader or group succeeded in unifying and pacifying the country. Under the leadership of the new dynasty, the country flourished, often expanded its borders, and extended its influence far abroad. However, after some time, in most cases a century or two, the country's foreign influence began to decline and the domestic unity and well-being began to disintegrate. Finally, the dynasty came to an end amidst social disorder, rebellion, and war, out of which, sooner or later, another group established a new dynasty to start the process all over again.

Confucianism had a convenient explanation for this process. A dynasty could rule as long as it held the "Mandate of Heaven," but when the Mandate was withdrawn, the dynasty came to an end. In the Confucian scheme of things, the ruler's behavior determined the relations between the natural and the supernatural, between the things of this world and the forces of the other world, of Heaven. As long as the emperor ruled in a moral fashion, Heaven approved, and manifested that approval by good harvests, absence of floods, and similarly happy conditions. Under such conditions, the people were well off and content. If, however, the ruler were immoral, Heaven would disap-

prove, would withdraw the Mandate, and there would be various ominous signs of Heaven's displeasure: drought, plague, erratic comets, and the like. Under these conditions, the people would be distressed and miserable. The well-being of the people thus became the chief standard for judging the morality of the ruler, and when a dynasty declined and finally collapsed it was attributed to the ruler's evil character.

While it is important to understand the Confucian view of the dynastic cycle, the explanation for dynastic change must finally come in political and economic terms. The general level of official competence and morality was likely to be high at the beginning of a dynasty, not only because the founders sought to demonstrate that they had acquired the Mandate of Heaven, but also because only competent men, with effective organizations, could win out over their rivals to found a new dynasty.

Once the new dynasty was consolidated, however, things began to change. The financial drain of defending expanded borders required frugality at home, and the development of new sources of funds. Yet successive monarchs tended to become increasingly extravagant as the court became accustomed to the luxuries that went with power. Officials gradually became corrupted by the power they wielded and the opportunities it provided to amass wealth. To support their extravagance and corruption, the officials and the wealthy class generally exploited the peasant ever more mercilessly, driving more and more peasants to banditry and revolt.* To put down these revolts, the court gave great power to a few generals, and this effectively reduced the authority of the monarch. Finally, the dynasty collapsed amidst the struggles of generals and peasant revolutionaries.

* See *Readings in World History*, "China Is Defeated by the West," p. 485.

* See *Readings in World History*, "Peasant Poverty," p. 424.

Perhaps the most striking feature of this cyclical process is that each dynasty so closely resembled its predecessor. Despite the revolutions, wars, and political disorder out of which new dynasties arose, there was a remarkable continuity in the basic elements of Chinese culture. What were those elements, and what accounts for the apparent lack of innovation in China's social and political order?

Cords to the past. Confucian ideology justified the power structure in traditional China.* Prestige and power came with position in the official bureaucracy, which was obtained by passing through an examination system that tested the applicant's knowledge of the Con-

* See *Readings in World History*, "Confucian Indoctrination of the Masses," p. 425.

While passing the Confucian examinations might in fact testify to little more than a good memory, in theory it proved a man's right to public authority.

CULVER PICTURES

fucian classics.* Confucianism taught men to look to the past; it said that authority should be in the hands of moral men, that the men of antiquity exemplified morality, and that the classics contained the thoughts of the men of antiquity. This implied that knowledge of the past was tantamount to cultivation of morality, and therefore the proper prerequisite to government position.

Confucianism also held that all men could be educated, that cultivated men were made, not born. In accord with this, the examination system was open to all groups, with only minor exceptions. Consequently no important group in Chinese society felt that it was deprived by the system of an opportunity to get ahead. In fact, the way to improve one's station was not to change the system but to become one of the manipulators of the system, an official.

Other elements of traditional society also encouraged the Chinese to look to the past. Reverence for the ancient wise men or sages led to a general exaltation of the past as a golden age; China did not seek to progress to a new and better future, but to return to an old and better past. Even in relations between individuals, age always took precedence over youth. In the family, which was the basic unit of the whole social system, this took the form of control by the oldest male over a family hierarchy ranked according to age and sex. On a small scale, the family was thus an authoritarian system similar to the monarchy on a national level.

Traditional China was primarily an agrarian society. The overwhelming majority of Chinese made their living directly from the soil, and most of the remaining were supported indirectly by agriculture. China's entire value system stressed agriculture; in Confucian terms, agriculture was the "root," while commerce and other activities were

* See *Readings in World History*, "The Civil Service Examinations," p. 419.

"branches." Confucian orthodoxy considered commerce socially disruptive, and merchants little better than social parasites.* Everyone wished to own land, not only because the Confucian value system stressed agriculture, but because it was the most secure form of wealth. Merchants, who were of low social status, invested their commercial profits in land. By becoming landowners they rose in status, and could hope to educate their children or grandchildren to take the examinations, and ultimately bring the family into the elite class of officials. Thus even the merchants aspired to rise in the system rather than change it.

China's relations with other peoples also provided almost no stimulus to change. The Chinese considered their civilization to be the only civilization, and those not a part of it were considered uncultured barbarians. This was not a feeling of racial superiority, but cultural superiority, and was nourished by the fact that the peoples with whom the Chinese had close and sustained contact were indeed less culturally developed. China's foreign relations were therefore not conducted on the basis of equality, but within the framework of the tribute system; other nations periodically sent missions bearing tribute, samples of local products, to express their political inferiority and their subordination to the Chinese emperor. This system tended to preserve China's faith in the superiority of her traditional system, as did the eagerness of adjacent people to learn about and adopt Chinese ways. On several occasions, conquerors from the north and west were assimilated into Chinese culture, which accounts for the idea that China has always "absorbed" her conquerors.

Finally, China's isolation from other major civilizations was of crucial importance. Confucian ideology indicated that dynasties fell

* See *Readings in World History,* "Economic Values in Traditional China," p. 450.

The kowtow, a form of respect, is performed by kneeling and touching the forehead to the ground.

because of abuse by officials, thus seeming to argue not for a new system but for new officials. Therefore, since there were no compulsions for innovation within the system, alternative forms of social and political organization could only be presented from without. But since China's contact with other major cultures was severely limited, no such alternatives ever appeared.

Over the course of many centuries, these elements of traditional Chinese society worked together into a smoothly operating, stable system. Each institution, value, and custom was inextricably linked with a whole complex of others by which it was supported and which, in turn, it bolstered. Inevitably, innovation was an enemy. Change in any one area threatened repercussions throughout the closely interrelated system. More important, it threatened those who profited most from the system. Consequently, China changed only very slowly. This was true throughout the period of traditional China until the 19th century, when the West challenged China in such a way that change became the only alternative to extinction.

Reviewing the Essentials

Geography

1. On a map of Asia, locate the protective barriers that isolate China from the rest of Asia and the world, i.e., mountains, deserts, oceans. How have these affected the development of China?

2. Compare China with the United States and the Soviet Union in respect to area, climate, and natural resources.

3. What are important geographical differences between north and south China? How have they influenced the way in which the Chinese make a living?

4. Locate the major river systems of China. How have they both promoted and retarded China's development?

5. How has China's coastline affected her development?

6. What do you conclude about the relationship of geography to the development of China?

Peoples

7. Give current figures for: (a) China's population; (b) annual increase; (c) percentage of population, rural and urban.

8. Name and locate on the map the autonomous regions of China. What percentage of the population is non-Chinese?

9. In spite of non-Chinese minorities, why does China have more racial unity than the United States or the Soviet Union?

Languages

10. How has language contributed to Chinese cultural unity?

11. What progress has been made in simplifying the written language?

12. What arguments can be made for changing China's writing system to employ an alphabet instead of characters? What good arguments can be made to oppose such a change?

Religions

13. Name the major religions of China.

14. What were the religious practices and beliefs of China's common people?

15. What are the essential elements of a religion? How does religion differ from philosophy?

Historical Periods

16. What characteristics of Chinese history are in marked contrast to those of other regional areas of the world?

17. Why was the discovery of the "dragon bones" so important to our understanding of the ancient period in Chinese history?

18. Account for the fact that although China could have competed with Europe in the 15th century for trade and colonies, it withdrew from trade with the West. What were to be the consequences of this policy?

19. What is the explanation for the rise and fall of Chinese dynasties? What elements seem to be common to all the dynasties?

20. How did the Confucian explanation of the dynastic cycle protect from blame the very group most responsible for dynastic collapse?

21. What is a "stable society"? Was traditional China a stable society?

22. "Continuity is a characteristic of Chinese history." Support this statement with evidence from your study of this section.

Explain, Identify, or Locate

1500 B.C.	1027 B.C.	Manchus	Hong Kong
bureaucracy	221 B.C.	Mongols	Canton
feudalism	Confucianism	Koreans	Yangtze River
empire	Buddhism	Great Wall	Pearl River
dynasty	Taoism	Manchuria	Amur River
imperial government	Shang Dynasty	Peking	Indochina
dragon bones	Tibetans	Shanghai	
ancestor worship	1644 A.D.	1912 A.D.	

无产阶级文化大革命万岁！

POLITICS: The Rebirth of China

PRESENT STATE

China today. It is quite possible that from the point of view of world history the most significant event since World War II is the triumph of communism on the mainland of China. All of Asia was affected by the Second World War that ended in 1945: India was reborn, and Pakistan came into being; the map of Southeast Asia was redrawn; Japan was occupied by American troops. In short, old-style imperialism of both the Western and

Japanese variety came to an end. But more far-reaching than any of these changes was the birth of Communist China. Within a few years China was transformed from a weak and divided nation to a strong united state.

It is true that China, unlike India, was not a newly independent nation, and that after 1945 both countries turned corners in their long histories. However an important difference must be kept in mind. As the Indian sub-continent was freed from colonialism, it split into two nations. But as China shook off the heavy influence of foreign powers, it achieved a stronger unity than it had ever known before. This statement holds true despite the existence of a separate Chinese government on Taiwan (Formosa).

Like India, China was profoundly affected by contact with the West. She was impressed by such things as the efficiency of railroads, the advantages of machine manufacturing, the superiority of steam power and electricity, and the usefulness of automobiles. Both China and India were determined to launch economic revolutions which would bring them the benefits of a developed economy in the shortest possible time. But because of the profound differences between the two civilizations, because of the different ways in which they were exposed to Western technology and ideas, and because of the accidents of history, China and India reacted differently to the West. As a result, China has taken the road of communism to the destination of a modern industrialized state while India has taken the road of capitalism.

Communist regime. On October 1, 1949, Mao Tse-tung, leader of the Chinese Communists, proclaimed a new government which was named the People's Republic of China. At the same time, the city of Peiping, which means "northern peace," was renamed Peking, or "northern capital," and was declared the capital of the new regime. Not until the spring of 1950 did the Communists complete their military victory. Yet already before that date they had begun to establish more effective control over the Chinese population and resources than any government in the history of the country, and to channel the energies of the people toward the development of a new society. The leaders have achieved this by using various organizations, one of the most important of which is the formal apparatus of government.*

Government. In 1954, the Communists instituted a new constitution. According to this constitution, the organs of government authority at every level are called people's congresses. A people's congress is simply a group of people who have the authority to govern a certain administrative unit, from the smallest village, township, or commune to the entire nation. The members of the lowest level people's congresses are directly elected by the people. These people's congresses then elect the members of the next highest level people's congress, who, in turn, elect the next highest, and on up to the highest organ of state power, the National People's Congress. Candidates for the people's congresses are nominated by the Communist Party, by any of the eight minority parties which are permitted to operate, and by various other organizations.

There are four very important features in this hierarchy of people's congresses. The first has already been mentioned: the use of indirect elections; only at the lowest level are delegates elected directly by the people. Second, the people's congresses normally meet for only a short time during the year, then delegate some of their number to conduct the business of the congress. These smaller groups are called standing committees, or people's councils, and in practice wield the authority that is vested in the congresses. Third, the entire system works in accord with the principle of *democratic centralism*, which is used in virtually all Communist parties and governments. Dem-

* It is important to note that the Cultural Revolution, which started in 1965, is still going on as this is being written. China is in turmoil, the situation is constantly shifting, and the outcome is not yet certain. The following discussion of party and government, therefore, relates primarily to the period before 1965. The Cultural Revolution will be discussed at the end of this section.

ocratic centralism means that policy may be debated thoroughly at all levels, and recommendations submitted from lower to higher levels, until a decision has been made. However, once the matter has been decided at the top, lower levels must accept it and carry it out. The decisions of any people's congress may be modified or vetoed by the people's congress at any higher level. The fourth important characteristic of the people's congress system concerns the role of the Communists. Members of the Communist Party are leaders at every level; thus, while at lower levels Communists may not constitute a majority of the congress, they will probably be a majority of the standing committee, and thus dominate the work of the congress. In addition, the higher the administrative organ, the larger the percentage of Communists.

The National People's Congress is at the apex of this system. It is the highest organ of state power, and the only body which exercises legislative power. It elects several important state officials, including the Chairman of the People's Republic, who is the official head of state. Mao Tse-tung held that position until 1959, when he was succeeded by Liu Shao-chi. The National People's Congress meets once a year, but like congresses at all other levels, it elects a standing committee that exercises general supervision over the government.

The executive arm of the National People's Congress is called the State Council. This is the highest administrative organ of the central government; it carries on the daily business of government, and very much resembles a cabinet in many Western governments. It is headed by a premier, a position

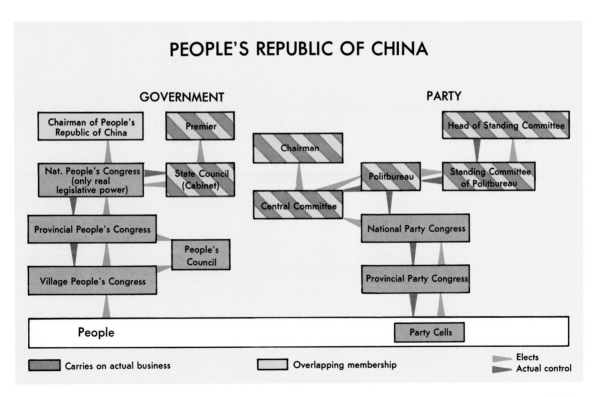

Premier Chou En-lai

tories, mines, and other enterprises, offices, schools, army units, and so forth. These elect delegates to higher Party units, which in turn elect higher levels, and so on up to the National Party Congress. All relations between Party congresses at the various levels are in accord with democratic centralism.

Near the top of the hierarchy is the National Party Congress, which the Communist Party constitution describes as "the highest leading body of the Party." The National Party Congress is supposed to meet briefly each year, at which time it elects a Central Committee which functions throughout the year. For some time, the Central Committee had consisted of about 90 full members, but in the spring of 1969 the number was raised to 170. The Central Committee constitutes the most important group in the National Party Congress. But the Central Committee, in turn, elects its chairman, several vice-chairmen, and, most important, a Political Bureau or Politbureau. It also elects the Standing Committee of the Politbureau. In the past six or seven years, the number in the Politbureau has varied between about 17 and 21, seven or eight of whom constituted the Standing Committee of the Politbureau. In 1969 this number was reduced to five. The Politbureau determines major government policy. Its members are the men who rule China. Mao Tse-tung has long been Chairman of the Central Committee, as well as head of the Standing Committee of the Politbureau. In other words, Mao stands at the very peak of the Communist Party pyramid.

How does the Communist Party keep control of the entire country in Communist hands? The simplest answer is that Party members are leaders in every other important organization and activity. We have already seen that Communists hold leading positions in the government apparatus. Of

long held by Chou En-lai, and includes a number of deputy premiers and other ministers.

The Party. The government, and all other organizations in China, exist to carry out the plans and programs of the central organization, the Chinese Communist Party. Although there are nine political parties, the eight "democratic parties" can recruit only from specified sectors of the population, and are limited in other ways. The Communist Party is the sole and unquestioned source of power.

The Chinese party is the largest Communist Party in the world. The last official figures were released in 1961, indicating a membership of 17 million. This probably increased at least to 18 million by the eve of the Cultural Revolution. The Party is organized in a hierarchy similar to that of the government. The basic, or primary units of the Party, called cells, are organized in fac-

Waving Quotations from Chairman Mao,
*Chinese students and teachers in Peking
surround Mao Tse-tung.*

course, they hold similar positions in the army and in the police organization, so that all agencies of organized coercion are in Party hands. Moreover, there are many nationwide mass organizations by means of which the Party can mobilize the support of the people. Through such organizations as the All-China Federation of Trade Unions, the All-China Federation of Democratic Women, the All-China Students' Federation, and many others, virtually everyone in the remotest village or the largest city has become involved in the tasks set by the Party.

The leaders in all these organizations are normally Communists. Thus the policies that are promoted and followed in the government and all other organizations are policies determined by the Party. And since Mao and a few men are at the head of the Party, and everything works according to the principles of democratic centralism, Mao and his associates can be said to rule China, and their decisions can rapidly be made effective throughout the nation.

The Communist Party's control of all propaganda media supplements and confirms these organizational aspects of control. Newspapers and many other publications, radio and television, lectures and study centers, are all used by the Party to argue for the correctness of Party policies and the foolishness of opposing them.

WESTERNERS IN CHINA

Napoleon once likened China to a slumbering lion which, he said, "will astound the world when it awakens." Today the lion is awake and roaring. China is a nation on the march. China, like the rest of Asia, is reacting to the tidal wave from the West. China's ancient civilization was undermined and overwhelmed during the course of the 19th century. Western goods and Western ideas penetrated to all parts of the country and set in motion a series of revolutions. Industrialism, nationalism, and communism became the driving forces which reunited China and made her once more a strong power.

Early Sino-Western relations. When the Westerners reached Asia by sea in the 16th century, and for the first time established close and sustained intercourse between the West and China, the Chinese looked upon them as simply another type of barbarian, in this case "long nosed barbarians." * Chinese attitudes of cultural superiority may have been strengthened by the fact that many Westerners seemed to share them. Europeans were enchanted with the richness, variety, wealth, and sophistication of China.

* See *Readings in World History*, "China's View of Westerners," p. 461.

EASTFOTO

During the 17th and 18th centuries, Westerners not only eagerly sought Chinese products, and diligently tried to copy Chinese manufactures, but Western philosophers extolled the wisdom of Chinese thinkers and the advantages of Chinese political organization.*

The imperial court sought to tax the barbarian traders and control their trade. To that end, from the middle of the 18th century, all foreign trade was limited to the single port of Canton, and only about a dozen Chinese merchants were authorized to deal with foreigners. Chinese rules forbade the traders from communicating directly with Chinese officials. All messages had to go through the Chinese merchants, even those complaining about the merchants themselves. Moreover, various rules governed the lives of the foreign traders in China: they could come and go only at specified times, they had to pay various fees, their recreation was strictly regulated, and there were numerous other restrictions. In addition, Westerners were subject to Chinese law, and several were executed for offenses that would have been treated much more leniently in the West.

By the early 19th century, Westerners angrily resented these restrictions. Europe had undergone the beginnings of the industrial revolution, and Westerners with 19th century technological knowledge saw little to admire in "backward" China.† Many became unsympathetic to the achievements of Chinese civilization. Yet Chinese assumptions of superiority still flourished, and the Chinese consequently made little effort to master the achievements of Western science. Even daily communication was difficult for neither the Westerners nor the Chinese made an effort to learn the other's language; the chief means of communication was "pidgin English," a strange hybrid that sounded a bit like exotic baby talk.*

Despite these irritations, the British East India Company, as well as American and other traders, developed a flourishing and extremely profitable trade, especially in tea and silk, but including other Chinese goods.† However, the Westerners had little that the Chinese wanted in exchange for their goods, and through the 18th century they had to supplement their cargoes of woolens and other items with substantial amounts of gold and silver. Then in the late 18th century, opium was added to the cargo. Although the Chinese government prohibited the import of opium, the Westerners brought it into the country in ever larger quantities. The British grew opium in India for this purpose. In the early 19th century, the Westerners sold so much opium in China that the balance of trade shifted. The sale of opium provided enough money to buy a cargo of tea and silk, and have silver left over to ship to London. Chinese officials became concerned over the harmful effects of opium on the Chinese people, and the drain of silver from the Chinese economy, and they determined to stop the trade.

In 1839, an official sent by the Chinese court to stop the opium trade seized foreign opium stocks. This triggered a chain of events which resulted in war with England later in that year. To the Chinese, this was a war over opium. To the British, it was a war not only over opium, but over the unsatisfactory conditions of trade and diplomacy in China. The war ended with British victory in 1842.‡

---

* See *Readings in World History,* "China's Impact on Europe," p. 429.
† See *Readings in World History,* "Westerners' View of China," p. 430.

* See *Readings in World History,* "Pidgin English," p. 431.
† See *Readings in World History,* "England's Tea Trade with China," p. 432.
‡ See *Readings in World History,* "China is Defeated by the West," p. 485.

Unequal treaties. China and England spelled out the peace terms in the Treaty of Nanking in 1842. Immediately afterwards, a number of other Western nations, including the United States, concluded similar treaties with China. These treaties are called the First Treaty Settlement. They contained a number of provisions which proved to be extremely disadvantageous to China, but China agreed to them partly because of her military inferiority and partly because she did not fully understand the implications of acceding to Western demands for commercial and other privileges.

China fought another war from 1856 to 1858, with a last flareup in 1860, and at that time the Second Treaty Settlement was drawn up. This expanded and clarified the privileges won in the 1840's, and through the rest of the century the Westerners wrung concession after concession from the Chinese to expand steadily the scope of the treaties. It was within the framework of the treaty system that Western imperialism exploited China, and that Western culture made its way into China. To the Chinese, these have long been known as the "unequal treaties," and their abolition was a major goal of 20th century Chinese nationalists. The last of the unequal treaties was eliminated only in 1943.

What were the treaties' most important provisions? First, they opened an increasing number of Chinese ports to foreigners. With the various treaties, the number of open ports were expanded to more than 80 by the end of the century. At these ports, Westerners paid a fixed tariff on goods brought into the country, and the treaties said that China could not raise the tariff without Western permission. By including opium on the tariff list, the opium trade was effectively legalized.

The "most-favored nation" clause was an extremely far-reaching privilege exacted by the West. Each nation included this clause in its treaties with China. It said, in effect, that the country concluding the treaty with China could claim all the rights and privileges that China had granted to any other nation, or would in the future grant to any other nation. In other words, each nation claimed the same privileges as those given to the most favored nation. Thus each time a nation extorted a concession from China, the same or an equivalent concession had to be given to all the other powers.

Another far-reaching privilege was that of extraterritoriality, more commonly called *extrality*. This meant, in essence, that Westerners in China were not subject to Chinese law. Each Westerner was subject to the laws of his own nation, as administered by his own consul.

Perhaps the most important of all privileges was the right of Christian missionaries to travel and own property throughout the country and to seek converts freely. The missionaries established many hospitals, schools, and other social welfare agencies, and doubtless took satisfaction in their contributions to China. Yet their activities offended Chinese sensibilities in numerous ways and at every level of society, and were a constant source of trouble for the Chinese.*

The treaty system naturally demanded that the Chinese cease treating Western diplomats as inferiors, and provided for equality of treatment between officials of equal rank. But as Western power began to give substance to the treaty system, this equality became increasingly formal. For practical purposes, the Westerners held the upper hand, and the Chinese increasingly were forced to acknowledge it.

China was also forced to give up territory. The English seized Hong Kong. Russia moved into some Chinese areas of Central

---

* See *Readings in World History,* "Christian Missionaries in China," p. 434.

Asia, and also took the region on the north bank of the Amur River and the area on the eastern seacoast today known as the Maritime Provinces of the Soviet Union. The Japanese annexed Taiwan and the Pescadores Islands. Korea and Vietnam, which had for centuries been close vassals of China, were seized by Japan and France respectively.

Until the middle of the 19th century, trade was the primary interest of the Western nations in China. Toward the end of the century, however, financial investment through loans and through the building and operation of mines, railways, industries, and other enterprises increasingly became goals of the imperialist nations. By the end of the century, it was widely believed that China would shortly be partitioned among

the powers. In anticipation of that event, and to facilitate exploitation in the meantime, each imperialist power asserted first claim to a particular portion of China where its economic and political interests were very strong. These were called spheres of influence. Russia, for example, gained the right to build and operate a railroad across Manchuria to Vladivostok, and also secured a lease on Port Arthur strategically located on the Yellow Sea. Germany seized Tsingtao and gained mining and railway rights in the province of Shantung. Britain dominated central China, and British gunboats patrolled the Yangtze as though it were the English Channel. In fact the British Navy at this time actually had an officer with the revealing title of Rear Admiral of the Yangtze. Finally, France dominated southern

A Chinese artist's conception of the port of Canton: the flags represent those nations granted permission by the emperor to trade with China.

TIME CHART FOR CHINA

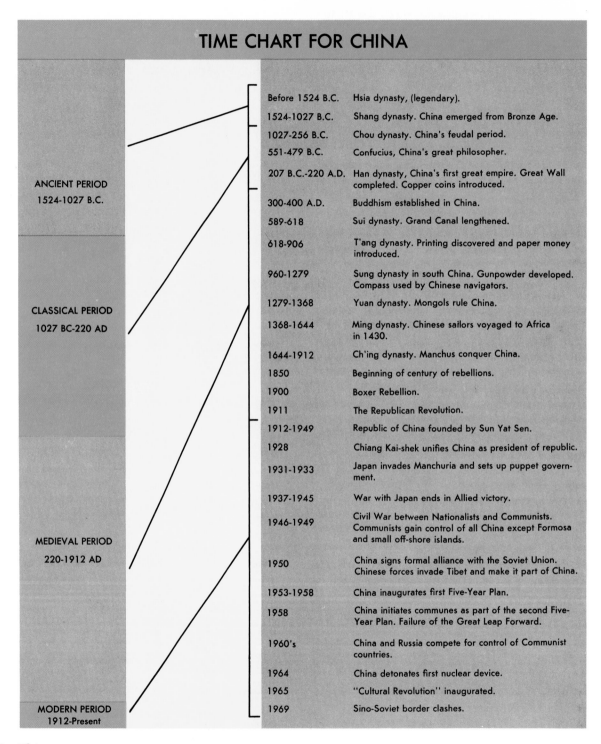

	Before 1524 B.C.	Hsia dynasty, (legendary).
	1524-1027 B.C.	Shang dynasty. China emerged from Bronze Age.
	1027-256 B.C.	Chou dynasty. China's feudal period.
	551-479 B.C.	Confucius, China's great philosopher.
ANCIENT PERIOD 1524-1027 B.C.	207 B.C.-220 A.D.	Han dynasty, China's first great empire. Great Wall completed. Copper coins introduced.
	300-400 A.D.	Buddhism established in China.
	589-618	Sui dynasty. Grand Canal lengthened.
	618-906	T'ang dynasty. Printing discovered and paper money introduced.
CLASSICAL PERIOD 1027 BC-220 AD	960-1279	Sung dynasty in south China. Gunpowder developed. Compass used by Chinese navigators.
	1279-1368	Yuan dynasty. Mongols rule China.
	1368-1644	Ming dynasty. Chinese sailors voyaged to Africa in 1430.
	1644-1912	Ch'ing dynasty. Manchus conquer China.
	1850	Beginning of century of rebellions.
	1900	Boxer Rebellion.
	1911	The Republican Revolution.
	1912-1949	Republic of China founded by Sun Yat Sen.
	1928	Chiang Kai-shek unifies China as president of republic.
	1931-1933	Japan invades Manchuria and sets up puppet government.
	1937-1945	War with Japan ends in Allied victory.
MEDIEVAL PERIOD 220-1912 AD	1946-1949	Civil War between Nationalists and Communists. Communists gain control of all China except Formosa and small off-shore islands.
	1950	China signs formal alliance with the Soviet Union. Chinese forces invade Tibet and make it part of China.
	1953-1958	China inaugurates first Five-Year Plan.
	1958	China initiates communes as part of the second Five-Year Plan. Failure of the Great Leap Forward.
	1960's	China and Russia compete for control of Communist countries.
	1964	China detonates first nuclear device.
	1965	"Cultural Revolution" inaugurated.
MODERN PERIOD 1912-Present	1969	Sino-Soviet border clashes.

China as much as Britain did central China and Russia northern China.

The Open Door Policy. Meanwhile, the United States enjoyed what has been described as "hitchhiking imperialism." That is, without seizing Chinese territory, it gained many of the concessions China was forced to make to the other foreign powers. Through a diplomatic plan known as the Open Door Policy, the United States tried to keep the bitter rivalry of the competing imperialist powers under control. The policy also served American interests. It called for the treaty powers to refrain from staking out exclusive trading rights in certain parts of China or, in other words, to leave the door open to all for trade. It also asked other nations to respect the sovereignty of China.

Many nations gave lip service to the Open Door Policy. Perhaps this policy even slowed the process of cutting China into many different colonial areas. More likely, however, it was the bitter rivalry among the European powers that saved China from complete partition.

Age of rebellion. The Manchu Dynasty was caught in a hopeless situation. Not only was it unable to protect the country against foreign aggression, but it was losing control over the internal situation. By the 19th century, the normal workings of the dynastic cycle were intensified by a phenomenal increase in population since the beginning of the dynasty. This created a large number of landless people, extremely poor and without hope. By the early decades of the century, agrarian revolts were breaking out in all parts of the country. By mid-century, these scattered uprisings merged into the enormous wave of the Taiping Rebellion.

Taiping Rebellion. The ideology and socioeconomic program of the Taipings dif-fered from all earlier peasant revolts in China. Taiping ideology was a mixture of Confucianism and Christianity, but each was so distorted that the combination was acceptable neither to Western Christians or Confucian scholars. The leader of the movement, who had been briefly exposed to Christian teachings, claimed that divine visions had revealed him to be the younger brother of Jesus Christ, and that he was to save the world from evil. The Taipings destroyed Buddhist, Taoist, and Confucian temples, monasteries, and idols wherever they went. Despite the influence that Confucianism clearly had on their own movement, they condemned Confucian philosophy and put thousands of scrolls and books to the flames.

Although Taiping followers accepted the Christian religion, at least nominally, many adherents were far more interested in the social and economic reforms declared by the leaders. These included equal distribution of land, communal ownership of other wealth, equality between the sexes, and prohibition of foot-binding, prostitution, tobacco and opium-smoking, and wine-drinking. Unfortunately, the leaders did not have the ability to implement such far-reaching innovations. Many leaders were concerned primarily with personal gain, and they fell to fighting among themselves. As a result, the vigor and spirit of the Taipings declined, and though they held vast territories for several years, the government forces finally destroyed the rebels. Foreign troops gave some aid to the Manchus in hope of preserving the gains of the first and second treaty settlements.

The alien Manchus would not have been able to suppress the Taiping rebellion without the help of the Chinese scholar-official class. The scholars and officials worked for the government because the Manchus completely supported the Confucian social order which the scholar class wanted to preserve and which the Taipings sought to destroy. When the Manchu armies proved too corrupt and weak to put down the rebellion, Chinese officials organized regional armies, loyal to themselves, with which they suppressed the Taiping movement. This was a mixed blessing for the Manchu court; the rebellion was put down, but the new regional armies were more powerful than the armies of the central government. From this time until the end of the dynasty, behind the facade of Ch'ing centralization lay the reality of regional armies and regional political power.

Continued imperialist encroachments upon China during the last three decades of the 19th century prodded some regional officials to recognize that only by modernizing, at least in a limited way, could China avoid more defeats and losses. Some measures were taken along these lines, but they were inadequate for two reasons. First, they did not have the full support of the central government, and were strongly opposed by many powerful conservatives. Second, the only measures that might have strengthened China to the point where she could have resisted imperialism were so drastic as to destroy Confucianism, yet the preservation of Confucianism was the chief goal of the reformers. This contradiction was not resolved until well into the 20th century, when the threat to the existence of the Chinese nation replaced the threat to Confucianism as the chief concern of politically conscious Chinese.

Boxer Rebellion. Conservative court officials not only opposed reform, but finally, in 1900, tried to resist the West by force. In the last years of the century, famine in north China created pockets of banditry and disorder, the beginnings of rebellion. An old Chinese secret society, the Boxers, emerged to give the movement leadership and a combined anti-foreign and anti-dynastic bias. Conservative officials, however, persuaded the Boxers to bolster the dynasty and focus all their antagonism on the foreigners. Finally, the imperial court itself gave support to the Boxers, in effect leading them in a war against the West.

The Boxers especially hated missionaries and Chinese converts to Christianity, and killed many in north China. When foreigners and converts fled for safety to Peking, the Boxers besieged them in the legation quarters for two months. Finally, an international force was able to reach the capital and rescue them, ending the Boxer rebellion and enabling the Westerners to impose another harsh treaty on China.

The fiasco of the Boxer Rebellion finally convinced court conservatives that some reforms were essential, and for the first time the central government took the lead in promoting innovation. But the Manchu reforms were much too limited and too late.

Company of "Boxers" after defeat, 1900

Ironically, one of the most successful measures worked against Manchu rule. The Manchus sent thousands of students abroad to get a modern education. Many of these young people became convinced from their foreign experiences that the Manchu government was hopelessly obsolete, and that China's only hope was revolution and the creation of a Western-style government.

Republican Revolution. By the first years of the 20th century, revolutionary groups had come into existence in China and overseas, particularly in Japan, dedicated to the forcible overthrow of the Manchu monarchy. In 1905, several of these groups came together to form a new revolutionary organization under the leadership of Sun Yat-sen. In the following six years, this organization attempted several revolts, but failed in every case until October 10, 1911, when success came almost by accident. On that day, a small group of revolutionary soldiers loosely associated with Sun's organization, fearing that the police had discovered their identity, suddenly revolted in Wuchang, a large city in central China. Instead of moving promptly to suppress the revolt, the Manchu authorities in the city fled, and the revolutionaries were able to take control of Wuchang. This marked the beginning of the Revolution of 1911, the Republican Revolution.

The success of the Wuchang rebels sparked discontented elements throughout the country to seize local power. By mid-December, virtually all of the provinces in south and central China had declared their independence of the Manchu government. These declarations were made by local groups made up of revolutionaries, members of provincial assemblies that had come into being as part of the late Manchu reforms, and, perhaps most important, army officers in charge of provincial troop units. Faced by this widespread disaffection, the Manchu

Yuan Shih-k'ai

court gave all power to General Yuan Shih-k'ai, commander of the government's most powerful and modernized army. Yuan, however, made a deal with the revolutionaries whereby he was made first president of the Chinese republic in return for his forcing the Manchu Emperor to abdicate. The abdication occurred in February, 1912, bringing the Manchu Dynasty to an end and clearing the way for the Chinese republic which the revolutionaries had already proclaimed.

Unfortunately, the new state was a republic with very few republicans. The revolutionaries in Sun Yat-sen's party had only a superficial understanding of the needs and functioning of parliamentary government. Even more important, Sun's followers had very little power after 1912. Genuine power was in the hands of the local and regional military leaders, and while Yuan Shih-k'ai's personal army was strong enough to keep these local militarists fairly well under control, he was unable to eliminate them. Thus when Yuan died in 1916,

Politics 415

his army broke up, all semblance of unity ended, and China fell to the warlords.

The Warlords. Provincial and local military leaders were called warlords. Each warlord controlled an armed following and a certain amount of territory, from a few villages to several provinces, from which he drew revenue. Although a few of the most powerful warlords had national political aspirations, most of the warlords were concerned only with adding to their personal wealth and power. In attempting to do this they naturally came into conflict with one another, and local and regional warfare became commonplace. The Chinese people suffered incredible hardships through these continual wars and through the ravages of the warlords and their troops. Moreover, the disunity of the warlord period made China more vulnerable than ever to foreign imperialists who virtually controlled China's state finances, and interfered in various ways in Chinese affairs.*

Imperialism and Chinese youth. It was Chinese youth who reacted most vigorously to the extension of imperialist privileges in their country. High school and university students concluded that China's national weakness showed China's tradition and national culture to be obsolete and irrelevant to the modern world. They therefore condemned and rejected Confucianism, the family system, traditionalism, reverence for the aged, and all the other major elements of traditional Chinese culture. This was called the "New Culture Movement," because they sought to replace these Chinese attitudes and institutions by institutions and values taken from the modern West, with particular emphasis on cultivating science and democracy.† These young Chinese believed particularly in the general principles of democracy and self-determination laid out by the Western democracies in World War I.

Early in the war, Japan had seized the German concessions in China's province of Shantung. However, China had entered the war on the side of the Allies in 1917. Therefore, the Chinese were confident that the Allies would see that this territory was returned after the war, in accordance with Allied principles. Certainly she would not be abandoned by her partners when her cause was so obviously just. Yet that is what happened; the peace conference at Versailles did not return the Shantung concessions to China, but confirmed Japan's possession.

This flagrant act of imperialism aroused furious demonstrations and strikes by Chinese students and intellectuals in 1919, and the nationalistic indignation also spread to other elements of the Chinese population.* Anti-imperialist agitation was directed against Japan specifically, and the Western nations generally, but not against the Soviet Union. For one of the first acts of the revolutionary Russian regime was to cancel all of the unequal treaties that the tsars had exacted from China, an act which young Chinese greeted with enormous enthusiasm and appreciation. Moreover, Lenin's consistent emphasis on the evils and dangers of imperialism made very good sense to the Chinese, who were thus drawn to Marxism through Leninism.

The student demonstrations, however, as widespread and sincere as they were, could only be indirect weapons against imperialism. That is, the students hoped to influence their own government to resist imperialist encroachments. But the Chinese government at that time was a warlord government, which could not make its authority felt far outside of Peking. In fact, the warlords of

* See *Readings in World History*, "Warlords," p. 436.
† See *Readings in World History*, "Young China Arises," p. 439.

* See *Readings in World History*, "Christian Missionaries in China," p. 433.

Peking, like warlords generally, were greedy for foreign favors, and thus made it easier for foreigners to fish in China's troubled waters. It therefore became apparent to Chinese nationalists that the warlords had to be destroyed, and a genuinely united nation created, before China could hope to struggle successfully against imperialism. To achieve this, a revolutionary army and effective political organization were necessary. These were supplied by the Chinese Communist Party, and by Sun Yat-sen's party, the Kuomintang or Nationalist Party.

Sun Yat-sen. The Chinese Nationalists call Sun Yat-sen "Kuo Fu," which means the "Father of the Country," and hail him as the great revolutionary of modern China. Some skeptics have said that Sun owes his fame in history to the fact that he died at just the time that the Nationalists needed a hero rather than to the greatness of his achievements. Be that as it may, it is true that Sun's successes have frequently been exaggerated.

Sun was born in south China, grew up in Hawaii, and was trained as a doctor in Hong Kong. He absorbed many Western political ideas and became a rebel against his own society. In 1895 he fled to England to escape punishment for revolutionary activities in Canton. In London he was kidnapped by the Chinese embassy and held prisoner, but an English friend, to whom he smuggled out a note, secured his release. This episode was important, not only because his well-publicized rescue gave him a reputation which aided him in his work, but also because Sun was convinced he had been saved in order to carry out a great mission for China.

Wherever Sun travelled outside China, he stirred up national sentiment among the overseas Chinese and persuaded them to join or support his movement. This was important because by this time there were a considerable number of Chinese who lived abroad in

Sun Yat-sen

countries such as the United States, the Philippines, Siam, Indonesia, Burma, and Malaya. Many of these emigrants had become prosperous as farmers, merchants, laundrymen, and moneylenders. So their financial support helped Sun in his campaign against the old dynasty.

Although Sun is often credited with the success of the 1911 Revolution, we have seen that the series of provincial defections which deprived the Manchus of any power base was at least as much the work of provincial military leaders as of Sun's party. And it was Yuan Shih-k'ai's duplicity more than revolutionary force that brought about the abdication of the Manchus. The revolutionaries did not have clear and practicable plans for government after the revolution, and they were so weak relative to Yuan's military machine that they could not carry out the plans they had. Less than two years after the Revolution of 1911, Sun's party tried to overthrow Yuan Shih-k'ai. Yuan easily put down the attempt, and ordered the dissolution of the Kuomintang. Sun Yat-sen once again had to flee abroad, just as he had under the Manchus.

Sun returned to China after Yuan's death, but found it impossible to cope with warlords by political means. An army was necessary, and Sun therefore made alliances with some warlords against others. However, warlords proved to be unstable allies, more concerned with their own goals and interests than those of Sun Yat-sen. Despite his prestige as a pioneer revolutionary, by the beginning of the 1920's the influence of Sun and his party had reached its lowest point.

Soviet aid. On several occasions, Sun appealed for Western aid and support, but he was ignored. The Soviets, however, were not so short-sighted. By the beginning of the 1920's, agents of the Communist International, usually called the Comintern, were in China to establish friendly contacts with political groups with whom they hoped to cooperate, and to help Chinese Marxists organize a Chinese Communist Party. In 1921, the Chinese Communist Party was formally created under Soviet guidance. Two years later, Sun Yat-sen reached an agreement with the Soviets whereby they would also help his party, the Kuomintang, with advisers, money, and weapons. Moreover, Soviets used their influence in the two parties to bring about cooperation between the Communists and the Kuomintang. Communists were permitted to join the Kuomintang, and the two parties agreed to strive together to achieve their common goals: overthrow the warlords to unify the country, and oust imperialism from China.

As a result of the Soviet help, the Kuomintang became a much more effective revolutionary party. First, it was remodelled along the lines of the Russian Communist Party to make it a more cohesive and disciplined organization. In addition, Soviet and Kuomintang leaders set up the Whampoa Military Academy to train officers for a revolutionary army. Chiang Kai-shek was the first director of the academy, and much of his later power derived from the contacts and friendships he made at Whampoa. The Soviets also urged that the Kuomintang develop a consistent ideology to replace the amorphous and often unrealistic ideas that had characterized party thinking up to that time. Sun Yat-sen's chief response to this was to rework his earlier ideas about the Three Principles of the People.

Three Principles of the People. It was at the beginning of the century, before the 1911 Revolution, that Sun Yat-sen first proposed his Three Principles of the People, often called Nationalism, Democracy, and Livelihood. The principle of Nationalism at that time was essentially anti-Manchuism. To make it more relevant to the conditions of the 1920's, Sun gave it a new emphasis: anti-imperialism. The principle of Democracy had originally been tantamount to the demand for a republic. Sun retained the goal of a republic, but he worked out a system of popular control that seemed to have little connection with the actual conditions in China. However, that was a long-range goal in any event, for Sun had a three-stage theory of revolution which envisaged military seizure of power as the first stage, Kuomintang dictatorship to teach the people constitutional methods as the second stage, and the realization of constitutional government as the final stage. The principle of Livelihood called for what Sun termed equalization of the right of property. This, in a vague way, sought to protect the state and people from excessive accumulation of land by landlords. Sun also called for state control of industries.

Sun died in 1925, before he finished reworking his Three Principles. Ever since that time, these principles have been hailed by the Nationalists as the heart and substance of their social and political programs. This has been a source of Nationalist weakness as much as strength. The slogan "Nationalism, Democracy, Livelihood" may elicit some support, but Sun's detailed elaboration of these slogans is confused and confusing, causing the ideological weakness that has plagued the Kuomintang from that day to this.

Northern Expedition. Sun's death occurred just as his revolutionary army was taking shape. In the context of warlordism, where military power was crucial, it is not surprising that leadership of the Kuomintang fell into the hands of Chiang Kai-shek, director of the Whampoa Academy and head of the National Revolutionary Army.

In 1926, the Revolutionary Army finally began its campaign against the warlords, marching northward from its Canton base towards Peking, with the aim of gaining control of the entire nation in between. This so-called Northern Expedition moved swiftly not only because the army fought well, but because political organizers and agitators, mostly Communists who had joined the Kuomintang, preceded the troops and prepared the people to side with and assist the Revolutionary Army. The Communists achieved this by preaching a genuine social revolution, including seizure of land from the landlords. This struck fear into the hearts of many Kuomintang officers who came from landlord families. Many were against the warlords, and for national unification, but not at all interested in social revolution. Chiang Kai-shek, who recognized that the Communists planned to try to take over the Kuomintang, seized the opportunity to move against them. With the backing of conservative elements in the Kuomintang, and the support of financial interests in Shanghai, in the spring of 1927 Chiang suddenly turned his troops against the Communists, killed large numbers of them, and almost shattered the Communist Party. Chiang then resumed the Northern Expedition, and in 1928 finally captured Peking. He declared the country unified, the military phase of the revolution completed, and established a new government in Nanking to carry out the second phase, preparation of the country for constitutional government.

Nationalist weaknesses. Chiang's government had several significant weaknesses. Most important was the fact that the unification of the country was more nominal than real. Many warlords, when they saw the enthusiasm and the fighting capacity of the Northern Expedition, decided not to oppose it and not to flee. Instead, they and all their troops joined the National Revolutionary Army! Chiang gave the warlords high office in the government and Kuomintang, and made their armies new units in the Revolutionary Army. When the Northern Expedition began, it consisted of eight armies; it consisted of over fifty armies a few months later when it reached the Yangtze River. And, since the warlords were permitted to retain their regional political and military authority, although under a new title, it meant that behind the apparent unification of 1928 there remained in actual fact a large measure of warlord rule and regional independence.

The Nationalist government was also weakened by its aversion to genuinely revolutionary change. From the time of the New Culture Movement, progressive Chinese recognized that the modernization of China required social change as well as technological change. Yet Chiang Kai-shek's supporters now included landlords, conservative business circles, and ex-warlords. These groups would not permit progressive social changes.

Therefore badly needed land reform programs were neglected. Instead of tutoring the people in constitutional government, as Sun Yat-sen's plan envisaged, the Kuomintang's one-party rule increasingly stifled all evidences of political liberty. Moreover, Sun Yat-sen's Three Principles, which had a generally progressive thrust despite their shortcomings, were paid only lip service by the Nationalists who gave more emphasis to a revival of Confucian values. Chiang Kai-shek proved to be more interested in social order than social change.

Despite these weaknesses, the Nationalist government made some progress in the decade after 1928. The authority of some independent warlords was reduced, a unified currency replaced the monetary confusion that had previously existed, and improvements were made in tax collecting and other administrative processes. Moreover, the Western nations, which until 1927 had opposed the Nationalist-Communist movement for fear that it would oust them completely from China, now found it possible to do business with Chiang Kai-shek. However, they did have to return to China some of the privileges gained by the unequal treaties; thus the Nationalists regained control of the tariff, and treaties began to be made on a basis of equality. The final remnants of extrality were removed in 1943.

Civil war and invasion. After Chiang Kai-shek's devastating attack upon the Communists in 1927, remnants of the Communist Party regrouped in the mountainous interior of South China under the leadership of Mao Tse-tung. They organized their own Red Army, and created a government for a region containing some eight million people. The Nationalists repeatedly hurled their armies against the Communists, but were invariably resisted and thrown back. Finally, in 1934, the Nationalists surrounded the Communist area with fortifications manned by nearly a million men. About 100,000 Communists managed to break through this encirclement and begin what turned out to be a 6000-mile trek of incredible hardship. Thousands perished, but the survivors reached northwest China a year after the march began, and there, at Yenan in the province of Shensi, they established a new base. The Communists steadily increased their following among the peasants by introducing genuine land reforms, and among intellectuals and students by their call for a united national resistance against Japan.

Chiang Kai-shek's inability to subdue the Communists was closely related to his failure to prevent Japan's aggression. The Japanese attacked China in 1931. They overran Manchuria and penetrated down into North China. Chiang recognized the danger of Japan, but he preferred to remove the Communist menace before confronting the Japanese threat. His decision to put out the fire within his own house before battling the flames threatening from the neighboring house became increasingly unpopular. Communist calls for a united effort against Japan won more and more popular support. Finally Chiang gave way and in 1937 accepted Communist cooperation for common resistance against the Japanese.

Japan retaliated by beginning in the same year an all-out invasion of China. The Chinese could not resist such a powerful attack and were forced to retreat. Chiang followed the strategy of trading space for time, and fell back in stages to Chungking in the western part of the country. The Japanese were left in control of all north China, the coastal lands, and the rich Yangtze valley.

By 1940 China was divided into three sections. The eastern areas were controlled by the Japanese and administered through a puppet government at Nanking. The Nationalist government from its capital in

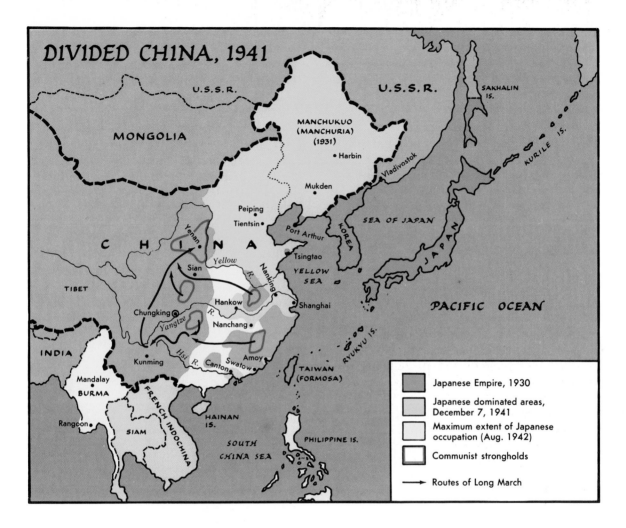

DIVIDED CHINA, 1941

�(dark)	Japanese Empire, 1930
▢ (medium)	Japanese dominated areas, December 7, 1941
▢ (light)	Maximum extent of Japanese occupation (Aug. 1942)
▢ (white)	Communist strongholds
→	Routes of Long March

Chungking dominated the west and southwestern areas. In the northwest, the Chinese Communists, nominally under the authority of the Nationalist government, ran their own territory from their capital of Yenan. In the Japanese-occupied zone, troops garrisoned the major cities and guarded the main lines of communications between them. But they never became the masters of the countryside, where Chinese guerilla bands kept up the fight.* This prevented the Japanese from

* See *Readings in World History*, "Communist Guerrilla Tactics," p. 442.

fully exploiting the economic resources of the territories they occupied.

In the Kuomintang areas the Chinese faced a bitter trial. The rural southwest was hopelessly inadequate as a base for supporting the government and the armies. Industries had to be built up from scratch, transportation systems developed, and universities resettled. Faced by the formidable problems of sustaining the armies and supporting a huge population, the government became highhanded and corrupt. The conservative landlords in the Kuomintang territories became increasingly oppressive. The population suffered cruel hardships. Goods were scarce, inflation ruined incomes, and open discontent was harshly handled by the secret police. Despite this ordeal the Kuomintang armies somehow held on and the government remained intact.

The Communists fared much better. By organizing extensive guerilla operations against the Japanese in the north, the Communists succeeded in fighting the invader and simultaneously spreading their own influence and reputation. By the time of Japan's surrender in 1945, the Communists had bases scattered over much of north China, and had organized a population of about 90,000,000 people. The Communist army was not corrupt, its morale was high, and it enjoyed widespread popular support.

The surrender of Japan set off a wild scramble in which Communists and Nationalists raced to take over Japanese-occupied China. The Nationalist government re-established itself in Nanking and recovered all the main cities. The Communists occupied the countryside around the major cities and gained a major advantage when the Soviets turned over to the Chinese Red Army the arms which the Japanese had surrendered in Manchuria. The Nationalists had the advantage of a larger military force, command of the major cities, and liberal aid from the United States. But morale and leadership had been so weakened by the long years of the war that they could not cope with the economic and financial problems of reconstruction. When civil war seemed imminent, the United States sent a mission under Gen-

Chinese Communist guerrillas wait along the Great Wall to repel Japanese advances.

PIX INC.

eral George Marshall to attempt to negotiate a settlement between the two major factions. But neither faction could overcome its fear and suspicion of the other and the American efforts to mediate proved hopeless. By 1947 the final showdown was at hand.

The first result of the renewed civil war was the loss of Manchuria by Chiang Kai-shek. He had placed many of his best troops in Manchuria but in indefensible positions. They were surrounded by the Red Army and, unable to withdraw, they surrendered. The chain of military disasters followed in quick succession. The Communist armies swept through North China and by 1950 had control of all of the the mainland. The Nationalists withdrew to the island of Tai-wan and with U.S. support established a stable exile government, the Republic of China, which is officially recognized as China's legal government by many nations.

Why did the Communists win? Many factors account for the Communist success. In one sense, it was basically a military victory; the Communists simply out-fought the Na-tionalists. Although substantially outnum-bered by the Nationalists at the end of War War II in 1945, the Communist army was experienced, well-trained, with high morale, and most effectively organized in a structure that reached all the way down to the village militia. Nationalist units, on the other hand, were permeated with cor-ruption, and were poorly led.

There is some disagreement about the extent to which popular support accounted for the Communist victory. Some writers say that the people's approval of the Commu-nist program was the major factor in Mao's success, while others maintain that the people were generally neutral, and passively acquiesced in a Communist victory that they could not prevent. However, it seems fair to say that, at the very least, Communists enjoyed a measure of support from all classes of the population. The peasants approved the Communist program for land reform, par-ticularly since it was actually put into effect. Perhaps even more important, the Commu-nists were not corrupt; it was corruption that deprived the Chinese peasant of his property and his dignity, and the honesty that was universally acknowledged to be a characteristic of the Chinese Communists inevitably drew approval.

Intellectuals liked the Communists' un-compromising anti-imperialism, and were perhaps also attracted by the idea that Marxism was the wave of the future, and its adoption would put China at the head of world history. Moreover, the intellectuals were alienated by the Kuomintang's rever-sion to Chinese tradition. Confucianism, in their view, clearly had no relevance to their problems, and they could only suspect the government that promoted it. While they possibly had many doubts about Com-munist ideology, it was at least a genuine attempt to deal with current problems.

Even the business class was not com-pletely opposed to the Communists. Busi-nessmen could not do business in the infla-tion and economic chaos that existed in the last years of Kuomintang rule, so they saw more hope in an efficiently run Communist state that declared private capitalists would have a role to play for some time. Thus each class found something attractive about the Communists, and that was sufficient when the only alternative was the Kuomintang which was increasingly distasteful to all classes.

In more general terms, we can say that the Communists won because they re-sponded more effectively to the needs of China in the mid- 20th century. Nationalism was the most powerful single force in China. It was fired by indignation against over a century of imperialism culminating in the brutal Japanese invasion, by a fierce national pride grown out of the traditional belief in cultural superiority, and by recognition that in a world of nation-states China could only exist as a strong nation. From this basic nationalism, many implications flowed. In the 20th century, a powerful nation had to be industrialized. Industrialization, as well as other elements of national pride and power, demanded widespread education and a general rise in the cultural and economic level of the agrarian masses. The achievement of all these ends demanded effective organization, the capacity for self-sacrifice, and an orientation towards the future instead of the past. The Communists met all of these requirements more effectively than the Nationalists.*

Nationalist government on Taiwan. Taiwan was a part of the spoils of war taken by Japan after defeating China in 1895, and one of China's goals during World War II was the recovery of that island. Therefore, as soon as Japan surrendered in 1945, the Chinese Nationalist government sent troops to reoccupy Taiwan. Although the Taiwanese at first viewed the Nationalists as liberators, coming to free them from Japanese colonialism, their welcome quickly turned to hate because of the Nationalists' brutal and rapacious policies. The new Nationalist government mercilessly exploited the island and its people, producing resentment among the Taiwanese that resulted in a revolt in February 1947. The revolt was put down by Nationalist troops who massacred thousands of Taiwanese, including virtually all of the island's leaders and potential leaders.

In 1949, the Nationalist central government fled to Taiwan. In all, about two million people fled from the mainland to the island. Although it was generally expected that the

* See *Readings in World History*, "American Policy in China," p. 443.

Communists would pursue the Nationalists, and ultimately conquer the island, the United States prevented this by sending a naval fleet to the Taiwan Straits in 1950, at the outbreak of the Korean War. Since that time, the United States has supported the Nationalist Government as it has attempted to build a stable economic and political base to support a campaign to return to the mainland.

One of the first major programs launched by the Nationalists was a land reform which forced landlords to sell their surplus land to the government, which then offered the land on easy terms to the tillers. When they were on the mainland, the Nationalists avoided land reform because it would have alienated their landlord supporters. Since they had no ties to Taiwanese landlords, such obstacles no longer existed, and the land reform was pushed through successfully. The result was a radical reduction in the number of tenant farmers, and the creation of a relatively stable base of small landowners. With the help of American economic aid, the Nationalist government continued to improve agricultural practices, promote foreign trade and foreign investment, and stimulate the growth of industry. Since 1951, Taiwan has had the highest rate of economic growth in Asia, outside of Japan. The best indication of this achievement is the cessation of American economic aid in 1965. However, the United States continues military aid to the island, and this, of course, helps the Taiwanese economy indirectly.

Although Taiwan has a constitution, real power is still wielded by the Kuomintang and, ultimately, by its still unchallenged leader, Chiang Kai-shek. The legal reason given for Chiang's continued dictatorship is the fact that the Nationalists consider themselves still at war with the Communists, and therefore emergency powers are necessary. Since Chiang is over 80 years old, there is much speculation about who his successor will be. Most informed opinion is that power will go to Chiang's son, Chiang Ching-kuo, who is now Minister of Defense. Another fundamental political problem is the character of Taiwanese-mainlander relations. The Taiwanese would like a greater share of political power, but this would mean a lessening of the authoritarian Nationalist rule which has been unacceptable to the Kuomintang. There is also a Taiwanese independence movement, but its leaders are overseas, and it is impossible for an outsider to know how extensive their following is in Taiwan.

Communist China. On October 1, 1949, in Peking, Mao Tse-tung proclaimed the establishment of the Central People's Government of the People's Republic of China. He solemnly hoisted the new national flag, a red flag with five stars. The years since that event form the final period in the story of the Communist revolution in China, a revolution that is still going on.

The most conspicuous characteristic of the past two decades has been the fantastic tempo of change. In the economy, for example, small independent land-holdings gave way to cooperatives, collectives, and communes in a bewilderingly rapid sequence. At the same time, giant efforts were made to industrialize the country and to nationalize the entire economy. And all the while the Communist regime promoted drastic innovations in social, intellectual, and cultural life. Most recently, China has been shaken by the extraordinary upheaval known as the Cultural Revolution. We must examine this before turning to a survey of economic and cultural history since 1949.

"National Day" parade in Peking, 1950.

The Cultural Revolution. In 1966, the world watched incredulously as millions of Chinese teenagers roamed across their country extolling "the thought of Mao Tse-tung," and denouncing a wide variety of practices and attitudes they labelled "bourgeois." This was part of a movement officially labelled "The Great Proletarian Cultural Revolution," yet nobody outside of China seemed to know who was revolting against what. The turmoil has continued into 1969, and we have gradually learned enough to understand the main issues, although we do not yet know what the outcome will be.

In general terms, the Cultural Revolution is an attempt on the part of some of China's leaders, chiefly Mao Tse-tung, to prevent China from settling into a social order that falls short of genuine communism. It involves an attempt to revolutionize the nation's youth, and a profound struggle between the Maoist group and those who feel that the rate of social change should be slower.

Events at the end of the 1950's and in the early 1960's led Mao Tse-tung to think that the goals of the Communist revolution

were in danger. Until 1958, the country seemed to be moving towards communism as rapidly as anyone could hope. By that time, agriculture was completely collectivized, business was nationalized, and the Communist government had created new political, legal, and educational systems. It had also effected far-reaching changes in art, literature, and Chinese culture generally. The political system seemed to function smoothly. But all of this steady progress suffered several setbacks at the end of the 1950's.

In 1958, the Communist government launched the "Great Leap Forward" and the commune movement. The Great Leap was an attempt to catch up economically with the West almost overnight by means of a frenzy of work and effort. The result, however, was to dislocate the economy and interfere with production. At the same time, the communes involved such regimentation that peasants objected vigorously, and agricultural production declined. Growing disagreements with the Soviet Union led to the withdrawal of Soviet economic and technical aid in 1960. Finally, unfavorable weather further disrupted agricultural production to the point where the nation was threatened by famine.

Faced by these circumstances, the government reversed its policies. The Great Leap was abandoned. Although the communes were nominally retained, in fact rural organization returned to roughly what it had been under the collective farms. Peasants were even given small plots of land for private cultivation. Moreover, the government had to shift the focus of its energies from the development of heavy industry to the improvement of agriculture.

As a result of these reverses, and the end of the tense efforts of the Great Leap projects, a general let-down and relaxation took place at the beginning of the 1960's. The peasants gave much attention to their private plots, thus diverging psychologically as well as practically from the principle of collectivism. Many technical personnel interpreted the recent failures as signs that political enthusiasm could not substitute for technical expertise, and concluded that indoctrination should be reduced to make way for more technical training. Intellectuals had been skeptical about the Great Leap and the communes, and the failure of both encouraged a tendency for intellectuals to criticize the government and leaders, although still in guarded terms. Finally, many party and public officials at all levels seemed to show more concern for their status, income, power, and comforts than for public welfare. This was probably not the result of the failures of the late 1950's as much as the fact that by the early 1960's the officials had been in office long enough so that their earlier revolutionary enthusiasm had worn off, and they had become accustomed to the pleasures of office.

Mao Tse-tung considered all these trends unhealthy and dangerous for the future of the revolution. In 1962, he launched a movement designed to improve the caliber of basic level officials and party workers in the countryside. When this proved unsuccessful, Mao concluded that the unhealthy trends were more widespread than he had thought, and extended into the very top levels of leadership. Moreover, some of the top leaders clearly disagreed with Mao's policies. They thought that the failure of the Great Leap Forward and of the communes proved that China should progress more slowly and methodically, and they feared Mao's tendency to push for drastic and rapid change. Thus the leaders, who had so long maintained a solid unity, began to split over policies. Struggle for the authority to implement a particular set of policies is, of course, a struggle for power.

This power struggle first took place within the Communist Party, but Mao was unable to dislodge his opponents. Because of this,

Workers in Tachai walk to the fields past signs with quotations from Mao. Note that the workers, adults and children, carry their little red book with them even into the fields.

EASTFOTO

427

At a demonstration in 1966, young Chinese salute the revolution and the thought of Mao Tse-tung.

and because Mao believed that the Party itself showed many of the ills he wanted to eliminate, he sought help outside the Party, and made a cleansing of the Party one of his major targets. Mao first sought the support of the People's Liberation Army, and the alliance between Mao and the army was symbolized in the autumn of 1966 when Lin Piao, Minister of Defense, became the second man in the Communist heirarchy, Mao's heir apparent. Moreover, Mao closed the schools and mobilized millions of Chinese youth to force local officials out of office, or compel officials and Party workers to shape their actions and policies after a more revolutionary model. This tactic not

only gave Mao a means to pressure the Party from the outside, but it gave him the backing of the "masses," even if the masses were largely teenagers. It also offered an opportunity to cultivate among Chinese youth revolutionary attitudes through particpation in revolutionary action.

In the autumn of 1966, millions of Chinese youths, called Red Guards, went to Peking, where Mao Tse-tung addressed them at monster rallies. Thus inspired by their leader, they went forth to battle the enemies of the revolution, all those who would slow the pace of change, or who saw anything good in Western society. During the last several months of the year, they roamed the cities, attacking every vestige of the Chinese past and the Western "bourgeois" present, from miniskirts to leather shoes, from Shakespeare to hair styles. They renamed so many streets "Anti-imperialist Avenue" that finally nobody knew his address, and the old names had to be restored.*

By the early months of 1967, some Red Guard groups and other Maoists managed to seize control of a few cities from the regular Party and government officials, but they found administration difficult in face of the growing social turmoil, passive and active resistance, and their own inexperience. Finally, Mao summoned the army to help them. In essence, the army became responsible for administration and public order until new organs of governing authority, called revolutionary committees, could be created. When these were finally formed, they consisted of representatives from the army, from Party factions that supported Mao, and from various mass organizations. But the army was clearly the dominant element. From 1967 to 1969 has been a time of much confusion and conflict as local party and government agencies resisted the establishment of revolutionary committees. However, by 1969 such committees were set up in all provinces, and the Maoists seemed to be in control.

China as a world power. The Communists have made substantial progress towards their goal of restoring China to a position of leadership in East Asia and of great power in world affairs. In 1950, China concluded a treaty of friendship with the Soviet Union. The Chinese have gained formal recognition from about 50 nations, and played a leading part in several important international conferences. Chinese military prowess was displayed by successfully reasserting Chinese rule in Tibet, and effective intervention in

*See *Readings in World History*, "Red Guards," p. 446.

the Korean war when American troops approached the Chinese border. In recent years, the Chinese have begun the development of nuclear weapons. China has even undertaken a program of economic aid to selected Asian and African countries, her own desperate need of resources notwithstanding.

Despite these achievements, China continues to suffer from several basic weaknesses in her quest for great power status. Most conspicuous is the burden of China's enormous population, by far the largest in the world and growing at the rate of 40,000 people a day. Because of the huge number of people, the nation's standard of living is low. And because of the continued rapid increase, much, if not all, of any gain in production is immediately cancelled out by the additional mouths to feed. The Communists have viewed rapid industrialization as a partial solution to their economic problems as well as a key to great power status, but an agricultural nation such as theirs has little surplus capital to invest in industry. As a consequence, industrialization cannot come as rapidly as the Chinese would like.

China's international position has also been profoundly affected by a rupture in Chinese-Soviet relations which has become increasingly serious since the end of the 1950's. Although complicated by questions of prestige and the leadership of world communism, the split was basically caused by differing views of proper Communist policy towards the United States, and by differing ideas about how to achieve communism. The Soviet Union, confident of its own great power and the superiority of the Soviet system, argues for peaceful coexistence with the United States, competing economically but avoiding war. China, on the other hand, cannot compete with the United States at present. China's leaders therefore argue that Communists should encourage a militant anti-Americanism throughout the world, but especially in the non-Western portions of the world. The Chinese also believe that the Soviet Union's willingness to coexist with the United States, the greatest capitalist power of the world, is one of several indications that the Soviets are no longer truly Marxists. The Russians, say the Chinese, have "revised" Marxism, and this revisionism has become one of the chief targets of the Cultural Revolution.

THE FUTURE

Although the turmoil of the Cultural Revolution makes it unusually difficult to foresee the shape of China's future, we can at least discern some of the major political problems that the country will face during the next few years. Certainly the most important issue will be the fate of the Communist Party. Attacks by Cultural Revolutionaries have drastically weakened the Party, and the seizure of authority by the army and by the revolutionary committees have badly undercut its power. However, there is little reason to think that the Maoists will destroy the Party and create a new organ of power. The revolutionary committees will probably prove to be a temporary device, and attempts will be made to complete the difficult and lengthy task of bringing the Party back to its former preeminence. In the meantime, it is possible that there will be continued conflict on the local level between those attempt-

ing to restore the Party's authority and those who have won status during the Cultural Revolution by acting outside of the Party.

In foreign affairs, there is unfortunately little reason to expect a change in China's hostility to the United States. As long as the United States bolsters Chiang Kai-shek's government on Taiwan, and has troops on China's borders in Vietnam, the Chinese will see this country as the chief threat to their security. Moreover, the Chinese leaders condemn American values and institutions, and view this country as the leading example of the bourgeois society they loathe.

The future of Sino-Soviet relations seems less certain. There will be hostility between the two nations as long as they hold different visions of the Communist future and of policies to follow towards the Western world. However, some bureaucratic and professional men in China still hold views close to those of the Soviets, and it is not out of the question that China's policy towards the Soviet Union might change quickly if they were to come into power.

This possibility raises still another issue: the future leadership of China. Mao and his associates are already old men, and it will not be long before a new generation of leaders takes over. Whether this new generation will be as uncompromising as the Maoists, or will backtrack and imitate the Soviet Union in domestic and foreign policies, can not be prejudged. We must wait for this next stage in the development of China.

Reviewing the Essentials

Present State

1. How did World War II affect China and India? Why did India and China react differently to Western influence?
2. When and under whose leadership did the People's Republic become the new government of China? What were the objectives of the leaders?

3. What are the main political supports of the People's Republic? How do they operate to achieve the objectives of China's leaders?
4. Explain the organization and rule of the Chinese Communist Party, including: (a) structure; (b) membership; (c) how party policy is

made; (d) how the Party remains in control of the government.

5. How is the government of China organized? How is the business of government conducted, i.e., who determines and enforces policy? How does "democratic centralism" hold the government together?

6. What is democracy? Is "democratic centralism" democratic?

7. How has the Cultural Revolution weakened China? Is it possible that the Cultural Revolution may in the long run strengthen China? How?

8. What accounts for the hostility between China and the United States?

9. What is the function of the Red Army?

Historical Origins

10. Historically, how did China view the West? Why? With what results?

11. Explain how each of these helped to open China to the West: (a) British East India Company; (b) Opium War, 1839–1842; (c) Treaty of Nanking, 1842; (d) "most-favored-nation" clause; (e) extraterritoriality; (f) the treaty system; (g) Open Door Policy.

12. On a map locate those areas of the Chinese Empire that became spheres of influence claimed by England, France, Germany, Russia, and Japan.

13. What internal crisis confronted the Manchu dynasty during the last half of the 19th century? What reforms were introduced by the Taiping rebels? Why do the Communists today identify themselves with the Taiping rebels?

14. What conditions culminated in the Boxer Rebellion? What were the immediate and long-range results of the Boxer Rebellion for China?

15. Were the "unequal treaties" genuinely unequal? If so, in what ways? If not, why were they called unequal?

16. Discuss the Republican Revolution of 1911 in terms of: (a) conditions that prompted it; (b) goals; (c) roles of Sun Yat-sen and Yuan Shih-k'ai; (d) outcome of the Revolution; (e) immediate and ultimate results for China.

17. What events and conditions culminated in the Nationalist Revolution of 1926–1927? What did Sun Yat-sen and Chiang Kai-shek do to strengthen the Kuomintang in preparation for revolution?

18. What reforms and changes were introduced by the Kuomintang? What important reforms were not achieved? How did the failure to achieve certain of these reforms serve to aid the Communist Party?

19. Trace the development of Chiang Kai-shek's program to cope with (a) the Chinese Communists and (b) the Japanese invasion.

20. How did Mao Tse-tung and the Chinese Communists strengthen their position during the period after 1937, in preparation for their conquest of China in 1947–1949? What factors are responsible for the Communist victory?

21. Review major political changes made by the Chinese Communists since 1949. What appear to be underlying weaknesses of Communist China? Politically, what is the outlook for the future of Communist China?

22. How does Chinese history of the past century illustrate a traditional dynastic cycle? How does it differ from a traditional dynastic cycle?

Explain, Identify, or Locate

Politbureau	1917	1927	National People's
democratic centralism	Communist Revolution	Sun Yat-sen	Congress
extraterritoriality	Kuomintang	Yenan	Central Committee
Taiping Rebellion	Liu Shao-ch'i	Chungking	Three Principles
Treaty of Nanking	Mao Tse-tung	Taiwan	of the People
Republican Revolution	Chou En-lai	1934	Northern Expedition
1911	Yuan Shih-k'ai	1949	Red Guards

ECONOMICS: Great Leap and a Stumble

China's economic life since 1949 falls roughly into two periods. The first, to 1958, was a time of steady and rapid progress in both agriculture and industry. The second, since 1958, has seen several economic crises. A major problem is the competition between industry and agriculture. The Communists want to focus all energies and resources on industrialization in order to transform the economy of the country quickly. Yet most of the nation's resources are needed merely for subsistence, leaving little to devote to modernization. The Communists have not yet been able to resolve this iron dilemma, a dilemma rooted in the age-old agrarian nature of China.

HISTORICAL ORIGINS

Traditional Chinese economy. The most important feature of China's economy has always been the predominance of agriculture. Over three-fourths of the people were crowded on the cultivable land. A typical peasant spent his whole life on the land and lived in a village he rarely left. When he did leave he went no more than a few miles to the market town to sell his crops. Often he did not own his land. In the wheat-growing regions of the north only about one-fourth of the peasants were forced to rent their land, but in the rice-growing regions of the south more than two-fifths were tenant farmers. Whether he owned or rented the land there was never very much of it. The average-sized farm was rarely more than two acres, and one-third of the peasants worked less than one acre. With so little land available, the peasants and all the members of their families had to work long and hard to keep body and soul together. They encouraged the tired soil to yield more by irrigating it and fertilizing it with human waste, or "night soil." But success was always in the laps of the gods of nature. The frequent floods and droughts, and the appalling famines which followed, showed that the gods were not always kind.

A second major characteristic of China's traditional economy was its low productivity. Such a large part of the population was engaged in agriculture that the production per person was extremely low. Human labor was plentiful but land was scarce. The small plots were used quite efficiently and crop yields per acre were high. But so many people worked one plot of land that the yield per person was low.

A third general feature of the Chinese economy was the dense population. If there had been fewer people, and if so many of them had not been farmers, China could have raised its standard of living. But China has always had a larger number of people than any other nation in the world. It is estimated that there were about 350 million Chinese by the year 1850, which was an increase of four times from the year 1650. Today, as we have already seen, China's population is about 780 million, a figure far higher than that for any other nation.

The huge size of its population has always been an important factor in keeping China's economy at a low level. Furthermore the oversupply of manpower has discouraged the use of inventions and machinery for labor-saving purposes. This is one of the important reasons why there was no Industrial Revolution in China as there was in Western Europe. Also the dense and constantly increasing population, together with the limited amount of available land, led to extreme exploitation of the peasants. The landlords could demand and collect very high rents, while the usurers charged outrageous interest rates for the money they loaned to desperate peasants. This meant that grinding poverty and cruel misery were all too frequently the fate of China's hardworking villagers.*

All of these features of China's traditional economy—the predominance of agriculture, low productivity, dense population, and dependence on human energy—caused China to fall behind the industrialized nations of the world. It made China an underprivileged nation of poverty-stricken peasants. Few Chinese could accumulate even a small margin of reserve to meet emergencies. Failure of crops in any one year led to famine and economic disasters that took years to repair.† But the fact that China's civilization was based mainly on the soil gave it a fundamental stability. It kept the standard of life low but it enabled the Chinese to continue for century after century their ancient ways of earning a living. All this was rudely and suddenly changed when the Western Europeans burst into China. They brought science, technology, and new economic theories and practices which gradually undermined China's traditional economy and finally swept it away.

Beginnings of modern industrialism. The treaties which China was forced to accept after 1842 opened the country to Western economic penetration. Foreigners appeared in the treaty ports, and before long were

* See *Readings in World History,* "Peasant Poverty," p. 424.
† See *Readings in World History,* "Famine in Honan," p. 451.

establishing industries in the coastal areas and constructing railways into the interior. In China, as in India and other non-Western regions, these developments, by opening domestic markets to the West, shattered the traditional economy.

In the first place they ruined the old village handicraft industries. For centuries the peasant families had depended on the sale of their handicrafts to supplement their earnings from the land. These home crafts provided a part-time occupation which filled in the long winter days in the north when the fields could not be worked. Cotton cloth, shoes, cooking utensils, nails, and many other things were turned out in this way from the peasant huts. But the new railway now brought in vast quantities of Western machine-made goods which often were less expensive and almost always were of better quality. For example, making nails by hand is a slow process, but with a machine one man can turn out thousands each day. Cotton thread produced in the mills of the cities was of far better quality than that which was spun in peasant households. In this way the handicraft industries of the countryside were steadily ruined, and as a result the peasants became even poorer than they had been in the past.[*]

Another effect of the West's economic offensive was to make many of the peasants dependent on world markets. In order to buy the machine-made goods the peasants had to have cash. Now they grew crops that could be transported on the new railways and steamships to the factories of Western Europe. No longer did the peasants raise foodstuffs for themselves and their village. Now they grew commercial crops that could be sold on the world markets: tea, silk, soybeans, cotton, and hides. Thus the Chinese village, like the Indian and many others, lost its traditional self-sufficiency and became entangled in the world market.[*]

A few far-sighted Chinese leaders realized that their country must adopt Western science and technology if it was to hold its own in the 20th-century world. They did make some efforts but with little success. One obstacle was the extreme reluctance among all classes to change the old ways of making a living. Another was the lack of engineers and managers to run the factories filled with machines. The unequal treaties were still another obstacle which prevented the Chinese from setting up protective tariffs to stop the flood of goods from the West. Finally there was the corruption and instability of the Chinese government which was unable to provide the necessary funds and leadership.

All this does not mean that the industries in China were owned totally by foreigners. Gradually a few Chinese-owned shipyards, textile mills, mines, and other enterprises began to appear. This was especially true in the 1930's when China regained control of its tariffs. Now she was able to raise duties in order to protect her industries and collect revenue. Small rural industries began to sprout up in the interior of the country. Thus China did have a modest industrial structure by the beginning of World War II. But it was extremely modest in relation to the tremendous natural and human resources of the country. Also China's industries often were geared to foreign trade rather than to the over-all development of the national economy. Consequently they had little effect on agriculture, which continued to absorb the great bulk of the labor power of the country, and with a miserably low return. Obviously China needed a coordinated development of agriculture and industry, the one stimulating the other. But this the Nationalist government was never effectively able to do.

[*] See *Readings in World History*, "Plight of the Artisan," p. 455.

[*] See *Readings in World History*, "Plight of the Peasant," p. 458.

Five-Year Plans. When the Chinese Communists conquered the mainland and regained possession of Manchuria, they controlled an economy which was made up of three parts. The first was the largely self-sufficient agricultural sector which absorbed the energy of three-quarters of China's population. The second was the industries developed in the coastal cities and along the main lines of communication in the interior. These were geared largely to foreign trade, and were mostly light industries such as textile mills and food processing plants. The third was the heavy industrial area in Manchuria, which had been built mainly by the Japanese after they took over the area in 1931.

All three of these subdivisions of China's economy were largely in a shambles after the 12 years of foreign and domestic wars. Industrial production was only a fraction of its prewar peak. Trade was almost non-existent, public works were neglected, railways destroyed, and inflation was out of control. Consequently, the Communists first had to restore the national economy.

By 1952 the Communists had been sucessful in reviving the economy. After they had firmly established their political authority and put the economy back on its feet, they launched an economic program. This consisted of a series of Five-Year Plans which were modelled after those of the Soviet Union and which were started in 1953.

The first Five-Year Plan (1953–1957) called for a crash program in industrialization and socialization. The emphasis was placed on the construction of heavy industry, the socialization of commerce, and the collectivization of agriculture. Production goals were set for every sector of the economy, and land was redistributed in order to squeeze out the maximum agricultural surplus. An essential feature of the plan was the close economic cooperation between China and the Soviet Union.

By 1958, Soviet-aided projects totalled 211 and required over two billion dollars' worth of Soviet equipment. By 1959 the Soviet Union had sent many thousands of experts, mostly technicians, to China to assist in building and operating these projects. It should be noted, however, that Soviet aid was given on the basis of a loan and not a gift. China was to pay for this vital assistance by exporting goods to the Soviet Union. So it was primarily the Chinese peasant who paid

Machines are increasingly used for tasks that were traditionally done by hand. Here commune workers thresh rice.

EASTFOTO

CHINA – LAND USE

Peking

Hong Kong

Nomadic herding

Livestock ranching

Commercial agriculture

Paddy rice

Subsistence agriculture
(including some shifting cultivation)

Industrial areas

No use made of land

Miles

0   500   1000

for the Five-Year Plans. Their produce was exported to pay for Soviet machinery and technicians, and their crops were used to feed the workers and to supply the raw materials for manufacturing. Consequently the entire Communist economic program depended on increasing the productivity of the land.

Collectivization of agriculture. To increase the crop yield as well as to control the peasants with greater efficiency, the Communists carried out three great agricultural revolutions during their first decade. The first was a land-redistribution program which had actually begun in Communist controlled areas before 1949. Land was taken from the rich farmers and distributed among the landless or those with tiny plots. This reform naturally won the support of millions of

peasants and helped the Communists to rise to power.[*]

The second revolution was the collective-farm system which was introduced stage by stage. At first the peasants who had acquired land were organized into mutual-aid teams in which farmers helped each other cultivate the land but still held ownership of their own plots and tools. The next stage was that of producers' cooperatives, in which the boundaries between plots were removed and tools and land were owned in common. The result is known as the collective-farm system. The third and most extreme of the agrarian revolutions was the commune system inaugurated in 1958 during the second Five-Year Plan. But before considering the communes, what progress was made during the first Plan?

Results of the first Plan. The Communists claim to have fulfilled their first Plan by the end of 1957 despite inexperience, mistakes, lack of trained personnel, and bad crop years. The output in grain, cotton and sugar, and in industrial products such as coal, steel, crude oil, electricity, and cotton cloth rose sharply, but less than claimed.

In addition to expanding the output of consumer and industrial goods, 6000 miles of new railway track had been laid, and water conservation projects for irrigation and flood control had been completed. Equally important was the development of new strategic industrial bases deep in the interior of China, particularly in the northwest area.

Up to 1958, the Chinese made giant strides toward their goal of industrialization. Four factors made this possible. First was the aid which the Soviet Union and other Communist nations gave to China. This aid included technological information, training of specialists, modern machinery, and the like. Second, Chinese Communists have succeeded in im-

[*] See *Readings in World History,* "Peasant Life in the 20th Century," p. 460.

posing far greater control over their people than Lenin and Stalin were able to impose on the Soviet citizens. Collectivization in the Soviet Union was accompanied by dislocation and disorder, whereas in China far-reaching agricultural revolutions were completed in half a decade without major dislocation. Third, China has a huge pool of manpower to work with. All the people were put to work and, as it has been said, "it may well be that never in history have so many people worked so hard for so little pay as in China this last decade." [2] Fourth, by industrializing at a later time than the other major powers of the world, China benefited from a much higher world level of technology than did the Soviet Union.

The Great Leap Forward. In 1958, the Second Five-Year Plan began. However, in the same year the Great Leap Forward and the commune movement were launched, creating such economic turmoil that the Plan became virtually meaningless from the outset.

The Great Leap Forward was an attempt to solve a basic dilemma: the need to finance industrialization from agricultural production. The Communists were determined to industrialize as rapidly as possible, for this was the key to modernization at home and power abroad. But since China was primarily an agrarian country, only agriculture could provide the money for the purchase of machines, the construction of factories, and all the other expenditures involved in creating new industry. And, since there was not usually a large agricultural surplus after meeting the subsistence needs of the country, the leaders wanted to expand agricultural production in order to increase investment in industry.

The usual way to boost agricultural production is to invest more money in that portion of the economy. That was unacceptable

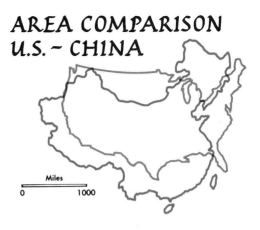

AREA COMPARISON
U.S. ~ CHINA

Miles
0   1000

to the Chinese, however, since it would automatically reduce the amount available for industry. That was the dilemma: the Chinese wanted to push forward rapidly in both industry and agriculture, but there seemed only resources enough to finance one, not both.

The solution was the Great Leap Forward. This was an attempt to mobilize the population to work harder in order to raise agricultural production and also to develop local industries to meet local needs. Huge work forces were organized for tasks such as building dams and irrigation facilities, reclaiming land, tree-planting, and the like. The Chinese set themselves the goal of overtaking England within 15 years; from every side they were exhorted to work harder, faster, longer, better.

The creation of the communes was associated with the Great Leap. By the beginning of 1957, rural China was organized in collective farms, which averaged about 175 households each. This was not a large enough unit to administer the huge work teams envisaged

The chessboard pattern of rice paddies in the Muya People's Commune is found widely throughout South and Central China.

by the Great Leap, and, in any event, it did not have the political authority to organize and assign workers. Therefore groups of collective farms were brought together to create larger units called communes. The commune had about 4,000 households, and the administration of the commune managed not only agricultural matters but all other economic as well as political and social affairs. This system also had the advantage of using the labor power of agricultural workers more efficiently. This labor was normally idle for part of the year, because agricultural work is seasonal. But since a commune might include forests, mines, or rivers, commune authorities could organize and employ all labor on a year-round basis for work in mines,

local foundries, lumbering, fishing, and other necessary work, as well as for the usual farm chores.

In order to handle the large work forces efficiently, and also to release the labor power of millions of women, various public facilities were set up, such as communal kitchens, mess-halls, nurseries, and the like, and the pattern of daily living became highly regimented. One gains a rough idea of a commune if he imagines a town of about 10,000 people in which the town authorities not only manage political and social welfare matters, but assign jobs and oversee all economic activities, and arrange the life of society in a highly organized and communal fashion.

438 *China*

The Great Leap and the commune movement both failed. The undeniable enthusiasm of many Chinese could not substitute for technical knowledge and improved equipment. Moreover, frenzied efforts to produce quickly often resulted in a drop in quality, and made rational planning and organization difficult or impossible. In the communes, the peasantry objected so strenuously to the extraordinary regimentation that the government immediately began to modify commune regulations. Before long the countryside was again organized in collectives for most practical purposes, although the facade of the communes continues to exist. In order to stimulate food production, the peasants were even given small plots of land for their personal use. The difficulties of the Great Leap and the communes were compounded by several years of bad weather. This combination of circumstances made a shambles of the Chinese economy, and produced a near famine.

In the face of this economic crisis, the Communist leadership, in 1961, laid down a new policy which gave primary emphasis to the development of agriculture. Industry was considered important, of course, but no longer could it lay first claim to the lion's share of available resources.

A peasant, too old to work in the fields, hand-threshes corn outside Canton.

THE FUTURE

Despite China's acknowledged progress in industrialization during the 1950's, and the remarkable success in developing nuclear power in the 1960's, the future clearly holds very formidable economic problems. One of the most important is certainly the rapidly increasing population, which continues to keep the standard of living low and to act as a brake on the industrialization process. Linked with this is the perennial problem of agricultural production. Official policy now proclaims "agriculture as the foundation and industry as the leading factor," but it is still uncertain that this concentration on agriculture can expand productivity to the point where it can support massive industrialization efforts while still feeding the nation. Indeed, a failure in agriculture may easily threaten the stability of the regime.

Inadequate natural resources could also prove to be a serious problem. For example, China seems to have only limited supplies of petroleum. However, the country has not yet been thoroughly explored geologically, and the vast territory may yet reveal rich holdings in oil and other resources.

Economics 439

The greatest problem of all could turn out to be political stability, or the absence of it. The balanced program of economic development undertaken since 1961 seems reasonable and constructive to most Western observers. But to Mao Tse-tung and his supporters, that program is much too bourgeois; it promises more commodities, more wealth, more things. The Maoists fear that more wealth could transform sturdy peasants and virtuous workers into greedy and selfish bourgeoisie. In Mao's view, economic progress at that cost is not success, but defeat. The creation of a new Communist man comes first. If Mao succeeds in that, presumably it will open the door to accelerated progress throughout the economy. If he fails, on the other hand, depressed economic conditions of the country will clearly reveal this failure.

Reviewing the Essentials

Present State

1. List as many reasons as possible why the Chinese Communists want to industrialize rapidly.
2. What are the chief obstacles in the way of achieving China's major economic goals?

Historical Origins

3. Explain why the characteristics of China's traditional economy caused her to fall behind the industrializing nations of the West. Account for the stability of the traditional economy.
4. How did Western penetration of China undermine and ruin the traditional economy? Compare with India.
5. What obstacles retarded and prevented China from introducing and adapting Western technology to develop an economy based on a coordinated agriculture and industry?

6. What was the condition of the economy when the Chinese Communists took over in 1949?
7. Examine the first Five-Year Plan in terms of: (a) date; (b) goals; (c) sectors of the economy that received priority; (d) extent and nature of outside aid; (e) outcome.
8. How does the commune differ from earlier reforms in Chinese agriculture? Why were the communes established?
9. What problems presently confront the Chinese economy and will determine whether or not it achieves its goal of modernization and industrialization?
10. What are some of the economic implications of the Cultural Revolution?
11. What problem was the Great Leap Forward designed to solve?

Explain, Identify, or Locate

"great leap forward"
commune system

collectivization of
living

collective-farm system
land-redistribution

handicraft industries

CULTURE: Anti-Western Westernizers

CHINA AND WORLD CULTURE

We have seen that China enjoyed social stability for many centuries before the arrival of Europeans. As a result of this stability, Westerners have tended to think of China as a country of no change. And since China has been technologically behind the West during the past century, Westerners have carelessly assumed that China was always backward. Nothing could be farther from the truth. Until a few centuries ago, China was generally abreast of or in advance of the rest of the world. Despite her relative isolation from other world centers, China's inventions, ideas, and products spread across Asia to stimulate and enrich other cultures.

Inventions. Many Chinese inventions and techniques are now used throughout the world. Silk, for example, was imported from China to the Roman Empire, until in the sixth century the Romans finally learned to make it themselves. The origin of porcelain is shown clearly by the name we usually give it, "China." Paper and printing, both of such incalculable significance for the development of civilization, were invented by the Chinese. Paper money and playing cards also originated in China, and the list could go on and on.

Plants. China also provided us with a number of fruits and other plants which are now commonly grown in the West, including peaches, apricots, lemons, oranges, and grapefruit. Most of these were introduced to Europe by way of the Arabs, although the grapefruit comes from a plant taken directly across the Pacific to the Western hemisphere. A more recent import is the soybean, which

ALAN BAND

Advanced production-line methods created these porcelain bowls, now drying in the sun before being painted.

is used to make a host of products, from edibles to steering wheels.

Probably the most important plant from China is tea. Although tea grew wild in both China and India very early, tea drinking probably originated in China, where it was known at least as early as the third century. Tea was taken from China to Europe in the 17th century, and was first sold publicly in London in 1657, where it was advertised as having such "particular virtues" as making one's body "active and lusty," "strengthening the weakness of the Ventricle or Stomack," and relieving "griping of the guts and looseness." In time, tea became popular throughout Europe, and virtually the national drink of England. It became an important item of international trade, and played a major role in the British economy.*

Science. Only in the past few years have we begun to learn about Chinese scientific achievements, largely because of the brilliant research of a British scientist, Joseph Needham. Although still a little-known subject, even a short list of some of China's scientific achievements speaks eloquently of the intellectual greatness of traditional China.

The Chinese have for thousands of years accurately observed and recorded heavenly phenomena. The earliest records of eclipses in the history of the world were made in China in the 14th and 13th centuries B.C. The Chinese recorded the kind of stellar explosion we call a nova as early as the 14th century B.C., more than a thousand years before the reports of the European Middle Ages. Chinese records of comets are by far the most complete of any civilization in the world. For example, Halley's comet was named after an English astronomer of the 17th and 18th centuries who used Western records from the 16th century to determine its periodicity. Yet the Chinese recorded this comet at least as early as the third century B.C., and from that time every appearance of the comet, which appears every 76 years, is described in Chinese records. Chinese records of sunspot activity also date from about two thousand years ago; the European discovery of sunspots was left to Galileo in the 17th century.

The Chinese invented clockwork at least three centuries before it was developed in Europe. The Chinese were evidently the

* See *Readings in World History,* "England's Tea Trade With China," p. 432.

A model of the observatory which was built at Peking by Kublai Khan in 1279 A.D. *The instruments in the foreground date from the seventeenth century.*

first people to use place value in numbers, and they certainly dealt with negative numbers earlier than any other civilization. The Chinese made relief maps some centuries before they appeared in the West, and also used the grid system for maps earlier than the West.

It would be possible to continue the list, but the point is clear: before modern times, Chinese observational and intellectual achievements in fields which we think of as primarily scientific and technological were far more advanced than we generally assume.

This raises some interesting and important questions. For example, since so many concepts and devices appeared in China earlier than they developed in Europe, what is the possibility that the European innovations somehow derived from China? This question cannot be answered with a single generalization. First of all, the whole process of cultural diffusion is still obscure. In any event, each device and idea must be separately examined. When that is done, we will doubtless find that some innovations were achieved independently in each civilization, with no influence from one to the other. In other instances, we may find that inventions or ideas that we thought were rooted completely in Europe were indirectly shaped or prompted by Chinese achievements. We already know that this happened with such items as paper and playing cards, so there is every reason to expect the future to reveal more such cases of Chinese influence on the West.

A still more important question is this: In view of China's inventive genius and intellectual power, why did the Chinese never develop modern science? Why was there never a genuine scientific revolution in China, or, for that matter, anywhere in Asia? We do not really know enough about China, or about the prerequisites for a scientific revolution to answer this question in a comprehensive way. But we can at least point out that the total orientation of Confucian society was anti-scientific.

Intellectually, Confucianism looked to the past, to tradition, and frowned upon innovation; science is innovative. Moreover, Confucian moralistic assumptions encouraged an anti-scientific reasoning. To a Chinese scholar, it might be a truism to say that the state would be well-governed if the emperor was personally virtuous, but this might not be acceptable to a more rigorous logic. Moreover, Confucian society did not reward scientific achievement, or attempts to put inventions to new uses. The scholar was honored, but scholarship meant study of the Confucian classics, not study of the real world. In addition, scholars considered it demeaning to work with their hands, an attitude that militated against working with tools and natural materials such as scientific experiments require. The long fingernails affected by Chinese scholars were supposed to testify that the wearer did not have to work with his hands.

Businessmen hesitated to invest money to put new inventions to commercial use not only because of the ingrained skepticism about the value of innovation, but also because the precarious position of the merchant in Chinese society made him wary about investing in anything that did not promise quick profit. Consequently, while artisans of genius might produce great inventions or discoveries in the course of practical work and trial and error experimentation, there was neither an intellectual elite nor a wealthy business class prepared to appreciate and apply them to practical problems.

NEW WAYS AND OLD

Rapid change is today the chief feature of Chinese culture, as it is also of politics and economics. Again the explanation is to be found in the violent intrusion of the West into old China, and the revolutionary repercussions that followed. China was hit almost simultaneously by the equivalents of the French Revolution, the Industrial Revolution, and the Russian Revolution. Young Chinese were introduced to Rousseau, the steam engine, Darwin, mass-producing industries, and Marx all at the same time. The revolutionary influences of nationalism, industrialism, communism, and science changed Europe gradually over a period of centuries. But today they are telescoped in China, so that they are turning that country upside down and inside out.

Some observers indirectly deny these far-reaching changes by emphasizing the parallels between the new and the old society. They say that the absolute rule of former emperors has its present counterpart in the preeminence of Mao Tse-tung, that members of the Communist Party correspond to the earlier ruling groups of bureaucrats, and that Marxism rationalizes the present order just as Confucianism did the earlier society. Yet every society has its elite, its intellectual justification, and its leaders. These parallels do not show that China is unchanging, unique, eternal. Indeed, it is clear that today's China differs profoundly from China of only a century ago.

Today Communist organization gives Mao Tse-tung far greater control over the people of China than the traditional monarchs ever had. The ideology of Confucius directed China's attention to the past, to the re-creation of the glories of previous periods, while Marxism, the Communist leaders say, turns the people toward a future of unlimited promise. The spread of education, inter-course with other nations, the new tools and new tasks that come with mechanization and industrialization, all are acting to change the relationships between individuals and groups in China, and the entire fabric of Chinese civilization. Some of this will become clear as we examine conflicts between the new ways and old in the family, the position of women, and the social classes.

THE FAMILY

The tradition of solidarity. No feature of China's traditional culture was more striking than the importance attached to the family. Family relationships were worked out so elaborately in China that the social system and the family system could be regarded as

one and the same thing. The family was the heart of the peasant's society in the villages and of the gentry's life in the cities. An individual found his place in society through his position within his family, to which he was subordinate.

This subordination of the individual to the group was one of the major characteristics of the Chinese family system. Other features included the absolute authority of the father, the subordination of wife and children, the general inferiority of the female to the male, and the domination of age over youth. Marriage was not looked upon as a love match to bring happiness to two young people. Rather its primary function was to produce sons through whom the family could be carried on. Sons remained in the household after marriage while the daughters left home at the time of the wedding. Marriages were always arranged, and men were permitted to take second wives or concubines, though only the wealthy could afford this luxury.

The Chinese family was a tightly knit group. Each member had certain rights and obligations according to his sex, his age, and his generation. The heavy stress laid upon loyalty to the family and, in particular, the loyalty of a son to his father, or filial piety, was the cement which held the family together.* Together the family shared the work in the field and the many hardships. But at the same time the family as a whole would gain great prestige by the success or fame of any of its members. The family also represented a religious unit which honored a common ancestry. This ancestor worship was another way of maintaining continuity of the line and perpetuating the good name of the family.

The ancient Chinese classics are full of references to the all-important role of the family in Chinese life. In the *Book of Poetry*

* See *Readings in World History,* "Family: Traditional and Modern," p. 463.

it is said, "No one is to be looked up to like a father. No one is to be depended on like a mother." Likewise during those early times, certain "criminals" were held to be worse than murderers. These "criminals" were:

> The son who does not serve his father respectfully, but greatly wounds his father's heart; and the father who cannot cherish his son but hates him; and the younger brother who does not bear in mind the evident intention of Heaven, and will not respect his elder brother; and the elder brother who forgets the tender regard in which he should hold his younger brother, and is unfriendly to him.[3]

This strong family solidarity gave the individual economic and social security and a stable life. But the price of this stability was often the highhanded bossing by a father of his wife and children, the friction between a mother-in-law and a daughter-in-law, and the frequent practice of nepotism. Another high price was the weakening of the state, since man's duty was first and foremost to his family rather than to his country.

Old ties weaken. For these reasons the family has been the prime target of reformers throughout the modern period of China. In fact, the changes brought about by the Communists are merely a great acceleration of changes which began a century ago with the impact of the West. These changes took place for various reasons. For one thing, modern culture was oriented more and more toward youth, toward young leadership which could provide the new ideas and the new methods needed. As younger leaders took over, the respect, prestige, and authority of elders dwindled and an essential bulwark of the old system weakened.

The growth of factory production also weakened the old family system. The economic tie of each member of the family to the family group was broken when the son or daughter of a peasant went to the city to work in a factory. For example, a daughter sent to work in the textile mills in Shanghai would receive direct wages. Usually she took most of it back to the family head, but she normally kept a little for herself and enjoyed making purchases possible only in the cities where the factories were located. Under such a system it is clear that a former village girl, and, even more, a village boy, would gradually begin to feel independent of the tight family system. Improved transportation and communications also loosened family ties. It made it easier for people to move from rural homes into the cities to look for work. The shift in population divided homes and broke up kinship groups. Thus the accent on youth, industrialization, and the growth of urban centers doomed the old family system.

Specific reforms accelerated the process of transformation already begun by these trends.

Young timbermill workers celebrate the establishment of the "Peking Municipal Revolutionary Committee." Here the mill's propaganda team carries news of the committee to the workers.

After the establishment of the Republic in 1912, attacks began to be made on the narrow family and clan loyalties, and on the all-important concept of filial piety. A unified nation, it was argued, could only be brought about by replacing narrow loyalties with a broader national loyalty. It was charged that individual initiative, self-expression, creativeness, and the adventurous spirit were being stifled by tight family controls. So the old institutions and customs had been under heavy attack long before the establishment of the Communist regime.

The many reforms and changes initiated by the Communists when they came to power further weakened the family system. For example, collectivization of agriculture undermined familial ties because possession of land had always been the economic basis for family solidarity. With the collectivization of land and animals, the individual family head lost his control over the means of production and the right to pass on family property to his descendants. In fact, with the appearance of the communes it seemed that the significance of the family as an economic unit would disappear completely, although this was prevented by the restoration of small plots to the peasants after the failure of the communes. The social function of the family has been further diminished by state welfare activities. For example, the establishment of nursery schools, orphanages, old-age homes, and the like, weakens the family by depriving it of some of its former functions.

THE POSITION OF WOMEN

In the disintegration of the old family system, nothing has been more conspicuous than the freeing of women from their centuries-old restrictions. Again this did not occur suddenly with the coming of the Communists to power. Thanks to the numerous Western influences, the position of women had been

Members of the women's militia practice drill routines within the walls of the imperial palace.

improving for some time. The New Culture Movement that emerged about the time of World War I laid great stress on the equality of the sexes and demanded an end to arranged marriages. As early as 1931 a Nationalist government law said that marriage should be based upon the consent of both parties and that the principle of equality should prevail with regard to divorce. Actually these radical notions were largely ignored in the countryside where the great majority of the people lived. In the cities, however, women did win more freedom because of the opportunities for education and for employment.

When the Communists became the rulers they drastically speeded up a trend that already was under way.* Their marriage law of May 1950 provided that: "Marriage shall be based upon the complete willingness of the two parties. Husband and wife are companions living together and shall enjoy equal status in the home." [4] In addition to equality

* See *Readings in World History,* "Marriage and Divorce," p. 471.

of status, women now were given equality of opportunity. They were allowed and encouraged to take jobs which hitherto had been reserved for men. Women became Communist Party leaders, government ministers, engine drivers, and managers of plants, as well as ordinary laborers. They were able to do all these things because of the government nurseries and common kitchens which freed them from their traditional duties. In the case of the communes we have seen that the women perhaps were freed more than they wished. But so far as the government was concerned, the new position of women meant a tremendous increase in the amount of labor power available to the Communists for the building up of China.

In summary, women have experienced extraordinary changes in a remarkably short time. The Chinese woman of today lives a different life and thinks different thoughts than she did only one or two decades ago. How great the difference is can be seen in the following poem composed by a woman worker who was illiterate at the time of the

Culture 447

Communist Revolution. Her lines were painted in ochre characters on the wall of the mess hall in the factory where she worked.*

> The machine is my husband,
> The factory is my family,
> The fruits of my labor are my children,
> The party is my father and my mother.[5]

SOCIAL SYSTEM

The Confucian ideal. The traditional Chinese notions of an ideal society have undergone equally far-reaching changes. The ideal society was one in which all groups or classes lived harmoniously together. Each individual recognized and accepted his place within that society and acted in a responsible manner according to certain principles. These principles were laid down by Confucius. Confucius taught that the father of the family as well as the father of the nation, the ruler, should exercise his authority with tolerance and benevolence. Members of the family, like the common people of the country, were supposed to be respectful and obedient. According to the Confucian scheme of social classes, there was a ladder of classes which, in descending order, included the scholars, farmers, artisans or craftsmen, and merchants.

This was the theory; actual conditions were quite different. In reality there were two classes: the small, educated ruling class and then the overwhelming majority of the population who worked the land. The upper, or, as it has usually been called, the scholar-gentry class, provided the leadership in the political, economic, and cultural life of the nation. Only the upper class enjoyed an education, and this education consisted largely of the classic literature. Thus political position, wealth, and education tested through the examination system, distinguished the ruling

* See *Readings in World History,* "Women: Traditional and Modern," p. 467.

group, while the illiterate masses worked hard, lived simply, and supported this ruling elite.

New classes emerge. During the last half of the 19th and the first part of the 20th century, the old class system gave way to a far more complex organization of society. The imperial examination system was abolished in 1905, a step which removed one criterion separating the two broad strata of the population. At the same time new economic opportunities resulting from Western influences made it possible for new social groups to emerge.

One of the first of these to emerge was a new military class which based its official political authority on military training and education. Second, a new Chinese middle class emerged around the foreign concessions or international settlements along the coast. Unlike the merchants and artisans in the hinterland, this new class developed relatively free from official interference. Third, urbanization resulted in the increase in the number of storekeepers and retail traders whose lives were tinged with Western influences and who understood the importance of China's modernization. Fourth, the growth in the number of industries produced a larger industrial working population in the cities. Fifth, there emerged a Western-oriented intellectual class in a position to carry on the tradition of a political elite.

Thus, before the Communists seized power, the social structure had already undergone some changes. For the vast majority of peasants, life remained a struggle with nature, tax-collectors, landlords, and warlords.* But the scholar-gentry no longer ruled the country; that role was now divided among militarists, party bureaucrats, Westernized intellectuals, and businessmen.

* See *Readings in World History,* "Peasant Life in the 20th Century," p. 460.

Although every aspect of Chinese life is changing rapidly, some traditional methods must for a time necessarily remain. A water buffalo is still used to plow rice fields near Canton.

The situation changed again under the Communist regime. The intellectuals and other leaders of the Nationalist period were forced to "reform themselves through labor," and "work with the masses" to acquire understanding of the life and values of the common people.* A new social elite emerged as members of the Communist Party took over the most important positions of responsibility and authority. Peasants and workers became celebrated as the heroes of the new society, exemplifying virtue, strength, humanity, and dedication to building a new society.

Since the early 1960's, much publicity has been given a new variant of the proletarian hero: a young person who excels in utter self-sacrificing devotion to the masses, to the Communist Party, and especially to the thought of Mao Tse-tung. The best-known example is Lei Feng, a young soldier whose every thought and act was for the Party and the people, and who has been glorified as the embodiment of the highest socialist virtues since his accidental death a few years ago. The whole nation was exhorted to "learn from Lei Feng," and national propaganda campaigns have idealized several other young heroes, all very similar to Lei Feng.*

LITERATURE

Together with radical change in the social system of China has gone radical change in the arts. The literary works produced under the Communist regime are strikingly different from those produced during past centuries. China has from early times been celebrated for a variety of literary forms. Outstanding among these were the great imperial histories which recorded carefully the achievements under the various dynasties. These historical works remain to the present day a valuable source for the study of China's past. Philosophical writing, especially the Confucian classics, set the standard in literary style. In

* See *Readings in World History*, "Work With the Masses," p. 473.

* See *Readings in World History*, "New Communist Heroes," p. 479.

Anti-American feeling is fostered by a play-demonstration in provincial China.

poetry, the Chinese did not produce great epics like those of the Indians or the Greeks. But they did write much poetry which frequently expressed a deep love of nature. In drama also, the Chinese were outstanding, creating plays based on historical and religious themes. Music was always prominent in their plays, providing an accompaniment to the rhythmic gestures and dances of the actors. So important was the role of music that Chinese plays might be compared with Western opera. Novels were traditionally considered to be vulgar, and not a form of art. Nevertheless, a number of magnificent and world-famous novels were produced.

These various types of Chinese literature were written in the literary language, which was very different from the simple spoken language of the mass of the people. Consequently this literature was written by, and for, the small class of scholar-officials and the educated merchants and landlords. With the passage of time this literature tended to become increasingly artificial and static. The same old subjects and the same ways of expression were repeated over and over again.

Long before the Communists came to power there was a movement against the stagnant literature of the past. A group of leading scholars in 1917 urged the use in literature of the simpler people's language rather than the traditional literary language. At the same time, a large number of Western works now were being translated into Chinese. With the new literature from abroad came new ideas concerning the purpose of literature. Now it began to be regarded as a means for social reform rather than for merely personal amusement or reflection.*

Today the Communists have taken over this literary trend but have carried it much further. They insist that all literature must have some social purpose. It must be designed specifically to help in the building of the new Communist society. Nor is this mere theory on paper. No literature is now being published in China unless it actually does make some contribution to the achievement of Communist goals.

The Communist government has been able to impose this extraordinary regimentation in various ways. One is its control of all magazines and publishing houses, so that nothing can appear in print without official approval. Another means is the establishment of the Central Literary Institute in Peking for the training of young writers from the working class. The intensive two-year course in the Institute gives not only training in writing but also a thorough indoctrination in communism. For this reason the students at the Institute include, in addition to the young apprentices, older established writers who are considered to be in need of indoctrination. Finally, the government requires writers to participate actively in the building of the new society by going out to the communes or the factories, or by taking part in mass campaigns for wiping out illiteracy or killing flies or planting trees.

As a result of all these controls, Chinese writers today are faithfully following Mao's orders that there can be no art for art's sake.

* See *Readings in World History,* "Literary Reform," p. 482.

Literature is a political weapon and an instrument for social building, just as much as tractors on the land or machines in the factories. So present-day authors are writing not about willows in the mist or beautiful court ladies or Confucian ethics. Rather they are calling on their readers to fight against "Western imperialism" or to help in a harvest campaign or to participate in an irrigation project. Consider, for example, the following two poems. The first, written about a thousand years ago, expresses the traditional Chinese love of nature. The second, written under the Communist regime, also refers to nature, but only to boast that even mountain tops shall be forced to yield crops.

> Amidst the mist-like autumn showers,
> Shallow the stony rapids flow;
> Its sprays besprinkle one another
> Up and down the egrets go.[6]

> Don't scowl, you naked mountain!
> We shall make you a set of new clothes.
> With a green gauze cap, and garlands of red
>   blossom,
> You'll have to change your name from "Bald-
>   Top"
> To "Flower-Fruit Eminence." [7]

FATE OF CONFUCIANISM

It is impossible to speak of the culture of China without emphasizing the influence of the main ideology of her civilization. The Chinese way of life was held together by the ideas of Confucius. The discarding of Confucian ideas in modern China has been in many ways more profound than the death of the old family system, the destruction of the traditional classes, and the abandonment of the old literature. This is true because the philosophy of Confucius provided the basis for the family and social system and literary tradition. The substitution of the ideas of Marx, which govern the new China, in place of the teachings of Confucius, which was the cement of the old society, is perhaps the most revolutionary change of all.

In our discussion of religions in China we saw how Confucianism was only one of many rival philosophies. Yet while Taoism and Buddhism, and later Christianity, became part of the stream of Chinese life, it was the beliefs of Confucius that provided the bedrock of Chinese thought and life. To understand why the Communists today are attacking Confucius, it is necessary to know what the old master taught.

Confucius believed that a society would function properly only if its members knew their places and acted accordingly. The proper social relationships between people of different stations in life were defined so that conduct according to these rules would assure proper behavior for the individual. If the individual acted properly, Confucius taught, then the family would be orderly, and when the family was right the state would be peaceful and all would be right under Heaven. Thus the first principle was "every man in his place." *

Confucianism provided the Chinese with a philosophy of government. It called for the subordination of the individual to the family and the family to the authority of the Son of Heaven. The emperor was expected to set an example of benevolent fatherhood. He and his officials, who were schooled in the teachings of Confucius, were presumed to be morally superior to the people. It was their duty to govern by the ethics of Confucianism rather than by a system of law. The aim of government was not to apply laws but to persuade the people to live in harmony and contentment. Moderation and respect for human relations were social and moral ideals but they also set the tone of Chinese political life.

* See *Readings in World History*, "The Thought of Confucius," p. 418.

In this case, as in so many others, we find that the Communists were not the first to attack Confucianism. During the 1920's many critics denounced it for smothering the individual in a web of family and social obligations. It was accused of paralyzing the initiative and enterprise of the people. The conservatism of Confucianism, with its stress on the past, was pointed to as the major cause holding up the progress of China.

Today the Communists are completing the uprooting of Confucianism as a living force: by weakening the traditional family system, ending the inferior position of women, and substituting a new class system for the old, all of which were supported by Confucianism. In their campaign against the old Confucian way of life, the Communists are using all the modern instruments of propaganda, including schools, newspapers, mass meetings, and radio.* The great gap separating the Communist China of today from the Confucian China of yesterday is evident in the following description of what 780 million people now are being taught and how they are being taught:

No one can escape the ubiquitous radio and loudspeaker. It started when I boarded the train at Chumchun, the frontier station, taking me to Canton. The radio haunted all my waking hours until I left the same frontier station on my way out of China, six weeks later.

The voice blares away at you in the bus, in the train, in the trolley, in sleepers and dining cars, on street corners, in villages, towns and cities—just about everywhere.

Even in a most backward and traditional village I saw a loudspeaker hidden in a treetop. You can escape the sun and the moon, but you cannot escape the radio and the loudspeaker. . . .

This is the most important medium for approved news—news for the nation's prog-

* See *Readings in World History*, "Schools: Traditional and Modern," p. 476.

ress, industrial output, how to make a smelter, how to defeat the American "imperialists," how to be a good Communist, how to be neat, how to denounce the rightists, how to behave in a train, how to kill a rat or a sparrow, how to cook a sweet potato—and a thousand other things, interspersed with traditional Chinese opera with its deafening gongs and cymbals and martial songs. . . .[8]

THE FUTURE

The judgment of Westerners on China has shifted back and forth. Matthew Ricci, a 16th-century Jesuit missionary, was dazzled by the rich culture and the efficient political and economic life of China. The accounts he wrote impressed the Europeans of his day with the high level of Chinese civilization.* By contrast, Europeans who travelled to China in the 19th century wrote of the decay of the government, the corruption of officials, and the poverty and backwardness of the people. In the 20th century prominent Chinese confirmed these unfavorable reports. One wrote in 1935 that China was "undoubtedly the most chaotic, the most misruled nation on earth, the most pathetic and most helpless, the most unable to pull herself together and forge ahead." [9] Today, judgments on China are mixtures of admiration and anxiety.

Out of the chaos of the past century a new civilization has been born in one of the great movements of history. One-fourth of mankind has been unified, regimented, and driven to catch up with the world. Material achievements have been remarkable. A child born in China today is likely to live longer, have more to eat, and enjoy a much better education than a child born a century ago. On the other hand, the same child is bound to be cut off from the rich heritage of an ancient civilization and subject to the

* See *Readings in World History*, "China's Impact on Europe," p. 429.

heavy pressures of a totalitarian government.

In the past century, the impact of Western armaments, machines, and ideas caused the breakdown of old China. Today the Communists have reunified the people and built a powerful state bent on achieving a century of progress in a few decades. We have seen some of the enormous difficulties they met in that ambitious task. Yet we have also seen the Chinese muster deep resources of strength and determination to overcome or adjust to those obstacles. We cannot know what the future holds for China, but of one thing we can be sure: whatever the future holds for China, China will have much influence on the future of the world.

EASTFOTO

Reviewing the Essentials

New Ways and Old

1. Explain: China was hit almost simultaneously by the equivalent of the French, Industrial, and Russian Revolutions.

2. Discuss this statement: No revolution, no matter how sweeping, can completely stamp out the effects of thousands of years of tradition.

The Family

3. Describe the family system of traditional China, noting distinguishing characteristics.

4. What price did the Chinese pay for the stability the family system gave their culture?

5. How and why did the penetration of Western nations in the 19th century change the family system?

6. What changes in the family system were initiated by the Kuomintang in 1931?

7. How have the Communist Chinese accelerated change in the family system as a means of achieving their objectives? Why has the family as an economic unit almost disappeared in China today?

The Position of Women

8. The status of Chinese women changed with the legislation passed by the Nationalists in 1931 and by the Communists in 1950. Cite important changes and describe the new Chinese woman.

Social System

9. Describe the social structure of traditional Chinese society. How did the Confucian ladder of classes differ from actual practice? Who were the elite? What advantages did they have?

10. What new social groups developed as a result of Western influence? Who became the new elite?

11. Who comprise the elite in Communist China? What advantages do the elite enjoy?

12. Who are the heroes of the New China? Why does the government publicize them?

Literature

13. What contributions did China make in literature and drama? What purpose did literature and drama serve in traditional Chinese society? What important change in purpose came as a result of Western ideas?

14. How are the Chinese Communists using literature and the arts as a means to achieve Communist goals?

Fate of Confucianism

15. Describe the Confucian way of life, including the (a) place of the individual as a person and citizen; (b) purpose of government. Why was it criticized as a barrier to progress and modernization? What modifications were introduced with the Revolution of 1911?

16. Why are the Communists attacking Confucianism? What means are they using?

The Future

17. Prepare a summary statement on the impact of cultural change on China and future prospects.

UNIT ACTIVITIES

1. We often read of the "greatness" of a civilization. Several teams of students should independently draw up criteria for "greatness." Applying this criteria, is there any justification for calling China's pre-modern civilization "great"?

2. Prepare for class discussion on this question: In what ways was Confucianism an appropriate philosophy to justify the social and political institutions of an agricultural society? This can lead into another and related problem: How was Confucianism incompatible with efforts at modernization? For information, see: *Readings in World History* (Boston: Allyn and Bacon, Inc., 1970); "The Thought of Confucius," pp. 418–419; "Confucian Indoctrination of the Masses," pp. 426–427; "The Civil Service Examinations," pp. 419–422; "Economic Values in Traditional China," pp. 450–451; "Peasant Poverty," pp. 424–426; "Family: Traditional and Modern," pp. 463–466; and "Women: Traditional and Modern," pp. 467–471. See also, H. G. Creel, *Chinese Thought From Confucius to Mao Tse-tung* (Chicago: University of

Chicago Press, 1953); and Kung-chuan Hsiao, *Rural China: Imperial Control in the Nineteenth Century* (Seattle: University of Washington, 1960).

3. Organize a debate or panel discussion in which one side argues that Western policies in China during the 19th and early 20th centuries were imperialistic and exploitative, and the other side defends Western policies.

4. Appoint two reporting teams, one to analyze the Kuomintang's relation to Chinese nationalism before 1949, and the other to present the Communist Party's relation to nationalism in the same period. Both teams should be sure to note that Chinese nationalism was not unchanging; it had different emphases, and involved different people, at different times. For information, see: *Readings in World History* (Boston: Allyn and Bacon, 1970); "American Policy in China," pp. 443–446; "Communist Guerrilla Tactics," pp. 442–443; "Young China Arises," pp. 440–441. See also, John King Fairbank, *The United States and China* (Cambridge, Mass.: Harvard University Press, 1958); "Modern China in Transition, 1900–1950," by Mary C. Wright; Albert Feuerwerker's (ed.), *Modern China* (Englewood Cliffs, N.J.: Prentice-Hall, 1964); C. P. Fitzgerald, *The Birth of Communist China* (Baltimore: Penguin Books, 1964); and Chalmers Johnson, *Peasant Nationalism and Communist Power: The Emergence of Revolutionary China, 1937–1945* (Stanford: Stanford University Press, 1962), particularly Chapter 1.

5. Analyze the role of Marxist ideology in the history of the Chinese Communist movement to 1949. To what extent has ideology served as a guide to action, and to what extent has it been used merely to justify action taken on other grounds? How have the Chinese modified Marxism, if at all? For information, see: Benjamin Schwartz, *Chinese Communism and the Rise of Mao Tse-tung* (Cambridge, Mass.: Harvard University Press, 1952); Maurice Meisner, *Li Ta-chao and the Origins of Marxism in China* (Cambridge, Mass.: Harvard University Press, 1967); John K. Fairbank, Conrad Brandt, and Benjamin Schwartz, *A Documentary History of Chinese Communism* (Cambridge, Mass.: Harvard University Press, 1952); and Stuart Schram, *The Political Thought of Mao Tse-tung* (New York: Praeger, 1963).

6. Imagine that you are in charge of the "China desk" of the State Department at a time when the Secretary of State comtemplates a major review of America's China policy. Prepare for the Secretary a memorandum explaining briefly but pointedly:

a) The general character of American policy toward China to 1945.

b) American objectives in China between 1945 and 1949, and the reasons for failure to attain them.

c) The chief premises of American policy toward China since 1949.

d) Present American objectives toward China.

e) What policy options are open to the United States to pursue those objectives?

f) What policy you recommend, and why.

In addition to your long experience at the China desk, you may find the following helpful: Robert Blum, *The United States and China in World Affairs* (New York: McGraw-Hill, 1966); John King Fairbank, *The United States and China* (Cambridge, Mass.: Harvard University Press, 1958); Akira Iriye (ed.), *U.S. Policy Toward China: Testimony taken from the Senate Foreign Relations Committee Hearings—1966* (Boston: Little Brown & Co., 1968); and Fred Greene, *U.S. Policy and the Security of Asia* (New York: McGraw-Hill, 1968).

7. Divide into two sides, one to take the Taiwan view of the mainlanders and the other to represent the view of the mainlanders toward the Taiwanese. Explore as completely as possible the attitudes and considerations that each must have when regarding the other. For information, see: George Kerr, *Formosa Betrayed* (Boston: Houghton Mifflin, 1965); Mark Mancall (ed.), *Formosa Today* (New York: Frederick A. Praeger, 1964); and Neil Herman Jacoby, *U.S. Aid to Taiwan* (New York: Frederick A. Praeger, 1967).

8. It has been said that the Chinese Communist government has mixed feelings about the intellectuals: it needs them badly, but does not trust them. What truth is there in this? For information, see: Fu-sheng Mu, *The Wilting of the Hundred Flowers: The Chinese Intelligentsia Under Mao* (New York: Frederick A. Praeger, 1962); Theodore H. E. Chen, *Thought Reform of the Chinese Intellectuals* (Hong Kong: University of Hong Kong Press, 1960); Robert Jay Lifton, *Thought Reform*

and the Psychology of Totalism, A Study of "Brainwashing" in China (New York: Norton Co., 1961); and Roderick MacFarquhar, The Hundred Flowers Campaign and the Chinese Intellectuals (New York: Praeger, 1960).

9. Read several descriptions of Red Guard activities. What evidence can you find that Red Guard activity was prompted by a genuine upsurge of revolutionary feeling? What evidence is there that the Red Guards are being manipulated? For information, see: Robert Trumbull (ed.), This is Communist China (New York: David McKay Co., 1968); and Hans Granqvist, The Red Guard (New York: Frederick A. Praeger, 1967).

10. Read at least one Chinese short story or novel written before 1900, and one written after that date. Discuss the differences in the literature of the two periods, with particular attention to the assumptions and premises with which authors approached their work. A few of the many translations available are: Pre-modern: Cyril Birch, Stories From a Ming Collection (London: Bodley Head, 1960); The Dream of the Red Chamber, translated by Wang Chi-chen (New York: Twayne, 1958); and All Men Are Brothers, Pearl Buck's translation of China's great novel of virtuous bandits (New York: John Day, 1933). Wu Ching:

tzu, The Scholars (Peking: Foreign Languages Press, 1957) is a satirical novel translated by Gladys Yang and Hsien-yi Yang. After 1919: Anything written by Lu Hsun (or Lusin), Pa Chin, Mao Tun, or Lau Shaw. Wang Chi-chen has translated a collection of Contemporary Chinese Stories (New York: Columbia University, 1944).

11. A few students interested in art might attempt to prepare a report for the class about art in Communist China. For information, see A. C. Scott, Literature and the Arts in Twentieth Century China (New York: Doubleday, Anchor Books, 1963); and Michael Sullivan, Chinese Art in the Twentieth Century (Berkeley & Los Angeles: University of California Press, 1959). The selected works of Mao Tse-tung contain some essays pertaining to art questions, and the writings of recent travellers often contain observations on art. However, all of these sources are unsatisfactory because they are largely writing about art rather than art itself from which the class and the reporters can make their own judgments. The task is for the reporters to use their imagination to find illustrations of recent Chinese art work. They might try magazines, propaganda pamphlets, papers, books of photographs, advertisements, and every other conceivable source.

SELECTED READING

● H. G. Creel, The Birth of China (New York: Frederick Ungar Co., 1937, 1961) is over thirty years old, but still not surpassed as a simple and fascinating introduction to Chinese antiquity. A very readable history of pre-modern China is Rene Grousset, The Rise and Splendor of the Chinese Empire (Berkeley and Los Angeles: University of California, 1953). A briefer and more general overview, including modern China's relation to the past, is Ping-chia Kuo, China (London: Oxford University Press, 1963). Robert Goldston, The Rise of Red China (New York: Bobbs-Merrill Co., 1967) sketches recent Chinese history, with particular emphasis on the 20th century.

● For modern China several pamphlets offer brief, readable, but knowledgeable surveys: The Foreign Relations Series pamphlet Chinese Dilemma, by John Armstrong (Chicago: Foreign

Relations Project, 1956); and Nos. 99, 136, and 179 in the Foreign Policy Association Headline Series. Also good are China and the World (1953) by Tillman Durdin; Mao's China (1959) by Peggy Durdin; and Communist China: Crisis and Change, by John Wilson Lewis. Oliver Bell, The Two Chinas (New York: Scholastic Book Services, 1962) introduces the two Chinas.

● Works of literature provide a convenient and entertaining way to enter the world of China old and new. Pearl Buck's classic work The Good Earth (New York: John Day, 1931) offers an unsurpassed view of Chinese peasant life. The same author's My Several Worlds: Abridged for Young Readers (New York: John Day, 1954) recounts her experiences in China. Life of the poor classes in the city is glimpsed in Lau Shaw's Rickshaw Boy (New York: Reynal & Hitchcock, 1945). John

ALAN BAND

Hersey tells of life on the Yangtze River in *A Single Pebble* (New York: Knopf, 1956).

There are quite a few volumes of photographs available. One very recent and excellent such volume is by Emil Schulthess, *China* (New York: The Viking Press, 1966), and includes essays by Edgar Snow and Henry Hamm. For the Life World Library, Loren Fessler and the editors of *Life* have written a readable book with many excellent illustrations, *China* (New York: Time Incorporated, 1963).

FURTHER READING

● The best all-round introduction to Chinese history is John King Fairbank's *The United States and China* (Cambridge: Harvard University Press, 1958). L. Carrington Goodrich, *A Short History of the Chinese People* (3rd rev. ed., New York: Harper, 1959) presents much information on pre-modern material culture in very few pages. C. P. Fitzgerald, *China: A Short Cultural History* (New York: Frederick A. Praeger, Inc., 1961) emphasizes cultural patterns of pre-modern China. An excellent synthesis of the latest scholarship on China is in the two-volume encyclopedic textbook *A History of East Asian Civilization* (Boston: Houghton Mifflin). Volume one, *The Great Tradition* (1960) is by John King Fairbank and Edwin O. Reischauer, and covers the period to the coming of the Europeans. Volume two, *The Modern Transformation* (1965), is by Fairbank, Reischauer, and A. Craig. O. Edmund Clubb, *Twentieth Century China* (New York: Columbia University Press, 1964) is a clear and excellent treatment of recent history. Franklin W. Houn, *A Short History of Chinese Communism* (Englewood Cliffs, N.J.: Prentice-Hall, Inc., 1967) is a straightforward account. *Anatomy of China: An Introduction To One Quarter of Mankind* (New York: Weybright and Talley, 1968), by Dick Wilson, is an excellent contemporary introduction.

● Following are a few of the many excellent works dealing with special aspects of China. The standard geography text is George B. Cressey, *Land of the 500 Million* (New York: McGraw-Hill, 1955). Alexander Eckstein, *Communist China's Economic Growth and Foreign Trade: Implications for U.S. Policy* (New York: McGraw-Hill,

1966) is informative, and the bibliography is a good guide to more specialized economic studies. Harold C. Hinton, *Communist China in World Politics* (Boston: Houghton Mifflin, 1966) offers a comprehensive and detailed survey of China's foreign affairs. C. K. Yang, *Chinese Communist Society: The Family and the Village* (Cambridge, Mass.: The MIT Press, 1965) contains two volumes in one: one deals with the Chinese family in the Communist revolution, and the other is about a Chinese village in early Communist transition. Jean Chesneaux, *The Chinese Labor Movement 1919–1927* (Stanford: Stanford University Press, 1968) is excellent, and virtually the only study of the labor movement. Joseph Needham is producing a monumental work in many volumes on *Science and Civilization in China*, which is being published by Cambridge University Press; six volumes have already appeared.

● The most comprehensive survey of Chinese philosophy is by Fung Yu-lan, *History of Chinese Philosophy* (Princeton: Princeton University Press, Vol. I 1952, Vol. II 1953). The same author has a shorter treatment titled *A Short History of Chinese Philosophy* (New York: The Macmillan Company, 1953); Derk Bodde translated both works. The clearest and simplest introductory survey of Chinese thought is probably H. G. Creel, *Chinese Thought From Confucius to Mao Tse-tung* (Chicago: University of Chicago Press, 1953). Creel has also written *Confucius: The Man and the Myth*, which was later published in paperback as *Confucius and the Chinese Way* (New York: Harper Torchbook, 1960).

● Many fine collections of documents are now available. William Theodore de Bary (ed.), *Sources of Chinese Tradition* (New York: Columbia University Press, 1960) includes translations from Chinese antiquity to modern times, mostly from works of Chinese philosophers and political and religious writers. *The Essence of Chinese Civilization*, by Dun J. Li (ed.) (Princeton: D. Van Nostrand Co., Inc., 1967) treats only traditional China, but contains a wide variety of materials relating to society, government, economics, law, and other areas. Ssu-yu Teng and John King Fairbank, *China's Response to the West, A Documentary Survey 1839–1923* contains some very interesting translations recording the reaction of Chinese to the Westerners. Franz Schurmann and Orville Schell have edited a three volume series published by Vintage Books in 1967 under the general title *The China Reader*. The first is titled *Imperial China: The Decline of the Last Dynasty and the Origins of Modern China, the 18th and 19th centuries*. The second is *Republican China: Nationalism, War, and the Rise of Communism, 1911–1949*. The third is *Communist China, Revolutionary Reconstruction and International Confrontation, 1949 to the Present*. These three volumes contain some original translations, and also readings taken from the studies of Western scholars. Theodore H. E. Chen (ed.), *The Chinese Communist Regime, Documents and Commentary* (New York: Frederick A. Praeger, 1967) is a good collection of material relating to the government, the Communist Party, and social institutions of contemporary China, accompanied by brief but knowledgeable commentary.

● There are still surprisingly few biographies of Chinese notables, although a number are in preparation. The best study of Sun Yat-sen is Harold Schiffrin, *Sun Yat-sen and the Origins of the 1911 Revolution* (Berkeley: Univ. of Calif., 1969). Chiang Kai-shek is described in Emily Hahn, *Chiang Kai-shek: An Unauthorized Biography* (Garden City Doubleday, 1955). Only two of the many warlords have received book-length treatment: *Chinese Warlord: The Career of Feng Yu-hsiang*, by James E. Sheridan (Stanford: Stanford University Press, 1966); and Donald Gillin, *Warlord: Yen Hsi-shan in Shansi Privince, 1911–1949* (Princeton: Princeton University Press, 1967). Maurice Meisner, *Li Ta-chao and the Origins of Chinese Marxism* (Cambridge, Mass.: Harvard University Press, 1967) is an excellent account of the life of the first Chinese Marxist. Several volumes have appeared on Mao Tse-tung: George Paloczi-Horrath, *Mao Tse-tung: Emperor of the Blue Ants* (New York: Doubleday, 1962); Robert Payne, *Portrait of A Revolutionary: Mao Tse-tung* (New York: Abelard-Schuman, rev. ed., 1962); Jerome Ch'en, *Mao and the Chinese Revolution* (London: Oxford University Press, 1965); and Stuart Schram, *Mao Tse-tung* (New York: Simon & Schuster, 1966).

● The book earlier cited by Franklin Houn, *A Short History of Chinese Communism*, is the most convenient brief survey of Chinese Communism. There are many books on specialized aspects of this subject, although many become quickly dated. A. Doak Barnett, *China After Mao* (Princeton: Princeton University Press, 1967) sums up current trends to see what they foreshadow. The Sino-Soviet dispute is analyzed, and many supporting documents translated, in two volumes by William E. Griffith, *The Sino-Soviet Rift* (Cambridge, Mass.: The MIT Press, 1964); and *Sino-Soviet Relations, 1964–65* (Cambridge, Mass.: The MIT Press, 1967). Hu Chang-tu, *Chinese Education Under Communism* (New York: Teachers College, Columbia University, 1962), contains translations with commentary. John Wilson Lewis, *Leadership in Communist China* (Ithaca: Cornell University Press, 1963), examines the theory and practice of leadership in China.

● Taiwan has not attracted much scholarly attention. *Formosa Today* (New York: Frederick A. Praeger, 1964) edited by Mark Mancall, contains essays on various aspects of life and politics in Taiwan since 1949. George Kerr, *Formosa Betrayed* (Boston: Houghton Mifflin, 1965) is a passionate book by a knowledgeable writer; it is strongly anti-Nationalist. Neil Herman Jacoby, *U.S. Aid to Taiwan* (New York: Frederick A. Praeger, 1967) studies the success of American aid programs in Taiwan.

● On the subject of Sino-American relations, the work by John King Fairbank earlier cited, *The United States and China,* covers the whole history of Chinese-American contacts in broad terms. Herbert Feis, *The China Tangle: The American Effort in China From Pearl Harbor to the Marshall Mission* (Princeton: Princeton University Press, 1953) makes some sense out of that confused era. The State Department's White Paper has been published by Stanford University Press (1967): *The China White Paper, August 1949,* edited by Lyman P. Van Slyke. Robert Blum's, *The United States and China in World Affairs* (New York: McGraw-Hill, 1966), edited by A. Doak Barnett, is a thoughtful volume on the present and the prospects of Chinese-American relations. Akira Iriye has edited a small volume, *U.S. Policy Toward China: Testimony taken from the Senate Foreign Relations Committee Hearings—1966* (Boston: Little Brown & Co., 1968). Fred Greene,

U.S. Policy and the Security of Asia (New York: McGraw-Hill, 1968).

● Michael Sullivan, *An Introduction to Chinese Art* (Berkeley & Los Angeles: University of California Press, 1961) is an excellent introduction, although not as well illustrated as an art book should be. The same author has treated a smaller period in *Chinese Art in the Twentieth Century* (Berkeley & Los Angeles: University of California Press, 1959). A standard study is Laurence Sickman and Alexander Soper, *The Art and Architecture of China* (Penguin Books, 1956).

● A number of pre-modern novels have been translated, and many short stories. A convenient collection is *Anthology of Chinese Literature From Early Times to the Fourteenth Century* (New York: Grove Press, 1965), edited by Cyril Birch. *The Dream of the Red Chamber,* perhaps China's greatest novel, has been translated from a German version by Florence and Isabel McHugh (New York: Pantheon Books, 1958), and another version is Wang Chi-chen's translation from the Chinese (New York: Twayne, 1958). *All Men Are Brothers* (New York: John Day, 1933) is Pearl Buck's translation of a celebrated Chinese novel. Pearl Buck's own novel, *The Good Earth* (New York: John Day, 1931) is one of the few works by a Western writer that deserves a place in a list of Chinese fiction. Harold Shadick has translated a late 19th-century Chinese novel of social commentary, *The Travels of Lao Ts'an* (Ithaca: Cornell University Press, 1952), and has included an informative introduction. Cyril Birch has translated some famous Chinese stories in *Stories From a Ming Collection* (London: Bodley Head, 1960).

● Lu Hsun is certainly the most celebrated Chinese writer of the 20th century. Wang Chi-chen has translated several of Lu's stories in *Ah Q and Others* (New York: Columbia University Press, 1941). Wang has also translated stories by various authors in *Contemporary Chinese Stories* (New York: Columbia University Press, 1944). Translated works by Mao Tun include *Midnight* (Peking: Foreign Languages Press, 1957) and *Spring Silkworms and Other Stories* (Peking: Foreign Languages Press, 1956). *Rickshaw Boy* (New York: Reynal & Hitchcock, 1945) is by Lao Shaw, a Chinese writer well known in the West.

INDIA

...India is a very distinctive country with distinctive ways of looking at things. Its...philosophy of life is gradually changing in the changing world, is being affected by other countries, by other factors, and by our own inner development. India has shown in its past history a great capacity to adapt itself to changing conditions. Sometimes the adaptation has been slow and that has been harmful, but it has been adapting itself.... Today we face the world, influenced very greatly by what has happened in Europe and in America, by the tremendous scientific and industrial development...which we wish to have in our own country, but with the distinctive outlook of India.

Jawaharlal Nehru

BASIC FACTS: The Spirit That Endures Conquest and Conflict

For centuries, India has been known as a land of contrasts and paradoxes. American images of India reflect some of these contrasts: the mental picture of the gaunt face and matchstick limbs of the famine-stricken peasant contrasted with the traditional image of the bejeweled maharaja with his palaces and elephants;* the millions of uneducated people side by side with the historic respect for education and learning.

One of the most difficult paradoxes to explain about India concerns the co-existence of social inequality on the one hand with social stability and parliamentary government on the other. Caste has been responsible for extreme inequalities of wealth, power, and status. Yet few countries have had fewer social revolutions or greater continuity in their history. Moreover, India is one of a few countries in Asia or Africa which has so far succeeded in adopting parliamentary democracy and universal suffrage.

Occasionally, Indian and American interests and problems seem similar. Both India and the United States have democratic governments. Both have had stormy relations with Communist countries. Both have serious problems with large minority groups. College students in both countries have been very impatient and have caused many disturbances. Yet in spite of these similarities, the differences between the two countries are profound. It is not simply that India is largely rural and the United States urban and industrialized. It is deeper than that. Indian values, thought patterns, and customs are unlike our own. The visitor to India begins to sense the differences even as he first hears the sounds of the Indian city: the hubbub of bargaining in the bazaar, the rhythmic

call of the street hawkers, the creaking wheels of carts carrying goods from the factories, the high pitched voice from a minaret summoning Muslims to morning prayer, the bells ringing in a Hindu temple.

The special character of India's culture is the product of many historical developments. In many cases, these historical developments have resulted in contemporary problems unknown to Americans. Before looking at these contemporary problems and their historical antecedents, however, one must understand certain basic facts about the human and physical geography which has helped create the environment in which Indians live.

GEOGRAPHY

What is India? Before we can talk about India, we must first decide what India is. This is a problem of definition. If we define India as being that area of the world where Indian ideas and culture have predominated at various times in the past, then India would be very large. Some scholars once called this area "further India" or "greater India," and it encompassed most of Southeast Asia, including Indonesia, Indo-china, Burma, and Thailand. If, however, we limit ourselves to a strict geographic definition we might say that India consists of a very large, triangular peninsula that juts out from the Asian land mass and is bounded on two sides by water and on the third by the Himalayas, the highest mountains in the world. The modern term for this area is South Asia. Finally, we might restrict ourselves even further and define India as a nation-state. From this point of view, India is one of the two major states which compose the Indian Peninsula. The other is Pakistan, and

*See *Readings in World History* (Boston: Allyn and Bacon, Inc., 1970), "Land of Contrasts," p. 488.

The diversity of the Indian subcontinent—its varied languages, peoples, and technology, is illustrated by the city of Karachi in West Pakistan.

both nations came into existence in 1947 when almost two hundred years of British rule of the Indian Peninsula came to an end. In this unit, we shall use the word India when discussing the pre-1947 period to mean the whole peninsula. In discussing the peninsula since 1947, we shall refer to India and Pakistan as separate states which together are called South Asia.

Geographic divisions. There are three main divisions of the Indian subcontinent or peninsula. First are the mountain barriers of the north: the Himalayas, the Hindu Kush, the Karakorams, and many lesser ranges. They form a mighty arc of still largely unexplored mountains over 2500 miles in length. Here are the highest mountains in the world, the Greater Himalayas, which have an average altitude of four miles over a distance of 1000 miles. They taper down in the east to the almost impenetrable tropical rain forests of Assam and in the west to the burning deserts of Seistan and barren badlands of Makran. These towering ramparts, steaming jungles, and barren deserts have served to isolate India from the rest of Asia. The northwest area is populated by restless frontier tribes who, until a few years ago, carried on clan warfare with terrible ferocity and frequently raided the fertile plains to the south of the mountains.

The second geographic division of India is the great Indo-Gangetic Plains. These form a great arc at the foot of the mountain barriers and stretch from the Arabian Sea to the Bay of Bengal. Averaging about 200 miles in width, they extend for more than 2000 miles and form one of the largest areas of continuously cultivated agricultural land in the world. This is the cradle of Indian civilization and the political and economic heart of the subcontinent. Delhi is the political center of this area and Calcutta and Karachi are the major regional ports. Almost two-thirds of the people of the subcontinent live along the mainstreams and tributaries of the Indus, the Ganges, and the Brahmaputra which rank as the region's principal rivers as well as rating among the world's greatest. Where the combined waters of the Ganges and Brahmaputra flow into the Bay of Bengal there is some of the most densely populated land in the world, the density reaching over 1000 persons per square mile in some areas.

Running through the Indo-Gangetic Plains from the north-west frontier eastward to Calcutta is the Grand Trunk Road, the crowded highway described so vividly in Kipling's *Kim*. Travelling east on the Grand Trunk Road, one moves gradually from the dry, sandy, and barren terrain characteristic of the Middle East and north-western Pakistan into the humid, moist, and lush landscape of monsoon Asia. Camels and wheat fields become fewer and finally disappear, to be replaced by water buffalo, rice paddy fields, palm trees, ponds, and rivers. But west or east, the stream of carts, pilgrims, merchants, peasants and hill people, Hindus and Muslims, continues in its endless variety. As Kipling said, it is "such a river of life as nowhere else exists in the world." [1]

The third great geographic division of India is the Deccan Plateau. It is a raised and tilted block of ancient rock that slopes gently from west to east. The generally hilly land of the plateau is bordered by narrow coastal plains which are somewhat wider on the east coast than on the west. It is separated from the Indo-Gangetic Plains by the relatively low but heavily forested Vindhya Mountains. The interior of the Deccan was at one time heavily forested but now, because of its continued occupancy by man and animal, the plateau takes on the aspect of a short-grass savanna with scattered trees. Along the eastern and western coasts of the Deccan there are deltas and coastal plains with fertile rice fields and lush tropical foliage.

The climate. Although India extends across almost thirty degrees of latitude, temperature does not vary much throughout the country. India is shielded from the cold, continental air of Central Asia by the mountain barriers of the north. The weather is generally hot and humid during the wet season of the southwest monsoon and dry during the northeast monsoon period. Rainfall is controlled by the prevailing winds of the monsoons. The southwest monsoon beginning in June blows across thousands of miles of warm ocean, so that it is heavily moisture-laden when it reaches India. It sheds its rain when mountains, such as the Western Ghats and the Himalayas, force it to rise. As it rises, the air cools, the moisture condenses, and the rain falls. The Indian farmer looks to the gods for this gift from heaven each June. Without it, his main crop will not grow, for about 90 per cent of the annual rainfall comes during the monsoon. Hardly a year passes when the southwest monsoon does not fail in some part of the subcontinent and in some years it fails over large areas, as in 1965 and 1966. It retreats from the end of September until around the beginning of January. At that time the northeast monsoon takes over and blows from the land toward the sea. Since it can pick up very little moisture except as it blows over the Bay of Bengal, it yields very little rain.

Rivers and coastline. It should be noted that vast areas of India are inaccessible by water. This is in marked contrast to Europe which is crisscrossed with rivers and has a coastline composed of an endless number of gulfs, inlets, and bays. As a consequence, Europe has one of the longest coastlines in

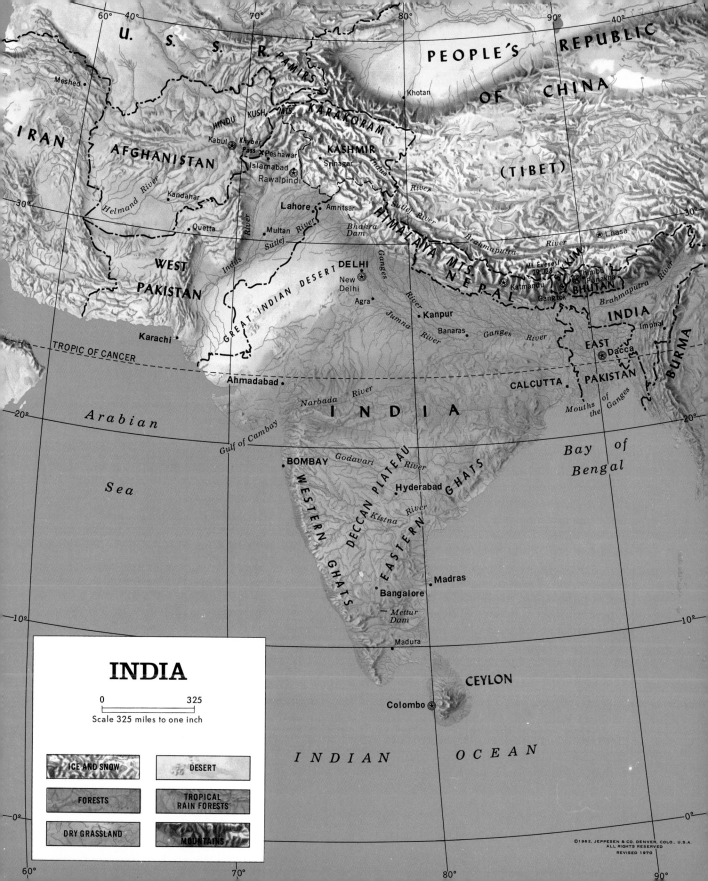

U. S. S. R.

IRAN

AFGHANISTAN

Meshed

Kabul

Kandahar

Quetta

Karachi

WEST PAKISTAN

PEOPLE'S REPUBLIC

OF CHINA

(TIBET)

Khotan

Lhasa

HINDU KUSH MTS. KARAKORAM

PAMIRS

KASHMIR

Khyber Pass Peshawar
Islamabad
Rawalpindi

Srinagar

Lahore Amritsar

Multan

Bhakra Dam

Sutlej

Indus River

Sutlej River

HIMALAYA MTS.

NEPAL

Mt. Everest 29,028

Katmandu

SIKKIM

Thimbu Punakha

BHUTAN

Gangtok

Brahmaputra River

Brahmaputra River

INDIA

Imphal

GREAT INDIAN DESERT

DELHI
New Delhi
Agra

Ganges

Ganges River

Jumna River

Kanpur

Banaras

Ganges River

EAST PAKISTAN

Dacca

BURMA

TROPIC OF CANCER

Ahmadabad

CALCUTTA

Mouths of the Ganges

Arabian

Sea

Gulf of Cambay

Narbada River

INDIA

Bay of Bengal

BOMBAY

Godavari River

DECCAN PLATEAU

Hyderabad

EASTERN GHATS

WESTERN GHATS

Kistna River

Bangalore

Madras

Mettur Dam

Madura

CEYLON

Colombo

INDIAN OCEAN

INDIA

0   325

Scale 325 miles to one inch

ICE AND SNOW	DESERT
FORESTS	TROPICAL RAIN FORESTS
DRY GRASSLAND	MOUNTAINS

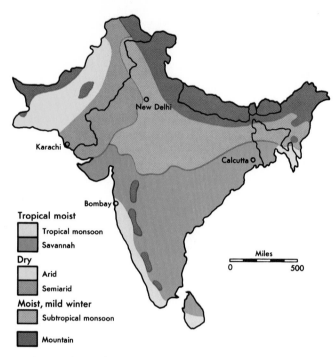

SOUTH ASIA - CLIMATE

Legend:

Tropical moist
- Tropical monsoon
- Savannah

Dry
- Arid
- Semiarid

Moist, mild winter
- Subtropical monsoon
- Mountain

the world, measuring over 50,000 miles. India, on the other hand, has a very smooth and short coastline only 3400 miles in length. Europe also has many rivers flowing in every direction and opening up the whole continent to water transportation. India, by contrast, has only three navigable rivers. These are the Indus with its five tributaries; the Ganges and Jumna which together flow into the Bay of Bengal; and the Brahmaputra which supplies water transportation to eastern India and Pakistan. The rest of India's rivers are seasonal. They are not fed by mountain snows but instead depend on the monsoon rains which strike in June and again in October. The rest of the year these rivers dry up completely or become tiny streams.

Geography and history. We must now ask how geography has influenced the course of Indian history. The most obvious effect of

India's geographic position has been to make her both accessible and inaccessible to the rest of Asia. The almost impenetrable mountains of the north, the desert region of the west, and the tropical jungle of the east have cut India off from the Asian mainland. Thus for long periods of time India has been isolated, although never to the extent of Australia which was almost completely separated from the main currents of Asian civilization.

Despite such formidable barriers, there are, high up in the Hindu Kush mountains, passes that open into the northern plains of India. The most famous of these is the Khyber Pass, which leads directly into the Indus Valley. From here it is an easy step to the Ganges and the whole of northern India. Consequently, the northern plains have been repeatedly invaded by the peoples of Central Asia, who were attracted by the wealth and fertility of the Ganges and Indus Valleys. The invaders from Asia, however, hardly ever succeeded in conquering all of India. So the North of India saw the periodic rise and fall of empires, but the Deccan and the South were rarely included in these states.

AREA COMPARISON
U.S. - SOUTH ASIA

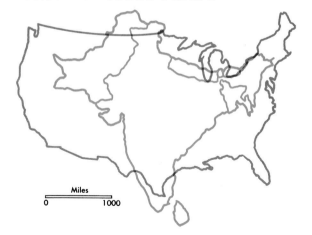

The reason for this brings us to another important effect of geography, the lack of communications in India.

Communications. The empires of the North often tried to conquer the lands to the South, but they rarely succeeded. Most of central India can only be entered on foot, and the hills and forests of the central Deccan formed an effective barrier to invading armies from the north. In fact, it was not until the arrival of the British in the 18th century, and the development of railroads in the 19th century, that India achieved any degree of unity of communications. Even so, it was not until 1928 that Delhi in the far north was connected directly by rail with the southern coastal city of Madras. This is as if New York and San Francisco had not been connected by railway until 1928; they were in fact joined in 1869.

Politically speaking, we might conclude then that India has tended to become neither like Europe with its multitude of independent nation-states nor like China with its single political and cultural empire. Instead, India has tried to achieve full unity, but without success until modern times. And one reason is the influence of the geographic forces we noted above. So political and economic solidarity was not attained until the arrival of the British with their control of sea power and their development of roads and railroads. India today, however, even after two hundred years of English political rule, is still not completely unified. As we shall see, this is due to the great variety of peoples, languages, and religions.

PEOPLES

The peoples of South Asia are as varied as their land. The total population of the peninsula in 1970 was over 650 million, of whom almost four-fifths live in India. Together the countries of South Asia have more people than all of Africa, South and Central America, and Australia. The three main races of mankind, the Caucasoid, the Mongoloid, and the Negroid, are represented in South Asia's population; although the great majority of the people are predominantly Caucasoid. Of these the darker Dravidians in the South are of the Mediterranean type, whereas the lighter northerners belong to the proto-Nordic branch. In the Himalayan and sub-Himalayan area, tribal peoples exhibit certain Mongoloid characteristics.

The regions of South Asia are perhaps as culturally diverse as the countries of Europe. Although the regions share caste and Hinduism, each has a special language and culture. Indians and Pakistanis often classify and stereotype their countrymen according to their region and community. And over the centuries the various regional types have not fused into a single people. Instead, each group has tended to develop its own culture, customs, and language.

The Khyber Pass.

EDITORIAL PHOTOCOLOR ARCHIVES

LANGUAGES

Language reflects the diversity of modern India and the frequent invasions and political fragmentation of the past. There is no single language understood by all or even half the population. Instead, there are 14 major languages comprising over 500 different dialects. These languages are divided into two main groups. First are the Indo-European or Aryan languages of the North which are related to the classical language of Sanskrit and are thus very distant cousins of English. Here are some words which reflect their common origin:

| Aryan Hindi | mata | na | tu |
| English | mother | not | thou |

Second are the Dravidian languages of Southern India. The most widely spoken Aryan languages are Hindi, Bengali, and Marathi, and the most common Dravidian languages are Telugu and Tamil. Today the government of India would like to establish Hindi as the one language for all India. There is, however, serious rivalry between languages, and this rivalry divides some regions from others. Many Indians object to Hindi as the language of all India; thus the government has been forced to retain English alongside Hindi as an official language.*

RELIGIONS

South Asia is not only a land of many tongues; it is also an area of many religions. Most South Asians are Hindus and most Hindus live in India. When we discuss the lack of social and political unity in India in the following pages, it is important to remember that Hinduism spread almost everywhere and provided an underlying cultural unity. The major exception to the generalization

* See *Readings in World History,* "India's Language Dilemma," p. 490.

about cultural unity is the Muslim community. About one-fourth of all South Asians are Muslims, most of whom live in Pakistan. Even so, India today has the third largest Muslim population in the world, exceeded only by Pakistan and Indonesia. In addition to Hindus and Muslims, there are many other smaller religious groups such as the Jains, Parsis (Zoroastrians), Sikhs, and Christians.

India also was the home of one religion which no longer plays a vital role in the country, except for the new untouchable converts, but which is still the dominant faith in vast areas of Southeast Asia. That is Buddhism, which was founded by the Indian Prince Gautama (563–483 B.C.), who was known to his followers as the Buddha or the Enlightened One. We have already seen that this religion started in India, spread widely through Asia, and then virtually died out in the country of its origin.

Outside of these organized religions, there are many tribesmen who live in the hills and forests and worship spirits. Unlike the priests and leaders of the other religions, the tribal priests, medicinemen, and sorcerers are usually illiterate and their philosophies are unsophisticated. For many centuries the tribesmen of the hills and forests were isolated from the more advanced cultures of the plains and coasts. But during the last century, many tribals have been partially Hinduized or Christianized. The 1961 Census estimated that only about 30 million of India's 439 million people were still outside the organized religious groups.

SOCIAL ORGANIZATION

Caste is a social institution peculiar to India. There are thousands of castes in India. Traditionally a member of one caste could not eat with or marry a member of another caste.

Moreover, some castes had great prestige and high status, others were regarded as little better than animals, while most castes fell somewhere in between. The caste system was based on a deep and emotional fear of contamination. Each caste thought contact with other castes, occupations, and foods (such as meat) was contaminating. The fear of close contact with other castes helps explain India's diversity and lack of unity. Today caste is changing but is far from dead.

HISTORY

Reasons for diversity. India is one of the oldest civilizations in the world. Between 3000 and 2500 B.C., Indians developed their social organization and agriculture sufficiently to maintain a technically advanced, urban culture in what is now West Pakistan. The growth of Indian culture may be traced from that time to the present. But until the British conquered the entire subcontinent, India was never politically united for more than a few years at a time. India's political history is the story of frequent unsuccessful attempts to build large empires. In this respect India's history has been the opposite of China's. Unity has been the rule rather than the exception in the case of China; with India it has been the other way around.

Why was India rarely united until the coming of the British? One reason, we have suggested, is the separation of people into castes. A second explanation is to be found in geography. We have seen that the Vindhya mountains and forests of the northern Deccan made penetration into southern India difficult. So there were many empires in northern India and many in southern India but few included both parts of the peninsula. Another explanation is to be found in the Indian ideal of conquest. Customarily, a conqueror did not displace a defeated raja but instead left him to rule provided he paid tribute and

Pakistani Muslims pray at a mosque.

acknowledged the superiority of the imperial power. This decentralized form of government contributed to the frequent political fragmentation.

Religion may hold still another clue to political disunity. Many of the best Indian minds were drawn to religious speculation and practices. The spiritual well-being of the individual seemed more important than the political and military achievements of the state or the material progress of society as a whole. In contrast to the Chinese who were interested in problems of government and personal conduct, many Indians concentrated on increasing religious insights and

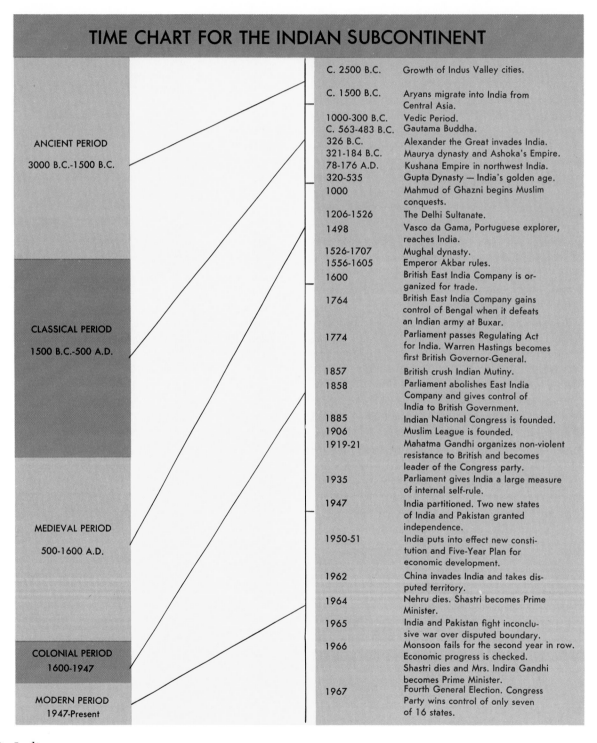

TIME CHART FOR THE INDIAN SUBCONTINENT

ANCIENT PERIOD 3000 B.C.-1500 B.C.		
CLASSICAL PERIOD 1500 B.C.-500 A.D.		
MEDIEVAL PERIOD 500-1600 A.D.		
COLONIAL PERIOD 1600-1947		
MODERN PERIOD 1947-Present		

C. 2500 B.C.	Growth of Indus Valley cities.
C. 1500 B.C.	Aryans migrate into India from Central Asia.
1000-300 B.C.	Vedic Period.
C. 563-483 B.C.	Gautama Buddha.
326 B.C.	Alexander the Great invades India.
321-184 B.C.	Maurya dynasty and Ashoka's Empire.
78-176 A.D.	Kushana Empire in northwest India.
320-535	Gupta Dynasty — India's golden age.
1000	Mahmud of Ghazni begins Muslim conquests.
1206-1526	The Delhi Sultanate.
1498	Vasco da Gama, Portuguese explorer, reaches India.
1526-1707	Mughal dynasty.
1556-1605	Emperor Akbar rules.
1600	British East India Company is organized for trade.
1764	British East India Company gains control of Bengal when it defeats an Indian army at Buxar.
1774	Parliament passes Regulating Act for India. Warren Hastings becomes first British Governor-General.
1857	British crush Indian Mutiny.
1858	Parliament abolishes East India Company and gives control of India to British Government.
1885	Indian National Congress is founded.
1906	Muslim League is founded.
1919-21	Mahatma Gandhi organizes non-violent resistance to British and becomes leader of the Congress party.
1935	Parliament gives India a large measure of internal self-rule.
1947	India partitioned. Two new states of India and Pakistan granted independence.
1950-51	India puts into effect new constitution and Five-Year Plan for economic development.
1962	China invades India and takes disputed territory.
1964	Nehru dies. Shastri becomes Prime Minister.
1965	India and Pakistan fight inconclusive war over disputed boundary.
1966	Monsoon fails for the second year in row. Economic progress is checked. Shastri dies and Mrs. Indira Gandhi becomes Prime Minister.
1967	Fourth General Election. Congress Party wins control of only seven of 16 states.

on achieving internal serenity and spiritual salvation. This emphasis may have lessened men's interest in the affairs of government.

Finally, an important reason for the disunity of India is the great gap that has separated the government from the people. Foreign conquerors penetrated into India much more frequently and deeply than they did into China. These foreign rulers often did not establish close relations with the millions of peasants who lived in the villages. The ethnic pride of the conquerors and the Indian caste system limited the number of marriages between the conquerors and the indigenous people. Moreover, India lacked a Chinese-type examination system for recruiting local people into government. These factors limited access to the ruling class. In addition, local groups were largely self-sufficient. Village and caste institutions assumed many governing functions which in other societies belonged to the territorial state. The rulers, therefore, concentrated on collecting as high taxes as possible, while the peasants preferred to be left alone to live according to their age-old customs.* So far as the peasants were concerned, government often meant ruthless taxation and few services, thus the less contact with the government the better.† This gulf between the rulers and the ruled was a great weakness for India. It left the country open to invasion since the mass of the people felt no desire to fight for any government. This explains in part why so many invaders were able to enter India and why a handful of British could conquer and rule a vast peninsula with hundreds of millions of people.

Turning to the various stages in the development of India, we can use the familiar divisions of the ancient, classical, medieval, and modern periods.

* See *Readings in World History*, "Village Life," p. 495.
† See *Readings in World History*, "Fruits of Despotism," p. 492.

Ancient period, 3000–1500 B.C. The ancient period in India is the time of the mysterious Indus Valley civilization of the dark-skinned Dravidians. We noted earlier that this civilization began about 2500 B.C. and reached a very high level before it was overwhelmed, probably by Aryan invaders from the north. The Aryan conquest was part of a vast migration of peoples that brought the Greeks into Greece, the Persians into Persia, and the Latins into Italy. The Aryan or Indo-European speaking tribes filtered into India about 1500 B.C. By that date they had made themselves the masters of most of northern India. This date marked the beginning of the classical period of Indian history.

Classical period, 1500 B.C.–500 A.D. The Aryan invaders were barbarians in comparison to the original inhabitants of the Indus Valley. But they were better fighters and they had superior metallurgy. Gradually they settled down and developed a civilization that was a fusion of Aryan and Dravidian elements. The basis of this civilization was Hinduism, which was not only a religion but also a philosophy of life and a social system. Later in this unit we shall consider the nature of Hinduism, which remains to the present day the foundation of Indian society.

Here we should note that the distinctive Hindu social institution, caste, seems to have developed out of the Aryan conquest. The light-skinned Aryan rulers tried to preserve the purity of their culture by discouraging intermarriage between different classes. The Brahmin priests classified the population into four *Varna* (literally, colors). The *Kshatriyas* (rulers and warriors) and *Brahmins* (priests) were at the top. Next came the *Vaishyas* (farmers and merchants). At the bottom were the *Shudras* who served the upper three Varna. During the classical period, these four categories lost much of their meaning with the multiplication of exclusive castes which would not interdine or intermarry. In theory Indian society is made up of the four Varna plus the untouchables; in reality it is divided into thousands of castes for whom Varna has little meaning.

We do not have exact information concerning events in India during the two thousand years of the classical period. The Hindus did not keep full historical records as did the Chinese. So there are long centuries of Indian history that still remain largely unknown. We do know, however, that numerous empires rose and fell, though none of them, as we have seen, was able to unite the entire peninsula. The three most important of these empires were the *Maurya* (325–184 B.C.), the *Kushana* (50–220 A.D.), and the *Gupta* (320–647 A.D.).

The Maurya Empire was founded by Chandragupta Maurya following the death of Alexander the Great in 322 B.C. Alexander had invaded India in 326 B.C. and occupied the northwestern part of the peninsula. But only four years later Alexander died and, in the confusion that followed, Chandragupta Maurya established his kingdom. It grew rapidly and reached its height during the reign of Emperor Asoka (273–232 B.C.). Asoka, famous for his devotion to the Buddhist religion, tried to govern his great empire according to the rules of Buddhism, and he also helped to spread Buddhism to surrounding countries. His services to Buddhism may be compared to Constantine's to Christianity. Buddhism was also popular with Indian merchants. The merchants had profited from the unification of India under the Mauryas. Travel and trade were safer, commercial exchange was easier. As the merchants increased their wealth, they began to resent the low place assigned to them in the caste system. Because Buddhism was implicitly opposed to caste, many merchants promoted it and sought higher status outside of Hinduism.

The third reason for Buddhism's spread was its association with popular religious cults. Prior to Asoka's time, Hinduism had been a religion of the highest castes only. Common village folk worshipped earth spirits at sacred spots near their villages and were largely ignored by the Brahmin priests. The Buddhists identified themselves with these popular sacred spots by burying the Buddha's ashes and other holy relics there. In this way, Buddhism became a mass religion. Soon after Asoka's reign the Maurya Empire began to decline, until finally it fell apart into warring fragments. When the last Maurya emperor was slain in 185 B.C., India experienced one of its many periods of disorder and invasion. Buddhism no longer had powerful royal backing and Hinduism, perhaps in competition with Buddhism, also began to absorb popular religious practices. A Central Asian dynasty named the Kushana was able to conquer and rule an empire for over two centuries, but this was limited to the northwestern part of the country. Not until 320 A.D. were the Ganges and Indus Valleys again united, this time under the Gupta Dynasty.

The Gupta Empire marks the high point of India's classical period. Arts, medicine, and literature all flourished. Gupta mathematicians and astronomers discovered the approximate value of *pi* as 3.1417. Great universities, probably the first in the world, offered instruction in various subjects and provided free tuition, board, and lodging to talented students. In short, this period of Indian history is like the Periclean Age in Greece. But eventually the Gupta Empire, like the others before it, began to deteriorate. Foreign invaders speeded the decline, so that long before the last Gupta ruler died in 647 A.D., India was in the midst of another period of chaos. For this reason the end of India's classical age is arbitrarily set at 500 A.D. By that time foreign barbarians had

Indicative of the magnificent art of the Gupta period is this sixth-century fresco from the Ajanta Caves in Maharashtra, India.

overrun the Gupta Empire, just as they were overrunning at the same time the Roman Empire in the West.

Medieval period, 500–1500 A.D. During this period, caste grew stronger, perhaps in reaction to conquests by foreigners; Hinduism completed its triumph over Buddhism; and devotional and mystical religious cults gained at the expense of formal scholarship and philosophy. The most important single development in India during the medieval period was the appearance of the Muslims. This occurred in three stages. First Arab Muslims occupied Sind at the mouth of the Indus River in 712. They made little impression upon their Hindu neighbors but Islam at least had a foothold in India. The second stage began about 1000 when Turkish Mus-

lims from Central Asia, including Afghanistan, started raiding India to plunder. Most famous of these marauders was Mahmud of Ghazni, whose destruction of Hindu temples and idols was honored in the Islamic world for centuries.

During the 12th and 13th centuries, Mahmud's successors altered the policy of hit-and-run raiding to one of permanent conquest and colonization. The word of India's wealth spread among the peoples of Central Asia. Adventurers descended onto the plains to fight or convert the infidel, idol-worshipping Hindus and to serve in the Muslim administrations and armies. Five Turkish and Afghan dynasties, known collectively as the Delhi Sultanate, ruled in Delhi from about 1200 until 1526 A.D. Once in India, the Muslims were often threatened

Basic Facts 473

by rival clans in Central Asia. The most famous invader was Timur, known to Europeans as Tamerlane or Timur the lame. In 1398 Timur sacked Delhi, massacred thousands of Hindus and Muslims, and deported many artisans to his central Asian capital, Samarkand, to beautify the city.

The result of these invasions and rivalries was that not one but many Muslim kingdoms were established in northern and central India. In the South, various Hindu states succeeded in resisting the Muslim advance long after the North was conquered. During Muslim expansion in the North, the South became the home of a revitalized Hinduism, based upon a theology stressing the closeness of man's soul to god, popular devotional songs composed by poet-saints, and an elaborate missionary organization.

Almost the whole of India fell under Muslim rule during the third stage of Muslim penetration. This final, brilliant period was that of the Mughal Dynasty (1526–1707). The word Mughal is a corruption of the term Mongol. The founder of the Mughal Dynasty, Babur, was descended from the two greatest Central Asian conquerors, the Mongol Genghis Khan and the Turkish Timur.

Mughals and Europeans, 1500–1763. Both the Mughals and the Europeans began to arrive in India at about the same time. The Mughals came by land as powerful conquerors and the Europeans came by sea as humble merchants. The Mughals had an immediate impact upon India. Their army-administrators imposed a greater degree of governmental centralization than India had previously experienced. By contrast, the Europeans made little impression on India at first. They were concentrated on the sea coasts, far from the inland capitals of the Mughals. But after the disintegration of the Mughal Empire in the 18th century, the European influence was profound.

Akbar the Great is represented with symbols of strength and wisdom. Compare this interpretation of Akbar with that on page 139.

The Mughals. The founder of the Mughal Empire was Babur who, from his headquarters high in the Hindu Kush Mountains, swooped down on India with a host of 12,000 warriors. At first satisfied with mere plundering raids, in 1526 he conquered Delhi and made it his capital. His sons extended the empire until it reached its height during the reign of his famous grandson, Akbar, who ruled from 1556 to 1605. Akbar was not merely a great conqueror whose empire stretched from Central Asia to southern India and from Persia to the Ganges; he was also an outstanding administrator, artist, and patron of learning. Every day he held three meetings; one for dispensing justice, the second for routine administrative business, and the third for discussing literature, art, religion, philosophy, and politics. One reason for Akbar's success was his religious tolerance, which won him the support of influential Hindu subjects. As part of his policy of broadening the base of Mughal power, he married three Rajput Hindu princesses from north-west India. He also invited Jesuits, Zoroastrians, Hindus, and Muslims to debate in his presence the merits of their respective religions. In his statesmanship, military successes, and intellectual curiosity, Akbar was comparable to contemporary monarchs such as Elizabeth I of England and Philip II of Spain.

The Mughal Empire was efficiently governed by a well-paid civil service. Most officials were Muslim, and of these the majority under the early Mughals were new immigrants from Persia and Central Asia. But Hindus, especially Rajputs, also served as governors, generals, and finance ministers in the Mughal administration. An elaborate system of taxation provided revenue for the royal treasury which during Akbar's time received annually about £40 million compared to Elizabeth of England's £.5 million. The Mughal Empire was outstanding in its cultural as well as its material achievements. It was during this period that the Taj Mahal was built, that a school of artists produced delicate and well-known miniature paintings, and that poets wrote verses which were recited in many parts of the Muslim world. In short, the Mughal court was a brilliant center of culture which spread its influence over the whole of South Asia.

Akbar's successors failed to adhere to his high standards. Some lacked ability and energy, others lacked his religious tolerance.

For example, the last of the great Mughal emperors was Aurangzeb (1658–1707), a man of great courage and talent. But he was an orthodox and puritanical Muslim who felt that Muslim rule in India was threatened by laxness in observing Islamic practices. He needlessly alienated the Rajputs with whom Akbar had allied himself and he wasted years in South India trying to subdue the independent Muslim sultans. Gradually he lost the allegiance of the Muslim aristocracy. When the Marathas of western India and other Hindu groups rebelled, Aurangzeb's demoralized army and administration failed to give him adequate support. Large areas of India sank into strife and anarchy as Mughal governors, army officers, subordinate rajas, and even landlords declared independence.

European merchants. Political chaos was not new to India. What made the breakup of the Mughal Empire particularly important, however, was the fact that Europeans with superior military technology and organization were present to exploit the Mughal disintegration. When the first Europeans had come, beginning with Vasco da Gama in 1498, the technological and political gap between the European countries and India was not yet wide. For 250 years after da Gama came, most Europeans were mere visitors in a few Indian ports. They humbly begged for permission to carry on trade, and the Mughal emperors allowed them to do so because they seemed harmless and insignificant. For example, in 1712, more than 200 years after the first appearance of the Portuguese, a British merchant in India, John Russell, sent an appeal to the Mughal emperor that began with these groveling words: "The request of the smallest particle of sand, John Russell, President for the English East India Company, with his forehead at command rubbed on the ground, and reverence due from a Slave. . . ."[2]

But even at this time the Mughal Empire was weakening. Emperor Aurangzeb's attempt to turn India into an orthodox Muslim state had hastened the decline. In the Deccan, the Hindu Marathas, under their great leader Shivaji, represented a powerful opposition which Aurangzeb had spent many years in fighting. After his death the Mughal Empire began to fall to pieces; civil war broke out; and independent principalities sprang up in many parts of India. In the turmoil of the times, only the Marathas were able steadily to extend their power and make a bid for empire, only the Marathas and the European trading companies. The more the Mughals and the Marathas fought, the better chance the Europeans had to establish themselves in the ports and to push inland. The most successful were the British. In a series of campaigns they defeated their French rivals as well as some local Indian rulers. By the Treaty of Paris of 1763, the French agreed to limit their activities in India as well as get out of Canada. The British now had a firm hold on Calcutta and began spreading out over the rich province of Bengal. During the following decades the British extended their control more and more until the 1840's, by which time they were the masters of the entire peninsula. For the first time India was under one rule, and it remained so until 1947 when the British departed and two new states, India and Pakistan, took their place.

In the remainder of this unit we shall see how the British conquered India and how their rule left a deep imprint that remains to the present day.

Reviewing the Essentials

Geography
1. In what ways do Western people have conflicting ideas concerning India? Why do Westerners know so little about the real India?
2. Study the map of India and give the following information:
   a. Locate and explain what is meant by Greater India, the subcontinent of India, India the nation-state.
   b. Name and locate the three main geographical divisions of the Indian subcontinent, and give the characteristics of each.
   c. Locate India's three major rivers and compare them with those of Europe.
   d. What are the distinctive features of India's coastline? Compare it with the coastlines of Europe, the Soviet Union, and the United States.

People
3. Give the present population of the Indian Peninsula; India; Pakistan. Compare the present population of India with that of the United States, the Soviet Union, and China.

4. What are the main racial types in India's population? Name and locate the more important regional types of people living in India.
5. An important characteristic of India's population is the tremendous variety of people. In what ways is this both a strength and a weakness for a young nation?

Language
6. Explain this statement: "The lack of historical unity is apparent in the languages of India."
7. Name the major languages spoken in India. What problem does the multiplicity of languages create for India? What are the official languages of India today?

Religion
8. Name the two major religious groups in India today with the approximate number in each group. Name other religious groups in India. What great world religion which originated in India is no longer a major religion in the country?

History
9. India, one of the oldest civilizations in terms

of history, was rarely united until the British came. Explain why.

10. On a map locate the center of India's ancient civilization. When did it reach its height? What people conquered it? When?

11. What was the basis for the new civilization that developed in India during the classical period?

12. Locate on an outline map of India the three major empires of the classical period: (a) Maurya, (b) Kushana, (c) Gupta. What conditions marked the rise and fall of each of these great empires?

13. The medieval period in Indian history was the period of Muslim invasions. When did these occur? What effect did they have on India's development and history?

14. Why is the early modern period important in Indian history? Who were the important rulers of this period? Show the territorial extent of their empires on the map of India.

15. What achievements of India's Muslim rulers give evidence of a high degree of civilization in the Indian Peninsula before 1500 A.D.?

16. When did Europeans arrive in India? How were they received by the Mughal emperors? Account for this attitude toward Western Europeans.

17. What events in India gave Europeans the advantage they needed to gain control of India?

18. What nations were rivals for the control of India? What is the importance of the Treaty of Paris, 1763, in the history of India?

Explain, Identify, or Locate

Alexander the Great	Hindu Kush Mountains	Madras	Indo-Gangetic Plain
Tamerlane	Khyber Pass	Karachi	Deccan Plateau
Babur	East Pakistan	Lahore	Punjab
Aurangzeb	Ceylon	Indian Ocean	Assam
Vasco da Gama	Delhi	Arabian Sea	Seistan
Dravidians	2500 B.C.	Ganges	Makran
Aryans	326 B.C.	Jumna	Sind
Mughals	712 A.D.	Indus	
Hindus	1526 A.D.	Brahmaputra	
Himalayas	1763 A.D.	Northern Mountain Barrier	

POLITICS: British Rule and the Indian Response

PRESENT STATE

When we talk about the impact of the West upon the rest of the world, it is important to realize that there have been two kinds of influences. First, there has been science and her companion, the Industrial Revolution. Faith in science means that man has confidence that he can improve his environment through the use of reason and the scientific method. This faith has had revolutionary effects everywhere it has spread. Americans may take scientific enquiry for granted but it is this scientific attitude which most clearly distinguishes a modern from a traditional society. In traditional India, for example,

man believed that his status and his environment were predetermined by the gods or by events in a previous life or reincarnation. Therefore, he did not ordinarily believe that he was capable of improving his surroundings. In India today, however, the belief that through inquiry, experiment, and scientific method, man may improve his material and political condition is challenging the old resignation and fatalism. Indians are applying steam and atomic power to tasks which man alone could not perform; they are testing new seeds and fertilizers, and they are searching for ways to bring

Modern methods to reduce the age-old threat of malaria include spraying insecticides on fly-breeding spots such as garbage heaps and scattering lime in the open sewer systems.

WHO (PAGE)

isolated villagers into the mainstream of national life.

The other Western influence of great importance to India is the belief in equality and liberty. Again, Americans tend to accept this belief as something no longer revolutionary because it has been part of our culture since the 18th century. However, the American belief in the equality of all men was qualified, and originally not all Americans were treated equally or guaranteed the right to vote. India, however, did not wait for education to spread or for caste discrimination to lose its grip before introducing universal suffrage and compensating for past discrimination. Instead all adults, most of whom are illiterate, have been given the right to vote; and untouchables and other "backward classes" have received special help and privileges. This confidence in the judgment of her people and this commitment to the rights and dignity of the individual distinguish India from many other countries.

Before taking up the story of modern India, it is important to hold a number of ideas firmly in mind. First, as we have already mentioned, India is not an entirely united nation, being divided by geography and a variety of races, languages, and religions. Second, India, of all the countries of Asia, has had the longest exposure to Western ideas and institutions. She had been subject to British rule for almost two hundred years, and so she has been greatly influenced both by Western technology, such as railroads, telegraph, and factories, and by Western ideas, such as liberalism, nationalism, and individualism. Third and finally, India may usefully be contrasted and compared with the second colossus of Asia: China.

Both India and China have borrowed heavily from the West, although not always the same ideas and institutions. For instance, India is adapting liberalism and democracy

to her needs, but China is adapting another Western idea, communism. Both countries are in the process of becoming vast industrial nations. Both face many of the same problems, such as the feeding, clothing, and housing of their countless millions who constantly live on the verge of starvation. Both nations are trying to adapt their ancient cultures to the demands of industrial and urban life and to new concepts of social justice. Both, in short, are engaged in an immense struggle to achieve a common end, although the means used to attain that end are very different.

Independence. Both India and Pakistan were created when the British Parliament passed the Indian Independence Act on June 3, 1947. By this act, India and Pakistan became independent states, though they remained within the British Commonwealth of Nations as Dominions, similar to Canada and Australia. The change from British rule to independence took place formally on August 15, 1947, when the Union Jack was hauled down and the crescent of Pakistan and the wheel of India took its place.

The Constitution. Independence brought many challenges in its wake. Indians had to agree among themselves how they would govern their country. Nationalist leaders of the Congress Party had to redirect the energies which had been devoted to opposition and obstruction of British rule to the task of building a nation. Having consistently attacked the British for their authoritarian ways, the politicians now set out to fulfill their promises of democracy. They began with valuable assets such as 25 years of experience with Indian majority rule in the provinces and a dedicated, honest national civil service. With remarkably little opposition or debate, a constitution was accepted which extended the right to vote to all

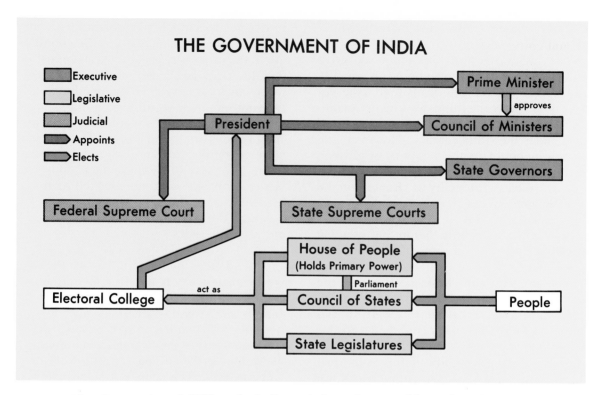

THE GOVERNMENT OF INDIA

Executive
Legislative
Judicial
Appoints
Elects

Prime Minister
President
approves
Council of Ministers
State Governors
Federal Supreme Court
State Supreme Courts
House of People
(Holds Primary Power)
Parliament
Electoral College
act as
Council of States
People
State Legislatures

The Constitution of 1950 made India an independent republic within the British Commonwealth, but India does not recognize the British monarch as do most other members. The President is chosen by an electoral college composed of members of parliament and the state legislatures. The Prime Minister, chosen by the President, but actually the head of the majority party of Parliament, wields the real power granted to the President by the Constitution. However, the President can dismiss the Prime Minister if he feels he or she has lost the confidence of the majority of Parliament, or he can dissolve Parliament and call new elections.

adults, provided for separation of church and state, and guaranteed a wide range of democratic freedoms. The constitution took effect on January 26, 1950, and gave India a federal republican type of government.

The Indian political system. India today is a federal state governed by a constitution which owes much to both American and British sources,* although the Indian federal

* See *Readings in World History*, "Constitution of Independent India," p. 508.

system differs from our own in several ways. When the 13 American colonies rebelled and broke away from the British Empire, two things were uppermost in the minds of our constitution-makers. First was to limit the power of the central or federal government; and second was to protect the rights and independence of the 13 colonies who still thought of themselves as semi-sovereign states. Thus our country is a federal system in which the authority of the central government is severely limited and the states retain all powers not specifically reserved to the federal government.

The authors of India's Constitution were influenced by different considerations. When she broke away from the British Empire, India was not revolting against the extreme central authority of the English crown and parliament. Instead, she was rebelling against foreign domination. Nor was there a long heritage of independence in the various Indian states. As a result, the framers of the Indian Constitution vested most of the power in the central government and left the state governments weak in theory. This principle is developed in three ways. First, the residual powers are specifically given to the central government. This means that all powers not stated as belonging to the various state governments automatically belong to the federal government. Second, in case of an emergency the central government can seize and assume the functions of the state governments. This happened on a number of occasions, including 1959 and 1964 when the national government at Delhi dissolved the legally elected Communist governments of Kerala. "President's Rule," as it is called, was also imposed on other unstable states in the late 1960's.

A third power of the federal government is its recruitment and control of the all-India Administrative Service. I.A.S. officers occupy chief posts in the state as well as federal governments. Finally, the Constitution gives to the federal government control over defense, foreign affairs, currency, internal communications, and commerce.

Political reality, however, is very different than the formal language of the Constitution in some important respects. The balance of power between each state and the federal government is bound to be somewhat different in India with only 17 large states than in the United States which is divided into 50 units. More importantly, most of the Indian states have distinctive cultures and languages, which create strong feelings of separate identity. In some regions, notably in the South and the Northeast, separatist movements threaten national unity. In the 1967 General Election, the *Dravida Munnetra Kazagham,* a regional party founded to resist "Aryan imperialism" from the north, defeated the ruling Congress Party in Madras so decisively that the Congress won only 49 of the 234 seats in the state Legislative Assembly. The extent of state autonomy was demonstrated during the 1966–67 famine when states with surplus food refused federal government requests to release extra food for the states suffering from famine. Thus India faces the danger of disintegration unless her leaders can find a balance between federal authority and state autonomy.

Government structure. Today India consists of 17 states, 9 federal territories, 2 protectorates, with the central government located in New Delhi. The federal government is composed of two houses of unequal power. The weaker upper house, or *Rajya Sabha,* is something like our Senate since it represents the various states of India. Almost all its 250 members are elected by the state legislatures and not by the people directly. The lower house, called the House of the People or the *Lok Sabha* is much more powerful. It has 521 members, almost all of whom are elected by universal suffrage throughout India.

Besides the two houses of the Indian parliament there is the president of the Republic who is elected by the members of the state and central legislatures. The great difference between the Indian president and our own is that the Indian president does nothing without the advice of his ministers. He somewhat resembles the king of England, who is little more than the symbolic head of state. The real head of government in India is the prime minister, who is the leader of the majority party in the *Lok Sabha.*

Finally, there is the judiciary. India has a Supreme Court which has the power to decide if laws and their interpretation by lower courts are consistent with the constitution. However, India's Constitution is easier to amend than the American Constitution. As a result, it is sometimes possible for the ruling party to change the Constitution if the Supreme Court rules that its program violates the Constitution.

Elections. India held its first general election in 1951–52 when 176 million voters had the right to go to the polls, most for the first time. Twenty thousand candidates stood for elections to the *Lok Sabha* and the State Assemblies. The difficulties of an election on such a scale were enormous.* The balloting had to be spread out over four months. In the Himalayas, it had to be held in October

* See *Readings in World History,* "Election in Independent India," p. 509.

before winter set in. In eastern India the monsoon season had to be considered, since some parts of the Assam Valley get as much as 425 inches of rain during the wet season. Language was also a problem. The ballot had to be printed in 14 different tongues, and in some cases no printing type existed for the native script. It has been calculated that if the Indian electoral roll were printed, 40 names to a page and bound together, the whole would form a book 600 feet thick!

To meet the needs of India, the democratic process has had to be changed and modified. National parties have to be identified by symbols since so few can read. For instance, the yoked oxen and plow is the symbol of the Congress Party, and when the voter sees that sign on the ballot he places his X mark under it if he desires to vote for that party. The people also have had to learn what democracy means and how it operates, and the records are filled with cases similar to that of the elderly peasant farmer who promised his vote to all 12 candidates. He kept his promise by tearing his ballot into 12 equal

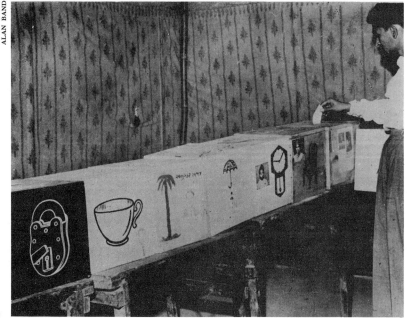

Ballot boxes in the Pakistan national election of 1960 included candidate's photographs and party symbols as identification— a necessary measure where many citizens are not yet able to read.

parts and placing one in each ballot box. Possibly never before has democracy had to face such difficulties.

Congress Party rule. The Congress Party dominated Indian politics during the first 20 years of independence. As the party of Gandhi and the freedom movement, and as the champion of democratic socialism, it won large majorities in the *Lok Sabha* not only in 1952, but in 1957 and 1962 as well. Some observers were distressed by the dominance of the Congress Party and the failure of a two-party system to develop. There was considerable opposition to the Congress Party (the opposition won between 52 and 55 per cent of the vote for the *Lok Sabha* in each of the first three general elections), yet the opposition was so fragmented that the Congress Party consistently won an overwhelming majority of the *Lok Sabha* seats. The Communist Party was the only opposition party to win as many as 29 *Lok Sabha* seats in any one of the three elections.

Why did the opposition parties not combine? One reason was that they represented a wide spectrum of political views, left and right, religious and secular. Important differences in outlook and emphasis separated the Communists from the free enterprise *Swatantra* Party and the Socialists from the Hindu revivalist *Jan Sangh* Party. Moreover, the possibility of electoral victory seemed remote while Nehru led the Congress Party and as a result, the incentive for combinations was missing. With time, though, opposition to the Congress Party stiffened as it lost its early sense of mission. The series of setbacks suffered by India in the 1960's, moreover, crystalized some of the opposition. The Chinese rout of the Indian army in 1962, the levelling off of food production, the 1966–67 drought, and the rise in the cost of living disenchanted former supporters. When Jawaharlal Nehru died in 1964, the Con-

Indira Gandhi presides over the Indian National Congress in New Delhi. Members customarily sit on the floor to conduct business.

gress Party lost a popular leader who had been both the hand-picked successor of Gandhi and a statesman of world stature. Nehru was succeeded first by Lal Bahadur Shastri, and then in 1966 by his daughter, Mrs. Indira Gandhi (no relation of Mahatma Gandhi's). Mrs. Gandhi continued the basic policies of her father, non-alignment in international politics and a mixed socialist and free-enterprise economy at home. She led the Congress Party in the 4th general election in 1967.

Politics 483

The 1967 watershed. The major difference between the 1967 general election and the previous three was that the opposition parties formed electoral alliances. Although the Congress Party's share of the vote declined by less than 4 per cent in 1967, the party's share of *Lok Sabha* seats was reduced from an average of 70% in the previous three parliaments to 54%. The opposition parties were even more successful in the state assemblies. Opposition parties captured 9 of 17 state governments, although only in Madras did a single opposition party win a clear majority. In the other eight states, opposition parties joined united front governments, some of which proved highly unstable. Legislators in states with narrow majorities shifted allegiances in return for appointment to ministry (cabinet) posts and other favors. Four legislators each changed parties four times within a year of the election! Frequent party defections turned majorities into minorities, forced state ministries to resign, demoralized the state administrative services, and brought accusations of unprincipled opportunism. Unless the political parties are able to enter lasting partnerships and prevent frequent defections, the parliamentary system in India will be further discredited. The multi-party chaos in several states since 1967 has cast serious doubt on the future of the present system of parliamentary democracy.

The political instability of 1967–68 was preceded and accompanied by a wave of lawlessness. Prime Minister Indira Gandhi's nose was badly broken by a rock thrown during a campaign speech. A communist-led uprising of tribesmen with bows and arrows near the Chinese and Pakistan borders caused concern. The Indian government was nervous about possible aggressive military cooperation between China and Pakistan. Striking workers in Calcutta and elsewhere locked their employers into factories and offices in order to force them to make concessions. There was a growing restlessness among students, teachers, transportation workers, dockers, taxidrivers, and the 2.8 million government employees. On different occasions, demonstrators marched on the legislatures, fought the police, and burned trams, trains, buses, and government buildings. Some of the issues were food rationing, cow killing, the proposed adoption of Hindi as the sole official language, and the detention without trial of left-wing politicians. In the late 1960's, an increasing number of people seemed to feel that the normal political institutions were unresponsive to public opinion. Some blamed the unrest on the failure of the political old guard to open its ranks to younger members while others believed that the Congress Party was not giving firm, decisive leadership. In any case, non-Congress Party politicians increasingly were turning to direct action in the streets.

Violence and national unity. Violence in India, as in other societies, indicates that certain groups lack confidence in their fellow citizens and peaceful political methods. This absence of trust is understandable in view of the age-old gap in India between castes, regions, and the rulers and the ruled. The average Indian peasant thinks in terms of his village and his family rather than his country. It is true that he leaves his village on many occasions. He goes to neighboring villages to arrange marriages for his children. He goes to a market to buy a few items not available in his village. Occasionally he will make a pilgrimage to sacred rivers and temples. And he may need to take a property dispute to the district court. But rarely do these activities take him out of his linguistic region.

City-dwellers, too, are often isolated from their fellow citizens for whom they feel little concern. Hindus and Muslims do not

Discontent over food shortages in India manifested itself in angry nationwide demonstrations throughout 1964–65. The sign reads: "Give cheap food grains to people, arrest hoarder-thieves."

mix easily. Hindi-speakers cluster in their sections of cities, Tamil-speakers in the Tamil-speaking section, and so on. In private social gatherings, persons from different regions and from castes far apart in the caste hierarchy rarely meet. Without integration, people lack sympathy and understanding for the problems of other groups.

Although Indian society is deeply fragmented today, it is much more unified than it was when the first European ship dropped anchor off the west coast in 1498. Europeans, and the English in particular, played a major role in giving India a measure of unity.

HISTORICAL ORIGINS

We must now ask how the present state of India came into existence. Very simply the answer is that the modern Indian state and its political institutions are the product of English rule. It was the English who united India and brought parliamentary government. It was they also who introduced many Western ideas and techniques. And it was the English who provoked the nationalist efforts to modernize India and to unite in order to expel foreign rule.

The East India Company. The English, along with other European peoples, were first attracted to India for reasons of trade. They sought the spices, silks, precious jewels, and luxuries of both India and Southeast Asia. In the year 1600 Queen Elizabeth of England granted to a group of 125 businessmen and merchants exclusive right to trade with the East Indies. To take advantage of this monopoly, the merchants and businessmen of the city of London raised £72,000 in order to finance the first English ships to sail to India. This was the humble origin of the English East India Company. Possibly never has an original investment of £72,000 paid off so handsomely in dividends, for the Company grew from a small trading venture into the ruler of all India. This was a most surprising change, for the Company's few ships and soldiers were nothing compared to the huge armies of the great Mughal emperors in Delhi.

The English advantage. What were the underlying reasons for the extraordinary English expansion? One explanation is to be found in the superior technology of the English. They had better artillery and muskets than did the Indians. Also they had control of the sea, so were able to move their troops freely from one part of India to another.*

More important than this technological difference, however, was a political difference. The Indian people were divided among themselves. They had no sense of nationalism, no feeling of national unity, as did the English and other Europeans. Instead, when the fighting began, many Indians fought with the British against their Mughal rulers and other Indians. The English had no trouble hiring large numbers of Indian soldiers, and these soldiers formed the great majority of their forces. In other words, the English were able to conquer India because of Indian help; without it they would have been nearly powerless.†

A third and final reason for the English victory was the rapid decline of the Mughal Empire. We noted earlier that Emperor Akbar was one of the great rulers of all time,

---

* See *Readings in World History*, "The Lack of Scientific Progress," p. 494.
† See *Readings in World History*, "Fruits of Despotism," p. 492.

great for his statesmanship and military strength. But after his death in 1605, he was succeeded by men who often lacked his abilities. The Empire remained intact for some decades because of the strength of the system established by Babur and Akbar. But after Aurangzeb (1658–1707), violence replaced law and order in many areas.

The 18th century was a period of rapid decline for the Empire. Hindus took advantage of this situation to rise against the Mughal rulers who were Muslims. The Marathas organized a Confederacy, which consisted of independent Hindu rulers in western and central India. In other parts of India, other independent rulers appeared, some of them Hindu and some Muslim. So we see that the decline of Mughal power left India a hodgepodge of many little states, often at war with each other. This made it easier for the British to conquer these states one after another until they had control of the whole peninsula.

The English conquest. The English won their rich prize through a combination of diplomacy and armed force. Both the English and the French found that their small Company armies, composed of Indian soldiers trained by European officers, were a valuable asset. They offered the services of their armies to local Indian rulers and would-be-rulers in return for trading concessions and grants of cash and territory. Once an Indian ruler had defeated a rival or usurped power with the aid of the Europeans, he often found himself entangled in a web of obligations to his European allies. For example, an ambitious Muslim noble promised Robert Clive and the British sizeable rewards for help in overthrowing the *nawab* or ruler of Bengal. Once in power after the British victory at Plassey in 1757, the new nawab tried to pay off his debts to his British allies. However, the British refused to pay him

CULVER PICTURES

Under Robert Clive, victory at Plassey made the British supreme in Bengal. From this base they were able to dominate the rest of India.

any taxes on their trade while Indian traders paid a tax of 40 per cent. The nawab rebelled against British restraints on his independence. In 1764 the British defeated him at Buxar, on the Ganges, and appointed a puppet ruler in his place. With this victory the British became the masters of the province of Bengal, with its fertile soil and profitable handicraft industry. Now they had a strong base which they used for the conquest of the rest of India.

In similar fashion, the British secured a foothold at Madras on the southeast coast. Using both alliances and military strategy, the British forced the French under the Treaty of Paris in 1763 to give them almost a free hand in India.

British territorial expansion continued piece by piece for the next one hundred years, usually with the object of removing a threat to British privileges and supremacy. The kingdom of Mysore in the South was defeated in 1799, the Marathas in the west were finally conquered in 1818, and the Sikh state in the Punjab was annexed in 1848. After 1848, the political map of India changed little until independence in 1947. The British ruled three-fifths of India directly and they ruled the other two-fifths indirectly through alliances with more than 550 subordinate princes. It was in this way that a small trading company became the overlord of a vast subcontinent with great riches and hundreds of millions of people.

Government in whose interest? The conquests of the English East India Company were a remarkable achievement, but they did create a serious problem. It soon became clear that a mere trading company was not suitable for governing a subcontinent. The purpose of any company, after all, is to make as high profits as possible for its shareholders. This was exactly what the officials of the East India Company set out to do, and they succeeded brilliantly. They made handsome profits for their shareholders, and they won fabulous fortunes for themselves. In fact, this was one reason why the Company expanded its domains as rapidly as it did. Conquest proved much more profitable than mere trade. Each new province promised more dividends and more private fortunes.*

With each of the early conquests, the English made great fortunes by taking over the trade from native merchants, by com-

* See *Readings in World History,* "The British Exploit India," p. 498.

Politics 487

pelling the princes to pay heavy tribute, and by forcing weavers and other artisans to produce goods for the Company. All this meant such a heavy burden on the Indian people that many were ruined and large numbers died from starvation.* Robert Clive himself described the situation in Bengal as "a scene of anarchy, confusion, bribery, corruption, and extortion," and concluded that never had so many fortunes been "acquired in so unjust and rapacious a manner."[3] So terrible were the conditions that protests were made even in England. A British writer, Horace Walpole, commented at this time, "We have outdone the Spaniards in Peru. They were at least butchers on a religious principle, however diabolical their zeal. We have murdered, deposed, plundered, usurped—nay what think you of the famine in Bengal, in which three millions perished, being caused by a monopoly of the provisions by the servants of the East India Company?"[4]

Because of this ruthless exploitation of India, the British government gradually took over control from the Company. The first step was taken in 1773 when Parliament appointed a governor-general who was given much of the Company's political powers. From then on the government of India was gradually transferred from Company agents to officials of the British government.

The Indian Mutiny. The final transfer of power to the government took place following the Indian Mutiny of 1857. This revolt began when a new kind of cartridge was adopted for use by the British Army in India. The army consisted of British officers and Hindu and Muslim soldiers. These soldiers were disturbed by the fact that the new cartridges were smeared with grease and had to be bitten between the teeth before being

* See *Readings in World History*, "Indian Traveller in England," p. 499.

placed in the rifle. The story spread that the grease was a mixture of cow and pig fat. For religious reasons Hindus could not touch cow fat, and Muslims, pig fat. So the new cartridges were the spark that set off the mutiny.

At the center of the revolt was something more important. Many Indians joined the rebellious soldiers because they hated changes that the British were making in India. Mughal aristocrats and Maratha chiefs resented having been displaced by the British and they hoped to recover their lost power and prestige. Soldiers from the disbanded armies of the aristocrats and chiefs were angry at their loss of employment. Orthodox Hindus were upset by Christian missionary attacks on their religion. And learned Brahmin priests and Muslim scholars felt threatened by technological innovations which were undermining people's respect for the sacred knowledge and ceremonies. How could a peasant believe that all knowledge worth possessing was in the head of a Brahmin when he saw a steamboat on the Ganges or a railroad with its shrieking iron horse which belched flames and smoke?

On many sides the traditional Indian elite classes were being challenged by the British, as well as by the small number of English-educated Indians, some of whom were advancing in the East India Company's administration and ridiculing the ways of their ancestors. The mutiny, in other words, was a desperate last effort by Indian conservatives to stop the changes introduced by the British. It was something more than a mere uprising of soldiers, for in some areas peasants rallied behind their dispossessed landlords and rulers, while in others Hindus joined Muslims in fighting the British. Many Indians regard the mutiny of 1857 as the first national war of independence, although wide sections of the population remained inactive and passive.

British regulars put down the rebellious Sepoys in this 19th-century engraving.

After some hard fighting the mutiny was put down. The next year, in 1858, Parliament in London abolished the English East India Company and transferred control of India to the British government. From then until 1947, the Government of India was responsible to Parliament through the British viceroy. During the 90 years between 1858 and 1947, British rule brought gradual change to India, although the experience of the mutiny discouraged radical experiments.

Political unification. One of the most important results of British rule was political unification. From the start this was the British aim. In 1865 one Englishman wrote home that they were "making a people in India where hitherto there had been hundreds of tribes but no people."[5] Political unity is an important part of nation-building. The British contributed to unification in six ways.

Government—First the English established a single government that directly or indirectly ruled all of the peninsula. Britain ruled the three-fifths of India known as British India directly through the Indian Civil Service headed by the Viceroy. The Indian Civil Service was a well-paid and largely British bureaucracy selected in London by rigid examination. It was responsible for collecting taxes, administering justice, and supervising the large staff of subordinate Indian officials.* It set a high standard of honesty and hard work, and it introduced a uniform administration throughout British India. The other two-fifths of India was ruled indirectly through semi-independent princely states. There were 562 of these scattered throughout the peninsula, and between Bombay and Delhi, a distance of 845 miles, a traveller would have to cross 36 frontiers. These kingdoms ranged in size from Hyderabad, which was about the area of Idaho or of Britain without Scotland, down to petty principalities no larger than a few city blocks. The link between British India and the princely states was the viceroy, who not only headed the bureaucracy which governed British India, but also represented the British crown in its relations with the princely states. These states were independent, at least in theory, except in matters of defense and foreign policy. In fact, the viceroy stationed British residents at the princely courts and these residents often advised the princes about their internal affairs. Thus all of India was united under a single power, that of the viceroy who lived at Calcutta until 1911 and then at Delhi.

The restoration of order—Another way in which the British helped unify India was by restoring internal order. During the twilight years of the Mughal Empire in the 18th century, large areas experienced anarchy. Villages, by necessity, had to protect themselves with armed guards and high walls. Robber bands roamed the countryside, taking protection money, looting, and killing. Local chiefs and landlords became warlords and raided their neighbors. It was unsafe to travel without an armed escort, and in places only the rich and the powerful could find either justice or security. These chaotic conditions discouraged commerce and travel, without

* See *Readings in World History*, "The Rise of the Color Bar," p. 500.

which unification was impossible. However the British gradually restored order, first by martial law enforced by the army, and then through the creation of a police force. By the middle of the 19th century, political and internal security had been restored though many people continued to suspect that the police were corrupt, that the shepherd was more terrible than the wolf.

One law for all—A third unifying force was the establishment of what is called the rule of law, which means that the British enforced a single law for all Indians. Thus rich and poor, outcastes and Brahmin, Hindu and Muslim, all were theoretically subject to one law. Before British rule, Indian law had been a jumble of customs, varying from religion to religion and region to region. Low caste people had often been subject to more severe penalties than high caste people. At first, the English simply tried to curb the worst examples of what the English had come to regard in recent centuries as barbarism. They tried to prevent brutal punishments, such as cutting off the hand of a thief, impaling a convicted robber, or turning over murderers to the vengeance of the dead man's family. Likewise, they tried to correct inhumane aspects of Hindu family law whereby a husband had the right to cut off the nose of an unfaithful wife, and to marry off his daughters as child brides.

In 1859 the British decided to abolish the old hodge-podge of ancient laws and to establish a single, uniform code of law for all. The principle that this law should be the same for everybody and should be administered honestly, without favoring the rich and the powerful, was one of Britain's greatest contributions to modern India. However, Indian and British ideas were often far apart on these matters, as can be seen in the reaction of a wealthy Indian who bitterly opposed the introduction of English law into India. His chief complaint was that poor men would receive the same treatment before the law as men like himself. In the old days, he said:

If any man without a well-established reputation ventured to go into court and lodge a complaint against a respectable person like myself, if he did not make good his accusation, he knew very well that he would probably have both his ears cut off and be turned out of court. Hence, in those days no such men ever ventured to make such a complaint or show their faces in any place near a court; but now see how it is. Any low-caste man cannot only go to the English court and lodge a complaint against me, but he can compel me to meet him in open court face to face and answer his questions as if I were a common man of no standing whatever. It is this that we complain of. There is no honor, no sense of right, no justice left. That which you call justice and impartiality is really wrong and oppression.[6]

Introducing the principle of equality before the law was a step toward the social unification of India.

Communications—The British also unified India by improving transportation. We have already seen that India has only three river systems that can be used for navigation. Food and supplies which were shipped inland had to be moved by ox cart or human carrier. Consequently until very recent times, terrible famines occurred in India because food could not be transported from regions of surplus to regions of scarcity. The British met this problem by (1) building a network of roads, such as the Grand Trunk to the Northwest frontier; (2) constructing an extensive canal system; and (3) building railroads which became India's substitute for rivers. In 1870, there were 4000 miles of

The British outlawed suttee, an Indian ritual which demanded that a widow, sometimes only a young child, climb willingly onto a funeral pyre and be burned with the corpse of her husband.

CHARLES PHELPES CUSHING

491

track; by 1939, the mileage had risen to 41,000.

Language and education—The English language and an English educational system contributed to the unification of India. In 1835 English was established as the official language of administration, replacing Persian. Also, beginning in 1858, a string of universities modelled after those in England was established. The British needed English-speaking Indians to work in the administration and commercial companies. They hoped to create, as Thomas B. Macaulay put it, "a class of persons, Indian in blood and color, but English in taste, in opinions, in morals and in intellect" who would in turn Westernize the rest of the population.[7] Just as Latin had once been the language of culture in medieval Europe, Persian and Sanskrit had been the languages of educated men in India. But few Englishmen respected or believed in the value of Persian and Sanskrit learning. Therefore, English was made the language of education in the new universities. And when Indians from different parts of India came together, for example, in the Legislative Councils and the Indian National Congress, English was the usual language of communication. At the same time, however, all but a few Hindus kept their traditional culture; they did not become, as Macaulay had hoped, "English in taste, in opinions, in morals and in intellect."

Legislative Councils—Finally, Parliament created Indian Legislative Councils in 1861 to pass the laws which the government wanted. At first, the Councils had little influence because the government chose the members and regarded the Councils as little more than an extension of the executive branch of government. However, a few Indians did participate in the Council discussions beginning in the 1860's. In 1892, Parliament enlarged the Councils and gave Indians the right to choose members for the first time. Step by step, Indian participation was increased. In 1909, 1919, and 1935, the Councils were again enlarged, their powers increased, and the right to vote extended. After the 1919 Council reforms, seven million people had the right to vote and the Indian majorities in the provincial Legislative Councils chose Indian Ministers to head certain government departments. In other words, Cabinet Ministers became responsible for the first time to the will of the elected representatives, rather than to the British executive. In 1935, full self-government was given, with safeguards, to the provinces but not to the central government. After 1935, 35 million people had the right to vote. The provincial and central Legislative Councils brought people together from different parts of India to discuss problems of common concern. They also gave Indians practical experience with democratic institutions. When independence came, millions of Indians had voted, many hundreds had served as legislators, and many dozens had acted as Ministers in charge of administrative departments. The transfer of power had been a gradual one.

Nationalism. Indian nationalism, like nationalism in other countries, is a complex phenomenon. It grew gradually, feeding on a belief in the superiority of Indian culture as well as on a dislike of British rule. However it reached different groups at different times, being slowed by regional, religious, and caste divisions which continued to hinder nation-building.

In the early years of the British rule, many English-educated Indians were embarrassed by caste, superstition, and poverty. But as they reformed and reinterpreted Hinduism and Islam, they found much of which to be proud. With this new pride came the confidence that Indians were capable of building and ruling their own nation, without British masters. Educated Indians began to demand a greater share in governing India. They also insisted that the administration should be conducted in the interests of India rather than of Britain. Nationalists wanted to Indianize the civil services, to have their own parliament, and to build their own industry. The British, on the other hand, wanted to keep India as a source of raw materials, as a market for their own manufactures, and as a military base for their colonial activities in the rest of Asia and East Africa. Out of the growing Indian confidence and this clash of interests emerged the Indian National Congress.

The Indian National Congress. The Congress party was founded in 1885 by a small group of Westernized Indians. They did not ask for independence at first. In fact, early Congress leaders were grateful to the British for their role in uniting India and in introducing ideas of liberalism, individualism, and democracy.* What they did want was a larger share in governing India. The British made concessions, we have seen, by expanding the size and powers of the legislative councils in 1892, 1909, 1919, and 1935, but in the eyes of most nationalists the concessions were inadequate. The nationalist movement grew in size and militancy and in 1907 it split between moderates and extremists. In that year, young students began to join secret societies and use terrorism in an effort to drive the foreign oppressors out of the country.

Mahatma Gandhi. By World War I, there was widespread disillusionment with both the moderate politics of the Congress and the bomb-throwing of the students. The Congress had remained a small party of up-

* See *Readings in World History,* "The Rise of Indian Nationalism," p. 502.

per class lawyers, journalists, teachers, and businessmen without appeal for the masses. The secret societies though small were bringing repression and other hardships on Indians without loosening the British grip.

In 1915, a wiry, bespeckled man named Mohandas Karamchand Gandhi returned to India from South Africa where he had been leading a struggle of the Indian community for better treatment. Within a few years he transformed the Indian National Congress. For the next three decades, Gandhi dominated nationalist politics and, more than any other man, engineered India's independence.

Although he was trained in London as a lawyer, Gandhi turned his back on a profitable law career and followed instead the ascetic life style of a Hindu holy man. That is why Gandhi is usually referred to as Mahatma Gandhi, Mahatma meaning literally great soul. Jawaharlal Nehru, Gandhi's disciple and India's first prime minister, described the coming of the Mahatma as a "powerful current of fresh air that made us stretch ourselves and take deep breaths, like a beam of light that pierced the darkness and removed the scales from our eyes, like a whirlwind that upset many things but most of all the working of people's minds." [8]

Gandhi has had few rivals in modern history as either a practical political tactician or a moral leader. Under his leadership, the Congress was converted into a mass organization almost overnight. The membership grew from under ten thousand to over two million in several years. In order to make the meetings more popular, English was replaced by Hindi as far as possible as the language of debate. The number of Muslims of the Congress executive committee rose from 11 to 25 per cent, and the number of lawyers on the committee declined from 64 to 21 per cent, as Congress leadership became more representative of the population as a whole.

Gandhi and non-violence. In addition to these organizational changes, Gandhi introduced the political tactics he had developed in South Africa. He called upon his countrymen to follow him in non-cooperation and civil disobedience. He asked Indians to renounce their titles and to boycott the law courts and schools, and British imported goods.

Gandhi always insisted that his followers be non-violent but passions rose, tempers flared, and violence was committed by nationalists as well as by the police. Gandhi led three great campaigns to gain more independence from Britain, and each campaign, in 1920–22, 1930–34, and 1942, ended in violence. Between campaigns, Gandhi withdrew from politics and devoted himself to constructive social work. He taught people spinning in order to encourage economic self-reliance and emphasize the dignity of manual labor. He worked to increase the rights and status of untouchables. He also used the periods of withdrawal to prepare himself and his followers to be non-violent in their next confrontation with the British.

Gandhi insisted on non-violence for two reasons. Non-violence or *ahimsa* was a Hindu concept with which most Indian villagers were familiar. Hindus avoided killing animals because of the belief that the soul is divine and that it is reborn in animals in many cases. *Ahimsa* was a particularly influential concept in the area of western India and among the shopkeeper caste from which Gandhi came. It was typical of Gandhi's genius that he introduced new methods and tactics in a form which would be familiar to the average Indian. Gandhi had a shrewd instinct for finding ideas and grievances which would appeal to large numbers of people.

The other reason Gandhi emphasized non-violence and the sacredness of all life reflected Gandhi's view of truth. Just as men differed about the nature of god, men had varying notions of truth. How could any human be certain that his idea of truth was absolutely correct and the next man's wrong? Gandhi believed that truth was so complex that man should not use violence to enforce his views on others. Non-violence was a more moral means of settling a dispute because there was a built-in limitation upon its use. While the victim of non-violent action might suffer, the user would also be inconvenienced. A man committing civil disobedience had to suffer because if he broke a law, he was subject to arrest and jail, if he walked off his job or shut down his store, he lost income, and if he boycotted, he had to do without the object or service he boycotted. Gandhi knew that only people with a good and moral cause would be likely to subject themselves to prolonged inconvenience or suffering in this way. Moreover, Gandhi thought the object of civil disobedience or non-cooperation should be to arouse the conscience of the opponent, to make the opponent see the justice of the cause. He said he opposed the use of civil disobedience to hurt or coerce an opponent.

The most famous demonstration of civil disobedience came in March of 1930 when Gandhi demanded the end of the state tax on the sale of salt. The salt tax had been collected for centuries before the British arrived. Nevertheless it was hated because it hurt the poorest people of the country. Every person needed about the same amount of salt, so they all paid about the same amount of salt tax, regardless of whether they were beggars or princes. Gandhi decided to use this tax to dramatize India's poverty and the British responsibility for it.

To do this he organized a salt march to the sea, where thousands of people illegally produced their own tax-free salt by boiling the ocean water. It was through tactics such as this that Gandhi transformed the Con-gress Party from a small group of upper-middle-class intellectuals into a vast popular crusade. In the eyes of his followers, Gandhi was a saint, uniting the poverty, asceticism, and devotion of the Hindu holy man, with the education and knowledge of the Western-trained lawyer and journalist. To publicize his boycott of English industrial goods and to encourage local village industry, he set aside machine-made cloth, dressed himself in a homespun loincloth, and lived mainly on goat's milk. To embarrass the British

The policy of civil disobedience practiced by Gandhi in the salt march was influenced by studying Henry Thoreau and was later followed by Martin Luther King.

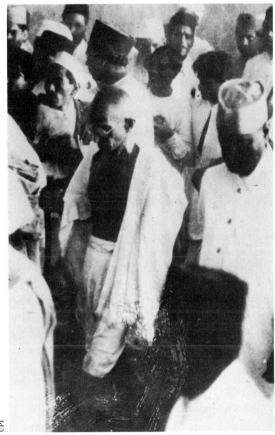

UPI

At the time of the partition, millions of Hindus and Sikhs moved from Pakistan into India, and millions of Muslims crossed the border in the opposite direction. The crowded condition of this Pakistan-bound train indicates why casualties were so heavy when the trains were attacked. The absorption of these refugees was the first problem both countries faced.

further, he went on hunger strikes, threatening to starve himself to death unless the British did as he demanded.

Under the leadership of Mahatma Gandhi the Congress became the party of most politically conscious Indians, whether high caste or low, socialist or conservative. The nationalists spread the idea that Indians were citizens of a single country and that they shared responsibility for the well being of fellow Indians. By the end of World War II, the nationalists had demonstrated that foreign rule could be continued only at an unbearable cost to the British.

In 1947 the Congress achieved its major goal when the British handed over the reins of government. But the transfer of power was not the joyous occasion toward which

the Congress had looked. The Congress had failed to persuade most Muslims that their future would be secure in a united India with a Hindu majority. On August 15, 1947, India was partitioned into two new states, India and Pakistan. And five months later, Gandhi was assassinated by a Hindu fanatic who opposed Gandhi's efforts to calm the religious hatred.

The Partition. The explanation for the division of the Indian Peninsula along religious lines goes far back into Indian history. During the centuries of Muslim control of India, a considerable number of Muslim conquerors settled down and remained in the peninsula. In addition, a much larger number of their Hindu subjects gave up their traditional religion and adopted the Islamic religion of the rulers. Some did so because of force or the threat of force, others because of Islam's egalitarianism and simplicity. It is true that the great majority of the people remained Hindus, but more than one-fifth of all Indians before 1947 were Muslims, and in the northwest and north-east, Muslims were a majority. As independence approached, Muslims felt that their interests would not be safe in a united India after the British left. The insecurity of the Muslim minority in the face of majority rule led Muslim leaders to insist upon the 1947 division into separate states.

This division had tragic consequences. The boundaries between India and Pakistan were drawn, wherever possible, along religious lines, but Hindus and Muslims were everywhere mixed so that millions of Hindus found themselves in Pakistan and millions of Muslims were still in India. Fear swept both communities as unspeakable atrocities were committed, in many cases by religious fanatics. Numbers can not measure the horror of the partition riots but clearly it was immense. Between one quarter and one million people died and about seventeen million people migrated. Something of the terror of the partition can be sensed from the experience of a Muslim professor at the University of Karachi:

> There was no bad feeling between us. The Muslims and Hindus lived peacefully together. Then suddenly hell broke out. People ran for their lives. I served as commissioner for refugees. Train after train arrived in Karachi, packed with men and women insane from fear. I met each train at the railroad station. One train arrived with only two men alive, the engineer and the fireman. All the cars were packed with dead bodies—men, women, children, all with throats cut. Blood everywhere, not a single child left alive.... My people did the same thing, ambushed caravans, ... murdered any Hindu who fell into their hands....[9]

Apart from the legacy of bitterness, the partition created numerous problems. Rail, highway, and irrigation systems were severed. The richest jute and cotton growing areas went to Pakistan but the great majority of the jute and cotton mills, as well as coal and iron deposits remained in India. Government assests, ranging from the materials of war and railroad rolling stock down to rubber bands and stationery, had to be partitioned. Even prisoners, lunatics, and war debts were divided.

Kashmir. The division of territory is still not settled. Both India and Pakistan claim the province of Kashmir in the Himalayas, the larger and richer part of which is in Indian hands. Pakistan claims Kashmir and demands a plebiscite on the grounds that four-fifths of the population is Muslim and will almost certainly vote against becoming a part of India, while India retains most of Kashmir on the grounds that its Hindu ruler legally chose to join India, that Pakistan illegally invaded Kashmir, and that the

Kashmir is called the "Roof of Heaven" because of its beauty and location in the Himalayas. More important, each of the main rivers of West Pakistan has its source in Kashmir.

LEON KOFOD

majority Muslim party in Kashmir sanctioned the subsequent Indian occupation and war against the Pakistani invaders. The Kashmir dispute led Pakistan to seek arms from the United States through the SEATO and CENTO military pacts. Kashmir was also the major cause of the Indo-Pakistan war of 1965 and of Pakistan's recent informal alliance with China against India. Both India and Pakistan continue to spend a major portion of their budgets on military defenses against the other. Until the issue is settled, India and Pakistan will continue to lose potential benefits of trade and economic cooperation, benefits both countries need. And the positions of the large Muslim minority in India and the Hindu minority in Pakistan are likely to remain precarious.

The Princely States. Kashmir was only one, although geographically the largest, of the 562 princely states which had owed allegiance to the British crown yet had not formally been a part of British India. Most of the States were ruled by rajas and nawabs who regarded their state's taxes and resources as a private possession rather than as a public trust. The wealthier rulers often owned fleets of automobiles, stables of race horses, and numerous palaces and concubines. In 1947, most rulers agreed to surrender their political authority to either India or Pakistan in return for generous pensions. The Nizam of Hyderabad, however, tried to keep his state as an independent kingdom. India would not tolerate a body of foreign territory within its borders, and in 1948 the Indian army occupied Hyderabad, putting down a Communist rebellion in the process. In recent years, some former princely rulers have been elected to public office, suggesting that many former subjects continue to venerate them. This in turn has produced demands that their large pensions be abolished.

Pakistan. Of the two major states of South Asia, India is by far the larger and more powerful. Nevertheless, Pakistan is an important state in its own right, and is important also in the strategic considerations of India, China, and the United States.

One of Pakistan's most serious problems arises from the fact that the Muslim majority areas out of which the country was formed are far apart. Almost one thousand miles of India separate West from East Pakistan, and this imposes a unique problem upon Pakistan's efforts to build a nation. Due to continuing hostilities with India, the land route is closed and all transportation must be by air or by the 2500 mile sea route. West Pakistan is larger and its people dominate Pakistan's government, armed forces, and business life, but East Pakistan has more people and richer soil. The problems created by the physical separation of the two areas are increased by regional rivalries and resentments. The language, culture, and ethnic background of East Pakistanis differ considerably from those of the West, and many easterners believe they are discriminated against in the distribution of jobs and public projects. It remains to be seen whether the bonds of Islam and mutual distrust of India will continue to offset these internal differences. In recent years East Pakistan has received a larger percentage of development funds though political freedoms remain restricted.

Pakistan has followed a political path similar to many other countries of Asia and Africa. An attempt was made after independence to establish parliamentary institutions but the elected politicians were widely discredited by accusations of corruption, selfishness, factionalism, and incompetence. The army therefore seized power, banned political parties, and selected the Commander-in-Chief, General Ayub Khan, to rule. From that time until 1968, Pakistan was

West and East Pakistan are separated by 1000 miles of India. Because they have Islam in common they form a single country. However, the people of the West and East speak different languages, eat different foods, have different customs and different ways of earning a living. The West is more industrialized and commercial, the East more agricultural. There is some question as to whether they will be able to work out their difficulties and remain together.

Grand Trunk Road, West Pakistan

Terraced Fields, East Pakistan

Within minutes of this modern textile factory which supplies a world market can be found women still using traditional spinning wheels to produce cloth for their own families.

relatively stable. However members of the educated classes increasingly resented being excluded from politics. East Pakistanis in particular charged that not only were they denied democratic representation, but they were also discriminated against in development spending and in administrative and military employment. Unrest and student riots grew during 1968 and 1969 in both East and West Pakistan and brought the administration and economy to a standstill. Finally in March of 1969, Ayub resigned in favor of General Yahya Khan. Rioting stopped, but the grievances of eastern regionalists, of Pakistanis seeking political reform, and of workers and cultivators asking for a larger share of profits remained.

Under Ayub Khan's firm hand, Pakistan made moderate economic gains which somewhat exceeded India's in both the agricultural and industrial sectors. The government has divided up many of the largest estates, distributing the land to the peasants who pay the former owners on an installment plan over a 25-year period. The government is also trying to raise agricultural productivity by providing more fertilizers, teaching new cultivation methods, introducing new crops, sinking wells in dry areas, and afforesting wastelands. Also, the fishing industry is being modernized and expanded in order to provide more food for the country's rapidly growing population. Finally, the government is working to encourage the growth of industry, both publicly and privately owned. It has been so successful in textiles that Pakistan is now self-sufficient, although the country began with almost no industry and still has a long way to go in meeting its other needs.

Reviewing the Essentials

Present State

1. According to the author, what three ideas must be held firmly in mind if we are to understand modern India?
2. When did India and Pakistan become separate states?
3. Explain what is meant by a dominion. What is the relation between England and India today?
4. On the map, locate Pakistan. What problems have faced this new nation since independence?
5. India is a federal state. Explain what is meant by a federal system of government. How is the Indian government organized? Point out similarities and differences between the structure of the governments of the United States and India.

Historical Origins

6. What were the circumstances and events that led to British rule over India? Why did the British government feel it necessary to gradually take control of India away from the British East India Company?
7. How did England bring about the political unification of India? Explain why, in doing this, England promoted a sense of unity and national feeling among the Indian people.
8. How did the British prepare India for political independence? economic independence?
9. What conditions brought about the organization of the Indian National Congress in 1885? How did the party goals change over the period 1885–1947?
10. Review the events in the life of Gandhi. How did Gandhi make the Indian National Congress a party of all India instead of one whose membership was limited to educated middle-class Indians?
11. Why did Gandhi insist upon non-violence?

The Future

12. Locate the present boundaries of India and Pakistan. Why are relations between India and Pakistan poor?
13. What are the difficulties India faces in attempting to make democracy operate successfully?

Explain, Identify, or Locate

Indian Mutiny of 1857	viceroy	Jawaharlal Nehru	Kerala
Battle of Plassey	boycott	salt march	Hyderabad
Battle of Buxar	nonviolent disobedience	Robert Clive	Bengal
Indian National Congress	*Lok Sabha*	Thomas Pitt	Mughal Empire
British East India Company	Mahatma Gandhi		

ECONOMICS: Breaking the Vicious Circle of Underproduction

PRESENT STATE—THE STATISTICS OF STARVATION

Poverty is the most important single fact about India today. The first several years after independence were taken up with immediate problems such as adopting a constitution, integrating the former princely states, and absorbing the refugees from Pakistan. But the problem of poverty overshadowed everything else during those years, and still does so today.

Most of us who live in the United States cannot really imagine the extent of misery in India. Statistics, charts, and figures do not tell us much about what it feels like to starve or be without a roof over our heads. Nevertheless, the statistics of human suffering are terrifying evidence of the economic crisis which confronts modern India.

The average per capita income in India in 1966 was $79 compared to $3,153 in the United States. A skilled industrial worker may earn as much as $250 a year but a farm hand receives as little as $25 for an entire year's work! Probably five million persons are unemployed and possibly three or four times this number are what is called under-employed which means that they do not have full-time jobs. A million or more persons live and sleep in the streets, without any shelter. An average of 2.6 persons live in each room in India compared to .7 persons in the United States.

The accompanying table shows some comparative figures between the United States and India.

Indicators of Living Standards	U.S.A.	India
Doctors per 100,000 inhabitants	149	16
Dentists per 100,000 inhabitants	56	.9
Percentage of the population over ten years of age which is literate	97	25
Students in higher education per 10,000 inhabitants	260	23
Radios per 1000 inhabitants	1000	7
Motor vehicles per 1000 inhabitants	454	13
Millions of tons of steel produced in 1966	121.6	6.6
Percentage of the population which lives in urban or suburban communities	70	18

These are the figures of what is called underdevelopment, which is an easy way of saying that India is still a land which is overwhelmingly agricultural and where 80 per cent of the people do not have enough housing, food, medical care, and education.

Nutrition. Walking hand in hand with underdevelopment is undernourishment. India faces the terrible fact that many of her people are near the starvation level. A healthy diet for man averages 2500–2750 calories daily (3100 in the United States). Below 2000 puts man at a level approaching starvation. The Indian diet averages 2110 calories. This means that many are below that dangerous level. Even this is misleading since most of their diet is cereal grains, principally rice and wheat. The average Indian eats only 4 pounds of meat a year. This means that his diet is deficient in animal protein and lacks balance in vitamins and minerals. A former Minister of Food estimated that 35–40 per cent of the children may have suffered brain damage because of protein deficiency. India produces enough food to feed her population but much of it never reaches the consumer. Perhaps one-fourth is eaten by rats. A United Nations Food and Agriculture report says that altogether, one half of India's food is wasted by rats, rot, birds, and insects. The value of this loss is twice the size of India's national budget. Proper storage and transportation arrangements could eliminate the food deficit. But those arrangements are beyond India's financial and administrative capacity at this time.

Millions of Indians live in constant want but few actually die of starvation. The climate is mild and people have adapted to poverty. But survival without good health means constant misery. Undernourishment leaves the average Indian vulnerable to many illnesses and infectious diseases which a healthy person could resist. Malaria, for

ALAN BAND

example, struck almost half the population until DDT recently brought it under control. Many other deadly diseases beset Indians: tuberculosis, cholera, and dysentery, and each adds its toll to the extremely high annual death rate. Life expectancy is now about 50 years, compared to about 70 in the United States.

Even this is a great improvement over pre-independence figures. Twenty years ago half the children born in India died before reaching the age of 10 and the life expectancy was about 30. DDT and antibiotics have given people a better chance to live; at the same time they have sent the population skyrocketing. If standards of sanitation could be improved, the disease rate could be cut. But few people understand the relation between disease and dirt. Sewage facilities and clean drinking water are not available for most Indians. The city of Howrah, for example, which is across the river from Calcutta and is the size of Boston, has no closed sewerage system.

What do all these facts and figures mean in terms of human suffering and productivity? It means that millions of children are unable to concentrate or learn in school, that workers in the fields and factories tire easily and are often absent, that a major part of the population is listless and lacks the energy necessary for efficient work or creative leisure. Hundreds of thousands are forced to make their living by begging. In parts of India the unemployed even search cow dung for undigested grain with which to supplement their diet.

We must emphasize, however, that poverty and the ignorance which contributes to it are not universal. India is one of the major industrial powers of the world and she has, in absolute numbers, a huge class of well educated people, including thousands of graduates from British and American universities. It is the persistence of poverty alongside the small pockets of modernization which perplexes many people. Modernization has not spread much from one place or group to another. Jawaharlal Nehru, an ardent supporter of modern science and technology, once said in exasperation, referring to the almost universal use of cow dung for cooking fuel and plastering of house walls, "we are talking about the atomic age while living in the cow-dung era." [10] If India, despite its jet airplane and atomic energy industries, is still living in the cow-dung era, we must now ask why this is so. Why is India so far behind the countries of Europe and North America?

HISTORICAL ORIGINS

Age-old poverty. Poverty is not new to India. Even in the days of the great Mughal emperor, Akbar, Western travellers were horrified at the wretchedness and degradation of many of the emperor's subjects. A 16th century visitor wrote that the people of India "live very poorly, go naked and are so miserable that for a penny they will endure to be whipped and they eat so little that it seems as if they live by the air." [11] However, the standard of living in India during Akbar's time was not greatly inferior to Europe's. Technology in Asia approached the European level in agriculture, textile manufacture, warfare, and navigation. And European merchants found that Indian banking, exchange, and insurance facilities were sophisticated. The extreme contrast between India and the West, then, is a relatively recent development. While the standard of living in the West has shot upwards during the last 150 years, the position of the Indian peasant in 1947 was not much better than it was in the 16th century.

Britain's role. Many people, chiefly Indians, blame the British for India's economic condition. They claim (1) that the British deliberately slowed down the rate of India's industrial growth, and (2) that the economic result of British rule was an actual increase of poverty and human suffering. The Indian critics of the British support these claims with three arguments.

First, it is argued that the English destroyed the ancient landholding system of India and created a class of ruthless and absentee landlords and money-lenders who loaded the peasantry with debt. In the days of the Mughal Empire, the peasants had rented their land, in theory from the state, by paying a land tax. The amount was highly elastic, averaging about one-third of the crop in Akbar's day and varying from year to year depending on the needs of the empire and the nature of the harvest. It was collected by the village as a unit, and the individual farmer could not be thrown off the land. The agent who collected the taxes from the village was called a *zamindar*. He gathered the taxes and kept one-tenth as his own share. He was also responsible for the peace and security of the countryside, and his office was often hereditary, passing from father to son.

In 1793 the British converted the *zamindar* from a tax-gathering agent into a landlord. They made him the owner of all the lands from which he formerly had collected taxes for the state. And being the landlord, the *zamindar* now could charge the peasants rents as high as he wished, while he continued to pay the same taxes to the state. This meant that the *zamindar* and his agents became richer and richer while the peasant became poorer and poorer. Furthermore, the peasant was now at the mercy of the *zamindar* because he could be ousted from the land if he did not pay whatever rents were demanded. So the new landholding system not only lowered the peasant's standard of living but also destroyed his security and dignity.

In this Rajasthan village dung is used to plaster walls and is piled up to use as fuel.

The *zamindari* system operated in about half of the agricultural land, but the lot of the peasant was not much better in the rest of India. Where the villagers continued to pay taxes directly to the state, the old way of life was destroyed by the English insistence that the peasants pay their taxes in cash with little consideration for a good or a bad harvest. Many peasants had to mortgage or sell the rights to their land to money-lenders in order to pay their taxes.

Economics 505

British efforts to make land a transferable and saleable commodity were a radical departure from Indian custom. In pre-British India, peasants had been unable to mortgage or sell the land which they cultivated. Land was held by the community, or at least by the community of the dominant castes. Individual rights of private property as we know them did not exist. The British ignored the customary joint ownership of land and introduced a new and complex property law which gave legal titles of ownership to individuals. The law was too complicated and its principle too novel for uneducated peasants. When illiterate peasants needed cash for taxes, seeds, or plow animals or for a wedding or dowry, money-lenders offered them money and got them to sign mortgages. The peasants, being unable to read or understand the complicated document, committed themselves to pay back the principal sum plus 35 per cent, 50 per cent or more annual interest. When the peasants failed, the lenders could foreclose through the British courts and take the land or they could keep the peasants on the land in a state of hopeless debt.

The indebtedness of the peasants rose steadily throughout the 19th and 20th centuries. In 1911 it stood at £255 million and by 1939 it had risen to £1350 million, or roughly two and one-half billion dollars. The peasant with an impossible debt lacked incentive to increase his output. When the money-lenders gained control of the land, they rarely improved its productivity. The dominant rural classes generally looked to rents rather than to improved productivity for their profits. Therefore, when the British created a market for land, they failed to

Madras, in South India, has long been famous for its distinctive textile patterns.

JACQUES JANGOUX

change agricultural techniques or instill profit-making habits among the actual cultivators.

The second argument against the British is that they destroyed the domestic handicrafts of India, especially the spinning and weaving industries. Cheap manufactured cloth flooded the country from the English industrial centers of Birmingham and Manchester. The Indian hand-spinners and weavers could not compete with the cheap machine-made goods and were driven out of work. In 1832 it was reported that millions of "Indo-British subjects have been totally ruined in their trade . . . while thousands of men and women have perished of want." [12] The ancient textile cities of India slowly decayed. Dacca, one of the largest, which at one time had a population of 150 thousand, withered away to 30 thousand.

This kind of technological unemployment and suffering was partly inevitable because manufactured cloth was cheaper and of better quality. The English working classes also suffered during the Industrial Revolution. But the big difference is that in England the displaced handicraftsmen could find work in the factories of the new industrial cities. In India this was not possible because there were no factories there; instead they were located six thousand miles away in England. England protected its own industry by taxing or prohibiting competitive imports while it opened India to duty-free importation of British textiles. For a while England even prohibited the export to India of certain manufacturing machinery which would have helped India to industrialize and would have decreased the Indian market for British manufactured articles.

By the mid-19th century, when the British adopted laissez-faire policies, Indian industry had little chance of catching up and competing without government aid and protection. Since Indians did not control their government, they could not assist the early industrialization process with protective tariffs, subsidies, and tax incentives as the governments of Britain, Germany, the United States, and Japan did. So India's jobless weavers, spinners, tanners, shipwrights, and smelters were driven back into agriculture or swelled the ranks of the unemployed.

According to the Indian Census, the percentage of people engaged in farming steadily increased from 61 per cent in 1891 to 73 per cent in 1921. And since the amount of land was limited, this influx into agriculture meant underemployment and declining living standards for the peasants. India was to be kept as an "agricultural farm" and a controlled market for British industrial products. Railways were built to bring British goods into India and to carry raw materials out but not to stimulate Indian industry. Universities were established to train clerks, administrators, and lawyers but not businessmen or engineers. Banks, insurance companies, and shipping lines existed primarily to serve the needs of British, not Indian, business.

The third argument against British rule of India in the 19th century is that England drained the land of wealth. When Englishmen referred to India as being the "priceless jewel of the imperial crown," the critics of England claim that what the British really meant was that India was the most profitable part of the empire. They argue that money which should have been used to start Indian industrial growth and to raise the standard of living was constantly drained off into British pockets.

The credit side. All these arguments are justified to a certain extent. The *zamindars* and money-lenders did exploit the peasants, the British did take much wealth out of India, and at times they did discourage the establishment of Indian industries. But, like most

Oxen still power many irrigation wells in rural India.

arguments, there is also another side that should be noted. Britain gave India significant benefits, such as the rule of law, and political and internal unity. Moreover, the record of Britain's economic achievement in India is not altogether bad.

When India achieved independence in 1947, the country had made a start along the road to industrialization. India was the second-ranking industrial power in Asia, leading China, and taking second place only to Japan. India was the seventh greatest producer of iron in the world, surpassed only by the United States, the U.S.S.R., France, Sweden, Great Britain, and Canada. India was behind only the U.S.S.R. and the United States in the output of cotton yarn and cloth, and second only to the United States in the filming of motion pictures. The railroad network was 34,000 miles, which placed her fourth in the world, exceeded only by the United States with 223,400 miles, the U.S.S.R. with 76,600 miles, and Canada with

41,300. Finally, India is the most heavily irrigated nation in the world, with almost 90 million acres of land under irrigation, which is more than in the United States, Mexico, Japan, Egypt, Spain, Italy, France, Chile, and Java combined.

The truth about England's role in India is difficult to estimate. It is a complex mixture of failure and success rather than all bad or all good. The British regarded India as a colonial possession and did little to speed up industrial growth. They educated the upper classes of India because it was to their interest to have a small English-speaking and English-thinking group with which they could cooperate and who could fill the minor civil service positions. But the British did almost nothing to end the illiteracy of the masses of the people. They gave India the blessings of unity and law but rarely tried to change the ancient methods of farming through the introduction of modern agricultural techniques. British rule set off a population explosion without providing enough new economic opportunities or food to meet the new demand. The case against Great Britain is not so much that she crippled Indian industry and ground helpless millions into poverty, but that she did not do enough to improve or change the existing economic conditions. What India would have been like without British colonial rule, we cannot know. It is possible that without colonial rule, India would have modernized herself more rapidly before World War II, as Japan did. It is also possible that traditional Indian values and institutions, like China's, would have failed to adjust to the needs of modernization. It is less important now to fix blame for past stagnation or to speculate about what might have happened than it is to identify the conditions and policies which now impede or stimulate economic growth.

THE FUTURE

Productivity and population. The obvious obstacles to development are low productivity and rapid population growth. There simply is not enough food reaching the market to feed all Indians without importing from abroad. India's agricultural productivity is one of the lowest in the world. Her two most important crops are rice and wheat. India's low yield per acre may be judged from the following chart.

Crop Yield in 1965					
	India	*China*	*Japan*	*U.S.A.*	*World*
Rice (pounds per acre)	1438	2504	4306	4265	1581
Wheat (bushels per acre)	13.3	12.9	40.2	27.2	17.6

There are various explanations for this poor performance. Inequalities in the social structure undermine the initiative of the less privileged. Many farms are uneconomical in size, often being under three acres. Many have been fragmented through inheritance into widely spaced strips and this prevents efficient cultivation. Many cultivators lack the capital and knowledge necessary for the use of proper fertilizers, seeds, insecticides, and irrigation. Also many are outside the market system so that profit incentives are lacking. Instead of producing as much as possible to earn as much as possible, they are satisfied if, after paying taxes and debts, they have enough left over to live on until the next harvest. For many cultivators who are part of a market system, irregular monsoons and fluctuating prices wipe out profits, discourage risk-taking investment, and encourage the traditional fatalism.

Low productivity per acre would not be serious if India were not densely populated. However, most of the Ganges Plain has over 800 persons to the square mile and in parts of Bengal the density reaches over 1000. Population is growing at the rate of 24 persons for every thousand of the population each year, or at a rate 50 per cent higher than in the United States. Every month, India's population increases by more than a million, far more than the economy has jobs for. Without effective family planning and increased agricultural output, economists see little hope for India.

Five-Year Plans. Poverty, starvation, unemployment, disease, and suffering, these are the stark realities which India faces today. If she is to survive, India must give to her millions the hope and the reality of a better life. The constitution of India clearly promises justice and an adequate livelihood for all. The key to the future of India lies in her ability to reach these goals.

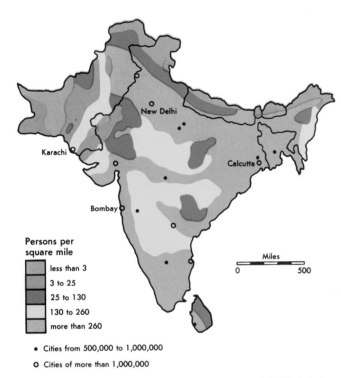

Persons per
square mile

- less than 3
- 3 to 25
- 25 to 130
- 130 to 260
- more than 260

• Cities from 500,000 to 1,000,000

○ Cities of more than 1,000,000

SOUTH ASIA – POPULATION

India's Five-Year Plans propose to do three things: (1) to make two stalks of wheat grow where only one did before; (2) to have only one baby where before two had been born; and (3) to build new industries that will first of all give immediate employment to the army of unemployed, and secondly produce a higher standard of living for all Indians. The first Five-Year Plan, which started in 1950, concentrated on agriculture, irrigation, power, and transport. Agriculture and irrigation received about one-third of the budget, and almost as much was allocated to transport and communications. In the second Five-Year Plan (1955–1960), the emphasis shifted to heavy industry, which received one-fifth of the outlay, as compared with the first Plan, during which industry received only a token consideration (less than

one-twentieth of the outlay). During the period of these two plans, India's output from agriculture rose by 36 per cent, from industry by 43 per cent, and from commerce, transportation, and services by 57 per cent. Altogether, India's total output rose 44 per cent during those ten years, or by 3.6 per cent per year. This growth rate was comparable to the United States' growth rate. However, agriculture, on which most people depend, improved less than expected and the population rose an alarming 21.5 per cent or from 361 million to 439 million. Consequently, the per capita output grew only 18 per cent during the two plans, or 1.6 per cent per year. Real progress had been made, but not enough to start the self-sustaining growth the planners had hoped for.

Major setbacks came during the third Five-Year Plan (1960–65). In 1962, the Chinese army occupied large areas of disputed boundary territory in the north-west and north-east. India's relations with Pakistan became worse as they fought a brief but costly war over their Punjab boundary. As a result, India increased her defense budget 2.8 times between 1961 and 1964. In the same period, food grain production stagnated at about 80 million tons. The harvest in 1964–65 was a bumper one of 89 million tons but it was followed by two years of serious drought with food grain crops of 72 and 80 million tons. The drought depressed the whole economy. During the severe food shortage, a larger share of the family budget was spent to buy the high-priced food, leaving less for manufactured goods. In addition to a decline in demand for its goods, industry suffered from a shortage of power. Without water, the hydro-electric dams could not generate electricity sufficient to keep many factories running. Government tax revenues declined while its expenditures for relief and for food imports increased, leaving less for the Five-Year Plan. Per capita income

Throughout India there are placards with propaganda for smaller families. This sign states: "A Planned Family is a Happy Family."

dropped 8.2 per cent in 1965–66. The droughts of 1965–66 and 1966–67 coincided with American decisions to cut back aid to India although American surplus wheat saved India from a devastating famine.

The discouraging events of the 1960's forced a re-thinking of development plans and the adoption of what some people call a "new realism." In the early years of independence, Jawaharlal Nehru and other leaders had counted upon friendship with China and foreign aid from the United States, and, to a lesser degree, from the Soviet Union. During the 1960's, India discovered that she must depend largely upon her own resources for development and defense. During the late 1960's, national self-reliance became a favorite theme of Indian planners, politicians, and intellectuals. In particular, village development and family planning received new emphasis.

Village development. The villages hold the key to India's economic growth. If agriculture prospers, the villages will buy manufactured goods, feed the cities, and generate the private capital and tax revenues necessary for further investment and growth. A large fraction of development funds and effort have been devoted to agricultural

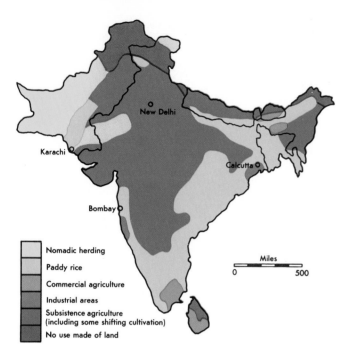

SOUTH ASIA ~ LAND USE

Map legend:
- Nomadic herding
- Paddy rice
- Commercial agriculture
- Industrial areas
- Subsistence agriculture (including some shifting cultivation)
- No use made of land

Map labels: New Delhi, Karachi, Calcutta, Bombay

Miles 0 500

development since the first plan was launched in 1950. Both land reforms and the Community Development Program were designed to step up food production.

During the independence movement, "land to the tiller" became a popular Congress Party slogan. After independence the Indian states passed new legislation to fix ceilings on the size of individual land holdings and to remove the intermediaries between cultivators and owners. The large *zamindar* landlords lost most of their land, for which they received compensation of a billion dollars. By contrast, the landowners in China were paid nothing when their land was taken from them. The end of the *zamindars* meant little change for the many Indian peasants who now pay rents to small landlords. However, peasants enjoy greater security of tenure and agricultural taxes are lower. The removal of the *zamindars* and intermediate rent collectors is expected to leave the actual cultivator with a larger share of the crop. This, in turn, should serve as an incentive to increase production.

Many cultivators lack the capital necessary for cash crops, fertilizer, and improvements. To meet this need, the government has set up cooperatives which advance credit, seeds, and fertilizer. Well-to-do landlords and cultivators who can offer security for their loans benefit from the cooperatives far more than the majority of small cultivators who are regarded as poor risks. Little progress has been made in consolidating fragmented holdings. Some pooling of land, capital, and labor is needed. However, mass collectivization of the farms by force, as in Russia and China, has been ruled out. Instead, the leaders of India are trying to raise productivity with the voluntary cooperation of the peasants themselves. This is the aim of the Community Development Program by which the government gives advice, materials, and grants or loans; the peasants are free to decide for themselves whether they will accept or reject these services. The government tries to arouse their interest by showing the peasants the greater effectiveness of the new farming methods. If even one peasant who is respected in his village for his farming ability can be induced to adopt the new methods, he may have a valuable demonstration effect on the rest of the village. The task is difficult because peasants are wary of outsiders and the government. Also, peasants are generally better agriculturalists than the inexperienced government development officers. However, peasants are anxious to increase their income, and will try new methods if convinced that they will work.

In addition to demonstrating new techniques, the government is trying to increase economic efficiency and welfare by building roads, digging wells, and constructing reservoirs to water the cattle and irrigate the fields during the dry season. Government experts in animal husbandry, agriculture, irrigation, and education are being sent to the four corners of India. The government offers improved seed, cement and pipe for the new wells, tools and wheelbarrows for the reservoirs. A revolutionary new hearth, or simple fireplace, is being introduced; in it the farmer no longer burns the precious cow dung so badly needed for fertilizer but uses coal briquettes as fuel for cookery. Almost all of India's 500,000 villages have been reached by the Community Development Program.*

The results of the Community Development Program have been mixed. In eastern India, agricultural productivity has increased very little. But the Punjab area of India and Pakistan, taken together, has experienced an increase in per acre output that compares favorably with any other poor region of similar size in the world. Moreover, there is a technical improvement which may revolutionize Indian agriculture. New hybrid rice and wheat plants have been developed which under proper conditions yield two and three times as much as older types. The limited use of these new plants and of greater quantities of fertilizers combined with a good monsoon in 1967–68 to produce a record food grain crop of 95 million tons. Many persons believe that the new seeds may bring a dramatic improvement in the food supply situation. It must be remembered, though, that similar hopes in the past have been disappointed. The new seeds will not be successful unless more fertilizers and pesticides are used and unless they can resist plant diseases.

Prospects. India's future depends upon the success of her economic development efforts.

* See *Readings in World History,* "New Hope in the Indian Village," p. 518.

Laborers in Bengal work to construct a more adequate water supply for Calcutta. To demonstrate new farming methods, Nehru had the grounds of his official residence planted with wheat. The yield was 32 bushels per acre rather than the 8 which was then typical of India.

COMPARATIVE GROWTH OF INDIA AND CHINA			1950-1968		
YEARLY OUTPUT	**INDIA**			**CHINA**	
	1950	1968	1950		1968
All Goods and Services (In Million US Dollars)	N.A.	$52,000	N.A.		$75,000
Steel (In Million Tons)	1.5	7	3.6		9
Oil (In Thousand Barrels)	1,867	42,190	730		86,300
Electric Power (In Billion Kilowatt Hours)	6.7	32	5		60
Food Grain (Pounds per Person)	306	400	330		500
Area	1,261,813	1,261,813	3,691,502		3,691,502
Population	339,000,000	511,115,000	580,000,000		750,000,000

Time is an all-important factor because many Indians may reject democratic methods if they do not bring rapidly the better world the Indian National Congress has promised. Many persons question the value of liberty when it provides such meager material benefits. The Indian Communists promise greater prosperity and a more dedicated leadership. They criticize the Congress for not requiring greater sacrifices, especially from the privileged classes. And they point to the economic successes of the Soviet Union and China as proof that communism provides effective solutions to the problem of poverty.

The attraction of the Soviet Union and China is a powerful one for some Indians because these two countries have developed their industry and promoted equality at a faster rate than India. Many Indians regard the Russian and Chinese experiences of modernization as more relevant than the experiences of the United States and Western Europe. India, like Russia and China, is trying to telescope the industrial revolution into a few decades. Many people compare

the rates of growth of China and India because these two countries, with approximately equal resources, started their development programs at about the same time but by different routes. Many people regard the comparison as a test of the democratic and communist paths to modernization.

The painful truth is that India fell behind China during the 1950's. When they started, India was the greater industrial power. But during the 1950's, China forged ahead in both food and industrial production. In addition, China poured a higher percentage of her national income back into the economy for the sake of future growth. China now seems to have a commanding lead in industrial production, military strength, and scientific education and development. However, the attraction of China and communism has decreased for several reasons. First, China failed in the 1960's to maintain the high growth rate of the 1950's. The 1958 "Great Leap Forward" in China proved to be somewhat more like a step than a leap. The Chinese economic troubles and the disorders accompanying the "Cultural Revolution" helped to place India's accomplishments in a far better light. Second, many Indian friends of China were shocked by China's invasion in 1962. Indian Communists who defended the invasion were denounced as traitors. Finally, Communist or Communist-led governments have been elected in two Indian states. In neither state were the Communists more successful than previous governments in solving problems.

In the long run, the appeal of non-democratic and dictatorial solutions to India's problems will probably depend not upon China's successes and failures as much as upon India's own experiences at home. If Indian parliamentary institutions are able to moderate conflicts and if the economic situation improves, violent, radical, and totalitarian changes will presumably have fewer supporters.

India's economic experiment has inevitably produced a clash between old and new ways of living and of doing things. Traditional institutions such as the joint family and the caste system are being challenged by new ideas and practices that are coming in with the steel mills and the tractors. In India, as elsewhere, economic change has led eventually to cultural change. This cultural change and the conflict that it has inspired are the subjects of the next section. While reading it, it will be convenient to keep in mind the difference in the philosophies which underlie the cultures of India and China as discussed in Unit Three. Recall that China has always been concerned with propriety and practical matters in this

Political and economic changes have revolutionized much of Indian society. Will the traditional religious and cultural philosophies, so far mostly unchanged, be able to withstand the onslaught?

ALAN BAND

life. It has traditionally had unity of purpose and culture. The proper conduct of the individual has always been of paramount importance, and duty, formerly to the family and now to the state, has always borne great emphasis. India's culture emphasized religion, a religion which directed man's attention away from society and the state and stressed individual religious experience. Indian society has been decentralized and often fragmented under hundreds of petty states. Its unity has only recently been achieved. Will its cultural background aid or impede further progress?

Reviewing the Essentials

Present State

1. What do the comparative figures on India and the United States tell about the level of living of the Indian and American people?
2. What do we mean when we speak of a country as underdeveloped? Specifically, what makes India an underdeveloped country?

Historical Origins

3. What evidence is there that poverty is not new to India? What reasons are given for India's poverty and underdevelopment?
4. What did England do to develop India economically? What did she fail to do for India?
5. How did Indian and English conceptions of property differ?
6. How did the Industrial Revolution affect India?
7. Compare the annual increase of population in India with that in the United States. Given the same rate of increase, what will India's population be in 1975? What is the number of unemployed in India today? Is overpopulation a sufficient explanation of Indian poverty?
8. Compare Indian and American agriculture in respect to output of wheat and rice per acre.
9. How has the division of the Indian Peninsula into Pakistan and India aggravated the problem of underdevelopment?

The Future

10. Contrast and compare the first, second, and third Five-Year Plans in respect to: (a) goals; (b) major emphasis; (c) cost; (d) resources; (e) outcome (successes and shortcomings in terms of goals).
11. What is the purpose of the village Community Development Program? Its underlying philosophy? How does the Indian government carry out the plan? What changes have come to the Indian village? What is the immediate and long-range importance of the Community Development Program?
12. Compare the methods used by India, China, and the Soviet Union in carrying out their modernization programs.
13. Why is the outcome of the economic race between China and India so important? Where did the two countries stand in this race in 1947? In 1968? Account for the difference.

Explain, Identify, or Locate

zamindari	agricultural surplus	technological unemployment	overpopulation
caloric consumption	productivity	vicious circle of	
Five-Year Plan	economic growth	underproduction	

CULTURE: Caste and Hinduism

An American visitor to India may go from the snow-capped mountains of the north to the palm-fringed beaches of the south. He may go from the rocks and deserts of the northwest to the steamy deltas of eastern India. But everywhere he will see stone statues and temples devoted to Vishnu and Shiva, the major Hindu gods. Everywhere he will find groups of people divided into castes. Caste and Hinduism are native to India; they give India a uniformity which government and language failed to provide.

Caste. A caste is a group of people with a relatively fixed position in a social hierarchy or pyramid. Membership in a caste is hereditary. Castes avoid contact with inferior castes and occupations out of pride and fear of contamination and defilement. Contamination may be cleansed by penances, rituals, bathing, or prayer. Extreme pollution may lead to temporary or even permanent expulsion from the caste.

Caste does separate people. But traditionally it also brought them together for certain purposes. Each caste performed a function which other castes needed. In other words, each person had reciprocal relations with members of other castes. The potter made pots, the blacksmith made plowshares and tools, the barber cut hair, the sweetmaker produced candy, the leatherworker removed dead animals and made sandals, and the priest performed sacrifices. Each of these persons was attached by heredity to a landowner's family which gave him a share of the annual crop and sometimes some land in return for his products and services. This web of reciprocal relations based upon exchange of services is called the *jajmani* system. Without the reciprocity of the *jajmani* system, it is doubtful if the low

Shiva. A bronze statue from the 14th century.

castes would have endured their inferiority as long as they did. Over the last century, many of the hereditary relations between landowners (*jajmans*) and their dependent artisans and laborers (*kamins*) have been severed and replaced by non-hereditary, cash relationships. The industrial revolution has weakened the inter-dependence of the artisans and other villagers, in particular; villagers increasingly prefer machine-made goods to the local hand-made products.

The flexibility of the caste system. Although caste has been the most rigidly stratified so-

Culture 517

The precepts of Hinduism create varied scenes. Two Faqirs (holymen believed to have miraculous powers) meditate for long hours in yoga positions. A high-caste bride, with caste marks on hands and forehead, waits to be married. An office worker, member of one of the many newly emerging castes, transacts business in Bombay.

cial system in the world, historically it has shown flexibility. Foreign conquerors, tribesmen, and other non-Hindus have entered the caste system at a variety of levels. Many Rajputs, for example, are believed to have been warriors from Central Asia who overran areas in northern India, accepted the services of Brahmin priests, and adopted Hindu gods and myths. In return, the Brahmins legitimized their political authority and gave them *Kshatriya* status just below themselves. Others, with less political power and prestige, entered at lower levels. The Hindu social and religious system has been absorbing new groups and ideas in this way through most of its history.

Limited group mobility, especially during the last century, has also been possible through a process called *Sanskritization*. Sanskrit, we have seen, is the classical language of the high culture of the Brahmins. Brahmins give Sanskrit prayers and chants at weddings, funerals, festivals, and temple ceremonies. Brahmin handbooks on mythology, ritual, and philosophy are written in Sanskrit. *Sanskritization* is the adoption of these values and customs. Castes hoping to improve their status and move up in the caste hierarchy have followed the Brahmin practice of avoiding meat, liquor, and widow-remarriage, and of using Sanskrit rituals in the worship of Brahmin gods. By imitating elite behavior, some castes have slowly elevated their status. This "levelling up" has reduced the social distance between Brahmins and some lower castes. However, other castes, especially in the South, have strongly rejected Brahmin values in the process of raising themselves politically and economically. Members of the "self-respect" movement in Madras have refused to employ Brahmins for their marriages.

Caste associations. Many Indians have turned to their caste associations in their search for social, economic, and political power. In certain areas, caste associations have put up candidates for office and persuaded their members to vote as a block. The caste associations have introduced many persons to democratic politics. Lower castes, organized by their leaders, have used their numerical strength to defeat high caste candidates, especially in the South, and to win concessions for the less privileged classes. Major political parties pay careful attention to caste when selecting their candidates in some areas in hopes of winning the votes of the larger castes.

Caste consciousness and caste solidarity seem to have grown since independence. But, paradoxically, this does not mean Indian society is becoming less democratic. Instead, some caste associations are attacking inequality and the traditional privileges of the high castes. By winning new rights for the poor and by helping people to understand democratic ideas and political processes, caste is once again adapting and transforming itself to meet changing conditions. In this case, the traditional and the modern are not diametrically opposed. Rather, political modernization is taking place through the traditional institution of caste, as well as outside it.

Rise of the intermediate castes. The caste associations have benefitted the intermediate, agricultural castes far more than the low castes and the untouchables. The middle-ranking peasant castes, the tenants and small landowners, have gained in many rural areas at the expense of the highest castes. Formerly, most villages were dominated by one or two high castes who controlled the affairs of the village, owned most of the land, and collected rents from their tenants without cultivating the land themselves. Now it is becoming legally and economically more difficult to live off rents. Most states limit a man to 25 acres of irrigated land. With the growth of the population, land has been subdivided each generation. Plots of land are often too small to make it feasible for owners to have tenants or laborers do the work. Yet high caste landowners often regard the actual work of farming as socially degrading and they therefore rarely take up the plow themselves. Some of these landowners have sold their land and invested the money in urban education for their children, leaving former tenants in control of the land. Even where the highest castes are still dominant, their position is being challenged. The intermediate, agricultural castes are learning their rights and freeing themselves from their economic and psychological bondage. These castes generally lack education but many are good agriculturists and many are discovering the opportunities offered by the right to vote. High caste politicians who might once have treated them as servile and inferior beings are now soliciting their votes and promising them local development projects.

The low castes. The low casts are often the artisans, small tenants, and landless laborers. Without land or education, they have not gained much from the right to vote or improved agricultural methods. However, they are numerous and the intermediate castes are providing an example of the advantages to be gained through community organization.

The untouchables. Untouchability is the aspect of caste Westerners find most difficult to understand. The caste system has operated on a belief that some activities, people, and things are pure and the rest are in varying degrees polluted. Untouchable castes were untouchable because they traditionally followed contaminating occupations, such as leather working, removing the dead, or cleaning up animal and human wastes. Untouchables were despised, avoided, and deprived of education. The British did not dare risk the political unpopularity of moving decisively to abolish untouchability. Gandhi, on the other hand, regarded untouchability as a corruption of Hindu institutions and a disgrace to India. He renamed untouchables *Harijan* or God's children. Under Gandhi's leadership, the Indian National Congress committed itself to the eradication of untouchability. After independence, a prominent untouchable, B. R. Ambedkar, was appointed Law Minister. Ambedkar drafted the Indian constitution which provided for the elimination of untouchability and for special measures to protect and assist untouchables, tribal peoples, and other "backward" classes. Approximately one-seventh of the seats in the national and state legislatures have been reserved for them and a 12.5 per cent quota has been fixed for government jobs.

Despite the preferential treatment, most untouchables remain in the villages in a depressed and subordinate position. Rarely do they exert pressure through the courts or the ballot box. There are several reasons for the slowness of their rise. Generally they are uneducated and economically dependent. Independent behavior may bring reprisals by more powerful villagers. Untouchables are geographically spread out and isolated from each other. Even within a local area untouchables practice untouchability among themselves. Not only are they treated as pariahs but they also regard themselves as degraded. Psychologically they *feel* inferior. Although the number of educated untouchables is growing rapidly, most of the quotas for government jobs with educational qualifications remain unfilled. In 1948, perhaps .5 million untouchables attended school while now the number is 7 or so million. Progress has been greatest in the primary schools.

Untouchability is still widespread in rural India. Many more village schools are admitting untouchables to sit with high-caste children. Many villages still have separate wells which must be used by untouchables. This young untouchable boy will follow the trade of sweeper, one of the few open to his caste until recent times.

ALAN BAND (TOP AND LEFT)

EDITORIAL PHOTOCOLOR ARCHIVES (DORANNE JACOBSON)

High caste villagers, especially of the older generation, find it difficult to accept the idea of equality. Discrimination, therefore, does persist despite laws which forbid it.* People's ways of thinking and behaving have not caught up with the law in most villages. Although untouchables are finding new opportunities and self-respect in the cities, it will be many years before the majority have the education, economic independence, knowledge of their legal rights, and the political leverage necessary to become full citizens.

Some untouchables resent the discrimination they still experience. About 2.5 million Mahars in western India have converted to Buddhism as a protest against discrimination. Buddhism seems to have given many Mahars a pride which other untouchables lack. However, the Government of India has placed an obstacle in the way of conversion by ruling that Buddhists do not qualify for the special privileges provided for the lower classes.

Caste in the cities. We have seen that caste is still strong in the villages. In the cities, caste solidarity has been eroding at a faster rate. High caste families with several generations of secular education and urban living show little concern for pollution, ritual, genealogy, and traditional occupation. Caste is still important to these families when arranging their children's marriages and perhaps when hiring and promoting persons in their offices and factories. Otherwise, their lives are largely caste-free. In fact, concern for traditional caste practices is often weaker in the cities among high castes than among low castes. This is because high caste families were the first to take advantage of Western education. As a result, many gained economic and educa-

* See *Readings in World History*, "The Lynching of an Untouchable," p. 543.

tional advantages which seemed more important than high ritual and caste status. Moreover, they accepted the nationalist argument that ability and achievement, rather than birth and race, should determine a man's opportunities.

While one hundred years ago, almost all the college graduates came from the Brahmin and a few other high castes, today a wide range of castes compete for education and employment. In the South, where Brahmin dominance was most extreme, non-Brahmins have captured political power and have legislated quotas which favor themselves over Brahmins in the distribution of scholarships and jobs. In many other areas, members of the middle castes are entering professions which were once high caste.

Caste is the social institution of the Hindus. Until recently, it would have been impossible to be a Hindu without also being part of the caste system. What else does it mean to be a Hindu? What values do Hindus have?

Hinduism. Most Indians today are Hindus and many non-Hindus in South Asia have been influenced by Hindu values. Hinduism is far more than a religion; it is also a way of life. It enters every aspect of human experience: washing, cooking, harvesting, giving birth, marrying, and dying. These are all religious and ceremonial actions and must be done with the proper ritual. An orthodox Hindu believes that to ignore the ritual invites misfortune.

Hinduism has been compared to a sponge which absorbs everything around it. Like a sponge, it has no clear outline, and it is extremely difficult to say exactly what Hinduism is or is not. It is not a church in the Western sense of a church which has an organization of bishops or elders and a precise creed which must be accepted. Instead, Hinduism and its offshoots represent a culture contain-

In Jaipur an extremely wealthy Hindu couple are married in a ceremony which takes over 21 hours to perform. To set a date for the ceremony, most likely astrologers were consulted to determine the correct month, day, and hour. The couple will probably name their children after Hindu gods so they can pronounce those holy names as often as possible.

ing a bewildering variety of beliefs and practices. For example, there have been atheist, monotheist, and polytheist sects. There are sects, such as the Jains, whose reverence of all forms of life lead some devotees to stay in at night and to wear masks so that they will not step on or inhale insects. On the other hand, the worshippers of the goddess Kali sacrifice buffaloes and goats.

The origins of Hinduism are obscure but it may safely be said that in its present form it is the product of interaction between Dravidian and Aryan religions. The easiest way to understand Hinduism is to distinguish between three levels: Hinduism as Brahmin philosophy, Hinduism as the devotional worship of the gods, and Hinduism as the popular spirit worship.

Brahmin philosophy has three important aspects: (1) the doctrine of a single god which permeates all living creatures,* (2) the belief in transmigration or rebirth of souls, and (3) the related concept of *karma* which holds that a man's soul will be reborn into a higher caste if his behavior has been good and into a lower state if he has been bad. Belief in monotheism, transmigration, and *karma* seems to have entered Aryan religion only after the Aryans settled in India. The early Aryan tribal invaders worshipped a number of male sky gods, many of whom were connected with war and the powers of nature. The Aryans approached their gods through animal sacrifices.

As the Aryans turned from nomadism and cattle-raising to settled agriculture, their priests developed more complex sacrifices with hymns, chants, and elaborate rituals. The sacrificial hymns and chants were gathered between 1500 and 900 B.C. in a collection known as the *Rig Veda*. The *Rig Veda* is the world's oldest religious text still in use. The hymns of the *Rig Veda* were explained and interpreted in subsequent works which are known collectively as the *Vedas*. Hindus revere the *Vedas* as the source of their religion although actual religious practice often bears no resemblance to the Vedic literature.

Gradually the Aryan hymns, chants, and rituals of the sacrifice grew in significance. The act of sacrifice and the Brahmin priests who performed it became as important as the gods themselves. Men thought that the cosmic order would collapse without correct performance of the sacrifices. The role of the Brahmin priests was so important that Brahmins were elevated above the rulers and warriors in social esteem.

Increasingly after about 900 B.C., people believed that there was a basic identity of the sacrificer with the gods. Men thought that

*See *Readings in World History*, "Hindiusm," p. 527.

the souls of living things were one with the gods, that everything was part of a universal god or soul. People and animals die and plants decay, but their souls are immortal and are reborn in different shapes. The form of the rebirth is determined by *karma* or the effect of one's deeds in a previous life. Proper behavior would lead to higher status in the next life, perhaps as a *Kshatriya* or a Brahmin, while accumulation of bad *karma* meant rebirth in a lower caste or perhaps as an animal or insect. The doctrine of *karma* explained and justified the social inequalities of the caste system. Brahmins persuaded people they deserved their inferiority because of misdeeds in a former life; on the other hand, Brahmins and other high castes promised the lower castes that proper observance of caste *dharma* or duties in this life would be rewarded in the next life.

The doctrines of transmigration of souls, *karma*, and the basic oneness of all creatures survived as integral parts of Hindu philosophy. However, Hinduism developed different ways for men to reach and communicate with god. Between 900 and 500 B.C. large groups of Indians reacted against the dominance of the Brahmin priests and the complicated, expensive ritual. Gautama Buddha was a product of that reaction. Like the leaders of the Protestant Reformation in Europe, reformers argued that if god was within each man, man could contact god directly, without the help of priests and rituals. Thinkers distinguished between the physical and the spiritual world and taught that material wealth distracted man's attention from spiritual concerns and prevented man's understanding of the basic mystical identity between his own soul (Atma) and the universal soul (Brahma). Many Indians turned to asceticism, living alone as hermits or in monastic communites in search of the god each believed was within himself. The ultimate goal of these ascetic holy men or *sadhus* was to merge their individual consciousness with that of god. That union would bring eternal bliss and an end to the long chain of rebirths. For this reason, the aim of Hindu philosophy could be said to escape from the suffering and illusions of worldly existence.

Christianity has also had ascetics who sought mystical union with God through meditation, prayer, and penances, but Hinduism has given more attention than any other religion to ascetic and mystical practices. Even today, many educated Indians consider renouncing their worldly possessions after they have fulfilled their obligations to their families in order to seek spiritual harmony. Great respect is given to men who, like Gandhi, surrender material comforts. It is thought that private wealth and physical desires cause selfishness and blind an individual to the real identity between himself, all other living beings, and god. The *sadhu* who walks on burning coals or lies on a bed of nails is trying to prove that he has triumphed over his physical needs and feelings, that he is selfless, that he is one with god.

Worship of the gods. Hinduism recognizes differences in human needs and development. Hindu philosophers have not insisted upon a single religious dogma. They recognized that the notion of a single, impersonal, all-pervading god would be too abstract for some people to understand and emotionally unsatisfying for others. Many people need concrete images and symbols to help them to worship and understand god. Most Hindus worship god not as an abstract principle but as symbolized by concrete images. It is sometimes said that there are millions of Hindu gods, one for each member of the faith. Because there are many gods, Hinduism may be described as polytheistic. But most educated Hindus believe that there is really only one

An Indian holy man.

god although the single god reveals himself to man in many shapes and consequently he is worshipped in many different forms. Krishna, Rama, Vishnu, Shiva, and Kali are either different names for the same god or different aspects of the ultimate divine force. Hindus who believe there is only one god are monotheists.

Almost all the gods are associated in mythology with either Shiva or Vishnu. Shiva worshippers generally are devotees of one of his wives, such as Kali, Durga, or Parvati. Shiva and his wives are identified with the forces of destruction. People exposed repeatedly to the destructiveness of invading armies, droughts, floods, and diseases understandably were awed by the dark forces of death and misfortune. They prayed and sacrificed to the gods of those forces in hope of controlling them.

Vishnu devotees usually worship Vishnu's avatars or incarnations, such as Krishna or Rama. Vishnu and his incarnations represent the forces of preservation. Vishnu is believed to have incarnated himself on nine different occasions to save the world from destruction.

Hindus worship the gods' images in temples and in the *puja* (prayer) rooms of their houses. They celebrate the mythical events of the gods' lives in annual religious festivals. It is through frequent festivals, pilgrimages, story-telling, and dramatic performances that the values of caste, chastity, obedience, and loyalty to parents are inculcated. When villagers watch Rama fight the demon Ravanna to recover his kidnapped wife, they are entertained while at the same time they see a model of the good Hindu husband and the righteous Hindu king. When devotees gather in the courtyard of a temple and sing about Radha's passionate longing for Krishna, they sing about a deep adoration which symbolizes human love for god. When devotees enter the temple and lay an offering of food before an idol, they know the idol will not actually eat the food. But by giving something away, they are bringing themselves closer to the god.

Spirit worship. Less educated Hindus are animists. They believe that their surroundings contain numerous spirits, some evil, some friendly. The evil spirits must be placated, or else they may cause trouble. Animism is a widespread phenomenon among people who do not understand the scientific explanation for disease, drought, and other disturbing occurrences. Villagers use sacrifices, *pujas*, charms, astrologers, medicine men, and priests to understand, appease, and neutralize the spirits.

Hinduism's tolerant and sponge-like quality has made it possible for many different races and sub-cultures to co-exist side by side. When a new group of immigrants or tribesmen came into contact with Hindus, usually they entered the Hindu fold. Respect for Brahmins, practice of caste, and belief in the sanctity of the cow would make a man a Hindu.

In the process of absorbing non-Hindu groups, Hindus accepted many new influences. For example, one of the most popular Hindu gods, Krishna, was probably not Hindu originally. He seems to have been worshipped exclusively by a group of dark-skinned, non-Hindu tribes at one time. Krishna is now portrayed in Hindu myths as a dark-skinned god who was a companion of the cowherds and a great warrior who destroyed a troublesome demon. (Historically he probably was a tribal leader who was deified for his exploits.) The Brahmins, in accepting these tribes into Hinduism, incorporated the Krishna cult into the Brahmin religious system. Krishna is recognized as the eighth and most popular avatar or incarnation of the god Vishnu.

Thus, India had religions which met the religious needs of different levels of society before the Europeans first reached India. Hinduism and Islam provided explanations of life and death as well as good and bad. Hinduism and Islam offered people moral guides for their behavior. Moreover, they were flexible enough so that when they were challenged by Christianity and science, reformers persuaded millions of Hindus and Muslims that reform of traditional culture was preferable to total abandonment of their ancestors' values.

Today, Hindu culture shows great vitality, although it is becoming more secular and popular. Myths which were once recited in scholarly Sanskrit by Brahmins at religious festivals are now made into movies in the

ALAN BAND

vernacular languages. "Mythologicals," like our "westerns," are popular and are shown even in the villages. Religious dances once confined to temple courtyards are performed now in concert halls by professional entertainers. A new mass culture is emerging. Because this culture is not limited to the high castes, it is helping to unify India. It is being spread by the new communications media: newspapers, cheap books, and radio and television sets.

Hindu revivalism. Many Brahmins regret the recent trends towards secularism, democracy, and special assistance for non-Brahmins, although other Brahmins have helped lead the struggle for these objectives. Conservative Brahmins are nostalgic for the days when they were rarely challenged as the custodians of sacred knowledge. Indian nationalism contains a strong streak of revivalist Hinduism. Militant Hindus have demanded a tougher policy against Pakistan. The Brahmin who assassinated Gandhi in 1948 resented Gandhi's generosity to Muslims. More recently, Hindu holy men have led a sometimes violent agitation for a ban on the slaughter of cows.* They, like many other Hindus, are disturbed by the influx of foreign influences which threaten older values. Some of the disputed influences concern morality as much as modernity. For example, Hinduism encourages people to avoid excessive wealth and contact with the opposite sex. The Indian film industry, the second largest in the world, is not permitted to show people kissing. Hindus object to the kissing, nudity, drinking, and the glorification of materialistic living which are shown in imported films, most of which come from the United States.

The Hindu revivalists often influence the course of public policy, even though their

* See *Readings in World History,* "The Sacred Cow," p. 530.

political parties do not win a major share of the vote in most states. Hindu nationalists are among the leaders of the agitation to make Hindi the sole official language. It would be extremely difficult for the government to compromise with Pakistan over the Kashmir issue in view of their opposition to a plebiscite in or neutralization of Kashmir. Judging from both the Hindi and cow-protection agitations and the growth of their political parties, the Hindu nationalists have gained in strength as the Congress Party has weakened. However, few argue publicly against the changes taking place in the caste system.

Conclusion. India's greatest achievement since independence has been the successful operation of democratic institutions, including fair elections and protection of freedom of speech, assembly, and movement. But these institutions are not working smoothly in some states and they are under attack from both the left and the right of the ruling Congress Party. India has also made modest progress in solving her economic problems. After several decades of stagnation under the British, food-grain production rose from 55 million tons in 1950–51 to 95.6 million tons in 1967–68. Her industrial production rose even more impressively during the first three 5-year plans, reaching in 1965–66, two and one-half times the 1950–51 level. Yet the problems India faces are staggering. Its people are still desperately poor and undernourished. Population growth has been so great that per capita income increased relatively little. Will the government be able to stem the rise in population? Will people tolerate such a slow improvement in living

The Ganges River is considered the "Mother" of India and is sacred to all Hindus. Each year thousands come to bathe at holy spots along the river. Some hope to cure ailments and others to die in the Ganges waters and thus be carried to Paradise.

CARL E. OSTMAN

standards? Gradualism marked the transition from British rule to self-government. Changes in the status of the lower castes are real but they are also gradual and slow. Social, political, and cultural change in India, in contrast to China, has so far been evolutionary rather than revolutionary. The question remains, therefore, will the present system satisfy the rising demand for more dramatic progress?

Reviewing the Essentials

Caste
1. How does caste separate people?
2. In what ways does caste bring people together?
3. How is the caste system changing? What government policies are causing it to change? What other factors are bringing change?
4. Distinguish between the upper, intermediate, and lower castes.
5. Why were untouchables regarded as untouchable?

Hinduism
6. What are the different levels of Hinduism?
7. What are the *Vedas?*
8. How did Krishna become a Hindu god?
9. How is Hinduism changing?
10. What grievances do Hindu revivalists have?

Conclusion
11. What achievements has India made in economics, politics, and social reform?
12. What are the prospects for India's future?

Explain, Identify, or Locate

jajmani	*puja*	*Sadhu*	Shiva
Kshatriya	*Harijan*	ascetic	Vishnu
Sanskrit	*Rig Veda*	polytheism	avatar
vernacular	karma	monotheism	

UNIT ACTIVITIES

1. Have students read or act out *the Ramayana* before the class. Then ask the class to discuss the behavior idealized in the roles of Rama and Sita. *The Ramayana* has appeared in many translations: R. C. Dutt's *The Mahabharata and The Ramayana* (condensed) (New York: E. P. Dutton, 1953), is one of the most readable versions.

2. Examine reproductions of Mughal and Rajput miniature paintings, together with the descriptions of the paintings and discuss what the paintings reveal about Indian customs and values. The following books have excellent reproductions and texts: Douglas Barrett and Basil Gray, *Painting of India* (Skira 1963); Mohinder Singh Randhawa and John Kenneth Galbraith, *Indian Painting: The Scene, Themes, and Legends* (Boston: Houghton Mifflin, 1968); and Stuart C. Welch, *The Art of Mughal India* (New York: The Asia Society, 1963). Consult W. G. Archer, *The Loves of Krishna* (New York: Macmillan, 1957) for the appealing and popular Krishna myth and paintings.

3. Compare the development and teachings of Hinduism, Buddhism, and Islam. See Joe David Brown and the Editors of *Life, India* (New York: TIME, Inc., 1967); A. L. Basham, *The Wonder That Was India* (New York: Macmillan, 1954); William de Bary (ed), *Sources of Indian Tradition* (New York: Columbia University Press, 1958);

and Nancy Wilson Ross, *Three Ways of Asian Wisdom* (New York: Simon and Schuster, 1966).

4. Estimate the effects of British rule on the Indian caste system and on Indian agriculture and industry. For background reading, see M. N. Srinivas, *Social Change in Modern India* (Berkeley: University of California Press, 1967); Daniel and Alice Thorner, "India and Pakistan" in *Most of the World,* edited by Ralph Linton (New York: Columbia University Press, 1949); and Martin Deming Lewis (editor), *The British in India: Imperialism or Trusteeship?* (Boston: D.C. Heath, 1962).

5. Read *Gandhi's Autobiography: The Story of My Experiments With Truth* (Boston: Beacon Press, 1957) and explain what Western and what Indian ideas influenced Gandhi on violence, sex, cows, non-Hindu religions, and industrialization.

6. Several students should read Harold Issac's *India's Ex-Untouchables* (New York: John Day, 1965) and lead a class discussion of the similarities and differences between the untouchable problem in India and the racial problem in the United States.

7. Compare the Indian and American political systems, including the constitution, parties and their ideologies, and federal-state relations. Consult W. H. Morris-Jones, *The Government and Politics of India* (London: Hutchinson University Library, 1964); Beatrice B. Lamb, *India: A World in Transition,* 3rd edition (New York, A. J. Praeger, 1968); and Norman D. Palmer, *The Indian Political System* (Boston: Houghton Mifflin, 1961).

8. Have two groups of students debate the Kashmir issue, with one group presenting India's case, the other Pakistan's case, and the rest of the class attempting to find a solution. The Kashmir conflict is discussed in Lord Birdwood *A Continent Decides* (London: Hale, 1953); Michael Brecher. *The Struggle for Kashmir* (Toronto: Oxford University Press, 1953); and Josef Korbel, *Danger in Kashmir* (Princeton, N.J.: Princeton University Press, 1954).

9. Prepare a set of recommendations for U.S. foreign policy in South Asia. Consider relations between India, Pakistan, and China; the economic problems of India and Pakistan; Indian and Pakistani attitudes towards the United States; and general American foreign policy objectives. Consult current newspapers; Beatrice P. Lamb, *India: A World in Transition,* 3rd edition (New York: A. J. Praeger, 1968); and Norman D. Palmer, *South Asia and United States Policy* (Boston: Houghton Mifflin, 1966).

10. Contrast the process of social change in an Indian and a Chinese village, using Andre Beteille, *Caste, Class, Power: Changing Patterns of Stratification in a Tanjore Village* (Berkeley: University of California Press, 1965); and William Hinton, *Fanshen: A Documentary of Revolution in a Chinese Village* (New York: Vintage Books, 1969).

11. Make a resource map of India locating major natural resources, irrigation projects, hydroelectric power, and industrial centers developed under Five-Year Plans to date.

12. Make a resource map of Pakistan locating major cities, natural resources, and industries being developed under Pakistan's Developmental Programs. Write a statement summarizing similarities and differences in the resource bases of India and Pakistan. What are implications for the economic development of both nations?

SELECTED READING

• Joe David Brown and the Editors of *LIFE, India* (New York: TIME, Inc., 1967) is a beautifully illustrated and well written survey of present day India, its culture, problems, and historical background.

• Walter A. Fairservis, Jr., the well known archaeologist-anthropologist, gives a vivid picture of Indian civilization in his *India* (New York:

World Publishing Co., 1961). Sir Mortimer Wheeler's *Civilizations of the Indus Valley and Beyond* (New York: McGraw-Hill, 1966) is a profusely illustrated survey of archaeological discoveries through the Mauryan Empire.

• One of the best brief, general histories is Percival Spear's *India, Pakistan, and the West* (New York: Oxford University Press, 4th edition,

1967). Also short and readable are Robert E. Frykenberg, *India* (Boston: Ginn and Company, 1968); Emil Lengyel, *The Subcontinent of India* (Englewood Cliffs, N.J.: Scholastic, 1961); and Manorama Modak, *The Land and People of India* (Philadelphia: Lippincott, 1963).

● A short biography of Gandhi is Jeanette Eaton's *Gandhi: Fighter Without a Sword* (New York: William Morrow, 1950). Also see Louis Fischer's *Gandhi: His Life and Message for the World* (New York: New American Library, 1963).

● Nehru's story is told through pictures in Michael Edwardes', *Nehru: A Pictorial Biography* (New York: Viking Press, 1963). The best biography of Nehru, as well as an excellent political history, is Michael Brecher's *Nehru: A Political Biography* (Boston: Beacon Press, 1962).

● A valuable study of changes taking place in rural India is William and Charlotte Wiser's village study, *Behind Mud Walls, 1930–1960* (Berkeley: University of California Press, 1963). Taya Zinkin's *Caste Today* (New York: Oxford University Press, 1962) is brief and readable.

● One of the easiest ways to get a feeling of the texture of Indian life is through the novel. Kamala Markandya's *Nectar in a Sieve* (New York: New American Library, 1956) dramatizes a peasant woman's suffering and appeals strongly to many high school students. The breakdown of trust between Hindus and Muslims in a village during the partition of India in 1947 is described in Khushwant Singh's *Train to Pakistan* (also published under the title *Mano Majra*) (New York: Grove Press, 1956). India's leading writer in

ALAN BAND

English, R. K. Narayan, has many fine and humorous novels, including *The Financial Expert* (New York, Farrar, Straus, 1959); and *The Guide* (New York: New American Library, 1966). John Masters' *The Deceivers* (New York: Ballantine Press, 1966) is perhaps the most exciting of his novels about India. It is about the suppression of the Thugs who straggled and robbed their victims for the sake of religion. Also excellent is E. M. Forster's *Passage to India* (New York: Harcourt, Brace and World, 1949).

● Personal accounts are sometimes useful. Cynthia Bowles, the daughter of the American Ambassador to India, wrote about her experiences in *At Home in India* (New York: Pyramid Books, 1959). Ruth Gallup Armstrong's *Sisters Under the Sari* (Ames: Iowa State Press, 1964) is an account of an American's visit to her Indian "adopted sister." Santha Rama Rau, who was educated in England, writes interestingly about her travels in India in *Gifts of Passage* (New York: Harper & Row, 1966).

FURTHER READING

● There are many general histories of India but Percival Spear's *India: A Modern History* (Ann Arbor: University of Michigan Press, 1961) is imaginatively written and not too detailed for most high school students. Beatrice Pitney Lamb's *India: A World in Transition* (New York: Praeger, 3rd edition, 1968) analyses caste, regional and linguistic conflict, foreign policy, and economic development in historical perspective. W. Norman Brown's *The United States and India and Pakistan* (Cambridge: Harvard University Press, 2nd edition, 1963) is the leading American Indologist's lucid and scholarly account of the same problems although it does not cover the last decade or so.

● Autobiographies provide insights into Indian life and culture. Especially good are *Gandhi's Autobiography: The Story of My Experiments With Truth* (Boston: Beacon Press, 1957); Jawaharlal Nehru's *Toward Freedom* (New York: John Day, 1941); and D. D. Karve (editor), *The New Brahmans: Five Maharashtrian Families* (Berkeley: University of California Press, 1963).

● High school students should be able to make interesting comparisons between India's untouchable problem and the United States' race problem after reading Harold R. Issac's *India's Ex-Untouchables* (New York: John Day, 1965). Gandhi's philosophy and political uses of nonviolence are discussed in Joan Bondurant's *Conquest of Violence: The Gandhian Philosophy of Conflict* (Berkeley: University of California Press, 1965). For politics, see Norman D. Palmer, *Indian Political Systems* (Boston: Houghton Mifflin, 1962).

● Ancient Indian history and culture are discussed in very considerable detail but authoritatively by A. L. Basham, *The Wonder That Was India* (New York: Hawthorn Books, 1963). Source materials on Indian culture (Hindu, Buddhist, and Muslim) from the *Vedas* to the present are collected and clearly interpreted in William Theodore deBary (editor), *Sources of Indian Tradition* (New York: Columbia University Press, 1958). A much shorter collection is O. L. Chavarria-Aguilar (editor), *Traditional India* (Englewood Cliffs, N.J.: Prentice-Hall, 1964).

● There are several short collections of conflicting historical interpretations. Among them are Ainslee T. Embree (editor), *1857 in India: Mutiny or War of Independence* (Boston: D. C. Heath, 1963); Martin Deming Lewis (editor), *The British in India: Imperialism or Trusteeship?* (Boston: D. C. Heath, 1962); and Martin Deming Lewis (editor), *Gandhi: Maker of Modern India?* (Boston: D. C. Heath, 1965). The roots and consequences of Hindu-Muslim antagonism are discussed in T. Walter Wallbank (editor), *The Partition of India: Causes and Responsibilities* (Boston: D. C. Heath, 1966). John R. McLane's *The Political Awakening in India* (Englewood Cliffs, N.J.: Prentice-Hall, forthcoming) contains source materials on the history of nationalism, regionalism, and communalism.

● Pakistan has not received as much attention from scholars as India has. However, Khalid B. Sayeed's *The Political System of Pakistan* (Boston: Houghton Mifflin, 1967) is a well written study of Pakistan's creation and development.

● India's economic problems are reviewed intelligently in Walter C. Neale's *India: The Search for Unity, Democracy and Progress* (Princeton: Van Nostrand, 1965). A perceptive Indian reporter spent a year touring and interviewing Indian peasants in an effort to discover what values and customs are restricting change. Her revealing case studies were published in Kusum Nair, *Blossoms in the Dust: The Human Factor in Indian Development* (New York: Praeger Books, 1962).

● The following books include good photographs of India: Madeleine Biardeau, *India*, translated by F. Carter (New York: Viking Press, 1960); Margaret Bourke-White, *Halfway to Freedom* (New York: Simon and Schuster, 1949); and Elizabeth Katz (compiler), *India in Pictures* (New York: Sterling, revised edition, 1965).

● The Asia Society provides invaluable assistance to people looking for teaching aids. It publishes guides to paperbacks, films, filmstrips, records, and maps related to Asian studies. Address: 112 E. 64th Street, New York, N.Y. 10021.

SUB-SAHARAN AFRICA

No responsible African leader would make much secret of the extent to which he needs outside economic assistance in the decades to come. One may sometimes wonder if the Western Powers fully understand the dilemma facing political leaders in the emergent lands. They have gained independence for their peoples. The hazards and excitements of the struggle lie behind. Ahead lies the workaday world in which people must live and eat and hope to prosper. Independence of itself ... does not supply all the economic and social tools. The leaders are now expected ... to work miracles. The people look for new schools, new towns, new factories. ... Construction must begin. There must be something to show for independence. And if there is nothing to show, popular discontent may split the country apart.

Kwame Nkrumah

BASIC FACTS: Vastness and Variation

A TV announcer advertises a program set in the grassland game reserves of East Africa as a "story of jungle adventure;" a magazine article refers to the "stone-age natives" in a West African country where Africans have been using iron for many, many centuries. Such inaccurate ideas persist in spite of Africa's increasing importance in world affairs. Millions of Americans still think of Africa South of the Sahara as a vast, steamy jungle, principally inhabited by man-killing beasts and naked hunters ignorant of the 20th-century world we share. Only by learning more about Africa can we begin to distinguish the facts from often long-held myths.

Africa has long been important to the world and to the United States. Mankind's first great technological revolution, in which people learned to shape stone into tools, occurred in Africa. Much later Africa, like Europe, contributed a large number of its people to pioneering the New World. About half of the world's people of European descent live outside of Europe, while about a third of the people of African background live on other continents. Now that most of Africa has regained its independence, Africa has more votes in the United Nations than any other continent.

From the very first decades the American colonies were built through the efforts of Africans as well as Europeans, and these two groups have played the predominant roles in American history ever since. A long history of trade existed between the United States and pre-colonial independent African states; and after the slave trade was outlawed, Americans in their clipper ships became the leading Western traders along the coast of East Africa. Today more than 11 per cent of Americans have some African ancestors, and in their struggle for equality they are testing whether within a Western culture liberty and justice can encompass all races.

Why Sub-Saharan? The Sahara Desert ceased to be a desert about 6000 years ago when Africa entered the most recent of its "wet phases." For about 2000 years people were able to settle in the area that is now desert, and Stone Age peoples were able to move between "Sub-Saharan" Africa, North Africa, and the Middle East. As the rains decreased, after 2000 B.C., most of the people had to move south or north to find areas of sufficient rainfall. Movement over the desert became more difficult, while migrations between the Middle East and the northern coast of Africa continued as before. To the Greeks and Romans, North Africa was part of their Mediterranean world. The sea and the coastal plain that circled it provided highways for trade, ideas, and people, thus connecting North Africa with the Middle East and southern Europe. With the expansion of Islam in the seventh century, Arab armies conquered North Africa, and later large numbers of Arabs migrated there. Thus the peoples, language, and Islamic religion came to be like that in Arab Asia.

While the drying up of the Sahara tended to separate Sub-Saharan peoples from those along the northern coast, contact continued. By Roman times there were well-established trade routes crossing the desert. As a result of trade with Islamic North Africa, the independent kings in the savanna belt south of the desert adopted Islam as their religion. Hence, like North Africa, their empires were thought of as part of the Islamic world during the Middle Ages, even though they had not been conquered or settled by Arabs.

Oldman Pass in Ethiopia illustrates one of the vast areas of savanna vegetation.

North Africa, then, has ties both with the Arab world and with Africa South of the Sahara, and today North African countries belong both to Arab and African international organizations. North Africa, though, still shares its language, religion, and people with the Middle East. Africa South of the Sahara, on the other hand, developed independently of the Mediterranean empires and large-scale Arab invasions. So we focus on the area of Africa lying south of the Sahara.

GEOGRAPHY

Isolation? Westerners tend to think of Africa as having been lost until Europe found it in the 15th century. This is as much a reflection of Europe's as of Africa's isolation to that time. Plants of African origin long ago found their way to many parts of the world. At least from the time of Greece, bold seamen had traded between India and the coast of East Africa.* About the time of Christ, people from Indonesia had reached the island of Madagascar and the east coast of the continent with the aid of equatorial winds and currents. Ancient Chinese coins and porcelain have been discovered buried in Africa. Chinese paintings dating from the 15th century show giraffes, and giraffes are not native to any area but Africa. Long before Europe "discovered" Sub-Saharan Africa, the trans-Saharan trade routes had connected this part of Africa with the Mediterranean world. Africa then must have been trading with Arabia, India, and China before northern Europe "explored" these areas.

* See *Readings in World History,* "East African Trade in Roman Times" (Boston: Allyn and Bacon, Inc., 1970), p. 548.

Yet, though Africa South of the Sahara was not isolated in the same sense as the Americas or Australia, it does have features that at times have made movement to, from, and within it difficult. Africa has few good natural harbors, especially on the west coast. Tropical rain forests and large swampy areas have often presented barriers as difficult as the Sahara; moreover, Africa's rivers, with their frequent rapids and fluctuating flow, cannot be used as great inland-to-ocean highways like the Rhine and Mississippi. Steep mountains and valleys add to the difficulty of transportation and help to cause the abrupt differences in climate which tend to separate the areas within Africa.

Physical geography. Look at the physical map of Sub-Saharan Africa. South of the Sahara, Africa consists principally of a great plateau, tipped so that the highest part is in the east. The plateau ranges from a height of about 3000 feet in the west to 6000 feet in the east. In late geologic times, there was an era of faulting on the eastern part of the plateau caused when the Indian Ocean subsided. This resulted in the fracturing of the plateau's surface, and the dropping down of long, relatively narrow segments of land, which became the great rift valleys of East Africa.

The greater of these stretches all the way from the Zambezi River in the south to the Ethiopian coast in the north; it extends further to form the Red Sea and the Dead Sea. It is in these East African rift valleys that we find deep lakes such as Tanganyika, Nyasa, Edward, and Albert. Lakes Tanganyika and Nyasa are both larger than two of the Great Lakes, Erie and Ontario.

There are no great areas of plains and mountains in Sub-Saharan Africa. Although the Congo is a vast interior basin, it is not similar to the great interior plain of North America. It is a plateau covered by tropical rain forests in many areas and also containing large areas of tall grass. Some high mountains may be found in the Republic of South Africa, Tanzania, Rwanda, Burundi, Kenya, Uganda, and Ethiopia. Lesser mountains can be found in South-West Africa, Angola, and Guinea. Plains areas are found all along the coast. They are narrow, frequently less than 20 miles wide and reaching over 100 miles inland only at very few locations.

Four great rivers have been especially important to Africa. In the northeast is the Nile which empties out of Lake Victoria. (Victoria is the second largest body of fresh water in the world, exceeded only by Lake Superior.) Its most important tributary is the Blue Nile, which rises in the Ethiopian highlands. In the northwestern part of Sub-Saharan Africa lies the Niger; in the center, the Congo; and in the southeast, the Zambezi. The great curve of the Congo is even longer than the Mississippi and drains a larger basin than the Mississippi-Missouri system.

The only parts of Africa South of the Sahara that lie below 1000 feet are parts of the Niger basin and the narrow coastal plains that extend around Africa between the ocean and the steep slopes which rise to the plateau. The sudden drop from the plateau to the coastal strip explains why all African rivers have rapids or waterfalls.

The Zambezi is a good example of the difficulties of penetrating the interior of Africa via the great rivers. The delta of the Zambezi has four separate mouths on the Indian Ocean in Mozambique, and each is obstructed by sand bars. For a distance of 400 miles to the edge of the great East African Escarpment (the edge of the interior plateau), the river is broad (2 to 5 miles) and flows through the relatively level coastal plain. There are few difficulties to navigation once within the sand bars except in the dry season when the river is low. At the

NORTH ATLANTIC OCEAN

Mediterranean Sea

Strait of Gibraltar

Algiers
Tunis
Tripoli
Benghazi
Alexandria
Port Said
CAIRO
Suez Canal
Dead Sea
SYRIA
ISRAEL
ASIA

Rabat
MOROCCO
ATLAS MTS.
TUNISIA

ALGERIA
LIBYA
UNITED ARAB REPUBLIC (EGYPT)
Karnak
Aswan
Aswan Dam

SAUDI
ARABIA
Riyadh
Mecca
Persian Gulf

El Aiun
SPANISH SAHARA
TROPIC OF CANCER

THE SAHARA

AFRICA

MAURITANIA
Nouakchott

REPUBLIC OF
Timbuktu Niger
Niamey

NIGER

Lake Chad
CHAD
Fort Lamy

SUDAN
Khartoum

Red Sea

Arabian Sea

Dakar SENEGAL
Bamako
MALI
Ouagadougou

Kano

NIGERIA

Blue Nile River
Lake Tana
FR. AFARS AND ISSAS
Djibouti

GAMBIA
Bathurst
PORTUGUESE GUINEA
Bissau
GUINEA
Conakry
Freetown
SIERRA LEONE
Monrovia
LIBERIA
UPPER VOLTA
IVORY COAST
GHANA
TOGO
DAHOMEY
Lome
Abidjan
Accra
Porto Novo
Ibadan
Lagos
BIAFRA
Port Harcourt

Jos
Benue
River

CAMEROON
Yaounde

CENTRAL AFRICAN REPUBLIC
Banqui

White Nile River

ETHIOPIA
Addis Ababa
Hargeisa

SOMALI REPUBLIC

EQUATOR

SOUTH ATLANTIC OCEAN

EQUATORIAL GUINEA
RIO MUNI
PRINCIPE
SÃO TOMÉ

GABON
Libreville
CONGO
REPUBLIC
Brazzaville

Congo River

REPUBLIC OF THE CONGO

Lake Albert
Lake Edward
UGANDA
Kampala
Kigali
RWANDA
BURUNDI
Bujumbura
Lake Victoria

KENYA
Nairobi
Mogadishu

INDIAN OCEAN

CABINDA
Kinshasa
Luanda

ANGOLA

KATANGA

Lake Tanganyika
TANZANIA
ZANZIBAR
Dar Es Salaam

MALAWI
Lake Malawi
Zomba

MOZAMBIQUE

ZAMBIA
Lusaka
Kariba Dam

Zambezi River

Salisbury
RHODESIA
Tananarive
MALAGASY REPUBLIC

TROPIC OF CAPRICORN

SOUTH-WEST AFRICA
Windhoek

BOTSWANA
Gaberones

Pretoria
Lourenco Marques
Mbabane
SWAZILAND
Johannesburg
REPUBLIC OF SOUTH AFRICA
Kimberley
Maseru
LESOTHO

Cape Town
Cape of Good Hope

AFRICA

Scale 700 miles to one inch

| 0 | 350 | 700 |

DRY GRASSLAND

DESERT

SAVANNA

TROPICAL RAIN FORESTS

MOUNTAINS

Victoria Falls in Zambia. Although the Falls impede navigation of the Zambezi River, they are proving to be a source of great amounts of hydro-electric power.

edge of the East African Escarpment the Kebrabasa Rapids are a formidable bar to navigation. From this point to the great canyon of the Victoria Falls, a distance of 800 miles, the river is navigable, although sometimes dangerous at low water.

It is on this middle stretch of the river that the Kariba Dam was built. The dam created a great lake upstream and the area is now being developed for industry. The generators of the dam supply electricity to the cities of Salisbury and Bulawayo, and to the copper belt of Zambia.

Above Victoria Falls, the upper part of the Zambezi, about 1000 miles in length, is navigable although obstructed at points by stretches of rapids. Stream flow decreases greatly during the dry season since the river receives very little water from the intermittent tributaries flowing from the arid and desert lands of South-West Africa and Botswana.

The Congo and the Niger Rivers also have extended stretches of rapids at the edge of the coastal plain, though they are navigable for hundreds of miles once the high inland plateau is reached. These navigational hazards have been an important factor in holding back Africa's development because they obstruct or impede passage to the interior. In this respect Africa is very different from North America where the Mississippi, the St. Lawrence, and the Great Lakes provide easy access into the heart of the continent.

Climate and vegetation. Some parts of Africa South of the Sahara have less annual rainfall than Arizona, while one area gets an annual rainfall of at least 400 inches. This is more than three times as much rain as falls upon the state of Washington, which has 120 inches per year, more than any other state in the continental United States. During April the average high temperature in one part of West Africa is 105°, while in the East African highlands night temperatures will fall to 20° in the warm season.

Why are there such vast differences in climate in Africa? If one keeps in mind the plateau and the equator, it is easy to understand.

The equator cuts across the middle of Africa a bit north of the mouth of the Congo River. The southern edge of the Sahara Desert lies about as far from the equator as Puerto Rico or Bombay, India, while the southernmost tip of the African continent is about as far from the equator as Little Rock, Arkansas, or Santa Barbara, California. Of course, since South Africa is on the opposite side of the equator in the Southern Hemisphere it has its winter during our summer.

From its location, then, most of Africa should have a very hot climate. But the influence of its location astride the equator is balanced, in many ways, by the effects of the elevation of the plateau. Because temperatures are lower at high altitudes, snow may be found on the peaks of the mountains on the equator in East Africa, and due to elevation, much of the continent is somewhat

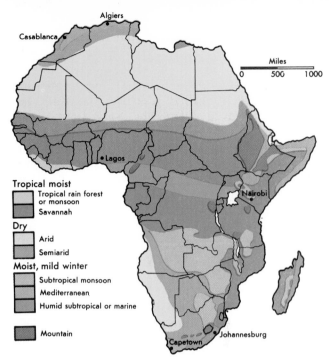

AFRICA - CLIMATE

cooler than it otherwise would be. Of course, the coastal plains and the lower river basins near the equator are hot and steamy.

There are five major types of climate in Sub-Saharan Africa. The first type is the tropical rain forest. Contrary to the popular conception of Africa as a land of jungles, rain forest climate covers only about 15 per cent of the area. This type of climate occurs in a large part of the Congo River basin, along the Guinea-Ghana coast, and on the east coast of the Malagasy Republic. These areas are characterized by heavy rainfall and high temperatures throughout the year. The air is hot, steamy, and damp, the humidity is always high, and winds are weak if not entirely absent. Minimum rainfall exceeds 60 inches a year and there is no period that can be classified as dry. Most of this rainfall is convectional; that is, it is caused by thunderstorms resulting from the intense heating of the earth's surface by the direct or nearly direct rays of the equatorial sun.

This type of climate has produced the great equatorial forests which are frequently and incorrectly called jungles. The trees are broadleaved evergreens. Seen from above, the rain forest looks like a vast green sea. Within the rain forest, the trees rise to well over 100 feet and form a canopy that shuts out the sunlight. When the layers of vegetation are dense, they prevent the growth of bushes and weeds and one can walk at ease in open ground between the great pillars of the leafy canopy. Jungles, on the other hand, occur only at the edges, along river banks, or in locations that have been cleared, that is, in areas which may be reached by the sun.

The second type of climate in Africa is the savanna, which prevails in about half of Sub-Saharan Africa. It occurs in areas where rainfall is still relatively high, but where there is a well-defined dry season of appreciable length. The natural vegetation is high grass because the dry season prevents the growth of forests. However, where moist monsoon conditions prevail within the savanna zone, a mixed grass-forest vegetation, called parkland savanna, occurs. It is found primarily north of the equator in the wide east-west belt called the Sudan. South of the equator the southern savannas are also marked by scrub and thorn forests mixed with grass. All trees in the savanna zone are deciduous, that is, they shed their leaves during the dry season.

The third major climatic area of Sub-Saharan Africa is the semiarid. It resembles the savanna in many ways but has one important difference. Both have marked wet and dry seasons. In the semiarid areas, however, the dry season is much longer and the rainfall is considerably less. The typical vegetation resulting from the relative scarcity of water is low grass. Trees are few in number and are species which can survive a prolonged dry

season. A large part of the Republic of South Africa and South-West Africa and a small section of Angola have a semiarid climate. In addition, there is a relatively narrow strip of semiarid land stretching completely across the widest part of Africa. It runs from the Atlantic to the Indian Ocean and is the transitional zone from the savanna to the arid desert climate of the Sahara.

The fourth type of climate is the arid. Since the Sahara Desert is excluded, the only arid regions in Sub-Saharan Africa are found in Botswana, South-West Africa, Angola, and the Republic of South Africa. Rainfall is scanty or nonexistent. For example, rainfall is less than one inch a year in the Namib Desert along the coast of South-West Africa. There are periods of severe and prolonged drought. Temperatures reach very high figures during the day but drop rapidly at night. Rivers are dry most of the time, but an occasional storm will send floods sweeping down the dry stream beds. Vegetation is scanty and is the type that can stand long periods without water.

The last major type of climate in Sub-Saharan Africa is the mediterranean. It is the only climate type in the region which is not tropical and covers only a relatively small area in the Republic of South Africa. Rainfall is not heavy and is concentrated in the winter months. Winters are cool; the rest of the year it is sunny and the summers are hot. In general, vegetation is scrubby and consists of species that can stand a long period without adequate rainfall.

The climates of Sub-Saharan Africa are, in general, not favorable for supporting agriculture or a large population. As we have seen, large areas are too dry or too wet. Population tends to be small in the rain forest and arid regions. In the rain forest, shifting cultivation is practiced. A village moves to a new area, cuts down the forest, burns the vegetation to make ashes for fertilizer, and begins a

The rain forest comes right to the edge of the Niger River. Because of the density of the vegetation and the width of the River, a bridge is not feasible in the area. Ferries, therefore, provide transportation for both pedestrians and vehicles; on this ferry the conductor exacts one egg as toll for each passenger.

primitive agriculture. After a few years of farming, the soil is mined of its important minerals and produces less and less. Finally, the village deserts its lands, moves to another area, and begins the process all over again. In the semiarid regions, most of the people are nomadic herders. The regions having a savanna climate are the most favorable for agriculture and supporting a large population. Even in these areas, however, some shifting cultivation is practiced.

There is evidence that the climate of Africa is changing. One of the most significant instances has been the shrinking of the rain forest areas which have turned into man-made savannas. For example, it is known that the greater part of Uganda lay within the great equatorial rain forest. Today, this forest has retreated westward to the Congo and only isolated islands of it are left in Uganda. This is thought to be the result of more intensive use of land for farming and grazing.

Resources. Over the long years of man's history probably the most important natural resource has been the fertility of the soil on which he lives. In general Africa does not have good soil. African soils may look like the rich brown and black soils of the American Middle West, but they do not have the same wealth of minerals and organic matter. One would think that the lush growth of the tropical forest indicated rich soil, but this is not true. Rain forests are seldom fertile. Heavy rains dissolve the minerals out of the soil, and the baking sun destroys other soil elements. This does not mean, of course, that farming is impossible in Africa. People

Basic Facts 543

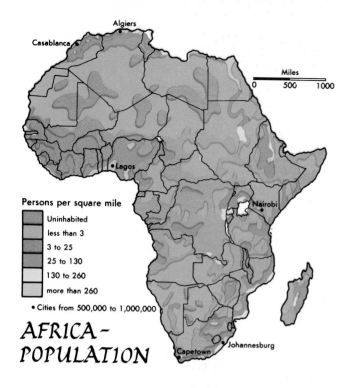

Persons per square mile

- Uninhabited
- less than 3
- 3 to 25
- 25 to 130
- 130 to 260
- more than 260

• Cities from 500,000 to 1,000,000

AFRICA – POPULATION

The distribution of African mineral resources is very uneven, however. Some territories are outstandingly rich in resources, but others must depend on only one mineral product or none at all. Thus the Katanga area in the Congo (*Kinshasa*) has a wealth of copper, diamonds, uranium, and gold. The copper in the Katanga formations continues into bordering Zambia, providing Zambia's chief export. Yet, Kenya has no significant mineral resource. Similarly, Gabon is rich in minerals, but neighboring Congo (*Brazzaville*) has very little.

Another problem is that coal has seldom been found near the iron or other mineral resources. This means that either the bulky mineral ores or the coal has to be transported long distances. Since the rivers seldom provide the cheap transportation needed, too often the cost of getting ores to a place where they can be refined or sold has made it too expensive to even begin such types of operation.

African rivers, as they fall from the plateau, provide invaluable power resources which can, at least in part, make up for the lack of easily available coal. Africa's potential for hydroelectric power has been estimated at several times that of the United States. A number of dams have been built to harness this potential. Water-power development plays an important part in almost every area's plans for economic development. Continued development of Sub-Saharan Africa's potential hydroelectric power will speed the industrialization of the region.

As for the timber necessary for economic development, the tropical rain forests do not provide the same temperate forest hardwoods and pulpwoods that industrialized countries have become accustomed to using. However, certain special tropical woods such as mahogany can be exported, and research is likely to reveal industrial uses for other products of the rain forest.

have farmed there for thousands of years. It does mean that Africans could not farm by the same methods as farmers in fertile and temperate regions like Europe or the American Middle West.

Although Africa seems poor in soil, it has proved to have mineral wealth valuable to the whole world. Africa had been famed for gold since before the legends of King Solomon's mines. Even today Africa is the world's greatest producer of gold. Most of the world's diamonds are mined in that continent; moreover, it has iron ore, oil, and good-to-excellent reserves of copper, lead, zinc, tin, bauxite, and abestos. It provides several of the minerals that have become increasingly important in producing high-grade and special-purpose steels: manganese, cobalt, chromium, vanadium, and columbium. Since much of Africa remains to be surveyed, the prospects for discovering additional resources are good.

PEOPLE

Africa's 320 million people vary widely in both way of life and physical type. Africa includes a greater number of different peoples than any other continent except perhaps Asia. Tanzania alone has more than one hundred groups who speak languages as different from each other as French is from English.

Language and culture. We can best understand the great differences among Africa's peoples by looking at the languages they speak, for a language reveals a people's culture and how it grew. Naturally people who live together and share the same culture have to use the same words and ways of putting words together to explain things. This is the only way they can understand each other. The language of a culture has a word for every thing or idea which the people who speak the language think is important. Thus when a new food or a new way of counting is introduced into a culture, a name is given to this item; so as a culture changes its language also changes. If a people who share a common culture separate and the two groups live apart, the language will change differently in two places as they create words for their new experiences. This is why American and British English differ from each other. If the groups are largely isolated from each other, they eventually develop separate languages that are "related," as are English, German, and Hindi. In addition, "loan words" tell us about outside influences upon a culture. For instance words of African origin in the American language, such as jazz, yam, and cola show some ways in which Africa has influenced our culture.

What do we find out about African peoples when we look at their languages? One scholar has divided all of the languages native to Africa into four large families: the

CARL E. OSTMAN

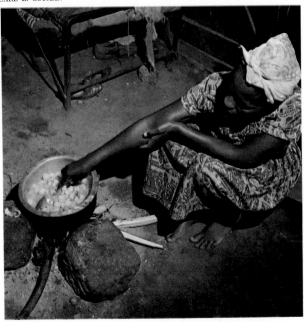

Any innovation in a society brings a concomitant addition to the language. New utensils introduced in Kenya require "loan" words to describe them.

Koisan, Nilo-Saharan, Afro-Asiatic, and Congo-Kordofanian. This means that the cultures of the many different indigenous African peoples of today come from four distinct cultures which existed thousands of years ago. Each of these four language families is divided into several sub-families which include groups of closely related languages.

The largest number of peoples who live south of the Sahara speak languages of the Congo-Kordofanian family. Within this family the Bantu sub-family is especially important because so many peoples south of the equator speak one of the closely related Bantu languages. Since the Bantu languages are similar to West African languages of the Congo-Kordofanian family, we believe that some people of a West African culture thousands of years ago migrated to the Katanga area south of the rain forest, and from there they later grew and separated to develop the many Bantu-speaking cultures.

When we look at African language patterns, we also notice that Swahili, a Bantu language originally spoken on the coast of East Africa, has many words of Indian or Arabic origin. These "loan" words point to objects and ideas that have been introduced to Africa through the Indian Ocean trade. The significance of Indian Ocean influences is also seen in the fact that the chief language spoken in the Malagasy Republic is an Indonesian, rather than an African, language. More recent history is reflected in the fact that many Africans speak Arabic or a European language as well as their own, for this suggests the effect on African cultures of Islam and European colonial rule and settlement. Moreover, there are groups of people born in Africa who speak Indian or European languages as their mother tongue. This is evidence of immigrant groups that have to a large extent maintained their separate cultures while living in Africa.

HOW DO WE KNOW ABOUT AFRICA'S PAST?

Until recently most Westerners knew very little about Africa's past, often feeling that "Africa had no history." This was partly because, having made slaves and colonial subjects of Africans, Westerners found it hard to imagine that anything worth knowing had happened in Africa's past. But also, because Western culture values writing so highly, historians used to believe that history should be the story of the past based on written records only. Since many African peoples did not adopt writing until the coming of the Europeans, it was assumed that until that time they "had no history." Gradually however Western historians have come to believe that history should provide a picture of man's past everywhere, using any evidence through which past cultures can be understood.

Of course the use of written evidence is one of the ways of knowing about Africa's past. Many African societies in the Nile Valley, the Sudanic Belt, and along the East Coast did adopt writing centuries before the Europeans arrived, and their written records, as well as written descriptions based on the experiences of travellers in Sub-Saharan Africa from other parts of the world, are used by historians.

But other kinds of evidence have to be used too. We do not have pre-European

LANGUAGES OF AFRICA

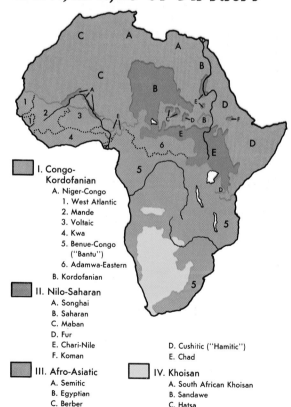

I. Congo-Kordofanian
  A. Niger-Congo
    1. West Atlantic
    2. Mande
    3. Voltaic
    4. Kwa
    5. Benue-Congo ("Bantu")
    6. Adamwa-Eastern
  B. Kordofanian

II. Nilo-Saharan
  A. Songhai
  B. Saharan
  C. Maban
  D. Fur
  E. Chari-Nile
  F. Koman

III. Afro-Asiatic
  A. Semitic
  B. Egyptian
  C. Berber

  D. Cushitic ("Hamitic")
  E. Chad

IV. Khoisan
  A. South African Khoisan
  B. Sandawe
  C. Hatsa

written records from the forests and southern plateau where African societies did not adopt writing prior to the arrival of Europeans. But these peoples *did* keep records of their past, histories that were memorized by specialists and passed on for generations. The memorizing of these "oral traditions" has proved to be about as accurate as the repeated copying of ancient manuscripts. As with written records, the historian must analyze these oral records very carefully to determine how much of what was recorded can be accepted as fact by 20th-century historians. For some societies oral traditions can give us important facts as far back as six centuries.*

Linguists can tell us certain things about the kind of culture a language group previously had, where they came from, and which other language groups they have learned from. Archaeologists, by systematic digging for the objects left by previous inhabitants can construct a story, just as detectives can by using circumstantial evidence. Anthropologists who study current cultures can gain some ideas about what is likely to have occurred in the past by comparing customs, art styles, and forms of music. Even botanists and zoologists have contributed by determining where certain plants and animals were domesticated, where they were later taken, and some effects they have had on human societies.

What, then, are the main outlines of the picture that historians, using many kinds of evidence, have drawn of Africa's past?

HISTORICAL PERIODS

It is important to remember that the present diversity of Africa's peoples reflects a past in which Sub-Saharan Africa has never had a single dominant culture to bring unity out

* See *Readings in World History*, "Sundiata: An Oral Source," p. 549.

of its diversity. In this way Africa is different from East Asia, a large part of which was unified by Chinese culture, or the Middle East, which developed a common culture through the expansion of Islam. Because Africa had no single dominant culture through which we can trace change over the centuries, its past can seem very complicated. We can more easily understand, however, if we fit the facts into a pattern of six periods of major developments. However, because similar developments occurred in different African societies at different times, the dates of the periods can only be approximate, and they have to overlap.

The development of man and agriculture, 2,000,000–500 B.C. At Olduvai Gorge in the East African Rift Valley archaeologists have discovered the remains of a man-like creature that they call *Zinjanthropus*. The evidence indicates that he lived about 2,000,000 years ago. The pebbles that he split and shaped to use for tools were also found. Since this is the oldest toolmaker we now know of, we say that man developed in Africa. Only in Africa have archaeologists found places where they can see the gradual change from these pebble tools to the more complicated "hand axes" of the early Old Stone Age; so until some 300,000 years ago Africa appears to have led the world technologically.

According to botanists farming is very ancient in Africa. As early as 2,500 B.C., cotton and sesame, African plants that already had a long history of domestication, had spread to Asia. After about 3000 B.C. many farming communities in the Sahara, which was then still a vast grassland because of Africa's last long "wet period," were using cattle and neolithic farming tools from the Middle East. In the drier centuries that followed, people of the fertile Nile Valley, capitalizing both on their African culture

and on what they had learned from the Middle East, created Africa's first urban civilization, Egypt. Despite the growing desert, Egypt maintained relations with the lands to the south. Also, regular contacts between the Sudanic Belt and North Africa as early as the first millenium B.C. are indicated by rock paintings in the Sahara showing horse-drawn chariots.

The expansion of Bantu-speaking peoples and iron working, 500 B.C.–1000 A.D. After about 400 B.C. an important iron smelting industry developed in the Kingdom of Meroë south of Egypt, and iron was also being worked in the area of the Nok culture 1500 miles to the west. Copper, tin, and gold, which require less advanced technologies, were also used. By 500 A.D. these metals were being mined and worked in many parts of the southern savannas. Linguists think that it was during approximately

the same period that farmers who spoke the "proto-Bantu" language from which the Bantu languages developed began to migrate out of the Katanga region. As they moved into new areas they gradually became separate peoples with separate Bantu languages and different cultures. Indonesian root crops, more productive than the African varieties, and bananas were probably introduced to Africa during this time as well. This combination of the expansion of pioneering peoples, the spread of metal mining and working, and the use of more productive crops led to the political and economic changes of the next period.

The development of African states, 750–1500 A.D. During this period people in many parts of Africa became organized into states, that is, into independent political systems with an organized government including various officials ruling a definite body of people. A state had existed in the upper Nile Valley as early as the eighth century B.C. and another in the Ethiopian highlands soon after. But not until approximately the eighth century A.D. were there states in several other parts of Africa South of the Sahara. By this time the beginnings of states appeared in three widely separated areas: the Sudanic Belt, the coast of East Africa, and the southern savannas.

Many states developed in the western Sudan as first the use of the camel in the desert and then Islamic rule in North Africa increased opportunities for trans-Saharan trade. The most famous were the empires of Ghana, Mali, and Songhai which successively rose to power by exporting gold to and importing salt from the north. During the same period, further east in the Lake Chad area, the empire of Kanem-Bornu lasted through various changes until its defeat by the Europeans at the end of the 19th century. At its greatest this thousand-year empire was larger than present-day France and England combined.

Ghana, Mali, and Songhai became famous largely because of Muslim travellers' descriptions of their wealth in gold, power, and learning. The story of Mali illustrates the development of such states. In the 10th century Mali was probably a subject country of the Ghana Empire whose traders carried gold from the mining people to the capital. As Ghana declined in power, Mali began to grow. About the time that it began this gradual expansion in the 11th century, its rulers were converted to Islam through their trade contacts across the desert. Sundiata,* a 13th-century ruler, conquered the capital of Ghana, incorporated the gold-producing regions into his empire, and systematically organized the government. But the Mali ruler whose name became known to Europe

* See *Readings in World History*, "Sundiata: An Oral Source," p. 549.

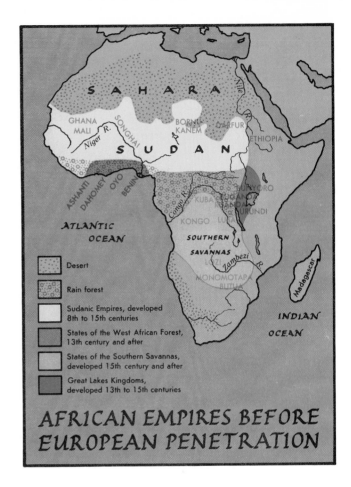

AFRICAN EMPIRES BEFORE EUROPEAN PENETRATION

was Mansa (King) Musa who, on his religious trip to Mecca in the 14th century, spent his wealth so generously that he deflated the Cairo gold market. The Muslim world was so impressed that Mali even began to appear on medieval European maps. As Mali began to decline in the 1400's one of its tribute paying kingdoms, Songhai, in turn became dominant.

The second area where states developed was along the coast of East Africa.* As Indian Ocean trade increased after the eighth century, the coastal towns began to

* See *Readings in World History*, "East African Trade in Roman Times," p. 548.

The "Great Enclosure" was one of three divisions of Zimbabwe, capital of an early state in the southern savannas. Later known as the Kingdom of Monomotapa, its people earned their wealth by mining gold which was exported from the coast of East Africa.

develop into city-states. Later, Islamic powers such as India, Persia, and Egypt came to dominate the Indian Ocean, and, beginning in the 13th century, their African trading partners along the coast adopted their Muslim religion. These Swahili-speaking city-states reached the height of their splendor in the years just before the Portuguese arrived along the coast in the 15th century.

Trade with the coast of East Africa was probably a major stimulus for state development in the third area, the southern savannas. Archaeologists have found evidence of a major trade route leading to the ocean from the Katanga copper mining region of the present-day Congo (*Kinshasa*) along the Zambesi River. A vast cemetery discovered in Katanga suggests that this area was the nucleus of a trading state by the eighth century. When the Zambesi trade reached the gold mines to the south of the river, states began to grow there. One of them built famous Zimbabwe for its capital.

By the end of this period people had also begun to organize themselves into states in the coastal forests of West Africa, in the area around the East African Great Lakes, and on the southern savanna near the mouth of the

Congo River. Thus, by 1500, states had been created in much of Africa. After 1500 similar states continued to draw more and more Africans into larger societies.

Independent trade with Western nations, 1450–1900. This is the period in which African states included Europeans and Americans in their trading. In the 15th century Europe began to break out of its isolation when Portuguese explorers sailed down the Atlantic Coast of Africa. They were looking for the famed Sudanic gold, Christian allies for their struggles with Islam, and a way to break the Islamic monopoly on trade with the East. Along the coast of present-day Ghana they found people who could bring them gold. At the Congo mouth they discovered the impressive Kongo Kingdom which they hoped would help to deliver Europe from its Islamic enemies. And in 1498 Vasco da Gama proved the possibility

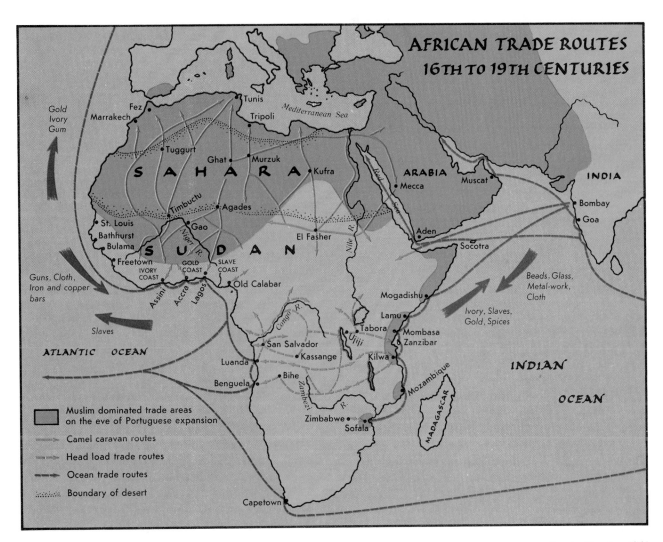

AFRICAN TRADE ROUTES
16TH TO 19TH CENTURIES

Gold
Ivory
Gum

Fez
Marrakech
Tunis
Tripoli
Mediterranean Sea

Tuggurt
Ghat
Murzuk
Kufra
ARABIA
Mecca
Muscat
INDIA

S A H A R A

Timbuctu
Agades
Bombay
Goa

St. Louis
Bathurst
Bulama
Gao
El Fasher
Aden
Socotra

Freetown
GOLD
COAST
SLAVE
COAST
IVORY
COAST
S U D A N

Guns, Cloth,
Iron and copper
bars

Old Calabar
Mogadishu

Beads, Glass,
Metal-work,
Cloth

Assini
Accra
Lagos

Slaves

Congo R.
Lamu
Ujiji
Tabora
Mombasa
Zanzibar

Ivory, Slaves,
Gold, Spices

ATLANTIC OCEAN

San Salvador
Kassange
Kilwa

INDIAN

Luanda
Bihe

OCEAN

Benguela
Zambezi R.
Mozambique
MADAGASCAR

Muslim dominated trade areas
on the eve of Portuguese expansion

Zimbabwe
Sofala

Camel caravan routes

Head load trade routes

Ocean trade routes

Boundary of desert

Capetown

The earliest existing painting of Westerners at the Cape of Good Hope is this one by Van Rhijn, 1720.

of a sea route to India by sailing around the Cape and following the ancient monsoon route up the coast of East Africa and across the Indian Ocean.

On the coast of West Africa the Portuguese negotiated with African rulers to set up trading stations where they bought gold, ivory, and pepper to sell in Europe.* In the 16th century other European states began to take part in this trade, although by the second half of the century buying people was becoming more important than the trade in goods. This was because Africans had begun to be used as laborers in the profitable mines and sugar plantations of the New World. Centuries later, due to the growing belief that slavery was wrong and the decreasing importance of both Caribbean sugar and profits from the slave trade, England made slave trading illegal in 1807. Other European nations and the United States followed suit soon after. But the volume of slaves exported from West Africa did not taper off until after 1850.

* See *Readings in World History*, "The Portuguese Bargain with an African Chief," p. 555.

On the coast of East Africa, the Portuguese found prosperous Swahili-speaking cities which gained their wealth by being part of the Islamic monopoly of the Indian Ocean trade. The Portuguese were determined to break this monopoly, and those cities that refused Portuguese control were sacked. Thousands of inhabitants were killed. But the Portuguese were unable to maintain control. By the 18th century these city-states were free, and Swahili trade routes were penetrating further and further into the interior. As the Dutch, French, and British became more involved in trade around the Cape to the East, the Dutch established the tiny settlement at the Cape which, only after more than a century, became significant as South Africa.

During four hundred years of expanding trade, African kingdoms used European technology, especially guns, to develop stronger governments and conquer neighboring peoples. Thus by the mid-19th century there were several empires that included large areas and numbers of people.

European penetration and colonial rule, 1800–1960. Before about 1800 Westerners traded with Africans as equals, and except for Portuguese and French traders in a few areas, they did not attempt to enter the interior. But by 1900 the major African states had lost their independence.

At the beginning of this period, African Islamic states were expanding their territory and influence far more rapidly than Europeans. However, three developments in Europe caused Europeans to become more interested in the interior of Africa and involved in the internal affairs of African states. In the first place, Europeans had become interested in the science of geography; new geographical societies sent men to Africa to explore the interior which had remained unknown to Europe during centuries of coastal

TIME CHART FOR SUB-SAHARAN AFRICA

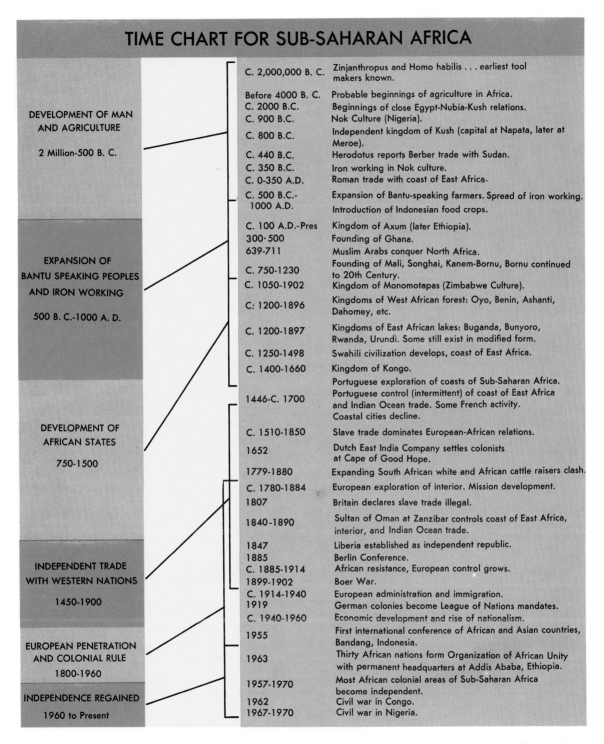

DEVELOPMENT OF MAN AND AGRICULTURE 2 Million-500 B. C.	C. 2,000,000 B. C.	Zinjanthropus and Homo habilis . . . earliest tool makers known.
	Before 4000 B. C.	Probable beginnings of agriculture in Africa.
	C. 2000 B.C.	Beginnings of close Egypt-Nubia-Kush relations.
	C. 900 B.C.	Nok Culture (Nigeria).
	C. 800 B.C.	Independent kingdom of Kush (capital at Napata, later at Meroe).
	C. 440 B.C.	Herodotus reports Berber trade with Sudan.
	C. 350 B.C.	Iron working in Nok culture.
	C. 0-350 A.D.	Roman trade with coast of East Africa.
EXPANSION OF BANTU SPEAKING PEOPLES AND IRON WORKING 500 B. C.-1000 A. D.	C. 500 B.C.- 1000 A.D.	Expansion of Bantu-speaking farmers. Spread of iron working. Introduction of Indonesian food crops.
	C. 100 A.D.-Pres	Kingdom of Axum (later Ethiopia).
	300-500	Founding of Ghana.
	639-711	Muslim Arabs conquer North Africa.
	C. 750-1230	Founding of Mali, Songhai, Kanem-Bornu, Bornu continued to 20th Century.
	C. 1050-1902	Kingdom of Monomotapas (Zimbabwe Culture).
	C: 1200-1896	Kingdoms of West African forest: Oyo, Benin, Ashanti, Dahomey, etc.
	C. 1200-1897	Kingdoms of East African lakes: Buganda, Bunyoro, Rwanda, Urundi. Some still exist in modified form.
	C. 1250-1498	Swahili civilization develops, coast of East Africa.
	C. 1400-1660	Kingdom of Kongo.
DEVELOPMENT OF AFRICAN STATES 750-1500	1446-C. 1700	Portuguese exploration of coasts of Sub-Saharan Africa. Portuguese control (intermittent) of coast of East Africa and Indian Ocean trade. Some French activity. Coastal cities decline.
	C. 1510-1850	Slave trade dominates European-African relations.
	1652	Dutch East India Company settles colonists at Cape of Good Hope.
	1779-1880	Expanding South African white and African cattle raisers clash.
INDEPENDENT TRADE WITH WESTERN NATIONS 1450-1900	C. 1780-1884	European exploration of interior. Mission development.
	1807	Britain declares slave trade illegal.
	1840-1890	Sultan of Oman at Zanzibar controls coast of East Africa, interior, and Indian Ocean trade.
	1847	Liberia established as independent republic.
	1885	Berlin Conference.
	C. 1885-1914	African resistance, European control grows.
	1899-1902	Boer War.
	C. 1914-1940	European administration and immigration.
	1919	German colonies become League of Nations mandates.
	C. 1940-1960	Economic development and rise of nationalism.
EUROPEAN PENETRATION AND COLONIAL RULE 1800-1960	1955	First international conference of African and Asian countries, Bandang, Indonesia.
	1963	Thirty African nations form Organization of African Unity with permanent headquarters at Addis Ababa, Ethiopia.
INDEPENDENCE REGAINED 1960 to Present	1957-1970	Most African colonial areas of Sub-Saharan Africa become independent.
	1962	Civil war in Congo.
	1967-1970	Civil war in Nigeria.

trade. Normally these "explorers" relied on African guides with whom they travelled Africa's well-established trade routes. Those who survived Africa's diseases brought back reports that aided trading companies and missionaries in their planning for expanded activity in the interior.

Secondly, the slave trade was made illegal. The anti-slavery movement had brought about the founding in 1787 of the first British colony in Africa, Sierra Leone. The abolitionist investors who founded the colony wanted both a place to send England's poor, freed blacks and to prove by the success of such an agricultural colony that farm products could replace slaves in Africa's trade. In 1821 Americans established a similar settlement for black freedmen that was the beginning of Liberia.

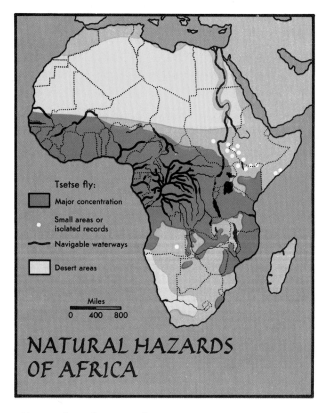

NATURAL HAZARDS OF AFRICA

Tsetse fly:

Major concentration

Small areas or isolated records

Navigable waterways

Desert areas

Miles
0   400   800

It was in trying to stop the slave trade at its source that England became deeply involved in the internal politics of some African coastal states. No longer legally allowed to compete in the slave trade themselves, the British made treaties with African governments to stop Africans from selling slaves to other Western traders. Then, with increased competition for trade in "legitimate" African products, French and British merchants tried to establish firmer control over their trade areas. A few key towns along the coast of West Africa came under colonial rule as officials found that only by using force or the threat of force could a local situation that favored their country be maintained.

Finally, Western Christianity had become eager to send missionaries to other parts of the world. And missionaries often encouraged both traders and governments to become more involved in Africa. The protection of a European government would make missionary activity easier. Moreover missionaries hoped that an increase of legitimate trade and the influence of European governments would bring about the end of slave trading within Africa.

During these years, Western uses for African products other than slaves were increasing. Trade flourished in palm and peanut oils to make soap and lubricate machinery and in ivory for piano keys and things for which we now use plastic. When diamonds were discovered in South Africa, people began to hope for great new mineral wealth yet to be discovered. At the same time, Africa became more accessible, for in the middle of the 19th century Europeans learned how to use quinine to prevent and cure malaria. Now large numbers of Europeans could penetrate into Africa without most of them dying.

Yet only toward the end of the century did the real "scramble for Africa" occur, as imperialism developed in the West. Then na-

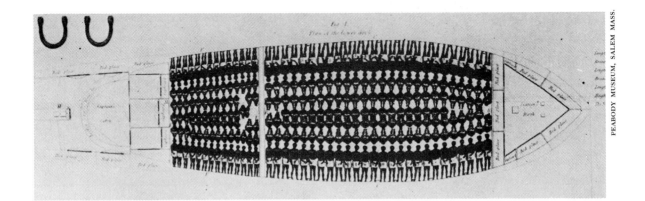

A plan of a French ship drawn in 1822 illustrates that some ships were designed to accommodate the slave trade. The lower deck provided for the maximum number of bodies. A double layer of bodies was made possible by extending shelves from each side. The slaves were forced to spend most of the "middle passage" in this position; for a few hours each day they were chained on the deck to get air.

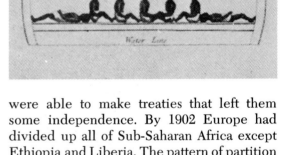

tional rivalries within Europe made each nation try to gain control of potentially valuable parts of Africa to prevent other nations from getting them first. To avoid international conflicts, the Berlin Conference in 1885 set up ground rules for making claims to African territory. Nations were required to have "effective occupation" of the areas they claimed; thus officials and troops were sent to Africa to set up colonial governments of some sort.

African governments resisted the encroachment of the Europeans in what seemed the best ways possible in their situations. Some, not understanding Western ideas about selling land permanently, signed treaties giving up their territories. Frequently they later rebelled in attempts to regain the freedom they had unknowingly lost. Many states used force to resist and were defeated. A few

were able to make treaties that left them some independence. By 1902 Europe had divided up all of Sub-Saharan Africa except Ethiopia and Liberia. The pattern of partition was the result both of diplomacy within Europe and of African governments' relations with Europeans in Africa.

Actually, the colonial period, during which European states ruled Sub-Saharan Africa, was very short in most places. Until World War I, the colonial powers were primarily concerned with "pacifying" the areas they claimed, putting down wars of resistance and making their rule effective. Consequently in the period between the two World Wars, the colonial powers consolidated their positions, administering their colonies in the confidence that the colonial system would last for centuries, perhaps forever. Most of the features we consider typical of colonialism in Africa existed during this period of about twenty years. Most of the European immigrant communities became established during this time.

After World War II, African nationalist movements became increasingly strong, first in British, then in French, Belgian, Portuguese, and Spanish colonies. By the end of the 1960's most of the Sub-Saharan colonies had gained their independence or were on the verge of achieving it.

Independence regained, 1960– . The period of independence regained can be said to have started when many Africans had once more come under African rule. In most, but not all, cases, the colonial governments did not return power to the rulers of the traditional states which they had defeated less than a century before. Instead, Western-educated Africans gained control of the government of the whole colony, which usually included a number of defeated traditional states and peoples.

Although we can speak of the time that Africa is now experiencing as a period of independence regained, we must remember that in southern Africa people are still not living under African rule. This is true in the Republic of South Africa, Rhodesia, and the Portuguese-ruled areas.

This, then, is a pattern of Africa's past, but we should expect it to change as new facts are uncovered by the various specialists who contribute to our understanding of African history.

Reviewing the Essentials

Geography

1. How is Africa north of the Sahara different from the area south of the Sahara? How similar?
2. Locate on a map Africa's four most important river systems. What have been the advantages and disadvantages of their rapids and waterfalls?
3. Locate on a map the areas where each of Africa's five major types of climate prevail. What kind of vegetation is produced in each of these climate areas?
4. How have Africa's climates affected its soils? What method of farming was developed as a result?
5. Locate on a map Africa's important mineral deposits. Why has it been expensive to develop these resources?

The People of Africa

6. What does a language tell us about the people who speak it?
7. What four language families developed in Africa? To which family and sub-family do most of the languages of Sub-Saharan Africa belong?
8. How do historians find out about the past of peoples that until recently did not use writing?

Historical Periods

9. What is the most important development in each of the periods of African history, and what are the approximate dates of each?
10. Locate on a map the four areas in which states first developed in Sub-Saharan Africa.
11. Why did Europeans become more interested in entering Africa after about 1800 A.D.?

Explain, Identify, or Locate

rain forest	Songhai	Zimbabwe	Meroë
savanna	Kanem-Bornu	Zinjanthropus	Ghana
Sudanic Belt	Mali	Nok	Katanga
rift valley	Bantu	Sundiata	Swahili

ECONOMICS: A Swiftly Changing Structure

PRESENT STATE

Subsistence agriculture. Although their ways of life may vary widely throughout the continent, most African families live by farming or herding or a combination of the two. Well over 70 per cent of Africans depend primarily on agriculture for their living. The typical African family is first of all concerned with growing what food it needs, although everyone looks forward to market day for fun as well as for bartering or buying such things as sugar, salt, or cloth. The family must also grow something extra to pay taxes and school fees. Certain manufactured goods, kerosene for its lamps, a hoe, or a metal pail for water, may seem essential, and the family will have to sell part of its produce for these things. Yet the African is primarily a subsistence farmer; that is, he himself produces most of what he needs. If he lives far from any town, he may know little about the goods that money can buy. If he knows about manufactured luxuries like corrugated iron roofs, bicycles, and sewing machines, he may try to produce enough to buy these things, or he may feel that his leisure is more important than the things that extra crops could buy.

Africans who live this way have security as long as there is enough land. They usually live in villages with relatives. Every African has very clear-cut obligations to help his kin at certain times with work and wealth. He will have to provide for his aged relatives, but he isn't expected to "save for a rainy day" because he will then be taken care of by his kin.

Generally the land is not owned by individuals who may buy and sell it. Instead, each village or kin group has traditional rights to use an area of land, and all the families that make up the group have the right to use a part of this land as long as they farm it.

This way of life does not make high production a goal, so per acre production in Africa is the lowest in the world. Yet even if Africans wanted to produce a large surplus, as some do, it would be difficult if not impossible. Most of Africa's soil is poor.

Africans customarily allow the land to "rest" so it may regain fertility, but in many places there is no longer enough land. The population of Africa has been growing rapidly. Many parts have more people than can live adequately according to present ways of using resources. In parts of southern Africa European immigrants have taken over large areas of land. The extreme example of this is the Republic of South Africa where 86 per cent of the land is saved for the descendants of Europeans who account for only about 18 per cent of the total population. Another example is Rhodesia, where 37 per cent of the land is reserved for the whites who form only 5 per cent of the total population.

Farmers must consistently take larger crops out of the land, land that was never really fertile, because they have to produce some surplus in order to pay their taxes. Moreover, the land must support more people than before. As a result of constant use, the minerals and organic matter are mined out of the soil, the fertility of the land decreases, and less food per acre is produced. Lower yields push the people to till even more fields that should be permitted to lie fallow. When the thick natural cover is stripped from the land, either by overgrazing or by planting crops, harsh rains erode the soil. As erosion further decreases fertility, Africans find themselves forced to use the land still more intensively, and the vicious circle of soil destruction continues. Poor soil, with unfavorable climate and frequent drought, makes crop yields poor compared with other parts of the world. And with increased population the situation will worsen.

Commercial agriculture. Because there is often not enough land to support everyone in the villages, many Africans go to work on large farms or plantations which grow the crops that the rest of the world wants to buy:

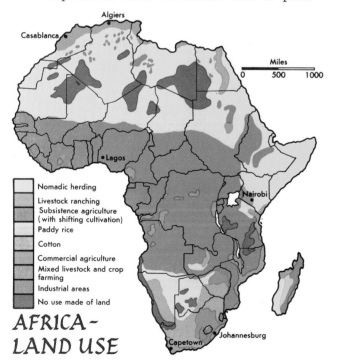

Miles
0   500   1000

Nomadic herding
Livestock ranching
Subsistence agriculture (with shifting cultivation)
Paddy rice
Cotton
Commercial agriculture
Mixed livestock and crop farming
Industrial areas
No use made of land

AFRICA - LAND USE

rubber, palm oil, cocoa, peanuts, sisal, coffee, tobacco, and cotton. Some of these large farms are owned by African individuals or governments, but many are owned by people of European descent or foreign corporations that are better able to provide the capital for large-scale agriculture.

Territories without mineral wealth must depend almost entirely on commercial crop exports to pay for the manufactured goods that they import. For this reason, all African farmers, large and small, are being encouraged to grow some commercial crops in order to speed economic development. In 1965 peanuts and peanut products accounted for 94 per cent of Gambia's exports; cocoa made up 60 per cent of Ghana's sales; while Chad depended on cotton for 77 per cent of the value of its exports.

Working in cities. Every year hundreds of thousands of Africans travel to the cities to work in mines, factories, or at various other jobs. Like farm people in all industrializing societies they go looking for greater freedom and opportunity. Many young men with a few years of classroom education believe that reading and writing qualify them for more than a hard life of farming. Some go to bring back either money so that they can get married or luxury goods to impress their friends in the village; others go to escape an irksome situation at home.

Most Africans who go to the city still think of themselves as members of the village community and try to return from time to time.* The village is where their people are, and as long as they are part of it they have a right to use a share of village land if they need it. This security is important to people in the city where things that are free in the village cost money: food, a place to live, and fuel for the cooking fire. If a man cannot find a

* See *Readings in World History,* "Cultural Change: Questions for Josephine," p. 629.

Heavy seasonal rains have caused severe erosion in parts of Africa where the cover of vegetation has been destroyed by overgrazing or constant use of the land for farming.

job or becomes too old to work, it is almost impossible to find food or shelter in the city. When the city worker returns to visit his home village bringing money, gifts, stories, and city attitudes, his rural family and friends are also affected by the city.

Although increasing numbers of Africans go to live in the city more or less permanently, hundreds of thousands of others go only for short periods as migrant workers. They often travel hundreds of miles, crossing national boundaries to cities where jobs are to be found, often in mining. Their wives and children stay at home to care for the family's piece of land which usually is not large enough to support them all by traditional farming methods.

This pattern of life is especially common in the countries in southern Africa ruled by European immigrant communities, where a white minority have taken a large portion of the best land, and Africans cannot take their families to the city. In South Africa almost all African men must at some time work outside the areas where they and their families have the right to live permanently.

The Africans' share. Africans are less well off than they otherwise might be because the profits from what they produce and buy often go to foreigners rather than to other Africans. Africa's modern mines, trading companies, and large plantations were for the most part developed by Westerners who were able to provide the necessary capital investment and technology. Thus a large share of the profits leave Africa. In addition, because there is little industry in most countries, products must usually be sold at the low prices of unprocessed materials while Africans have to pay the higher prices for imported manufactured goods.

In areas such as South Africa, Rhodesia, Kenya, and the Ivory Coast, where there are substantial numbers of European immigrants, considerable money and skills for development have been provided by these Europeans. So such countries are often more highly developed in terms of the modern world economy. But European immigrant communities have been able to save the wealth to reinvest largely by using cheap African labor, so Africans have not shared fully in the higher level of development in

such countries. In some countries immigrants from the Middle East, India, and Pakistan have provided the skills and capital for much of the small scale trade and business. Thus wherever there are minority populations of European and Asian descent, the Africans see even more clearly that the profits from their country's resources, their own labor, and their own buying power, are going to "foreigners."

The Republic of South Africa. Unlike the other states of Sub-Saharan Africa, the Republic of South Africa is considered economically developed. It is industrialized and has a higher per capita income than any other Sub-Saharan country. South Africa's industrial development results from its vast resources of gold and diamonds and its climate that have over the years attracted huge foreign investments as well as European immigrants with the skills required for developing local industry. As the European population has increased, it has been able to provide both capital and local markets to encourage further development. The European immigrant groups that have ruled South Africa have also controlled the lives of the African people in such a way as to provide a large supply of cheap African labor for European-owned farms, mines, homes, and factories. This has allowed savings that in turn have paid for further development. The standard of living of most Africans in the Republic, however, remains low. Their average per capita income is probably only about one-tenth that of the average of South African whites. Even so, Africans' per capita earnings are higher there than in most other Sub-Saharan countries. They have to be, however, because Africans have so little land that they cannot depend on subsistence farming to the extent that most Africans elsewhere do. So in South Africa more than anywhere else Africans have been drawn into the money

Park benches in Durban, South Africa, are reserved for whites only, as stated explicitly by signs in both English and Afrikaans. South African blacks are not permitted to sit or remain in any area so restricted.

economy, but many do not earn enough to live adequately.

Level of living. If we compare the material possessions and social services that most people of Sub-Saharan Africa have with what we take for granted in Western Europe and North America, the majority of Africans would seem to be appallingly poor. Most of them live in small huts with earth floors. Often they don't have furniture or the everyday manufactured goods that are necessities from our point of view. In the sprawling African areas of the cities, people often live in conditions that are very crowded both as compared with our standards and with what they are used to in their villages. In cities it is common for whole families to live in a single room. Sanitation and electricity are lacking in many districts, for they cannot be

extended as fast as the cities grow. Schools and hospitals are few. There are more than 30,000 people for each doctor in 13 countries where about half of the people south of the Sahara live. Even with the rapid growth of schools, however, only about one in every five primary school-aged children is able to be in school.

Better or worse? Authorities are not agreed on whether the African level of living is rising or falling. Their decision rests on how they measure human wealth and welfare. A person may choose to sell food that he needs for a balanced diet in order to buy a flashlight or a pretty piece of manufactured cloth for his wife. Does having the flashlight show a higher standard of living? One thing can be said with some certainty: more Africans have a greater range of choice in the things they now have than they did a generation ago.

Per capita income figures don't tell us much about how well off Africans are, while dependable statistics on life expectancy do not even exist. But estimates of childhood mortality suggest that most parents still watch at least one of their children die, and many lose several. Some of the devastating "tropical" diseases, like malaria and sleeping sickness, have been brought under control in some parts of Africa. Smallpox no longer wipes out such huge numbers as it once did. But Europeans have brought their occupational diseases, and urban slums present new health problems in Africa.

While there are not yet many Africans who go hungry most of the time, serious malnutrition is usual in some areas, especially where there is not enough land or where the tsetse fly makes stock raising impossible. In many regions a major cause of child deaths, even when there is no war or major famine, is kwashiorkor, a protein-deficiency disease that often follows weaning. Parasitic worm diseases, such as bilharziasis and hookworm, disfigure people, weaken them, and allow what we think of as "minor" diseases, such as measles, to become fatal. Despite disease and malnutrition, though, the African population has been increasing because Western science has reduced the death rate.

Looking at Africa with the ideas of Westerners, we conclude that Africa is economically underdeveloped. Productivity per person is low; national incomes are corre-

A mother from a bush village in Nigeria holds her five-year-old son who is afflicted with yaws. About 50 million people are thought to be infected by this disease which causes painful disfigurement— but which can be cured by a single shot of penicillin. Fortunately this child was able to be treated and in ten days had completely recovered.

WHO (ERIC SCHWAB)

spondingly low; life expectancy is short; housing and diet are poor by our standards; and illiteracy is predominant.

The governments of Africa and educated Africans who tend to value some things that Westerners value, also often see economic development as one of the major needs of Africa. The large majority of Africans, however, probably do not think of themselves or their land as "underdeveloped." As far as we can judge, most don't *feel* poor. Still many Africans do find it harder to make a living than they once did and would like to have more of the things that are sold. Increasing numbers of Africans are beginning to question why they should not live as well as the white people or the wealthy Africans. These people, frequently those who have lived in a city, often *do* feel poor. But they do not usually see their poverty as being the result of low production or "underdevelopment." In areas of white rule and settlement, they tend to see their loss of the use of the land as the basic cause of poverty, and they know that the white man's "color bar" prevents achieving security and a desirable level of living. In independent African-ruled countries, discontented young Africans sometimes blame the problems of their poverty on the new "politicians," especially if these leaders are wealthy or are too dependent on the old colonial powers. In the new nations where all adults vote, governments have to take these attitudes about the causes of poverty into account as they try to solve the problems of poverty and discontent.

HISTORICAL ORIGINS

Adjustment to environment. Westerners have often thought of African economies as rather primitive and illogical, mainly because Africans made their living quite differently than did Western Europeans. However, when European methods were tried in Africa, they often proved to be ineffective. And economists have come to realize that over the years, by trial and error, the Africans had evolved economies that were well adjusted to their difficult physical environment. The African continent does not make it easy for its people to make an abundant living; the soil is poor in most areas, and rainfall is generally inadequate and undependable. The Africans had to do what they could with what nature had given them. And although Africa may seem somewhat inhospitable to those of us used to a different climate, man has been making a living in Africa for a very long time.

Farming and herding. Africans have been growing crops and herding sheep and cattle for thousands of years. These two ways of making a living have formed the economic bases of most of Africa's cultures.

The choice of farming or herding was due partly to geography and partly to different peoples having their own ideas about what kind of life is more enjoyable and worthwhile.* In eastern and southern Africa, where much of the area is high grasslands, and in parts of the Sudanic Belt there have been many herding cultures. The Congo Basin and western Africa are the regions where farming has been general. These areas are mostly tropical rain forest or warm savanna where the tsetse fly, which carries a disease deadly to horses and cattle, made cattle raising impossible. In regions free of the tsetse fly, farming and herding peoples have often lived in the same area, each using different gifts of their environment.

In the savanna area, the African farmer had to adjust to the problem of infertile land and unreliable rainfall. In the tropical rain forest he had infertile soil and enough, or too much,

---

* See *Readings in World History*, "An African Farming Culture in the Eighteenth Century," p. 560, and "A Boy's Life in a Cattle Culture," p. 574.

Much of the culture of the Masai is built around the possession of cattle.

rainfall. In both instances, to cope with in-fertile soil the African farmer has followed a system of shifting agriculture. The soil was used as long as it remained fertile, often for three or four years; then it was allowed to return to grass or forest until it regained its fertility. Sometimes a period of 20 years was required for the land to regain its fertility. Whole villages would move from time to time over wide areas. At any given time much of the land a village claimed was not in use.

Crops developed thousands of years ago from native wild plants were grown in the savanna areas, for example: millet, sorghum, cotton, rice, and sesame. Adopting plants from Indonesia, and later from Central America, allowed farming populations to expand despite the heat and rain of the tropical forest. Southeast Asia contributed yams more productive than the native African types and plantain bananas. Over the centuries of slave trading, corn and manioc from Central America also became staple food crops in many forest areas.

In the eastern and southern grassy high-lands, safe from the tsetse fly, many peoples worked out a way of life in which not only their economy but also their religion and political life centered around their herds. A man measured his wealth and prestige by the number of cattle he had. Giving cattle made important contracts and relationships binding. For example, in marriage the groom gave cattle to his bride's family both as a proof of his good intentions and as a seal of the marriage contract. Milk and blood drawn from the cattle were important foods, and cattle were eaten when they died or after they had been killed for religious sacrifice. For, since live cattle proved their owner's worth, they were seldom killed simply in order to be eaten. The women grew enough crops to meet the family's additional food requirements, or the men bartered with neighboring farming people for foods they needed. Here, too, a system of shifting agriculture was used in order to maintain the fertility of the soil. Villages moved periodically, and pastures that had been grazed were left to grow up again. The area of land used by a village over many years was even greater in the highlands than in the agricultural regions. Because large herds were of the greatest value to the people of these East African cattle cultures, they had no reason to want to trade their cattle except for basic necessities, so they did not become trading people.

Trade, crafts, and cities. Trade has long been an important part of the traditional life of many African peoples. As well as local markets where people within one cultural group exchanged their goods, there were regional markets where different peoples met to exchange their special products. Market day was so special that people measured their "weeks" as the period between regular market days. In regional markets people might exchange gold from their mines for another group's salt or high quality cloth. A series of regional markets brought ivory, Katanga copper, and Rhodesian iron and gold to the East Coast at Sofala. Another series carried gold, ivory, and kola nuts (a stimulant much used by Muslims) from the West African forests to the Sudanic cities where they started the desert crossing.

The importance of trade to these cities and the prosperity it brought them is suggested in a description of Timbuktu written by Leo Africanus, a 16th century Muslim traveller.

Here are many shops of artificers [craftsmen] and merchants, and especially of such as weave linen and cotton cloth. And hither do the Barbary [North African] merchants bring cloth of Europe. ... The inhabitants, and especially the strangers there residing, are exceeding rich, insomuch, that the king that now is, married both his daughters to two rich merchants. ... Corn [grain], cattle, milk, and butter this region yields in great abundance; but salt is very scarce here; for it is brought hither by land from Taghaza which is five hundred miles distant. When I myself was here, I saw one camel's load of salt sold for 80 ducats. The rich King of Timbuktu has many plates and scepters of gold, some whereof weigh 1300 pounds: and he keeps a magnificent and well furnished court.[1] *

Because of Africa's forests, mountains, and deserts, and also the tsetse fly, transportation of African goods was difficult and expensive. Where transport animals could not survive and where there were no navigable rivers for canoes, people had to carry the goods on their heads. So only goods that were very highly valued were carried these long distances. Slaves could walk, of course, and could help to carry goods. They were part of this trade, just as slaves were part of the trade of Asia and early Europe. Most African craft products were traded only regionally because of the great cost of long-distance transportation. Still, what Europeans prized as "Moroccan" leather goods actually were the product of the Sudanic Belt, and the Hausa city of Kano was sending locally woven and dyed cotton cloth thousands of miles at the time the first European travellers arrived there.

Regional and long-distance trade could only prosper where African governments regulated the markets and insured the safety and just treatment of traders. This is why peoples of many cultures and languages were

* For a fuller description, see *Readings in World History,* "The Kingdoms of the Western Sudan," p. 552.

willing to be part of such empires as Ghana, Mali, Songhai, and Kanem-Bornu as long as the governments could keep the peace and maintain trade relations. As early as 1067 A.D. a Spanish Muslim geographer described how the ancient government of Ghana regulated the economy:

> The king levies a tax of one *dinar* of gold for each donkey load of salt which is imported and 2 *dinars* on any exported. He takes 5 *mithquals* for each load of copper and 10 for each load of merchandise. . . . If any nuggets of gold are found in any of the mines of his country the king appropriates the best of them, leaving only the dust for the people, otherwise gold would be so abundant that its value would depreciate.[2]

Thus we see that from very early times the growth of trade was related to the development of states that could protect it.

The period of independent trade with western nations. The East African cities never gained as much wealth from the Portuguese monopoly as they previously had from the Indian Ocean trade. As the Portuguese were driven out, the cities extended their traditional trade further into the interior and dealt with Western as well as Indian Ocean powers at the coast.

One might say that the trade with Europe allowed West Africa to face a new direction. Previously it had faced northward toward a desert "ocean" with such desert port cities as Gao, Kano, and Timbuktu trading with port cities of Egypt and North Africa. Now West Africa began to face toward the Atlantic Ocean as well as toward the desert. Regional trade routes that pushed through the forest to the Atlantic became more important. New states such as Dahomey and Ashanti were organized, creating conditions that allowed Africa's wealth to reach the European buyers. On the southern savannas the Lunda empire grew and organized the export of slaves both to Islamic markets on the East Coast and to the Portuguese markets of Angola.

With the growth of ocean commerce, trade across the Western Sahara declined. The cities of the western Sudan became smaller, and their involvement in the world of Islam somewhat decreased.* For two centuries after Songhai's defeat around 1600, no empire equally great rose to take its place. This was partly because the forest people were sending more of their gold and ivory to the coast, rather than trading it northward. Also, due to political difficulties in North Africa, the trade routes were no longer well maintained in the north. Overland trade never disappeared, however, and a 19th century European explorer in Bornu described the route northward as "a regular trading route along which a child might travel. . . ."[3]

Trade with Europeans brought new products to Africa. Of special importance were guns which Africans imported all along both coasts. More constructively, the Atlantic trade introduced a number of American crops, such as corn, peanuts, sweet potatoes, and manioc, which have become very important over large areas of Africa. But one cannot discuss the effects of African trade with the West without considering that for most of the period of 1550 to 1850, the overwhelming proportion of African exports was slaves.

The slave trade. Why did the slave trade begin? Actually, there was nothing strange about the fact that Europeans took some captives from Africa as slaves. Slaves were bought and sold in many parts of the world in the 1400's. A few Europeans were being sold into Islamic slavery by fellow Europeans, and two centuries later some European Catholics were still condemning European Protestants to lives as galley slaves.

* See *Readings in World History,* "René Caillié Finds Timbuktu," p. 569.

What was strange about the African slave trade, however, was the way it developed. In the first place, plantation slavery, especially in North America, came to allow the slave fewer opportunities and rights than slaves in any other contemporary society. Second, the huge number of people taken from Africa affected the histories of North and South America as well as that of Africa.

How did the trade work? In a European port a ship would take on a cargo of such things as guns, beads, cloth, and metal bars (an African currency). In West Africa these would be traded for young, able-bodied slaves. They would be packed as tightly as possible onto the ship that would then take them on the dreadful "middle passage" across the South Atlantic to the New World. There they would be traded for sugar or other products worth many times the original cargo loaded in Europe. This pattern was repeated many thousands of times.

The Europeans did not normally capture the slaves themselves. African traders brought them down the trade routes to the coast.* Before the Atlantic slave trade began, African societies, like societies in most parts of the world, had included some people who were not entirely free. Prisoners of war were sometimes forced to become part of the victorious group. Criminals or debtors could be sentenced to work off their obligations to the people whom they had wronged. Men who had broken the law could run away from their rulers and offer themselves to another king in exchange for protection. In the Sudanic states, where there were considerable class differences, serf groups had special labor obligations. Although these various people were not free, they had the rights of human beings, and often their children were born free. We have no reason to think that in most of Africa it was usual to buy or sell any of

these people prior to the Atlantic trade. But as European traders began to insist on buying slaves instead of ivory or pepper, some of these unfree people came to be sold increasingly. At the height of the trade in the 18th and 19th centuries most of the people sold were prisoners of war, criminals, or people kidnapped or caught in slave raids by foreign Africans.

A bronze figure of a Portuguese cast in Benin about 1600. By studying the accoutrements of the figure one can see what the African found most dominating about the Portuguese. The Portuguese, however, did not originally come as conquerors and for many years had traded with the Africans as equals.

BRITISH MUSEUM

* See *Readings in World History,* "Joseph Wright Loses His Freedom," p. 565.

Kongo. The fate of the kingdom of Kongo near the mouth of the Congo River shows us how the slave trade affected one African state. When the Portuguese first became familiar with Kongo in the late 1400's, they were impressed by the similarity between Kongo and the feudal kingdoms they knew in Europe. The Portuguese government, which was looking for allies in Europe's struggle with Islam, hoped for an alliance that would extend Christianity and Portuguese trade deep into Africa. The ruler of Kongo accepted Portugal's offer of missionaries, builders, and traders, and his eldest son was baptised and educated by the missionaries.

This son, Nzinga Mbemba, who took the Christian name of Alfonso I, ruled for over 30 years. During this time his country lost much of its strength. For, at the same time that Portugal was building an alliance with Kongo, it was allowing its trader settlers on the nearby island of São Tomé complete freedom to deal in Kongo slaves. The slave trade had begun, almost unnoticed, by the custom of the king turning over a number of captives to his Portuguese ally. But by 1526 at least four or five thousand people were being taken yearly from Kongo. Nzinga Mbemba appealed repeatedly to the Portuguese king to control the São Tomé traders. Then he asked the king to sell him ships so that he, rather than São Tomé traders, could control Kongo's Portuguese trade. Finally in 1526 he tried to stop the slave trade entirely. Nzinga Mbemba wrote to the Portuguese king saying:

> We cannot reckon how great the damage is, since the above-mentioned merchants daily seize our subjects, sons of the land and sons of our noblemen and vassals and our relatives. . . . Thieves and men of evil conscience take them because they wish to possess the things and wares of this Kingdom. . . . So great, Sir, is their corruption and licentiousness that our country is being utterly depopulated. . . . We

need from [your] Kingdoms no other than priests and people to teach in schools. . . . It is *our will that in these kingdoms* [of Kongo] *there should not be any trade in slaves nor market for slaves.*[4]

But the Portuguese king, ruler of a far-flung empire, could not have controlled his São Tomé traders if he had wanted to. Nor could the Kongo king any longer control his vassals who had gained wealth and guns from selling slaves. Slave trading continued, civil wars increased, and by 1700 Kongo had broken into a number of insignificant chieftaincies.*

Effects. What, then, were the effects of the slave trade? For one thing, the trade caused slavery to increase in Africa. It brought slavery to many African societies that had not previously had slaves; "surplus" slaves came to be used for labor while waiting to be shipped; and slaves even came to be saved up as currency in some places. In the second place, the slave trade encouraged wars and problems within societies. The increasing value of captives made wars more worth fighting and court cases more frequent. Peoples who had lived without organized armies or guns had to join a state that could protect them, or else they would see their people taken in raids. Third, because the slave trade was so necessary for European development of the Americas, African states were discouraged from developing products and crafts that would have been valuable to them. For instance, when some people along the coast of present-day Ghana began to grow cotton, the British government wrote to its representative there, saying:

> The introduction of culture and industry amongst the Negroes is contrary to the known established policy of this country, there is no

---

* See *Readings in World History,* "An African Farming Culture in the Eighteenth Century," p. 560.

saying where this might stop, and that it might extend to tobacco, sugar, and every other commodity which we now take from our colonies; and thereby the Africans, who now support themselves by wars, would become planters and their slaves be employed in the culture of these articles in Africa, which they are employed in in America.[5]

Because in most places the Westerners wanted to buy only slaves, Africans had no reason to try to develop improved products or technology.

Finally, the West Coast and Central Africa lost a huge number of its healthiest young people. About 70,000 slaves were exported yearly in the 1700's, and by the 1830's the average had soared to 135,000. Other hundreds of thousands were lost to East Africa through the Muslim Indian Ocean trade which was also increasing in the 18th and 19th centuries. More died in slave raids or on the way to the ships. Many of these people were skilled soldiers, farmers, and craftsmen. Some were political leaders or Muslim scholars. Some African groups lost very few, if any, people, but who can tell how this loss affected the productivity and creativity of those societies from which most of the captives were taken?

The changing balance after 1800. The period from about 1800 to 1900 marks the time during which African control of Africa's economies began to shift to control by others. Until then African merchants had done almost all of the trading in the interior of Sub-Saharan Africa. African governments had controlled the markets and currency.* When after 1807 various European nations decided to stop the slave trade, many African states lost their chief means of making the money to buy the guns they needed as well as other European products they had come to rely on.

Some Africans were perplexed by the fact that the trade that Europeans had begun and had encouraged for centuries had now suddenly become "wrong." But Africans adjusted their internal trade to provide the new products Westerners wanted.

The European traders, however, could not make the huge profits on "legitimate" trade that they had on the slave trade. So they tried to get into the interior where they could buy African products more cheaply than at the coast. The work of the European "explorers" and the drug for malaria made going into the interior easier than it had been before. In this way the African coastal states that had protected the trade routes were bypassed and lost business. Some European companies, as they came to have more ships and guns in Africa, refused to let African traders continue to trade in their customary ways.*

Whenever a part of Africa came to be ruled by a European country, the African rulers naturally lost control of their economies. Much of the trade that had been carried on by the Africans for their own sake came to be controlled by Europeans to benefit their trading companies and the economy of the European ruling countries.

Colonial rule. As colonial rule was extended to the more remote parts of the continent, Africans' loss of control of their own economies was completed. An African ruler could no longer control the use of his people's land, the currency used by Europeans, or the movement of European traders or their goods through his lands. Traditional local trade, and even some regional trade, was left in the hands of Africans, because the profits were too small to be worth foreign investment. But European capital and technology made it possible to build railroads and use

* See *Readings in World History*, "Trade and Politics on the West African Coast," p. 558.

* See *Readings in World History*, "The Case of the Brass Chiefs," p. 598.

steam boats on the rivers and lakes. European companies could transport more goods much more cheaply than African caravans could by the traditional long-distance head-load routes. Thus the wealthy African merchants and kings of earlier centuries were replaced by foreign trading companies.

While scholars are not agreed about whether European countries divided up Africa primarily for economic gain, it is clear that the colonial powers did not want to pay out money to support the colonies. They had to get at least enough money from a colony to make it worth the cost of paying the salaries of colonial officials and soldiers. Thus trading companies from the country that ruled a colony were encouraged to come in and do business. European companies were allowed to buy land very cheaply for plantations, especially where African farmers were not raising cash crops that the European trading companies wanted. In the high plateaus of East Africa, where Europeans found the weather pleasant, settlers were helped to buy large farms so that they could support the new railroads and also export products to the "home" country. The mines that Africans had long used were usually sold to European corporations that were able to increase production through the use of modern technology and cheap African labor. The colonial powers also expected colonies to bring wealth to home industries, so the development of industry in Africa was discouraged. Africa sent its raw materials to Europe and, in turn, bought Europe's manufactured goods.

At the beginning of the colonial period, governments, companies, and settlers all had one major problem in developing Africa's resources for Europe's benefit. Africans generally preferred to work on their own farms rather than for the Europeans at the wages offered. This was particularly true further away from the coast, where fewer people had been involved in long-distance trade and European money and goods were not highly valued. Various policies were adopted to solve the labor "shortage." In some colonies African families were required to pay taxes in European money so that someone would have to work for wages. In other areas systems of forced labor were used. Those Africans who did want to work for wages had little opportunity for advancement. This was particularly true wherever Europeans came to live permanently. By law or custom the European settlers saved the jobs that paid well enough to support a "European" standard of living for their own people.

Africa experienced a spurt of rapid economic development following World War II. High war-time prices for African products continued for some years, and with increasing production many colonies earned more money than ever before for investment in economic development. In addition, the major European colonial powers for the first time began to contribute money from their own taxpayers for African economic development. Thus educational opportunities were expanded, basic power and transportation facilities were extended, some industries were established to process African products for local use, and Africans began to be trained for technical responsibilities. With this economic boom, cities that were centers for mining, small industry, and trade with Europe mushroomed. After 1955, however, there was a sharp decrease in world prices for the agricultural products that Africa exports. The most drastic price reductions were in coffee and cocoa. In 1965 the average price of Ghanaian cocoa in London was only 40 per cent of the 1958 price. Although production of commercial crops increased, it was difficult to make up for the lower prices. New mineral resources were discovered, but prices for many minerals also fell. Economic aid was not enough to make up for falling

The Kariba Dam on the Zambezi River created the largest man-made lake in the world. The combined discharge of the six floodgates can provide hydroelectric power for large areas of Zambia and Rhodesia.

prices, and after 1961 developed nations began to contribute less for African development. During these years prices for the manufactured goods that Africa must buy went up. Yet in spite of these recent setbacks, between 1938 and 1965 Sub-Saharan Africa's share in the total value of world exports increased somewhat.

Under the colonial system, then, Africans lost control of their economies, and new forms of economic development controlled by foreigners came into existence. Africa was drawn further into the world of Western technology and world trade, but this "modern" part of the African economies was very unbalanced, for colonies had to produce what their ruling country wanted rather than what they needed for themselves. More and more people began to use some money, and people increasingly measured value by money. But

Economics 571

Africans very seldom had the opportunity to become wealthy, and almost everyone suffered when prices for their exports fell.

Independence regained. African governments came to independence with serious economic problems. First, there were the basic problems of difficult soil, climate, and terrain. Second, there were the problems created by the way in which colonial rule brought Africa into the modern world economy. A very high percentage of the produce that was sold by Africans was exported, so their incomes were directly dependent on the prices offered by the developed nations. Moreover, the various companies that to a large extent controlled the modern economy in Africa were usually owned by foreigners. Finally, world prices for African raw materials were falling. During the colonial period many Africans had learned to want some of the things that can be bought through the modern money economy. The push for independence made them hope for a higher economic level when that goal was achieved. Instead, lower prices threatened the gains of the post-war period. The new African states have generally been unable to achieve the rapid economic growth they had hoped for. The most important single reason for this has been the fall in world prices; but political instability, the inexperience of new governments, and decreases in foreign aid have contributed to the problem.

The approaches of African-led governments to economic development have varied,* but they also share some basic ways of attacking their problems. In the first place, the political leaders believe that it is part of the government's responsibility to plan and guide economic development. There are so

* Compare in *Readings in World History,* "Self-Reliance: From the Arusha Declaration," p. 606, with the approach to development shown in "Ivory Coast Education: Brake or Spur?" p. 632.

few trained people that in many places most of those who could manage major modern enterprises are in the government. Few Africans have the money to invest in private enterprise; and the governments do not believe that African economies can afford the waste of unplanned development. Second, all governments are making some effort to increase the control of Africans over their modern economies. Some governments have required foreign corporations to train African managers or have set up cooperatives to bypass the dominance of foreign corporations in trade or have bought out key foreign companies. Third, independent governments have encouraged, or have themselves set up, two particular types of industries, those that will process Africa's exports to make them more valuable and those, such as cigarettes and cement, that can replace expensive imports. They have also taken various steps, often not very successfully, to increase agricultural production. Finally, all African governments have to take into account the hopes and dreams of their people. Thus, for instance, in most places educational facilities have increased several times over since independence.

THE FUTURE

Africa is still in the process of moving from a largely subsistence economy toward an exchange, or money, economy. This change will probably continue, with more farmers producing more for sale and larger numbers of Africans selling their labor for wages. As more people become dependent on the money economy, we can expect increased demands for an improved economic level which will provide the security the traditional village economy had provided. If these needs are to be filled, and the demands satisfied, there will have to be rapid economic growth in Africa.

We need to keep in mind that the prospects for economic development vary immensely from country to country, due to differences in their resources, histories, and cultures. The Republic of South Africa is the only Sub-Saharan country that is already considered economically developed. All the economic factors point to continued rapid growth there, provided South Africa can progress toward solving the problems of relations among its races. Some other countries show promise of economic growth without too much difficulty. For instance, Uganda can build on its well-developed agriculture and its appeal to tourists, while Gabon is rich in forests, mining, and water power. At the other extreme, however, Mali, despite its great past, is burdened in the modern economy by being landlocked, having a poor climate for agriculture, and lacking significant mineral or forest resources. And Mali shares these problems with a number of the other new nations. The advantages of accessibility, mineral resources, and climate and soil favorable to agriculture are very unevenly divided among the African nations. It is likely that the rich among them will become richer and the poor will become poorer.

Looking at Africa as a whole, we can see that it has many handicaps in the race for economic development. Africa's geographical features obviously cannot be changed. Yet concentrated research on tropical soils could make them less a disadvantage to African agricultural production, and investment of money and skills could similarly modify other "liabilities." Africa's problems of dependence on unprocessed exports, dominance of its economies by foreign corporations, and falling prices for primary products are problems shared by all of the "underdeveloped" world.

Unfortunately, nations that are handicapped in these ways tend to fall even further behind the already industrialized nations of the world. Industrial wealth breeds more industry and wealth. Poor areas without the money to invest to produce more wealth, thus tend to lag further and further behind. Increasing population means that production must increase even more rapidly in order for people's level of living to improve at all.

More and more African countries are providing training for their own people and are now able to rely less heavily on European technicians. Here Angolans lay pipe in a trench.

CHARLES BONNAY (BLACK STAR)

Although Africans are developing confidence in "Western medicine," many in rural areas go to both a scientific and a traditional doctor. A modern Dahomean physician has been able to overcome the animosity of his village traditional healer. This has not always been the case; conflict over medical methods has often occurred.

Africa's economic problems can be solved only by a combination of wise leadership within Africa and cooperation from the world's wealthy nations. Some economists see certain traditional values of African cultures as a major handicap to economic growth: the responsibility to share with the family; the fact that a man's status often is shown more by what he gives away than by how much he produces; the value put on cooperation rather than competition. It is not really clear yet whether economic development requires that people take on the individualistic values of the West. Some African groups have used their traditional kinship ties to provide a basis of capital and security that allowed them to increase their productivity and move into the money economy. Obviously Africans will be eager to take the steps necessary for increased production only if they see that this will strengthen rather than weaken what they see as good in life.

In this respect the independent African governments are in a better position to promote economic growth than were their colo-

nial predecessors. While the educated political leaders may seem very different from the
peasant farmers, they still usually share their
most basic attitudes toward family, land,
and work. African governments, moreover,
for political reasons must pay more attention
to the desires of their people than did the
colonial governments. So with independence, development programs are likely to
be better designed to gain the support of

the people involved.* Thus, while the coming of independence slowed economic gains
in some places because less experienced
people were brought into some jobs, in the
long run African governments may be better
able to find forms of development that will
effectively use the energies of their people.

* See *Readings in World History*, "Farmer Power and
Agricultural Development," p. 610.

Reviewing the Essentials

Present State

1. Why do Africans in traditional villages often
have very little money but still feel quite secure
so long as there is enough land?

2. What are some reasons that African farmers
go to cities to work?

3. In what ways is the Republic of South Africa
economically different from the rest of Sub-
Saharan Africa? In what ways similar?

4. What are the characteristics of underdeveloped areas, and which of these apply to Africa?
Why do many Africans not think of their poverty
as a result of underdevelopment?

Historical Origins

5. What was the major *economic* change that
occurred in each of the historical periods into
which African history was divided in "Basic
Facts?"

6. What are some reasons that many African
peoples lived by farming, while other peoples
had economies based on herding? What are some
of the chief crops that have been grown by
African farmers?

7. Why did long distance trade and cities prosper in the same areas where there were strong
African governments? Show on a map the areas
where the chief trading cities existed before trade
with the West began.

8. In which parts of Sub-Saharan Africa did
states become more powerful from about 1500 to
1800? Where did states generally become weaker
in these centuries? Why?

9. How did the slave trade affect African societies?

10. How did colonial rule affect African economies in regard to (a) control of the use of land;
(b) control of trade and traders; (c) forms of money
and extent of its use; (d) control of labor; (e) forms
of technology.

11. What steps are the new independent African
governments taking to develop independent
economies that can provide their people with an
adequate economic level? What problems stand
in the way of achieving these goals?

Explain, Identify, or Locate

traditional economy	tsetse	Dahomey	legitimate trade
subsistence economy	regional markets	Ashanti	settlers
money economy	Sofala	Lunda	
shifting agriculture	Timbuctu	Kongo	
commercial agriculture	Kano	Nzinga Mbemba (Alfonso I)	

CULTURE: Old Traditions, New Ways

PRESENT STATE

Reaction to change. A rural chief in the Congo *(Kinshasa):*

> I have tried to keep my dignity. I have tried to remain a man in the eyes of my father. ... But for my children it is different. They do not know good and bad as I know it. . . .[6]

A Luyia university student from Kenya:

> True it is that our children today are born and bred in an unsettled environment. But I believe that the prevalent forces of change are, or can be channelled to be, for the better.[7]

An old village woman:

> You Europeans think you have everything to teach us. You tell us we eat the wrong food, treat our babies the wrong way, give our sick people the wrong medicine; you are always telling us we are wrong. Yet, if we had always done the wrong things, we should be all dead. And you see we are not.[8]

An unschooled urban worker in Zambia a few years before independence:

> It is true that we should copy some of the things Europeans have brought, but good ones

only. It is right for me to learn to speak Bemba, Nyanja, or any other tribe's language, because we are of the same country, like water in the same jar. . . . Therefore, we people in Northern Rhodesia should be one, and not say, "I am a Bemba, or Ngoni, or such and such."[9]

A prosperous shoemaker in a Nigerian city:

> On Sunday the family will come, you know we Yoruba are not like white people, we do not wait to be invited. If I have a brother in Abeokuta, his son may come, let us say, or a cousin. So in the afternoon there is fried yam, beer for an aged person, Coca Cola for the children. It is because of our belief that in this way they will help us when we are old, and when you die, they will remember their uncle who did this or that for them. That is why we are careful never to offend them, and treat them like that so they will never forget it.[10]

Each of these Africans was expressing a reaction to Africa's changing cultures. The Congolese chief and the old village woman cherished the old ways and resented the changes they saw; the urban worker and student hoped that what was good in the changes would be adopted by Africans. The city shoemaker served his visitors a new beverage as a means of maintaining traditional family ties. These individuals suggest the diverse ways in which Africans are responding to their rapidly changing cultures.

The nature of change. Everyone's culture changes. Parents everywhere explain how ways of doing things were different when *they* were young. Yet African cultures are changing more rapidly than most. Children born in tiny huts in African villages with the help of traditional midwives have grown up to become surgeons, lawyers, teachers, and prime ministers. While the lives of millions of others show less spectacular changes, they have experienced new patterns of work, customs of marriage, forms of dress, and ways

of handling sickness. And when a people take on new ways of making their living, new forms of family life, and different ways of coping with crises like illness and death, they begin to think new thoughts, to speak new words, and to cherish new hopes. That is to say, their culture changes.

African cultures are changing because new situations are requiring that people make new kinds of decisions. Every culture reduces the choices that people have to make. For instance, you don't have to decide whether to eat dog meat because your culture has given you a ready-made answer by teaching you that it is disgusting. In the same way, traditional African cultures provided their people with answers to most of the problems that came up in the course of life. But economic and political changes of the past half century have brought new kinds of education, places to live, jobs, laws, and methods of taking part in government decisions. Faced with these unfamiliar situations, Africans have to make crucial choices for which the traditional cultures provide no clear answers.* In making these myriad new choices, Africans are developing the new customs that will form their new cultures.

Yet when people make brand new choices, they make these choices based on the way that their traditional culture taught them to see things. So while many Africans have chosen a way of life that looks radically different from that of their parents, no African group has abandoned its traditional culture. On the basis of the cherished values of their culture, people have made the changes that they thought best.†

The direction of change. The changes which result as Africans make new decisions in new

---

* See *Readings in World History,* "Cultural Changes: Questions For Josephine," p. 629.
† See *Readings in World History,* "The Life of Women in a West African Village," p. 626.

situations are as varied as the people of Africa themselves. It may help you to understand the patterns of change, therefore, if you think about the two chief stimuli that are making change necessary. First, every African culture is having to adjust to meet the changes brought by Africa's involvement with the West in the 20th century. The money economy, scientific medicine, the custom of voting, and classroom education are requiring every African people to make new decisions. This does not mean, however, that Africans are simply "taking on Western ideas and ways." Rather, Africans are modifying their own cultures to adjust to the new situations introduced by the West, while retaining the cherished values of their traditional culture. Thus some things that Africans do look the same as what Westerners do, but their purpose in doing them is based on traditional values. For instance, an African will take a job in a factory to earn wages just as he would in the United States, but he might use a large share of the money to help his younger brothers get married. The money earned in a "Western" way is used in a traditional one.

In the second place, change in African cultures is being stimulated by the growth of larger national cultures. There are many things that the various people within a nation are coming to share. Individuals travel and share life in the cities. People from many cultures meet in the army and share the same training. People of different cultures have the bond of voting for the same president, and their representatives meet in the same legislature. The governments are encouraging those things that will help their people to develop shared ways of life and values. Most important, perhaps, they are putting a very large part of their budgets into expanding opportunities for classroom education.* Thus more and more children from

* See *Readings in World History*, "Ivory Coast Education: Brake or Spur?", p. 632.

different cultures are coming to share a background of similar education that is in part designed to help them become one people. Those who are most likely to become leaders in their nations get to know one another and understand each other's customs as they study in the same universities. Yet, while it seems clear that the many diverse peoples of Africa in some ways are becoming part of new national cultures, this does not mean that the traditional cultural groups are about to disappear. Africans still love their own languages and the ways of their own people. They are changing their cultures only as much as they need to in order both to make the most of what they see as best in the modern world and to participate in their nation's political life.

HISTORICAL ORIGINS

Traditional cultures. There are three things we should keep in mind when we speak of Africa's "traditional" cultures: they were well organized; there were a lot of different ones; and they continually changed.

Like all human cultures, Africa's cultures had been organized to offer their people ways of life that made sense. Thus they were highly developed in politics, music and art, human relations, and religion because these were things that were important to them. On the other hand they did not develop their technology as the West did, for most cultures did not especially want to produce a big surplus for sale.

Some of the Westerners who went to Africa saw nothing good in African ways of life, calling them "savage," "barbarous," or "primitive." This was partly because they assumed that the European way of life was naturally the best and measured everybody else's culture by their own. Beyond this, the slave trade probably influenced Westerners to expect little that was good out of Africa,

The non-naturalistic style demonstrated in much modern African art, both painting and sculpture, has influenced such artists as Picasso, Klee, and Matisse. The National Institute of the Arts, Ivory Coast, is training specialists (lower right) to preserve the artistic and cultural traditions, including oral literature, music, and dance.

(TOP) SOUTH AFRICAN INFORMATION SERVICE; (BOTTOM) WIDE WORLD

The Tswana traditionally built circular homes composed partially or completely of reeds. Modern and traditional ideas blend in a trading post in Botswana. The reed roof and circular shape are combined with modern windows, doors, and hardware.

and as colonial rule developed, Europeans were more comfortable as rulers if they believed that Africans were inferior. Mungo Park, who in 1795 was the first European to explore the Niger, was surprised by the city of Segu, even though Europeans of that time knew about Muslim reports of great cities in the Sudanic Belt. Notice that he admired it for the ways in which it was like the culture to which he was accustomed.

> The view of this extensive city; the numerous canoes upon the river; the crowded population, and the cultivated state of the surrounding country, formed altogether a prospect of civilization and magnificence which I little expected to find in the bosom of Africa.[11]

Regardless of what Westerners thought, though, African cultures were organized to help their people reach the goals which the African people themselves valued.

The second thing we must keep in mind in talking about traditional African culture is that there were many different cultures with different goals. For instance, the Masai nomadic herders of East Africa spoke a Nilo-Saharan language. Among them children belonged to their father's family and inherited through it. They could not marry any first cousins. The Masai had no aristocracy, and there was nobody beyond the village or neighborhood whom we would recognize as rulers, although some religious leaders had influence over a group of settlements. Cattle were the center of their lives and religion, and they believed that their lives were far more interesting and worthwhile than the lives of neighboring agricultural people. The Hausa people of northern Nigeria, on the other hand, were an agricultural people among whom there were many full-time traders and craftsmen. They spoke an Afro-Asiatic language. Their large city-states were ruled by strong governments made up of a king and numerous officials chosen from the various classes in their society. Cavalry armed with swords imported from across the desert formed the core of the army. Islam was their religion. They inherited through their father's family, and parents preferred that their children marry cousins on their father's side. In another culture, the Suku, who lived on the southern savannas east of the old Kongo kingdom, depended largely on farming, although their men also hunted. While there was a king, and people believed that the health of the land and people depended on his health, he had few officials and no regular army. Real political power was held by the lineages, that is, the large groups of people who counted their descent from common ancestors. People inherited through their mother's family and belonged to her lineage. These examples show only a few of the ways in which Africa's hundreds of cultures varied. Obviously people whose laws and customs were so very different often thought of neighboring cultures as foolish or foreign, as the West often thought of Africa.

The third thing we should remember in speaking of "traditional" cultures is that, like all cultures, they changed over the years. When people describe "traditional" African cultures, they are usually describing about what the colonial rulers found when they arrived on the scene not very long ago. But each of these cultures had become what it then was as the result of a long history. For example, Hausa towns only began to develop into the famous city-states with strong governments between 1350 and 1500 A.D. as they became important in the trans-Saharan trade. They followed indigenous African religions until their ruling families adopted Islam in the 1400's. They came under the rule of the conquering Fulani in the 1800's. Other groups also changed, moving from place to place, changing their forms of government and inheritance and many other customs.

Even though African traditional cultures varied widely and had a long history of change, there were also some similarities among most of them that are striking to people accustomed to Western culture.*

Importance of people and family. In African cultures people and control of people were generally more important than control of things. Whereas a Westerner tends to measure how well off he is by how big a house he has, how well he eats, and what kind of car he drives, an African usually measured his satisfactions by how many people were dependent on him. The chief's house was seldom very much different from any other in the village, but chiefs generally had more wives and children, and many people depended on them and owed them special duties.

A man got his sense of worth from belonging to groups and from the positions he held in them. Other people were always involved in his major decisions; if others were going to put up money for his bride, for instance, a man could not very well insist on one they didn't like. We can say, then, that most African cultures were less "individualistic" than the culture we are used to. Certainly individual persons were loved and respected in African cultures; but as most Africans viewed life, an individual could achieve happiness only by carrying out his responsibilities to the groups of which he was a part. An African political scientist has put it this way:

> Western liberal democracy used to start from the axiom that what the individual needed above all else was his liberty. Indigenous African systems, on the other hand, have seemed to start from the premise that what was most important for the individual was in fact a sense of being needed.[12]

* Compare in *Readings in World History*, "An African Farming Culture in the Eighteenth Century," p. 560, and "A Boy's Life in a Cattle Culture," p. 574.

The most important groups to Africans were usually family and kinship groups that often lived together to make up a village. Children were educated through these groups. The "family" generally included at least the grandparents and uncles, aunts, and cousins on either the mother's or father's side. The lineage was a much larger group descended from a common ancestor, and often the whole people, or "tribe," was thought of as related through a common an-

The entire village participates in bringing in a catch. Young boys watch carefully to learn their father's techniques. The women will clean the fish and carry it back to the village.

TWENTIETH CENTURY FUND

cestor in the distant past. Kin groups included the dead who had lived before, the living, and all those yet to be born in that line of descent. Marriage meant that one kin group enriched another with a wife and the possibility of children; in return the groom's kin group would give bridewealth (specific things of value) to the family of the bride. This exchange made the marriage legal and helped to keep it stable. In many cultures, if the marriage didn't work out well the bride could just go home. But if the breakup had been her fault, her family would have to scrape together enough to return the bridewealth to the ex-husband. If, however, it had been the husband's cruelty that had spoiled the marriage, he got nothing back and would have to go to his relatives again for enough bridewealth to afford another wife.

Polygyny, which is the custom of men having more than one wife, was generally the preferred form of marriage because it made the kin group large and strong with many children. But only a minority of men could actually afford more than one wife. Women often preferred to be part of a polygynous family because it gave them status; there were other women to help them; and children were not left without a mother if the real mother died young, as she often did. There were customs that encouraged husbands to treat co-wives fairly, and each wife had a separate hut for herself and her children.

Unity of life. Africans, like most people who are not part of industrialized societies, tended to see life as one unit. Working life was not separated from leisure by hard-and-fast hours. Work was part of family life, not a thing to be sold. Art was not a separate activity, but a way of making more lovely the things one would do anyway. Religion did not happen in church, but rather was in the land and family and all the mysterious forces that made things happen in the world around. Land was not a *thing* to be mapped or sold. Like the air man breathed, land was part of the universe to be used by the group for the good of all its people.

Since land was not a thing to be owned or inherited, there was relatively little difference in wealth among Africans of the same village. This, along with the fact that a man did not measure position by the collection of the things he had, may in part explain why trade and industry did not develop to the extent that they did in the West. Few Africans were wealthy enough to invest. When they did get some wealth it was invested in influence over people.

Religion. Religion played a very important part in the lives of most Africans. There were well-developed theologies by which they explained how the universe came to be, what man was like, and man's relationship to the spiritual power of the universe. From this understanding Africans derived clear ideas and laws about a man's proper relationship to other men as well as about man's obligations to the spiritual power or powers.

Africans usually believed that behind everything there was a single creative power. Sometimes this power was thought to be rather vague and distant, so humans contacted it through their ancestors and other spirits that they believed inhabited the world. Problems were solved by influencing the spirits who were able to bring about changes. The rituals required for managing the spirits have been called magic. While Africans believed that the "spiritual" force within people and behind events was more powerful than the aspects of things that could be seen and touched, this did not lead them to concentrate on some better future "spiritual" existence. The world of here and now was where these forces acted, so it was this life that mattered.

Ancient brass heads from Ife (Nigeria) were realistic portrayals done from life. The holes bored into the figures once held human hair.

Art and music. Art and music were highly developed in most African cultures. These are also areas in which modern Western culture has been profoundly influenced by Africa.

The form of African art that has become best known outside Africa is sculpture: masks, ancestor figures, and decorated objects. Since the masks and ancestor figures were created to represent spirits rather than individual human personalities, the artists adjusted features to emphasize what was important to them rather than copying nature. This expressive sculpture inspired such European artists as Picasso and Modigliani who, at the beginning of the 20th century, were looking for something more meaningful than the European tradition of imitating nature. Africans could also, of course, show features naturalistically as they did several hundred years ago in the Ife brass heads.

Senegalese villages participate in a "jam session" (an Anglicized phrase originating in Africa). The music and dancing of Africa have found a secure place in American culture.

Most African sculpture is wood. Since wood deteriorates rapidly, most of the sculpture in museums is from the past century. We know, however, that African sculpture is very old because more durable materials were sometimes used. The oldest Sub-Saharan sculptures that we know of are the many fine terra-cotta (pottery) figures from about 200 B.C. which were found in the area of the West African Sudanic belt where Nok culture flourished. These ancient sculptures look strikingly like some African works from more recent centuries. Ife brass heads and the famous bronzes made in Benin several centuries ago also indicate the continuity of this tradition.

Of course African cultures had many forms of art besides sculpture. One that has been generally neglected by Westerners is architecture. As with sculpture, there is not a great deal of ancient African architecture remaining because Africans seem not to have considered it important to build enduring monuments. Yet we get some idea of the sense of form and technical skill of their architecture from southern Africa's huge dry stone-walled structures such as Zimbabwe and the unique centuries-old mosques built of mud in the Sudanic Belt.

Africa's music has probably influenced the 20th century world even more than its art has. Like art, music was very much a part of African life, adding richness to everyday work and play or solemnity to special occasions. African music actually "talked" with the rhythms of speech, so that those who heard it knew what it meant. Usually there were several rhythms going at the same

584   *Sub-Saharan Africa*

time. When Africans danced a different part of the body responded to each of the rhythms in the music. It is this rhythmic complexity that has influenced modern music throughout the world. Many people think of the jazz elements in modern music as coming from America, as they do. But they became part of the culture of America, then of the world, through the contributions of Americans of African descent.

The early development of African cultures. Africa's traditional cultures were the results of many thousands of years of internal development and relationships among African cultures as well as relationships with cultures outside of Sub-Saharan Africa. But since historians have not yet developed the tools to work out a very clear or detailed picture of what was happening many centuries ago within Africa's many different non-literate cultures, we know less about their pasts than about Africa's relations with neighboring areas that used writing.

It is reasonable though to say that human culture emerged in Africa. The tools early man left behind do not tell us how these people communicated or how they were organized to live together, but clearly man made his first huge cultural strides there. Since African Old Stone Age techniques later reached into Europe and Asia, all mankind is in this sense the inheritor of African culture. We also know that far later, at some time in the last millenia before the Christian era, a number of farmers from the West Sudanic Belt gradually made their way to the southern savanna and that the population sharing this Proto-Bantu culture of West African origin later expanded to produce the Bantu-speaking populations of Sub-Sahara Africa. This rapid Bantu expansion in part explains the similarities in art, religion, and values that we see in many otherwise different African cultures.

The period of the development of African states and the coming of Islam. Beginning in the 11th century, after several centuries of contact with Muslim traders, most of the ruling families of the western Sudan adopted Islam as their official religion. The East Coast city-states became Islamic two centuries later.

Islam remained mostly a religion of the trading towns. Few rulers tried to enforce the Islamic laws throughout their empires, although Islamic law did gradually affect local laws and customs. For instance, the new religion encouraged the capture of slaves in neighboring cultures since Islamic law allowed Muslims to enslave and sell infidels. But the adoption of Islam was significant chiefly because it drew these areas into the dynamic Arabic-speaking world culture of that time. Travellers came from China, the Middle East, Spain, and North Africa, and African governments set up hostels in Mecca and Cairo so that their pilgrims and students would have places to stay. Islamic centers of learning developed in mosques in Gao, Djenne, and Timbuktu. Leo Africanus observed that books were the most valuable import to Timbuktu when he visited there in the 16th century.* The spread of Islamic education provided African governments with a class of literate people who became very useful as government officials and record keepers.

The impact of independent trade with the West. Over the long period during which African states controlled their trade with the West, they also maintained control of their own cultures.† Increased trade, and the export of millions of people, doubtless influenced the changes going on within

---

* See *Readings in World History*, "The Kingdoms of the Western Sudan," p. 552.
† See *Readings in World History*, "Trade and Politics on the West African Coast," p. 558.

African cultures. But these changes were within the traditional religions and patterns of family life and government. Few Christian missionaries had yet come to Africa.

Because Islam was primarily a religion of the trading towns, it lost ground as trade and cities declined in the western Sudan following the growth of the Atlantic trade. Fewer states maintained Islam as the religion of the rulers, and those people who thought of themselves as Muslims probably practiced fewer of the teachings of Islam as contacts with major Islamic centers became less regular.

European penetration and Islamic revival. After about 1800 both the Islamic and Western cultures began to grow in influence in Sub-Saharan Africa. Toward the end of the 18th century Muslim reformers in the Sudanic Belt began to draw together groups of followers who wanted to purify the practice of Islam among Africans and extend the faith

The continued strength of Islam in Africa is reflected by the number of children being educated in Muslim schools. Here children study the Koran.

UNESCO

to non-believers. A number of these groups gained political and military power and created several huge Islamic empires that in the 19th century extended across the Sudanic Belt from the Atlantic Ocean to Lake Chad. At the same time, the Islamic Swahili city-states were pushing their trade routes deeper into East Africa and even establishing Islamic trade settlements at key points in the interior. Egypt, too, was pressing its borders south into the present-day Republic of the Sudan.

Next to this many-sided growth of Islam, the Western explorers, traders, and missionaries who began to come to Africa seem few in number and slight in influence. For the first time, though, Westerners began to enter the interior of Africa. With the increased personal contacts between individual explorers or missionaries and Africans, there was more room for misunderstanding between these people of different cultures.*

Where missionaries preached, taught, and advised African rulers in foreign policy, Africans were exposed to some aspects of Western culture. But African governments were primarily concerned with survival in an increasingly difficult situation in which many were threatened by competing European powers as well as by enemy African states. In most cases African governments welcomed missionaries for contributions they could make in international relations more than for the faith and culture that the missionaries themselves wanted to give. Yet explorers and early missionaries had an additional effect on Africa. For it was largely their writings that formed the ideas of Europeans about Africa and Africans, thus influencing European attitudes as colonialism developed.†

* See *Readings in World History*, "Stanley Meets a Flotilla of African Canoes," p. 571, and "A White Man Comes Down the River," p. 573.
† Compare the above articles with "A Boy's Life in a Cattle Culture," p. 574.

Thus while some Westerners were present in Africa in the 19th century, they did not really much change the lives of Africans. Only in South Africa and in the coastal cities of West Africa had the missionaries by the end of the century produced a tiny group of Africans well-educated in the Western way. In most other places only the changes brought about by colonial rule made Western influence significant.

Colonial rule: "keeping order." The colonial rulers did not usually try very hard to change African cultures. Even though they talked about such things as their responsibilities to bring "civilization" to Africa, this was usually limited to outlawing certain customs they found especially objectionable, such as the slave trade. Their main task was to keep order.

But the way the alien rulers went about "keeping order" deeply affected African cultures even though the Europeans did not necessarily intend it that way. African chiefs and elders could no longer be the final authorities in whom their people's religion, laws, sense of family, and government centered. Often they had to act merely as officials imposing the perplexing laws of their foreign rulers upon their own people. Some laws even tried to keep them from their basic job of protecting their people. For instance, laws prohibited the killing of twin babies, which in some cultures were a sign of terrible danger to the whole group. Moreover, to help keep order and maintain justice, Europeans wrote down the traditional laws of African peoples. But one of the ways in which the Africans had gradually changed their cultures was through the flexibility of unwritten laws based on court decisions. Thus the European attempt to keep order prevented the flexibility traditional to African societies and brought a rigidity which had not been there before.

Colonial rule: Missionaries. The only people who came to Africa with the principal purpose of changing the traditional cultures were the Christian missionaries. Also, because they lived close to Africans for a longer time than most other Europeans, Africans saw the missionaries' way of life as an example of what Western culture was like. With European governments in power, the missionaries were no longer so dependent on the good will and support of African rulers, and they were able to start work in many new places. Besides, colonial governments encouraged missionaries because they carried out the "civilizing" task that Europeans believed was part of the purpose of colonial rule.

The missionaries' chief instruments of change were education, medicine, and religion. Mission stations included schools offering a Western type of education and Western ideals. Since all but the French colonial governments continued to leave education in the hands of the missions, this is the area in which missions probably affected the largest number of Africans. In mission schools, Africans were taught reading and writing, tools that opened the door to a different culture and helped them to cope with the changes their people were experiencing. Often though, they were taught that their parents' way of life was primitive and wrong. Schools used European books and generally taught more about Europe than Africa. It is said that history books in France's colony of Senegal began by teaching African children about "our ancestors, the Gauls." Individualism was admired and encouraged in contrast to the African emphasis on the welfare of the family group. Africans who had several years of education often looked for jobs with the colonial governments, missions, or businesses, thus moving further away from their traditional ways.

Missionaries brought medicine and education to many Africans. However, their major interest was in spreading Christianity. Occasionally, entire villages converted at the same time as was the case in this 1904 baptism in the Belgian Congo.

The missions brought medical facilities that saved the lives of many Africans, but while medicine saved lives, it also forced Africans to question their traditional ideas of what caused illness and death. White people proved sometimes to have power to cure disease even when proper handling of the spirits had not worked. The traditional religion no longer provided all the answers that people needed. Most Africans continued to follow Islam or African traditional religions; yet every important change in attitude, whether toward illness, family, or agriculture, made religion a less cohesive force in the African's way of life.

Some Africans, of course, became Christians. When this was an individual decision, the convert became separated from his people, at least to the extent that he could not participate in the group's religious rites. Converts were also told that they could not continue some of their old practices because they were wrong. African Christians were sometimes expected to wear more clothes than their people found attractive or necessary. The husband in a polygynous family had to send away all but one wife, repudiating his responsibility to the others.

So we see that missions did not simply affect the religion of some Africans and leave the rest of their culture the same.* In a sense, the missionaries explained and prepared the way for the changes that occurred as Africa became more involved in the 20th-century world. Through education, medicine, and Christianity of a Western type, the missionaries affected the thinking, family relationships, and everyday life of those Africans who came under their influence.

The missionary influence, however, was uneven. Fewer missionaries were sent to Islamic areas than to the areas of indigenous African religions, so far fewer people in Muslim cultures received Western educations, although of course they continued to learn to read and write Arabic. As in centuries before, African Muslim traders continued to spread their faith, but now colonial roads and rail systems increased their movement. Thus Islam as well as Christianity grew during the colonial period.

Colonial rule: The color bar as a limit to Westernization. Even though there was some Western education available to Africans, nowhere were large numbers of Africans encouraged to adopt Western culture so wholeheartedly that they would live like Europeans and do the work of Europeans. If they had done the work of Europeans, this would have promptly ended colonial rule and settler privilege. Moreover, by the end of the 19th century a great many Europeans actually believed that people of different "races" were born to be unequal, with whites being the superior race that should rule. Thus racial discrimination set the limits. Africans were aware of this, as an urban worker in a settler territory made clear when

* See *Readings in World History,* "The Coming of Christianity," p. 613.

he said, "I do not know how to read or write because my father told me it was useless for me to go to school. . . . And he told me that even if you are educated, you will not be a white man." [13]

The French and Portuguese did speak of encouraging their subjects to give up their African cultures and become black Frenchmen or Portuguese. But only the tiniest number of Africans in their colonies received the education that would make this possible. The new cities had separate neighborhoods where the white people lived, and white farmers and businessmen were given various kinds of help that was not available to their African counterparts. The British followed a policy of letting the Africans "develop along their own lines." This meant that they tended to support traditional ways and did not expect Africans to be drawn into the upper-level jobs of Western-style business or colonial government.

Although there generally were more opportunities for Western education in British colonies than in French and Portuguese colonies, the firmly held "color bar" kept Africans "in their place." In West Africa there were somewhat greater opportunities for Africans than in other parts of British Africa. This was both because of the long tradition of West African trade, wealth, and independent relations with Westerners and because there were few Europeans who wanted to live and work in the "white man's grave." In eastern and southern Africa, however, special obstacles were put in the way of Africans, for the white settlers wanted to keep their control of jobs, land, and governments.

White missionaries, settlers, businessmen, and colonial officials all thought that Africans should do some things differently from their traditional ways, whether it was trading in different products, worshipping a different god, or working the same number of hours every day for someone beyond the family. So Africans were encouraged to take on *some* Western ways at the same time that they were kept from really living like Westerners as equals.

Colonial rule: Economic changes and city living. The economic changes which affected more and more Africans in the colonial period also brought cultural changes. With a money economy, ideas about what was valuable changed. Whereas before a man had worked simply because it was part of family life, now he often "sold" his labor for money. Things that traditionally had come to a man because of his place in a kin group, such as status, wives, or use of land, could now sometimes be gotten simply if one had enough money. As an old West African complained in the 1930's:

> The old men and chiefs are much poorer than the young men today. Children were more obedient to their parents than at present. ... The young men lived in their fathers' compounds and worked for them. They might work for others and have some money but they could not make use of it without the knowledge and consent of the old men. ... Now they look after their own interests. Sometimes they will give assistance if there is any big trouble. But at present, it is very hard for some people to get a helping hand if they have no money, for every small piece of work needs payment.[14]

While the traditional organization and values of some cultures seem to have been weakened by colonial economic changes, other cultures looked upon these changes as an opportunity to strengthen their traditional system.*

* Compare in *Readings in World History,* "Economic Change: Oil Mills and the Family," p. 601, and "Economic Change: The Money Economy and the Tribe," p. 603.

Colonial trade brought the growth of cities. It was in the new cities that all the changes of the colonial period affected African cultures most sharply. During the early part of the colonial period, these new cities, such as Kinshasa (formerly Leopoldville), Salisbury, and Dakar, grew slowly. But with the rapid economic development after World War II, they grew by leaps and bounds. Kinshasa, with only 26,000 people in 1935, had grown to 13 times that size by 1955. Unlike the old African trading cities that were governed by African states and often organized around kin groups, the new cities were centers of foreign trading companies, mines, and colonial governments. The people who ran the most important affairs of these cities were white people. Africans came to these cities as foreigners, and they lived under strange laws, worked at new jobs, and had to have money for everything that they needed.

City living brought new patterns of family life. Often men went to the city alone, but even when they were able to take their wives and children, they were separated from their larger family and lineage. Urban Africans had to make far more decisions without depending on their families. In short, city living encouraged a certain amount of "individualism." Some people felt terribly lonely and insecure without the constant sharing of village life, and they yearned to go home. Others found the new opportunities exciting. Yet even those who liked the city kept their ties with their people as close as they could. They tried to go home for important occasions, and in the city they banded together with others of their own people in "tribal associations." By providing companionship and help in times of need, these associations gave people in the city some of the security they had known in the traditional groups they belonged to back home. Thus, while city life required Africans to change some very basic ways of doing things, it did not cut their ties to their traditional values or their own peoples.*

Colonial rule and cultural change. During the colonial period, then, Africans found themselves facing new situations and unfamiliar choices. As peoples decided what to do, their cultures gradually changed. Some groups, such as the Pygmies, Bushmen, and herding peoples of East Africa, avoided contact with Western ways as much as they could. Their lives were good, and the West offered nothing they wanted. Some more individualistic cultures, like that of the Ibo of Nigeria, were eager for Western education, and many Ibos became clerks in the colonial government or teachers in the new schools. Each group made its decisions on the basis of what, if anything, their traditional values and the situation they found themselves in made them see as good. But even in groups that eagerly adopted much that was Western, the African ideal of the close family, through which a man was made secure by being needed by his kin and his people, continued.

Independence regained. With independence, the power to govern, rather than being given back to what remained of the traditional states, was transferred to new governments led by people who had proved themselves "ready" for self-government by doing certain things in Western ways. They had run elections and had formed Western-type parties and cabinets. These "Westernized" Africans had learned two different cultures and valued both. What did these new governments want that would affect their peoples' cultures? First, they wanted to keep what was good in Africa's traditional ways of life. At the same time, they wanted

* See *Readings in World History*, "Life in an African City," p. 616.

WIDE WORLD

Internal disturbances erupted into civil war in the Congo and Nigeria during the 1960's. Many suffered in the turmoil. Here a child wanders, homeless and confused, during the Nigerian civil war.

their nations to be respected by the whole world, including their former rulers. They also wanted to increase the economic development that had already required so many cultural changes. Most important, perhaps, they had to create a single loyalty out of their many cultures, if these new nations were to survive.

Often these goals seemed in conflict with each other. Economic change seemed to threaten valuable traditional ways in art, religion, and family life. To maintain African traditions meant supporting the diverse customs that cause people to feel strange toward each other, thus making national unity more

Culture 591

difficult. Moreover, to some people such customs as traditional dress * and polygynous families seemed to stand in the way of respect in the modern world. Some governments have developed new national codes of law to bring about national customs of behavior. All have emphasized expanding those aspects of modern African life that provide common experiences for all of their people: schools, armies, youth groups, the press, and radio broadcasting. Most of the new governments are also planning economic development through various forms of socialism and village cooperatives which they hope will encourage the traditional African group solidarity and sharing.

* See *Readings in World History,* "Trousers for the Masai," p. 636.

THE FUTURE

All African leaders want to keep the best of their peoples' African ways at the same time that they guide their countries toward becoming modern nations. Some believe that unity requires eventually giving up separate customs and loyalties. Others believe that their peoples can keep their differences and expand their feeling of "family" to include the whole nation, just as in the past a number of lineages joined together to become one state and thought of themselves as a single great "family."

However this may be, national governments are themselves strong forces toward creating national cultures. Economic development and the improved communications

View of Kinshasa, Democratic Republic of Congo

EDITORIAL PHOTOCOLOR ARCHIVES

required for it also will tend to make Africans from different cultural groups live in similar ways and learn from each other. At the same time, if economic development comes unequally to various ethnic groups within a nation, it can increase the differences, too. Even so, it seems likely that the new African national cultures will become more and more important and, for instance, Lozi will more and more frequently think of themselves as Zambians. How much of the different traditional cultures remain may depend on how much Africans can keep and still reach their other goals. But African cultures will remain deeply African in those values held in common over the centuries.*

* See *Readings in World History*, "African Contrasts," p. 619, and "The Life of Women in a West African Village," p. 626.

Reviewing the Essentials

Present State
1. What causes cultures to change?
2. What two major aspects of present-day African life are making it necessary for African cultures to change?

Historical Origins
3. Why did Westerners often fail to see that African cultures were well organized?
4. What features are common to most traditional African cultures? What aspects of modern African life are likely to demand changes in each of these? Why?
5. What major *cultural* changes that we know of occurred in each of the six historical periods described in "Basic Facts"?
6. What is the significance for African cultures of the rapid expansion of the Bantu-speaking peoples and of the area from which they originally migrated?
7. What were some ways in which the acceptance of Islam affected African societies? What parts of Africa were chiefly affected?

8. Why did Western culture have relatively little direct influence in Africa until the late 19th century?
9. What changes did colonial officials and missionaries hope to bring about in African cultures? What unintended changes came about from the influence of each?
10. How did racial discrimination affect the extent to which Africans adopted Western customs in the colonial period?
11. In what way is the value of goods, land, and services measured in a "money economy"? How does this differ from Africa's traditional ways of measuring the value of such things?
12. When did the rapid development of "new" African cities occur? How were they different from the old cities? Cite some changes that life in the new cities demanded of Africans.
13. What factors in modern African life encourage the growth of African national cultures? What factors still stand in the way of such developments?

Explain, Identify, or Locate

national culture	spiritual force	color bar	Gao
traditional culture	Benin	polygyny	jazz
Hausa			

POLITICS: The Challenge of Nation-Building

PRESENT STATE

The line that Europeans drew on their African maps creating the northern borders of Angola, Rhodesia, and Mozambique have special importance for African politics today. With the exceptions of Portuguese Guinea and the French enclave called the Territory of the Afars and Issas, the countries north of this line are independent states in which citizens of all "races" share the same political rights. With the exceptions of Botswana and tiny Lesotho and Swaziland, which are free politically but very dependent on South Africa economically, the territories and nations south of the line are still ruled by whites.

AREA COMPARISON U.S. - AFRICA

Miles
0   1000

The independent states. The challenge that faces the independent African states was expressed by Mamadou Dia, a former prime minister of Senegal, when he wrote:

> It would be a factual error . . . to think that the struggle ends with the proclamation of independence. This admittedly is an important phase of the struggle, but it is only a first step that allows us to face up to basic tasks and crucial questions, and to apply bold solutions.[15]

What are these basic tasks and crucial questions that African nations now are facing? President H. K. Banda of Malawi spoke of this period as one of "hard work, reconstruction, and building up of a nation of people who can walk with their heads high, knowing and realizing their importance as human beings." [16]

There is considerable agreement among African leaders about the goals that must be reached to build nations of self-confident Africans. In relation to the rest of the world all agree that African states must increase their independence of action. To do this they need to develop stronger and more independent economies. They need to develop greater unity with one another in order to present a stronger united voice in world affairs. They also want to see the end of whites ruling blacks in southern Africa.

Within each individual country, the chief task of the government is to help people achieve more satisfying lives. First of all, they must unify their countries enough to be able to govern them effectively. Also, if there is to be a higher material level of living, there must be economic development. But Africans want to have economic development without creating the great class differences that exist in most economically developed societies. Africans refer to this government-led combination of development and equality as "African socialism." Finally, to live well also means returning to the democratic tradition of everyone participating in political decisions. African leaders want their people to have the best the modern world has to offer without losing traditional African values.

The new African states have tried various ways of achieving these goals in the few years since independence. The approach of any single country has depended on the nature of its traditional cultures, its experiences in the colonial period, its resources, its relations with other nations, and the personalities of its leaders. Thus one can see great differences among the new states. In a few, the traditional rulers play a major role in new governments, although in most cases their influence has decreased. In some countries only one political party is allowed, while in others minor opposition parties continue to exist. The army has taken over a number of governments, but in other countries civilian rule continues. Some governments allow their citizens far more freedom to criticize the government than others do. Yet, with all their differences, there are broad similarities in the political situations of Africa's independent states because they all face the basic problems of unification and economic development.

Southern Africa. White-ruled southern Africa is made up of two territories ruled by Portugal and three ruled by the descendants of European immigrants. Portugal considers Angola and Mozambique to be "overseas provinces," just like the European provinces of Portugal, even though they are each several times the size of all of Portugal in Europe. In Portuguese territories there is much less obvious racial discrimination than in the rest of white-ruled Southern Africa,

although being born to a Portuguese father does open up opportunities in education and other areas that are rare for Africans. Because Portugal has not had a democratic regime in recent decades, neither the Portuguese settlers nor the Africans have a significant part in governing. Decisions are made by the central government in Europe.

The white governments of South Africa and Rhodesia consider themselves to be democracies in the Western tradition. But their democratic rights apply only to whites. This ruling class based on race makes decisions about the destiny of the African majority without Africans having any significant part in the decisions. The majority has no legal way of organizing to change these decisions. The Rhodesian government has allowed some Africans to vote and participate in the government, but this participation has been regulated in such a way as to guarantee that the power to make decisions will still lie with the whites. The white South Africans have developed a system of *apartheid* (literally, apartness, or "separate development"). Thus by law race counts for everything. Whites, "coloured" (mixed race), Asians, and "Bantu" (Africans) each have separate and unequal neighborhoods, hospitals, schools, political parties, and job opportunities.* Though Africans are the majority in .the "white" cities, they have no political rights in the Republic's government. They are limited to participation in politics in the underdeveloped Bantustans, or rural reservations, still under the final control of the white South African government.

Whereas most of the politically aware citizens of independent African countries agree about the basic goal of nation-building, there is no such agreement in white-ruled southern Africa. For the basic political goal of the ruling white group, whether born in Afri-

* See *Readings in World History,* "Apartheid and Sandra Laing," p. 592.

ca or part of the Portuguese government, is to keep their control over the black African majority. On the other hand, the goal for politically aware Africans in these countries is freedom, freedom to have a full part in the governing of the land of their people. Only when this problem is resolved can they begin the task of nation-building.

Yet despite the very different political situations that exist in independent Africa and southern Africa, all of Sub-Saharan Africa shares the fundamental problem of having diverse cultural or ethnic groups within its countries. So most governments feel threatened by certain types of political opposition and suppress it. Because the goals of the major groups in white-ruled Africa are so completely at odds with each other, there is more suppression of opposition there.

HISTORICAL ORIGINS

Traditional political systems. African traditional political systems varied just as widely as did other aspects of African cultures.* Some cultures had states with kings and complex bureaucracies that ruled large areas, while at the other extreme some "stateless" societies had no rulers beyond the heads of families.

To say that Africa had stateless societies, however, does not mean that these people had no political systems. Because human relations were important to Africans, politics, which regulates human relations, was important in every African culture. Stateless societies actually had very complicated systems for solving problems by negotiation between independent kinship groups, somewhat like international negotiations in the modern world. While stateless societies have existed

* Compare in *Readings in World History* the political aspects of "Sundiata: An Oral Source," p. 549, "An African Farming Culture of the Eighteenth Century," p. 560, and "A Boy's Life in a Cattle Culture," p. 574.

in Africa for thousands of years as they have in other parts of the world, we know less about their pasts than we do about the histories of states.

African states were usually headed by kings, sometimes called paramount chiefs, who were answerable to the spiritual powers and the ancestors of all of the people for the welfare of their people and the land they used. They were helped by various officials and advised by councils that usually represented important groups within the states. Some states were made up of a single language group. Others, like old Mali, included a number of peoples of different languages and cultures that gave the king allegiance and taxes in return for justice and protection.

In a great many African political systems, both those with highly centralized states and those with "less" government, age sets were important. When each boy was initiated into adult society, he became part of a kind of brotherhood of boys in the community who were initiated at the same time. After a period of education in the ways of their people, the young men often spent some time together in the army. Then they moved together into a period when they married and were active in farming or whatever economic activity their people depended on. As their own first sons grew old enough to be initiated, the men moved into the position of being "elders," the people who formed the council that made political decisions for the community. Because kinship ties were very important and lineages often formed the major political groups, the age sets provided a unity that cut across kinship lines. They also allowed every male citizen to have a voice in local government when he reached the proper age.

Present-day African leaders often speak of their traditional societies as democratic. This does not mean that they had regular state-wide elections, which are a very new thing even in European countries. It does point up two very important things about African government. In the first place, most cultures provided that *all* men upon reaching a certain age would take part in political decisions, at least at the local level. In addition, the authority of rulers was strictly limited. Kings and other rulers were usually chosen from a number of eligible men by a council representing lineages or other groups in the society. Rulers were required to follow the unwritten law of their people, and major decisions usually had to have the consent of the ruler's council.

As early as the 10th century an Arab traveller visiting the coast of East Africa described the limitations on an African ruler. He wrote:

> [The Zanj] have a king called the Waqlimi, which means Supreme Lord: they call him this because they choose him to govern with equity. From the moment he begins to tyrannize over them or depart from the established laws, they kill him and exclude his posterity from succession to the throne, for they say that behaving thus he has ceased to be the son of the Master, that is the king of heaven and earth. . . .[17]

The democratic qualities of African government were disapprovingly commented upon by a Portuguese observer, who in 1837 said of one of the people of the Angolan plateau:

> The government of the Bailundu is democratic. These heathen mix with the infamous humiliations of the orientals, the coarseness of the English people at election time in England. The kings defer to and flatter their counsellors: these are they who elevate the king to the throne and also cast him down again.[18]

Dispensing justice was a major responsibility of rulers and their councils. One authority, commenting on the law of the Lozi people of Zambia, said:

> On the whole, it is true to say that the Lozi judicial process corresponds with, more than it differs from, the judicial process in Western society. Lozi judges draw on the same sources of law as Western judges— . . . custom, legislation, precedent, equity, the laws of nature and of nations, public policy, morality. They assess evidence in the same way. . . . Lozi judges expect cross-examination. . . . They will dismiss a case if the evidence is not conclusive enough. They do not convict on a past bad record. . . . A person is innocent until he is proved guilty.[19]

Justice was also tempered with mercy. Africans generally wanted a guilty man to make good the harm he had caused someone else; they had little desire to make him suffer. Their greatest concern was the welfare of the group as a whole. A missionary who worked for many years among the Shona people of Rhodesia described their approach this way:

> When a case is heard there is a tradition of free speech, and the parties are allowed to say their say at length, and friends and witnesses intervene. . . . In the case of a homicide, it is not at all in accordance with our tradition that the killer must be killed. The court will probably hear all the details of the quarrel, but the general attitude is that the tribe has already lost one man, and there is no sense in losing another. When the noise and anger have died down a little, somebody will make an appeal. *"Tese tiri wanhu,"* he will begin. "We are all men."[20]

When the missionary explained the Law of Moses, these people replied, "Ah no! We don't want to do like that. That is too hard."[21]

The growth of African states. How did Africa's "traditional" political situation develop? The earliest Sub-Saharan states for which we have clear evidence developed in the Nile

An early 18th-century Ethiopian manuscript portrayed a battle between Ethiopian Christian warriors and Muslim invaders. In the lower frame the Muslim, who was always shown in profile, has discarded his rifle and taken up an Ethiopian spear.

Valley and Ethiopian highlands. During the first millennium B.C., Kush, Egypt's province to the south, gained in power. In a period of Egyptian weakness it proclaimed its independence, then conquered Egypt to rule a reunited Egypt. When the Assyrians defeated the Kushite pharaohs of Egypt, the state turned its expansion southward and came to be known as Meroë. At about the same time the ancestors of today's Ethiopians organized a state called Axum. From the highlands it traded with India and the Mediterranean during the first to seventh centuries A.D. and defeated neighboring Meroë

in the fourth century. Ethiopia's ancient tradition of Christianity began in this period through its close relations with the Byzantine Empire.

The striking development of states in several parts of Africa came in the period from 750 to 1500 A.D. when increasing opportunities for trade developed, following the spread of metal working and of the Bantu-speaking people. It appears that most states started as fairly small groups with decentralized governments. As they took advantage of mines or trade routes they became stronger and gained control of neighboring peoples.

Thus states developed early in the Sudanic Belt, on the East African coast, and on the southern savannas. With increasing trade and wealth and larger numbers of people to control, the authority of the rulers tended to grow, numbers of officials increased, and armies became bigger. Yet limitations on the king's power remained.

The increased trade that followed the coming of Europeans to Africa's coasts naturally encouraged the growth of states, especially those, such as Lunda, Dahomey, and Ashanti, that could control trade routes to the Atlantic. Coastal states, regulating the activities of European traders for the benefit of their people,* charged rents for land used by the Europeans, and levied tariffs on goods traded. Europeans who broke African laws went before African courts; and when European trading posts proved uncooperative, African governments closed off the trade or drove them out.

The fact that the trade came to be predominantly trade in slaves no doubt increased both internal and international instability in Africa.† Possibly the hardest hit by the slave trade were the stateless societies that had no armies to protect them. Some formed states; others were drawn into existing states for protection; some may have disappeared. In remote areas many were able to survive as stateless societies.

The strengthening of nineteenth-century African states. A striking development of the 19th century was the growth of larger-scale African political systems, based in part on the technologies learned through centuries of contact with the West. For example, in the north Egypt expanded through

present-day Sudan into the border areas of what is now Uganda. Emperor Menelik unified the provinces of Ethiopia and armed his soldiers with Italian guns. In East Africa the influence of Swahili traders centered in Zanzibar penetrated into the Congo Basin where allied trader-rulers came to control large areas. In West Africa the Islamic empires led by the Fulani people drew together many diverse people under the banner of Islamic reform, and armies were reorganized on more modern lines. In the south the expanding Zulu nation caused wide-spread migrations and political change.

Other smaller African states such as Dahomey also used foreigners to give them technical and political advice. Some looked to Islamic advisers, others to missionaries or to returned slaves from Brazil or Sierra Leone. Just before they were drawn into colonialism, then, Africans were making moves toward developing larger states such as those that were later imposed upon them by European rule.

The colonial period: The system. The basic fact about the coming of colonial rule was that Africans could no longer control their own destinies through their own political systems. Decisions that affected the lives of millions of Africans were made by people in distant European capitals on the basis of politics in their own countries. The policies were then carried out by European officials in Africa. Because Europeans and the Africans they ruled had been raised in different cultures, they understood each other's words and actions differently. A district officer who saw his kind plans for building a road resisted was likely to see the Africans as ungrateful or stubborn, lazy, and stupid. The Africans probably saw a tyrant forcing busy men to do slaves' work to build his road. Misunderstandings in cases such as these were inevitable.

---

* See *Readings in World History,* "Trade and Politics on the West African Coast," p. 558.
† See *Readings in World History,* "Joseph Wright Loses His Freedom," p. 565, for a personal experience of a war in which the capture of slaves was a goal.

Colonial governments saw their first job as "keeping order," that is, maintaining their control. They had to depend somewhat on Africans to do this, for Europe could not provide enough people to rule every village. The British tried to gain the cooperation of Africans by "indirect rule," allowing traditional rulers to stay in their jobs so long as they would carry out British policies. Other colonial powers initially deposed the traditional leaders, hoping to eliminate African resistance by destroying the political systems. They set up as chiefs "cooperative" Africans, usually people who were not eligible to rule under traditional laws. Some were even foreigners. Africans ignored these usurpers whenever they could, so colonial officials could not accomplish what they wanted done. Therefore as time went on there were increasing attempts to establish indirect rule. Even in stateless societies "chiefs" were appointed. But naturally Africans who had never obeyed anyone beyond the village elders saw these chiefs as tyrant tools of the white rulers.

Even in states where traditional rulers were kept in their jobs, political systems came to be very different. Under colonialism only Africans who would carry out colonial policies were allowed to rule, and they depended on the power of colonial officials to keep them in office. Because Africans were no longer entirely free to choose their rulers or depose them, rulers often became autocratic, and Africans found it hard to change their societies as they had before. International relations among traditional states also could no longer be managed in normal ways. Keeping "order" meant keeping people in predictable places, so migration, which had been a common way of solving problems, was discouraged. Wars among African peoples were prohibited, so rivalries were no longer solved by conquest or negotiation, but just frozen to become thawed at independence.

Two characteristics of the colonial political system were especially important in the way they affected the reactions of Africans at the time and continue to influence African politics. In the first place, everywhere it was an authoritarian system. Generally, until the last months of colonial rule, Africans were allowed neither democratic participation in the government of their colonies nor freedom of speech, press, or assembly. In the second place, the system in many ways worked against the development of unity among Africans. Strong states could no longer use war to create bigger nations as European states did in becoming the unified nations we know. At the same time, indirect rule supported traditional systems, thus maintaining the divisions within each colony. Moreover new movements that drew together Africans of different cultures were frequently discouraged or suppressed because colonial officials feared that they could develop into unified resistance. Finally, colonial economic and cultural changes often increased ethnic and regional differences because peoples in areas of European economic development, along the coast for instance, became richer and better educated than peoples in more remote areas.

The Colonial period: White settlers. In 1652 a few Dutch settlers had come to the Cape of Good Hope, a very remote part of the African world, isolated by deserts, mountains, and an angry ocean. Unlike the West Africans, whose states had maintained control of the Europeans, the Hottentots and Bushmen at the Cape had stateless societies that were unable to resist the Europeans. They fled or were enslaved. These early centuries had also brought a few Portuguese traders, adventurers, and landowners to Angola and Mozambique. These people often cooperated with African states and accepted many African ways. Some founded powerful

A section of the city of Kano in Nigeria today. The buildings are all constructed of mud baked dry by the sun. Like most of the Hausa states, Kano has been an urban center based on trade since before 1500.

Afro-Portuguese families that continued to play important roles in these areas.

Although during the 19th century Cape Colony farmers expanding eastward had already begun to come into conflict with African states in the area, European settlers really became important in African history only as imperialism extended European interest in Africa and colonial rule. Thus the diamond and gold discoveries in South Africa fired colonial enthusiasms which, supported by Cecil Rhodes's business ventures, brought the first large influx of European immigrants. More came to other parts of

Africa only when they could depend on the protection of European companies or governments. Laborers from India were brought to work on railroads and plantations, and many stayed on to join the old Indian communities of traders, creating another level in the racial economic-political hierarchy.

The largest concentration of people of European descent was in South Africa. Next in size was the group in Rhodesia, then that in Kenya. There also came to be significant numbers of Europeans in Tanzania, Zambia, Malawi, Uganda, Angola, the Congo (*Kinshasa*), and in some cities of French West

Leopold Senghor, poet-president of Senegal

Africa. In all of these areas the Europeans were a minority and in most places a tiny minority. But the settlers had a special relationship to the colonial governments. In the first place, they came as part of European policies for developing Africa's resources for Europe's benefit. In return for their money and technological skills which made possible more economically productive use of Africa's resources, the settlers were given special help, often beginning with large tracts of free or cheap land. Second, because the settlers shared the same culture as the colonial officials, they shared the same view of Africans, seeing them as primitive people whom they should rule and protect rather than as their countrymen or equals. The settlers pressed for a role in governing their territories but assumed that Africans should be

satisfied with participating in their traditional systems, which were of course controlled by the colonial governments.

When Britain in 1910 granted independence to the white South African government, and in 1924 gave internal self-government to the Rhodesian settlers, there were protests from Africans. But in those days few Europeans could imagine Africans ruling states in the modern world, and the British hoped that the settlers would gradually give political rights to individual Africans who obtained Western education. North of Rhodesia, the settler communities were not yet large or strong enough to take on the job of governing their colonies. By the time they reached this strength, the world, and large numbers of Africans within the colonies, no longer accepted the idea that a white minority should rule far larger numbers of Africans.

Colonial rule: Resistance. From the beginning of European penetration, African societies resisted courageously and usually chose wise methods of doing so. Stateless societies like the Bushmen, knowing they could not win, often retreated to remote areas where the strangers could not follow. Some states, like Zulu, Dahomey, Ashanti, and the Boer Republics of South Africa, fought the thrust of imperialism militarily but lost. These were not always quick defeats. Samori Touré, who ruled a huge Sudanic empire stretching from present-day Guinea to northern Ghana, held out against the French for 12 years until he was captured in 1898. Some who fought were able to insist on advantageous peace terms. The Basuto state of South Africa, for instance, was able to win concessions that in the long run allowed it to re-emerge as independent Lesotho in 1966.

Other African states chose to use diplomacy to preserve their freedom, balancing one European nation against the others. In time these African nations usually had to offer certain privileges to one European power for "protection" from the others. In time many of these states came to be treated like conquered territories, but some, like Buganda and Barotseland, retained considerable control over their affairs throughout the colonial period.

Liberia was left politically independent because of its ties to the United States, but Ethiopia retained its independence through a combination of military and diplomatic resistance. As one of the states that during the 19th century became more centralized, expanded, and adopted certain aspects of Western technology, Ethiopia was able to defeat the Italian invaders in 1896.

As Africans began to experience colonial rule, many peoples began to cooperate with their neighbors to resist.* For example, in 1896 the Shona of Rhodesia joined their Ndebele oppressors in a widescale rebellion against the white man's rule, which had proved to be more degrading than Ndebele overlordship. In Tanzania thousands of Maji Maji "soldiers of God" were drawn together from many different peoples by leaders of the traditional religions who saw that this new threat required new ways of acting. Between 1905 and 1907 at least 75,000 died as the Germans suppressed the revolt. However, such rebellions inspired Africans to continue to resist, although new ways had to be found that would not cost so many lives.

Intertribal religious groups based on traditional religious ideas continued to develop, but their promise of freedom from oppression began more often to be for a vague future date. The independent Christian churches that were also organized taught about the Kingdom of God, offering a similar hope for a better time. Both types of new religious movements, Christian and indige-

* See *Readings in World History,* "Early Resistance in South West Africa," p. 579.

nous African, offered Africans a freedom otherwise rare under colonial rule, for they were able to organize in new ways and develop leadership to accomplish what was important to their African members. In a few cases revolts were even organized through such religious movements. Religious groups of these types were especially common where white settlers blocked Africans' education and involvement in the new life under colonial rule.

Workers on mines and railroads sometimes struck against conditions that left their families poor and insecure. Because colonial governments regulated African labor, industrial strikes were also a form of resistance against the whole system. Where unions were allowed, they became early supporters of nationalist movements.

The people who were eventually able to lead the successful movements to freedom were those who had gone to school. Villages often sent their sons to mission boarding schools so that their people would be in a better position to manage colonial rule to their advantage. They wanted the knowledge that made their conquerors strong. As well as reading and writing, these boys learned the ideas and attitudes of the strangers who ruled them. The Protestant mission schools, in particular, emphasized the idea of individualism and freedom. The danger of this new outlook was understood by one Portuguese commentator in Angola:

> To tell a person he is able to interpret the Bible freely is to insinuate in him an undue autonomy and turn him into a rebel. ... A Protestant native is already disposed towards— not to say an active agent in—the revolt against civilizing peoples.[22]

The ideas of the French Revolution that Africans learned about in the secular schools of French Africa were equally dangerous. African boys wondered why they should not have the equality and freedom that their books held up as ideals for Europeans.

Young graduates, frustrated by being neither needed in their traditional governments nor wanted in the colonial hierarchy, organized clubs to provide social life with others like themselves. Such clubs began to ask for greater opportunity for educated Africans to take part in the new ways of life introduced by the Westerners. In French Africa there was some opportunity in the local levels of the colonial government due to France's policy of replacing the traditional rulers. In British Africa, on the other hand, although more boys went to school there was no place for them in the new political system, for the traditional rulers often could give no special preference to young men who had gone to school. Because political opportunities for educated Africans were so limited in the British colonies, early nationalist protests were centered there.

Educated Africans struggling for equality found support in the activities and writings of some West Indians and Americans of African descent. Many Afro-Americans felt that it was their responsibility to help their brothers in Africa. Some missionaries from black American churches encouraged Africans in their yearning for equality and freedom, and young Africans were helped to get educations at Negro American colleges. W. E. B. DuBois, along with other black people from the Americas and Africa, organized Pan-African conferences with the purpose of improving the situation of all peoples of African background. Marcus Garvey's weekly newspaper circulated widely in several African languages, inspiring Africans with hope for freedom and equality. Worried colonial governments banned it.

From the early days, then, movements among educated Africans toward equality and freedom were tied to the goal of unity of all Africans, with each other and with Afro-Americans. At that time, though, they had to accept goals of gradual rather than revolutionary change, for it appeared that colonialism was a fairly permanent pattern of world organization. Therefore they pressed for Africans to be as free as Europeans to participate in the colonial government on the basis of their Western-style education rather than their race. The leaders of these movements were people who felt at home with Western ideas and individuals, as well as with their African cultures. They did not expect Africa's resurgence to come through a revival of traditional African states. Rather they hoped that Western-educated Africans might eventually lead Africa into the modern world.

Events occurring during and after World War II gradually brought together the various forms of resistance among both educated and illiterate Africans, and they started to demand independence. The war-time situation turned huge numbers of rural Africans into soldiers and urban workers, and they quickly learned much about Western culture and the colonial system. Soldiers who were sent to Europe saw Europeans doing menial work that only Africans did back home; they saw Europeans fighting their tribal wars and being defeated in spite of their technology; and often they experienced respect from whites that they had never known in the colonial world. Urban workers experienced new patterns of work and often joined tribal associations through which they came to know about movements for African freedom. Both soldiers and workers came to know many Africans of different cultures who lived under the same colonial government with them. These people formed a large discontented group that now could understand the demands of the middle-class educated Africans and in turn explain them to the people in their home villages.

Despite the decreasing importance of Britain in Africa, there are still occasional reminders of colonial rule.

A new, much more radical generation of educated leaders emerged to build on this support. As the colonial countries of Asia began to gain their freedom, it became realistic for Africans to demand *immediate* equality or independence. In French and Belgian Africa, educated leaders pressed their governments to turn their promises of equal justice and opportunity into action. In British Africa, the leaders had come to realize that there would never be equality without self-government. So where there were no settlers to veto their hopes, Africans demanded that the British turn over the machinery of colonial government to them. The slogan became "Self-government, *now!*" *

The British had intended at some time in the dim future to turn power in West

* See *Readings in World History*, "Nationalism in British West Africa," p. 582, and "Nationalism in the Belgian Congo," p. 583.

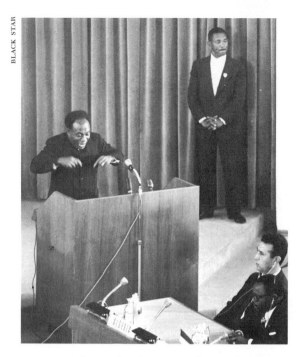

Kwame Nkrumah, first president of Ghana, worked hard to help bring independence to his country. He was later removed from office.

Africa over to the traditional rulers in some modernized form of government. But now the new educated nationalists, such men as American-educated Kwame Nkrumah of Ghana and Nnamdi Azikiwe of Nigeria, had the support of the masses. Strikes and boycotts proved that the real political power lay in the hands of these new men rather than with the traditional rulers, so as pressure increased, the British turned the government over to them.

The first Sub-Saharan country to gain its independence was actually Sudan in 1956. But since its ruling group was Arabic-speaking Muslims with historic ties to Egypt, the world tended to think of this as part of North Africa. Sub-Saharan Africa's rush to independence was begun by Ghana, which won internal self-government under

Prime Minister Nkrumah in 1954 and full independence in 1957. French-ruled Guinea followed when its people voted for complete independence in 1958; although the other French territories preferred to remain and accept the promise of the rights of Frenchmen and economic aid. In 1960 several of the United Nations' trust territories attained their carefully prepared freedom, and, under the pressure of rising disorder in the Congo, Belgium suddenly gave in to its vast colony's demand for freedom. In that same watershed year the rest of French Africa reversed itself to follow Guinea into complete independence, and Nigeria became free as a huge federation of widely different nationalities.

In the years that followed, Africans in the white settler territories continued their struggles for equal political rights against the steadfast opposition of most white settlers. Within a few painful years all of the British settler territories except Rhodesia were free under African governments. Britain's very tiny colonies and the territories surrounded by South Africa also required extra time to work out their special problems sufficiently to take on independence.

Independence regained. When the newly independent states of Africa won their freedom, their governments were basically the colonial governments placed in African hands. Now, however, they had such democratic institutions as parliaments, political parties, and prime ministers. Two things about the way these governments were set up have had important effects on what has happened since independence. In the first place, these were forms of governments invented over the centuries by Europeans for their needs rather than by Africans for the needs of their specific societies. In the second place, the democratic aspects of these governments were only a few weeks or years old when independence came. Most of the colonial period had been an experience of autocracy for Africans.

Under these circumstances, one would expect some political change and instability, and this has occurred. Each African state is made up of many peoples, but European democratic forms of government were usually developed in states composed of a single people. Many African countries have felt the need for a stronger chief executive to help to unify the country. So they have changed from having a prime minister to having a popularly elected president. Legislatures, which were set up to represent regions and thus emphasize the diverse peoples within each country, have in many cases decreased in power. Opposition parties have sometimes become the rallying point of angry ethnic groups who want their own people to replace those in power, so in some countries opposition parties have been outlawed, and in others they have been limited. At the same time these modern governments and political parties have had to adjust to the fact that they need the support of the variety of traditional rulers who command the loyalty of many people.

With independence has come the need for systems of defense. So armies have been strengthened, and the young educated officers know that they have the power to overthrow their civilian governments if the masses of the people do not feel that the government is important to them.

Many changes in African governments have come about through constitutional changes. There have also been a large number of *coups*, many of them with little or no violence, through which army officers have replaced the civilian governments. In some cases, such as Nigeria and Sudan, where divisions between different peoples and regions are especially great, civil war has broken out. What are the stresses behind these events?

Obstacles blocking the achievement of African goals. Stresses in the new states have developed largely because the goals of independence, unity, economic development with equality, and democratic participation have been blocked by certain situations inherited from Africa's past as well as by circumstances in the world as a whole.

As the first Prime Minister of Kenya, Jomo Kenyatta had a leading role in unifying and stabilizing his country. One attempt at economic reform involved resettlement of 2500 landless families from areas dominated by white farmers. Here Kenyatta hands out land titles to the relocated families.

JOHN MOSS (BLACK STAR)

The world patterns of international relations by which a few great nations compete for dominance still leaves African states at the mercy of the rich and powerful nations. When, from 1953 to 1960, the United States and the Soviet Union competed for the support of the Africans, Africa gained help for its freedom movements and economic aid as well. But as the U.S.S.R. and the United States moved toward greater cooperation after 1960, aid fell off and freedom movements were given less support. African countries have had to plan their economies and their votes in the United Nations partly according to international rivalries rather than just according to what they think is best for their countries. Even more basically, the huge amounts spent for defense and competition in space constantly limit the money the rich nations can spend on other things, including economic development in the poorest nations of the world.

Certain situations that have grown out of Africa's past also block the achievement of the goals of independence. Three factors of special importance have been the unbalanced modern economy, ethnic-regional problems, and the differences between educated "modern" Africans and their rural countrymen who still live in their traditional worlds.

While traditional African economies did not offer their people a wide choice of material goods, they provided pretty much what their people wanted and expected. During the colonial period, Africans learned to want the products of a modern technological economy. But since the modern economies of African colonies were designed to be dependent on European nations and their trained people, African governments could not immediately upon independence provide the advantages of economic growth that their people had come to expect. Because their economies were still so dependent on Eu-

rope, African leaders could not be as independent as they wished in making decisions in international affairs. Nor did they have the money or manpower to give very much help in the struggle to free southern Africa.

Ethnic-regional divisions, sometimes called "tribalism," have also created problems in achieving the goals of independence.* When the European countries put the various African "nations" together in colonies, what had previously been international rivalries became problems inside the new boundaries. Where the Europeans divided a single African people, like the Somali, among several different territories, they sowed the seeds of later boundary problems. In addition, changes during colonial rule often increased the differences among the peoples within a colony. These widely different peoples were usually able to agree on the goal of ending European rule, but afterwards many found themselves struggling to get a fair share under the new system. The smaller, less Westernized peoples became afraid that they or their cultures would be destroyed by their more powerful neighbors or by those in control of the new government. The goal of unity and with it all of the other goals of independence have been threatened by such divisions.

A third problem left by the past is the wide differences that exist between middle-class "modern" Africans, educated in the Western way, and Africans who live largely by the subsistence economy in traditional cultures.† It is easy to overemphasize these "class" differences. There are still few extremely wealthy Africans, and there are literate wage-earning Africans who fall between the extremes. Also, through their large families with mutual obligations, educated

* See *Readings in World History*, "'Tribalism': Its Promise," p. 586, and "'Tribalism': Two Examples," p. 587.
† See *Readings in World History*, Part II of "African Contrasts," p. 619.

Africans maintain ties with and obligations to people in the traditional rural areas.

Yet the fact remains that recent years have brought vast opportunities to those who have secondary-school or university educations, while limited economic growth has kept uneducated people at a fairly constant economic level. With independence, educated Africans moved into positions in government and the professions that had been held by Europeans who had had to be very well paid to live away from home. While most Africans were glad to see blacks getting the same pay that the whites had, uneducated Africans saw no similar improvement in their fortunes. The gap is maintained by the continued importance of European languages in Africa. Because the colonial language is usually the only language by which all the cultures within an African state can communicate, people must have had enough education to learn the colonial language well in order to get ahead in politics, the civil service,

and many other high level jobs. Africans at all levels of society are terribly eager for education because they know it is the way to get ahead. Since independence, governments have responded by expanding educational facilities very rapidly, but the school systems have not been very effective in preparing young people for the large numbers of semi-skilled jobs that could improve the level of living of the majority of urban and rural Africans. Where the lives of the mass of Africans have not improved noticeably, people are resentful if they see that their leaders have taken on all of the wealth and most of the manners of the European elite they replaced.

Each of these three problems interacts with the others. If the distance between political leaders and farmers leads governments to make plans for agriculture that seem pointless to the farmers, economic development is slowed. Without adequate economic growth the division between the

In 1960, at the time of independence, there were no Congolese doctors. By 1965 there were 20. Much effort is therefore being placed on training the technicians, nurses, and doctors which are so desperately needed.

WHO

educated middle class and the masses is made more serious because there is little opportunity for new people to move into the middle class. If, in such circumstances, certain ethnic groups have received more education than others, they have most of the advantages and power, and people from other ethnic groups are not moving up. That is when ethnic-regional splits become acute.

African governments have taken various approaches to solving these problems. For instance the Ivory Coast, led by President Houphouet-Boigny, emerged from colonialism as one of the richer African countries; and it has built on the advantages it already had. By allowing itself to remain dependent on France, its colonial ruler, for economic aid and trained personnel, it has maintained a relatively high level of economic development. As prosperity has reached the villages, it has tended to unify the country. But at the same time the Ivory Coast has not taken independent steps in foreign policy that would risk France's displeasure.

In contrast, Tanzania (the union of colonial Tanganyika and Zanzibar), which came into existence poor, has worked under the leadership of President Nyerere to solve its problems through very basic government-led political and economic changes. Tanzania has tried first of all to free itself from dependence on the West. The government has taken specific actions, such as using the Swahili language throughout the schools, to bring about cultural unity. By the unified hard work of all its citizens, Tanzania hopes to achieve economic development and independence of action as well.*

African unity: dream and reality. Modern nationalism and pan-Africanism (the move-

ment toward African unity) grew as part of the same hope for equality. After all, all Africans, whatever their ethnic group or colonial rulers, shared the experience of a recent past dominated by the white Westerners. Moreover, a unified Africa would offer greater hope for economic development and provide greater strength in the attempt to win for Africans a fair share of the world's respect and wealth.

But the way in which independence came made it hard to unify Africa. Each nationalist movement had been organized to work for support within the boundaries of one colony created by the Europeans so that it could win control of the colony's government. The European governments decided to grant independence to different colonies at different times, so African governments usually did not have the chance to unite before independence started them on their separate paths. Moreover, there were few economic ties to bind African countries together except between some neighboring territories that were under the same European colonial power. Colonial trade between African countries had been slight; roads, railroads, and telephone systems led to the oceans and Europe rather than to African neighbors.

Thus African states came to independence wanting unity but with little but their hopes to build on. With the overwhelming needs within their own countries and decreasing support from the wealthy nations, the new African governments were forced to concentrate on providing adequate governments within their own boundaries.

For most governments, therefore, the idea of creating a "United States of Africa" was replaced by gradually increasing cooperation among independent African states. Thus while the dream of unity has not brought about a single continent-wide African state, the dream, backed by the reality of Africa's relative poverty and weakness,

* Compare in *Readings in World History,* "Ivory Coast Education: Brake or Spur?", p. 632, with "Self-Reliance: From the Arusha Declaration," p. 606, and "Trousers For the Masai," p. 636.

has brought about a degree of cooperation unusual among recently independent nations in other parts of the world. Yet, most African leaders are convinced that the dream of unity cannot become a reality and that African freedom will not really be secure so long as the world powers allow minority rule to continue in southern Africa.

White-ruled southern Africa. When African colonies began their rapid move to independence in the 1950's the Union of South Africa had one of the oldest and strongest African nationalist movements. For decades educated Africans had supported the African National Congress, a movement that worked through South African laws to try to win equality for the African majority. During the 20th century, as increasing numbers of Africans moved to the cities and gained the skills to take part in the "white" world of skilled labor, the professions, and politics, more legislation was passed to be sure that whites would keep their privileged position. In 1948 white South Africans voted into power a party that offered the policy of *apartheid*. With the increase of discriminatory legislation and the surge toward independence in colonies to the north, more and more Africans at all levels of society began to support the protests of the African nationalists. Every group in the population, including the whites, had their freedoms limited in the attempts to control growing African resistance.* In 1960, Africa's freedom year, the world heard about Sharpville. In this much publicized case of South African police firing into a crowd of demonstrating Africans, 67 Africans were killed and 186 wounded, many of them shot in the back. Shortly after, the white South African parliament outlawed the African nationalist parties which had been organizing non-violent resistance.

* See *Readings in World History*, "Apartheid and Sandra Laing," p. 592, and "African Contrasts," p. 619.

Resistance was thus driven underground and sabotage began. The government increased its spending on police and armed forces. The rate of legal executions continued to increase to the point that in the mid-1960's nearly half of the world's legal executions took place in South Africa. At the same time, the government moved ahead slowly with plans for Bantustans. It hoped that some Africans would be satisfied by more opportunities in the separate areas set aside for them and that foreigners who criticized its racial policies might accept this as an improvement in the lives of the African majority. The policies of South Africa have been extended to South-West Africa, a territory that was mandated to South Africa following World War I.

In the first six months of the rebellion that broke out in Angola in 1961 an estimated 50,000 Africans and 2,000 Portuguese died. While the revolutions in Portuguese Guinea, Angola, and Mozambique have continued, Portugal has responded by a combination of force and persuasion. Portugal's military manpower and equipment has been concentrated on putting down the revolts, and education has been expanded to try to make African children into loyal subjects sharing the Portuguese language and Catholic culture.

As Africans in Rhodesia saw their brothers to the north emerging into independence they hoped that they could finally gain their right to participate fully in the government of their own country. The British insisted that the Rhodesian government should gradually allow increasing African participation until Africans could be a majority in the government as they are in the country. Rhodesian whites, fearful of being ruled by Africans, decided that the only way to maintain their minority rule would be to break with England before being forced to turn power over to Africans. So the white minority government of Rhodesia declared its independence from Britain in 1965. Since the Rhodesian government had made it clear that it did not intend to give Africans their share of power in the government, there was no longer any reason for Africans to work within the laws set up by the white dominated government. Again, the whites made violence the only way for Africans to achieve freedom.

THE FUTURE

When most of Africa first gained independence, there was great optimism on the part of some African leaders as well as of people in other parts of the world. They hoped that Africa, which had suffered so much injustice,

could make a fresh start in nation-building, avoiding many of the problems of other new and economically underdeveloped countries.

But Africans are like other people, and there has been no way to avoid the long, difficult, unstable years of building new societies, economies, and nations. And these years are not over. What kinds of societies are built will depend primarily on the leadership and values within each African state. Yet the world is very small now, and decisions of the nations that have wealth and power often determine the possibilities among which African leaders must choose. For instance, southern Africa's white rulers have been able to resist the African freedom movements largely because of British and American investment in their economies and

because of arms supplied to Portugal by NATO. What choices do African leaders have when their fellow-Africans call for help against such odds? Similarly, the choices Africans can make were affected after 1960 by relaxation of the Cold War and with it the decrease in economic aid. Thus, what Africa is likely to become is related to some extent to the development of patterns of world politics as well as to the leadership within Africa itself.

Yet despite all the problems that threaten to overwhelm African states along with other poor nations of the world, many Africans still hold to the conviction that Africa has something unique to offer the world in human relations.* Such convictions also have some part in shaping cultures and nations. A Senegalese put it in poetry, saying:

> Listen comrades of the struggling centuries
> To the keen clamor of the Negro from Africa to the Americas
> It is the sign of dawn
> The sign of brotherhood which comes to nourish the dreams of men.[23]

* See *Readings in World History*, "An African President Speaks," p. 593.

Reviewing the Essentials

Present State

1. What is the significance for politics of the northern borders of Angola, Rhodesia, and Mozambique?
2. What are some of the differences in the political systems of the new African states?
3. What are some differences and similarities between the goals of the governments of white-ruled southern Africa and those of most independent African-rule states?

Historical Origins

4. What were the differences between traditional African "stateless" societies and those organized as states?
5. Prepare a list of practices that suggest elements of democracy in traditional African political systems.
6. What was the most important *political* change in each of the historical periods discussed in "Basic Facts"?
7. Locate on a map the areas in which large-scale African states developed in the 19th century.
8. What were some effects of indirect rule upon (a) traditional political systems (b) the newly independent African states?
9. Why did the white settlers identify with the colonial officials rather than with their African neighbors? What were the results of this attitude?
10. Give some examples of the different ways in which African societies resisted European penetration.
11. What were some forms of resistance to colonial rule before World War II? How did resistance change after that war?
12. What are the chief obstacles which make it difficult for the new African leaders to gain their goals for their countries?

Explain, Identify, or Locate

apartheid	Fulani	Basuto	Kwame Nkrumah
Bantustan	Dahomey	Menelik	Felix Houphouet-Boigny
"coloured"	Zulu	Maji Maji	Julius Nyerere
age sets	Cecil Rhodes	W. E. B. DuBois	pan-Africanism
Kush	Samori Touré		

UNIT ACTIVITIES

1. On an outline map of Africa locate and label the following: rift valleys; mineral deposits; deserts; major rivers; types of vegetation; herding and farming cultures; major crops.

2. Prepare a map that shows by shading which European nation governed each Sub-Saharan territory after 1919. Label each with its name both under colonial rule and after independence, also indicating the date of independence.

3. A group of students might prepare a report comparing three or four traditional African states, for instance: Ghana, Mali, Songhai, Dahomey, Ashanti, Benin, Oyo, Kongo, Bunyoro. Consider how and when they came into being, their economies, religious practices and beliefs, values, systems of government, and changes that occurred within these societies. Consult: Margaret Shinnie, *Ancient African Kingdoms* (New York: St. Martins, 1966); Basil Davidson, *African Kingdoms* (New York: Time, Inc., 1966); and *A History of West Africa to the Nineteenth Century* (Garden City: Doubleday, 1966); Lavinia Dobler and William Brown, *Great Rulers of the African Past* (New York: Doubleday, 1965); A. A. Boahen, *Topics in West African History* (New York: Humanities Press, 1966); Norah Latham, *The Heritage of West Africa* (London: Hulton, 1964); Daniel Chu and Elliott Skinner, *A Glorious Age in Africa* (Garden City: Doubleday, 1965); R. A. Oliver, ed., *The Dawn of African History* (London: Oxford University Press, 1968); and *The Middle Age of African History* (London: Oxford University Press, 1967); and John Beattie, *Bunyoro* (New York: Holt, Rinehart and Winston, 1965).

4. Prepare a report on childhood in colonial Africa drawing on evidence in the autobiographies in the lists of books for Selected and Further Reading.

5. Several students might do some research and report back to the class concerning the impact of Africa and its cultures on (a) 20th century world culture; (b) the culture of the United States as a whole; (c) Afro-American culture.

6. Prepare a report on cultural change in Africa, drawing on evidence from: *Readings in World History* (Boston: Allyn and Bacon, Inc., 1970),

"Life in an African City," pp. 616–619, "Cultural Change: Questions for Josephine," pp. 629–631, "Life of Women in a West African Village," pp. 626–629; Colin Turnbull, *The Lonely African* (New York: Doubleday, 1962); and Noni Jabavu, *Drawn in Color* (New York: St. Martins, 1962). Consider especially: (a) reasons for cultural change; (b) aspects of life in which Africans are accepting major changes; (c) aspects of life in which Africans are maintaining traditional values and ways.

7. Prepare a report comparing the attitudes and achievements of two recent African leaders who have written about their lives. (See "Further Readings.") Consult their autobiographies and books about their countries in the "Modern Nations in Historical Perspective" series.

8. A group of students might prepare a report on white-ruled southern Africa, comparing the Republic of South Africa with the Portuguese ruled territories. Focus on (a) resources; (b) historical background; (c) economic development; (d) forms of government; (e) racial composition and racial policies; (f) African freedom movements; (g) governmental relations with other African countries. Consult: Ronald Chilcote, *Portuguese Africa* (New York: Prentice-Hall, 1967) (Modern Nations in Historical Perspective series); Leo Marquard, *A Short History of South Africa* (New York: Frederick A. Praeger, 1968); Marion Friedman, ed., *I Will Still Be Moved* (Chicago: Quadrangle Books, 1963); recent issues of *Africa Report;* and African issues of *Current History.*

9. The whole class might study the question: What are the implications of Africa's development for United States foreign policy? Reading on the following policy problems might be done by all members of the class or the class may be organized into groups, each working on a single problem.

    a. What position should the United States take when an African region tries to secede from the country of which it is a part?

    b. What, if anything, should the U.S. do about white minority rule in southern Africa?

c. What should be United States' policy in regard to economic development in Africa? For background reading consult: Arnold Rivkin, *The New States of Africa* (Headline Series, no. 183, New York, the Foreign Policy Asso., June 1967). L. G. Cowan, *The Dilemmas of African Independence* (New York: Walker and Co., 1967); *Africa Report;* and issues of *Current History.*

SELECTED READING

● A good general history for secondary school students is G. W. Kingsnorth, *Africa South of the Sahara* (New York: Cambridge University Press, 1962). Basil Davidson's *A Guide to African History* (Garden City: Doubleday, 1965) emphasizes pre-European Africa and is very easy to read. *Africa Past and Present* by Elizabeth Bartlett Thompson (Boston: Houghton Mifflin, 1966) is absorbing and generally accurate in what it describes, although it leaves out some important things and overemphasizes others. Olivia Vlahos, *African Beginnings* (New York: Viking, 1967), provides an introduction to recent discoveries in the earliest periods, while Margaret Shinnie, *Ancient African Kingdoms* (London: Edward Arnold, 1965); and Basil Davidson, *African Kingdoms* (New York: Time, Inc., 1966) are excellent descriptions of African states. Lavinia Dobler and William A. Brown, *Great Rulers of the African Past* (Garden City: Doubleday, 1965), describes earlier leaders; while Rex Niven, *Nine Great Africans* (New York: Roy Publishers, 1964), emphasizes 19th-century figures. The relationship of Europe and Africa since 1880 is stressed in D. D. Rooney and E. Halladay, *The Building of Modern Africa* (London: George Harrap, 1967). C. R. V. Bell, *The Road to Independence* (London: Longmans, Green, 1966), is a good history of East Africa; and Tom Hopkinson, *South Africa* (New York: Time, Inc., 1964), gives the background to South Africa's unique problems.

● A number of traditional rural cultures are described by the anthropologist Colin Turnbull in *The Peoples of Africa* (Cleveland and New York: World, 1962; and *Tradition and Change in African Tribal Life* (Cleveland and New York: World, 1966). Autobiographies of young Africans give considerable insight into traditional village life and the impact of colonial rule. Some good ones are Legson Kayira, *I Will Try* (New York: Double-

day, 1965), which deals with Malawi; the Guinea childhood of Camara Laye, *The Dark Child* (New York: Noonday, 1954); the South African life of Dora Magidi in John Blacking, *Black Background* (New York: Abelard-Schuman, 1964); Joseph A. Lijembe, *et. al., East African Childhood: Three Versions* (Nairobi: Oxford University Press, 1967); and Sahle Sellassie, *Shinega's Village: Scenes of Ethiopian Life* (Berkeley:University of California Press, 1966). Glimpses into the dreams and frustrations of city life can be gained from Barbara Hall, ed., *"Tell Me, Josephine"* (New York: Simon and Schuster, 1964).

● Literature reveals African culture past and present in John Reed and Clive Wake, *A Book of African Verse* (London: Heineman, 1964); and Richard Rive, *Modern African Prose* (London: Heineman, 1964). Shirley Glubok's *The Art of Africa* (New York: Harper and Row, 1965) is a fine, simply stated presentation, while Elsy Leuzinger, *Africa: The Art of the Negro Peoples* (New York: Crown, 1960), goes into much greater detail. Betty Warner Dietz and Michael Babatunde Olatunji, *Musical Instruments of Africa* (New York: John Day, 1965), is a superb introduction to African music which is accompanied by a small record. It can be supplemented with the record *Africa South of the Sahara* (Ethnic Folkways, FE4503) with notes by Alan Merriam.

● For recent developments with some historical perspective, Pierre E. Dostert, *Africa 1968* (Washington: Stryker-Post, 1968), which is to be revised annually, provides a valuable reference work. Andrew Boyd and Patrick van Rensburg, *An Atlas of African Affairs* (New York: Frederick A. Praeger, 1967), includes a good selection of maps with comments. Louis R. Salkever and Helen M. Flynn, *Sub-Saharan Africa: Struggle Against the Past* (Chicago: Scott, Foresman, 1963), is still valuable for economic resources and basic problems of development; while Arnold Rivkin, *The New States of Africa* (New York: Foreign Policy Association, 1967), emphasizes recent politics.

● West Africa provides an excellent area for concentration because of the wealth of reading at different levels on many subjects. The two small volumes of *West Africa in History* (London: Allen and Unwin, 1965-1966) by W. F. Conton are a general history for students in West Africa. *Topics in West African History* (New York: Humanities Press, 1966) by A. Adu Boahen is an absorbing collection of essays by a prominent African historian. Traveller's accounts are found in Norah Latham, *The Heritage of West Africa* (London: Hulton, 1964). Basil Davidson's *A History of West Africa to the Nineteenth Century* (Garden City: Doubleday, 1966) is detailed but well written. Daniel Chu and Elliott Skinner, *A Glorious Age in Africa* (Garden City: Doubleday, 1965) is a lively account describing Ghana, Mali, and Songhai. D. J. Niane's *Sundiata* (London: Longmans,

Green, 1965) is an oral history recounting the legendary deeds of Mali's founder. A little knowledge of Nigeria's early relations with the British will make *Eminent Nigerians of the Nineteenth Century* (Cambridge: Cambridge University Press, 1960), edited by K. O. Dike, easy to understand. Richard Adloff, *West Africa: The French-Speaking Nations Yesterday and Today* (New York: Holt, Rinehart, and Winston, 1964), emphasizes the politics of recent decades. Enjoyable introductions to West African literature are provided by Paul Edwards, *West African Narrative* (London: Thomas Nelson and Sons, 1963), and Cyprian Ekwensi, *Lokotown and Other Stories* (London: Heineman, 1966). Chinua Achebe's famous novel, *Things Fall Apart* (New York: McDowell, Oblensky, 1959), tells how the coming of Westerners in the early 20th century affected an Ibo village. Dilim Okafor-Omali, *A Nigerian Villager in Two Worlds* (London: Faber and Faber, 1965), is the true story of an Ibo's life in that same period.

FURTHER READING

● For a clear description of events, Robert Rotberg's *A Political History of Tropical Africa* (New York: Harcourt, Brace, and World, 1965) is excellent. Where they occurred can be found in J. D. Fage, *An Atlas of African History* (London: Edward Arnold, 1965). Basil Davidson's *The Lost Cities of Africa* (Boston: Little, Brown, 1959) emphasizes pre-European Africa. Many pre-colonial periods and peoples are ably described in short essays for radio broadcasts in *The Dawn of African History* (London: Oxford University Press, 1968); and *The Middle Age of African History* (London: Oxford University Press, 1967), both edited by Roland Oliver. *The African Past* (Boston: Little, Brown, 1964) by Basil Davidson includes a wide selection of short readings on Africa before the 20th century. Davidson's *Black Mother* (Boston: Little, Brown, 1961) stresses the impact of the slave trade on Africa, while Olaudah Equiano, *Equiano's Travels* (New York: Frederick A. Praeger, 1966), is the remarkable autobiography of an Ibo who was enslaved as a child.

● The African subseries of "The Modern Nations in Historical Perspective" (Englewood Cliffs: Prentice-Hall, 1964—) includes a number of recent and forthcoming books on closely related states: Ghana and Nigeria, Egypt and the Sudan, Portuguese Africa, the former French states of West Africa, Central Africa, the Congo, Sierra Leone and Liberia, and Ethiopia, Eritrea and the Somalilands. Leo Marquard, *A Short History of South Africa* (New York: Frederick A. Praeger, 1968), explains the background of *apartheid;* while Marion Friedmann, ed., *I Will Still Be Moved* (Chicago: Quadrangle Books, 1963), forcefully shows its impact on individuals. The history of South Africa's "mandate" is told in Ruth First, *South West Africa* (Baltimore: Penguin Books, 1963).

● An anthropologist's insight is provided by Paul Bohannan, *Africa and Africans* (New York: Natural History Press, 1964). John Beattie's *Bunyoro: An African Kingdom* (New York: Holt, Rinehart, and Winston, 1960); and Mary Smith's *Baba of Karo: A Woman of the Muslim Hausa*

(New York: Philosophical Library, 1955), are two different approaches to understanding traditional African state cultures. Mature readers will deepen their understanding of contemporary cultural change in *The Lonely African* (New York: Simon and Schuster, 1962), written by Colin Turnbull, an anthropologist; and *Drawn in Color* (New York: St. Martin's Press, 1962), by an African writer, Noni Jabavu.

● Thomas Hodgkin, *Nationalism in Colonial Africa* (New York: New York University Press, 1957), remains a good analysis of the roots of independence movements in the colonial period, while Rupert Emerson and Martin Kilson, eds., *The Political Awakening of Africa* (Englewood Cliffs: Prentice-Hall, 1965), is selections from writings of nationalist leaders. Among these leaders who have written autobiographies are Obafemi Awolowo, Sir Ahmadu Bello, Kenneth Kaunda, Albert Luthuli, Tom Mboya, Oginga Odinga, and Kwame Nkrumah.

● William A. Hance, *The Geography of Modern Africa* (New York: Columbia University Press, 1964), provides an excellent background for recent economic and political developments. These are thoughtfully discussed in L. Gray Cowan, *The Dilemmas of African Independence* (New York: Walker and Co., 1968), which includes a reference section of useful charts, tables, and maps. *Current History* and *INTERCOM* periodically have valuable issues on Africa, but the best current articles are in *Africa Report*.

618

MIDDLE EAST

Our real crisis in my view is that we are going through two revolutions, not merely one. Every people on earth goes through two revolutions—a political revolution by which it wrests the right to govern itself from the hand of tyranny and a social revolution involving the conflict of classes which settles down when justice is secured. ... Peoples preceding us on the path of human progress have passed through two revolutions, but they have not had to face both at once; their revolutions in fact were a century apart in time. But as for us, the terrible experience through which our people is going is that we are having both revolutions at once.

Gamal Abdel Nasser

BASIC FACTS: A Crossroads for Ideas, Trade, and Armies

GEOGRAPHY

The Muslim world. The Middle East is a part of the Muslim world, a huge area stretching from Morocco to Indonesia, and from Central Asia to Central Africa. Although the peoples of this world have different languages and customs and belong to different races, the majority of them share the Islamic religion. We shall not try to study all these peoples in this unit. Instead we shall deal only with those who live in the region called the Middle East. Here, the Islamic religion began; here on the Arabian Peninsula is located the holy city of Mecca, revered by all Muslims because it is the birthplace of Mohammed, their founder, just as Jerusalem is sacred to Christians because it is the place where Jesus Christ lived.

The Middle East. Exactly what do we mean when we talk about the Middle East, or the Near East, as it is sometimes called? These terms have not been used very precisely, with the result that they mean different things to different people. When the term Middle East is used in this book, it designates the territory lying between the Soviet Union in the north, Afghanistan and Pakistan in the east, the Indian Ocean and the Sudan in the south, and Libya in the west. In size it is about 2,808,000 square miles and includes about 125 million people. Its area, then, is a little more than three-fourths that of the United States, while its population is about five-eighths as much.

There are 17 countries in the Middle East, but only 9 of them are important for our purposes. These may easily be kept in mind if we think of five small countries in the center of the area, with four large countries surrounding them. The map of the Middle East shows that the large countries are the following: Turkey in the north, Iran in the east, Saudi Arabia in the south, and the United Arab Republic in the west. The small countries in the center are Iraq, Lebanon, Jordan, Israel, and Syria.

The Middle East has two natural land regions, the northern mountains and the southern plateaus. The northern mountain region covers most of Turkey and Iran. This mountainous region serves to wall off the Middle East from the Soviet Union and is the source of the Tigris and Euphrates Rivers which water the Fertile Crescent.

Covering most of the other countries of the Middle East, the plateau region lies to the south of the mountain region. It consists largely of barren deserts except for thin strips of green vegetation along river valleys and certain coastal areas.

Climate. Throughout the Middle East there is a rhythmic pattern of rainy winters and dry summers. The amount of precipitation during the rainy season is never great and it declines in amount from north to south. This has resulted in an absolute aridity in the south with some areas receiving absolutely no rainfall at any time in the year.

If you were to fly over this vast region, you would see almost all brown earth beneath you, dotted rarely with green vegetation. The only real stretch of green would be in that long curve known as the Fertile Crescent, so named because the area is the shape of a crescent moon. Beginning at the mouth of the Tigris-Euphrates River, the green belt goes up the valley of the river, which has plenty of water for crops. Then it extends around to the Mediterranean coast of the

The Nile River has for thousands of years been the single most important source of irrigation in Egypt.

Syrian region and Israel, which is also kept fertile by rain brought in on breezes from the sea. Finally the Crescent reaches south into the Nile River valley of Africa, where the soil is rich because of the river's annual flooding. The famed Fertile Crescent has impressed, attracted, and nourished the people of the Middle East all through history. It is here that the Biblical Garden of Eden is thought to have flourished, and the "land of milk and honey" described by Moses.

A few other sections of the Middle East receive enough rain to be fertile and green. Most important are the west and north coasts of Turkey, which benefit from rain-laden breezes off the Mediterranean, the Black and the Aegean Seas, and a few mountain areas in east Turkey and west Iran, which are high enough to trap winds from the coast. With the exception of these regions, however, the rest of the Middle East receives little rainfall and is almost all desert.

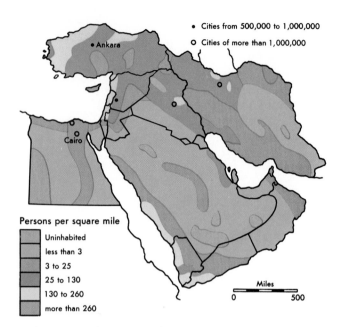

Cities from 500,000 to 1,000,000
○ Cities of more than 1,000,000

Ankara

Cairo

Persons per square mile
Uninhabited
less than 3
3 to 25
25 to 130
130 to 260
more than 260

Miles
0   500

MIDDLE EAST - POPULATION

Very few people live in the desert, only the Bedouin nomads who wander by camel from oasis to oasis. By far the greatest concentration of population is in the Fertile Crescent and along the coasts. This fact underscores the vital importance of rainfall in the Middle East. Where there is enough rain, there are many people; where there is little rain there are few people, with the exception of Egypt and Iraq where the Nile and Tigris-Euphrates supply water for irrigation.

Resources. Most regions of the Middle East are undersupplied with minerals as well as with rain. The sole exception is Turkey, which has a good supply of coal, iron, copper, chrome, and salt. Other minerals are scattered throughout the region, but most of them cannot be mined economically. But the Middle East is very rich in one of the world's most important mineral resources, oil. Iraq, Iran, Saudi Arabia, and some of the small countries along the coast of the Arabian Peninsula have tremendous supplies of oil beneath the earth. One-half of the world's known resources are in the Middle East. Since the Arabs do not have the technical knowledge to operate their oil fields, they allow foreign companies to do so. In return, the Middle East governments receive well over two billion dollars annually in the form of royalties. This is a boon for those countries lucky enough to have oil deposits, but some of the largest countries with the greatest populations have no oil and receive no money. Most of the crude oil is exported, but there are refineries in Iran, Saudi Arabia, and some of the smaller states.

Location. The final point to be made about the geography of the Middle East is the strategic location of the area. Its central position at the crossroads of three continents: Africa, Asia, and Europe, has deeply affected the region all through history. It explains why so many world trade routes, such as the medieval spice route and the modern Suez Canal route, pass through the Middle East. It explains also why so many invading armies, such as the Mongols from Central Asia and the Crusaders from Western Europe, overran Middle East lands. Finally the central location, plus oil, explains why the area is so often in the headlines today. Since it is the land bridge linking three continents, the power blocs of the world are very much concerned with what goes on there. If one bloc appears to be gaining influence the other immediately tries to check it. An international crisis develops; the Middle East is once more proclaimed a "trouble spot."

PEOPLE

Origins. We have seen that the Middle East has been frequently overrun by various invaders, many of whom stayed on and min-

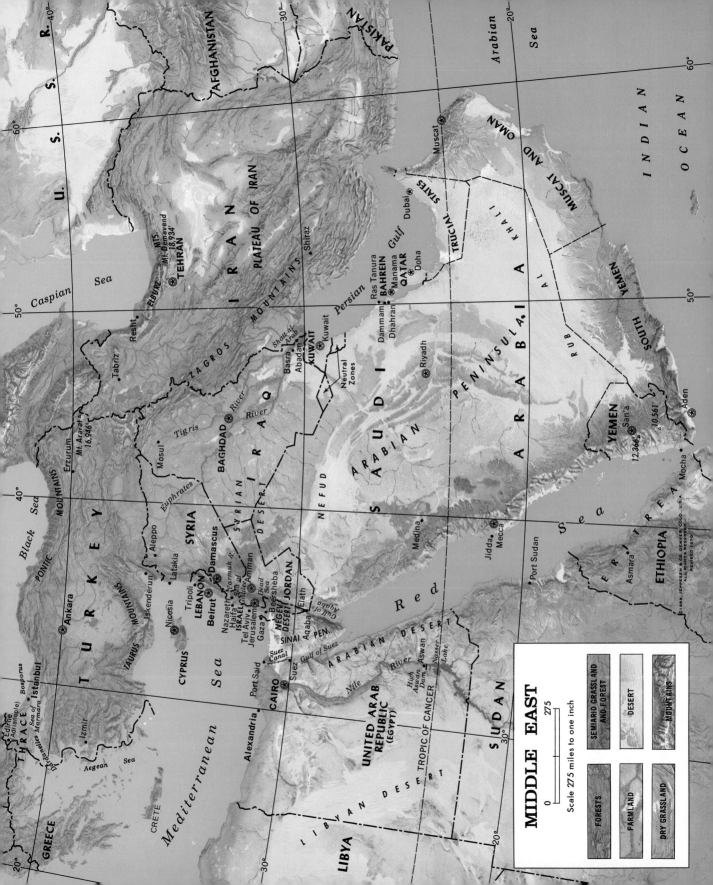

MIDDLE EAST

Scale 275 miles to one inch

0   275

SEMIARID GRASSLAND AND FOREST

DESERT

MOUNTAINS

FORESTS

FARMLAND

DRY GRASSLAND

© 1966, JEPPESEN & CO. DENVER COLO., U.S.A.
ALL RIGHTS RESERVED
REVISED 1970

Labels

U. S. S. R.

AFGHANISTAN

PAKISTAN

Arabian Sea

INDIAN OCEAN

Caspian Sea

Black Sea

Aegean Sea

Mediterranean Sea

Red Sea

Persian Gulf

Gulf of Aqaba

Gulf of Suez

IRAN
PLATEAU OF IRAN
ZAGROS MOUNTAINS
ELBURZ MTS.
Mt. Demavend 18,934'
TEHRAN
Resht
Tabriz
Shiraz

TURKEY
PONTIC MOUNTAINS
TAURUS MOUNTAINS
Ankara
Erzurum
Mt. Ararat 16,946'
Izmir
Istanbul
Bosporus
Sea of Marmara
Dardanelles
Edirne (Adrianople)

THRACE
GREECE
CRETE
CYPRUS
Nicosia

IRAQ
SYRIAN DESERT
BAGHDAD
Mosul
Basra
Abadan
Shatt al Arab
Tigris River
Euphrates River

KUWAIT
Kuwait
Neutral Zones

SYRIA
Aleppo
Latakia
Tripoli
Damascus
Yarmuk R.

LEBANON
Beirut

ISRAEL
Haifa
Nazareth
Tel Aviv
Jerusalem
Gaza
Beersheba
NEGEV DESERT

JORDAN
Amman
Dead Sea
Sea of Galilee
Elath
Aqaba

SINAI PEN.
Suez Canal
Suez
Port Said

UNITED ARAB REPUBLIC (EGYPT)
CAIRO
Alexandria
Nile River
High Aswan Dam
Aswan Dam
Lake Nasser
TROPIC OF CANCER

LIBYA
LIBYAN DESERT
ARABIAN DESERT

SUDAN
Port Sudan

ETHIOPIA
ERITREA
Asmara
Mocha
Aden

SAUDI ARABIA
ARABIAN PENINSULA
NEFUD
RUB' AL KHALI
Riyadh
Medina
Mecca
Jidda

YEMEN
San'a 10,561'
12,366'

SOUTH YEMEN

MUSCAT AND OMAN
Muscat

TRUCIAL STATES
Dubai

QATAR
Doha

BAHREIN
Manama

Ras Tanura
Dammam
Dhahran

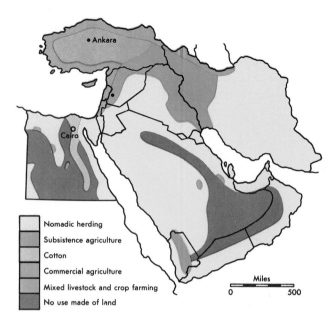

Nomadic herding
Subsistence agriculture
Cotton
Commercial agriculture
Mixed livestock and crop farming
No use made of land

Miles
0   500

MIDDLE EAST ~ LAND USE

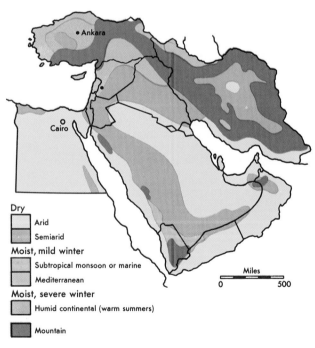

Dry
Arid
Semiarid
Moist, mild winter
Subtropical monsoon or marine
Mediterranean
Moist, severe winter
Humid continental (warm summers)
Mountain

Miles
0   500

MIDDLE EAST ~ CLIMATE

gled with the local populations. As a result the Middle Eastern peoples today are of very mixed origins. We can distinguish four major groups; in the heart of the region are the Semitic Arabs who occupy most of Arabia, Iraq, Syria, Lebanon, Jordan, and the nomad lands of Egypt. To the north of this Arab bloc are the Turks, to the east the Persians, and to the west the Egyptians. The upper classes of Egypt are a mixture of Turkish and Arab blood, but the peasants, who compose most of the population, are the same as their ancestors who lived under the pharaohs of Biblical times. These people, however, speak an Arab dialect and consider themselves to be Arabs as much as the Syrians and the Iraqi do.

Classes. If we divide the Middle Eastern peoples on the basis of occupation, we find that about 70 per cent are fellaheen, or peasants, tilling the soil, about 25 per cent are city-dwellers, and the rest are nomads in the desert. These proportions, however, vary from country to country. The urban population is no more than 10 per cent in the Arabian Peninsula, which is mostly desert, but is over 40 per cent in Lebanon and 78 per cent in Israel. Likewise the nomadic population varies from zero per cent in Lebanon to 10 per cent in the Arabian Peninsula and 40 per cent in Jordan.*

The peasant, the townsman, and the nomad live very different kinds of lives. The nomad is a wandering herdsman whose only home is his tent. He is usually illiterate, fiercely independent, and willing to support his tribal chief rather than his country's government. The peasant is a little higher on the social scale than the nomad. He works hard on his little plot, growing such crops as cotton if he has irrigation, or various grains if he does not. Finally, the townsman is

* See *Readings in World History* (Boston: Allyn and Bacon, Inc., 1970), "The Arab Bedouin," p. 655.

likely to be a merchant or artisan. He usually is better educated than the peasant or nomad, and knows more about the world. Most of the leaders of the Middle Eastern countries come from the towns rather than the rural areas or deserts.

HISTORICAL PERIODS

In considering the main periods of Middle Eastern history, we can use the same divisions that we did earlier when we summarized the entire history of man. These divisions were the prehistoric, to 3700 B.C., the ancient, from 3700 to 1000 B.C., the classical, from 1000 B.C. to 500 A.D., the medieval, from 500 to 1500 A.D., and the modern from 1500 to the present.

Prehistoric, ancient, and classical periods. During the first two periods the peoples of the Middle East were the most advanced in the world. In the prehistoric period they were the first to discover how to practice agriculture, about 8000 B.C. This discovery, which gradually spread to other regions of Eurasia, enabled prehistoric man to settle down, to live in villages, and to increase in numbers. In the ancient period it was Middle Eastern man again who first discovered the arts of civilization: the building of cities, the invention of writing, and the development of political organization, of literature, and of science. The first center of civilization was in Mesopotamia, but Egypt followed close behind, and other centers developed in Asia Minor, Syria, and the Aegean Islands. From the Middle East, civilization, like agriculture, spread gradually to India, to Europe, and probably to China.

In the classical period a number of great empires were organized which, for the first time, united the Middle Eastern lands. First was the Persian Empire of the sixth century B.C., which included Egypt and a part of the

The architecture of ancient Egypt, such as the sphinx and pyramids, is famous throughout the world. The Great Temple, built in the 12th century B.C., is decorated with four colossuses representing Ramses II. Each is 67 feet high. The width of each face, from ear to ear, is 14 feet.

Balkans in the west and stretched eastward to India and Central Asia. In contrast to the local differences of earlier times, the whole of the Middle East was now a unit, both culturally and politically. In 332 B.C. the Persian Empire was overthrown by Alexander the Great of Macedon. His short-lived empire was even larger than that of the Persians, for it included Greece in the west and the Indus Valley in the east. Alexander's empire is important in Middle Eastern his-

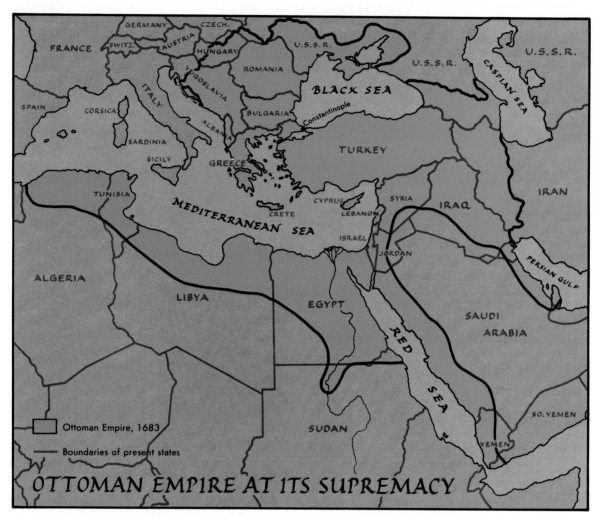

OTTOMAN EMPIRE AT ITS SUPREMACY

Ottoman Empire, 1683
Boundaries of present states

tory because it made possible the spreading of Greek civilization over the entire region.

But Hellenistic civilization, as we saw in Unit Three, did not sink deeply into the life of the region, especially in the eastern part of the Middle East, beyond Egypt, Syria, and Asia Minor. Thus after the death of Alexander and the overthrow of his generals who had divided the empire among themselves, the Middle East split into two parts. The western part, which first was conquered by the Roman Empire and later became the East Roman or Byzantine Empire, was largely Greek in culture and Christian in religion. The eastern part, ruled first by the Parthians and then by the Sassanians, was more Persian in culture and Zoroastrian in religion.

Islam is born. The medieval period began when the greater part of the Middle East was overrun and conquered by a handful of Arabs fired by the new religion of Islam. (The word "Islam" means submission to the will of God.) The division between the eastern and western parts of the Middle East now disappeared. The entire region again became a unit; Islam was the cement binding it together. This is the case to the present day when the Middle East possesses a natural unity because of its Islamic religion and culture. During most of the medieval period the Middle East was under the rule of the Arab Muslim conquerors. But in time their strength declined, and they gave way to Turkish invaders from Central Asia. These invaders were pagans at first but, under the influence of the Arabs, they gradually became Muslims. One branch of the Turkish people, the Seljuk Turks, captured the capital, Baghdad, in 1055, and thereafter controlled most of the Middle East.

The modern period. The modern period of Middle Eastern history falls naturally into two parts, the Ottoman and the national. The Ottoman era began when a new branch of Turks, the Ottoman Turks, crossed the Straits to Europe and captured the city of Constantinople in 1453. The fall of this city marked the end of the Byzantine Empire. The Ottoman Turks then continued to expand until their empire included North Af-

rica, southeastern Europe, and the entire Middle East except Iran. The Ottoman Empire at this time was one of the greatest in the world. Western Europeans regarded it with much respect and fear, especially because of its efficient administration and powerful army.[*]

By the 18th century, however, the Ottoman Empire was on the downgrade.[†] First Austria seized some Ottoman provinces along the Danube River, and then Russia conquered other Ottoman provinces on the north shore of the Black Sea. During the 19th century the various Balkan peoples: Greeks, Serbians, Bulgarians, and Rumanians, all won their independence one after the other. By the end of the century the Turks had lost all their lands in Europe except for Constantinople and its environs.[‡]

The final disaster was the decision of the Turks to enter World War I on the side of the

[*] See *Readings in World History*, "The Ottoman Empire at Its Height," p. 647.
[†] See *Readings in World History*, "Decline of the Ottoman Empire," p. 650.
[‡] See *Readings in World History*, "On the Eve of Partition," p. 653.

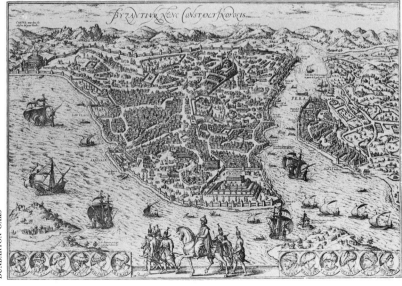

Map of Constantinople during the Byzantine Empire.

DUNBARTON OAKS

Central Powers; they were defeated and their empire was partitioned. Asia Minor, together with the Constantinople region, became the new republic of Turkey under the leadership of its great founder, Mustapha Ataturk. The Arab lands to the south were divided into mandates which were given to the victorious Allies, Britain and France under the guidance of the League of Nations.

This partition began the national period of Middle Eastern history that has continued to the present. In contrast to the past, no one empire controls the Middle East today. Instead, the region is divided into many nation-states, and loyalty to the nation rather than to an empire is the strongest feeling of most people. Hence this present period is known as the national period.

Reviewing the Essentials

Geography

1. On a map, locate the boundaries and name the countries of the Muslim world. Give the total population of the area. Locate the Middle East, as the term is defined in the text. Give its boundaries. What countries are included in the Middle East? What is its population? Compare with the population of India, the Soviet Union, and the United States. Why is the Middle East important to the Muslim world?

2. Describe the climate of the Middle East. Locate those parts of the Middle East that have enough rainfall to be fertile and green. What effect has climate had on the concentration of people in the Middle East? (Use a map.)

3. Name and locate the resources of Middle Eastern countries. What resources essential to industrial development are lacking in much of the area?

4. Explain the great importance of geography as one factor influencing the history of the Middle East.

People

5. Name and locate on the map the four major groups of people in the Middle East.

6. In terms of population, what percentage of people in the Middle East live in cities? are farmers? are nomads? What inferences do you draw from this?

Historical Periods

7. Why was the Middle East the most advanced part of the world during ancient times?

8. From its center in Mesopotamia to what areas did civilization spread?

9. Name and locate the extent of the great empires that were organized and dominated the Middle East during the classical period. What was the effect of empires as a form of political organization on the Middle East?

10. What people ruled the Middle East and influenced its culture during the medieval period?

11. Distinguish between the Ottoman and national periods of the Middle East.

Explain, Identify, or Locate

Bedouin	Zoroaster	Fellaheen	Asia Minor
nomad	Alexander of Macedon	Seljuk Turks	Ottoman Empire
Hellenistic civilization	Parthians	Persian Empire	Fertile Crescent
8000 B.C.	332 B.C.	1055 A.D.	1453 A.D.

POLITICS: A Surge of Nationalism in the Middle East

PRESENT STATE

Nationalism is by far the strongest force influencing Middle Eastern politics today. What this means exactly may be seen in the experience of an American correspondent who visited the small country of Kuwait on the east coast of the Arabian Peninsula. This is a very rich country because much oil has been found there, and the government is receiving large sums of money from the foreign companies who have leased the oil rights. As a result the people of Kuwait are much better off today than they were several years ago before oil was discovered. And yet the American correspondent found that the best-educated young men in Kuwait were dissatisfied with their ruler and wanted to join with President Gamal Nasser of Egypt to form a great united Arab state. When the correspondent asked these young men why, he received these replies:

A poster for El Fatah (an Arab guerrilla force dedicated to recapturing Palestine) shows an Arab nationalist fighting for victory.

It is a question of dignity. Arabs want to feel equal to other nations and must unite to do so. President Nasser has shown us how we can look you in the eye.

We want to belong to a larger movement with a sense of purpose and direction. We cannot be happy when others about us in the Arab world are miserable.

Our day is coming. Nothing can stop the Arabs from uniting. You will see.[1]

We see from these answers that, for the young men in Kuwait, nationalism is the desire to unite with all other peoples who speak the same language and have the same culture. It is also the belief that if the Arab peoples can unite, life will be better for all

of them. As citizens of a great and powerful state, they will feel themselves the equal of citizens of other great nations.

Despite its tremendous appeal to the people of the Middle East, nationalism appeared in that region only recently. A mere fifty years ago, which is a short time historically speaking, an observer who had travelled widely in Asia, wrote: "Religion absorbs the intellect of the Asiatic; it is stronger than his feeling for nationality, the latter is almost everywhere of second importance."[2]

This was most certainly true of the people of the Middle East. We know this to be the case for two reasons. One is the fact that all of these people, with the exception of the Iranians, were under foreign Ottoman Turkish rule. They showed no strong desire to set up independent nation-states. Instead they accepted their place as subjects of the Ottoman Sultan in Constantinople.

The other sign of weak nationalism in the Middle East is to be found in the highhanded actions of the Great Powers of Europe. In 1904, for example, Britain and France signed an alliance which provided, among other things, that France should recognize Britain's occupation of Egypt, and Britain in return should recognize France's special interests in Morocco. Likewise in 1907 Britain and Russia reached an agreement by which northern Persia was regarded as a Russian sphere of influence, and southern Persia as a British sphere. Thus, we see the Great Powers dividing the Middle Eastern lands, and, more important, we see the Middle Eastern peoples accepting this division with little protest because a national feeling was largely absent.

Today, less than 70 years after these events, the situation is very different. The Ottoman Empire has disappeared and in its place are several nation-states: the Turkish Republic, Syria, the United Arab Republic, the kingdom of Saudi Arabia, and others.

Legionaries in Morocco in 1910. Romantic legends surround the French Foreign Legion. Actually it was a life of tedium and oblivion, dedicated to maintaining control of French colonies.

HISTORICAL PICTURE SERVICE

President Gamal Nasser of Egypt is the spokesman for Arab nationalism—based primarily on his reputation for driving the British out of Egypt.

Furthermore, these states are intensely nationalistic. Their citizens are extremely proud of their newly-won independence and fiercely opposed to any control from the outside.

Nasser. One of the most popular leaders in the Arab world today is the President of the United Arab Republic, Gamal Abdel Nasser. Nasser's popularity is high because he removed the last traces of British control in Egypt. First he persuaded the British to give up their military base in the Suez Canal zone, and then he took over full control of the Canal and nationalized it. Thus, Nasser stands out in Arab eyes as a great leader who finally has won for his people full independence after many centuries of foreign rule. Almost all Egyptians agree enthusiastically with the views that President Nasser set forth in a book which he wrote, entitled *The Philosophy of the Egyptian Revolution*. In this book he described how Egypt had been over-run by the European Powers, and he expressed his determination to create a free and united Egypt.

For us, everything came at once. We had been living behind an iron curtain (before the nineteenth century), and suddenly it collapsed. We had been cut off from the world and had withdrawn from its affairs, especially after commercial traffic with the East began to use the sea route around the Cape of Good Hope. And then suddenly we became the object of European ambition and the springboard for European colonization. . . .

I look at this, and can feel a deep understanding of the confusion we are in and of the disorder besetting us. And I say to myself: This society will crystallize, it will take hold, it will become powerful, united, and homogeneous.

Pan-Arabism. This growing nationalist movement does not mean that the political situation is the same throughout the Middle East. In fact, very different political conditions and institutions prevail in the various countries. Saudi Arabia, for example, is an absolute monarchy with a king who has no parliament to check him. Iran, by contrast, is a constitutional monarchy and the king must rule with the aid of an elected parliament, or *majlis*, as it is called. Turkey, Syria, and the United Arab Republic are republics with elected presidents instead of kings.

Despite these differences in the forms of government, the tide of nationalism is so strong that a Pan-Arab movement has developed among the peoples of the various Arab countries. This movement seeks to combine all Arab peoples into one state that is more or less unified. Many obstacles stand in the way of this movement. For example, the rulers of the various Arab countries would lose their positions if a single Arab state were formed; for this reason many of them are not enthusiastic about Pan-Arabism. There are also religious differences dividing Arabs; most of them are Muslims but a few are Christians. In fact, the majority of the population of the small Arab state of Lebanon is Christian. Even among the Muslim Arabs there are differences just as there are among Christians. Some Muslims are Sunnites and others are Shiites, in the same manner that some Christians are Roman Catholics or Protestant or Greek Orthodox. Such religious differences may not seem important to Americans who live in a country where people of many religions get along together with little trouble. But we should remember that a few centuries ago bloody wars were fought in Europe between Protestants and Roman Catholics. It is true that religious differences are not as important today in the Middle East as they were in the 19th century, but they still are more serious than in the Western world. Some of the religious and dynastic differences which affected Pan-Arabism during the interwar years are discussed later in the book.

Finally, the Arab peoples are divided also by great differences in social and cultural conditions. Lebanon, for example, with its comparatively high living standards, its low rate of illiteracy, its relative freedom for women, and its democratic form of government, is poles apart from Saudi Arabia with its extremely low living standards, its high rate of illiteracy, its strict segregation of the sexes, and its absolutist type of monarchical government. Thus we find much greater differences between the Arab countries of Lebanon and Saudi Arabia than we find between two British Dominions such as Canada and New Zealand.

Despite this diversity and dissension among the Arab peoples, the Pan-Arab movement still remains strong. Its outstanding leader at the present time is President Nasser because, as we have seen, he won spectacular victories for the cause of Egyptian nationalism. Nationalists throughout the Arab world regard him as the great hope of their cause. This is especially true of young people who are impatient and want radical change and want it quickly. We noted an example of this feeling in the case of the Kuwaiti nationalists interviewed by the American correspondent.

On the other hand Nasser faces serious economic troubles at home, and was also disastrously defeated by Israel in June 1967. Unless he copes successfully with his domestic and foreign problems, the Arab nationalists may well be following another leader in the future.

HISTORICAL ORIGINS

The roots of nationalism. After this survey of the political situation in the Middle East today, we turn now to trace the historical origins. We shall try to find answers to two questions in particular. The first is why nationalism did not become strong in the

Santa Sophia in Istanbul, built by Justinian in the sixth century, is an example of the best of Byzantine architecture. Its splendor has been the inspiration for imitations all over the world. It was the cathedral of Santa Sophia which so impressed Vladimir's emissaries that the Orthodox faith was chosen to be the official religion of Russia.

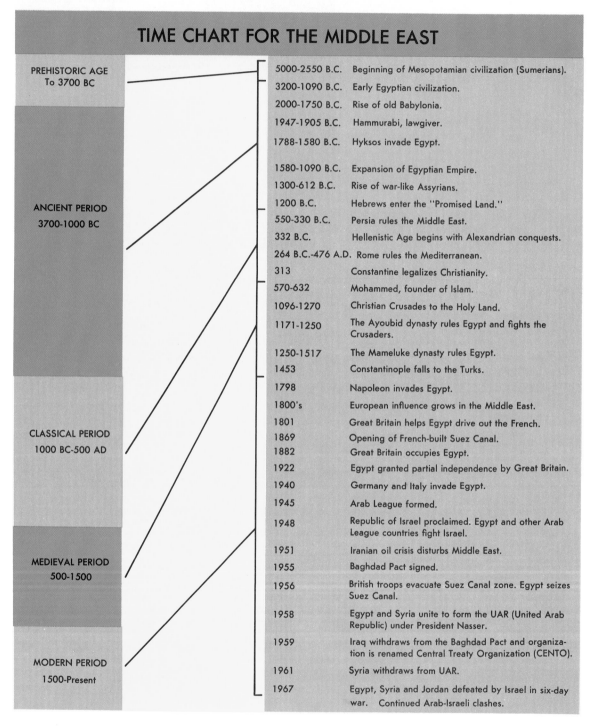

TIME CHART FOR THE MIDDLE EAST

PREHISTORIC AGE To 3700 BC	5000-2550 B.C.	Beginning of Mesopotamian civilization (Sumerians).
	3200-1090 B.C.	Early Egyptian civilization.
	2000-1750 B.C.	Rise of old Babylonia.
	1947-1905 B.C.	Hammurabi, lawgiver.
	1788-1580 B.C.	Hyksos invade Egypt.
ANCIENT PERIOD 3700-1000 BC	1580-1090 B.C.	Expansion of Egyptian Empire.
	1300-612 B.C.	Rise of war-like Assyrians.
	1200 B.C.	Hebrews enter the "Promised Land."
	550-330 B.C.	Persia rules the Middle East.
	332 B.C.	Hellenistic Age begins with Alexandrian conquests.
	264 B.C.-476 A.D.	Rome rules the Mediterranean.
	313	Constantine legalizes Christianity.
	570-632	Mohammed, founder of Islam.
	1096-1270	Christian Crusades to the Holy Land.
	1171-1250	The Ayoubid dynasty rules Egypt and fights the Crusaders.
	1250-1517	The Mameluke dynasty rules Egypt.
	1453	Constantinople falls to the Turks.
CLASSICAL PERIOD 1000 BC-500 AD	1798	Napoleon invades Egypt.
	1800's	European influence grows in the Middle East.
	1801	Great Britain helps Egypt drive out the French.
	1869	Opening of French-built Suez Canal.
	1882	Great Britain occupies Egypt.
	1922	Egypt granted partial independence by Great Britain.
	1940	Germany and Italy invade Egypt.
	1945	Arab League formed.
	1948	Republic of Israel proclaimed. Egypt and other Arab League countries fight Israel.
MEDIEVAL PERIOD 500-1500	1951	Iranian oil crisis disturbs Middle East.
	1955	Baghdad Pact signed.
	1956	British troops evacuate Suez Canal zone. Egypt seizes Suez Canal.
	1958	Egypt and Syria unite to form the UAR (United Arab Republic) under President Nasser.
	1959	Iraq withdraws from the Baghdad Pact and organization is renamed Central Treaty Organization (CENTO).
MODERN PERIOD 1500-Present	1961	Syria withdraws from UAR.
	1967	Egypt, Syria and Jordan defeated by Israel in six-day war. Continued Arab-Israeli clashes.

Middle East until the 20th century, whereas in Western Europe it began in the 17th century and reached its full development by the 19th. The other question is why, after such a late start, nationalism is such a powerful and growing force in the Middle East today.

Retarded nationalism. One reason why nationalism developed in the Middle East centuries later than it did in Western Europe is the nonnational character of the Islamic religion. Muslims do not care whether a person lives in China or India or Nigeria, or whether his skin is yellow, white, brown, or black. They care only about one thing: whether a person is a believer or a nonbeliever, whether he is a Muslim or a non-Muslim. This attitude helps Islam in certain respects. It explains, in some part, why it is spreading much more rapidly today in Africa than is Christianity. On the other hand, the fact remains that this attitude has discouraged the growth of nationalism. People are not so likely to become nationalistic if they have been taught from infancy to think in terms of religion rather than of nationality.

The other main reason why nationalism came late to the Middle East was the antinational character of the Ottoman Empire. The emperor or sultan of the empire strongly opposed the growth of any national feelings. Instead he insisted that all citizens should think of themselves not as Turks or as Arabs, but as his subjects. It was understandable that he should insist on this, because if the citizens became too nationalistic they would want to set up separate nation-states with the result that the Ottoman Empire would be torn apart. In order to prevent the breakup of his empire, the sultan demanded that his subjects be loyal to him rather than to any nationalist idea. The attitude, and the power, of the sultan held back the development of nationalist feeling in the Middle East. And it did so for a long time, because the Ottoman Empire lasted for almost five hundred years, until 1918.*

The stirrings of nationalism. During the 19th and early 20th centuries the various peoples of the Middle East began to feel nationalistic for the first time. The people of Egypt started to think of themselves as Egyptians and wanted to be free of foreign rule; the people of Syria also began thinking of themselves as Syrians and wanted to be independent, and so on with the Iranians and the Iraqi and the rest. One reason for the rise of nationalism was the fact that the Middle Easterners were now being exposed much more to ideas and to people from the West. This was the time when Western missionaries were establishing schools and opening hospitals and distributing literature in various parts of the region. It also was the time when Western diplomats, merchants, financiers, and military men were appearing there in increasing numbers. As a result of these new contacts there was now a steady flow of goods and persons and ideas between the West and the Middle East. This made it possible for the Turks and Arabs and Persians to learn about Western science, literature, and history. They also became acquainted with the idea of nationalism, and started thinking in national rather than in religious terms as they always had in the past.

The other principal reason for the rise of Middle Eastern nationalism was the aggression of the West. During the 19th century the strongest powers in the world were those of Europe. This explains why Britain and France, as we saw earlier, divided Egypt and Morocco between themselves, and why Britain and Russia divided Persia. At the same time the European countries became stronger economically and were able to gain control of the commerce and finances of

* See *Readings in World History*, "The Lack of Nationalism in the Ottoman Empire," p. 659.

the Middle East. It is not surprising that this political and economic domination by the West caused the Middle Eastern peoples to turn nationalistic and anti-Western. They became determined to build up strong nation-states in order to protect themselves against the expanding West.

Turkish nationalism. The two groups that were first influenced by the Western idea of nationalism were the Turks and the Arabs. This does not mean that all of the Turks and Arabs, or even a majority of them, became nationalistic in this early period before the First World War. As a matter of fact, only a very small minority was affected by nationalism. This was the tiny group who had learned to read books and newspapers in European languages, or who had travelled in Europe or had met and talked with Europeans in the Middle East.

The Ottoman Empire long had had close relations with Europe; Western European nations enjoyed certain commercial and legal favors in Turkey. During the Crimean War (1854–1856), Turkey was the ally of Britain and France, the winners over Russia. However, the war disclosed the weaknesses of the Ottoman Empire just as it did those of tsarist Russia. Turkish reformers wished to remodel the state along Western lines.

In 1856, the government issued a reform edict under which the civil authority of religious leaders was abolished, equality of Christians and Muslims before the law was guaranteed, the army was desegregated, and prison conditions improved. For 20 years, liberal leaders tried to make this program work, but there was strong resistance, especially from religious leaders. Nationalism was growing along with liberalism, but during the latter part of the 19th century, both were stifled by the opposition of the ultra-conservative Sultan Abdul Hamid (1876–1909).

An 1897 interpretation of Sultan Abdul Hamid. What group would be likely to support this interpretation?

The pioneer nationalists were called Young Turks to distinguish them from the old leaders of the Ottoman Empire who opposed change. Many of these Young Turks were army officers who had studied military science in Western schools. While they were at these schools, they absorbed political ideas along with lessons in strategy and tactics. Dissatisfied with the rule of Sultan Abdul Hamid when they returned, they wanted to establish a new government that would strengthen and modernize the empire. One of the Young Turks wrote at this time, about 1900:

> When we look round in our own land and see how Adrianople, Brussa, Aleppo, Damascus, and Bagdad, all once centres of the empire, have failed to maintain their former

glory and beauty, and have become desolate through utter neglect of the spirit of modernisation, we pity them for the darkness and ignorance into which they have sunk. At Brussa and Adrianople, situated at very short distances from the capital [of Constantinople], we still find the primitive waggons pulled by oxen. ... But why quote instances from provincial towns? Let us take Constantinople itself, with its million inhabitants, and in point of natural beauty excelling all other capitals. On the roughly paved streets dirt and filth lie deep, and dogs prowl about. Stamboul [popular name for Constantinople] has no theatres, no botanical or zoological gardens—modern institutions which have found their way even into Australia and Siberia. ... For God's sake ... let us have done with this slowness, this negligence. ... Yes, and let us be governed, not by violence and tyranny, but by justice and wisdom![3]

As noted above, many of the Young Turks were army officers and thus had the power to put their ideas into practice. In 1908, using the soldiers under their command, they overthrew the old Sultan's government and established one of their own. Before they could modernize and strengthen the empire under their control, the First World War intervened. They decided to enter the war on the side of the Central Powers against the Allies. When the Central Powers were forced to surrender in 1918, the Ottoman Empire was doomed. The victorious Allies carved it up, leaving only Asia Minor (the region bordered by the Black, Mediterranean, and Aegean Seas) and the region of Constantinople to the Turks. Even in Asia Minor, which was populated mostly by Turks, the Allies tried to arrange spheres of influence in which they would have economic and political control.

Kemal Ataturk. At this point there appeared a brilliant and energetic man who was to help the Turks to rid themselves of Western domination and to win complete independence. His name was Mustapha Kemal, but he is always called Kemal Ataturk. Ataturk means "father of the Turks," a title which shows that the people of Turkey regarded Kemal as we regard George Washington.

Kemal fully deserves the honor. He aroused his fellow Turks and organized armies which he led to victory against the occupation forces of the Greeks, who were supported by the Allies. In 1923 he signed with the Allied Powers the Treaty of Lausanne which gave full independence to the new Turkish Republic. As President of the Republic, Kemal made many changes which transformed the country. He adopted Western-style legal codes. He outlawed

Kemal Ataturk demonstrates the Roman alphabet, part of his program of Turkish modernization.

HISTORICAL PICTURE SERVICE, CHICAGO

many symbols of the past. The wearing of the fez by men and the veil by women were abolished. Kemal reorganized the educational system and replaced the very difficult Arabic alphabet with the much simpler Latin alphabet. If you look at a Turkish newspaper or book today, you will recognize the individual Latin letters even though the words mean nothing to you. But if you look at a newspaper or book published in the United Arab Republic or any other part of the Arab world, you will find that the Arabic letters mean nothing to you.

Turkey today. These changes, and many others that Kemal introduced, made the Turkish Republic a much more modern and unified state than the old Ottoman Empire had been. Progress was the result largely of the triumph of the spirit of nationalism. No longer did this spirit influence only the small minority who read Western books and travelled in Western lands. Today the great majority of the Turkish people are nationalist-minded, thanks to the schools, which are attended by most of the children, and to the radio which reaches the peasants in the most isolated villages. As a result, Turkey has become by far the strongest and most stable country in the Middle East. Certainly it is very different from the rickety and anti-national Ottoman Empire of the past. How different it is can be seen from the following passage in a third-grade Turkish textbook: "The Turks are the oldest independent nation of history. . . . The Turks are the bravest and best-hearted nation in the world. To be brave, to be hospitable, and to pity those who have fallen are some of the most beautiful qualities of the Turk." [4] The extreme nationalism of the Turkish Republic is the exact opposite of the antinationalism of the old Ottoman Empire.*

* See *Readings in World History,* "Nationalism in the Turkish Republic," p. 660.

To establish the Turkish Front, British troops occupied Mesopotamia in 1917.

Arab nationalism to World War I. Arab nationalism, like Turkish, began during the period before World War I. It started first in Syria and in Egypt where Western influence and Western ideas were the most widespread. Arab nationalism at first was anti-Turkish because all the Arab lands before 1914 were a part of the Turkish Ottoman Empire. So the pioneer Arab nationalists who wanted independence had to win it from their Turkish rulers. They organized secret societies and carried on underground propaganda, but they were unable to arouse enough of their countrymen to force the Turks to give them their freedom. So the Arab lands remained a part of the Ottoman Empire until the First World War.*

* See *Readings in World History,* "Arab Nationalism Before World War I," p. 661.

We have seen that when this war began, the Turks joined the Central Powers. At once the Allies, and especially Britain, tried to persuade the Arabs in the Turkish Empire to join them against the Turks. One of the outstanding Arab leaders at this time was Sharif Hussein, a descendant of Mohammed the Prophet. Hussein negotiated with a British official, Sir Henry McMahon, and in October 1915 he agreed to lead his Arab people in a revolt against the Turks. In return McMahon made a promise, the McMahon Pledge, as it was later called. In this pledge the British stated that they would "recognize and support the independence of the Arabs" south of Asia Minor.

The Arabs carried out their part of the agreement and helped the Allies a good deal in the war against the Turks. But when the Ottoman Empire was forced to surrender, the Arabs did not receive the full independence that they expected. Instead the most important Arab lands were given by the League of Nations to France and Britain as mandates. Syria and Lebanon became the mandates of France, while Iraq and Palestine became the mandates of Britain. The provisions were that France and Britain should administer the mandates in the name of the League of Nations until the local peoples were ready for full independence.

The Arabs, as might be expected, insisted that they were ready for independence, and demanded that the terms of the McMahon Pledge be fulfilled. So far as they were concerned, the mandate system was simply a trick to deprive them of the freedom that they had been promised and that they had earned. Accordingly the Arabs strongly opposed the whole mandate arrangement that was established after World War I.

The Arabs also opposed violently the creation of a Jewish "national home" in Palestine. In November 1917, while the war was still in progress, the British government had is-

sued the "Balfour Declaration." This stated that Britain would help to establish in Palestine "a national home for the Jewish people." It is understandable that some Jews should want to go to Palestine, since their ancestors had lived there some two thousand years ago. On the other hand, the Arabs' reply was that two thousand years is a long time, that during that time they had occupied Palestine and made it their home, and that they certainly were not ready to step aside for any newcomers, whether Jews or anybody else.*

* See *Readings in World History,* "Origins of the Palestine Problem," p. 664.

Chaim Weizmann and Abba Eban raise the "Star of David" in Palestine, 1921.

CULVER PICTURES

It is clear, then, that the settlement at the end of World War I was quite unsatisfactory for the Arabs. They refused to accept either the mandate system or the Palestine arrangement. Thus it is not surprising that Arab nationalism grew very rapidly after the First World War. No longer was it a movement of a tiny minority as it had been before 1914. Now, after 1918, it attracted the support of a larger and larger percentage of the Arab people. So the period between the two world wars was a stormy one, as the growing Arab nationalist movement fought against British and French domination, and against the Jews in Palestine.

Arab nationalism between the wars. There are many similarities in the struggle of the Arabs against the British protectorate in Egypt and the British mandate rule in Iraq. First the Arabs took up arms against the British. The attempt failed in both countries and the British were able gradually to restore order and impose their authority. In 1922 Britain proclaimed the independence of Iraq and Egypt, but with many reservations and exceptions. Britain, for example, insisted on controlling the foreign affairs of the two countries and on keeping certain military bases and airfields. The Arab nationalists rejected these terms and continued their opposition to British rule.

Finally settlements were reached in Iraq in 1930 and in Egypt in 1936. Iraq became an independent state and a member of the League of Nations, and in return Britain was allowed to keep three air bases in the country. Likewise Egypt became independent and entered the League of Nations; in return Britain was permitted to keep a large military base in the Suez Canal Zone, and also to continue the joint British-Egyptian administration of the Sudan that had existed since 1899. These arrangements in Iraq and Egypt lasted until the Second World War, though the nationalists were far from satisfied. They accepted the terms only for the time being and were ready to demand more on the first opportunity.

Meanwhile the French had proven less flexible in dealing with the nationalist agitation in their Syrian and Lebanese mandates. Armed revolts had broken out in those countries also, and the French were able to assert their authority only after large-scale fighting. But then the French refused to make the concessions that the British had made in their mandates. As a result the conflict in Syria and Lebanon continued unsettled until World War II.

In the Palestine mandate the situation was even worse because the struggle there involved three parties: Jews, Arabs, and British. In an attempt to satisfy the Arab opposition to Jewish migration to Palestine, the British in 1921 divided Palestine into two parts. The portion east of the Jordan River was made into the independent state of Transjordan, to which no Jewish immigration was to be allowed. The western region, or Palestine proper, was to be open to Jewish immigration as promised in the Balfour Declaration of 1917.

At first there was little trouble over the immigration. In fact the Arabs welcomed the newcomers who brought with them money, energy, and skills. They did much to increase the prosperity of Palestine, and the Arabs benefited along with the Jews. But the trouble began when the number of Jewish immigrants rose to the point where the native Arab population felt threatened. This was especially true when Hitler started his persecution of the Jews in the 1930's. As a result, Jewish migration to Palestine jumped from 9553 in 1932 to 61,854 by 1935. Likewise the total Jewish population in Palestine rose from 65,000 in 1919 to 450,000 in 1939. This increase continued and was to reach 2,300,000 in 1965.

India, as part of the British Empire, sent troops to the Middle East in 1940.

The Arabs naturally reacted violently against this flood which appeared endless. They argued that there was no reason why they should suffer because of the evil of Nazi anti-Semitism in Europe. On the other hand the Jews also could argue, and did argue, that they should have refuge in Palestine because of the promise in the Balfour Declaration and because they had to find some escape from the ruthless Nazi persecution. In fact, the tragedy of the Palestine crisis is that both sides had much right and both fought righteously and passionately. The result was a bitter triangular conflict, with Jews fighting against Arabs, and the British trying to keep order and to find some

way out. Despite many investigations and proposals, no solution was found, and the Palestine crisis remained unsettled when the Second World War began in 1939.

Arab nationalism during World War II. The Jews were enthusiastically pro-Allied during World War II. This was only natural in view of Hitler's anti-Semitic policies before and during the war. The Arabs, on the other hand, were either neutral or openly hostile toward the Allies. This attitude also is understandable if we recall the unhappy experiences of the Arabs in the British and French mandates. In Iraq, Arab hostility developed to the point of an armed attempt in

May 1941 to drive the British out of the country. For a few weeks the British were hard pressed, but in the end they were able to keep control over the country. In Egypt also, the British had trouble with King Farouk who was generally uncooperative when the German and Italian Armies were nearing the Egyptian frontier. But with the final defeat of the Axis Powers, the Arabs no longer could hope to use the Germans and Italians in order to be completely rid of Anglo-French control.

On the other hand, World War II drastically changed the balance of power in the Middle East and the change was so much in favor of the Arabs that within a few years they were all able to win full independence. The first change was the exhaustion of both France and Britain. France had been easily overrun and occupied by the Germans, while the British had suffered a series of humiliating and costly defeats, even though their island kingdom had not been invaded. The net result was that Britain and France emerged from the war in a greatly weakened condition and with their prestige in the Middle East at low ebb.

Arab nationalism since World War II. This brings us to the second change in the Middle Eastern balance of power, namely, the growing strength and confidence of Arab nationalism. This was due in part to the influence of German and Italian propaganda, which for years had been calling on the Arabs to awaken and to become masters of their own destiny. It was due also to the series of Allied defeats, which left the Arabs much less impressed by the strength of Britain and France. Finally Arab nationalism was built up by the spread of modernization in the Middle East. The radio, the newspaper, and the cinema brought the masses for the first time into contact with the outside world they had previously little known.

No longer was the peasant aware only of what went on in his village. No longer did he regard his miserable lot as unchangeable and his leaders as divinely appointed. Instead he now became convinced that his life could be improved and that he himself could do something towards bringing about that improvement. The masses had awakened; from their new outlook came greatly increased strength for the Arab nationalist leaders. They now had a united people behind them rather than a minority.

The Arab leaders were further strengthened by a third change in the Middle Eastern balance of power following World War II. This change was the appearance of the Soviet Union as a major power in Middle Eastern affairs. In contrast to Britain and France, whose prestige had been weakened by the war, the Soviet Union emerged in a stronger position. This shift helped the Arab leaders tremendously. In the past they had to face Britain and France with no outside aid, but now they could turn to a state that was both able and eager to help them. Of course the Soviets had their own selfish reason for supporting the Arabs, namely, to weaken Western influence in the Middle East. But the Soviet motives did not concern the Arabs. They took advantage of the opportunity to win full independence by playing off the Soviet Union against the Western Powers.

We may conclude, then, that the remarkable triumphs of Arab nationalism since World War II were made possible by these new developments: the weakening of Britain and France, the awakening of the Arab masses, and the appearance of Soviet power.

The Arab League is formed. The first sign of growing Arab strength was the organization in March 1945 of the Arab League, consisting of seven countries: Egypt, Iraq, Lebanon, Saudi Arabia, Syria, Transjordan, and Yemen. (Six other nations joined later.)

The members agreed to cooperate in political, economic, and cultural matters.

The League won its first victory in May 1945 when the French tried to re-establish their control over Syria and Lebanon. The Arabs resisted, being determined not to return to the power mandate system, or anything like it. The French tried to break the resistance by shelling open cities. At once the Arab League protested that this was a violation of the United Nations' principle of national self-determination, that is, the principle that all peoples should have the right to rule themselves without interference from the outside. The British agreed with this argument of the Arabs and supported them. As a result the French were forced to leave the mandates that they had controlled since World War I. By the end of 1946 all foreign troops were out of Syria and Lebanon; for the first time in centuries these two countries became completely independent.

The issue of Palestine. The Arab League next became involved in the Palestine question, and here it suffered a humiliating defeat. Palestine became more and more a crisis spot during the war years because Hitler carried his anti-Semitic campaign to the point of murdering no less than six million Jews. The pitiful survivors naturally were anxious to flee to Palestine but the Arabs were strongly opposed. In August 1945 President Truman of the United States proposed that 100,000 Jews be permitted to enter Palestine. The Arab League replied that it would fight such immigration, even by armed force if necessary. Finally the General Assembly of the United Nations voted on November 29, 1947, in favor of dividing Palestine into two parts, one for the Jews and one for the Arabs. On May 14 of the following year the Jews proclaimed the independent state of Israel in that part of Palestine which had been set aside for them by the United Nations.* The next day the Arab League declared war on Israel and sent its armies to attack the new state and wipe it out.

To everybody's surprise, the Arab armies were defeated. Because they were disunited and jealous of each other, they did not cooperate effectively. The Jews, on the other hand, had no alternative but to win. They knew that if they lost, there was no place for them to go. Without a country of their own to which they could return, they had no choice but to win the war. And this is exactly what they did. They defeated the armies of the Arab states, and forced these states in 1949 to sign armistice agreements under UN auspices.

The armistice agreements ended the fighting, but they were not followed by regular peace treaties which would settle matters decisively. Two big issues continue to divide the Arabs and the state of Israel. One of these is the question of what to do with the Arab refugees who fled from Israel in the course of the fighting. Between three-quarters of a million and one million displaced Arabs are now living miserably in camps outside the borders of Israel. The Arab states insist that the refugees be allowed to return to their former homes. The government of Israel maintains that this is impossible for two reasons. One is that the refugees are, quite understandably, violently anti-Israel and would try to destroy the state if they were allowed to return. The other reason is that the areas in which the Arabs formerly lived are now occupied by Jewish refugees, some of whom fled from Arab countries where they were persecuted during and after the Israeli-Arab war.

In addition to the refugee question, there is also the question of frontiers which prevents a peace settlement between Israel and the Arab states. When the United Nations

* See *Readings in World History*, "Israeli Independence," p. 666.

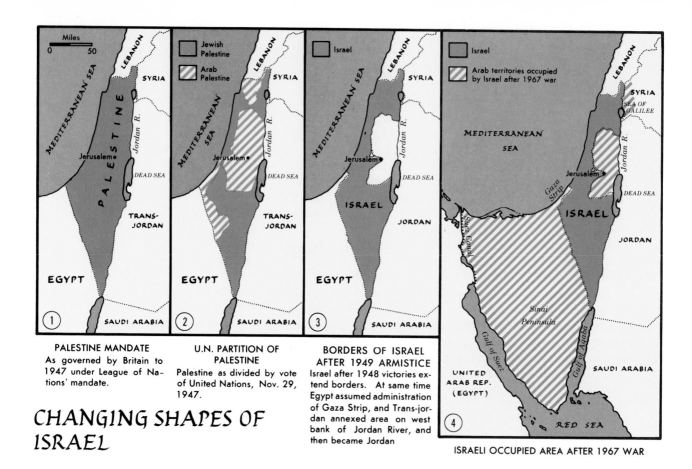

1 PALESTINE MANDATE
As governed by Britain to 1947 under League of Nations' mandate.

2 U.N. PARTITION OF PALESTINE
Palestine as divided by vote of United Nations, Nov. 29, 1947.

3 BORDERS OF ISRAEL AFTER 1949 ARMISTICE
Israel after 1948 victories extend borders. At same time Egypt assumed administration of Gaza Strip, and Trans-jordan annexed area on west bank of Jordan River, and then became Jordan

4 ISRAELI OCCUPIED AREA AFTER 1967 WAR

CHANGING SHAPES OF ISRAEL

voted in favor of dividing Palestine, it also drew the frontier that should divide the two parts. However, when the armistice agreements were signed in 1949, Israel, as the victor, was left with more territory than the United Nations had awarded. The Arabs insisted that they would accept no peace unless Israel gave up the extra territory. But Israel argued that she won the land in a war that the Arabs themselves started, and also that she needs the extra land for the hundreds of thousands of Jewish immigrants who continue to come from all parts of the world.

The result has been deadlock, with neither side being willing to compromise on these two basic issues.* The Israelis refuse to give up land or to accept the refugees, and many Arabs not only insist on having their way on these questions, but also are determined to wipe out the state of Israel altogether.

Triumphs of Arab nationalism. Arab nationalism suffered a setback in Palestine, but everywhere else it was victorious. The greatest triumphs were won in Egypt under the leadership of President Nasser. We noted above that the 1938 treaty between Britain and Egypt allowed Britain to keep her troops

* See *Readings in World History,* "The Arab View of Israel," p. 668.

along the Suez Canal and also to take part in the administration of the Sudan together with Egypt. These privileges left to Britain were very unpopular with the Egyptian nationalists. In July, 1952, they revolted against King Farouk and forced him to leave the country.

Two of the top leaders of the revolt against Farouk were General Naguib and Colonel Nasser. Naguib became the first President of the new Republic of Egypt. On February 12, 1953, he signed an agreement with Britain providing that the people of the Sudan should vote on whether they preferred to be independent, or to be united with Egypt, or some other arrangement. When the election was held, the majority voted for independence, so that both the British and the Egyptians have left the Sudan. The following year, Nasser replaced Naguib as President of the Egyptian Republic. On October 19, 1954, Nasser succeeded in persuading the British to give up their Suez Canal base. The agreement provided that the British troops should withdraw, though they had the right to return if Turkey or any of the Arab League countries were attacked by an outside power, meaning the Soviet Union. For the first time in many centuries Egypt was completely free of foreign domination. Nasser was hailed by his people as a national hero.

Nasser won an even greater victory when, on July 26, 1956, he took over the Suez Canal from the international company that owned it and made it Egyptian property. The canal had been built between 1859 and 1869 by the Suez Canal Company. Forty-four per cent of the shares in this company were owned by the British government and the remainder by private investors, mostly French. Nasser took over, or nationalized, the canal in order to hit back at the Western Powers because they had refused to help him build the High Aswan Dam across the Nile River.°

° See *Readings in World History,* "Arab Nationalism in the Mid-Twentieth Century," p. 662.

ALAN BAND

Because the new Aswan High Dam would inundate the present site, the colossuses of Ramses II had to be moved to higher ground. Each face alone weighs about 25 tons and had to be moved by crane.

An earlier Aswan Dam had been built in 1902. But the new dam was a much greater project. Nasser was anxious to build the dam because the population of Egypt was increasing very rapidly and more land was needed to feed the people. The dam would help Egypt meet her economic problems by providing enough water to irrigate 30 per cent more land and to increase the electric power supply eight times. In fact, it is estimated that the dam would make it possible to raise Egypt's national income by one-third.

The big problem was to find the huge amount of money necessary to build the dam. In December 1955, the United States and Great Britain offered to provide 270 million dollars to get the project started. Nasser left the offer dangling while he sounded out the Soviet Union and Soviet allies on the subject. He bought weapons in Czechoslovakia for which he promised to pay with Egyptian cotton. Dimitri Shepilov, Soviet foreign minister, visited Cairo, and rumors flew that he was making the Egyptians a better offer. But nothing concrete materialized, and Nasser decided to take advantage of the American-British offer, after seven months of indecision. When his ambassador came to inform John Foster Dulles, American Secretary of State, on July 19, 1956, he was shocked to learn that the offer had been withdrawn. There was no opportunity given to the Egyptians for face-saving or negotiation. Naturally they were angry and humiliated. Nasser struck back by announcing on July 26, 1956, that he was nationalizing the Suez Canal, lifeline for Britain and the West.

Britain and France were much more concerned over nationalization than was the United States. All of Western Europe depended on Middle Eastern oil, much of which was brought in tankers that used the canal route. France and Britain were also concerned because Nasser would become a great hero of the Arab world if he were allowed to get away with nationalization. Arab nationalism would become stronger and bolder and might next drive all the Western oil companies out of the Middle East, or try to force the French to get out of the predominantly Arab country of Algeria. Even more concerned than France and Britain was the state of Israel. Nasser had made it clear on more than one occasion that he planned to force Israel to accept peace on Arab terms, and that he perhaps intended to do away with Israel altogether. So the Israeli government was naturally interested in preventing Nasser from becoming strong enough to carry out his plans.

For all these reasons, Britain, France, and Israel suddenly invaded Egypt in October 1956, three months after the nationalization of the canal. They did not inform the United States of their intention ahead of time. Although they knew that the United States would be opposed to such violent action, they assumed that the American government would not try to stop them. But both the United States and the Soviet Union strongly opposed the invasion; they supported a UN resolution calling for the invaders to withdraw. Thus the attack halted before Nasser could be overthrown, and the effect of the invasion was not to get rid of Nasser but rather to make him a hero of Arabs everywhere. Most of the Arabs did not realize that the United States and the Soviet Union saved Nasser. Instead they were convinced that Nasser had won a great victory over the Arabs' old enemies, the British, French, and Israelis.

The next year, 1958, marked the high point of Nasser's influence. Revolutionaries in Iraq in that year deposed and assassinated King Feisal and established a republic under General Kassim. Since Feisal had opposed Nasser in Arab affairs, his removal was regarded as an advance for Nasser. In the same year, the government of Syria proposed union with Egypt, and Nasser agreed. The two countries combined to form the United Arab Republic (UAR) which was enthusiastically greeted as the nucleus of an Arab union that would steadily expand until it included all the Arab world.

This hope, however, was not realized. Kassim and Nasser did not get along together, so that the new Iraq republic proved to be a rival rather than an ally of Egypt. At the same time the UAR was torn by conflict because many Syrians resented interference in their domestic affairs by Nasser and his Egyptian bureaucrats and army officers. So bad was the friction that a revolution broke out in Syria in September 1961, and the tie with Egypt was broken. Nasser kept the name UAR which is still used, but it now consists only of Egypt.

Another setback for Nasser occurred in the primitive country of Yemen in the southwestern tip of the Arabian peninsula. An army revolt in September 1962 overthrew Yemen's new ruler who had just come to the throne. Nasser sent troops to help the army rebels, but the tribesmen in the mountainous interior remained loyal to the ruler and rallied behind him. The king of Saudi Arabia, who feared Nasser's influence in the Arabian Peninsula, sent money and arms to the Yemenite tribesmen. Thus Nasser, who had expected an easy victory in Yemen, found himself involved in a costly war which dragged on and from which he could not withdraw without losing face. As an Egyptian official remarked, "Yemen is our Vietnam."

Far more serious, however, was the stunning defeat of the UAR and other Arab states by Israel in a six-day blitzkrieg from June 5–10, 1967. The roots of the war go back to the basic problems left unsolved after the two earlier wars in 1948 and 1956. We have seen that the Arabs refused to recognize the state of Israel, while Israel refused to accept the return of the Arab refugees and to give up the lands she had won in 1948 beyond the frontiers drawn by the UN.

A crowd in Cairo wildly cheers President Nasser after his announcement of the nationalization of the Suez Canal. Many of the banners contain anti-Western, pro-Soviet slogans.

Thus Arab bands continued to raid Israeli settlements, and Israel hit back with reprisal attacks. The situation was particularly tense on the Syrian-Israeli frontier where a large-scale battle was fought on April 7, 1967. Nasser was in danger of being involved in these clashes because he had signed a mutual defense treaty with Syria in November 1966.

Apparently, in order to distract Israel from further attacks on Syria, Nasser demanded that the UN remove its 4,000-man Emergency Force (UNEF) from the UAR-Israel armistice line, and from the Straits of Tiran at the entrance to the Gulf of Aqaba where Israel's port of Elath is located. UN Secretary Thant complied with Nasser's demand and withdrew UNEF; legally he could not have kept UNEF on the armistice line against the wishes of Egypt, nor practically could he have done so because India and Yugoslavia, who supplied most of the men for UNEF, insisted that Nasser's demand be respected.

When UNEF departed, large Egyptian forces took their place along the line. This seemed reasonable as a move to help Syria by pressing Israel from the south. But then Nasser declared the Tiran Strait closed to all shipping to and from Israel. He said, "Recently we have felt strong enough that if we were to enter a battle with Israel, with God's help we could triumph. . . . The battle will be a general one and our basic objective will be to destroy Israel. . . ." Two days later he said, "Israel's existence in itself is an aggression." [5]

In May of 1967 King Hussein of Jordan flew to Cairo where he signed a mutual defense pact with Nasser. This was especially disturbing for the Israelis who had regarded Hussein as a moderate with whom they could negotiate. The next day Iraqi and Kuwaiti troops arrived in Egypt, and the Iraqi President told his soldiers: "Brethren and sons, this is the day of the battle to avenge your martyred brethren who fell in 1948. It is the day to wash away the stigma. We shall, God willing, meet in Tel Aviv and Haifa."[6]

The combination of the closing of the Tiran Strait and the concerted Arab mobilization led the Israeli government to decide on preventive war. Beginning with air attacks on June 5, the Israelis in a few hours destroyed half the air forces of Egypt, Syria, and Jordan. Then their armies quickly advanced, and by the cease fire on June 10 they had reached the Suez Canal and the Jordan River, and occupied Jerusalem, the Gaza Strip, and Sharm el-Sheikh on the Tiran Strait. Israeli losses totalled only 679, as against 10,000 to 15,000 Arab casualties. Once again the Israelis were the victors, thanks to their interior lines of communication, their superior officer corps, and their high morale born from the knowledge that they were fighting for sheer survival.

For the Arabs, their defeat was a severe psychological shock. They had been told that they were ready for war, yet the 1967 disaster was even worse than that of 1948. Nasser offered to resign, but there was no one else to take his place, and the crowds marched in the streets of Cairo in his support. In August 1967 Nasser met with leaders of the other Arab states in Khartoum, where they agreed not to recognize or negotiate with Israel, and to try by diplomatic means to get Israel to evacuate the occupied territories. Also it was agreed that the three rich oil producers, the conservative monarchies of Saudi Arabia, Kuwait, and Libya, should provide Egypt and Jordan with an annual subsidy of 379 million dollars. This was to make up for Jordan's loss of revenues from tourism and farmlands, and Egypt's loss from the blocked Suez Canal and the Sinai oil fields. The wealthy monarchs were willing to pay this large sum as a form of political insurance. So long as the radical

Israel achieved a rapid victory in the Six Day War of 1967. Arabs huddle in refugee camps after their homes were demolished. A Syrian bunker is abandoned at Golan Heights. An Egyptian soldier surrenders to Israeli forces.

Children at a refugee camp in Jordan receive guerrilla training under the supervision of members of El Fatah. The training is to encourage the refugee children against Israel, which El Fatah regards as the usurper of their homeland.

Nasser was financially dependent on them, so long he would be unable to challenge them.

Meanwhile the UN Security Council passed a resolution on November 22, 1967, which balanced the Arab and Israeli claims. It declared that peace should be based on two principles: "Withdrawal of Israeli armed forces from territories of recent conflict," and "Respect for and acknowledgment of the sovereignty, territorial integrity, and political independence of every state in the area and their right to live in peace within secure and recognized boundaries free from threats or acts of force." The resolution also called for "freedom of navigation through international waterways in the area," and "a just settlement to the refugee problem." Finally the resolution requested the Secretary-General to send a representative to the Middle East to seek a settlement along the above lines. Gunnar Jarring, Sweden's ambassador to Moscow, was sent by Thant on this mission in early 1968. Jarring remained in the Middle East until early 1969,

when he left without achieving success in arranging a compromise.

Meanwhile, through 1968 and into 1969, incidents of violence occurred on both sides. Several Arab guerrilla organizations, whose members call themselves *fedayeen* (fighters for the native land), were formed, comprised mostly of Palestinian refugees made homeless by the 1948 war. The guerrilla organizations, owing no fealty to any cause but the recovery of Palestine, can be controlled by none of the Arab governments. However, their frequent attacks on Israel, often in such crowded places as schools, cinemas, and shopping areas, have brought Israeli reprisals against the surrounding Arab countries. Although some of these countries have tried to curtail the activity of the fedayeen, the guerrillas have become such popular heroes that most Arab governments dare not speak out against them. The Lebanese government, in April 1969, actually was forced to resign after a clash between the Lebanese security forces and the fedayeen.

As tensions mounted and each side mobilized, neither side seemed willing to compromise. The Israeli's, entrenched along the Jordan River and the Suez Canal, refused to return any of the occupied territories without a formal peace settlement. The Arabs, on the other hand, demanded the restoration of the pre-1967 frontiers and also the return of the Arab refugees to their former homes in what is now Israel.

As the clashes increased and the seriousness of the Middle East crisis became more apparent, both the Communist Bloc and the West offered assistance in arriving at a peace settlement. In early 1969 the UN representatives of the U.S., the U.S.S.R., Britain, and France met to try to work out a settlement agreeable to both sides, and the U.S. and the U.S.S.R. also met in Washington to seek a solution.

Reviewing the Essentials

Present State

1. Define nationalism. Cite evidence that nationalism is a compelling idea in the Middle East today. Why was nationalism weak or non-existent in the Middle East until the 20th century? How did the spirit of nationalism reach the Middle East?

2. Explain what is meant by Pan-Arabism. What are its goals? Who is the acknowledged leader of the movement? Who opposes it?

Historical Origins

3. Turkish nationalism was an important factor in the political development of the Middle East. Who were the early nationalists in Turkey? What were their objectives? Why did they fail to achieve these goals? On a map, locate the boundaries of Turkey after World War I.

4. Describe Kemal Ataturk's program of reform for Turkey. What is his place in the history of modern Turkey?

5. Why did Arab nationalism develop more slowly than Turkish nationalism?

6. What was the McMahon Pledge? Why did it foster anti-Allied feeling among the Arabs after World War I? What was the Balfour Declaration? How did both the McMahon Pledge and the Balfour Declaration promote the growth of Arab nationalism?

7. What concessions did Britain make to Arab demands in the period between World Wars I and II in Egypt, Palestine, and Iraq? How did France deal with Arab demands in Syria? In Lebanon?

8. How did World War II change the balance of power in the Middle East? Why was Arab nationalism strengthened by the shift?

9. When and why was the Arab League organized? What nations are members? Where, since 1945, has the Arab League been most successful in achieving its goals? Where has it suffered setbacks? What are unresolved problems in the Palestine situation? Describe the events that culminated in Nasser's seizure of the Suez Canal. What has been the effect of these events on Arab nationalism in the Middle East? In the Muslim world?

The Future

10. Why has communism won support in the Middle East? What will determine the future of the Middle East?

Explain, Identify, or Locate

1917	Young Turks	Sharif Hussein	Transjordan (Jordan)
Pan-Arabism	Nasser	Farouk	Suez Canal
balance of power	Naguib	Ben-Gurion	United Arab Republic
McMahon Pledge	Kemal Ataturk	Kuwait	Arab League
Balfour Declaration	1947	1956	1967
1939			

ECONOMICS: Since the Middle Ages, a Downward Spiral

PRESENT STATE

Underdeveloped area. A traveller in the Near East would soon discover that this region is poverty-stricken. He would find that the peasants, who form two-thirds of the total population, are for the most part landless, deeply in debt, disease-ridden, and illiterate. If our traveller were interested in statistics, he would learn that the average annual income per person varied from about $1400 in Israel to about $50 in Yemen, and that the other countries are much closer to the Yemen level than to that of Israel, with most of them averaging between $100 and $200 a year. By contrast the average annual income in the United States is above $3000.

The conclusion that our traveller would have to reach is that the Middle East today is an underdeveloped region. All the typical symptoms are present: low national income, short life-expectancy, high rate of illiteracy, and substandard housing, clothing, and diet. What this means in terms of human beings and their everyday living has been revealed in a study of Egyptian villages that was made by the Rockefeller Foundation of New York. This study showed that all the people in the villages had amoebic dysentery, and 90 per cent had bilharziasis, a crippling disease caused by the bilharzia worm that enters the body through the feet of the peasants working in the irrigated fields. (We shall read of this disease's prevalence in Sub-Saharan Africa.) A pair of rubber hip boots would protect the peasants from this scourge, but most of them cannot afford to buy such boots.

The Rockefeller investigators also found that Egypt holds the world's record for eye diseases and blindness. Eighty-nine per cent of the villagers had trachoma, which is a painful inflammation of the lining of the eyelid and eyeball. If this disease is not treated, it leads to partial or complete blindness. And since most Egyptian peasants have had no opportunity for treatment, the Rockefeller scientists found that 6.4 per cent of the villagers were blind in one eye, and one per cent were totally blind. Other findings of their study were that life expectancy is 15 to 20 years, that half the children die before the age of five, and that two-thirds of the families have an income of less than $14.50 per month or about 48 cents per day.

Thanks to recent reforms introduced by President Nasser, conditions are somewhat better today than they were at the time of the Rockefeller study. Nevertheless it is shocking that millions of people in Egypt and the rest of the Middle East should be living under conditions almost as bad as those described above. It is equally shocking that they should be living in the Middle East, the region which for thousands of years led the entire globe in economic development as well as in other respects. What is the explanation for this complete reversal? Why has the Middle East declined from its age-old position of leadership to its present sad situation. Before considering this question we shall examine in more detail the present-day economic conditions and problems, first in agriculture and then in industry.

Agriculture. Near Eastern agriculture is of two types, irrigated and rain fed. The irrigated land amounts to only one-sixth of the total cultivated land, but it produces crops whose value equals two-thirds of the gross value of all crops. The reason for this discrepancy is that irrigation agriculture is much more intensive, and since water can be pro-

Zigana, Turkey. The west and north coasts of Turkey are examples of the few places in the Middle East which receive adequate rainfall. Because Turkey is so mountainous, however, much of the farmland is terraced.

vided whenever needed, it is possible to grow two, or even three, crops per year, instead of the one crop of rain-fed agriculture. The irrigated lands usually are used to grow cash crops such as cotton, citrus fruits, and sugar cane, whereas the rain-fed lands are sown with subsistence crops such as wheat and barley, grown for home consumption.

The productivity of the Middle Eastern peasant is extremely low, regardless of the type of agriculture he practices. He does not have the ideal combination of good soil and good climate, as do the farmers of Iowa and the Ukraine. In addition the population of the Middle East is growing very rapidly, and in some countries such as Egypt and Lebanon, there are now too many people and not enough land. This means that each peasant must compete for the available land, and usually he ends up with a plot that is too small for his family needs, and for which he must pay too high a rent to the landlord. Under such conditions the peasant cannot possibly increase his output. His plot is not large enough for efficient operation, and after paying one-half or more of his produce to the landlord, he has only enough left over to keep himself and his family from starving.

Economics 653

Certainly he does not have the surplus that is needed to improve the soil and to buy the equipment and fertilizers and improved seeds that are necessary for raising production.

This leads us to another reason for the low agricultural productivity, namely, the concentration of land in the hands of a few families. In countries such as Iraq and Iran, a handful of wealthy families own from 35 to 40 per cent of all the cultivated land. It is true that large holdings do not necessarily mean inefficient agriculture. In fact, the size of farms is now increasing every year in the United States, and the result is not lower,

but higher, productivity. This happens because the owners of these large farms use the latest machinery and agricultural techniques, and grow tremendous quantities of produce per man employed.

But the landowners of the Middle East rent small plots at high rents, a year at a time, so there is no chance for efficient mass production. We shall see that some countries such as Iran and Egypt have recently passed reforms dividing large estates among the landless peasants. The Shah of Iran has himself distributed some of his family's holdings. But the fact remains that most

Bedouin tribesmen on the Sinai Peninsula produce barely enough to survive.

ALAN BAND

Middle Eastern peasants are land-hungry and have a very low output.

All these factors: poor land and climate, population pressure, unequal distribution of land, and high rents with no security of tenure, explain why Middle Eastern agriculture is the least productive in the world with the exception of that of Africa. This low output is the main cause for the poverty of the Middle East, since more than two-thirds of the people are engaged in agriculture.*

The industrial lag. Turning to industry, we find that productivity here also is extremely low. One reason for this is that most families have incomes under $200 per year. Such families obviously can afford to buy only a few things, and this means a restricted domestic market for native industry.

Another factor holding back industry in the Middle East is the scarcity of raw materials in that region. Turkey alone has an abundant supply of minerals, including coal, iron, chrome, and copper. It is significant that Turkey, also, is the only country with a heavy industry of any size. Of the other countries, only Egypt and Israel have mineral resources worth mentioning; phosphates, iron ore, potash, and bromine. In the rest of the Middle East the only resource known at present is the vast oil reserves in the Persian Gulf area. We shall see shortly that, despite their world-wide significance, they have not so far created local industry.

A third factor hindering the growth of industry is the lack of skilled labor and of trained managers and technicians. This difficulty is now being partly met by sending young men abroad for training, and by employing foreign technicians to teach native workers. Also, the thousands of laborers and technicians who are working for the oil com-

* See *Readings in World History,* "Tradition in the Village," p. 673.

AREA COMPARISON U.S. – MIDDLE EAST

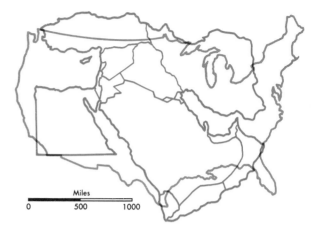

Miles
0   500   1000

panies in the Middle East are learning new skills that will be useful in other industries.

The fourth and final factor that has slowed down the growth of industry is the scarcity of capital. Most of the people do not have enough income to be able to save money and to invest it in industry. The few who are wealthy are not interested in industry; they have always preferred to invest their capital in farm land or to lend it at high interest rates to the peasants.

These various factors that have held back the growth of Middle Eastern industry are not equally strong in each country. Turkey, for example, has had the advantage of plentiful mineral resources and a government that has tried hard to develop industry. Likewise Egypt has plentiful cotton and some oil, iron, and hydroelectric power. On this basis, a number of industries, including textile plants, munition works, iron and steel mills, paper factories, and chemical plants have been started. Yet even in Turkey and Egypt manufacturing is responsible for only about 15 per cent of the Gross National Product. And in the other Middle Eastern countries there are only light industries geared to the

The oil rig is the monument of the Middle East—symbolic of past foreign domination and future prosperity.

restricted domestic markets, industries such as food processing, beverages, tobacco, and construction materials.*

Oil, the big plus. The one industry in the Middle East that is highly developed and of world-wide significance is the oil industry. About one-half of the world's oil reserves are to be found in the Middle East; and about one-fourth of the world's oil production and over one-third of the world's oil exports are from that region. This flourishing industry has been developed and is being operated by foreign companies, mostly American, British,

* See *Readings in World History*, "Tradition in the Town," p. 676.

French, and Dutch. In return for giving the companies the right to pump out the oil and to sell it in foreign markets, the Middle Eastern countries receive royalty payments. These payments usually are a certain per cent of the profit made by the companies. Between 1948 and 1965 the total royalties paid to the various Middle Eastern governments increased from about 100 million dollars to about 2,250 million dollars per year.

These are very large sums, and yet they are not helping the economic development of the Middle East as much as might be expected. One reason is that most of the oil discovered so far is located in the Persian Gulf area which is largely desert. Consequently most of the royalties are going to countries such as Saudi Arabia and Kuwait, which together have only about nine million in population. Also they have little agriculture and virtually no industry. Thus most of the oil money has not been used for the development of the region as a whole. The Arabs are aware of the need to use some of the oil revenues for over-all regional development. In recent years they have organized an Arab Petroleum Conference, Arab Common Market, Arab Tourist Union, the Kuwait Fund for Arab Economic Development, Arab Atomic Energy Organization, Arab Economic Unity Council, and the Arabian Gulf Fund—all organizations to aid development.

Our survey of economic conditions in the Middle East thus tells us that it is a typical underdeveloped area. By this we mean an area in which inadequate use is made of manpower and resources because of technological backwardness. Or, to put it in other words, the people lack know-how, and consequently have low productivity. This leads to low national incomes, low living standards, poor health conditions, and high illiteracy rates. All the typical symptoms of an underdeveloped area are to be found in the Middle East, as they are also in Sub-Saharan Africa, in Latin America, and in most parts of South and East Asia.

HISTORICAL ORIGINS

Ancient predominance. We come now to the question of why the Middle East should be underdeveloped today. This is particularly puzzling in view of the fact that for most of human history this region led the rest of the world in economic as well as cultural matters. We have already seen that it was in the Middle East that man first learned to grow his own food, to build cities, and to practice the arts of civilization. An American historian has described as follows the basic contributions that the Middle East made to all of mankind many centuries before Christ.

Written history is at least six thousand years old. During half of this period the center of human affairs, so far as they are now known to us, was in the Near East. . . . In this rough theatre of teeming peoples and conflicting cultures were developed the agriculture and commerce, the horse and wagon, the coinage and letters of credit, the crafts and industries, the law and government, the mathematics and medicine, the enemas and drainage systems, the geometry and astronomy, the calendar and clock and zodiac, the alphabet and writing, the paper and ink, the books and libraries and schools, the literature and music, the sculpture and architecture, the glazed pottery and fine furniture, the monotheism and monogamy, the cosmetics and jewelry, the checkers and dice, the ten-pins and income-tax, the wet-nurses and beer, from which our own European and American culture derive by a continuous succession through the mediation of Crete and Greece and Rome. The "Aryans" did not establish civilization—they took it from Babylonia and Egypt. Greece did not begin

Attempts are being made to insure that money derived from oil is utilized to raise the living standards of all Arabs.

civilization—it inherited far more civilization than it began; it was the spoiled heir of three millenniums of arts and sciences brought to its cities from the Near East by the fortunes of trade and war. In studying and honoring the Near East we shall be acknowledging a debt long due to the real founders of European and American civilization.[7]

The Middle East was predominant in the medieval period as well as in the ancient. At a time when Western Europe was a land of primitive agrarian manors with virtually no cities or commerce, the Middle East presented a dazzling contrast. This can be seen in the following description of Baghdad, the capital of the mighty Muslim Arab Empire, in the eighth century A.D.

> The Imperial Court was polished, luxurious, and unlimitedly wealthy: the capital Baghdad, a gigantic mercantile city surrounding a huge administrative fortress, wherein every department of state had a properly regulated and well-ordered public office; where schools and colleges abounded; whither philosophers, students, doctors, poets, and theologians flocked from all parts of the civilized globe. . . . The provincial capitals were embellished with vast public buildings, and linked together by an effective and rapid service of posts and caravans; the frontiers were secure and well-garrisoned, the army loyal, efficient, and brave; the governors and ministers honest and forbearing. The empire stretched with equal strength and unimpaired control from the Cilician gates to Aden, and from Egypt to Central Asia. Christians, pagans, Jews as well as Moslems were employed in the government service. . . . Traffic and wealth had taken the place of revolution and famine. . . . Pestilence and disease were met by imperial hospitals and government physicians. . . .[8]

Irrigation breakdown. We can see that in the Middle Ages the Middle East was developed and Western Europe underdeveloped. But several countries of the Middle East began to decline economically because of a combination of circumstances. One of these was the misuse of the great irrigation works which led to salination, sedimentation, and malarial swamps. Salination was produced by salts carried by the Tigris and Euphrates Rivers from northern mountains down to the plains. When too much water was used in the fields, the ground water level rose, bringing the salt to the root zone of plants or to the surface. High salt concentration prevents the growth of plants and, in severe cases, water evaporation leaves hard salt beds on which nothing can be grown. Vast areas in the Middle East have become "salt deserts" in this manner.

Equally disastrous was the sedimentation produced by the silt carried down from the mountains. As time passed, it became increasingly difficult to clear the silt from the clogged canals and they were allowed to fill up and become useless. This created marshes as the river waters spread out over the flat countryside. The marshes in turn bred malarial mosquitoes which diseased the peasants and made them even less capable of keeping up the irrigation works. In these various ways the formerly productive lands of the Middle East became the sterile deserts that they are today. These are the reasons why one encounters so often the ancient remains of great cities amidst waste lands that today can just barely support a few miserable nomads. The explanation can be found in the inability of the inhabitants to keep their irrigation systems in proper working order.

Mongol invasions. The decline was speeded up by a long series of catastrophic Mongol invasions into the Middle East in the mid-13th century. In 1258 a Mongol army appeared out of Central Asia, led by Hulagu Khan, grandson of the great conqueror, Genghis Khan. Hulagu captured and destroyed Baghdad, killing 800,000 people in a week of terror. Next Hulagu destroyed the

Hospitality is a Bedouin art; no matter how little one has it is always shared.

Syrian city of Aleppo, putting another 50,000 to the sword. The "peace" of a graveyard followed during the next one hundred and fifty years. Then appeared another Mongol conqueror, Timur Leng, also known as Timur the Lame and Tamerlane. Timur sacked Aleppo in 1400 and Damascus in 1401.

We noted earlier (Unit Three) that these devastating Mongol eruptions affected not only the Middle East but the whole of Eurasia. Both China and Russia, for example, were overrun by the Mongols and ruled by them for centuries. But the Middle East was particularly hard hit by the Mongols because they killed or carried off into slavery the learned men and the skilled craftsmen. Even worse was their wholesale destruction of the remaining irrigation canals and dams. This process turned more agricultural lands into deserts, and the local population was unable to reverse the process. Whole districts were left in ruins, never to recover their prosperity. This also helps to explain why in many parts of the Middle East, far fewer people live today than did a thousand or two thousand years ago, and at a lower standard of living than in the past.

Economics 659

Shifting trade routes. But in spite of the Mongol disaster, the Middle Eastern lands still had left one important source of economic strength. This was the flourishing trade between southern Asia and Western Europe, from which the Middle Easterners drew fabulous profits as middlemen. Arab merchants picked up cargoes of spices in the East Indies and transported them to India. Then other Arab merchants hauled these spices, together with Indian products such as fine textiles, precious stones, and perfumes, from India to ports in the Near East, and particularly to Alexandria. There they were received by Italian merchants who shipped the goods to various European countries where they were bought finally by consumers.

The Arab merchants who bought and transported the goods from the East Indies to the eastern Mediterranean made very high profits, ranging anywhere from 100 to 2000 per cent. But the merchants were not the only ones who gained from this commerce. In the course of the long journey to the Mediterranean ports, the goods had to be loaded and unloaded repeatedly from ship to caravan and back again. This was true regardless of whether the goods were taken from India to the Persian Gulf, up the Tigris-Euphrates, and across the desert to Syrian ports, or from India up the Red Sea, across the Egyptian desert to the Nile River, and down the river to Alexandria. In addition customs duties were levied at various strategic locations along these routes: at Aden, Mecca, Suez, Cairo, Alexandria, Ormuz, and Basra. Thus not only did the Arab merchants benefit from this East-West trade, but also the government treasuries and many sections of the population, including shipbuilders, sailors, brokers, camel-drivers, and stevedores. It can be seen why the economy of the Middle East depended a good deal on this ancient and highly profitable trade.

In 1498 this trade was suddenly undermined by Vasco da Gama's voyage from Portugal around Africa to India. We noted earlier that the new ocean route was much more economical than the old route through the Middle East. A ship could now take a load of spices or textiles directly from South Asia to the consumer in Western Europe without the necessity of loading and unloading. Within a few years most of the commerce was routed around Africa instead of up the Tigris-Euphrates Valley or the Red Sea. Thus the Middle East, which for centuries had profited from its position at the crossroads of world commerce, now found itself on the side lines. Once the Europeans discovered and won control of new ocean routes, the Middle East was no longer a great trade center; instead it became a dead-end street. The decline of commerce inevitably hurt Middle Eastern civilization as a whole. Revenues declined, cities shrank, and all aspects of life, political and cultural as well as economic, were affected.

The West's economic domination. In an earlier unit we saw that the shift in world trade which undermined the economy of the Near East had the opposite effect on the economy of Western Europe. First Spain and Portugal obtained vast riches from the overseas commerce, followed by Holland, France, and Britain. To these countries poured profits from all portions of the globe: from the East Indian spice islands, from the African slave markets, from the Mexican and Peruvian silver mines, and from the West Indian sugar plantations.

This world-wide trade not only enriched the West's economy, but also transformed it into something new and unique. In order to take advantage of the opportunities offered by the overseas markets, joint-stock companies replaced the old merchant guilds, capitalist middlemen with their "putting out" system took the place of the craft guilds, and large banking houses overshadowed the former moneylender. In every branch of economic life, commerce, industry, and finance, Europe was now efficient, dynamic, and expansionist.

Meanwhile the Middle East, like other sections of the globe, remained unchanged in its ancient ways. Arab and Persian and Syrian merchants continued to trade as individuals and so were hardly a match for the Western trading companies. Thus it was not these merchants who journeyed to the ports of western Europe. Rather it was the Dutch, the French, and the English who organized their respective Levant Companies and gained control of the international commerce of the Near East. It was Western ships that sailed to the Levant ports with clocks, glass, guns, woolen goods, and sugar, and returned with wheat, corn, cotton, and dyestuffs.

Western control of commerce also led to Western control of industry. Middle Eastern industry continued to be in the hands of craftsmen who made and sold their goods in picturesque bazaars. Needless to say, these could not compete with the new large-scale industry of the West, particularly when labor-saving machinery was in use from the late 18th century onward. The result was that many native industries were wiped out by the flood of cheap machine-made products from Europe. An Englishman who visited Constantinople, the capital of the Ottoman Empire, in 1800, was most impressed by the poor quality of its products: "Let a foreigner visit the bazaars . . . he will see nothing but slippers, clumsy boots of bad leather, coarse muslins, pipes, tobacco, coffee . . . second-hand pistols, and the worst manufactured wares in the world. . . ."[9] Two centuries earlier, English travellers had been reporting just the opposite, the superior quality of Middle Eastern goods. But by 1800 the tables were turned: the West had pulled far ahead.

(DORANNE JACOBSON) EDITORIAL PHOTOCOLOR ARCHIVES

In Beirut, a cloth merchant bargains with his customer. Bazaars are still important in the economic system in much of the Middle East.

In the latter half of the 19th century, Western domination of commerce and industry was extended to finance. The Ottoman Empire, which included the whole Near East except Persia, began to borrow from European governments and private banks in 1854. By 1875 the Empire had piled up debts of over one billion dollars. Furthermore, it had borrowed the money at such high interest rates that it was unable to meet the payments as they fell due. In other words, the Ottoman Government became bankrupt, and the European Powers took over control of certain Ottoman revenues in order to collect the money that was owed to them. In

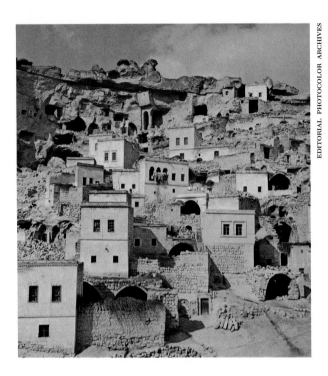

Houses and cave dwellings at Urgup, Turkey. Although many Turks live in poverty areas, conditions have vastly improved in the past decades.

slight. For example, an American expert who studied Turkey's economy in 1948, almost three decades after the founding of the republic, reached the following conclusions:

> This country remains, by the standards of Western Europe or the United States, largely underdeveloped. Twenty-six years of the Republic have seen sweeping reforms and an ambitious attempt at industrialization, but as yet the Industrial Revolution has barely touched the daily lives of the great majority of the Turkish people. Their levels of living have been improved little, if at all.[10]

The Israeli exception. We have seen that the Middle East is an underdeveloped region, and we have noted some of the reasons why it should be so. This does not mean, of course, that conditions are the same in all parts of the Middle East. Among the Arab states, for example, Lebanon is far more advanced economically than Yemen, while Israel is equally more advanced than any Arab country.

The reasons for the difference between Israel and her neighbors will become clear if we look briefly at her agriculture and industry. In agriculture, for example, the Israelis grow several crops instead of depending on one, as is the case in many parts of the Middle East. They have turned to poultry farming and dairying, for example, with profitable results. Whatever they do, they use much machinery and modern scientific techniques. They can do this because the Israeli government helps them by providing agronomists, model farms, experimental stations, and other agricultural services. Another reason is that the farmers themselves cooperate with each other closely. In fact, about two-fifths of them live in communes called *kibbutzim* (singular *kibbutz*). All the land in these communes is owned collectively, and the members work the fields together and share the

this way the Ottoman Empire, and thus most of the Middle East, passed under Western domination in financial matters as well as in commerce and industry.

At the end of the First World War the Ottoman Empire disappeared, but this scarcely affected the economic backwardness of the Near East. The majority of the people continued to till the soil and use the same old, unproductive methods. It is true that some Middle Eastern governments did try to develop some industry. This was especially true of the Turkish republic, which had the advantage of a good supply of natural resources. A certain number of industries were established in Turkey, and a smaller number in the other countries. But even in Turkey, the economic progress was rather profits. The majority of the farmers do not live in *kibbutzim* but they also cooperate with each other in various ways, particularly in buying machinery and in selling their goods.* Finally the Israeli farmers have the great advantage of owning their own land instead of renting it from absentee landlords on exorbitant terms. Thus, instead of handing over most of their produce to the landlords, they use it to live better and to improve their farms. The net result has been a rapid rise in the extent of the cultivated area and in the value of agricultural output.

The fact that the Israeli farmers can enjoy a reasonable standard of living is a great boost for their national industry. Since the farmers can afford to buy something more than bare essentials, Israeli industry has a flourishing domestic market. The industry also has been helped by the constant influx of immigrants, some of whom arrive with both capital to invest and technical skills.

* See *Readings in World History,* "Israel's Agricultural System," p. 687.

Jewish communities in foreign countries, and especially in the United States, also have helped by providing capital and other forms of help. So in industry, as in agriculture, we find rapid growth during the years since the winning of independence.*

Israel's growth has been achieved by a unique combination of government, cooperative, and private enterprise. The government operates the railways and communications, and also is responsible for road construction, irrigation and drainage, afforestation, and similar public works. In addition, the government owns more than half the shares of over 100 corporations engaged in the production of electricity, potash, bromine, phosphates, fertilizers, copper, ceramic materials, and so forth. In all, the government is responsible for about one-quarter of the total national product.

Another quarter is generated by *Histadrut* or the Israeli Federation of Labor. This is a

* See *Readings in World History,* "Science in Israel," p. 690.

The first kibbutz in Israel was composed of tents and quickly constructed buildings. Because of the fear of Arab attack, high walls and watch towers were necessary and vigilance was never relaxed.

KLUGER (BLACK STAR)

federation of trade unions that includes the great majority of Israeli workers. But it is also the country's largest single employer, for it owns and operates enterprises in agriculture, industry, commerce, insurance, banking, construction, transportation, education, and culture. *Histadrut* became involved in all these activities partly because of its socialist beliefs and partly in order to create employment for its members. Accordingly it established new enterprises of its own, encouraged its members to organize themselves into producers' cooperatives, and bought enterprises that were about to dissolve in order to save the employees' jobs. As a result, *Histadrut* now controls over 2000 Israeli businesses and farm cooperatives, employs a quarter of the country's 950,000 wage earners, grows 75 per cent of the food, and is responsible for one-fourth of the Gross National Product of nearly four billion dollars.

The remaining half of the GNP is the product of private enterprise. This is much more vigorous in Israel than in the surrounding countries, thanks to the capital resources

The children's house of an Israeli kibbutz reflects the improved living conditions since 1948.

ISRAELI CONSULATE

and technical skills of the immigrants, and to the initiative of the government in supporting comprehensive and compulsory general education and distinguished institutions of higher learning and research. Of a total labor force of 950,000, Israel has 55,000 professionals with higher degrees and 115,000 technicians. The Israeli government has had considerable success in attracting foreign industries because of this highly trained manpower and the various research institutes which are equipped with modern scientific equipment, including nuclear research reactors, computers, electron microscopes, and fermentation units.

The remarkable rate of Israel's economic growth in all fields is evident in the following statistics:

	(in thousands)	
	1948	1967
Population	657	2669
GNP	Negligible	$3,900,000
Exports	$29,680	$522,000
Imports	$253,120	$734,000
Agricultural Production		
Cultivated Area (acres)	412	1087
Irrigation (acres)	62	387
Afforestation (acres)	13	71

In 1966 and 1967 Israel experienced a fairly severe depression. Economic growth stopped and unemployment soared as the economy operated at only 70 per cent of capacity. About 50,000 citizens emigrated in 1966, and most were scientists, technicians, and doctors. This exodus is a serious problem, for Israel, with her limited natural resources, can prosper only if she develops science-based industries.

After the 1967 war, however, the economy again boomed forward. Unemployment not only was wiped out, but a manpower shortage forced the Israelis to truck in Arab laborers from the occupied territories to work on construction projects. The rate of economic growth in 1968 jumped to 13 per cent, and living standards approached those of the advanced countries of Western Europe.

Economic progress in the U.A.R. In justice to the other countries of the Middle East it should be noted that Israel has enjoyed a unique and vital advantage: the steady flow of capital and skilled immigrants from the outside. Without this stimulus the state of Israel would not have advanced as far as it has today.

It should also be noted that in the years since World War II the pace of development in Turkey, Iran, and the Arab lands has picked up a good deal. This is particularly true of Egypt, or the United Arab Republic, under the leadership of President Nasser. When he came to power in 1952, Nasser had no definite program for economic reform; for the next decade he was concerned more with foreign affairs. But finally, in May 1962, he issued the National Charter which stressed the need for radical change. Economic progress, the Charter stated, "cannot be left to desultory individual efforts motivated by private profit. . . . Political democracy cannot be separated from social democracy." [11]

Nasser first passed an Agrarian Reform Law limiting the amount of land that any individual could own to 200 feddans (one feddan = 1.038 acres), and this limit was later lowered to 100 feddans. At the same time, cooperatives were established to help the new owners use their land more efficiently. By the end of 1965 about one million acres had been distributed, representing about one-sixth of the total cultivated land of Egypt. The cooperatives provided quality seeds, fertilizers, livestock, and machinery, and also arranged for the storage and transportation of the crops. Thus between 1950 and 1965, the average yield rose from 30.1 to 40.6 bushels per acre for wheat, and 3394 to 4493 pounds per acre for rice. The cooper-

atives also invested the profits for socially useful purposes such as village clinics with doctors and nurses, and village social centers with radios and television sets. This was a marked improvement over the age-old custom of the Egyptian peasant, who, when he had a particularly good year spent his surplus on a new wife or in marrying off his daughter.*

The government also boosted industry by building steel mills and various factories, and also by locating and developing new oil fields and mineral deposits.† To stimulate the new industries there is a National Research Center with 200 full-time and 300 part-time research workers. These scientists are working on such problems as how best to exploit the mineral resources, how to harness the sun's energy, and how to get rid of the cottonworm moth which causes great damage each year. Progress has been made in several fields.

The most important single project is the High Aswan Dam, built with the aid of the Soviets who provided the technical skill and about one-third of the one billion dollars that it cost. It is a huge structure, two miles across and 131 feet wide at the top. It contains 17 times as much rock as the greatest pyramid, and as it dams the Nile River, it creates an enormous 310-mile long reservoir, known as Lake Nasser. Its gigantic generators eventually will have a 2,100,000-kilowatt capacity that will provide light for Egyptian homes and power for Egyptian factories. Also the thousands of engineers and technicians who are being trained during the building of the dam will be an invaluable asset for Egyptian industry. The most obvious benefit from the Dam is the great extension of irrigation, which will add about

* See *Readings in World History,* "Change in the Village," p. 679.
† See *Readings in World History,* "Change in the Town," p. 683.

1.7 million acres to the 6 million acres now being tilled.*

Economic needs. Despite this progress, the fact remains that the U.A.R. and the other Middle East countries still have far to go before they will be able to meet the economic needs of their people. In Lebanon and Egypt, for example, there is the urgent problem of population pressure. As in other underdeveloped countries, the problem has arisen because the birth rate has remained high while modern medicine has reduced the death rate by one-half. As a result, Egypt's population has doubled in the past half century to its present total of over 30 million. And at the present rate of increase it will double again

* See *Readings in World History,* "The High Aswan Dam," p. 685.

Outside Tripoli, Lebanon, workers produce salt from sea water, one of that country's many development projects.

CARL E. OSTMAN

in only a quarter of a century. This means that the population increase that occurs during the building of the High Aswan Dam will balance the increased productivity that the dam will make possible. Thus Egypt's biggest problem is Egyptians: it is the 3000 babies that are born each day.

An equally serious problem in most Near Eastern countries is the social inequality which has created a dangerous gap between the wealthy few and the poverty-stricken masses. A good example of this is in Iraq where, in 1954, out of a total agricultural population of 3,300,000, only 125,000 owned land. Thus over 96 per cent of the farm population had to work for the less than 4 per cent who owned the land. Since these landowners controlled the Iraqi parliament, they paid no land taxes or inheritance taxes whatsoever.

All this means that the public works built by the Development Board increased the productivity of the country, but the proceeds went to those who already owned the land. The effect of the construction, therefore, was to make the rich richer and the poor poorer. There was much talk about land reform, but by 1957 only 15,000 peasants had actually benefited from the reform. The conditions explain why a year later a bloody revolt broke out in Iraq. King Feisal and his chief minister, the pro-Western Nuri as-Said, were murdered, and, since then Iraq has been ruled by a succession of unstable military governments.

We may conclude that despite important progress since World War II, the Middle East remains largely underdeveloped. Many serious problems are still unsolved. We have seen that these are long standing and date back several centuries, and we cannot hope that they will be solved overnight. But we have also seen that the people of the Middle East are today awake as they never have been before. They now believe that

The Aswan Dam was at one time thought capable of providing sufficient water for irrigation for Egypt. Now, due to the large population density in irrigated areas and the increased growth rate, even the new Aswan High Dam will be inadequate.

poverty and wretchedness are not inevitable, and they expect relief in this world rather than in the paradise promised in the *Koran.*

The great question in the Middle East today is whether nationalist regimes, such as that of Nasser in Egypt, can satisfy these popular expectations. If not, the revolutions in Iraq are a warning of what must be expected.

The example of Israel. Finally, it should be noted that the Israeli experience is having repercussions far beyond the borders of the Middle East. The success of Israel in developing her economy is attracting the attention of the underdeveloped countries of Asia and Africa. Since most of these countries have won their political independence, they are now interested primarily in economic growth. To get this economic growth started, they frequently look for help from Israel rather than from the Great Powers of the East or West. They do not care for the help

of the former colonial powers because of unpleasant historical experiences. Nor do they wish to follow Soviet or Chinese models with their disregard for individual liberty. Israel attracts them since it falls into neither category.

Between 1961 and 1965 approximately 10,000 people went to Israel for training, more than half of them from African states. And since 1958, about 3,000 Israeli experts have gone abroad, two-thirds of them to African states. An African leader, who recently visited and studied in Israel, expressed this attitude as follows: "You have achieved outstanding social and technical progress without sacrificing human values. . . . Israel is the only valid alternative for us." [12] Coming from an African this statement is important and summarizes the significance of Israel's achievement for the world of the 1960's.*

* See *Readings in World History,* "Israel and the New Nations," p. 693.

Reviewing the Essentials

Present State

1. What symptoms of underdevelopment are present in Middle Eastern countries? Give specific evidence for each symptom cited. What differences exist among Middle Eastern nations, i.e., Lebanon, Saudi Arabia, Turkey, Israel, Yemen, Iran, Iraq, Egypt?

2. What types of agriculture are practiced in the Middle East? Why is productivity in agriculture the lowest in the world second only to Africa? Why is this a major factor aggravating underdevelopment?

3. Why is productivity in Middle Eastern industry also extremely low? Cite Middle Eastern nations that illustrate differences in extent of industrial development.

4. Cite data to show that oil is the most highly developed industry in the Middle East. What nations share in this development? To what extent is oil promoting the economic development of the Middle East?

Historical Origins

5. Prepare a list of the major contributions the Middle East made to civilization in the ancient and medieval periods. How did the invasions of the Mongols and Vasco da Gama's voyage to India contribute to the economic decline of the Middle East?

6. Formulate reasons for the decline of the Middle East as a center of civilization.

7. Explain why Israel is an exception to the symptoms of underdevelopment that exist in the Middle East. Support with evidence from statistical data given in your text.

8. What progress in economic development has been made since 1945 in Turkey, Egypt, Iran, and Iraq?

9. In spite of progress being made, what are urgent problems of Middle Eastern countries?

10. What will determine whether or not the Middle East wins in its war on poverty? What are the alternatives if it loses?

Explain, Identify, or Locate

1258	1400	1498	Tel Aviv
bilharziasis	Arab Petroleum Conference	Tamerlane	Aleppo
kibbutz	Agrarian Reform Law	Hulagu Khan	Baghdad
joint-stock company	population pressure	*Histadrut*	High Aswan Dam
capitalist middlemen	fellaheen	1948	1952

CULTURE: Islam and the Impact of Modernization

PRESENT STATE

The model is the West. The principal cultural trend today in the Middle East, as in other underdeveloped areas, is the impact of Western thought and technology upon the daily life of the people. This trend is known as modernization, which means simply that the Middle East is now experiencing the combination of changes that have revolutionized or "modernized" the West during recent centuries.

What changes did the West undergo that are now affecting the Middle East? One was rationalism, a new way of thinking based on logical thought rather than on the dictates of theology. Rationalism emphasizes reason rather than faith, and states that man can determine his own future by using his reasoning power. Rationalism is the foundation on which science rests; it is one of the West's outstanding contributions to the world.

The other major change in the West was individualism, an attitude that emphasized the individual rather than class or community. It is important to note that individualism was not something specific but rather a general attitude. In social affairs, individualism held that each person should be free to rise up the social ladder depending upon his own qualities and achievements rather than upon his titles and connections. In politics, individualism meant that each person should be able to participate in public life as an active citizen rather than being forced to accept rule from above. In education, individualism required that all citizens should have the opportunity to learn depending on their ability and desire rather than their money or class. This seems natural and proper to us today, but as late as 1807 a member of the British Parliament opposed

Students in downtown Tehran

education for the lower classes because, he said, it would teach them "to despise their lot in life instead of making them good servants in agriculture and other laborious employment to which their rank has destined them." [13]

These new concepts revolutionized Europe. And, as Europe's influence extended overseas, they gradually revolutionized the entire globe. In the mid-19th century, for example, a statesman of the Ottoman Empire declared frankly, "There is no means to save the Ottoman state save by imitating the West." [14] But until the 20th century Europe's influence was limited to a very small number of non-Europeans who could read Western books and newspapers, or who had travelled in Western lands. The overwhelming majority of the people were altogether ignorant of European culture.

Education. Since World War I, and particularly since World War II, Western ideas and practices have penetrated into every part of the Middle East. One reason for this is that the various governments have assumed responsibility for the establishment of schools for all citizens. The Middle East is still a long way from wiping out illiteracy, but important progress has been made, with far-reaching repercussions. The subjects of the pre-1914 Ottoman Empire, for example, were 99 per cent illiterate. But as soon as the Turkish republic was established, a campaign was started for the "suppression of ignorance." The percentage of illiteracy was reduced to 81.3 in 1935 and 68.1 in 1950. Today about one-half of the Turkish people can read and write. In the rest of the Middle East the rate of literacy varies widely, ranging from 90 per cent in Israel and 86 per cent in Lebanon, to 30 per cent in the U.A.R. and about 10 per cent in Yemen and Saudi Arabia.

The significance of this increase in education is that it has opened the way for new ideas and attitudes. In the past, age was believed to bring wisdom, and the elders were respected and listened to simply because of their years. But now the ability to read and write is considered to be more important than age, and illiterate elders are giving way to the young people who have been to school. For example, a 75-year old farmer in Lebanon, when asked for his opinion concerning a certain matter, replied, "When you ask a person like me, I don't know anything. . . . We have many educated young men in the village who will answer your questions very well." [15] Another older person in Lebanon replied to a similar question as follows: "Am I learned enough for you to take my opinion about this? Go to the person who goes to school and let him tell you. What do you want my opinion for?" [16] Thus we see that the spread of education in the Middle East not only has introduced new ideas to the people, but also has changed drastically the traditional relations between the older and younger generations.*

Industrialization. The Middle East is being transformed by economic as well as by educational development. The building of roads, for example, has brought the villages closer to the cities. No longer do the peasants live in isolation, concerned only with their crops and animals. Now they can travel to the city with relative ease, and their sons are more likely to find work in the city and break away from the age-old occupation of their forefathers. This again leads to new ideas and attitudes. The son who has a job in the city also has economic independence. He does not need to wait for his father to bequeath to him his share of the family plot. The son also acquires prestige because of his contact with the outside world and the news that he brings back with him. An illiterate

A cement factory in Saudi Arabia represents the upswing in construction as oil profits flow into the country.

ARABIAN AMERICAN OIL COMPANY

* See *Readings in World History*, "The New Education," p. 702.

peasant mother in Lebanon, for example, declared proudly, "When my son comes from the city, he feels like a lord among the neighbors because he reads the newspaper in the city, and he always has many new things to tell the people in the village." [17] This penetration of news and ideas from the outside naturally increases as economic development progresses. A textile plant, a steel mill, or an oil refinery will mean many more city workers. Eventually it will also mean a trade-union, which will introduce a whole set of new concepts and attitudes. A Middle Eastern worker who is a member of a trade-union and who is able to bargain with his employer and even to strike against him, is a very different person from the peasant who tills the land and meekly obeys the landowner's orders.

Mass communication. Finally Middle Eastern culture is being transformed by the rapid spread of telephones, radio, and television. The following figures concerning Egypt are typical of the region as a whole.

Growth of Communications in Egypt [18]		
	1956	1963
Telephones in use	180,000	264,000
Radio receiving sets	850,000	1,980,000
Television sets (1960)	50,000	197,000

This extremely rapid development of communications is having a profound impact on Middle Eastern society in many different ways. This may be best illustrated by repeating some of the replies received by a group of American scholars who studied the process of modernization in the Near East.[19]

Lebanese shoemaker–I have a son that works the whole day; in the evening he goes to the cinema. So now he wants to buy a hat, he wants long trousers, he wants to buy a revolver, and I don't know what else.

Young Syrian government clerk–When we see the lives of the people in the West, and then compare it with our own lives, we find that we still have a long way to go before attaining their level. The movies are . . . like a teacher to us, who tells us what to do and what not.

Young Lebanese Muslim girl–When they see a love story full of kissing, the young men or women get so excited as to go directly from the movie to practice what they have seen.

Lebanese peasant–Those who read newspapers . . . always have something of great importance to tell. . . . We who do not read the newspapers wait for others to amuse and fascinate us with what is happening in other villages and towns. A friend of ours always tells us amazing and strange stories . . . and he always says that he reads this in the newspaper.

President Gamal Nasser of Egypt–It is true that most of our people are still illiterate. But politically that counts far less than it did twenty years ago. . . . Radio has changed everything. . . . Today people in the most remote villages hear of what is happening everywhere and form their opinions. Leaders cannot govern as they once did. We live in a new world.

The new woman. Another example of the effect of modernization in the Middle East is to be found in the changing status of women. For many centuries women in the Muslim world have been secluded. Strangely enough, Islam at first raised rather than lowered their position in society. It permitted them to keep their family names after marriage, granted them the right to own and sell property, made them guardians over minors, and allowed them to enter trades and professions. But as the Muslim Empire became larger and richer, upper-class women secluded themselves in the pomp and ceremony of court life. They adopted the veil as a mark of distinction and superiority of their class. Gradually the custom spread to the women of other classes until the veil and seclusion became the lot of almost all Muslim women.

During the 20th century new ideas concerning the position of women came in from the outside world. Women's magazines and women's societies urged full equality for the female sex. Unveiled women took part in the struggle against British and French occupation following World War I. Unveiled women also held parades against Jewish immigration to Palestine. By 1929 the American University of Beirut graduated its first Muslim woman student, and in 1932 Cairo University gave a law degree to a Muslim girl.

Even more rapid change took place following World War II. For example, the United Arab Republic adopted a new divorce code on October 1, 1960. A Muslim husband no longer can divorce his wife simply by telling her, "I divorce thee." Now he must go to court and give good reasons. Also a husband no longer may beat his wife or abuse her with insulting language. If he does, she may be granted judicial separation for six months, with alimony. If her husband does it again, she may have a divorce. Finally, a man may still have four wives, in accordance with the 1300-year-old Islamic law; but the first wife now has the right to divorce her husband if he takes another wife.*

Total impact of the West. From the above we can see how mass education, economic development, and mass communication are revolutionizing the Middle East today as they did Europe in earlier centuries. This process of modernization is affecting all aspects of Middle Eastern culture: relations between generations, relations between men and women, and relations between rulers and ruled. The impact of the West which, in the

* See *Readings in World History*, "The Position of Women," p. 700.

ALAN BAND

19th century, affected only an infinitesimal upper class, is now reaching the masses. The result is a great awakening, a broadening of horizons, and a raising of expectations. Those countries that prove capable of satisfying these new expectations will experience healthy progress; those that do not will experience social conflict and turmoil. "Leaders," as President Nasser pointed out, "cannot govern as they once did." This is the promise and the threat of the modernization trend which is slowly developing in Middle Eastern countries.*

* See *Readings in World History*, "Changing Folk Cultures," p. 709.

HISTORICAL ORIGINS

Mohammed and Islam. The modernization process is not proceeding unchallenged in the Middle East. At every point it is meeting with resistance from the traditional culture. This culture is essentially Islamic; it is based on the teachings of the Prophet Mohammed. In many basic respects it represents the opposite of modernization; it emphasizes faith, community, and tradition in place of reason, individualism, and change.

Mohammed was born in Mecca in 570 A.D. At that time Mecca was a prosperous transfer point on the ancient spice route between India and Syria. It was also a religious center where pagan Arab tribesmen worshipped before a black meteorite housed in the Kaaba, or Cube. Mohammed developed a distaste for idolatry and often wandered into the hills to meditate, sometimes for days at a time. One night the Archangel Gabriel appeared to him in a vision and cried, "Recite!" For a decade or more the revelations continued, and Mohammed recited, or preached, in the city streets or beside the Kaaba. He felt himself selected by God to be the Arabian prophet of true religion, for the Arabs had had no prophet as other nations had.

The merchants of Mecca attacked Mohammed because his denunciation of idolatry threatened the pilgrim trade on which the city's prosperity depended. In 622 Mohammed fled to the friendlier city of Yathrib, now called Medina. The year of his Hijra or hegira (flight) is the year one of the Muslim calendar. At Yathrib, Mohammed built a model theocratic state, and by 630 he was strong enough to capture Mecca and destroy the detested idols. Two years later Mohammed died, but by that time his faith was consolidated, and his followers were ready to burst out upon an unsuspecting world.

The *Koran*. We do not know whether the *Koran* was set down in full during Mohammed's lifetime. But we do know that soon after his death an authoritative version was prepared by one of his secretaries. This was approved by a committee of his followers, and thereafter preserved as the accepted text. The fundamental teachings of the *Koran* are basically similar to those of the Bible. The basic doctrine is the Oneness of God or Allah as the sole creator and the sole judge. All Muslims must praise and glorify Allah, and submit to his will.

Mohammed did not establish either an organized priesthood or sacraments, but he did call on all Muslims to perform certain rituals known as the Five Pillars of Islam. They are: (1) Once in his life the believer must say with full understanding and absolute acceptance, *la ilaha illa'llah: muhammed rasulu'llah*, "There is no God but Allah; Mohammed is the Messenger of Allah." (2) Five times daily he must pray: at dawn, at noon, in midafternoon, at dusk, and after it has become dark. The prayers are said and are performed on a carpet with the worshipper's shoes removed, his head covered, and facing in the direction of Mecca. (3) The Muslim must give alms generously, as an offering to Allah and an act of piety. (4) The Muslim must fast from daybreak to sunset during the whole month of Ramadan. (5) Once in his life the Muslim, if he can, must make the pilgrimage, or Hadj, to Mecca. This pilgrimage has contributed greatly to the unity of the Muslim world. From the four corners of the globe the pilgrims come each year, nearly 200,000 strong before World War II. They are of all kinds, rich and poor, yellow, white, brown, and black. And when they complete the rituals they receive the title of Hadji, which gives to all, whether prince or pauper, great prestige.*

* See *Readings in World History,* "The Muslim Faith," p. 639.

Islam dominates the Middle East. In Istanbul, the faithful pray at sundown in the courtyard of the Blue Mosque. A copy of the Koran made in Iran in the 10th century. The Kaaba at Mecca houses a black meteorite worshiped by pagan Arabs but now part of Islam.

So far as moral teachings are concerned, Islam is very similar to Christianity and Judaism. For example, the following statement in the *Koran* is comparable to our Golden Rule: "Offer to men what thou desirest should be offered to thee; avoid doing to men what thou dost not wish to be done to thee."

A wave of conquest. One year after Mohammed's death the forces of Islam burst out of the Arabian Peninsula into an astonished world that hitherto had scarcely known of its existence. The Arab armies were led by caliphs, who were not religious leaders comparable to the popes, as is often assumed, but rather supreme commanders in the Holy War. Within two decades Islam was triumphant throughout the Near East. Syria fell in 635, Iraq in 637, Palestine in 640, Egypt in 642, and the Persian Empire in 650. The momentum of conquest carried the Arabs eastward to India, and westward across North Africa to the Atlantic, and thence across the Strait of Gibraltar to Spain. It was at this time that the peoples of the Near East adopted the Arab language and became Arabized. And the Muslim world as a whole was united by the bonds of a religion which was at the same time a social code and a political system. The Holy Law offered to the faithful not only religious commandments but also specific rules for private and public life. Thus it was quite possible for a learned man from Morocco to be made a judge in India, for the law was the same everywhere.

Islamic culture. With such free intercourse in the Muslim world, a common Islamic culture developed. This culture reached its height in the 9th, 10th, and 11th centuries. It was based on the Graeco-Roman, Byzantine, and Persian heritage of the conquered lands, but in every field the Muslims added something of their own. The result was a brilliant civilization that excelled in literature, art, architecture, mathematics, and medicine. It was a civilization that far surpassed that of the primitive agrarian society that existed in northwestern Europe at that time. In fact an Arab philosopher who lived in Muslim Spain in the 10th century described the Europeans further north as barbarians. "Their temper is slow," he wrote, "and their humors raw; their hair is long and their complexion pale. The sharpness of their wit, the perspicacity of their intelligence is nil; indolence and ignorance are dominant among them, as well as crudeness and lack of judgment." [20]

Many objects that we now use show by their names that they had their origin in Muslim lands. Grenadine was first woven in Granada, the Muslim stronghold in Spain. Taffeta was originally a Persian silk called *taftah*. Attab, a certain section of Baghdad, called the striped silk which was their specialty *attabi*; in time people in Europe began to call their striped cats tabby. And the sweets we eat today are called by names of Arabic origin: sugar from *sukkar*, and candy from *quandah*.

The Muslim world stands still. Muslim civilization, like others before it, gradually stagnated and declined. The invasions of the barbarian Turks and Mongols from Central Asia hastened the downward course. Thus, while the formerly backward Western Europe experienced a great transformation in early modern times, the Muslim world stood still. It fell behind not only in economic matters, as we have seen, but also in cultural. Authority and tradition were slavishly followed; originality and creativity in large part ceased.

The West moves in. This hardening of the arteries was not so serious as long as the world was left to itself. But when the dynamic West began to expand, the Islamic countries proved utterly incapable of holding their own. One by one they passed under Western domination, so that by 1914 two-thirds of the world's Muslims were ruled by Britain, France, Holland, Russia, and China. The only independent Muslim countries were Turkey, Persia, and Afghanistan, and even they were independent in little more than name. They were controlled economically by the West and were not annexed outright because of rivalries among the Western Powers rather than because of their own strength.

Islam is separated. This subjugation of the Muslim world to the formerly despised West naturally weakened the prestige of Islam. Hitherto Islam had been a complete "way of life," regulating both public and private affairs. But after the First World War, the Turks under Kemal Atatürk established a Western-type republic in which Islam and the state were completely separate. The Islamic Holy Law henceforth had no authority,

Al Azhar, the oldest university in the world, has been modernized to accommodate new students.

ALAN BAND

and religion became a purely private matter. Other Muslim countries moved in the same direction, though not as far as Turkey. This trend is clearly evident in education. Religion is taught in the schools of the Muslim world, but the teacher of religion is usually not also the teacher of the other subjects. Thus the religious and nonreligious fields are becoming independent of each other. In Egypt, for example, is to be found the famous al-Azhar University, founded in 930 A.D., and thus the oldest university in the world. Al-Azhar is a Muslim institution, devoted to the teaching of the faith. But during the past century, four modern universities have been established in Egypt, and these are Western in organization and in spirit. Furthermore, Al Azhar itself has been modernized since 1961. New colleges of business administration, engineering, agriculture, and medicine have been added to the three traditional colleges of religious doctrine, jurisprudence, and Arabic studies.

The former domination of Islam is being weakened not only by official actions but also by the unofficial infiltration of the entire Muslim world as a result of the modernization process. We have seen that schools, roads, factories, newspapers, radios, and cinemas are all undermining the traditional Islamic culture. Seclusion of women, deference to age, acceptance of tradition, obedience to authority; all these are now being questioned and frequently rejected.

The survival of Islam. Obviously Islam no longer is the all-embracing force that it was a mere half-century ago. Does this mean that it is on the way out and that it will soon be submerged by the wave of modernization? Muslim intellectuals, having had the most contact with the West, are the most divided on this question. Some believe that Islam is out of date, that it has nothing to offer toward the solution of modern problems,

In Cairo today Western dress has almost entirely replaced the traditional Arab robe.

and that the sooner it is dropped, the better off its followers will be. Others take the opposite view: that the troubles of the Muslim world have arisen because the pure faith has not been properly observed, and that the only way out is to restore the Holy Law to its former authority.

Between these two schools is a third one which believes that Islam should have a position similar to that of Christianity in the Western world.* One of the champions of this view, which is held by most educated Muslims, has pointed out that only 50 of the *Koran's* 6000 verses are concerned with law. "We should know," he concludes, "that the glorious *Koran* is not based upon the laws. . . . The *Koran* is concerned rather with the training of character and the cleansing and purification of the spirit." [21]

* See *Readings in World History*, "The Role of Religion," p. 698.

The masses of the people in the Middle East do not have these doubts and reservations concerning Islam. Despite the inroads of modernism, they are much more likely to accept the traditional faith than are the intellectuals. One reason for this is that although the peasants and city workers may listen to radios and attend movies, they are not familiar with Western science and political thought. Therefore they are not so likely to question the fundamentals of their Islamic faith. In fact, like most people throughout the world, they simply do not think of the fundamentals of their religion. Rather they observe its rituals, and we have seen that in the case of Islam these rituals are very impressive and binding. The prayers, the fasting, the almsgiving, and the pilgrimage to Mecca, all provide a cement that gives Muslims a strong feeling of unity and brotherhood.

Culture 677

Even the most casual traveller in the Middle East cannot help noting that Islam is still a much more powerful force in that region than Christianity is in the Western world. In Turkey, where Islam was officially separated from the state, hundreds of mosques were rebuilt during the past decade. Thousands of Turkish pilgrims are now going to Mecca each year, and in response to popular request, the state radio has started broadcasting religious events. In the country-side the village *hoja* or preacher still has a strong influence over the peasants. The nature of this influence can be seen in the fol-

lowing sermon preached by a *hoja* before a congregation of women whose morals he feared would suffer from contacts with the city:

> A certain army officer had a sister whom he allowed to live in evil ways. On her face she wore paint. Her hair was cut short and uncovered to the eyes of men. Her dress was indecent. She displayed bare arms and naked legs to the public gaze. This indecent woman soon sickened and died—a judgment of God. Her brother, who had failed to keep her from her evil ways, accompanied the corpse to the cemetery. Stooping over the open grave, he chanced to drop his wallet in it unawares, and the pocketbook was covered over when the grave was filled. After the service he wanted to pay those who had officiated, but his money was gone. He at once realized what had happened. The clergy-man in charge was appealed to and at once agreed that the grave should be reopened, and this was immediately done. But . . . in those few minutes . . . the arms and legs which that shameless woman had displayed naked to the common gaze had crumbled away. They were no more. The angel of God already had visited her. Hear, oh congregation, the moral of this event. . . .[22]

We may conclude that the balance between the traditional Islamic culture and moderni-zation depends on various factors. Women, in general, are more resistant to change than men, illiterates more than the educated, and country people more than the city dwellers.

So far as the future of Islam in the Middle East is concerned, it will depend on its ability to adjust to the changing requirements of modern times. Some Westerners wrongly assume that Islam is essentially a static faith. This is a conclusion that can be dangerously misleading. Islam has gone through many upheavals in the past and, in the future, may show itself able to adjust to the rapidly-changing Middle East of today. At times in

An Iranian woman in traditional Persian dress. The traditional Persian jacket has become a clothing fad in the Western world.

PIX INC.

their history, in the religious as well as the temporal realm, Muslims have 'broken through' to constructive innovations that show flexibility of thought and attitude. At other times Muslim thought has been characterized by stagnation and rigidity.

One of the strengths of Islam lies in its emotional appeal to many millions of people. Another is its concept of racial equality which has helped to free Islam from the smear of "the white man's burden." The non-Christian frequently associates Christianity with colonialism and racial prejudice.

The future of Islam will also depend on the course of political events, for Islam, like other religions, fares very differently under Communist rule than it does under non-Communist.[*]

[*] See *Readings in World History,* "The New Middle Eastern Man," p. 712.

Camels are still important work animals in the Middle East; they are often used to carry goods over long distances. Here, a camel driver rests in the local market.

Reviewing the Essentials

Present State

1. Explain (a) rationalism and (b) individualism. Why did these concepts revolutionize Europe? When did they penetrate and begin to influence the Middle East?

2. Give examples of how the culture of the Middle East is being changed by: (a) education; (b) economic development; (c) mass communication.

3. Cite examples to show that the position of the Muslim woman has changed during the 20th century.

4. Prove or disprove this statement made by President Nasser of the United Arab Republic: "Leaders cannot govern as they once did." You may want to select a particular country as a basis for your answer or answer the question in terms of the entire Middle East.

Historical Origins

5. Review the major events in the life of Mohammed and the development of the Muslim religion.

6. Explain the meaning and significance of The Five Pillars of Islam (Faith, Fasting, Almsgiving, Prayer, Pilgrimage to Mecca).

7. What was the extent of the Muslim world by the 11th century? Locate on a map.

8. Cite examples to illustrate the achievements of the Muslim civilization in the 10th and 11th centuries. Account for these achievements.

9. Why did the Muslim civilization, which had far outdistanced Europe by the mid-11th century, stagnate and decline, and by 1914 come largely under the rule of European countries?

10. Give evidence that the prestige of Islam, as a way of life, weakened with the conquest and expansion of Western control in the Middle East.

11. What is the role of Islam as a religion in the Middle East today? What is the source of its strength?

12. Why do the masses have fewer reservations about accepting the traditional faith of Islam than do the Muslim intellectuals?

13. Discuss the following statement: "Even the most casual traveller in the Middle East cannot help noting that Islam is still a much more powerful force in that region than Christianity is in the Western world."

14. In what respects is the Islamic culture opposed to modernization?

15. In what ways can it be said that the bonds of the Islamic faith are at the same time a social code and a political system?

16. How did Kemal's introduction of Western ideas into Turkey affect the rest of the Middle East?

Explain, Identify, or Locate

mosque	*sukkar*	*hoja*	Mecca
Hijra	Kaaba	Allah	Medina
Koran	Ramadan	Mohammed	al-Azhar University
570 A.D.	622 A.D.	930 A.D.	

UNIT ACTIVITIES

1. a. On an outline map of the Middle East locate: 1) Countries of the Middle East; 2) Rivers: Tigris, Euphrates, Nile, Jordan; 3) Bodies of Water: Persian Gulf, Red Sea, Mediterranean Sea, Black Sea, Caspian Sea, Gulf of Aden, Dardanelles; 4) Cities: Aleppo, Baghdad, Basra, Damascus, Jerusalem, Alexandria, Aden, Mecca, Medina, Cairo, Teheran, Tel Aviv, Beirut, Haifa, Ankara, Istanbul; 5) Others: Negev, Suez Canal, Aswan Dam.

b. On an outline map show the successive empires that controlled the Middle East during the classical and medieval periods. This may be done most effectively with overlays.

2. Prepare a chart that gives the major events, leaders, achievements, and problems of the Middle East, using the five historical periods as a framework for organizing and presenting information on the chart. Selected events might be graphic and pictorial.

3. Read and prepare a report on: "The Ottoman Empire at Its Height." Note reasons why it commanded the respect and fear of Christian Europeans and reasons for its decline in the nineteenth century. Useful sources of information are the section "Since Mohammed" in *Readings in World History*, Unit Ten, "The Middle East," pp. 639–658; and the bibliography.

4. Several students might prepare a pro and con discussion on the strengths and weaknesses of Arab nationalism. Look for news reports on affairs in the Middle East. See *Readings in World History*, "Nationalism in the Turkish Republic," p. 660; "Arab Nationalism Before World War I," pp. 661–662; and "Arab Nationalism in the Mid-Twentieth Century," pp. 662–664. See also "Arab Nationalism: Force for Good or Evil," in *America's Role in the Middle East* (Foreign Relations Series, River Forest, Ill.: Laidlaw); Sylvia G. Haim, *Arab Nationalism: an Anthology* (Berkeley: U. of California Press, 1962); Torrey's "Nasser's

Egypt," in *Current History*, May 1965; Hurewitz's "Regional and International Politics in the Middle East," in *The United States and the Middle East* (American Assembly) (Englewood Cliffs, N.J.: Prentice-Hall, 1964).

5. Plan and present to the class a panel discussion on the Arab and Israeli positions in the Arab-Israeli conflict. For preparation see *Readings in World History*, "Origins of the Palestine Problem," pp. 664–666; "Israeli Independence," pp. 666–667; and "The Arab View of Israel," p. 668. See also "The Arab-Israeli Conflict Today" in *The United States and the Middle East* cited in item 4.

6. Read Leonard Kenworthy's *Leaders of New Nations* (New York: Doubleday, 1959) for accounts of Ben-Gurion of Israel, Hussein of Jordan, and Nasser of Egypt. Note early life, rise to leadership, program, successes and failures.

7. On an outline map of the Middle East show the major oil deposits, refineries, and pipelines. Try to locate current figures on capital investment in the oil industry, royalties received by governments of the Middle East, oil companies involved in the development of resources, major markets and importance of oil to economic development programs.

8. Village development programs are as important to the Middle East as they are to India. Prepare a report on the topic: "Village Redevelopment: Key to Modernization in the Middle East." Read for information on: (a) life in a Middle Eastern village (housing, education, health, sources of income); (b) village development programs underway in Egypt (philosophy, government's contribution, points of attack, response of villagers); (c) outlook for the future. See *Readings in World History*, "Tradition in the Village," pp. 673–676; "Change in the Village," pp. 679–683; "The New Middle Eastern Man," pp. 712–715. See also Najmeh Najafi, *Reveille for a Persian Village* (New York: Harper, 1958), which is excellent on problems of village development.

9. Several students might prepare a symposium on "Israel: The Exception." Focus on reasons why a country lacking resources essential to industrial development has gone a long way to overcome the obstacles of its geography. Consult: Gail Hoffman, *The Land and the People of Israel* (Philadelphia: Lippincott, 1960). O. I. Janowsky, *Foundations of Israel;* Emil Lengyel, *Israel: Problems of Nation-Building;* Robert St. John, *Ben-Gurion, The Biography of An Extraordinary Man* (Garden City: Doubleday, 1959); *Readings in World History*, "Israel and the New Nations," pp. 693–697.

10. "The Muslim world as a whole was united by the bonds of a religion which was at the same time a social code and a political system." Discuss this statement, explaining why it is not a completely accurate appraisal of the role of religion in the Muslim world today. See John S. Badeau, "Religion in the Middle East," *Social Education*, January 1961.

11. Have the class prepare for discussion on the question: "What should be the United States' goals for Middle Eastern foreign policy?" The class might be divided into four groups, each making special preparation on these policy problems:

    1) How can we prevent the Soviet Union from extending her control in the Middle East?

    2) What should we do about supplying arms to the Middle East?

    3) What should we do to bring about a settlement of the Arab-Israeli dispute?

    4) How can we assure free passage of oil to the West?

For each policy problem, groups should be ready to explain the existing problem and circumstances that caused it; propose alternative courses of action that the United States might take; give the consequences of each alternative for the United States, Middle East, and world; give the policy position the group supports, with reasons.

Following presentation of each of the group recommendations, the class can draft a policy statement, outlining what they accept as the best course for the U.S. in the Middle East. If there is a minority position, it should be stated.

For information consult: Hanson W. Baldwin, "Middle East in Turmoil," Headline Series May–June 1957; *Middle East Proposals*, Department of State Publication 6440 (Washington D.C.: U.S. Government Printing Office, January 1957). Also consult the bibliography and *Readers' Guide to Periodical Literature* on United States, Middle East Foreign Policy.

SELECTED READING

● An old but still invaluable general survey of the Middle East is by J. S. Badeau, *East and West of Suez* (New York: Foreign Policy Association, Headline Book, No. 39, 1943). More recent general studies are by J. B. Christopher, *Middle East: Growing Pains* (New York: Foreign Policy Association, Headline Series, No. 148, July–August 1961); and E. Lengyel, *The Changing Middle East,* Oxford Social Studies Pamphlets (New York: Oxford Book Co., 1958). Specific countries are considered by the following two Foreign Policy Association pamphlets: M. H. Kerr, *Egypt Under Nasser* (Headline Series, No. 161, September–October 1963); and N. Safran, *Israel Today: A Profile* (Headline Series, No. 170, April 1965).

● An excellent analysis of the diplomatic situation in the Middle East is given by S. Shepard Jones, *America's Role in the Middle East,* Foreign Relations Series (River Forest, Ill.: Laidlaw, 1965). For the 1967 Arab-Israeli War and the repercussions, see M. H. Kerr, *The Middle East Conflict* (New York: Foreign Policy Asso., Headline Series, No. 191, October 1968). Finally there are two biographies: E. Lengyel, *They Called Him Atatürk* (New York: J. Day, 1962); A. MacLean, *Lawrence of Arabia* (New York: Random House, 1962).

Traffic jam in Cairo

PIX INC.

FURTHER READING

● Two invaluable reference works are *The Middle East and North Africa, 1968–69* (London, Europe Publications, 1969) which is periodically revised; and R. L. Cleveland, *The Middle East and South Asia, 1967* (Washington: Stryker-Post, 1967). A convenient atlas with informative text is by R. C. Kingsbury and N. J. G. Pounds, *An Atlas of Middle Eastern Affairs* (New York: Praeger, 1964). The best study of the geographic background is by G. B. Cressey, *Crossroads: Land and Life in Southwest Asia* (Philadelphia: Lippincott, 1960). Two standard textbooks on the Middle East are by P. K. Hitti, *The Near East in History* (Princeton: Van Nostrand, 1961); and S. N. Fisher, *The Middle East* (New York: Knopf, 1959). A useful collection of documents is available in L. S. Stavrianos, *The Ottoman Empire: Was it the Sick Man of Europe?* (New York: Rinehart, 1958).

● For the Arab world there are several excellent books: P. K. Hitti, *The Arabs: A Short History* (Gateway Editions, 1956), which concentrates on early Arab history; M. Berger, *The Arab World Today* (Garden City: Doubleday, 1962), an American sociologist's vivid picture of contemporary Arab life; W. R. Polk, *The United States and The Arab World* (Cambridge: Harvard University Press, 1965), which is a perceptive analysis of the evolution of the Arab world in modern times; and P. Mansfield, *Nasser's Egypt* (Penguin Books, 1965), an excellent study of Nasser.

● For the non-Arab parts of the Middle East, the best general work is L. V. Thomas and R. N. Frye, *The United States and Turkey and Iran* (Cambridge: Harvard University Press, 1952). On Israel, the historical background is presented in J. Parkes, *A History of the Jewish People* (Pelican Book, 1964); and the state and society of Israel are analyzed by N. Safran, *The United States and Israel* (Cambridge: Harvard University Press, 1963).

● The best studies of the process of modernization are by M. Halpern, *The Politics of Social Change in the Middle East and North Africa* (Princeton: Princeton University Press, 1963); and Rivlin and Szyliowicz, eds., *The Contemporary Middle East: Tradition and Innovation* (New York: Random House, 1965). For diplomatic developments, see G. G. Stevens, ed., *The United States and the Middle East* (Englewood Cliffs: Prentice Hall, 1967); and M. Kerr, *The Arab Cold War: A Study of Ideology in Politics, 1958–1967* (New York: Oxford University Press, 1967).

● Interesting materials are available free of charge from the following sources: Turkish Information Office, 500 Fifth Avenue, New York, N.Y. 10036; Arab Information Center, 757 Third Avenue, New York, N. Y. 10017; Government of Israel Office of Information, 11 East 70th Street, New York, N.Y. 10021; and Arabian-American Oil Company, 505 Park Avenue, New York, N.Y. 10022.

GLOBAL IV
HISTORY TODAY
AND
TOMORROW

OUR WORLD TODAY

Since Adam and Eve ate the apple, man has not refrained from any folly of which he was capable.[1] I think it probable that civilization somehow will last as long as I care to look ahead. ... I think it not improbable that man—like the grub that prepares a chamber for the winged thing it never has seen but is to be—that man may have cosmic destinies that he does not understand. And so beyond the vision of battling races and an impoverished earth I catch a dreaming glimpse of peace.[2]

[1] Bertrand Russell   [2] Justice Oliver Wendell Holmes

FORCES THAT UNITE THE WORLD

We have now completed our study of the various regions of the world. We have examined present-day conditions and institutions in these regions and have traced the development of these conditions and institutions over the centuries. Now the time has come to stand back and examine the world as a whole.* When we take this long look backwards, we see how our present situation has been shaped by the world history we have been studying. Certain forces are at work which tend to unite the globe while others are pulling in the other direction. In this unit we shall describe first those forces working toward global unity, then those producing disunity, and finally we shall study the United Nations, which is trying to reduce the amount of disunity.

TRANSPORTATION FACILITIES

One of the most obvious and spectacular ways in which the world is being united is through transportation. Man today is conquering space at a rate that is almost unbelievable. As a result, our world now has a physical unity that scarcely could have been imagined a century ago. How rapidly this unity is developing can be seen by comparing the circumnavigation of the globe in 1519–1522 by the Magellan expedition with the circumnavigation in 1960 by the American nuclear-powered submarine, the U.S.S. *Triton*.† The Magellan expedition took three years, during which time four of the five ships were lost and Magellan himself was killed. The crews suffered horribly from lack of food and drinking water. The men chewed on leather and hunted after mice, which came to be regarded as delicacies. By contrast, 450 years later the U.S.S. *Triton* covered the 30,000 miles of Magellan's expedition in just two months, from February 24 to April 25, 1960. During the whole of those days the submarine cruised under water, safe from the surface storms that wrecked most of Magellan's ships. Its crew of 183 officers and men enjoyed radio communication, which provided entertainment as well as news of the outside world. Nor did they need to worry about food and drinking water. When the *Triton* neared the end of its voyage, its crew held a party to celebrate the world's first submerged circumnavigation of the globe. According to the captain's log, "the cooks kept the party goers well supplied with a steady flow of pizza, popcorn and punch." [1]

Man has reached much higher speeds by plane than by submarine. Jet planes now reach speeds of over 1000 miles per hour, which means that they can cross the United States from coast to coast in three hours. How different this is from a century ago when a full week was needed to travel only half way across the country. Furthermore, scientists tell us we will soon be travelling by rockets, which will outstrip the jets as much as the jets already have surpassed the railway. Rockets can reach speeds of 10 or even 100 times greater than those of jets. So we soon will be able to circle the globe several times in a single day. Could Magellan's men even have dreamed of this as they wearily sailed their way across the Pacific less than five hundred years ago? All this means that we now live in one world.

---

* See *Readings in World History* (Boston: Allyn and Bacon, Inc., 1970), "Our World Today," p. 717.
† See *Readings in World History,* "The U.S.S. *Triton* and Magellan's Voyage," p. 718. See also the illustrated article by the commander of the *Triton:* Capt. Edward L. Beach, USN, "*Triton* Follows Magellan's Wake," *National Geographic,* Vol. 118, November 1960, pp. 585–615

NASA

COMMUNICATION FACILITIES

The world is being united by rapid and far-reaching developments in communication as well as in transportation. All of us use these new means of communication in our everyday life. We use them when we read a book or a newspaper, when we go to the theater to see a movie, when we pick up the telephone to speak to a friend, when we send a telegram to another city or country, when we turn on the radio to hear a broadcast, or when we sit before a television set to look at pictures transmitted from a station hundreds or thousands of miles away. Thanks to these facilities, it is easier for us today to send a message around the world than it was for George Washington to send information across the Potomac River.

The significance of this revolution in communications is that it is creating a revolution in the minds of men all over the globe. It is making it possible for hundreds of millions of villagers to learn for the first time about the outside world and to think for the first time about new and stirring ideas. The speed of the change taking place can be seen in the fact that in 1860 over 90 per cent of the world's adult population (over 15 years of age) was illiterate, compared to about 45 per cent in 1960. It is not surprising that today illiteracy remains highest in the regions that are economically underdeveloped: about 80–85 per cent in Africa, 60–65 per cent in Asia, 40–45 per cent in Latin America, 7–9 per cent in Europe, and 3–4 per cent in the United States and Canada.

The increasing numbers of literate people are being provided with an ever-increasing supply of books and newspapers. In 1960, for example, about 300 million copies of newspapers were being sold each day

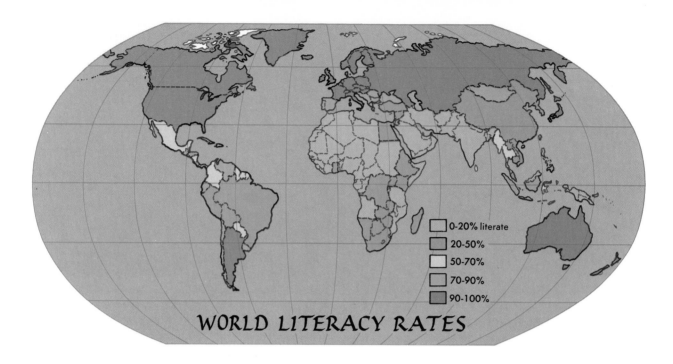

WORLD LITERACY RATES

0-20% literate
20-50%
50-70%
70-90%
90-100%

throughout the world. Also books are continually being translated for use in all parts of the globe. In 1956, alone, the works of William Shakespeare were translated in 25 different countries, of Chekhov in 23 countries, Tolstoy, Balzac, and Dostoevsky each in 22, and Jules Verne and Turgenev each in 20.

For the 45 per cent of the world's adults who cannot read books and newspapers, there are now available television, motion pictures, and, most important, the radio. In 1965 there were about 450 million radio sets in the world, more than the number of newspapers sold each day. Moreover, a radio reaches a much larger number of people; illiterate peasants, for example, can gather in village squares to hear music or news or weather reports from one radio. This is also true of television sets, of which there were a total of 161.5 million in 1965.

All this does not mean that the new means of communication are uniting the world by persuading all people to accept the *same* ideas. Rather it means that a large number of people now have *some* ideas. The exact nature of these ideas depends upon the region concerned. In Africa the ideas are likely to be nationalistic, in the Soviet Union and China communistic, and in Sweden socialistic. But whatever they are, the important point is that the masses of the people have *some* ideas, and *some* notion of what is going on outside their particular village. This is completely different from all past history, when the lot of the masses was not to think but to work and to obey. "It is true," said President Nasser of Egypt recently, "that most of our people are still illiterate. But politically that counts far less than it did twenty years ago. . . . Radio has changed everything. . . . Today people in the most remote villages hear of what is happening everywhere and form their opinions. Leaders cannot govern as they once did. We live in a new world." [2] In other words, this new world is in large part the product of the new means of communication we have been studying.*

ECONOMIC INTERDEPENDENCE

The world is being united not only by new transportation and communications facilities, but also by its increasing economic interdependence. This can be seen especially clearly in the tremendous amount of international trade. We noted earlier that worldwide trade did not begin until the great discoveries of the 15th and 16th centuries brought together all parts of the globe. But the trade which got under way at that time was limited to goods such as spices, tobacco, furs, textiles, sugar, and firearms. Today international trade is altogether different. Many more articles are exchanged, and in much greater quantities. During the past century the volume of international trade has spurted ahead especially rapidly, as is

* See *Readings in World History,* "Revolution in Communications," p. 724.

shown in the figures at the bottom of this page.

The meaning of these figures is that the world has become an economic unit; its parts are more interdependent than ever before in history. International trade is now essential for the economies of almost all countries. If the spice trade had been interrupted in the days of Christopher Columbus, it would have been inconvenient but not disastrous. Housewives would have grumbled, and the group of merchants who bought and sold the spices would have lost money. But the mass of people in Europe and in other regions would not have been vitally affected. Today, however, any interruption of international trade would mean closed factories, millions of unemployed, and, in some cases, outright starvation. The countries that would be hurt most are those that are economically advanced, such as the United States and Great Britain. They are the countries that must have raw materials for their factories from all corners of the globe. The United States is dependent upon

INCREASE IN WORLD TRADE		1950-1967		
	VALUE OF ALL EXPORTS	RR FREIGHT	SHIPPING FREIGHT	AIR FREIGHT
1967	$180,550,000,000	4.4 billion ton kilometers	1890 million metric tons	6.7 billion ton kilometers
1950	$56,500,000,000	2.0 billion ton kilometers	550 million metric tons	1.06 billion ton kilometers (1953)
% Increase	220%	120%	345%	650%

One hundred years ago, the words of a national leader, covered in the press, took weeks to reach all the nation. Today, with radio and television, there is an immediate reaction.

foreign trade, despite the richness of its own natural resources.

We may conclude that the globe has become an economic unit because of its dependence upon the world-wide exchange of raw materials and manufactured goods.* It also has become an economic unit because of the speed with which new inventions and techniques spread throughout the world. In the early days of man these developments spread with unbelievable slowness. Hundreds, and even thousands, of years were needed to pass on from region to region such discoveries as the grinding of stone tools, the growing of plants, or the use of the wheel. Today, by contrast, the invention of a new machine is known at once throughout

* See *Readings in World History,* "World Economic Interdependence," p. 728.

the world. Usually it is available for sale to any country with the money to pay for it and the technicians to operate it. This is why the Industrial Revolution is spreading so quickly to all continents.

COMMON WAYS OF LIFE

The spread of the Industrial Revolution has imposed upon the world not only new methods of production but also new and common ways of living. This stamp of uniformity is noticeable in the various parts of the United States as well as in the various parts of the world. Not too many years ago, the small town in New England was distinctively different from the small town in California, in the Mid-West, or in the South. Today the differences are being flattened out by the same highways, the same chain stores and drug stores, the same houses and clothes and entertainment. An American journalist has described this growing homogenization as follows:

The approach to every American city seems the same. The road widens and divides, traffic thickens, an intersection light appears—an outdoor movie, motels, a wrecked car dump with its most unbelievably flattened specimens next to the highroad. . . . Then, where through-route cement jolts into municipal maintenance macadam, spreads the new subdivision—cellar excavations going on at one end, baby carriages and ranch houses standing at the other. Then comes a city avenue in violent transition—gas stations, used car lots, down-at-heel mansions, the bankers' home of 80 years ago now the Aleppo Temple, the stately house where the cast-iron deer once stood now labeled "Tourists." Here are the older, maple-tree suburbs, a white church with many-paned windows, the new high school. . . . At the center of town they have cut down the elms to widen Main Street. Here is the row of chains: Woolworth, Sears, A & P; the familiar drugstore; the local hotel (run from Chicago); the corner diner by the depot; the high office buildings; the green square and the war monument.

Here are the inevitable groups of teenagers, all in blue jeans, slouching around the entrance to the drugstore or the movie house, their poses, their gestures stylized like figures from a ballet. Boys and girls in jeans, chewing gum, smoking, hanging around the drugstore in a terrible effort to be casual until one of them gets his first car and it's zoom-zoom-zoom with everybody else.

Across town you reach the river, the factories, the poorer homes, the slums. . . .

You can walk down the streets at night in the new suburban subdivisions and see six families to a block looking at the same picture after supper. How they ever passed the time before TV nobody can guess. Now they have everything, prize fights, religion, Westerns, breathless cash prizes. They have a tidal-wave of advertising, new desires and discounts —above all a feeling of identification, of belonging, and a common denominator of accent, clothes and viewpoint. . . .[3]

A comparable sameness is beginning to appear throughout the world, though at a much slower rate.* And the reasons are roughly the same as those we noted in the United States: the new road which for the first time has brought the village close to the city, the new factory that has brought together workers from the surrounding country-

* See *Readings in World History,* "Becoming More and More Alike," p. 735.

National brand names, chain drug stores, standard parking meters and waste barrels. What distinguishes one city from another?

MAGNUM

side, the new radio bringing the same entertainments and the same political teachings, the new machine-made clothes and knickknacks which the peasants for the first time can afford to buy, the new schoolhouse giving all pupils the same education, and the flood of new ideas pouring in from the radio, the city streets, the schoolroom, and the factory. What does all this mean in terms of human beings and their everyday lives? Here are a few examples:

Japan–At Tokyo's famed Nichigeki music hall screaming teenagers storm the stage to tug at Japan's latest rock-and-roll sensation. The putt-putt of tiny tractors echoes from a thousand valleys, shattering the pastoral quiet of centuries from Kanto to Kyushu. Billboards sprout like ugly mushrooms amid the green of rice paddies. . . .

Parking meters are installed. Supermarkets spring up almost overnight. Small shopkeepers contend they are being driven out of business, which indeed many of them are. . . .

Japanese children have developed a taste for Western food through the school lunch programs, which include milk and often meat instead of fish. . . . *(Chicago Daily News,* July 29, 1959)

Pakistan–The women of Pakistan are on the verge of achieving the legal right to choose their husbands and to divorce them. . . .

Under old laws, a woman has virtually no rights. As a girl she may be sold or given away. Once wed, she is the servant of her husband. He may take a second wife or any number of wives.

The proposed code would bar marriage of girls under 16 years old and boys under 18. The presence and consent of both parties would be required. Divorce would be permitted only upon presentation of grounds in court. Furthermore, a husband seeking another wife would have to prove in court his ability to support all his wives and children in the manner to which they had been accustomed. *(New York Times,* March 27, 1960)

Bolivia–The Prado La Paz, a central boulevard (in La Paz, Bolivia) looks almost like the main street of a southwestern United States city when school lets out, except for Indian women in brown bowler hats and babies slung over their backs in colored ponchos. Bolivian girls wear their hair in pony-tails, dress in toreador pants or skirts, bobbysox or saddle shoes. Boys by preference wear blue jeans and black leather jackets. In an Indian market place an Aymara girl tending her mother's stand solemnly chews what turns out with a pink pop to be not the traditional coca leaves but bubble gum. *(New York Times,* March 20, 1959)

Egypt–The government is trying to get Egyptian men out of their flowing robes and into trousers. Within the last few weeks the Central Ministry of Social Affairs has launched a campaign to popularize a loose-fitting blouse and slacks combination that looks like the casual outfits some American men wear for lounging in their backyards. Hussein el-Shaffei, Social Affairs Minister, hopes this costume will eventually replace the gallibiya, a loose cotton robe that falls from the shoulders to the ankles like a nightshirt. *(New York Times,* June 29, 1959)

Indonesia–Jakarta's teen-agers are running so wild even the army has trouble keeping order.

They have picked up every Western fad; from mod clothes to Beatle haircuts, to beat sounds, to drag racing and drug taking, and added a few of their own, including topless and bottomless street cruising.

Every day the papers are filled with reports on adolescent antics.

In one case a traffic police commander told a local newspaper he had witnessed a demonstration of topless fashions when a car filled with young girls wearing "nothing but the lower part of their dress" drove past him on a Jakarta street.

"I thought this was shocking," he said, "I should have been prepared for the next show. Some teen-age girls, this time wearing the top part of their dresses, but not the bottom part, whisked by, drinking liquor." *(New York Times,* August 8, 1967)

A mixture of diverse cultures is becoming more and more a part of cities all over the world. (Below) An African woman shops in Tema, Ghana. (Right) Veiled and westernized women stroll in Algiers.

(LEFT) ALMASY FOR WHO; (RIGHT) MARC RIBOUD FOR MAGNUM

Reviewing the Essentials

Transportation Facilities

1. List the means used by man since ancient times to conquer distance and space. What inventions accelerated this conquest? When and under what circumstances did these inventions and discoveries occur?

2. What, at mid-20th century, is the significance of man's achievements in transportation?

Communication Facilities

3. What discoveries and inventions have brought about a revolution in communication? How is this creating a more united world?

4. What relation is there between the developments in communication and the revolution of rising expectations that is sweeping the underdeveloped areas?

5. Give reasons why nations and people are increasingly interdependent.

6. Why, as nations become better developed economically, are they less self-sufficient? Cite examples for each of the major regional areas of the world.

7. What factors promote increasing cultural uniformity within and among nations?

Forces That Unite the World 695

FORCES THAT DIVIDE THE WORLD

RACE DIFFERENCES

It is true that in some ways the modern world is becoming more unified and homogeneous. More than ever before in history, the world is a neighborhood; most of its people are living and thinking and acting along increasingly similar lines. But there is another side; certain forces are dividing the people of the world and creating dangerous conflicts among them. One of the most serious of these conflicts is that between races. Headlines in the newspapers frequently announce race clashes; not only in South Africa where the racial situation is the worst, but also in countries such as the United States and Great Britain.

It has not always been so. In fact, racial conflict began only in modern times. The ancient Greeks and Romans looked down upon foreigners as "barbarians," but as people who were of an inferior culture rather than of an inferior race. During the medieval period the emphasis was on religion. The Church taught that all who were Christians were the same kind of men. Jews were persecuted and Muslims were fought because they were enemies of the Christian faith and not because they were of a different race than the Christians. Likewise the Muslim world traditionally has been "color-blind." Mohammed insisted on the equality of all believers, whatever their race or color.

Why, then, did race prejudice and conflict begin in modern times? One reason is the world-wide intermixture of races that occurred for the first time following the expansion of Europe. We noted in an earlier unit that before Europe's expansion, the Caucasoid, Mongoloid, and Negroid races were distributed over the world in fairly homogeneous blocks. The Negroids were in Africa, the Mongoloids in Central, North, and East Asia, and in the Americas, and the Caucasoids in Europe, North Africa, the Middle East, and India. But after Europe began her fateful push overseas in the 15th century, the racial map of the world changed radically. As a result there is today a high degree of racial intermixture in the Americas, and a lesser amount in Africa, Central Asia, and Siberia. Where there is such intermixture, there is much more likelihood of conflict than where there is little contact among the races.

A good example of this is the case of England since World War II. Before the war, England had experienced almost no interracial conflict. The English were very proud of their record and tended to feel superior whenever they heard of clashes in the United States. But after the war, a considerable number of black people came to England from the British West Indies. For the first time England had sizeable Negro settlements in certain urban centers. And for the first time England experienced outbreaks of violence between the two races. To the embarrassment of the English, the London district of Notting Hill and the city of Nottingham gained the same unpleasant international reputation as Selma in Alabama and Sharpeville in South Africa.

A second reason for racial trouble in the modern world is to be found in the dominant position that the white man has enjoyed for centuries. We have seen that it was the Europeans who first reached the relatively empty spaces in the Americas, Australia, and Siberia. So they became the masters of much of the best land of the globe. This aroused a good deal of bad feeling, especially when lightly-populated countries such as the United States, Canada, and Australia, passed immigration laws to keep out Chinese, Japanese, Indians, and other Asians or assumed a superior attitude to non-white minorities in their midst.

Martin Luther King in Atlanta, Georgia.

WIDE WORLD

Forces That Divide the World 697

Still another cause for racial difficulty arose from the colonial rule that Europe imposed on most of Africa and large parts of Asia. With the spread of nationalism all over the world, colonial peoples everwhere have arisen against foreign domination. And since the foreign master was a white man, the anticolonial movement sometimes has become a race movement of the non-whites against the whites. This happened particularly because the Europeans had used race arguments to justify their rule. That is, they had maintained that the white man was born superior and therefore was justified in ruling over the non-white. In fact, they maintained that it was to the advantage of the colonial peoples to accept European civilization. This was what the English poet, Rudyard Kipling, had in mind when he wrote about the "white man's burden." Another Englishman wrote:

> To us—to us, and not to others,—a certain definite duty has been assigned. To carry light and civilization into the dark places of the world, to touch the mind of Asia and of Africa with the ethical ideas of Europe; to give to thronging millions, who would otherwise never know peace or security, these first conditions of human advance.[4]

This attitude of white superiority antagonized the indigenous peoples as much as their economic exploitation by the whites.* In fact, one English writer maintains that the superiority attitude was resented more than anything else. "People do not like being exploited but they can put up with it. What they cannot put up with is being considered inferior." [5]

The resentment of the non-white peoples against white superiority claims has been strengthened by findings of science. Only in the past half-century have scientists in various fields gathered reliable data regarding the races of mankind. On the basis of these data, virtually all scientists are agreed that no race is superior in intelligence to any other race. Apparent differences in intelligence exist because of differences in environment or opportunity rather than because of differences in brain power.* One example of this is the experience in New York City when the educational authorities decided to set up a special school for gifted children. Five hundred promising children were selected on the basis of intelligence tests given in elementary schools throughout the city. When these five hundred children were examined as to racial, religious, and national backgrounds, the distribution was approximately the same as that of the population of New York City as a whole. About 10 per cent of the children were black, corresponding to the 10 per cent black population of the city. Likewise the proportion of intelligent children corresponded for Jews and for some national groups. It is because of large amounts of evidence of this sort that the well-known British historian, Arnold Toynbee, has written: "The so-called racial explanation of differences in human performance and achievement is either an ineptitude or a fraud." [6] An American anthropologist made the same point in a famous essay on the "100 per cent American."

> Our solid American citizen awakens in a bed built on a pattern which originated in the Near East but which was modified in Northern Europe before it was transmitted to America. He throws back covers made from cotton, domesticated in India, or linen, domesticated in the Near East, or silk, the use of which was discovered in China. All of these materials have been spun and woven by processes invented in the Near East. He slips into his moccasins, invented by the Indians of the

---

* See *Readings in World History,* "The Word 'Native'," p. 745.

* See *Readings in World History,* "Race and Intelligence," p. 741.

Eastern woodlands, and goes to the bathroom, whose fixtures are a mixture of European and American inventions, both of recent date. He takes off his pajamas, a garment invented in India, and washes with soap invented by the ancient Gauls. He then shaves, a masochistic rite which seems to have been derived from either Sumer or ancient Egypt.

Returning to the bedroom, he removes his clothes from a chair of Southern European type and proceeds to dress. He puts on garments whose form originally derived from the skin clothing of the nomads of the Asiatic steppes, puts on shoes made from skins tanned by a process invented in ancient Egypt and cut to a pattern derived from the classical civilizations of the Mediterranean, and ties around his neck a strip of bright-colored cloth which is a vestigial survival of the shoulder shawls worn by the seventeenth century Croatians. Before going out for breakfast he glances through the window, made of glass invented in Egypt, and if it is raining, puts on overshoes made of rubber discovered by the Central American Indians and takes an umbrella, invented in southeastern Asia. Upon his head he puts a hat made of felt, a material invented in the Asiatic steppes.

On his way to breakfast he stops to buy a paper, paying for it with coins, an ancient Lydian invention. At the restaurant a whole new series of borrowed elements confronts him. His plate is made of a form of pottery invented in China. His knife is of steel, an alloy first made in southern India, his fork a medieval Italian invention, and his spoon a derivative of a Roman original. He begins breakfast with an orange, from the eastern Mediterranean, a cantaloupe from Persia, or perhaps a piece of African watermelon. With this he has coffee, an Abyssinian plant, with cream and sugar. Both the domestication of cows and the idea of milking them originated in the Near East, while sugar was first made in India. After his fruit and first coffee he goes on to waffles, cakes made by a Scandinavian technique from wheat domesticated in Asia Minor. Over these he pours maple syrup, invented by the Indians of the Eastern woodlands. As a side dish he may have the eggs of a species of bird domesticated in Indo-China, or thin strips of the flesh of an animal domesticated in Eastern Asia which have been salted and smoked by a process developed in northern Europe.

When our friend has finished eating, he settles back to smoke, an American Indian habit, consuming a plant domesticated in Brazil in either a pipe, derived from the Indians of Virginia, or a cigarette, derived from Mexico. If he is hardy enough he may even attempt a cigar, transmitted to us from the Antilles by way of Spain. While smoking he reads the news of the day, imprinted in characters invented in Germany. As he absorbs the accounts of foreign troubles he will, if he is a good conservative citizen, thank a Hebrew deity in an Indo-European language that he is 100 per cent American.[7]

Although resentment and racial conflict are widespread, they are not found everywhere. In Brazil, for example, there is much racial intermixture and harmony. From the outset, the Portuguese settlers intermarried with the native Indians and the imported Negro slaves. This attitude persists to the present, with the firm support of the Roman Catholic Church. In Hawaii, racial intermixture has gone even further. The chief strains are the native Hawaiians and the Caucasoid, Chinese, Japanese, Filipino, and Korean immigrants. Present marriage trends indicate that individuals of mixed blood will be in the majority by the end of the century. In both Brazil and Hawaii there are no political or economic restriction on the grounds of race.

In South Africa, on the other hand, racial conflict is most acute and is becoming steadily worse. The British and Afrikaners, the descendants of the original Dutch settlers, have passed legislation designed to keep the large Negro majority in a permanently inferior position. These apartheid decrees discriminate against the Negro in virtually every field: schools, jobs, housing, politics, and civil rights. (See the unit on Africa)

In the United States, also, racial conflict has been worsening in recent years. The legal position of black Americans has been improving with specific legislation such as the Civil Rights Act of 1964, the Voting Rights Act of 1965, and a number of Supreme Court decisions against various types of racial discrimination. But the economic position of the blacks has not also improved; for some it has declined, which explains in large part the current unrest and riots

The root trouble is that black people have not benefited from the advances of technology; rather they have been the victims of that technology. First there were the labor-saving innovations in Southern agriculture which cut its labor force between 1940 and 1960 from 4.2 to 1.7 million persons. The Negro sharecroppers, who had worked on the southern farms, found themselves "surplus," so they flocked to the northern cities, attracted by wartime jobs and by fair employment practices legislation. (Whereas 77 per cent of black Americans lived in the South in 1940, by 1967 it was only 55 per cent.) When they reached the cities, black people, lacking education and vocational training, took unskilled or semi-skilled jobs. But these are the jobs now being eliminated by automation. Thus, the American blacks are now once again finding themselves "surplus."

In 1968 the Commerce Department reported that 41 per cent of all Negroes lived in poverty compared to 12 per cent of all whites. Also infant mortality amongst Negroes is twice as high as amongst whites, and maternal deaths four times higher. These were the conditions that led to the devastating riots in the 1960's in Harlem, Rochester, Watts, Hough, Newark, and Detroit. In these and other cities, entire neighborhoods were burned, looted, and left as though bombed in wartime. These riots in turn led to a reaction amongst whites who clamored for "law and order" and armed themselves with private weapons.

Battles with police in Selma, Alabama (p. 696), black men being jailed for leading marches (p. 697), "Resurrection City," Watts, and endless other triumphs and tragedies mark attempts to improve conditions for America's black people. Deprived of equal opportunity, many families must live in small, rat-infested, overpriced apartments. Rebellion and violence can only be the result until the American people seriously reconsider their values.

WIDE WORLD

The seriousness of the race problem facing the United States was emphasised in these findings of the National Advisory Commission on Civil Disorders appointed by President Johnson.

This is our basic conclusion: Our nation is moving toward two societies, one black, one white—separate and unequal.

Reaction to last summer's disorders has quickened the movement and deepened the division. Discrimination and segregation have long permeated much of American life; they now threaten the future of every American.

This deepening racial division is not inevitable. The movement apart can be reversed. Choice is still possible. Our principal task is to define that choice and to press for a national resolution.

To pursue our present course will involve the continuing polarization of the American community and, ultimately, the destruction of basic democratic values.

The alternative is not blind repression or capitulation to lawlessness. It is the realization of common opportunities for all within a single society.

This alternative will require a commitment to national action—compassionate, massive,

WIDE WORLD

and sustained, backed by the resources of the most powerful and the richest nation on the Earth. From every American it will require new attitudes, new understanding, and above all, new will.

In February of 1969, a follow-up report was published by the Urban Coalition and Urban America entitled *One Year Later.* In a study of actual progress made since the Commission's report, it was found that, except in a few major cities, no real effort had been made to end racial inequality and promote equal opportunities for black citizens, nor had resources been made available for low-income areas. In essence:

> Progress in dealing with the conditions of slum-ghetto life has been nowhere near in scale with the problems.... A year later, we are a year closer to being two societies, black and white, increasingly separate and scarcely less equal.

Not yet have American citizens aquired the understanding or the desire to make their country a true democracy.*

Prior to World War II, racial troubles were regarded as purely the business of the country involved, but today this is no longer the case. An outbreak in Little Rock or Johannesburg or Notting Hill at once attracts world-wide attention.† News of discrimination or violence arouses passionate feelings among not only Negroes but all non-white peoples. And these non-white peoples, representing two-thirds of mankind, are now extremely sensitive and militant because of the world-wide anticolonialism. A well-informed English writer has pointed out the dangers of this situation for the white man who has hitherto been in the saddle.

* See *Readings in World History,* "Is Prejudice in the U.S. Declining?", p. 742.
† See *Readings in World History,* "Race Conflict Divides the World," p. 738.

At present, most Westerners think of the race problem as being primarily one of whether men and women of African stock—in Africa or the United States—can achieve full equality of status. But this definition is probably already outdated. The question is no longer whether Africans can achieve equality. It is becoming the wider query whether men and women of white color shall lose it. There is no certainty that mankind will, after three hundred years of white dominance, move safely to race equality.[8]

CULTURAL DIFFERENCES

The world today is divided not only by differences in race but also by differences in culture. The term "culture," as used here, does not refer merely to the arts, such as painting, sculpture, or poetry. Rather it refers to a people's total way of life, to the way in which they think and believe and act.

During the long course of human history many thousands of different cultures have been developed. A large number of these have survived to the present day. If we were to take a trip around the world, we would see signs of these different cultures on all sides, in the variety of ways in which people eat, clothe their bodies, bring up their children, worship God, dance and sing and work and play. We noted above that some of these cultural differences are disappearing today because of the spread of industrialization and the improved means of transportation and communication. Nevertheless cultural variations still remain, and some of these are important enough to produce misunderstandings and even conflicts between nations and within nations.

Language. One of the most obvious of these cultural differences can be seen in the numerous languages of mankind. Linguists say that there are approximately three thousand languages spoken in the world today,

Cultures usually become modified by constant interaction. While these children of the Ivory Coast will continue to honor their individual cultural backgrounds, they will also experience a shared culture because of their common education.

and they don't pretend that they have finished counting yet. Some are spoken by hundreds of millions of people while others are used by tribal goups of only a few thousand or even a few hundred. The "Language Map of the Modern World" indicates the eight major language families. The geographic spread of a language family does not necessarily reflect the number of people who use it. For example, more people speak Sino-Tibetan than the Semitic-Hamitic languages.*

The existence of numerous languages did not cause much trouble in the early history of man because the various peoples had little contact with each other. Today, however, there is a serious problem because all peoples have become neighbors and frequently must communicate with each other. It is true that this constant communication has led to a good deal of borrowing between languages. For example, the French use English words such as "sandwich," "film," and "baby"; the Italians speak of "nylon," "football,"

* See *Readings in World History,* "Man Talks in 3000 Tongues," p. 747.

and "cold cream"; the Japanese say "busa" and "matchi," for "bus" and "match"; while Latin Americans drink "cocktails" and "ginger ale." In return, English-speaking peoples have taken "ski," "geyser," and "slalom" from the Scandinavian tongues; "Soviet" and "Sputnik" from Russian; "pizza" and "influenza" from Italian; "fooey" and "kibitzer" from Yiddish; "kowtow" and "typhoon" from Chinese; and "yogi" and "khaki" from Hindi.

Despite this borrowing of certain words, the numerous languages of the world remain quite different from each other. This creates serious trouble when peoples from various countries must communicate with one another. When the United Nations meets, for example, several interpreters must be present to repeat the words of each speaker in the five official UN languages: Chinese, English, French, Russian, and Spanish. Similar difficulties are encountered when a businessman wishes to trade with another country, when a scientist wants to learn of an experiment conducted in another part of the world, or when a tourist travels.

Forces That Divide the World 703

LANGUAGES AND LANGUAGE CONFLICTS

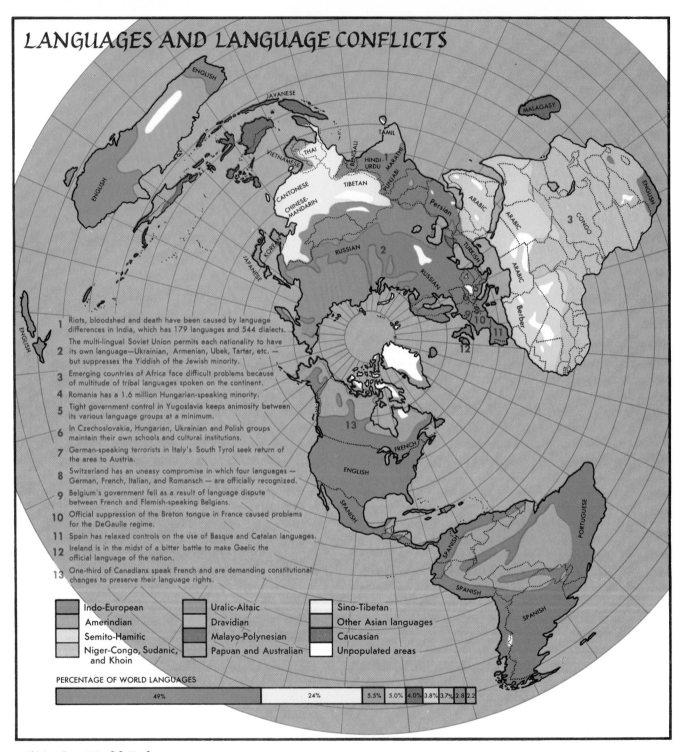

1 Riots, bloodshed and death have been caused by language differences in India, which has 179 languages and 544 dialects.

2 The multi-lingual Soviet Union permits each nationality to have its own language—Ukrainian, Armenian, Ubek, Tartar, etc. — but suppresses the Yiddish of the Jewish minority.

3 Emerging countries of Africa face difficult problems because of multitude of tribal languages spoken on the continent.

4 Romania has a 1.6 million Hungarian-speaking minority.

5 Tight government control in Yugoslavia keeps animosity between its various language groups at a minimum.

6 In Czechoslovakia, Hungarian, Ukrainian and Polish groups maintain their own schools and cultural institutions.

7 German-speaking terrorists in Italy's South Tyrol seek return of the area to Austria.

8 Switzerland has an uneasy compromise in which four languages — German, French, Italian, and Romansch — are officially recognized.

9 Belgium's government fell as a result of language dispute between French and Flemish-speaking Belgians.

10 Official suppression of the Breton tongue in France caused problems for the DeGaulle regime.

11 Spain has relaxed controls on the use of Basque and Catalan languages.

12 Ireland is in the midst of a bitter battle to make Gaelic the official language of the nation.

13 One-third of Canadians speak French and are demanding constitutional changes to preserve their language rights.

Legend:
- Indo-European
- Amerindian
- Semito-Hamitic
- Niger-Congo, Sudanic, and Khoin
- Uralic-Altaic
- Dravidian
- Malayo-Polynesian
- Papuan and Australian
- Sino-Tibetan
- Other Asian languages
- Caucasian
- Unpopulated areas

PERCENTAGE OF WORLD LANGUAGES

49%	24%	5.5%	5.0%	4.0%	3.8%	3.7%	2.8	2.2

Various suggestions have been made for the solution of this language problem. Some propose that we should all learn one of the languages already widely spoken in many parts of the world. But it is impossible to agree on what this common language should be. Certain languages, such as Spanish, French, and English, already have wide usage, but none of them could be accepted universally. Another proposal is that we should all learn one of the so-called artificial languages such as Esperanto or Interlingua, but these are combinations of Western tongues and probably would not be accepted by non-Western peoples. Despite much talk of an international language and the reported approval of most people in the world, governments so far have shown little interest in carrying out the extensive educational program required to put it into operation.

Finally we should note that the multiplicity of languages has created various problems within nations as well as between nations. A good example of this is the case of India; its nearly 500 million people speak 845 different languages and dialects. This has seriously held back the unification and the progress of the country. Some of the delegates to the Indian parliament speak only their provincial languages which are understood by a minority. One representative of a small northern tribe could understand no one but himself. Furthermore the people are fiercely loyal to their respective languages, so that the central government has had to redraw the boundaries of the various states along linguistic lines. India is an extreme example of the problem of language diversity within a country. Other countries, however, also face this problem, such as Ceylon with the Sinhalese and Tamil languages, Canada with French and English, Malaysia with Malayan, Chinese, and Tamil, and the Soviet Union with 125 languages and dialects.

Religions. The modern world is divided by religions as well as by languages. The map of the "Religious Population of the World" shows that Christianity has the largest number of members, followed by the

RELIGIONS OF THE WORLD

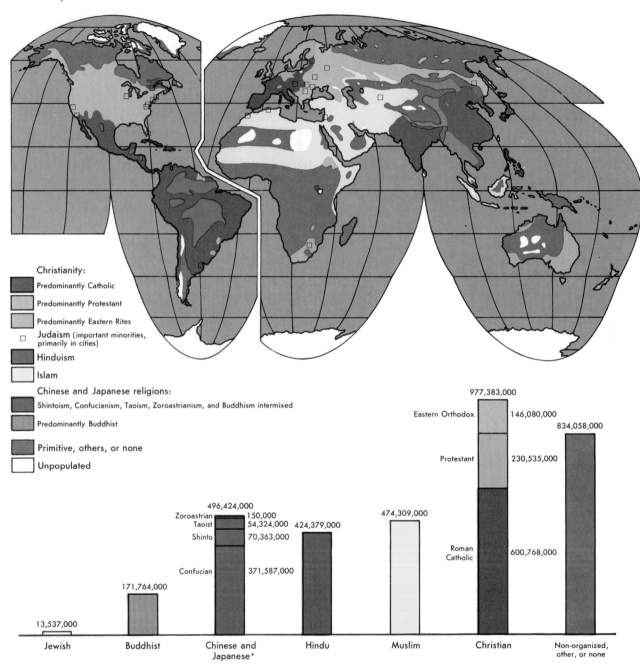

Christianity:

- Predominantly Catholic
- Predominantly Protestant
- Predominantly Eastern Rites
- □ Judaism (important minorities, primarily in cities)
- Hinduism
- Islam

Chinese and Japanese religions:

- Shintoism, Confucianism, Taoism, Zoroastrianism, and Buddhism intermixed
- Predominantly Buddhist

- Primitive, others, or none
- Unpopulated

Jewish — 13,537,000

Buddhist — 171,764,000

Chinese and Japanese* — 496,424,000
- Zoroastrian — 150,000
- Taoist — 54,324,000
- Shinto — 70,363,000
- Confucian — 371,587,000

Hindu — 424,379,000

Muslim — 474,309,000

Christian — 977,383,000
- Eastern Orthodox — 146,080,000
- Protestant — 230,535,000
- Roman Catholic — 600,768,000

Non-organized, other, or none — 834,058,000

*Usually intermingled or superimposed

706 *Our World Today*

intermixed group of Far Eastern religions, Buddhism, Confucianism, Taoism, and Shintoism. Then follow the Hinduism of India and the Islam of the Middle East and Africa. However, the statistics given in the map are only rough approximations. Aside from Christianity, few religions attempt to keep statistical records. Even the Protestants and Catholics employ different methods of counting members. All persons of whatever age who have received baptism in the Catholic Church are counted as members; in most Protestant Churches only those who "join" the church are numbered. Statistics are further complicated by the fact that many Japanese are both Buddhists and Shintoists. Likewise many Chinese are at the same time Confucians, Taoists, and Buddhists. Finally there is the unanswerable question of how successful the Communist governments of China, Russia, and other countries have been in persuading their citizens to reject all religions.

The great diversity in religious beliefs has affected world history profoundly in the past, and it still does so today. Most of us may assume that the way a man worships God is his own business. But this is a modern idea that has won wide support only in the past century or two. Most of human history has been darkened by bloody persecution of one religious group by another, or even of one sect by another within the same religion. In the medieval period, for example, Muslims fought against Christians during the Wars of Religion through the 16th century, Christian Catholics fought against Christian Protestants. Likewise the Sunnite and Shiite sects of Islam have frequently fought savagely against each other.

This religious intolerance unfortunately has persisted to the present day in certain parts of the world. One of the most shocking recent examples was the cold-blooded murder of almost six million Jews in Europe by

In Cambridge, Massachusetts, members of a Krishna Consciousness group chant Hindu lyrics. The religions of the East have offered an answer to many people of the West.

Hitler during World War II.* Another was the bloody fighting between Muslims and Hindus when the British left India in 1947. Between one and two million people were killed in the violence, and probably twice as many died from hunger and disease during

* See *Readings in World History,* "Religion and Scapegoats," p. 749.

Forces That Divide the World 707

the conflict. A total of 12 million people found it necessary to abandon their homes and to seek safety with their coreligionists in Hindu India or Muslim Pakistan. And today, the Arab-Israeli conflict is based partially in animosity between the Muslims and the Jews.

Finally we might remind ourselves that unfortunately religious bigotry is by no means dead within our own country.

Examples:

Religious discrimination in some fraternities and sororities

Existence of "restricted" neighborhoods, hotels, and country clubs

Periodic desecration and bombing of synagogues

Anti-Catholic propaganda during the campaigns of the presidential candidates Alfred Smith (1928) and John Kennedy (1960)

Other differences. Language and religion are by no means the only areas of division in the modern world. Numerous other cultural differences are at work, though they are perhaps not so important as the two already mentioned. One is the very different sense of time in various parts of the world. Because nonindustrial societies have no need for the time clock, punctuality means little to them. Villagers in such societies rarely own a clock or know the names of the days of the week or of the calendar months. Consequently it is futile to try to arrange for a precise meeting time or for a deadline by which a certain job must be finished. Such hard-and-fast time schedules seem unreasonable and unjustifiable to the people of many societies.

Another cultural difference is to be found in the relations between the sexes. We con-

Muslim refugees from India crowd into slum villages in Karachi, Pakistan. With no money for relocation, many are destined to spend years in squalor and misery.

ALAN BAND

sider it perfectly natural and proper for a boy and a girl to have dates and to walk hand in hand down a street. But in most Muslim countries this is regarded as scandalous and forbidden behavior. Conversely, we feel that it is degrading to require women to wear a thick veil whenever they are outdoors, but many Muslims still consider this to be simply proper and essential modesty.

A final example of cultural difference is in the matter of food habits. If we look around we soon see that one man's meat is another man's taboo. Hundreds of millions of people in East Asia and Southeast Asia regard milk and milk products as repulsive and unfit for human consumption. Likewise Muslims will not touch pork. Hindus will not eat beef, and we just as firmly turn down puppy steaks, ant larvae, insect grubs, and locusts, all of which are nutritious and are considered delicacies in other parts of the world.

It is true that differences in food habits or in time sense are not likely to start a world war. Yet is is important to bear in mind that these differences do exist, even in a world being united by the radio and the jet plane. And we should also remember the advice of anthropologists: that if "they" don't do it our way, "they" are not therefore queer or wrong. After all, if "they" don't do it our way, then we are not doing it their way either.*

ECONOMIC DIFFERENCES

We noted above that, with the tremendous increase in international trade, the world is fast becoming an economic unit. No country is completely self-sufficient. Each one is dependent upon the others for foodstuffs, for raw materials, for manufactured goods, and for innumerable technical services. Yet at the same time that the world is becoming economically united, it is also remaining

* See *Readings in World History,* "They Don't Do it Our Way," p. 752.

economically divided. Indeed, one can say that there exists today not one economic world but three. These three are the Western industrial world, the Communist world, and the non-industrial world. The Western world has approximately a billion people, the Communist world about a billion, and the non-industrial three-quarters billion.

Communist system. The Communist world is the easiest to define. It consists of the countries whose economies are run according to plans prepared at the top and carried out from the top. We noted in the unit on the Soviet Union that the economic system of that country had, in the past, paid little attention to the wishes of individual citizens. The emphasis was on rapid economic growth, so a large proportion of national income was plowed back into industry rather than being made available to consumers. That is, there was more interest in building steel mills and tractor plants than in turning out bicycles and radios. This disregard of consumer demand made possible the rapidly growing economic strength of the Soviet Union prior to the 1960's. It explains why the Soviet economy could grow at a faster rate than that of the United States. It is significant that, as the Soviet economy has shifted more to consumer goods, its rate of growth has slowed.

Western system. The economy of the Western world differs from that of the Communist world in two important respects. In the first place, it is based much more firmly on private initiative and desires than on governmental plans and controls. In the second place, it is more highly industrialized and has higher living standards. The Western countries have a long head start in industrialization since they were the pioneers of the Industrial Revolution. So at present they enjoy much higher personal incomes, even though their rate of economic growth is generally lower than that of the Communist countries. The average per capita income of the United States is more than three times higher than that of the Soviet Union, the income in Canada is more than twice as high, and in Great Britain more than 50 per cent higher.

Non-industrial countries. Turning finally to the non-industrial countries, we see on the map, "The World Today" (page 716), that they are almost all located south of the 30th parallel of north latitude. These countries are often called underdeveloped because they do not make full and efficient use of their human and natural resources. As a result they all have low living standards. How low these standards are can be seen in the fact that the average *annual* income in the underdeveloped world is less than $100 per person.

Strong efforts have been made since World War II to raise this unbelievably low level of existence. Some of the non-industrial countries have succeeded in increasing their productivity, but unfortunately this gain has usually been wiped out by increases in population. If a country succeeds in raising its food production by 10 per cent but at the same time has 10 per cent more mouths to feed, then obviously the living standard remains at the same level. This is why the unprecedented increase in the world's population that is now taking place is one of the most serious problems which has ever faced mankind.

The rapid increase of people. The growth of population has become so rapid that it is often referred to as the "population explosion." In 1966 the number of people in the world was increasing at the rate of nearly 60 million each year. In other words, the addition each year is greater than the total population of West Germany. Or, to put it another way, the number of people on this globe is increasing by about 6800 persons an hour or 113 a minute.

This population explosion is of very recent origin. During most of his history, man has increased in numbers *extremely* slowly. During the hundreds of thousands of years when he was a food gatherer, he could not multiply rapidly because he simply could not find enough food. So there were only about 10 million human beings on this planet when man learned to grow food about 8000 B.C. Then his numbers rapidly increased because agriculture will fill many more mouths than hunting and fishing. By the time Christ was walking the Palestinian hills, mankind totalled about 250 million. It took about 16 centuries for that figure to reach 475 million in 1650.

From then on the population of the world has risen at an ever-accelerating rate. One reason was the coming of the Agricultural and Industrial Revolutions, which increased productivity and made it possible to feed many more mouths than before. Another reason was the progress in medicine, which reduced deaths from various diseases and epidemics. In fact, the present population explosion is due not to an increase in the birth rate but to a decrease in the death rate. These factors explain the jump in the world's population from 475 million in 1650 to one billion in 1850, two billion in 1925, three billion in 1960, and an estimated four billion by 1980 and five billion in 1990. This unprecedented population growth presents serious problems to all peoples, but particularly to those of the underdeveloped countries.

Two important points about the population explosion should be noted. The first is the tremendous difference in the per capita income of the various continents. North America in 1950, with about 16 per cent of the earth's land surface, contained less than 9 per cent of the world's population but over

43 per cent of the world's total income. Asia, in contrast, with almost twice as much of the world's land surface (29 per cent), had 55 per cent of the world's population but only 12 per cent of the world's income. Consequently, per capita income in North America was 22 times greater than that in Asia and the difference has increased rather than decreased.

The second point is that, generally speaking, the continents with the lower incomes have, and will continue to have, rising birth rates, while the continents with higher incomes have, and will continue to have, falling birth rates. This is a serious matter because a continent with an annual per capita income of $2100 can easily support an increased population, whereas one with an income of $50 can scarcely do so. In other words the flood of babies is coming, and will continue to come, to precisely those people who can least support them.

Running fast to stand still. This means that the people of the underdeveloped world are like squirrels on a treadmill. They must work harder and harder merely to hold their own and to stay where they are. For example, Asia, in order to maintain her present level of living, must increase her aggregate product by 60 per cent between 1950 and 1975, and then by an additional 75 per cent between 1975 and 2000. The tragedy is that the existing living standard is so low that, even if these substantial increases in productivity are reached, it would still mean semistarvation and misery for the great majority of the people.*

It is difficult for us in the Western world to understand what it means when we read statistics such as $50 per capita annual income in Asia or $75 in Africa. Precisely what do such figures represent in terms of human lives?

* See *Readings in World History*, "Developed and Underdeveloped Lands," p. 755.

They represent:

–half the children of the world who go to bed hungry every night.

–hundreds of thousands of families in Bombay who have no home other than the city streets.

–a life expectancy of less than 45 years for people in India, compared to about 70 years in the United States.

–Bolivian tin-miners who chew coca leaves to still their hunger pangs, though they are a narcotic to which they become addicted.

–The Thai farmer who, for three years, had been unable to work because his hands were infected by yaws, which could be cured by a single shot of penicillin.

–the headman in the Dahomey coastal village who, asked how many children died from malaria, replied, "We don't count them; we just bury them."

What solution? With so many people living in such misery, and with their numbers increasing so rapidly, is there any hope for the future? Experts are by no means agreed on this question.* Many are very doubtful that productivity can be increased quickly enough to keep up with the rising populations and also to raise living standards appreciably. Furthermore they feel that even if billions more people could be kept alive, the planet would become so crowded that man would be forced into an unpleasant beehive existence. Even in a rich and relatively underpopulated country such as the United States, the population rise has created serious problems such as crowded schools, traffic jams, congested cities, and a vanishing green countryside. Accordingly many prominent organizations and individuals have advocated birth control to balance man's new

* See *Readings in World History*, "Man and Food: Can They be Balanced?", p. 9.

death control. This group includes scientists such as Sir Julian Huxley and Sir Charles Darwin (grandson of the famous Darwin), and organizations such as the World Council of Churches, which includes most of the world's major Protestant and Orthodox denominations.

On the other hand, some experts believe that productivity can be raised to meet the needs of future billions. This can be done by bringing under cultivation unused land that is tillable, and by increasing the yield of the land already in use. These experts point to the following as examples of what might be done:

–approximately 30 per cent of the United States is cultivated; the percentage could be raised to 45.

–only 40 per cent of the arable land of the Philippines is tilled; if it were all tilled efficiently, the islands could support six times their present population.

–only 15,000 of an estimated 41,000,000 acres of tillable land in Alaska are now worked.

–an additional one billion acres could be brought under cultivation in the tropical lands of the globe.

–productivity of land now in use throughout the world could be increased an average of at least 25 per cent if the most efficient methods *now known* were employed. This does not take into account important advances in agricultural techniques which continue to be made each year.

In view of the above, a British authority has concluded that, "the area of the world at present cultivated could support, if fully farmed by known best methods, at least three billion people on an adequate nutritional standard. If the lands at present unused or inadequately used could be brought into production on the same basis, potential world population could climb to over the ten billion mark." [9] The Catholic Church, which opposes birth control by artificial means or devices, emphasizes the possibilities of production potential. On November 25, 1959 the Roman Catholic bishops of the United States issued a statement in which they maintained that, "alarmists do not place in proper focus the idea of increasing the acreage yield to meet the food demands of an increasing population. . . . It seems never to dawn on them that in a chronic condition where we have more people than food, the logical answer would be, not to decrease the number of people but to increase the food supply which is almost unlimited in potential." [10] Pope Paul VI has reiterated these sentiments in an encyclical issued July 29, 1969, at which time he again stated the Churches position against birth control as the answer to the population explosion.

Reasons for optimism. So far as the people of the underdeveloped countries are concerned, they do not feel that their future is hopeless. On the contrary, they feel just the opposite. For the first time they look forward to the future. For the first time they feel that an improvement of their condition is a real possibility.

Why this optimism in the face of so much misery? The answer is that in the past man had little control over his environment. He had no choice but to accept a life of ceaseless toil, hunger, disease, and early death. But in the past few centuries he has broken these age-old bonds with his dramatic discoveries in science and technology. The industrially advanced countries have demonstrated this by the consistently decreasing poverty in their midst, brought about by establishing welfare programs which care for their citizens "from the cradle to the grave." The good news of the improved status of ordinary

COMPARATIVE STATISTICS FOR SELECTED COUNTRIES

	USA	USSR	CHINA	INDIA	BRAZIL	DEM. REP. OF CONGO	UAR (Egypt)
Land Area in Square Miles	3,615,211	8,649,489	3,691,502	1,261,813	3,286,473	905,563	386,100
Cultivable Land in Square Miles	723,042	1,375,000	781,251	630,906	179,200	52,075	18,025
Cultivable Land as % of Total Area	20%	16%	21%	50%	6%	6%	5%
Population	200,002,200	234,396,000	750,000,000	511,115,000	85,655,000	16,664,000	30,083,000
Population Density (people per sq. mile)	54.7	27.1	211.3	395.5	26.1	18.4	77.8**
Acres of Cultivable Land Per Person	2.35	2.40	.64	.83	.70	2.00	.40
Rate of Literacy	97.6%	98.5%	not available	25%	50%	17.4%	35%
Average Per Capita Income (in U. S. Dollars)	$3760	$1450.*	$85	$79	$273	$96	$144
Railway Mileage	241,645	80,815	19,500	35,970	20,806	3,225	3,265
Chief Exports	Machinery, Manufactured Goods, Food, Chemicals	Machinery Iron and Steel Crude Oil	Textiles, Metals and Ores, Meat, Rice, Tea	Jute, Tea, Manufactured Goods	Coffee, Iron Ore, Cotton	Copper, Palm Oil, Coffee, Rubber	Cotton, Rice

*Actual income would be higher as the Soviet government provides services which in other countries must come from individual income.

**Actual population density is closer to 2370 because all must crowd into the irrigated areas.

people has reached the peasants of Asia, Africa, and Latin America. It has given them hope to know that it is now possible for human beings to live a truly human life, freed from the endless struggle just to survive. This hope has led to what is called "the revolution of rising expectations." The great question of the future is whether these expectations will be fulfilled.*

Why should the United States be concerned whether or not these expectations of

* See *Readings in World History*, "Revolution of Rising Expectations," p. 759.

the people in the underdeveloped countries are met? One reason is that these countries are essential for our economic health because they provide markets for our manufactured goods, and they supply raw materials for our industries. We noted earlier how dependent we are upon them for such things as bauxite, rubber, tin, manganese ore, chromite, cobalt, and industrial diamonds.

As important as this economic reason is a political one, namely, the competition between the Communist and Western worlds for the friendship of the underdeveloped countries. This does not mean that if the United States gives aid to a certain country, it automatically gets a friend or an ally. Nor does it mean that aid should be given only with political strings attached. Experience has shown that this type of aid is likely to make enemies rather than friends.

But it does mean that a country with a healthy economy, and with the mass of its citizens reasonably well cared for, is not likely to turn to communism and against the Western world.

DIPLOMATIC DIFFERENCES

The map entitled "The World Today" on pages 616–617 shows that the globe is divided into three blocs in diplomacy as well as in economics. What factors explain this line-up of the powers of the world into three camps? Why do some of the powers find themselves in the Western camp, others in the Communist camp, and still others remain outside both camps as uncommitted countries?

One important factor is geographic location. Little Finland, located next to the Soviet giant, could not join the Western bloc even if it so wished. Likewise the small but strategic Panama Republic could not join the Communist bloc if it so desired.

Another important factor is economic ties. Canada and the United States, for example, are very closely connected economically. Canada exports raw materials to the United States; in return the United States provides manufactured goods and also has invested billions of dollars in Canadian enterprises. These close economic relations make it almost inevitable that Canada should be allied with the United States rather than with the Soviet Union.

Still another factor is ideology, or form of government. It is only natural that one Communist government should line up with another, rather than with a democracy. On the other hand this is not inevitable. The Communist government of Yugoslavia, for example, joined the Communist bloc at the beginning, but later dropped out because the Soviet Union wanted to be a master rather than an ally. So Yugoslavia today is an uncommitted country, even though it has a Communist government and economy.

A final factor explaining today's diplomatic blocs is historical background. The United States and Canada, for example, have a long tradition of friendly relations. Both countries are very proud of their mutual four thousand miles of unfortified frontier. With this historical background, it would be surprising and unnatural if Canada and the United States were not on the same side of the diplomatic fence. In other parts of the world the tradition is precisely the opposite. This is especially true of former colonies, where there are memories of domination and exploitation by European powers. This is why former colonies in Africa and South Asia are almost all in the uncommitted bloc.

These various factors explain why the world today is divided into three diplomatic groups. We noted in Unit Four that these blocs developed because of the outbreak of the Cold War following World War II. The leader of the Western bloc is the United States, who took the initiative in negotiating a number of regional treaties that hold together the members of the bloc:

–in Southeast Asia—Southeast Asia Treaty Organization (SEATO)

–in the Middle East—Central Treaty Organization (CENTO)

–in Europe—North Atlantic Treaty Organization (NATO)

–in the Americas—Rio Treaty, which set up what became the Organization of American States (OAS) (See map, pages 616–617, for the member nations).

At the same time that the Western bloc was being organized, the Soviet Union was forming its own bloc. By the Warsaw Treaty of 1955, several states in Eastern Europe formed a mutual protection agreement. Also the Soviet Union signed with China a treaty of friendship and of mutual aid in case of war.

Neither the Western nor the Communist blocs are one hundred per cent solid. Both have weak spots which continually need patching. For example, the Central Treaty Organization included the Arab country Iraq until 1958. In fact, this regional bloc was named the Baghdad Pact after the capital of Iraq. But in the summer of 1957 a revolution occurred in Iraq; the new government dropped out of the Baghdad Pact, which was then reorganized as the Central Treaty Organization. There is always the possibility of political revolutions of this sort, which lead to changes in diplomatic ties. This is especially true of countries where the governments face a good deal of opposition at home, and are not too firmly in the saddle. A number of such countries are to be found in the SEATO, CENTO, and Rio groups. It is quite possible, therefore, that some countries which were members of these Western blocs in 1965 will not be members in future years.

For example, the Rio Treaty in the Americas has been disturbed by Castro's Cuba, to the point of bringing the world to the brink of war in 1962, as noted earlier in Unit Four. Even though this crisis was settled peacefully, Cuba remains a danger point in the New World. The Organization of American States (OAS) voted on July 26, 1964 to end diplomatic relations with Cuba and to cut all trade relations excepting food and medicines. This resolution was supported by all OAS members except Bolivia, Chile, Uruguay, and Mexico. Even the Western Hemisphere treaty system is not truly solid.

The Communist bloc has at least as many weak spots as the Western. As early as 1948 a dispute developed between Communist Yugoslavia and the Soviet Union because Yugoslavia refused to take orders from Moscow. After a long and bitter battle of words, the Yugoslavs crossed over to the ranks of the uncommitted nations, where they remain to the present day. Equally serious were domestic revolts in 1956 against the Communist governments in Poland and Hungary. These governments had been set up by Soviet armies at the end of World War II. They remained unpopular with their own people, partly because of their policies at home and partly because of their kowtowing to the Soviets. The revolt in Poland was patched over by granting a new Communist Polish government more freedom from Soviet control. But in Hungary it

Refugees disembark at Miami airport after fleeing Communist Cuba. Many leave homes and businesses in Cuba but will be faced with poverty in the United States.

WIDE WORLD

THE WORLD TODAY

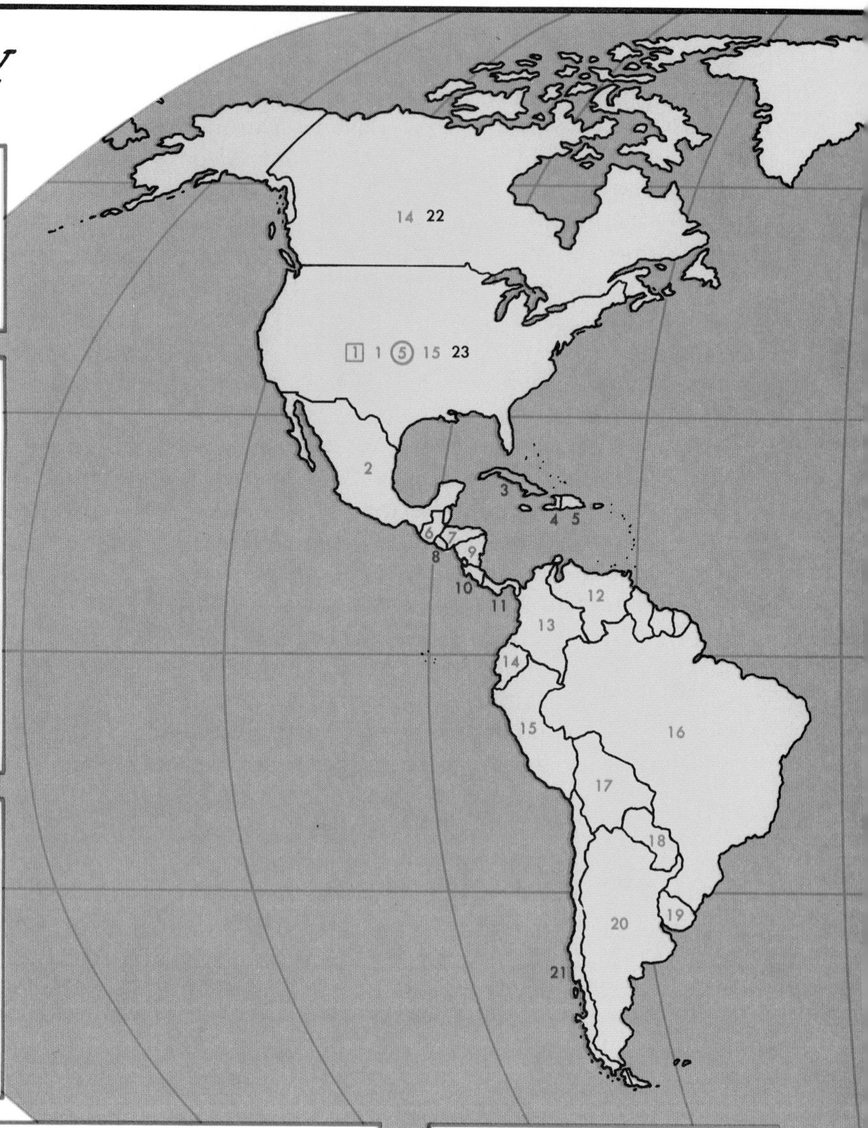

WARSAW PACT

1. Soviet Union
2. Poland
3. East Germany
4. Czechoslovakia
5. Hungary
6. Rumania
7. Bulgaria
8. Albania

ORGANIZATION OF AMERICAN STATES

1	United States	12	Venezuela
2	Mexico	13	Colombia
3	Cuba*	14	Ecuador
4	Haiti	15	Peru
5	Dominican Rep.	16	Brazil
6	Guatemala	17	Bolivia
7	Honduras	18	Paraguay
8	El Salvador	19	Uruguay
9	Nicaragua	20	Argentina
10	Costa Rica	21	Chile
11	Panama		

*Present government excluded

NORTH ATLANTIC TREATY (NATO)

1	Norway	8	France
2	Denmark	9	Portugal
3	United Kingdom	10	Italy
4	Netherlands	11	Greece
5	Belgium	12	Turkey
6	Luxembourg	13	Iceland
7	Federal Republic of Germany	14	Canada
		15	United States

COLOMBO PLAN

1	Afghanistan	7	Laos	13	Indonesia	19	Australia
2	Pakistan	8	Thailand	14	Philippine Rep.	20	New Zealand
3	India	9	Cambodia	15	Rep. Korea	21	United Kingdom
4	Nepal	10	Vietnam (South)	16	Japan	22	Canada
5	Bhutan	11	Malaysia	17	Maldive Is.	23	United States
6	Burma	12	Singapore	18	Ceylon		

CENTRAL TREATY (CENTO)

1. United Kingdom
2. Turkey
3. Iran
4. Pakistan
5. United States (observor)

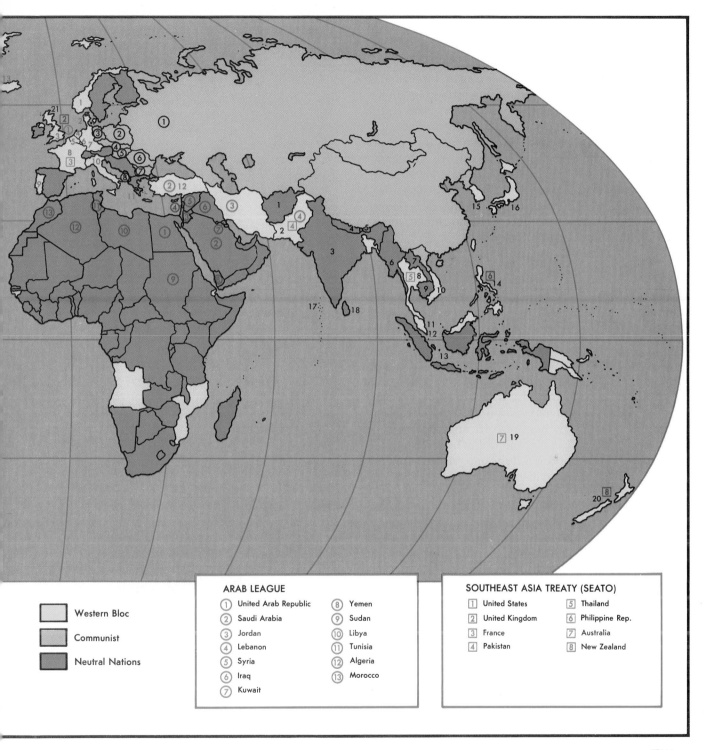

ARAB LEAGUE
1. United Arab Republic
2. Saudi Arabia
3. Jordan
4. Lebanon
5. Syria
6. Iraq
7. Kuwait
8. Yemen
9. Sudan
10. Libya
11. Tunisia
12. Algeria
13. Morocco

SOUTHEAST ASIA TREATY (SEATO)
1. United States
2. United Kingdom
3. France
4. Pakistan
5. Thailand
6. Philippine Rep.
7. Australia
8. New Zealand

Western Bloc

Communist

Neutral Nations

proved necessary to use 200,000 Soviet troops to smash the revolt and put the subservient Kadar regime in command of the country.

In 1968 the Soviet Union again intervened in the internal affairs of a neighboring Communist country when it sent an army into Czechoslovakia. This time the Soviets apparently feared that the democratic type of Communist society evolving in Czechoslovakia might create a demand for similar freedoms throughout Eastern Europe. So they forced the Czechoslovaks to accept Soviet occupation troops and to retract some of the new freedoms.

Perhaps the most serious trouble facing the Communist bloc is the problem of relations between the two giants, the U.S.S.R. and China. Deep-seated differences have developed between the two and these differences probably will increase rather than lessen in the future. One possible source of trouble is the colossal manpower of China. The U.S.S.R., with a population of 238 million, is increasing by 3 or 4 million a year; China, with a population of 780 million, is increasing by between 15 and 25 million each year. It is estimated that by 1975 China will have approximately one billion human beings. These statistics must give the Soviet leaders sleepless nights, expecially because they have a 3500-mile common frontier with China. And, uncomfortably for the Soviets, on their side of the frontier are the almost empty spaces of Siberia!

Another source of friction betweeen the two countries was the refusal of the Soviet Union to give nuclear weapons to China. This forced the Chinese into making their own, at the cost of great amounts of money. With her first atomic explosion in 1964, China joined the ranks of the superpowers which have nuclear weapons. By doing so, she added still another paragraph to her unwritten declaration of independence from Soviet leadership.

A protester outside the Soviet Embassy equates the 1968 invasion of Czechoslovakia with the Nazi invasion of 1938.

Perhaps the greatest controversy between the U.S.S.R. and China is their dispute over the inevitability of war between the Communist and capitalist worlds. The Chinese firmly believe that it is inevitable, and quote the following statement mady by Lenin in 1919: "the existence of a Soviet republic side by side with imperialistic states for a prolonged period is unthinkable. In the final end either one or the other will triumph. And before such an end is reached, a series of terrible clashes between the Soviet republic and the bourgeois states is inevitable." The Chinese not only believe that war must come, but also that such a war would destroy the capitalist states and not the Communist.

Nikita Khrushchev, on the other hand, held the opposite viewpoint. He criticized the Chinese for "repeating mechanically what Lenin said many tens of years ago." He argued that the situation was basically different now because war today would mean devastation for all peoples. "Only lunatics want war," said Khrushchev. And conceding that Western leaders are not lunatics, he concluded that, "under present conditions war is not inevitable." Khruschev's successors moreover, appear to hold similar views.

This dispute over "inevitable war" versus "peaceful coexistence" is more than a theoretical exercise. The Soviets are fearful that the Chinese, underestimating the consequences of modern war, may follow reckless policies that will actually bring about World War III. They are determined to avoid this risk if possible, because they have too much to lose. The U.S.S.R. has just begun to cash in on her great sacrifices of past years. Her people are starting to get better food, good clothing, more apartments, and luxuries such as television sets and automobiles. The Soviet leaders are unwilling to see all this go up in smoke. They are deadly serious in their opposition to the Chinese

Communists. Furthermore Moscow from the beginning has been the center of world communism, and the leaders of the Soviet Union have not been at all happy to see Peking's swift rise as a rival to Moscow.

We may conclude that both the Communist and Western blocs are in a very fluid state. Both undoubtedly will change drastically in organization and in membership in the years to come. Perhaps both will be challenged by a new Communist bloc with its headquarters in Peking.

The uncommitted. The third great bloc in the modern world is that of the uncommitted countries. We have seen that most of these are located in Africa and Asia and were colonial territories until a few years ago. For this reason most of them are very suspicious of the European powers that had ruled them for so long. On the other hand, they have no desire to throw in their lot with the Communist states. So they have formed an uncommitted bloc which tries to keep clear of the conflict between the other two blocs. They are impressed neither by arguments in favor of Western democracy and free enterprise, nor by arguments for the Soviet state and Communist economy. For example, President Gamal Nasser of Egypt has described this attitude as follows: ". . . the political neutralism which we advocate is not a compromise between East and West: it is, rather, an abstention from involvement in the cold war between the two camps. . . . The Cold War is a dispute between two blocs equally remote from us. In consequence, we can keep clear of their respective currents and decide for ourselves." [11]

The uncommitted countries, then, are interested only in meeting their own problems in their own way, and without outside dictation. To better do this, these countries of Asia and Africa have held a series of conferences. The first Asian-African Congress

Indian ski troops patrol the 1500-mile border which separates the disputed territory of Tibet from China.

met at Bandung, Indonesia, in April 1955. Twenty-nine countries participated, representing about half the world's population. The delegates to the conference enthusiastically condemned colonialism and racial discrimination, and recommended general disarmament, economic cooperation, and universal membership in the United Nations.

The new African states have gone further by establishing a permanent continent-wide organization. This is the Organization of African Unity created in May 1963 in Addis Ababa, Ethiopia. It provides for a General Secretary, a Secretariat, and periodic meetings of the African Heads of State. The Organization adopted a charter based on principles such as sovereign equality of all member-states, peaceful settlement of disputes, commitment to the emancipation of all remaining African colonies, and nonalignment in the Cold War.

The uncommitted states have further increased their influence in world affairs by using their voting power in the United Nations. When the UN was founded there were only 13 Afro-Asian states out of a total of 51 members; by 1968 there were 71 out of 126, or a full majority. This new balance of power in the UN became evident in 1961 when the post of Secretary General went to the Burmese U Thant.

The Afro-Asian states cooperate to attain common objectives but is should be emphasized that there are many differences within

Civil strife broke out in Cyprus when the Greek majority, feeling the Turkish minority had too much power, tried to amend the constitution. Most of the Turkish population took refuge in the hills.

their own ranks. Amongst the African states, for example, Somalia has territorial claims against Ethiopia and Kenya, Morocco likewise against Algeria, while the attempt of Biafra to break away from Nigeria precipitated a particularly savage and tragic war. Similarly, amongst the Asian states Cambodia has frontier disputes with both Thailand and South Vietnam; Ceylon and India have a long-standing quarrel over the rights of Indians living in Ceylon; while India and Pakistan feud bitterly over Kashmir. Most dramatic has been the 1962 border war between China and India, a war that is particularly ironic since Nehru and Chou En-lai had sponsored the "five principles of coexistence" at the Bandung Conference.

Equally ironic is the need of some of the newly-independent uncommitted states to call back troops of their imperial rulers in order to protect frontiers and to maintain domestic order. In 1964, for example, Britain had sent troops by invitation to Malaysia to resist aggression by Indonesia, to Cyprus to keep the peace between the island's Greek- and Turkish-speaking citizens, and to Kenya, Uganda, and Tanganyika to keep order against mutinous local soldiers. These paradoxical developments recall an incident that occurred during the official ceremonies held in Nairobi when Kenya became independent in 1963. Just when the British flag was about to be lowered and the new flag raised, Prince Philip, who was representing Britain, said to

Forces That Divide the World 721

DEFENSE COSTS IN SELECTED COUNTRIES 1966-1967

Defense Expeditures	USA	USSR	PEOPLES REPUBLIC OF CHINA	ISRAEL	UAR (Egypt)
Total (U. S. Dollars)	67,950,000,000	29,800,000,000	6,500,000,000	447,000,000	494,000,000
Per Capita (U. S. Dollars)	346	129	008	169	016
As per cent of GNP	9.2	8.9	10.0	12.2	11.1
Numbers of Mil. Personnel	3,400,000	3,220,000	2,736,000	71,000	180,000
As percent of Total Pop.	1.7%	1.4%	.3%	2.8%	.6%

GENERAL DYNAMICS CORPORATION

the new president, Kenyatta: "Sure you don't want to change your mind?"

We may conclude that just as the Communist and Western blocs are divided within themselves, so is the bloc of uncommitted countries. They are agreed in their opposition to racism and colonialism, and in their desire to keep clear of East-West conflicts. But at the same time they disagree, and disagree bitterly, over many other issues. So far as the future is concerned, however, they are united in their common desire for economic development. Since most of them have won, or are about to win, political independence, their chief goal now is economic growth. To achieve this, they are delighted to accept any help from either bloc, so long as no political strings are attached. And they have received a good deal of help from both the Soviet Union and the United States, thanks to the continuing Cold War.

The Cold War. "Every cloud has its silver lining." The silver lining of the Cold War is represented by the fact that the Soviet Union and the United States are competing with each other in their wooing of the uncommitted countries. A very considerable amount of aid was given to various countries by the Soviet Union and the United States in recent years. Since the uncommitted countries are almost all underdeveloped countries, they need all the assistance they can get from their suitors. On the other hand the silver lining should not be exaggerated. The cloud itself is much greater, and it is a grave danger to all mankind and a crushing expense to the nations involved in the Cold War.

The expense is made clear in the chart "The Cost of Military Forces" (see page 722). The money spent on armaments by the Western and Communist blocs almost equals the income of all the peoples of the underdeveloped world. If some way could be found to ease the Cold War and to spend a sizable percentage of this money in the underdeveloped countries, then they would not remain underdeveloped for long. And what this would mean in terms of human lives we have already seen above.

The conflict between the Western and Communist blocs is not only a great drain but also a terrible danger. The danger, of course, is that by accident, miscalculation, or deliberate design, the Cold War will become hot. In that case the distinction between Western and Communist blocs, between developed and underdeveloped countries, would become largely meaningless; there would be left only devastated countries and devastated peoples. The great destructive power of nuclear bombs can reduce even the largest cities to mere rubble. The amount of fallout can contaminate the atmosphere for years. Hiroshima and Nagasaki demonstrated what a catastrophe a nuclear bomb can produce. To prevent such a catastrophe is the purpose of the United Nations, to which we now turn.

Nagasaki, Japan, 1945. A street through a formerly congested residential area was reduced to rubble by the Atomic bomb. More than 200,000 people were annihilated by the explosions in Hiroshima and Nagasaki.

AIR FORCE PHOTO

Reviewing the Essentials

Racial Differences

1. Support this statement with evidence: "Race conflict began only in modern times."

2. Why is racial prejudice and conflict a development of modern times?

3. In what parts of the world is racial discrimination (a) most serious; (b) decreasing; (c) least serious or relatively rare? Account for the differences in these areas. Why is racial discrimination and conflict a problem that transcends national boundaries and causes world-wide concern?

Cultural Differences

4. Explain how language creates problems within and among nations. Give examples.

5. In terms of number of members, where do the major religions of the world stand? (See map, "Religious Population of the World.") Where are the largest concentrations for each religion?

6. Support this statement with evidence: "Religious tolerance is a modern idea." Where is religious tolerance *most* and *least* prevalent?

7. Cite other instances of cultural differences which contribute to misunderstanding among the people of the world.

Economic Differences

8. Give the distinguishing characteristics of (a) the Western industrial world; (b) the Communist world; (c) the non-industrial world.

9. What factors account for the increase in world population from approximately 10 million persons in 7000 B.C. to 2.5 billion in 1950 and an estimated 6 billion in 2000 A.D.?

10. Why are the people in underdeveloped countries optimistic about raising their standard of living in spite of the population explosion?

11. Why is it important to the United States that countries have healthy economies and make full and efficient use of their human and natural resources?

Diplomatic Differences

12. Into what blocs is the world divided diplomatically? Account for the formation of these diplomatic groups.

13. What regional treaties hold the members of the Western bloc together? What weaknesses have developed in the Western bloc?

14. What treaties hold the members of the Communist bloc together? What differences indicate weaknesses within the Communist bloc? Why is the most serious problem of the Communist bloc the differences that have developed between the Soviet Union and Communist China? What are the sources of tension and why are they of great concern to Kremlin leaders?

15. What nations belong to the uncommitted bloc? What do they have in common? What are their objectives? What differences exist within and among member nations of the uncommitted bloc?

16. Discuss this statement, relating it to the uncommitted countries: "The conflict between the Western and Communist blocs not only is a great drain but also a great danger."

Explain or Identify

economic independence	population explosion	SEATO	Western bloc
racism	Bandung Conference	NATO	Communist bloc
Cold War	Warsaw Pact of 1955	OAS	Uncommitted nations
	CENTO		

THE UNITED NATIONS

ORIGINS

The United Nations is not the first attempt made by mankind to prevent war.* For thousands of years and in all parts of the globe, war has been a constant scourge. Since 1500 alone, no less than three hundred wars have been fought. So we find that in every age

* See *Readings in World History*, "The Making of the First Peace Pipe," p. 763.

men have prayed for peace and have made plans to keep the peace. The Book of Isaiah, in the Old Testament, contains this passage:

> They shall beat their swords into plowshares,
> And their spears into pruning hooks;
> Nation shall not lift up sword against nation,
> Neither shall they learn war anymore.

These words are inscribed near the United Nations building in New York City.

Today war is a greater danger than ever before because it has become so much more destructive. The cost of World War I was 10 million soldiers and 180.5 billion dollars; while the cost of World War II was 15 million soldiers and 1500 billion dollars. And these figures do not include the loss of millions of civilian lives and the enormous destruction of civilian property!

In the hope of preventing a repetition of this staggering devastation, the League of Nations was organized after World War I. We noted earlier that the League was not successful in preserving the peace. The difficulty was not with the League itself, but rather with the failure of Great Powers; the United States for refusing to join, and others such as Britain and France for failing to support, the League in stopping the aggressions of Germany, Italy, and Japan. So in 1939 the Second World War began in Europe and it very quickly spread all over the globe.

During the course of World War II plans were made once more for the establishment of an international organization to prevent future wars. The general principles of this organization were drawn up in August 1941 when President Roosevelt and Prime Minister Churchill met aboard a battleship in mid-Atlantic. They prepared a declaration of principles now known as the Atlantic Charter. In this Charter, the two allies proclaimed that they sought "no aggrandizement, territorial or other," that they respected the right of all peoples to "choose the form of government under which they will live," and that nations must abandon the use of force to settle their disputes. Forty-five nations later accepted these principles, and called themselves the United Nations. Then representatives of these nations met in San Francisco and agreed upon a charter for the new international body. In this way the United Nations was born on October 24, 1945. At the time of its birth it had 51 mem-

The League of Nations convened in March 1936 to discuss the German occupation of the Rhineland. Discussion, however, failed to result in decisive action.

ACME PHOTO

bers. During the next 20 years its membership more than doubled as newly independent countries joined the United Nations.

ORGANIZATION

The central organ of the United Nations is the General Assembly, as can be seen in the chart on page 729. The Assembly draws up the UN's budget, elects members of the other organs, and receives reports from them. It may also consider any problem which it "deems likely to impair the general welfare or friendly relations" among nations. But in considering a problem, the Assembly can only discuss the issues and recommend a solution. It does not have the authority to take action. Every member nation, regardless of size, has only one vote in the Assembly. So the Assembly is a kind of town meeting of the world, or a sounding-board for world public opinion.

The UN body with responsibility and power for taking action is the Security Council. This is a small body, consisting of 5 permanent members: the United States, the Soviet Union, Great Britain, France, and China, and 10 other nations elected for a term of 2 years. Five of these must be from Africa and Asia, one from Eastern Europe, two from the Latin-American nations, and two from Western Europe and the rest of the world. According to the UN Charter, the Security Council must be ready to meet at any time. It may request disputing nations to settle their quarrel themselves through some peaceful means, or it may investigate a situation that endangers the peace and try to act as an umpire in getting a settlement. The Security Council may, if necessary, call upon members of the UN to cut off diplomatic or economic relations with an aggressor nation. Finally, if these measures prove inadequate, the Council has power to take "such action by air, sea, and land forces" as

U. Thant ponders the "brush-fire" war between Indonesia and Malaysia in 1964.

may be necessary to maintain or restore peace. UN members are supposed to contribute armed forces under the direction of a Military Staff Committee consisting of the Chiefs of Staff of the Big Five.

In carrying out these duties, the Security Council operates under what is called the Great Power veto. Decisions on important matters must be made by a vote of nine of its fifteen members, *including all five of the permanent members.* This means that each of the Great Powers has a veto and can prevent action by the Council, even in a dispute to which it is itself a party. The veto applies also to the admission of new members and to amendments or revisions of the Charter. The Soviet Union has frequently used this veto to prevent action by the Council. On the other hand the United States, as well as the

Soviet Union, originally insisted on including the veto in the UN Charter. The United States Senate might not have ratified the Charter if we did not have the veto to protect our sovereign power. Furthermore it has been pointed out that, regardless of the veto power, world peace can be maintained only if the Great Powers act together in harmony. If they do not, then it makes little difference whether the veto power does or doesn't exist.

A third important body of the United Nations is the Economic and Social Council. As its title suggests, its job is to fight against hunger, disease, ignorance, and prejudice. The scope of its work can be seen from the various specialized agencies whose work it coordinates. These agencies include the following:

–United Nations Development Organization

–International Labor Organization (ILO) Food and Agriculture Organization (FAO)

–United Nations Educational, Scientific, and Cultural Organization (UNESCO)

–International Civil Aviation Organization (ICAO)

–World Health Organization (WHO)

–International Telecommunication Union (ITU)

–World Meteorological Organization (WMO)

–International Bank for Reconstruction and Development

–International Monetary Fund (IMF)

The United Nations has three other major organs. One of these is the Trusteeship Council which is responsible for the World War I mandates which have not yet gained their independence and the various colonies taken from Japan and Italy during World War II. The duty of the Trusteeship Council is to make sure that the nations administering these colonial areas treat them as "sacred trusts" and prepare them for eventual independence.

The second body is the International Court of Justice, the principal judicial organ of the UN. Its 15 judges, elected by the Assembly and Council, decide treaty disputes and other questions of international law.

Finally there is the Secretary General and his Secretariat. The Secretary General is the chief administrative officer, in charge of the UN's day-to-day work. He and his staff of two thousand researchers, librarians, secretaries, and translators make up the Secretariat. For the first eight years of the UN's life, the Secretary General was Trygve Lie of Norway. His successors were, first Dag Hammarskjold of Sweden, and then U Thant of Burma.

The objectives of the UN are set forth in the beginning of its charter:[*]

> We, the peoples of the United Nations, determined to save succeeding generations from the scourge of war. . . .
> To reaffirm faith in fundamental human rights. . . .
> To promote social progress and better standards of life. . . .
> To practice tolerance and live together in peace. . . .
> To insure . . . that armed force shall not be used, save in the common interest. . . .
> To employ international machinery for the promotion of the economic and social advancement of all peoples, have resolved to combine our efforts to accomplish these aims.
> Accordingly . . . do hereby establish an international organization to be known as the United Nations.

From this we see that the UN has two main general tasks; to war against war, and to war against hunger, disease, and ignorance. We shall now see how successful it has been thus far with these two tasks.

[*] See *Readings in World History,* "The Charter of the United Nations," p. 766.

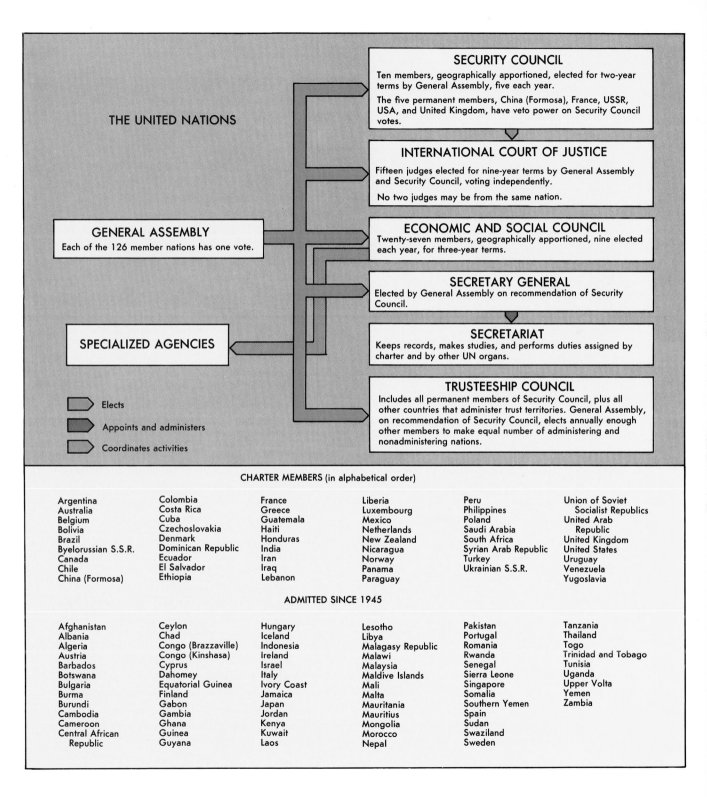

THE UNITED NATIONS

SECURITY COUNCIL
Ten members, geographically apportioned, elected for two-year terms by General Assembly, five each year.

The five permanent members, China (Formosa), France, USSR, USA, and United Kingdom, have veto power on Security Council votes.

INTERNATIONAL COURT OF JUSTICE
Fifteen judges elected for nine-year terms by General Assembly and Security Council, voting independently.

No two judges may be from the same nation.

GENERAL ASSEMBLY
Each of the 126 member nations has one vote.

ECONOMIC AND SOCIAL COUNCIL
Twenty-seven members, geographically apportioned, nine elected each year, for three-year terms.

SECRETARY GENERAL
Elected by General Assembly on recommendation of Security Council.

SPECIALIZED AGENCIES

SECRETARIAT
Keeps records, makes studies, and performs duties assigned by charter and by other UN organs.

TRUSTEESHIP COUNCIL
Includes all permanent members of Security Council, plus all other countries that administer trust territories. General Assembly, on recommendation of Security Council, elects annually enough other members to make equal number of administering and nonadministering nations.

Elects

Appoints and administers

Coordinates activities

CHARTER MEMBERS (in alphabetical order)

Argentina	Colombia	France	Liberia	Peru	Union of Soviet
Australia	Costa Rica	Greece	Luxembourg	Philippines	Socialist Republics
Belgium	Cuba	Guatemala	Mexico	Poland	United Arab
Bolivia	Czechoslovakia	Haiti	Netherlands	Saudi Arabia	Republic
Brazil	Denmark	Honduras	New Zealand	South Africa	United Kingdom
Byelorussian S.S.R.	Dominican Republic	India	Nicaragua	Syrian Arab Republic	United States
Canada	Ecuador	Iran	Norway	Turkey	Uruguay
Chile	El Salvador	Iraq	Panama	Ukrainian S.S.R.	Venezuela
China (Formosa)	Ethiopia	Lebanon	Paraguay		Yugoslavia

ADMITTED SINCE 1945

Afghanistan	Ceylon	Hungary	Lesotho	Pakistan	Tanzania
Albania	Chad	Iceland	Libya	Portugal	Thailand
Algeria	Congo (Brazzaville)	Indonesia	Malagasy Republic	Romania	Togo
Austria	Congo (Kinshasa)	Ireland	Malawi	Rwanda	Trinidad and Tobago
Barbados	Cyprus	Israel	Malaysia	Senegal	Tunisia
Botswana	Dahomey	Italy	Maldive Islands	Sierra Leone	Uganda
Bulgaria	Equatorial Guinea	Ivory Coast	Mali	Singapore	Upper Volta
Burma	Finland	Jamaica	Malta	Somalia	Yemen
Burundi	Gabon	Japan	Mauritania	Southern Yemen	Zambia
Cambodia	Gambia	Jordan	Mauritius	Spain	
Cameroon	Ghana	Kenya	Mongolia	Sudan	
Central African	Guinea	Kuwait	Morocco	Swaziland	
Republic	Guyana	Laos	Nepal	Sweden	

WORLD PRODUCTION OF GOODS AND SERVICES

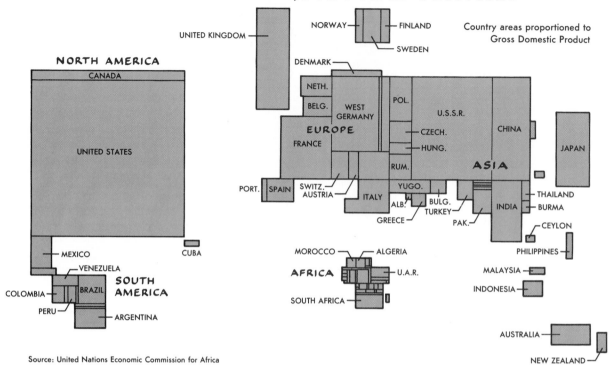

Source: United Nations Economic Commission for Africa

WAR AGAINST HUNGER, DISEASE, AND IGNORANCE

The UN, like the League of Nations, has been most successful in its second task, that is, the war against hunger, disease, and ignorance. The Economic and Social Council has carried on this war through the specialized agencies. Some of the specific aims of the Council are to: provide more food for the 50 per cent of human beings who are hungry; cure the 20 per cent of the world's population that has malaria; save the 40 per cent of the children who, in some countries, die before the end of their first year; teach the 45 per cent of the world's adult illiterates to read and write; and raise the incomes of the 70 per cent of the human race that earn less than $200 per year.

The various organs of the United Nations work towards these objectives in many ways. One is to send about three thousand technical experts to all parts of the globe. These highly trained men and women provide help for all sorts of projects: from flood control to fish-farming, from bridge-building to budget-balancing, from handicrafts to hydraulics. Most of these experts who work for the United Nations naturally come from the developed countries that are more advanced in technical matters. Yet this is by no means entirely a one-way affair. In one year India, which receives much help from the United Nations, in turn contributed 84 experts for service in other countries. Likewise Egypt provided 26 of its own specialists, Brazil sent 20, and Ecuador 10.

Even the United States in 1959 requested and received from the Food and Agriculture Organization the temporary services of Dr. Shao Wen Ling, Chinese authority on fish-farming. The story behind this arrangement is a good example of the constant exchange of technical know-how. The growing of rice had expanded rapidly in the Delta region of Arkansas, Louisiana, and Mississippi. The farmers prepare the land by building levees around each plot, filling the resulting reservoir with water, and letting it stand for a couple of years. The submerged decaying vegetation enriches the soil in which the rice is later planted.

Farmers soon discovered that numbers of local types of fish appeared in the water reservoirs. If better breeds of fish could be cultivated, then the farmers would be able to harvest a crop of fish together with their crop of rice. The Chinese are experts in combining rice and fish harvests, which they have been doing for centuries. In fact, Dr. Ling, as an FAO expert, helped fish-farming projects in Thailand, Burma, Indonesia, and Ceylon, before coming to the United States. In this country he gave advice on the most promising type of edible fish, on selective breeding and fish crop rotation, on fish disease and parasites, and on fish nutrition.

Another way in which the UN helps to spread technical knowledge is to provide fellowships to enable civil servants of one country to visit another where they might learn new techniques. An example of this is the case of the Technical Director of Public Works in Yugoslavia. He was responsible for the housebuilding program in his country, which was not progressing as rapidly as he

(TOP) ILO; (BOTTOM) WIDE WORLD

An Arab woman carries away her family's flour ration from the UN refugee center in the Gaza Strip. A teacher in Paraguay assists one of her 77 pupils. The school is part of a UNESCO–assisted Fundamental Education Program.

The United Nations 731

wished. So with the help of a UN fellowship he visited France where he learned about prefabricated building materials and prefabricated plumbing. Other civil servants have been able, with UN fellowships, to learn about controlling malaria, operating air transport services, improving farming in dry or mountainous areas, devising and administering tax systems, improving long-distance telephone operation, establishing weather-forecasting services, rehabilitating the blind and the crippled, and speeding up literacy campaigns.

The UN also helps to spread know-how by organizing international conferences of experts in various fields. These people meet to review the latest technical developments in their respective specialties, to exchange ideas, compare experiences and techniques, and sometimes to plan action programs. This method has been used, for instance, by the World Health Organization (WHO) as part of the battle against the "black death" or bubonic plague. In 1952 it arranged for a meeting in Bombay of six outstanding plague authorities from Argentina, Brazil, France, India, and the United States.

Examining the latest methods, the experts came to the conclusion that adequate dosages of new antibiotics like streptomycin reduced the death rate to less than 1 in 10, even in the most serious varieties of plague which had been regarded until recently as almost 100 per cent fatal. They also agreed that the most effective way to prevent plague epidemics was to improve housing so that rats,

ERIC L. BROWN (MONKMEYER)

carriers of the plague flea, could no longer live in close contact with humans. The experts also emphasized the value of insecticides such as DDT which destroy the chain of infection between rat and man by killing most of the fleas on infected rodents. Finally the conference drew up standard procedures for gaining the maximum advantage from all the modern anti-plague weapons: vaccinations, drugs, insecticides, and the latest rat poisons.

Still another way in which the UN spreads knowledge and techniques is through teaching equipment of various types, including books, bibliographies, journals, digests, films, and filmstrips. In Mexico City, UNESCO maintains the Scientific and Technical Documentation Center, which is an international clearing-house of knowledge. Each month, 1600 journals, treatises, reports, and reviews from all over the world pour into the Center. A staff of employees catalogue, sift, summarize, and translate this information, and make it available to all countries. Each month the Center issues a *Bulletin* which provides a summary of the information gathered from all the publications. In this way the results of world-wide research are publicized, and anyone can obtain at cost price a copy of the full text of any particular study.*

All this work of the United Nations against hunger, disease, and ignorance is of very great importance. How important it is was made clear in the following remarks by the then President Sukarno of Indonesia before the UN General Assembly on September 30, 1960:

> It has been said that we live in the midst of a revolution of rising expectations. It is not so. We live in the midst of a revolution of rising demands! Those who were previ-

ously without freedom now demand freedom. Those who were previously without a voice now demand that their voices be heard. Those who were previously hungry now demand rice, plentifully and every day. Those who were previously unlettered now demand education.

> This whole world is a vast power house of revolution, a vast revolutionary ammunition dump. No less than three-quarters of humanity is involved in this revolution of rising demands, and this is the greatest revolution since man first walked erect in a virgin and pleasant world. The success or failure of this Organization will be judged by its relationship to that revolution of rising demands. Future generations will praise us or condemn us in the light of our response to this challenge.

WAR AGAINST WAR

As exciting and constructive as all this work is, the fact remains that the most important duty of the UN is to war against war. If it fails in this task, then it will fail also in everything else. This was the case with the League of Nations, which did much valuable work in world health, education, and social services. But since The League failed to keep the peace, almost all its accomplishments went up in the fire and smoke of World War II.

How successful has the UN been so far with its main job? The answer is that it has been partly successful, but there have been serious failures. It has been able to prevent the outbreak of an all-out war between the Great Powers, which would have devastated the globe. On the other hand, it has not been able to forestall a series of local or "brushfire" type of wars, in Korea, Indochina, Indonesia, Algeria, Palestine, Egypt, Kashmir, and Vietnam.

Why has the UN not been able to prevent these local wars? The main reason is that all UN members remain sovereign states. That

---

* See *Readings in World History,* "U.N. War Against Hunger, Disease, and Ignorance," p. 768.

UN offices at El Kantara by the Suez Canal.

is, they are all independent, self-governing states, owing no allegiance to any higher authority, whether to the UN or any other organization. This means that the members of the UN have not surrendered any of their sovereignty to that body. It does not have the power to order; it can only try to persuade. It is not like a government. It cannot do what it wants; it can only do what its members wish it to do. If its members are in agreement, all goes well; if they are not, then there is trouble, and sometimes war. And

since the Great Powers have been divided by the Cold War, there have been disputes all over the globe, and in several places these disputes developed to the point of open warfare.

The Cold War not only has led to local wars but it also has affected the operations of the UN in various ways. An example is the stalemate that occurred in the General Assembly in 1964–1965, as a result of the refusal of the Soviet Union to pay assessments for peace-keeping operations in the Congo and the Middle East. The UN Charter provides that a member loses its vote in the General Assembly if it is in arrears on UN assessments for more than two years, and the United States insisted on invoking this provision. To avoid putting the issue to a test, no votes were taken in the General Assembly throughout the nine-month session. In the end a compromise solution was worked out and announced on the final day of the session.

Another result of the Cold War has been the failure to organize a UN army, as provided for in the Charter. Obviously the United States and the Soviet Union could not place their armed forces under the same international command when their political and military policies were so much in conflict. The Cold War also led to the rise of regional alliances. The various powers have entrusted their safety not to the UN, which had no army, but to alliances with friendly powers. So the world is divided, as we have seen, among several regional alliances such as the Warsaw Treaty, NATO, and SEATO. This regional grouping has showed up also within the UN, where the members have tended to vote in blocs. The most important of these blocs are the Latin-American, the Communist, the Arab, the Afro-Asian, and the British Commonwealth. Finally the Cold War has led to the decline of the Security Council because the Soviet representative has constantly used his power of veto. The voting record shows that by September 1964 the Soviet veto was employed no less than 102 times. In this way the Security Council has been blocked in almost every action it sought to take.

The weakening of the Security Council has led to increasing dependence upon the UN Secretariat, and particularly upon the Secretary General. Since a candidate for the post of Secretary General must be recommended by the Security Council and elected by the General Assembly, it is tacitly agreed that he not be a citizen of any of the Big Five powers. Consequently the three men who have held the post since the organization was founded have been a Norwegian, a Swede, and a Burmese. The Charter authorizes the Secretary General to bring to the attention of the Security Council "any matter which in his opinion may threaten the maintenance of international peace and security." He also carries out any tasks that may be given him by other organs of the UN.

The Secretary General is in a strategic position to find ways of settling a crisis so long as he has the goodwill and trust of the permanent members of the Security Council. Sometimes nations have taken a stand which they may be willing to modify but which they refuse to do publicly because of a fear of loss of face. Thus both sides in a dispute may actually be ready to reach a settlement but be unable to find a graceful way in which to do it. In such a deadlock, the Secretary General can step in and quietly work out a compromise that would be impossible in public meetings. Hammerskjold stated that his job was "blunting the edges of conflict" and removing problems from the "cold-war orbit." He was able, for example, through secret negotiation, to obtain the release of 11 American airmen held prisoners by Communist China in violation of the Korean armistice agreement.

Another example, however, shows that the Secretary General can do only so much and no more. This was the case of the Congo, which won its independence from Belgian rule in June 30, 1960. But with independence came virtual anarchy, including a mutiny by the Congolese Army and attacks on Belgian civilians. The UN promptly sent an army to restore order, and also a group of technicians to take the place of the Belgian technicians who had left. Hammarskjold directed these UN operations, but the Soviet Union was not satisfied with the manner in which he did his job. Khrushchev accused him of using the UN to help Western interests in the Congo. In fact, Khrushchev went further and demanded that the office of UN Secretary General be abolished and be re-

OWEN FRANKEN

placed by a three-man board, one each for the Western, Communist, and neutralist powers. His proposal was not accepted, but it does show that all branches of the UN are very much affected by the Cold War.

The effect was especially clear following Hammarskjold's death in an airplane accident in the Congo September 18, 1961. The question of a successor became a political football, with the Western and Communist Powers disagreeing sharply as to who should be the successor and how much power he should have. U Thant of Burma was elected acting Secretary General on November 1961 and has since been permanently appointed.

This raises the question of the future of the UN. Will it be able to keep the peace or will it disappear in another world war? To answer this question we must again remind ourselves that the UN is not an independent body or a government. Its members have kept their full sovereignty and always place their national interests first and foremost. The UN can provide machinery for settling disputes but it cannot itself force settlement of disputes. Consequently the fate of the UN, like that of the League of Nations, will be settled by the policies decided upon by the Great Powers. The League was doomed because certain Great Powers were willing to resort to war in order to gain their ends. If this happens again, then the organization inevitably will go the way of the League. Perhaps the knowledge that nuclear war will leave no victors will prevent a repetition of this dismal past. This is the world's biggest hope, and if this hope is realized, then the United Nations has a future.*

* See *Readings in World History*, "War or Peace?", p. 773.

Anti-war protesters picketing the induction center in Portland, Maine, are in turn picketed by Korean and World War II veterans.

Reviewing the Essentials

Origins

1. Compare the costs of World War I and World War II.
2. What attempts has man made to prevent war? Why have these failed?
3. Under what circumstances did President Roosevelt and Prime Minister Churchill draft the Atlantic Charter? Explain the importance of the Atlantic Charter's principles.

Organization

4. When and where was the United Nations Charter adopted? How many nations signed the Charter? State the purposes of the UN as presented in the Charter.
5. What is the function of the General Assembly? What nations are members? How many votes does each have?
6. What is the function of the Security Council? What nations are members? How may the Security Council deal with an aggressor nation?
7. Explain how the Big Power veto operates in the Security Council.

8. What is the nature and purpose of the Economic and Social Council?
9. Name and state the purpose and membership of the other organs of the UN.

War Against Hunger, Disease, and Ignorance

10. Show how the United Nations, through the Economic and Social Council and specialized agencies, has been successful in its program to deal with disease, hunger, and illiteracy.

War Against War

11. What is the UN's record in eliminating war among nations? Why hasn't it been able to prevent local wars?
12. How has the Cold War affected the operation of the United Nations?
13. Explain this statement: An important part of the Secretary General's job is to "blunt the edges of conflict and remove problems from the 'cold-war orbit'."
14. Why does the future of the UN depend on Great Power Policies?

Explain or Identify

United Nations Charter	specialized agencies	Security Council	International Court of Justice
Great Power veto	League of Nations	Secretariat	Trygve Lie
sovereign state	Fourteen Points	Trusteeship Council	Dag Hammarskjold
technical assistance	Atlantic Charter	Economic-Social Council	U Thant
	General Assembly		

UNIT ACTIVITIES

1. Several students might prepare for presentation to the class a panel discussion on the topic: Like it or not, for better or for worse, we are losing our differences and becoming more alike. Use the following selections: *Readings in World History*, "Revolution in Communications," pp. 724–728; "Common Ways of Life," pp. 730–734; "Becoming More and More Alike," pp. 735–737.
2. It has been said that, "It is easier now to smash an atom than to break prejudice." Use this statement as a basis for discussion, examin-

ing the causes of racial prejudice. For information consult: *Readings in World History*, "Race Conflict Divides the World," pp. 738–741; "Race and Intelligence," pp. 741–742; "The Word 'Native,'" pp. 745–747; A. H. Richmond, "The Colour Problem: A Study of Racial Relations," *UNESCO Courier*, October 1960.
3. Vera M. Dean in her article, "Three Decades of Crises: A Moment in History," *Foreign Affairs Bulletin*, June 15, 1961, reviews the mounting tensions and problems among the Western, Com-

munist, and uncommitted blocs. Several members of the class might report on the article, focusing on: (a) major points of tension and conflict among blocs; (b) significant changes on the world scene; (c) increasing commitments made by the United States.

4. Select a Specialized Agency and report on: (a) purpose; (b) member nations; (c) headquarters; (d) specific achievements in combating causes and problems of underdeveloped areas; (e) results of its work to date.

5. Class groups might prepare a report on these questions:

    1) Is the United Nations adequate to achieve its purpose as stated in the Charter?

    2) What are the pros and cons of Charter review and revision?

    3) Why is the immediate future a time of crisis for the United Nations?

    4) How can the UN help in crises now threatening the peace?

    5) What is the UN disarmament record?

    6) What has the United Nations done through the specialized agencies?

Consult the bibliography on the UN and these sources: "Issues Before the 20th General Assembly," *International Conciliation*, Sept. 1965; *The UN: The First Twenty Years* (New York: Harper & Row, 1965), by Clark Eichelberger; *The UN at Twenty and After* (Headline Series No. 173), by L. P. Bloomfield; 20th Anniversary Issue, *International Organization*, 27 articles (Boston: World Peace Foundation, Summer 1965).

SELECTED READING

● The problem of race relations in the United States and in the world as a whole is discussed in O. Handlin, *Race and Nationality in American Life* (Boston: Little, Brown, 1957); and, most interestingly, in the October 1960 issue of the *UNESCO Courier*. (UNESCO, Paris, France). For an understanding of present-day economic developments, three pamphlets of Curriculum Resources Inc. are indispensable: M. Daugherty, *Understanding Economic Growth;* M. Lovenstein,

Capitalism, Communism, Socialism; and J. D. Calderwood and H. J. Jones, *World Trade.*

● World economic conditions are analyzed in *World of Promise* (Dobbs Ferry, N.Y.: Oceana, 1965) by J. A. Joyce; *Man, Land, and Food,* Foreign Agricultural Economic Report No. 11 (USDA, Washington, D.C.: Government Printing Office, 1963) by L. R. Brown; and P. M. Hauser, *World Population Problems* (Headline Series No. 174, December, 1965). The same problems are discussed interestingly in two pamphlet series: *World Food Problems* published by the Food and Agriculture Organization of the United Nations, and *Food and People* published by UNESCO. Excellent studies of the problem of underdeveloped countries are: P. G. Hoffman, *One Hundred Countries* (1960), available from the Committee for International Economic Growth, 1028 Connecticut Avenue, N.W., Washington, D.C.; the same author's *World Without Want* (New York: Harper and Row, 1962); and R. Theobald, *The Rich and the Poor* (Mentor, 1961).

● The world diplomatic situation is discussed in pamphlets of the Foreign Relations Series (River Forest, Illinois: Laidlaw, various dates).

Another important source is the Headline Series pamphlets of the Foreign Policy Association.

● On the United Nations there is the fascinating account by J. Conway, *The U.N. in Action* (New York: Macmillan, 1965); and the pamphlet by E. J. Nolde, *The United States in the United Nations*, in the Foreign Relations Project series. See also the Headline Series pamphlets on the U.N.: L. P. Bloomfield, *The U.N. at Twenty and After*, No. 173, 1965; and Francis O. Wilcox, *The U.N. and the Nonaligned Nations*, No. 155, 1962. A fascinating overview of trends in various fields is published periodically as *Contemporary Civilizations* by Scott Foresman and Co., the latest is Issue No. 4, 1967.

FURTHER READING

● A very useful country-by-country fact book is *Other Lands, Other Peoples* (Washington: National Education Association, 1962). The best comprehensive studies of the problem of race relations are B. Berry, *Race and Ethnic Relations* (Boston: Houghton Mifflin, 1965); and G. Simpson and J. M. Yinger, *Racial and Cultural Minorities* (New York: Harper and Row, 3rd ed., 1965). The Anti-Defamation League (315 Lexington Ave., New York, 10016) has published noteworthy materials on this subject, including A. Montagu, *What We Know About "Race"*; M. M. Tumin, *Race and Intelligence;* and T. F. Pettigrew, *Negro American Intelligence.*

● Important books on world economic conditions are *Technology and Economic Development* (New York: A. A. Knopf, 1963), a paperback of articles from the *Scientific American*, September 1963; G. Myrdal, *Rich Lands and Poor* (New York: Harper, 1958); and K. and A. F. Organski, *Population and World Power* (New York: A. A. Knopf, 1961). An indispensable statistical reference work is *The Statesman's Year-Book* (New York: St. Martin's Press, annually).

● The American Foreign Policy Library series, published by the Harvard University Press, includes volumes on China, India, Japan, Russia,

Turkey and Iran, etc. There is a good summary of world developments since World War II in the paperback by G. Bruun and D. E. Lee, *The Second World War and After* (Boston: Houghton Mifflin, 1964).

● On the United Nations, see *Resources for Teaching about the United Nations* (Washington: National Education Association, 1962); the excellent collection of source material in C. A. McClelland, *The United Nations: The Continuing Debate* (San Francisco: Howard Chandler, 1960). The standard history of the United Nations is by C. M. Eichelberger, *U. N.: The First Twenty Years* (New York: Harper and Row, 1965). A convenient paperback on the subject is by D. C. Coyle, *The United Nations and How It Works* (Mentor Books, rev. ed., 1960).

● For stimulating interpretations of the historical forces moulding the world today, see E. H. Carr, *The New Society* (Boston: Beacon Press Paperback, 1957); V. M. Dean, *The Nature of the Non-Western World* (Mentor Paperback, 1957); Barbara Ward, *Five Ideas that Change the World* (New York: W. W. Norton, 1959); G. Barraclough, *An Introduction to Contemporary History* (Pelican Book, 1967); and R. L. Heilbroner, *Future as History* (Evergreen Books, 1961).

ACKNOWLEDGEMENTS

UNIT ONE

1. *What is Race? Evidence From Scientists* (Paris: UNESCO, 1952), p. 85.

UNIT TWO

1. R. Redfield, *The Primitive World and Its Transformation* (Ithaca: Cornell Univ. Press, 1953), pp. 8–9.

UNIT THREE

1. Cited by H. J. Muller, *Uses of the Past* (New York: Oxford University Press, 1952), p. 341.
2. Cited by R. Latham, *In Quest of Civilization* (London: Hutchinson & Co., 1946), p. 101.
3. Cited by Muller, *op. cit.*, p. 340.
4. Muller, *op. cit.*, pp. 105–106.
5. *Western Civilization. A Course of Selected Reading by Authorities* (London: Int. Univ. Soc., 1952), pp. 26–27.
6. Cited by Latham, *op. cit.*, p. 253.
7. Cited by De Bary *et al.*, *Sources of Indian Tradition* (N.Y.: Columbia Univ. Press, 1958), p. 149.
8. Cited by J. Needham, *Science and Civilisation in China* (Cambridge Univ. Press, 1954), I, pp. 209–210.
9. Cited by A. Mieli, *La science arabe* (Leiden: E. J. Brill, 1939), p. 376.
10. J. Needham, *op. cit.*, I, p. 219.
11. Cited by G. Vernadsky, *The Mongols and Russia* (New Haven: Yale University Press, 1953), p. 111.
12. Ata-Malik Juvaini, *The History of the World Conqueror*, tr., A. J. Boyle (Camb.: Harvard Univ. Press, 1958), I, p. 31.
13. Juvaini, *op. cit.*, I, p. 41.
14. Cited by G. F. Hudson, *Europe & China* (London: Edward Arnold, 1931), pp. 134, 156.
15. From C. R. Beazley, ed., *The Texts and Versions of John de Plano Carpini and William de Rubruquis* (London: Hakluyt Soc., 1903), pp. 109–111.
16. *The Travels of Marco Polo*, tr. from the text of L. F. Benedetto by Aldo Ricci (London: Routledge & Kegan Paul, 1931), p. 9.
17. *The Memoirs of the Conquistador Bernal Diaz del Castillo* (London, 1844), II, p. 390.
18. William Bradford, *Of Plymouth Plantation 1620–1647*, ed. by S. E. Morison (New York: Alfred A. Knopf, Inc., 1952), p. 25.
19. L. White, "Technology and Invention in the Middle Ages," *Speculum*, XV (April, 1940), p. 157.
20. Cited by Lynn White, "Dynamo and Virgin Reconsidered," *American Scholar* (1958), p. 192.
21. *Ibid.*, p. 192.

UNIT FOUR

1. E. G. Ravenstein, ed. and tr., *A Journal of the First Voyage of Vasco da Gama* (London: Hakluyt Society, 1898), pp. 69–70.
2. P. Zagorin, "The English Revolution 1640–1660," *Journal of World History*, II (1955), p. 908.
3. Cited, B. C. Shafer, *Nationalism: Myth and Reality* (New York: Harcourt, Brace & Co., 1955), p. 120.
4. J. S. Furnivall, *Netherlands India* (Cambridge: Cambridge University Press, 1944), p. 44.
5. Jawaharlal Nehru, *Toward Freedom* (New York: The John Day Company, Inc., 1941), pp. 29–30. Reprinted by permission of the publishers.
6. Cited, L. S. S. O'Malley, *Modern India and the West* (London: Oxford Univ. Press, 1941), p. 766.
7. Arthur Zimmermann, Undersecretary of State in the German Foreign Office, August 1, 1914.
8. Quoted in Goldwin and Zetterbaum, *Readings in Russian Foreign Policy* (Chicago: American Foundation for Pol. Educ., 1953), II, pp. 154, 156, 158.
9. R. Delavignette, *Freedom and Authority in French West Africa* (London: Oxford, 1950), p. 149.
10. United States, State Department, *Papers Relating to the Foreign Relations of the United States, With the Annual Message of the President* (Washington, D.C.: U.S. Govt. Printing Office, 1925), p. 799.
11. London *Times*, February 4, 1932.
12. Quoted in *Bulletin of International News*, XII (July 27, 1935), p. 7.
13. Quoted in M. Carlyle, ed., *Documents on International Affairs 1939–1946: Vol. II, Hitler's Europe* (London: Royal Inst. of Int. Affairs, 1954), p. 333.
14. Phillip P. Mosely, *Face to Face With Russia, Headline Series*, No. 70, New York, Foreign Policy Association, July–August 1948, p. 23.
15. *New York Times*, September 27, 1968.
16. A. J. Toynbee, "Encounter Between Civilizations." Copyright © 1947 by *Harper's Magazine*, Inc. Reprinted from vol. 194, April 1947, by permission of the author.

UNIT FIVE

1. Vera M. Dean, *Russia at War, Headline Series*, No. 34, New York, Foreign Policy Association, 1942, pp. 11–12.
2. Cited by R. M. Scammon, "Why the Russians Bother With Elections," *New York Times Magazine*, April 6, 1958, p. 63.
3. J. Curtis, *Church and State in Russia, 1900–1917* (N.Y.: Col. Univ. Press, 1940), pp. 30, 186–7.
4. Sir Bernard Pares, *A History of Russia* (New York: Alfred A. Knopf, Inc., 1953), pp. 119–20.

5. Cited by J. Kunitz, *Russia: The Giant That Came Last* (New York: Dodd, Mead, & Co., 1947), p. 55.
6. Cited by B. H. Sumner, *Short History of Russia* (New York: Reynal and Hitchcock, 1943), p. 96.
7. Anatoly Marchenko, in *New York Times, School Weekly*, November 4, 1968.
8. Edward Crankshaw, Chicago *Sun-Times*, January 21, 1968.
9. Cited by M. Paleologue, *An Ambassador's Memoirs* (New York: Doran, 1925), II, p. 34.
10. H. Schwartz, "The Organization Man: Soviet Style," *New York Times Magazine*, June 2, 1957.
11. From *U.S.S.R.: The Story of Soviet Russia* by Walter Duranty. Copyright, 1944, by Walter Duranty. Reprinted with permission from J. B. Lippincott Company.
12. Cited by A. G. Mazour, *Russia Past and Present*, p. 519. (Princeton, N.J.: D. Van Nostrand, 1951).
13. *Newsweek*, November 9, 1964.
14. *New York Times*, June 14, 1958.
15. *New York Times*, October 5, 1967.
16. Cited by R. L. Renfield, "Ivan doesn't learn more than Johnny," *New York Times Magazine*, November 11, 1962, p. 29.
17. Cited by T. W. Arnold, *The Preaching of Islam* (London: Constable & Co., 1913), pp. 243–244.
18. Cited by G. S. Franklin, Jr., "Off the Record Talks with Soviet John Does," *New York Times Magazine*, January 19, 1958, p. 69.
19. *New York Times*, October 9, 1967.
20. Cited by M. Slonim, "What the Russians Read," *New York Times Book Review*, Dec. 11, 1949, p. 6.
21. *The New York Times*, January 1, 1956.
22. *Life*, November 10, 1967, p. 43.

UNIT SIX

1. John A. Crow, *The Epic of Latin America* (New York: Doubleday and Co., Inc., 1946), p. 308.
2. James R. Scobie, *Argentina: A City and a Nation* (New York: Oxford University Press, 1964), p. 134.
3. J. Noval, "Guatemala: The Indian and the Land," *Américas*, March, 1964, p. 7.
4. "An Argentine's U.S.A.," *Américas*, Jan. 1954, p. 5.

UNIT SEVEN

1. Quoted in P. T. Moon, *Imperialism and World Politics* (New York: Macmillan Co., 1926), p. 321.
2. *New York Times*, January 31, 1960, p. 4E.
3. Quoted by S. Chandrasekhar, "Mao's War With the Chinese Family," *New York Times Magazine*, May 17, 1959, p. 21.
4. "Extracts from the Marriage Law," in *China Reconstructs*, July-August, 1952, p. 47.
5. Quoted by B. Ullmann, "China's Grim Winter," *New York Times Magazine*, Feb. 19, 1961, p. 50.
6. Quoted in Lin Yutang, *My Country and My People* (New York: The John Day Company, Inc., 1935), p. 249. Reprinted by permission of the publishers.
7. Chang Jen-hsia, "An Outburst of Popular Poetry," *China Reconstructs*, October, 1958, p. 26.
8. S. Chandrasekhar, "State Radio in Red China," *Chicago Sun-Times*, February 17, 1959.
9. Lin Yutang, *op. cit.*, p. 4.

UNIT EIGHT

1. Rudyard Kipling, *Kim* (New York: Dell, 1959), p. 60.
2. Quoted in R. Pearson, *Eastern Interlude: A Social History of the European Community in Calcutta* (Calcutta: Thacker, Spink & Co., 1954), p. 64.
3. Robert Clive, quoted in V. A. Smith, *The Oxford History of India* (3rd ed., New York: Oxford University Press, 1958), p. 472.
4. Quoted by J. Strachey, *The End of Empire* (New York: Random House, 1960), p. 42.
5. L. S. S. O'Malley, *Modern India and the West* (London: Oxford University Press, 1941), p. 80.
6. O'Malley, p. 632, quoted from Bishop J. M. Thorburn, *India and Malaysia* (New York: Hunt and Eaton, 1896), p. 69.
7. T. B. Macaulay, *Prose and Poetry*, ed. by G. M. Young (Cambridge: Harvard, 1958), p. 132.
8. Jawaharlal Nehru, *The Discovery of India* (New York: The John Day Company, Inc., 1946), p. 361. Reprinted by permission of the publishers.
9. Quoted in W. S. Woytinsky, *India: The Awakening Giant* (New York: Harper & Brothers, 1957), p. 9.
10. *Ibid.*, p. 4.
11. Sir Percival Griffiths, *The British Impact on India* (London: Macdonald Co., 1952), p. 477.
12. Quoted *Ibid.*, p. 398.

UNIT NINE

1. Leo Africanus, *The History and Description of Africa . . .*, trans. John Pory (London: Hakluyt Society, 1896), III, p. 824. Spelling and place names modernized.
2. Al-Bakri, quoted in J. Spencer Trimmingham, *A History of Islam in West Africa* (Glasgow: Oxford University Press, 1962), p. 54.
3. Gordon Laing, quoted in A. Adu Boahen, "The Caravan Trade in the Nineteenth Century," Journal of African History, III (1962), p. 351.
4. Quoted in Basil Davidson, *The African Slave Trade* (Boston: Little, Brown, 1961), pp. 147–148.
5. A. Adu Boahen, *Topics in West African History* (London: Longmans, Green, and Co., 1966), p. 113.
6. Chief Matungi, quoted in Colin Turnbull, *The Lonely African* (New York: Simon and Schuster, 1962), pp. 83–84.
7. Joseph A. Lijembe, "The Valley Between: A Muluyia's Story," in *East African Childhood: Three Versions*, ed. Lorene K. Fox (Nairobi: Oxford University Press, 1967), p. 36.

8. Quoted in Margaret Read, *Education and Social Change in Tropical Areas* (London and New York: Thomas Nelson & Sons, 1955), p. 7.

9. Quoted in Hortense Powdermaker, *Copper Town: Changing Africa* (New York: Harper & Row, 1965), p. 311.

10. Quoted in Peter Marris, *Family and Social Change in an African City* (Evanston: Northwestern University Press, 1962), p. 29.

11. Mungo Park, *Travels in the Interior Districts of Africa . . . in the years 1795, 1796, and 1797* (London: W. Bulmer and Co., 1799), p. 196.

12. Ali A. Mazrui, *The Anglo-African Commonwealth* (Oxford: Pergamon Books, 1967), p. 88.

13. Quoted in Powdermaker, *ibid*, p. 294.

14. The Rev. W. Groves, recorder, "The Story of Udo Akpabio of the Anang Tribe, Southern Nigeria," in *Ten African*, ed. Margery F. Perham (Evanston: Northwestern University Press, 1963), p. 57.

15. Mamadou Dia, *The African Nations and World Solidarity*, trans. Mercer Cook (New York: Frederick A. Praeger, 1961), p. 41.

16. David Rubadiri, "Africa: An African Evaluation," *Annals of the American Academy of Political and Social Science*, CCCLIV (July 1964), p. 84.

17. El Mas'udi, quoted in Basil Davidson, "The Tents of Kedar: Pre-European Africa," *History Today*, VII (1957), p. 652.

18. Quoted in Basil Davidson, "Letters to the Editor," *History Today*, VIII (1958), p. 135.

19. Max Gluckman, *The Judicial Process Among the Barotse of Northern Rhodesia* (Manchester: Manchester University Press, 1955), pp. 357, 360.

20. Reginald Smith, "Letters to the Editor," *History Today*, VII (1958), p. 59.

21. *Ibid.*

22. Thomas Hodgkin, *Nationalism in Colonial Africa* (New York: N. Y. University Press, 1957), p. 98.

23. David Diop, "Listen Comrades," in *Modern Poetry from Africa*, ed. Gerald Moore and Ulli Beier, 2nd ed. (Baltimore: Penguin Books, 1966), pp. 61–62.

UNIT TEN

1. *The New York Times*, May 2, 1959.

2. Cited by W. Z. Laqueur, *Communism and Nationalism in the Middle East* (N.Y.: Praeger, 1956), p. 7.

3. Cited by A. Vambery, *Western Culture in Eastern Lands* (London: J. Murray, 1906), pp. 343–344.

4. Cited by H. E. Allen, *The Turkish Transformation* (Chicago: Univ. of Chicago Press, 1935), p. 113.

5. From *Israel and World Politics* by Theodore Draper. Copyright © 1967, 1968 by Theodore Draper. All rights reserved. Reprinted by permission of The Viking Press, Inc.

6. *Ibid.* p. 67.

7. W. Durant, *The Story of Civilization* (New York: Simon and Schuster, Inc., 1935), I, p. 116.

8. Sir M. Sykes, *The Caliph's Last Heritage* (London: Macmillan, 1915), pp. 222–23.

9. E. D. Clarke, *Travels in Various Countries of Europe, Asia and Africa* (Cambridge, England, 1810), I, p. 690.

10. M. W. Thornburg, *Turkey: An Economic Appraisal* (N.Y.: Twentiety Century Fund, 1949), p. 253.

11. Mansfield, *Nasser's Egypt* (Penguin, 1965), p. 131.

12. Y. L. Kohn, "Israel and the New Nation States of Asia and Africa," *Annals of the American Academy of Pol. and Social Science*, July, 1959, p. 102.

13. Cited by J. S. Schapiro, ed., *Modern and Contemporary European History* (Boston: Houghton Mifflin Co., 1953, rev. ed.) p. 120.

14. Cited by R. N. Frye, ed., *Islam and the West* (The Hague: Mouton & Co., 1957), p. 61.

15. D. Lerner, *The Passing of Traditional Society* (Glencoe, Illinois: The Free Press, 1958), p. 188.

16. *Ibid.*

17. *Ibid.*, p. 189.

18. *Statistical Abstract of the U.S.*, 1958, 1962, 1965.

19. Lerner, *op. cit.*, pp. 189, 193, 195, 214, 283.

20. Cited in *What is Race? Evidence from Scientists* (Paris: UNESCO, 1952), p. 60.

21. Cited by I. Husseini, "Islam Past and Present," *Atlantic Monthly*, 198 (October, 1956), p. 172.

22. Cited, Thomas, "Recent Developments in Turkish Islam," *Middle East Journal*, VI (1952), p. 34.

UNIT ELEVEN

1. *USS Triton, SSRN586, First Submerged Circumnavigation, 1960* (Washington, D.C.: U.S. Government Printing Office, 1960), p. B–76.

2. D. Lerner, *The Passing of Traditional Society* (Glencoe, Ill.: The Free Press, 1958), p. 214.

3. T. R. B., "Washington Wire," *New Republic*, September 19, 1955, p. 2.

4. Cited, W. L. Langer, *The Diplomacy of Imperialism 1890–1902* (N.Y.: A. A. Knopf, Inc., 1956), p. 93.

5. W. R. Crocker, *Self-Government for the Colonies* (London: George Allen & Unwin, 1949), p. 8.

6. A. J. Toynbee, *A Study of History* (London: Oxford University Press, 1934), I, p. 245.

7. R. Linton, *The Study of Man* (N.Y.: D. Appleton-Century Co., Inc., 1936), pp. 326–27. By permission of Appleton-Century-Crofts, Inc.

8. Barbara Ward, "Race Relations as a World Issue," *New York Times Magazine*, Nov. 11, 1956, p. 12.

9. L. Dudley Stamp, *Land for Tomorrow: The Underdeveloped World* (Bloomington: Indiana University Press, 1953), pp. 218–19.

10. *The New York Times*, November 26, 1959.

11. President Gamal Abdel Nasser, "Cooperative Society," *Arab Review*, I (March, 1960), p. 11.

INDEX

Guide to pronunciation. The following phonetic symbols, with their corresponding sounds shown in parentheses, are used to indicate the pronunciation of selected words in the index:

a	(b<u>a</u>t)	eye	(<u>i</u>dentify)	g	(go)
ah	(f<u>a</u>ther)	o	(c<u>o</u>t)	j	(jump, legend)
ai	(<u>ai</u>r)	oh	(c<u>oa</u>l)	kh	(a<u>ch</u>: German)
aw	(c<u>au</u>se)	oo	(c<u>oo</u>l)	s	(<u>s</u>in)
ay	(d<u>ay</u>)	oy	(c<u>oi</u>l)	th	(<u>th</u>in)
e	(b<u>e</u>t)	ow	(cl<u>ou</u>d)	z	(do<u>z</u>e, no<u>s</u>e)
ee	(f<u>ee</u>d)	or	(h<u>or</u>n)	zh	(mea<u>s</u>ure)
ew	(f<u>ew</u>)	u	(f<u>u</u>n)	er	(h<u>er</u>, f<u>ur</u>, s<u>ir</u>)
ih	(t<u>i</u>p)	yoo	(c<u>u</u>be)	yah	(V<u>i</u>rginia)
y	(f<u>i</u>nd)	uh	(<u>u</u>p, at<u>o</u>m)		

173. *See also* Latin America; names of countries
American Revolution, 154, 156
Amur (ah·MOOR) **River,** 230
Ancestor worship (China), 79, 392
Ancient civilizations, 56–69; end of, 73; nature of, 64–67; significance of, 67–69; similarities of, 67
Andes, 302
Angles, 96
Angola (an·GOH·luh), 142, 170, 538, 594, 595, 600, 601, 603, 611. *See also* Africa; Sub-Saharan Africa
Angora (an·GOR·uh), **battle of** (1402), 109
Animism, 526
Apartheid (a·PAHRT·hyt) **system,** 595, 611, 699
Arab League, 642–643
Arabian Sea, 29
Arabs: invasions by, 101–102, 116; Islamic civilization and, 101–106; Israeli-Arab tensions, 208–209, 643–644, 647–651; nationalism and, 186. *See also* Middle East
Arbenz, Jacobo, 341
Argentina, 298, 299, 300, 302, 305–306, 308, 309, 310, 311, 321, 323, 326, 333, 334, 340, 343, 349, 350, 353, 355, 357, 370, 371, 372; independence, 320. *See also* Latin America
Armada, Spanish, 128, 135
Aryans, 62, 73, 75, 78, 80–81; India invaded by, 471
Ashanti (a·SHAN·tih), 602
Asia: Central, Russia and, 162; European empires in, 159–164; influence in Latin America, 372; South, 462–529; World War II and, 196–197, 199. *See also* Southeast Asia; specific countries
Asian-African Congress (1955), 719–720, 721
Asia Minor, 72, 74; Hellenism and, 86
Asoka, Emperor, 79, 90–91, 472
Assyrian (a·SEER·ee·an) **Empire,** 65, 72, 76
Assyrians, 72, 82
Aswan (ahs·WAHN) **Dam,** 645, 646
Ataturk, Mustapha (Kemal) (ah·tah·TEWRK moos·tah·FAH ke·MAHL), 628, 637–638, 676
Athens, 84–85
Atlantic Charter, 726

Atom bomb, 199
Audiencia (ow·DEE·en·see·ah), 328
Aurangzeb (OR·rung·zeb), **Emperor,** 475, 476, 486
Australia, 22, 32–33, 141; aborigines, 21, 32–33; culture, 173; Europeanization of, 170–173
Austria: German annexation of, 193; World War I and, 178–182
Austria-Hungary, 178
Austrian Succession, War of the, 139
Axis powers, 191
Ayub Khan (eye·OOB kahn), 498, 500
Azikiwe, Nnamdi (ah·zee·KEE·way NAHM·dee), 606
Aztecs, 31, 32, 129, 147, 311, 312, 313, 316, 362

Babur (BAH·ber), 474, 486
Babylonian Empire, 65, 74
Bacon, Roger, 117, 118
Baghdad, 658; captured by Mongols, 108
Baghdad Pact, 715
Bahama Islands, 128
Bahia (buh·HEE·uh), **Brazil,** 318
Balboa, Vasco Nuñez de, 316
Balfour Declaration, 639, 641
Baltic Sea, 226
Banda (BAHN·dah), **H. K.,** 594
Bandeirantes (BAHN·day·rahn·tays), 318
Barbados, 298
Barbarians, 71–73, 75, 77–79, 86, 95, 96, 99, 101
Barotseland (buh·ROT·sih·land), 603
Basuto (buh·SOO·toh) **state** (South Africa), 602
Batista, Fulgencio (bah·TEES·tah fool·HAYN·see·oh), 335, 340
Bay of Pigs, 341
Beagle, **H. M. S.,** 44
Bedouins (BED·oo·inz), 101, 622
Belgium: World War I and, 178–182; World War II and, 194
Bell, Alexander Graham, 152
Bengal (ben·GAWL), **Bay of,** 29
Bessarabia (bes·uh·RAY·bee·uh), 199
Biafra (bee·AH·fruh), 721
Birth control, 711–712
Black Sea, 226, 227
Blitzkrieg, 194
Blue Nile River, 538
Boers (boorz), 137, 169, 602
Bolívar, Simón, 320, 321, 331

Bolivia, 298, 302, 306, 307, 311, 321, 326, 330, 331, 333–343, 345, 347, 350, 357, 362, 365, 367, 368, 371, 711, 715; independence, 320. *See also* Latin America
Bolshevik (BOL·sheh·vik) **Revolution,** 157, 158, 184–185
Bolsheviks, 184–185, 238, 239, 248, 250, 251, 266, 281
Bonaparte (BOH·nuh·pahrt), **Joseph,** 319
Bonaparte, Napoleon, 319, 320; quoted on China, 408
Bosch, Juan (bohsh hwahn), 341
Botswana, 594
Boxer Rebellion, 414–415
Bradford, William, 115
Brahmaputra (brah·muh·POO·truh) **River,** 464, 466
Brahmans (BRAH·muhnz), 81, 82, 88
Brasília, Brazil, 319, 375
Brazil, 298, 299, 301, 305, 306, 308, 309, 310, 311, 318–319, 321, 323, 326, 330–331, 334, 340, 344, 349, 350, 353, 355, 359, 364, 365, 370, 371, 372, 373, 699; independence, 320. *See also* Latin America
Brazilian Highlands, 302
Brezhnev, Leonid (BREZH·nef lay·o·NYEET), 290
Britain, Battle of, 194
British East Africa, 168
British East India Company: India and, 485–489; China and, 409
Bronze, 72, 75, 80
Bronze Age, 72, 75
Bubonic plague, 732–733
Buddha (BOOD·uh), 90, 93
Buddhism, 24, 79, 81, 391–392, 396, 707; decline of, 91, 92; four great truths of, 90; India and, 468, 472, 522; Mongols converted to, 112, 115; significance of, 91; spread of, 88, 90–91, 93, 472
Buenos Aires (BWAY·nohs AIR·ez), **Argentina,** 373
Buffalo, water, 386
Buganda, 603
Bulgaria, 195, 210
Burma, 160
Burundi (boo·ROON·dih), 538. *See also* Africa; Sub-Saharan Africa
Bushmen, 30, 600, 602
Byrnes, James F., 340

722–723; UN and the, 734–736
Collective farms, 256, 258–260, 266, 268
Colonialism, 149, 158–174; Africa and, 554–556, 569–572, 586–591, 599–606; decline of, 210–211; revolt against, 185–186
Colonies: Belgian, 165, 601, 606; comparison of English and Spanish in Americas, 330; Dutch, 135–137, 169; English, 137–138, 159–161, 169, 330; French, 138, 168, 169, 606; German, 168; Italian, 168; Portuguese, 134; Russian, 140–141; Spanish, 133. *See also* under colonized area
Colombia, 298, 299, 301, 304, 306, 308, 321, 332, 334–338, 350, 352, 355, 359; independence, 320. *See also* Latin America
Columbus, Christopher, 128–129
Comintern, *see* Communist International
Commandments, 82, 83
Commonwealth of Nations, 213
Communication, global unity and, 689–691
Communism, 157, 158, 709, 714, 715, 718–719; China and, 403–408, 417–430, 443; containment of, 203; doctrines of, 249, 277; Latin America and, 341–342; rise of, 184–185, 186, 187; spread of, 211; U.S.S.R. and, 239, 241, 242–244, 249, 252, 253, 266, 277
Communist International, 158, 202; abolishment of, 200; China aided by, 418
Communist Party: Chinese, 404–408, 417–420, 427–428, 430, 443; U.S.S.R., 239, 241, 242–244, 252, 256
Confucianism, 79, 82, 88, 91, 391, 392, 396, 398, 399–400, 413, 414, 416, 423, 448, 451–452, 707
Confucius, 81–82, 395, 396, 444, 448
Congo, Belgian, 165, 601, 606; UN and, 735
Congo, Democratic Republic of (Kinshasa, kin·SHAH·suh), 550, 576; resources, 544; UN and, 735. *See also* Africa; Sub-Saharan Africa
Congo, French, 168, 606
Congo, Republic of (Brazzaville, brah·zah·VEEL), resources, 544. *See also* Africa; Sub-Saharan Africa

Congo River, 538, 540
Conquistadores (kon·KWIS·ta·dorz), 129–132, 316
Constantine, Emperor, 88
Constantinople, 97
Cooperatives: Indian, 512; Soviet, 256
Cortes, 328
Cortés, Hernán (kor·TEZ er·NAHN), 129, 301, 316
Costa Rica, 299, 308, 321, 326, 327. *See also* Latin America
Coups d'état (KOO day·TAH), 324, 326, 327, 334
Creoles (KHREE·ohlz), 319–320, 330, 369
Crete (kreet), 62, 65, 66, 72, 74; World War II and, 195
Crimean (kry·MEE·en) War, 264, 636
Cro-Magnon man, 40
Cromwell, Oliver, 154
Crusades, 114–115
Cuba, 298, 300, 306, 316, 338, 340, 341, 350, 715; crisis over (1962), 205; Revolution (1959), 335–337, 358. *See also* Latin America
Cultural Europeanization, 172–173
Culture: African, 545, 547, 576–593; American, 173; Canadian, 173; Chinese, 386, 388, 389, 390, 400, 441–453; civilization and, 56; differences in, causing global disunity, 702–709; defined, 56; European, spread of, 172–173; food producers and, 48–51; High, 69, 158; Iberian, in Latin America, 363–364; Inca, 314; India, 469, 517–529; Indian, Latin American, 362–363; interregional contacts and, 86–87; Islamic, 675; Latin-American, 172, 361–377; Low, 69, 158; Mayan, 313; Middle East, 669–673; Neolithic, 47–51, 56; U.S.S.R., 276–290
Cuneiform (kew·NEE·ih·form), 80
Cyprus (SY·prus), 721
Czechoslovakia (CHEK·oh·sloh·VAH·kee·yah), 182, 187, 210; German invasion of, 193; Soviet invasion of (1968), 209, 253, 718

Da Gama, Vasco (dah·Gam·ah VAS·koh), 29, 128, 132, 147, 475, 551, 660
Dahomey (dah·HOH·may), 599, 602, 711
Darwin, Charles, 44–45, 152

Darwin, Charles (grandson), 712
Dawes Plan, 187
D-Day, 196
DDT, 301, 504, 733
Dead Sea, 538
Deccan (DEK·uhn), Plateau, 464, 466, 469
Declaration of Independence, 154
Delhi (DEL·ih) Sultanate, 104
Delphi (DEL·fy), 83
Democracy: China and, 418; rise of, 84–85
Democratic centralism, principle of, 404–405
Denmark, World War II and, 194
Derthick, Lawrence G., 278
Dewey, John, 173
Dia, Mamadou (DEE·ah mah·mah·DEW), 594
Diamonds, 544, 601
Diaz, Bernal (DEE·ahs BAIR·nahl), 115
Diaz, Porfirio (DEE·ahs por·FEER·yoh), 335
Dictators, Latin American, 324–326, 335, 340
Diplomatic blocs, 714–723
Discovery, exploration and, 128–132
Dnieper (NEE·per) River, 230
Dominican Republic, 298, 299, 325, 337, 340–341. *See also* Latin America
Donatorias, 318
Dorians, 72, 84
Drake, Sir Francis, 135
Dravidians, 467, 471
Dübcek (doob·CHEK), Alexander, 209
DuBois (doo·BOYS), W. E. B., 604
Dulles, John Foster, 646
Dupleix (dew·PLEKS), Joseph, 139
Dust storms, 13–14, 15
Dutch East India Company, 136
Dutch East Indies, 136, 137, 160
Dvina (dvee·NAH) River, 230

Earth: age of, 40; land surface of, 12, 22; man and, 6–33
East Africa, 168
East China Sea, 29
East Indian Company. *See* British East India Company *and* Dutch East India Company
East Roman Empire, *see* Byzantine Empire
Economic Europeanization, 171–172